Volume 1

GITA
for GEN
A to Z

CHAPTERS 11 TO 18

RAM PRAKASH SINGHAL

INDIA · SINGAPORE · MALAYSIA

Notion Press

Old No. 38, New No. 6
McNichols Road, Chetpet
Chennai - 600 031

First Published by Notion Press 2019
Copyright © Ram Prakash Singhal 2019
All Rights Reserved.

ISBN 978-1-68466-884-7

||ॐ||

"Krishnam Vande Jagadgurum"

"मातृ देवो भव:"

Dedicated to My Mother

Late **Shrimati Bhanwari Bai**

(In spite of herself being illiterate, she invoked my interest in the study of Gita in childhood by making me to recite it aloud to her every morning)

||ॐ||

"Krishnam Vande Jagadgurum"

GITA for GEN A to Z

(In simple, Interesting, Practical Form)

अध्येष्यते च य इमं धर्म्यं संवादमावयोः ।
ज्ञानयज्ञेन तेनाहमिष्टः स्यामिति मे मतिः ॥

**"It is my firm opinion that whosoever studies this sacred
dialogue between you and Me that reveals the essence
of Dharm; he has worshipped Me by way of performing
Jnaan Yajn, the path to cultivate perfect knowledge."**

– Krishn in Gita 18/70

CONTENTS

BLESSINGS OF A GURU

*(**Guruji Shri G. Narayana** (77) is Chairman Emeritus of Excel Industries Ltd. and chairman and director of several other companies, but his life's mission is to channelize inner light & potential of people, especially the entrepreneurs and corporate managers, to work for bliss, peace & harmony in society. For this, he is actively associated with Management Associations of Ahmedabad & Baroda besides others. In spite of being honored with much recognition from global institutions for promoting world spirituality, his modesty and simplicity are unmatched. Presently, he stays at Vadodara and also serves at **Shri Sitarama Seva Sadan**, Mantrapuri, Telangana, India. He invests his time, energy and resources in the spiritual awakening of people and serving them. As such, he is **Jeevan Mukt**, a soul liberated in his life time, because all his activities are for **Lok Sangrah** i.e. for the good of people. In my opinion, he is an embodiment of accomplished Yogee of Gita.*

An author of more than 500 books, including some on Gita, he very kindly spared his valuable time to read few excerpts of this treatise on Gita and blessed it in following words)

"DEAR RAMPRAKASH JI,

Many thanks for sending few excerpts of your exhaustive work on Srimad Bhagavadgita, the inspiring guide light for humanity. This inspiring, innovative, insightful and integrated work will be of great value for learners, teachers, researchers as well as spiritual guides. The meaning, message, explanation and commentary of each shlok are of master class. The manner in which you have given cross-references and interconnections between spiritual thoughts of major world religions & Holy Scriptures as well as quotes of great personalities is commendable since it enhances Gita's universal spirit and scope of application to everybody's life in multi-dimensional ways. In addition, effective compounding of Sanskrit, Hindi and English makes the book to touch the hearts and souls of different people in a super-connective way.

Your inspiring writing is very valuable for all human beings across the globe irrespective of faith, culture and spiritual thoughtways, as you have put in great effort to forge unity and harmony amongst them. Readers shall achieve inner peace and fulfillment while studying and grasping its approach of spiritually integration and unification of world community into one family.

Your unique style of writing and its contribution is truly admirable.

With deep, hearty Congratulations to you, greetings and best wishes to readers, and,

With Aum and Prem"

Narayana

January 2019, Vadodara.

GOOD WORDS FROM LIKE-MINDED FRIENDS

"Wow! You have completed your herculean work – a Treatise on Gita. What a scholarly work of not only explaining the Shloks but also what they advocate to live a spiritual life, caring for duty and not the outcome. I am thrilled to read the e-mail and attached excerpts from the treatise. What a novel way to link Gita's teachings to the works of varied India's Sages and Sants! What a simple innovative work to bring attention of the world towards Gita! My unceasing respects, laudatory salutes and well-deserve kudos to you.

I am very fortunate to be your classmate and a friend."

Om P. Bahethi, Ph.D.

Vienna, Virginia, USA

————◆————

"I consider myself one of the few fortunate and privileged ones to whom you have thought to send a copy of Gita you have penned. It is, in fact, a herculean task to understand the message of a Great Scripture like Gita, which took place almost five thousand years ago, and explain it in a simple language, understandable by a common person. Your effort to substantiate subject matter by giving various similes, quotes, anecdotes, and relate it day-to-day life is very valuable for all human beings struggling for peace & happiness in today's world.

I highly appreciate and salute your arduous endeavor of putting forth Gita, and thereby enlightening & elevating mental level of the society to higher spiritual plane."

– Kedar Govind Tambe,

Executive Director,

K.B. Mehta Construction Pvt. Ltd. Ahmedabad

MY SUBMISSION

(If you can't explain it simply,
you don't understand it well enough)
– Albert Einstein

Dear Readers! Please accept my hearty compliments for completing the study of Volumes I & II of this treatise, and starting to read its last volume III now. With all my humility, I hope that my simple and practical style served you well you in your study so far. Henceforth it would be easier for you to grasp the concluding part of Gita because most of it deals with application of its teachings in practical situations of daily life.

I invoke God's benevolence blessings in our joint quest to give us patience to complete study of Gita by reading Volume III, and bestow wisdom on us to understand Samagr Yog, the complete knowledge of Gita. This study should certainly help us in attaining liberation from stress, anxiety, fear and grief; and leading a useful, contributory & peaceful life without renouncing duty, and the beauty of the world.

In His last sermon in 18/65-66, God beckons us towards our desired goal of freedom from grief in life, and attainment of permanent bliss of a **Yogee**:

"Be wholeheartedly engrossed in Me; unconditionally devoted unto Me; offer all sacrificial activities and adorations unto Me; and bow in reverence & obeisance before Me. You shall certainly attain Me in this way. This is My true & sincere promise to you for you are the dearest to Me.

Abandon all kinds of Dharm, that an ignorant person perceives as his personal Dharm, and seek shelter in Me alone. I shall deliver you from all sins.

You need not grieve anymore."

श्रीकृष्णार्पणमस्तु । (I offer my work to Shree Krishn, the God personified)!

– **Ram Prakash Singhal**
February 2019
Thane, Maharashtra, India

INTRODUCTION

(Understanding of life mapped out by Krishn in His scientific and logical discourse in Gita, does transform the thought pattern of its student, as he discovers for himself a new purpose and a clearer vision of the goal of his life)

– *Swami Chinmayaanand*

The picture that comes to one's mind immediately upon the mention of Gita is as below:

Take two minutes to absorb this picture and retain it in mind as long as possible

(We see the battlefield of Kuru Kshetr where two armies positioned on each side are eager to commence Mahaabhaarat, the Great

Indian War. Its dry, yellow colored ground is going to turn into red mud soon with the imminent bloodshed. The right side sky looks brighter compared to grayish on the left side as if reflecting the moods of both armies. Kauravs on the left look excited and aggressive because of superiority in numbers but Paandavs on the right are calm & confident in spite of low numbers. Parked in between the two armies, there is a grand chariot yoked with four spotless white horses impatient to charge. A two-tailed saffron flag flying atop this chariot bears the insignia of mighty ape god Hanumaan, the faithful servant of Raam, an avatar of God. The man seated in the chariot has a mixed expression of nervousness and confusion on his face though his body is fully protected with steel armor. Nevertheless, his eyes reflect hope of deliverance. He is Arjun, the owner of the chariot. His formidable bow is hanging loosely on his right shoulder, and the quiver is lying on the floor. With folded hands, he is making a request to his charioteer Krishn, easily recognized by His peacock feathered crown and Peetaambar, the simple yellow robe. A very bright circle of divine aura surrounds His slightly grey complexioned face aglow with eternal bliss and calm, as if casting the spell of a full moon in the backdrop of gloomy sky. With eyes full of compassion, He is looking backwards at Arjun, restraining impatient horses simultaneously with reins in left hand and a whip in the other.)

LEGENDARY BACKGROUND OF GITA

Since Gita is a part of the great Indian epic Mahaabhaarat scripted by sage Ved Vyaas, it is necessary to go through relevant part of Mahaabhaarat briefly as given below.

Vichitraveerya, the king of Hastinaapur, had two sons namely Dhrutraashtr and Paandu, born by a boon from Vyaas. Since Dhrutraashtr was born blind, the nobles made Paandu the king of Hastinaapur after the death of Vichitraveerya. Soon thereafter,

Paandu went to live in the forest for some time with his two wives, Kuntee and Maadree, with a hope to recover from some mysterious ailment. There, he had 3 sons named Yudhishthir, Bheem and Arjun from Kuntee; and the twin sons named Nakul and Sahadev from Maadree. Dhrutraashtr ruled Hastinaapur as caretaker in the absence of Paandu. However, when Paandu succumbed to his incurable disease in the forest, Maadree committed Sati* with his body after entrusting her sons to the care of Kuntee.

Kuntee, with five young sons collectively called Paandavs, returned to Hastinaapur after Paandu's death. She painfully realized it soon that Dhrutraashtr (supposed to act as a caretaker) was in full and firm command of the kingdom of Hastinaapur along with his ambitious and atrocious son Duryodhan and other 99 sons collectively called Kauravs. The latter started disputing legitimate claim of Paandavs on the throne. They made several vile attempts to eliminate them, even by killing, but never succeeded. Paandavs, in order to avoid a family feud, gracefully accepted partition of the Empire, left Hastinaapur and settled in Khaandavaprasth, a very hostile forestland allotted to them. By their dedicated hard work, they developed it into a very prosperous Empire and renamed it Indraprasth that outshined Hastinaapur. Krishn, their cousin and king of Dwaarikaa guided, helped and stood with them all along in their tragic times. They in turn, reposed full faith and love for Him. Jealous of newly created wealth of Paandavs, Kauravs conspicuously lured them into playing a *Game of Dice* and defeated them in it due to cunning maneuvers and trickery of Shakuni, the maternal uncle of Kauravs. Paandavs lost everything to Kauravs including their kingdom Indraprasth. They lived for 12 years in exile in the forests, followed by living incognito in the 13th year to fulfill pre-decided terms of the *Game of dice* sincerely. Upon expiry of the 13th year, they asked Kauravs to return Indraprasth to them in accordance with the Game agreement. Kauravs did not honor the agreed terms and refused.

All attempts to persuade Dhrutraashtr and Duryodhan for a peaceful settlement failed. Krishn Himself made the last attempt for peace with a proposal to allot five villages to Paandavs but Duryodhan refused pointblank saying he would not part with a land equal in area to even the point of a sharp needle without a fight. The result was inevitable. Paandavs, had no alternative but to fight and get back Indraprasth from Kauravs were not ready to part with their ill-gotten Empire. Then, Ved Vyaas blessed Sanjay, the friend cum attendant of Dhrutraashtr, with divine vision that enabled him to see the war while sitting in Hastinaapur, and narrate it to his blind master Dhrutraashtr.

A strong army of 18 Akshauhinee (equal to 40 million approximately), 11 of Kauravs and 7 of Paandavs, assembled in the battlefield of Kuru Kshetr to fight in the *'Great Indian War'* called Mahaabhaarat with determination to swing the result in their favor. Dhrutraashtr, anxious to know what was happening in the battlefield on the 1st day of the war, asks Sanjay in the first shlok of Gita *'Dharm Kshetre Kuru Kshetre ... Akurvat Sanjay'* i.e. *'What his, and Pandu's sons do after they assembled in the sacred place of Kurukshetr (now a battlefield)'*. Remaining 699 Shloks of Gita consist of narration by Sanjay of the divine, spiritual dialogue that took place between Arjun, bewildered about his duty, and Krishn, his charioteer cum teacher, teaching him his duty just before the beginning of war.

SYMBOLIC AND SPIRITUAL PERSPECTIVES OF GITA

Yam, the lord of death, gives the simile of **Rath,** a chariot, to Nachiketaa, a child aged 7 years, while imparting spiritual knowledge to him in Kathopanishad. He describes a person's body as a chariot, his Soul as **Rathee,** its owner, and his intelligence as **Saarathee,** the charioteer. The horses yoked to this chariot depict **Jnaanendriys,** the sensory organs like ears, tongue, eyes and nose that need to be reined by **Man,** the mind, from their natural tendency to gallop after the objects of passions and drag the chariot on the disastrous path of passions and pleasures.

Vyaas modified this simile of chariot with some more imagination and incorporated it into Gita. He replaced the soul with Arjun, a highly confused and stressed person unable to decide his duty. Then he substituted Buddhi, the intelligence, by Krishn, the God incarnate in charioteer's seat. Since Nachiketaa, a simple and pure hearted child, is the knowledge seeker in Kathopanishad, it was befitting for Yam to place his intelligence as his charioteer. However, Vyaas considered it fit to hand over to God the chariot of Arjun, also a seeker of knowledge in Gita, because **Moh,** the delusion, corrupts his intelligence. In Kathopanishad, Yam advises Nachiketaa to command his intelligence to control the horses from straying on the path of passion, and direct them on the path of knowledge. However, as Arjun, the **Rathee** of Gita is highly deluded; he must seek total refuge in his **Saarathee**, God and request Him to drive the chariot of his life on the path He considers best for him. Nachiketaa knew well his destination in Kathopanishad, but Arjun, in Gita, has no idea where he ought to go, *'to quit the battle or fight'*.

Let us extend the simile of chariot further keeping above picture in the battlefield of Mahaabhaarat in mind. Krishn is the inner conscience of a distressed individual Arjun and He is always available, sitting next to him, to give proper counsel and guidance. Mahaabhaarat depicts the battle between positive and negative thoughts going on in our mind in the Kuru Kshetr of life whenever we face battle like situations demanding quick & correct decision and action. The Paandav army on the left side consists of **Daivee Sampadaa,** the wealth of virtues and meritocracy, and Kauravs on the right depict **Aasuree Sampadaa,** the devilish, vicious wealth. Thus, the battle of Mahaabhaarat symbolizes the conflict between virtuous and vicious thoughts before we decide to act in real life situations. The decision distorts if mind lets loose reins of the horses of senses, allows them to run after passions and desires, and land the chariot of life in the gorge of **Vikaars**, the disorders that agitate our mind further. When disorders of **Kaam,** the desire, **Krodh,** the anger, **Lobh,** the covetousness, **Moh,** the bewilderment, **Mad,** the frenzy and **Matsar,** the envy forge an alliance with self-interests, they create a chaotic state of indecision and confusion described by Arjun in Gita in 1/29 & 30. Then, we are torn between **Daivee** and **Aasuree Sampadaa** as they pull us on their sides, rendering our physical and mental faculties dull. As a result, we sometimes become nervous and melancholic like Arjun, and at other times, we become egoist like Duryodhan.

Thus, Mahaabhaarat war is not only a legendary battle fought between Kauravs and Paandavs, but also a fight between **Dharm,** the Godliness, and **Adharm,** the ungodliness, in a person's life. At society level, it also symbolizes conflicts between positive, virtuous people on one side trying tooth and nail, to stop the negative, vicious people from realizing their evil ambitions on the other side; and thereby maintain law and order.

HISTORY OF GITA AS A SCRIPTURE

As mentioned above, Vyaas, the greatest sage contemporary of Krishn & Arjun, scripted Gita. Most historians estimate the period of Mahaabhaarat & Gita around 3200 B.C. Due to cultural and political upheavals, which subsequently took place in India, the original Gita or some of its portions might have been lost with passage of time; and its different versions might have appeared in the society. Then, Aadi Shankaraachaarya (788 to 820 A.D.) revived, compiled and presented Gita to the society in its most authentic form and named it Shreemad Bhagawad Gita, popularly called Gita, which is followed universally ill today.

COMPOSITION AND FORMAT OF GITA

Gita literally means **Geet**, the divine song sung by God. It is in Sanskrit language, written in Devanaagaree script. It contains 700 verses called shloks, spread in 18 chapters. The name of each chapter is suffixed with the word **Yog** e.g. first chapter is called **Arjun Vishaad Yog**. As explained earlier, Gita is in the form of a dialogue between Krishn and Arjun in the midst of the battlefield of Kuru Kshetr where the fight between Paandavs and Kauravs is about to begin on the first day of war. There are total 59 speeches in it, 1 by Dhrutraashtr, 9 by Sanjay, 21 by Arjun and balance 28 by **Shree Bhagawaan** i.e. Krishn, the God of Gita. Each shlok is composed and balanced metrically conforming to Sanskrit grammar.

THE PREMISES ON WHICH GITA STANDS

As Gita is a part of Mahaabhaarat, the greatest epic dealing with Hindu way of life, it is imperative that Gita also should have its premises on the four main ethos and beliefs of contemporary Hindu culture and religious practices. Though we would deal with various aspects related with these premises in our study later, let us know them now for better and faster understanding of Gita. they are:_

1. **First pillar is theism, the belief in God:**

   The thought of seeing God everywhere is the most soul satisfying one.

2. **Second pillar is Karm, the action and Karm Phal, the result of action:**

   It means that every person is responsible for his actions. He would get rewards for his good deeds and punishment for his evil deeds. Nevertheless, the beauty of Gita is that it lifts a person, from the physical, materialistic level of this concept, to the highest plane of spirituality by lending a great value addition to it with its unique doctrine of **Nishkaam Karm.** It teaches him to perform his prescribed duty without any consideration of self-interest; and remain detached from its result by leaving it to the divine justice of God

3. **Third pillar is Punarjanm, the repetitive cycles of birth and death:**

   Logically, it is an extension of the theory of **Karm** and **Karm Phal** described under point 2 above. According to it, all living beings, including humans and other species, are bound to take birth, die, and take rebirth to lead a new life again. These cycles of death and rebirth continue perpetually in order to make them consume (enjoy or suffer) the reactions of their actions in previous or current lives.

4. **Fourth pillar is Varn, the caste system:**

   Gita prescribes a social order consisting of four main castes: **Braahman, Kshatriy, Vaishya** and **Shoodr**, but it does not profess caste by birth or family lineage. It lays great emphasis on one's **Swadharm** i.e. his characteristic nature, professional skills, duties and responsibilities. Gita rejects the idea of *Caste by Birth.*

Nevertheless, Gita wholeheartedly welcomes even those readers who are skeptical about its founding principles, because its aim is to lead them from spiritual infancy to maturity; from impulsive irrationality to intelligent rationalism; from an agitated mind to serene tranquility. For this, I suggest readers, who feel uncomfortable with above-mentioned pillars, to substitute few words, as below, and continue their study:

1. Replace 'God' with unified force of nature that creates, sustains and destroys everything.

2. Replace **'Karm Phal'** with Newton's third law of motion *'For every action, there is an equal and opposite reaction'.* Applied to spirituality it simply means that there is always a force, which acts to create reaction of our every interaction with other entities; and its quality depends squarely on the quality of the intent behind our action.

3. Replace **'Punarjanm'** with our current remaining life. And,

4. Replace **'Varn'** system with professional groups that collectively strive to achieve excellence in their respective fields of activity by helping each other.

I hope this *introduction* is informative and useful to the students of Gita. Nevertheless, I wish to bring to their attention that Arjun too was full of doubts and prejudices in the beginning of Gita, but he became a fully enlightened soul after listening to teachings of Krishn. Gita would have served its purpose well if we can understand and practice its message. Gita and its teacher Krishn would thereafter, exist in our lives just for reference, and as a booster dose in times of need.

Gita first recognizes the existence of distress and sorrow in one's life, then it systematically analyses their causes and finally prescribes **Samagr Yog**, a total therapy to lead a moral, virtuous and purposeful life to achieve bliss in own life, and contribute simultaneously in building a happier society. Gita states it in 1st part of 6/23:

"Know it well that Yog is indeed deliverance from distress; and one can achieve it by isolating his self from conjunction & involvement in material world".

Readers belonging to religious faiths other than Hinduism might be under the impression that Gita is the Holy Book of Hindus, like other Holy Books of different religions in the world. Nevertheless, once they start studying it, they would certainly agree with the opinion of many world-renowned scholars, including followers of different religious faiths, who held Gita in very high esteem and found it of universal appeal and application. Mahatma Gandhi used to say:

'Whenever I am stuck up, I look towards Gita to find my path forward; it has never failed me in my belief'

Maharshi Aurobindo sums up well for us:

"if we steep ourselves in the spirit of this great Scripture (Gita) and, above all if we have tried to live in that spirit, we may be sure of finding in it as much real truth as we are capable of receiving, as well as the spiritual influence and actual help that, personally, we were intended to derive from it."

Let us request Krishn with folded hands to be our Guru, guide and mentor, seek His blessings to realize our **Dharm** and act accordingly in the battlefield of life.

'इक बंजारा गाए जीवन का गीत सुनाये ।
हम सब जीने वालों को जीने की राह दिखाये ॥'

(God, the nomadic wanderer, is singing divine song of life that shows us the right way of living)

Let us be ready with folded hands like Arjun and listen to divine song of Gita intently.

Note: Above *'Introduction'* is an abridged version of full *'Introduction'* of Gita, given in volume 1.

CHAPTER 11

VISHW ROOP DARSHAN YOG

(Birth and death are two sides of the coin of one's life. God judges the true value of this coin according to the value addition he does to this coin while it is in his hands).

PREAMBLE & CONTEXT

In chapters 8 & 9, Gita imparted us the deepest secret of spiritual knowledge, called **Adhyaatm**, about individual soul and its relationship with the Supreme Soul. Krishn continued His talk uninterrupted from chapter 8/3 until 10/11 without giving any chance to Arjun to express his gratitude for teaching him such knowledge. However, when he heard Krishn describing His 37 **Vibhooti** in 9/16-19, and 45 again in 10/4-6 he could not restrain his curiosity anymore and requested Him in 10/17-18 to tell all about His divine **Vibhooti**. Acceding to his request, Krishn devoted entire chapter 10 to describe His 127**Vibhooti** briefly. In the beginning of this chapter, Arjun sees an opportunity to show his gratefulness to Krishn for teaching **Adhyaatm** to him in chapter 9, and for disclosing His **Vibhooti**, the **Sagun Niraakaar** i.e. the invisible manifestation of His divine virtues in all outstanding entities of the universe in chapter 10. He is overwhelmed like a child who never met his grandfather, but once he learns of his virtuous qualities from his father, his immense desire to meet him grows out of bounds. Arjun would express his desire similarly to Krishn in 11/3-4 with great humbleness to manifest His universal form before him, if He thinks it proper.

WHY CHAPTER 11 IS NAMED VISHW ROOP DARSHAN YOG?

Vishw means universe, **Roop** means a physical form and **Darshan** means physical appearance. Thus, **Vishhw Roop Darshan Yog** means connecting with the physical appearance of God in His universal form. Chapter 10 was verbal description of God's quality of omnipresence in brief, and chapter 11 exhibits Him in entirety in physical form in which one can see every entity of this universe, and even other universes.

When Arjun heard vivid details of **Vibhootis** of God, he was awe struck by their expanse. On top of it Krishn said in 10/19 & 40 that it is mentioned them brief since they are endless. Hearing this, Arjun wants to see God in entirety in His universal form that encompasses, pervades and penetrates everything in the universe and even beyond. Since this chapter deals with manifestation of divine universal form of Krishn, and its description by Him to awestruck Arjun and Sanjay, it is titled as **Vishw Roop Darshan Yog** aptly. Some scholars have also titled this chapter as **Viraat Roop Darshan Yog.** Since **Viraat** also means the vast, splendid and imposing Universal form of God, this variance is acceptable.

✁❧

Arjun thanks Krishn for teaching him Adhyaatm and describing God's Vibhooti.

(11/1 & 2)

अर्जुन उवाच

मदनुग्रहाय परमं गुह्ममध्यात्मसंज्ञितम् ।
यत्त्वयोक्तं वचस्तेन मोहोऽयं विगतो मम ॥ ११/१ ॥
भवाप्ययौ हि भूतानां श्रुतौ विस्तरशो मया ।
त्वत्तः कमलपत्राक्ष माहात्म्यमपि चाव्ययम् ॥ ११/२ ॥

Arjun Uvaach

Madanugrahaay paramam guhyamadhyaatmasanjnitam I
Yattvayoktam vachasten moho∫yam vigato mam II (11/1)
Bhavaapyayau hi bhootaanaam shrutau vistarasho mayaa I
Tvatt: Kamalpatraaksh maahaatmyamapi chaavyayam II
(11/2)

Madanugrahaay (Your kindness for me) Paramam (ultimate)
Guhyam (esoteric secret) Adhyaatm (the spiritual study) Sanjnitam
(is called)I Yat (which) Twayaa (by you) Uktam (spoken) Vach:
(words, speech) Ten (by that) Moh: (delusion) Ayam (this) Vigat:
(dispelled) Mam (mine)II (11/1)

   Bhavaapyayau (appearance & disappearance) Hi (definitely)
Bhootaani (all beings) Shrutau (listened) Vistarash: (in detail) Mayaa
(by Me)I Tvatt: (from you) Kamal Patraaksh (Krishn) Maahaaatmyam
(majesty) Api (also) ch (and) Avyayam (inexhaustible)II (11/2)

Arjun said:

**"I am highly grateful to You for Your kindness in revealing
to me the most secret, esoteric and ultimate knowledge
called Adhyaatm, the knowledge of Embodied Soul and its
relationship with Supreme Soul. My delusion is now dispelled
by Your teachings. (11/1)**

   **O Kamal Patraaksh (lotus-leaf-eyed Krishn)! I am very
fortunate to have listened from You about the appearance and
disappearance of all the living and inanimate entities in this
universe; and about your inexhaustible greatness & majesty in
detail. (11/2)**

   Bhavaapyayau means appearance of all beings upon birth and
disappearance upon death i.e. the repetitive cycles of **Punarjanm**.
Maahaaatmyam Avyayam used by Arjun in 11/2 here refers to the
everlasting greatness, supremacy and majesty i.e. **Vibhooti** of God
described in chapter 10. Thus, Arjun acknowledges teachings of
Adhyaatm in 11/1-2 to the description of **Vibhootis** in chapter 10.

In response to seven spiritual queries raised by Arjun in 8/3-4, Krishn explained **Adhyaatm** as the spiritual education, which teaches us about soul, its source God, the Supreme Being, its relationship with Him, its repetitive coming and going i.e. **Punarjanm**, the cause of its separation from Him and how it can reunite with Him. I dealt with it there under *'What is Adyaatm'*. Krishn also identified **Adhyaatm Vidyaa** as His **Vibhooti** in 10/32, among all kinds of **Vidyaa** indicating that this is the highest kind of learning. This teaching continued through chapters 8 & 9, and was followed immediately by the description of God's **Vibhooti** in chapter 10. Arjun thanks Krishn in these two shloks for His kindness in imparting him the secret knowledge of **Adhyaatm** and **Bhavaapyayau** i.e. **Punarjanm** and for giving a brief account of His **Vibhooti**. Overwhelmed by the compassion shown by Krishn, he addresses Him as **Kamal Patraaksh** i.e. one with eyes like the leaves of lotus. Besides being the most beautiful and magnificent flower, Kamal, the lotus is also greatly revered in Hindu scriptures for its quality of remaining unaffected by water though staying all the time it. Gita also instructed likewise a Yogee in 5/10 to live in the world like **Padm Patram**, the petals of lotus.

Moh Ayam Vigat Mam literally means that my delusion is gone. Note that, after 10 chapters of Gita, Arjun accepts here for the first time that the bewilderment caused by his misplaced compassion towards relatives, was dispelled now due to the teaching of Krishn. Though he says so, its traces are still lurching in him. He would finally admit the same in most unequivocal words in 18/73 towards the end of Gita saying **Nasht Moh Smruti Labdhaa** when Krishn would ask him categorically whether he is finally relieved of delusion and ignorance by His teachings.

༺✦༻

Arjun requests Krishn to show him
His universal form of God.

(11/3 & 4)

एवमेतद्यथात्थ त्वमात्मानं परमेश्वर ।
द्रष्टुमिच्छामि ते रूपमैश्वरं पुरुषोत्तम ॥ १ १ / ३ ॥
मन्यसे यदि तच्छक्यं मया द्रष्टुमिति प्रभो ।
योगेश्वर ततो मे त्वं दर्शयात्मानमव्ययम् ॥ १ १ / ४ ॥

Evametadyathaatth twamaatmaanam Parameshwar I
Drashtumichchhaami te roopamaishwaram Purushottam II
(11/3)
Manyase yadi tachchhakyam mayaa drashtumiti Prabho I
Yogeshwar tato me twam Darshayaatmaanamavyayam II
(11/4)

Evam (thus) Etat (this) Yathaa (like) aatth (have said) Twam (you) Aatmaanam (by You) Parameshwar (Krishn)I Drashtum (see) Ichchhaami (I wish) Te (your) Roopam (form) Aishwaram (supremacy, majesty) Purushottam (Krishn)II (11/3)

Manyase (think) Yadi (if) Tat (then) Shakyam (possible) Mayaa (by me) Drashtum (see) Iti (it) Prabho (Krishn)I Yogeshwar (Krishn) Tat: (then) Me (my) Twam (you) Darshayaa (appear) Aatmaanam (your) Avyayam (inexhaustible)II (11/4)

O Parameshwar (Krishn)! I have no doubt about You being exactly the same as described by You but O Purushottam (Krishn)! It is my heart's desire to see the physical manifestation of the beauty of Your Supreme majesty & grandeur with my eyes. (11/3)

O Prabho (Krishn)! If You accept it as possible for me to see it with my own eyes, then please appear before me in Your inexhaustible universal form O Yogeshwar (Krishn)!" (11/4)

Prabho (same as **Prabhu**) means the master. Since God is the cause of vivid forms of universe in its all processes of creation, existence and destruction; and the soul residing in everyone's heart, He is addressed as **Prabho**, the Supreme Master. Arjun is relieved of his delusions and doubts to a good extent by now as admitted by him in previous shlok 11/2. Therefore, he has no doubt that Krishn, speaking to him right now, is **Prabho**, the supreme Master, **Parameshwar**, the Supreme Lord of all Lords and **Purushottam,** the Supreme Being manifested in personified form as the greatest person among all humans. Readers may refer to *'Some Additional thoughts on Purushottam'* expressed earlier in 15/18.

Clarification*: One should not understand here that Arjun is asking Krishn to show His universal form as a proof of what He told about Him. Actually, he looks upon this moment as an opportunity to see God physically in Universal form as Krishn described until now.*

Although Arjun is the closest friend and cousin of Krishn, he sheds off his illusion of regarding Him in this way; and addresses Him as **Parameshwar, Purushottam, Prabho** and **Yogeshwar** to disclose his heart's feelings and reverence for Him in these two shloks. Arjun would be repeating such addresses for Krishn henceforth very often in acknowledgement of Him being God. Look at the words and manner with which he makes his request. He first seeks His permission to put up his request, then submits it before Him adding that He should fulfill his desire only if He finds it practically possible, and considers him worthy & deserving to see Him in His universal form. It reveals the simplicity, submission and modesty filled in Arjun's heart. A practiser of Yog should pray to God in the same manner.

Note that the disposition of Arjun towards Krishn was casual, and to some extent even arrogant, in the beginning but it has now completely transformed into a humble, submissive, reverentially devoted person after listening to God's sermons in just 10 chapters of Gita. I hope some of us, who have carefully studied Gita so far, also get the same feeling. This behavior of Arjun sets an example for us how we should behave with a person, once we come to know of his latent qualities and greatness, irrespective of how we treated him in the past. When Sudaamaa visited his childhood schoolmate Krishn in Dwaarikaa, he praised the opulence of Dwaarikaadheesh with humbleness and modesty; and Krishn too showered the same childhood love and affection on His destitute, poor friend Sudaamaa by washing his feet by own hands. An exactly opposite example from Mahaabhaarat is that of another pair of childhood friends, Dron & Drupad, who became bitter enemies in grown up age.

Moral: *Howsoever one may become great in material possessions or knowledge in the course of life, he should never forget and look down upon his friends, relatives, and companions of his humble days. Similarly, a person who remains under-privileged and humble in later days, must never overlook, underestimate, or feel jealous of the greatness of his now well-accomplished friends and relatives.*

৺৽৻

Highly pleased with the modesty of Arjun, God briefly describes His Vishw Roop He intends to show.

(11/5, 6 & 7)

श्रीभगवानुवाच
पश्य मे पार्थ रूपाणि शतशोऽथ सहस्रशः ।
नानाविधानि दिव्यानि नानावर्णाकृतीनि च ॥ ११/५॥
पश्यादित्यान्वसून्रुद्रानश्विनौ मरुतस्तथा ।
बहून्यदृष्टपूर्वाणि पश्याश्चर्याणि भारत ॥ ११/६॥
इहैकस्थं जगत्कृत्स्नं पश्याद्य सचराचरम् ।
मम देहे गुडाकेश यच्चान्यद् द्रष्टुमिच्छसि ॥ ११/७॥

Shree Bhagawaan Uvaach
Pashya me Paarth roopaani shatashoʃth sahastrash: I
Naanaavidhaani divyaani naanaavarnaakruteeni ch II (11/5)
Pashyaadityaanvasoonrudraanashwinau marutastathaa I
Bahoonyadrushtapoorvaani pashyaashcharyaani Bhaarat II
(11/6)
Ihaikastham jagatkrutsnam pashyaadya sacharaacharam I
Mam dehe Gudaakesh yachchaanyaddrashtumichchhasi II
(11/7)

Pashyam (look) Me (My) Paarth (Arjun) Roopaani (of appearances) Shatash: (hundreds) Ath (now) Sahastrash: (thousands)I Naanaa Vidhaani (of different types) Divyaani (divine) Naanaa (various) Varnaa (colors) Aakruteeni (forms) ch (and)II (11/5)

Pashya (see) Aadityaan (12 sons of Aditi & Kashyap) Vasoon (8 Vasu) Rudraan (11 Rudr) Ashwinau (two Ashwineekumaars) Marut: (49 winds) Tathaa (and also; as well as)I Bahooni (many) Adrusht (never seen) Poorvaani (earlie) Pashya (see) Aashcharyaani (of surprises, wonders) Bhaarat (Arjun)II (11/6)

Ih (this) Ekastham (situated in a small place) Jagat (universe) Krutsnam (entire) Pashya (see) Adya (now) Sacharaacharam (entire creation with all its moving or stationary constituents)I Mam (My) Dehe (in the body) Gudaakesh (Arjun) Yat (whatever) ch (and) Anyat (else) Drashtum (see) Ichchhasi (wish, desire)II (11/7)

God said:

"O Paarth (Arjun)! Look now at hundreds of thousands of My divine appearances in different types, of various colors, classes, races & shapes. (11/5)

"O Bhaarat (Arjun)! Look at Aaditya, Vasu, Rudr, the duo of Ashwineekumaars and different kinds of winds. See many surprises and wonders in My universal form, never seen before by anyone. (11/6)

O Gudaakesh (Arjun)! You are now at going to see that this entire universe with all its moving or stationary; animate or inanimate entities is situated in one small place in My enormous body. And you shall also see in it whatever else you wish to see with your own eyes. (11/7)

God is so much delighted with the simplicity and modesty of Arjun that He immediately accedes to his request to exhibit His Vishw Roop before him. In His delightful mood, He very briefly tells Arjun what he is going to see in few moments:

1. His innumerable divine forms, each differing in shape, kind, color, class, race and shape,

2. 33 Kinds of Devs consisting of Aaditya, Vasu, Rudr and Ashwinikumaars,

3. Different kinds of winds,

4. Great surprises and wonders which nobody has seen before,

5. Entire universe and its moving or non-moving entities known to mortal beings, situated in just one small corner of His huge body, and,

6. Whatever else he wishes to see in it.

Arjun had wanted to know about all **Vibhooti** of God in detail in 10/17-18, but Krishn described them in brief saying it was not possible to describe them in detail. Now He tells him to see with his own eyes in His Vishw Roop whatsoever he wants to see and know about His divine existences. For example, God had already described Aaditya, Vasu, Rudr, Marut etc. in 10/21 & 23 as His **Vibhooti**; but He tells him now to see them physically along with other demigods like Ashwineekumaars, the twin Demigod doctors.

CLARIFICATIONS:

1. *12 Aaditya, 8 Vasu, 11 Rudr and 2 Ashwineekumaars together constitute the group of 33 Koti Devs i.e. 33 kinds of principal Demigods of Hinduism. Since the word Koti also means 10 million (one Crore) in Sanskrit there is a widely prevalent myth among Hindus and others that there are 330 million Devs in Hinduism. Every Hindu must know it well that Koti means kinds here, not crores, because Hinduism sometimes becomes a subject of mockery by followers of other religions due to this myth.*

2. *Though 49 kinds of winds are described as God's Vibhooti, they are excluded from 33 principal Devs. The reason for it seems that they were originally born from Diti, the mother of Daityas but opted later to be in the service of Indr to repay his obligation to save them from destruction. In energy and opulence, however, they are equal to other Devs.*

God sees sincerity on Arjun's face and calls Arjun Gudaakesh to express His happiness on regaining his mastery over sleep, symbolic of delusion. He also tells him in advance here about many wonderful things he would be shortly seeing in His universal form, which he or anyone else never saw before. This is a caution sounded by God to him to remain calm and unperturbed while seeing its ferocity and wonders.

৵ৡ

God says it is difficult to see His Vishw Roop,
and helps Arjun to overcome it.

(11/8)

न तु मां शक्यसे द्रष्टुमनेनैव स्वचक्षुषा ।
दिव्यं ददामि ते चक्षुः पश्य मे योगमैश्वरम् ॥ ११/८॥

n tu maam shakyase drashtumanenaiv swachakshushaa I
Divyam dadaami te chakshu: pashya me yogamaishwaram II
(11/8)

N (not) tu (but) Maam (to Me) Shakyase (possible) Drashtum (see) Anen (by these) Ev (certainly) Swachakshushaa (with your normal human eyes)I Divyam (divine) Dadaami (confer) Te (to you) Chakshu: (eyes) Pashya (look, behold) Me (My) Yogam Aishwaram (God's mystic prowess & supreme opulence)II (11/8)

Nevertheless, it is certainly not possible for you to see Me (in Universal form) by your these human eyes. I therefore, confer divine vision on you by which you shall be able to behold My Yogam Aishwaram, the supreme opulence, grandeur & majesty of My mystic prowess, energy, knowledge, and bliss." (11/8)

The phrase **Pashya Me Yogam Aishwaram** had appeared in 9/5 earlier, where God told Arjun to behold His supreme opulence and mystic prowess & energy of His Yog, but Arjun did not show much interest there because of deluded state of his mind. Now that Arjun expressed a sincere desire in 11/3-4 to see the vast expanse of His supremacy, God readily agrees and asks him to look intently at the manifestation of His **Yogam Aishwaram** in His Universal form. Note that **Vibhooti,** mentioned earlier, are only representative samples of God's full **Yogam Aishwaram.**

SOME ADDITIONAL THOUGHTS ON DIVYA CHAKSHU, THE DIVINE VISION

Arjun expressed a genuine doubt in 11/4 about his ability to see God's universal form. God confirms his doubt by informing him that it is certainly not possible for anyone to see His vast expanse with normal eyes because divine eyes are required for it; and the next moment, He very kindly alleviates his disappointment by enabling him with divine eyes.

As mentioned in *Introduction*, Vyaas had blessed Sanjay also with divine vision before the war started in order to enable him to visualize what was happening in the battlefield of Kurukshetr and narrate it to Dhrutraashtr while sitting in Hastinaapur located about 250 km away. Now Krishn blessed Arjun with the same power to see His supreme, divine form. Some enthusiasts try to justify this divine vision by equating it to television of today but such attempts are childish. The divine vision bestowed on both these characters of Mahaabhaarat is actually much beyond the range of TV, as it enables them to visualize all the happenings in the past, present or future simultaneously at any or all locations of universe in the vast panoramic view as a whole or in part. Sanjay would admit later in his last speech in 18/74-77 that he too is benefitted by seeing God's **Vishw Roop** besides Arjun.

Moral: *We need clear, virtuous vision, free from bias and prejudice, to feel divine presence within us, and outside in the universe.*

੭°੬

God then exhibits His divine form and Yog to Arjun.

(11/9)

सञ्जय उवाच
एवमुक्त्वा ततो राजन्महायोगेश्वरो हरिः ।
दर्शयामास पार्थाय परमं रूपमैश्वरम् ॥ ११/९॥

Sanjay Uvaach
Evamuktwaa tato raajanMahaayogeshwaro Hari: I
Darshayaamaas Paarthaay paramam roopamaishwaram II
(11/9)

Evam (thus) Uktwaa (having told) tat: (then) Raajan (king Dhrutraashtr) MahaaYogeshwar: (Krishn) Hari: (Krishn, incarnation of Lord Vishnu, emancipator of sins & troubles)I Darshayaamaas (displayed) Paarthaay (to Arjun) Paramam (supreme) roopam (appearance) Aishwaram (majesty, grandeur)II (11/9)

Sanjay said:

"O King (Dhrutraashtr)! Having spoken thus, Krishn, the Supreme Master and Lord of Yog and an incarnation of Lord Vishnu, immediately showed His Roopam Aishwaram, the supremely divine universal form displaying His splendor, majesty & grandeur to Arjun, the son of Pruthaa. (11/9)

Sanjay is thrilled so much of getting the unasked for opportunity to see God's universal form along with Arjun that in his zeal he adds **Mahaa** to an already superlative word **Yogeshwar** which would literally mean the greatest of the Masters and Lords of Yog. Later, when he would be better composed, he shall use **Yogeshwar** for Krishn in 18/78 the last shlok of Gita.

☙✶❧

Sanjay describes the majesty and beauty
of God's universal form to Dhrutraashtr.

(11/10, 11, 12 & 13)

अनेकवक्त्रनयनमनेकाद्भुतदर्शनम् ।
अनेकदिव्याभरणं दिव्यानेकोद्यतायुधम् ॥ ११/१ ० ॥
दिव्यमाल्याम्बरधरं दिव्यगन्धानुलेपनम् ।
सर्वाश्चर्यमयं देवमनन्तं विश्वतोमुखम् ॥ ११/११॥
दिवि सूर्यसहस्रस्य भवेद्युगपदुत्थिता ।
यदि भाः सदृशी सा स्याद्भासस्तस्य महात्मनः ॥११/१२॥
तत्रैकस्थं जगत्कृत्स्नं प्रविभक्तमनेकधा ।
अपश्यद्देवदेवस्य शरीरे पाण्डवस्तदा ॥ ११/१३॥

Anekvaktranayanamanekaadbhutdarshanam I
Anekdivyaabharanam divyaanekodyataayudham II (11/10)

Divyamaalyaambardharam divyagandhaanulepanam I
Sarvaashcharyamayam devamanantam Vishwtomukham
(11/11)
Divi sooryasahastrasya bhavedyugapadutthitaa I
Yadi bhaa: sadrushee saa syaadbhaasastasya Mahaatman: II
(11/12)
Tatraikastham jagatkrutsnam pravibhaktamanekdhaa I
ApashyaddevDevasya shareere Paandavastadaa II (11/13)

Anek (many) Vaktr (mouths) Nayanam (eyes) Anek (many) Adbhut (wonderful) Darshanam (appearances)I Anek (many) divya Aabharanam (divine ornaments) divya (divine) Anek (many) Udyataayudham (wielding weapons)II (11/10)

Divya Maalyaa Ambar Dharam (wearing divine garlands & garments) Divya Gandhaa (divine fragrances) Anulepanam (smearance)I Sarv (all sorts of) Aashcharya Mayam (full of amazements) Devam (God) Anantam (endless) Vishwtomukham (facing entire universe from all sides in Universal form) (11/11)

Divi (in the sky, heaven) Soorya Sahastrasya (of thousands of suns) Bhavet (be there) Yugapat (simultaneously, together) Utthitaa (rise)I Yadi (if) Bhaa: (brilliance, radiance) Sadrushee (matching) Saa (that) Syaat (be) Bhaas: (brilliance, radiance) Tasya (his) Bhaas: (brilliance, radiance)II (11/12)

Tatr (there) Ekastham (situated in one small place) Jagat (universe) Krutsnam (entire) Pravibhaktam (divided) Anek dhaa (into many)I Apashyat (could see) Dev Devasya (God of devs) Shareere (in body) Paandav: (Arjun) Tadaa (then)II (11/13)

Then Paandav (Arjun) saw there the universal figure of the Supreme God of all Demigods with whole universe including all of its divisions & diversities situated in a small place in His body. He has many mouths and eyes and many wonderful appearances. His whole body is smeared with divine fragrances. He wears many divine garlands & garments and is decorated with many divine ornaments. He wields many divine weapons in many hands. He is full of all sorts of amazements; and He is facing entire universe on all sides with His ultimate, endless universal form. The brilliance of this manifestation of Supreme

Soul is such that even if thousands of suns rise and shine simultaneously in the sky, the brilliance produced by them shall not match it at all. (11/11, 12 & 13)

The adjective **Divya**, the divine used repeatedly in this chapter depicts divinity of God, not of Demigods. It represents the supreme opulence of God to which none of other gods can match. As the glow of billions of stars cannot match the glow of sun in the space, similarly innumerable suns also can never match the brilliance of God's universal appearance. The radiance and heat of even the one sun, which shines on our earth, is unbearable especially in the summer months. Sunburns are very common even in people living in cold countries. It is therefore impossible for us to imagine the brilliance & heat generated if thousands of suns rise at the same time. God's glorious form outshines cumulative radiance of billion suns, but it is cool & soothing to the eyes of the beholder.

৵৽৽৶

Sanjay describes the condition of Arjun on seeing God in His Vishw Roop.

(11/14)

ततः स विस्मयाविष्टो हृष्टरोमा धनंजयः ।
प्रणम्य शिरसा देवं कृताञ्जलिरभाषत ॥ १ १/१ ४॥

Tat: s vismayaavishto hrushtaromaa Dhananjay: I
Pranamya shirsaa devam krutaanjalirbhaashat II (11/14)

Tat: (then) S: (he, that) Vismay Aavisht: (awestruck by amazement) Hrusht Romaa (body hairs raised due to thrill, ecstasy) Dhananjay: (Arjun)I Pranamya (bowing in obeisance) Shirsaa (with head & shoulders) Devam (God) Krutaanjali: (with folded hands) Bhaashat (began to speak)II (11/14)

Awestruck by amazement and with body hairs raised due to thrill, Dhananjay (Arjun) then bowed with head and shoulders bent in obeisance to the grand appearance of God and began speaking with folded hands." (11/14)

Hrusht Romaa means raising of body hairs of a person. It is same as **Rom Harsh** used by Arjun earlier in 1/29. The body hairs of a person raise under two types of emotions: one when fear possesses him, and the other when overwhelmed with joy on encountering something wonderful. Arjun's body hairs raised in 1/29 due to fear and horror of imminent destruction in war, but his body hairs raise now due to the ecstasy and pleasure of looking at the wondrous universal form of God. Similarly, Sanjay described Arjun in 2/1 as **Krupayaa Aavisht** i.e. possessed with cowardice and compassion towards his relatives, but now he sees him **Vismay Aavisht** i.e. awestruck by the vast expanse and beauty of God's universal form, bowing calmly with head & shoulders bent in devotion, and praying before Him.

Dev denotes Supreme God here, not any of the demigods here.

Morals:

1. *This exactly is the change one should feel within himself after studying 10 chapters of Gita. When an extremely stressed Arjun could get rid of his stress after listening to 10 chapters there is no reason why we, never subjected to such intense stress in life, should not benefit from it.*

2. *When a person bows head, he symbolically surrenders his ego. This body posture described above is the typical Hindu way of showing respect and devotion to great, venerable personalities or God by surrendering ego to Him with total humility and modesty. Since Arjun has realized Krishn as God by now, he bows before Him in this way.*

৶৹৵

Overwhelmed Arjun starts describing what he sees in the Grand Universal appearance of God with hands folded and head bent in humility.

(11/15, 16 & 17)

अर्जुन उवाच
पश्यामि देवांस्तव देव देहे सर्वांस्तथा भूतविशेषसंघान् ।

ब्रह्माणमीशं कमलासनस्थमृषींश्च सर्वानुरगांश्च दिव्यान् ॥ ११/१५॥
अनेकबाहूदरवक्त्रनेत्रं पश्यामि त्वां सर्वतोऽनन्तरूपम् ।
नान्तं न मध्यं न पुनस्तवादिं पश्यामि विश्वेश्वर विश्वरूप ॥ ११/१६॥
किरीटिनं गदिनं चक्रिणं च तेजोराशिं सर्वतो दीप्तिमन्तम् ।
पश्यामि त्वां दुर्निरीक्ष्यं समन्ताद्दीप्तानलार्कद्युतिमप्रमेयम् ॥ ११/१७॥

Arjun Uvaach

Pashyaami devaanstav dev dehe
sarvaanstathaa bhootavisheshasanghaan I
Brahmaanameesham Kamalaasanastham-
rusheenshch sarvaanuragaanshch divyaan II (11/15)
Anekabaahoodaravaktranetram
pashaami twaam sarvato∫nantroopam I
Naantam n madyam n punastawaadim
pashyaami Vishweshwar Vishwaroop II (11/16)
Kireetinam gadinam chakrinam ch
tejoraashim sarvato deeptimantam I
Pashyaami twaam durnireekshyam samantaaddeepta-
analaarkadyutimaprameyam II (11/17)

Pashyaami (look) Devaan (Demigods) Tav (your) Dev (God) Dehe
(in body) Sarvaan (all) Tathaa (and) Bhoot Vishesh Sanghaan (vivid
groups of living beings)I Brahmaanam (Brahmaas) Eesham (Shivs)
Kamalaasanastham (seated on lotuses) Rusheen (great sages) ch
(and) Sarvaan (all) Uragaan (serpents) ch (and) divyaan (divine)II
(11/15)

Anek (many) Baahu (arms) Udar (abdomens, bellies) Vaktr
(mouths) Netram (eyes) Pashaami (see) Twam (you) Sarvat: (on all
sides) Anant (endless) Roopam (forms)I N (neither) Antam (end)
n (nor) Madyam (middle) n (nor) Pun: (also) Tav (your) Aadim
(beginning) Pashyaami (see) Vishweshwar (Krishn, Lord of universe)
Vishw Roop (universal form)II (11/16)

Kireetinam (wearing a crown) Gadinam (holding a mace)
Chakrinam (having a discus) ch (and) Tejoraashim (extremely
lustrous with majesty) Sarvat: (on all sides) Deeptimantam (glittering

with brightness)I Pashyaami (see) Twam (you) Durnireekshyam (very difficult to see) Samantaat (from all sides) Deept Anal Ark Dyutim (blazing with fire & glowing like the sun) Aprameyam (immeasurable, unlimited; also that which does not need any proof & beyond argument)II (11/17)

Arjun said:

"O God! I see in your body all Demigods and similarly all the vivid groups of living beings; and Brahmaa, the Lord of creation, seated on a lotus as well as Shiv, the Lord of annihilation and also all the great sages and also all divine serpents. (11/15)

O Vishweshwar (Krishn, Supreme Lord of the world)! I see You with many arms, abdomens, mouths and eyes on all sides of Your endless form. O Vishw Roop (Krishn, Supreme manifestation of universe)! I see neither Your end, nor middle, nor the beginning. (11/16)

I see You wearing crowns on Your heads, holding maces and discuses in Your hands. You are glittering with brightness of Your extremely lustrous majesty on all sides. It is extremely difficult for me to see and discern Your immeasurable, incomparable form blazing with fire and glowing like sun. (11/17)

Besides seeing Brahmaa, Lord of creation and Shiv, Lord of destruction, Arjun also sees Lord Vishnu, the third among divine Trinity, holding His divine mace named Kaumodinee in one hand and His discus named Sudarshan Chakr in another hand, and wearing a crown on His head. Krishn too calls these divine weapons often to kill wicked, vicious people like Shishupaal, Dantavakr, Bhaumaasur, Paundrak etc. in Mahaabhaarat and Shreemad Bhaagawat. Seeing the trinity of Brahmaa, Shiv and Vishnu in God's Universal Form symbolizes that supreme Godhead is the primary source of creation, maintenance and destruction of the universe. Sanjay had seen God with many mouths and eyes in 11/10. Besides many mouths and eyes, Arjun also sees God having many arms and abdomens in 11/16.

Apramey means that which is dimensionless and therefore, immeasurable. It also means something incomparable, not needing any proof for its existence for it is self-proven, and which is beyond any kind of argument. God only, nothing else in the universe, is **Apramey**. Hence any debate about God's existence is as meaningless as someone questioning his mother about own birth and existence. To know God in entirety is as impossible as a fish trying to measure the expanse and depth of the ocean though it lives in it. Scriptures try to explain universal form of God to some extent with the simile of sky that also is without any beginning, middle or end. As no mathematician can find the value of infinity or zero, similarly God's Vishw Roop is inaccessible.

Clarification: *Though Krishn did manifest His grand form in the court of Hastinaapur to threaten Duryodhan and also at few more places in Mahaabhaarat, the universal form shown to Arjun here is the most outstanding, unique and complete than any other as stated by none other than Him from 11/5 to 8 in the beginning of this chapter. This shows His extreme love for Arjun, His dearest friend & devotee.*

ॐ

(11/18, 19 & 20)

त्वमक्षरं परमं वेदितव्यं त्वमस्य विश्वस्य परं निधानम् ।
त्वमव्ययः शाश्वतधर्मगोप्ता सनातनस्त्वं पुरुषो मतो मे ॥११/१८॥
अनादिमध्यान्तमनन्तवीर्यमनन्तबाहुं शशिसूर्यनेत्रम् ।
पश्यामि त्वां दीप्तहुताशवक्त्रं स्वतेजसा विश्वमिदं तपन्तम् ॥११/१९॥
द्यावापृथिव्योरिदमन्तरं हि व्याप्तं त्वयैकेन दिशश्च सर्वाः ।
दृष्ट्वाद्भुतं रूपमुग्रं तवेदं लोकत्रयं प्रव्यथितं महात्मन् ॥११/२०॥

Twamaksharam paramam veditavyam
twamasya Vishwasya param nidhaanam I
Twamavyay: shaashwatadharmagoptaa
sanaatanastwam Purusho mato me II (11/18)
Anaadimadyaantamanantaveeryam-

anantabaahum shashisooryanetram I
Pashyaami twaam deeptahutaashavaktram
swatejasaa Vishwamidam tapantam II (11/19)
Dyaavaapruthivyoridamantaram hi
vyaaptam twayaiken dishashch sarvaa: I
Drushtwaadbhutam roopamugram tavedam
lokatrayam pravyathitam Mahaatman II (11/20)

Twam (you) Aksharam (imperishable) Paramam (ultimate, extreme) Veditavyam (the only one worth knowing) Twam (you) Asya (this) Vishwasya (of universe) Param (extreme) Nidhaanam (repository, resting place)I Twam (you) Avyay: (inexhaustible) Shaashwat Dharm Goptaa (eternal protector of Dharm) Sanaatan: (primeval) Twam (you) Purush: (Supreme Soul) Mat: (opinion) Me (my)II (11/18)

Anaadi (without a beginning) Madya (middle) Antam (end) Anant Veeryam (with infinite vigor) Anant Baahum (with innumerous arms) Shashi Soorya Netram (with eyes of Moon & Sun)I Pashyaami (see) Twaam (from you) Deept Hutaash Vaktram (blazing with flames of fire emitting from Your mouths) Swatejasaa (with your radiant energy) Vishwam (to universe) Idam (this) Tapantam (burning)II (11/19)

Dyaavaa (from heaven) Pruthivyo: (to earth) Idam (this) Antaram (intervening space) Hi (only) Vyaaptam (are pervaded) Twayaa (by you) Eken (only one) Dish: (directions) ch (and) Sarvaa: (all) I Drushtwaa (by seeing) Adbhutam (wonderful) Roopam (forms) Ugram (fierce, terrible) Tav (your) Idam (this) Lok Trayam (three worlds) Pravyathitam (extremely distressed) Mahaatman (Krishn) II (11/20)

You are the ultimate, imperishable Supreme Spirit, the only One worth knowing. You are the ultimate foundation on which this entire universe rests. You are the eternal protector of Dharm. According to me, You are inexhaustible, eternal & most primeval person, the Supreme Soul. (11/18)

You are without any beginning, or end or middle. You have infinite strength and vigor. You have innumerous arms; and You have the moon and the sun as Your eyes. I also observe that the blazing flames of fire, emitting from Your (many) mouths due to Your own energy and vigor, are burning entire universe. (11/19)

O Mahaatman (Krishn, the Supreme Soul)! The heaven, the earth and the intervening space between them; and all the directions are pervaded by You, the only one. All the three worlds are extremely distressed by looking at Your very amazing and fearsome appearance. (11/20)

Dharm was explained in 4/7-8 as the eternal power, which a person lays hold of, and which holds together sacred institutions like law, justice, morality; and the role of nature; **Karm**, the action and all righteous, virtuous things in an individual's life, and in a society. **Shaashwat Dharm Goptaa** meaning the eternal promulgator & protector of **Dharm** confirms what God proclaimed in 4/7-8 saying that He would appear every time to protect eternal **Dharm** whenever it would be endangered to perish. Arjun did not show any enthusiasm to understand what God said there due to his deluded condition. He confesses his understanding of **Dharm** now.

Moral: *God is the ultimate protector of Dharm. Whoever is engaged in protecting Dharm, he is fulfilling the work of God with His power as per His supreme will.*

Buddh also is addressed very often as **Shaashwat Dharm Goptaa** in the scriptures of Buddhism as it believes that he revived eternal **Dharm** from the clutches of hypocrisy that prevailed in his time. Most Hindus therefore consider him as an Avatar of God.

Clarification: *I had described fourteen Loks in 8/16 as parts of three main categories called Urdhw, the upper, Madhya, the middle and Adh, the lower. In 11/20, Arjun also refers to the same three main categories of Loks as heaven, the upper worlds, the earth, and Paataal, the lower, subterranean worlds by using Lok Trayam i.e. the three worlds.*

God's omnipresence is beautifully described in **Dyaavaa Pruthivyaa ......Dishashch Sarvaa** which says that He is the only one who pervades everywhere i.e. this world; all the worlds above (and below) it; the space in between them; and also all the directions. **Dish: Sarvaa** meaning all the directions refers to ten directions known to human beings. They are East, South, West, North, northeast, southeast, south-west, north-west; and above & below. Mundak Upanishad emphasizes this idea in 2/2/11:

'ब्रह्मैवेदं अमृतं पुरस्तात् ब्रह्म पश्चात् ब्रह्म दक्षिणतः
उत्तरश्च । अधश्चोर्ध्वं च प्रसृतं ब्रह्मैवेदं विश्वमिदं वरिष्ठम् ॥'

(All that is in the front is nothing but Brahm, the Immortal One. Brahm is also at the back as He is on the right and the left. He extends above and below too. This world is nothing but Brahm, the Noblest One)

(11/21 & 22)

अमी हि त्वां सुरसंघा विशन्ति केचिद्भीताः प्राञ्जलयो गृणन्ति ।
स्वस्तीत्युक्त्वा महर्षिसिद्धसंघाः स्तुवन्ति त्वां स्तुतिभिः पुष्कलाभिः ॥११/२१॥
रुद्रादित्या वसवो ये च साध्या विश्वेऽश्विनौ मरुतश्चोष्मपाश्च ।
गन्धर्वयक्षासुरसिद्धसंघा वीक्षन्ते त्वां विस्मिताश्चैव सर्वे ॥११/२२॥

Amee hi twaam surasanghaa vishanti
Kechidbheetaa: praanjalayo grunanti I
Swasteetyukwaa maharshisiddhasanghaa:
stuvanti twaam stutibhi: pushkalaabhi: II (11/21)
Rudraadityaa vasavo ye ch saadyaa
vishve∫shwinau marutshchoshmapaashch I
Gandharvayakshaasurasiddhsanghaa
veekshante twaam vismitaashchaiv sarve II (11/22)

Amee (all those) hi (even) twaam (in you) sur (Demigods) sanghaa: (groups of) vishanti (entering into) kechit (some of them) bheetaa: (afraid) praanjalay: (with folded hands) grunanti (are praying)I Swasti (benedictions) Iti (like this) uktwaa (saying) maharshi (great sages) siddh (great accomplishers in spiritual realm) sanghaa: (groups of) stuvanti (singing hymns, praying) twaam (of you) stutibhi: (prayers, hymns of praise) pushkalaabhi: (abundant, excellent)II (11/21)

Rudr (group of 11 Rudrs) aadityaa: (12 Demigod sons of Aditi & Kashyap) vasav: (8 Vasus) ye (who) ch (and) Saadyaa: (groups of 12 Saadyaa) vishve (group of 10 Vishve Devs) ashwinau (twin Ashwineekumaars) marut: (49 Demigods forms of wind) ch (and) ooshmapaa: (7 groups of deceased forefathers) ch (and)I Gandharva (heavenly minstrels and musicians) yaksh (descendents & attendants of Kuber) asur (demonic people like Daityas, Raakshasas, Daanavs) siddh (accomplished in Yog) sanghaa: (groups of) veekshante (staring with eyes wide open) twaam (in you) vismitaa: (surprised) ch (and) ev (also) sarve (all)II (11/22)

Even all those groups of Demigods are entering into You and some of them, frightened by Your form, are praying to You with folded hands. Moreover, groups of great sages and other great spiritual accomplishers are profusely exclaiming benedictions like 'Victory to Thee', 'Glory to Thee', 'Peace to everyone' etc., and singing many excellent hymns in Your praise. (11/21)

All those groups of Rudr, Aaditya, Vasu, Saadyaa, Vishve Dev, the twin Ashwineekumaars, Marut, Pitr, Gandharv, Yaksh, Asur and Siddh also are staring at You with eyes wide open in amazement. (11/22)

Though God briefly told Arjun in 11/6 to see Aaditya, Vasu, Rudr, Ashwinwwkumaars and Marut in Him, Arjun also sees many others like Saadhyaa, Vishwe Dev, Pitr, Gandharv, Yaksh, Asur and Siddh besides them in the service of God. Among them, we have already discussed **Rudr** and **Vasu** in 10/23 & 11/6; **Yaksh** and **Raakshas** (called **Asur** here) in 10/23; **Aaditya** and **Marut** in 10/21 & 11/6; **Ashwineekumaars** in 11/6; **Pitr** (called **Ooshmapaa** here) in 10/29; **Siddh** in 7/3, and **Gandharv** in 10/26 earlier. Readers may like to refer there to refresh themselves. **Saadyaa**[1]

---

1 *Vaayu Puraan 66/15 & 16 mentions 12 Saadyaa as Man, Anumantaa, Praan, Nar, Yaan, Chitti, Hay, Nay, Hans, Naaraayan, Prabhav and Vibhu.*

are the groups of great people seeking salvation, and **Vishve Devs**[2] are the remaining demigods not named here but exist. **Ooshm** means hot; **Pitr** are called **Ooshmapaa** here since they accept only the freshly cooked hot food offered to them in oblation by their descendents on **Shraaddh** (death anniversary) days. Manu Smruti names them as Somasad, agnishwaatt, Barhishad, Somapaa, Havisgmaan, Aajyapaa and Sukalin. **Asur** are just the opposites of **Sur**, the Demigods i.e. the righteous people. This word, therefore, also includes **Daitya, Raakshas, Daanav** and all evil spirited, demonic, fiendish, wicked people who are enemies of Demigods, righteous people and sages. They always indulge in **Adharm** and destroy eternal **Dharm** by any means. Gita would describe their nature in chapter 16 as **Aasuree** wealth in many verses. We would go through them in detail there.

All people mentioned above, and others not mentioned above, are standing with hands folded in veneration before this fearsome form of God, never seen before by them; and praying to re-establish calm and peace allover. Upanishads describe one beautiful prayer quoted below for all-round peace:

ॐ द्यौः शान्तिरन्तरिक्षं शान्तिः
पृथिवी शान्तिरापः शान्तिरोषधयः शान्तिः ।
वनस्पतयः शान्तिर्विश्वेदेवाः
शान्तिर्ब्रह्म शान्तिः सर्वं शान्तिः
शान्तिरेव शान्तिः सा मा शान्तिरेधि ॥
ॐ शान्तिः शान्तिः शान्तिः ॥

{Unto the heaven be peace; unto the sky and the earth be peace; peace be unto the water; unto the herbs and the trees be peace; unto all the gods be peace; unto Brahm, the Supreme Being and unto all His creations be peace; and may we realize that peace. Om! Peace (to body) Peace (to mind & heart) and Peace (to Soul)}

ॐ

---

2   *Vaayu Puraan 66/31 & 32 also mentions 10 Vishve Devs as Kratu, Daksh, Shrava, Satya, Kaal, Kaam, Dhuni, Kuruwaan, Prabhwaan and Richwaan.*

Now, Arjun sees the fearsome part of God's Vishw Roop.

(11/23, 24 & 25)

रूपं महत्ते बहुवक्त्रनेत्रं महाबाहो बहुबाहूरुपादम् ।
बहूदरं बहुदंष्ट्राकरालं दृष्ट्वा लोकाः प्रव्यथितास्तथाहम् ॥ ११/२३॥
नभःस्पृशं दीप्तमनेकवर्णं व्यात्ताननं दीप्तविशालनेत्रम् ।
दृष्ट्वा हि त्वां प्रव्यथितान्तरात्मा धृतिं न विन्दामि शमं च विष्णो ॥ ११/२४॥
दंष्ट्राकरालानि च ते मुखानि दृष्ट्वैव कालानलसन्निभानि ।
दिशो न जाने न लभे च शर्म प्रसीद देवेश जगन्निवास ॥ ११/२५॥

Roopam mahatte bahuvaktranetram

Mahaabaaho bahubaahoorupaadam I

Bahoodaram bahudanshtraakaraalam drushtwaa

lokaa: pravyathitaastathaaham II (11/23)

Nabh: sprusham deeptamanekavarnam

vyaattaananam deeptavishaalanetram I

Drushtwaa hi twaam pravyathitaantaraatmaa

dhrutim n vindaami shamam ch Vishno II (11/24)

Danshtraakaraalaani ch te mukhaani

drushtvaiv kaalaanalasannibhaani I

Disho n jaane n labhe ch sharm

praseed Devesh Jaganniwaas II (11/25)

Roopam (form, shape) Mahat (stupendous) te (they) Bahu (multitudinous) vaktr (mouths) netram (eyes) Mahaabaaho (Krishn) Bahu (many) baahu (arms) uru (thighs) paadam (feet)I Bahu (many) udaram (abdomens, bellies) Bahu (many) danshtraa (teeth, especially the molars; also tusks) karaalam (fiercely projecting) drushtwaa (by looking at) lokaa: (all the worlds, people) pravyathitaa: (are terribly upset, extremely distressed) Tathaa (as well as) aham (I)II (11/23)

Nabh: (the sky) sparsham (touching) deeptam (brilliant, glowing) anek (many) varnam (colors, forms) vyaatt (gaping) aananam (faces, mouths) deept (brilliant, glowing) vishaal (broad, vast, huge, grand) netram (eyes)I Drushtwaa (by seeing at) hi (because) twaam (you) pravyathit (are extremely tormented) antaraatmaa (innermost self) dhrutim (steadfastness) n (not) vindaami (find) shamam (tranquility of mind) ch (and) Vishno (Krishn)II (11/24)

Danshtraa (teeth, especially the molars) karaalaani (fiercely protruding) ch (and) te (your) mukhaani (from mouths) drushtwaa (by looking at) ev (also) kaalaanal (the fire causing end of universe) sannibhaani (as if)I Dish: (directions) n (neither) jaane (sense) n (nor) labhe (get) ch (and) sharm (bliss, prosperity) praseed (be gracious, kind) Devesh (Krishn) Jaganniwaas (Krishn)II (11/25)

O Mahaabaaho (Krishn)! People in all the worlds as well as I also are terribly upset by seeing Your stupendous appearance which has multitudinous mouths, eyes, arms, thighs, feet, bellies and fiercely projecting teeth and tusks. (11/23)

O Vishno (Krishn, an incarnation of Lord Vishnu)! I am also losing my mental peace and steadfastness since my inner self is extremely distressed on seeing You in many colors and forms touching the sky and glowing with gaping mouths and very large, brilliant eyes. (11/24)

When I look at the teeth menacingly protruding from Your frightening mouths ablaze with fire as if ready to cause the end of universe, I neither have the sense of direction nor do I find any comfort. Please be gracious to me O Devesh (Krishn, the supreme Lord of all gods)! O Jaganniwaas (Krishn, the ultimate abode & refuge of the universe)! (11/25)

Arjun observed only the sober part of God's Vishw Roop until 11/22, but he becomes greatly disturbed when his eyes fall on the frightening part of His form now where he sees:

1. Many legs, chests, numerous teeth protruding fiercely from many mouths besides many hands, mouths, bellies and eyes seen earlier,

2. His multicolored body with multiple shapes piercing the sky, and emitting heat and flames,

3. Many mouths wide open, spewing fire to engulf everything in the fire,

4. His eyes widened with anger and blazing with fire and,

5. Death and fire are joining to annihilate everything together.

Though God had sounded a caution to Arjun in 11/6 to remain calm and quiet, it becomes impossible for him to maintain his balance of mind on seeing His universal form, which is fearsome, far beyond his imagination. He loses his bearings and composure and observes that even all the great **Devs, Siddhs** & others, whom he is seeing in the presence of God there, are perturbed greatly by it. He requests Krishn to be merciful and kind to him.

Mahaabbaaho: Mahaabhaarat says in 5/70/9, 'बाहुभ्याम रोदसी बिभ्रन्महाबाहुरिति स्मृतः' i.e. Krishn is the incarnation of God who holds earth and sky in their positions by His both hands. Hence He is called Mahaabaaho.

৵৹৻

Arjun sees more frightening and even hideous scenes in God's grand appearance.

(11/26, 27, 28, 29 & 30)

अमी च त्वां धृतराष्ट्रस्य पुत्राः सर्वे सहैवावनिपालसंघैः ।
भीष्मो द्रोणः सूतपुत्रस्तथासौ सहास्मदीयैरपि योधमुख्यैः ॥११/२६॥
वक्त्राणि ते त्वरमाणा विशन्ति दंष्ट्राकरालानि भयानकानि ।
केचिद्विलग्ना दशनान्तरेषु संदृश्यन्ते चूर्णितैरुत्तमाङ्गैः ॥११/२७॥
यथा नदीनां बहवोऽम्बुवेगाः समुद्रमेवाभिमुखा द्रवन्ति ।
तथा तवामी नरलोकवीरा विशन्ति वक्त्राण्यभिविज्वलन्ति ॥११/२८॥
यथा प्रदीसं ज्वलनं पतङ्गा विशन्ति नाशाय समृद्धवेगाः ।
तथैव नाशाय विशन्ति लोकास्तवापि वक्त्राणि समृद्धवेगाः ॥११/२९॥
लेलिह्यसे ग्रसमानः समन्ताल्लोकान्समग्रान्वदनैर्ज्वलद्भिः ।
तेजोभिरापूर्य जगत्समग्रं भासस्तवोग्राः प्रतपन्ति विष्णो ॥११/३०॥

Amee ch twaam Dhrutraashtrasya putraa:
sarve sahaivaavanipaalasanghai: I
Bheeshmo Dron: sootaputrastathaasau
sahaasmadeeyairapi yodhamukhyai: II (11/26)
Vaktraani te twaramaanaa vishanti
danshtraakaraalaani bhayaanakaani I
Kechidwilagnaa dashanaantareshu
sandrushyante choornitairuttamaangai: II (11/27)
Yathaa nadeenaam bahavoʃmbuvegaa:
samudramevaabhimukhaa dravanti I
Tathaa tawaamee naralokveeraa
vishanti vaktraanyabhivijwalanti II (11/28)
Yathaa pradeeptam jwalanam patangaa
Vishanti naashaay samruddhaveg: I
Tathaiv naashaay vishanti lokaas-
tavaapi vaktraani samruddhavegaa: II (11/29)
Lelihyase grasamaan: samantaallokaan-
samagraanvadanairjwaladbhi: I
Tejobhiraapoorya jagatsamagram
bhaasastavograa: pratapanti Vishno II (11/30)

Amee (all those) ch (and) twaam (you) Dhrutraashtrasya putraa:
(sons of Dhrutraashtr) sarve (all) sah (along with) ev (also) avanipaal
(kings) sanghai: (hordes, groups of)I Bheeshm: (Bheeshm) Dron:
(Dron) Sootputr: (Karn, the son of Saarathee) tathaa (and) asau (that)
sah (along with) asmadeeyai: (on our side) api (also) yodhmukhyai:
(chief warriors)II (11/26)

Vaktraani (in mouths) te (your) twaramaanaa: (hurtling, rushing
rapidly) vishanti (entering into) Danshtraa (teeth, the molars)
karaalaani (fiercely protruding) bhayaanakaani (very frightening)I
Kechit (some of them) vilagnaa: (stuck up) Dashanaa Antareshu (in
the gaps between your teeth) sandrushyante (are visible) choornitai:
(crushed) uttamaangai: (with heads, the best part of body)II (11/27)

Yathaa (like) nadeenaam (of the rivers) bahav: (many) ambu
(water) vegaa: (impetuous streams) samudram (ocean) ev (only)

abhimukhaa: (towards) dravanti (flow rapidly)I Tathaa (similarly) tav (your) amee (all those) nar lok veeraa (eminent warriors in the human society) vishanti (entering into) vaktraani (in mouths) abhivijwalanti (flaming, blazing)II (11/28)

Yathaa (as) pradeeptam (brilliant) jwalanam (flames) patangaa: (moths) Vishanti (flowing into) naashaay (for ruin) samruddh vegaa: (with full speed)I Tathaa (similarly) ev (also) naashaay (for destruction) vishanti (rushing to) lokaa: (people) tav (your) api (also) vaktraani (in mouths) samruddh vegaa: (speedily)II (11/29)

Lelihyase (licking relishly) gras Maan: (devouring) samantaat (in all directions) lokaan (people) samagraan (all) vadanai: (by mouths) jwaladbhi: (flaming)I Tejobhi: (by Tej) aapoorya (filling) jagat (universe) samagram (all) bhaas (light) 'tav (your) ugraa: (terrible) pratapanti (are scorching) Vishno (Krishn)II (11/30)

All those sons of Dhrutraashtr along with Bheeshm, Dron, Karn, the son of a Saarathee and hordes of other kings on their side, and the chief warriors on our side also; all of them are hurtling and entering into Your frightening mouths having fiercely protruding teeth. Moreover, some of them are stuck up in between your teeth with their heads crushed. (11/26 & 27)

As many impetuous water streams of rivers flow rapidly towards ocean, similarly all those warriors eminent in the human society are entering into Your flaming mouths. (11/28)

As moths rush speedily into the glowing flames of fire only to get destroyed in it, similarly all these people are also rushing into Your mouths for self destruction with full speed. (11/29)

O Vishno (Krishn, an incarnation of Lord Vishnu)! You are licking with relish all these people in all directions to devour them into Your flaming mouths. Your terrible energy is scorching entire universe; and the brightness is encompassing it with dazzle on all sides. (11/30)

Arjun first saw God's majestic form. Then, as he saw His fearsome form, he felt as if **Kaalaanal**, the fire of death has appeared before him. Even as he started speaking about it to God, **Kaalaanal** physically manifested itself before him in its most horrible, dreadful, obnoxious form. Arjun sees, not only all the Kauravs and their generals like Bheeshm, Dron, Karn etc., but also the kings and warriors on his side, in fact whosoever has come to fight in the war on either side[3], rushing hastily into God's gaping mouths with their once beautiful-looking heads and other body parts crushed, ground and stuck in His terrible teeth. They are flowing into God's blazing mouths as the rivers flow impatiently to meet their own end in the ocean; or as flying insects like moths etc. jump hastily into fire. God is putting them into His flaming mouths by licking them from all sides with his tongues, and chewing them with smack & taste. Everybody is terrified with God's terribly scorching energy and brightness spreading its dazzle and heat on all sides in whole world. Those, who feel emotionally disturbed on seeing a cat catching a dove and eating it, can realize the plight of Arjun on seeing his charming friend Krishn in this extremely dreadful unpleasant form.

Moral: *What does this loathsome description symbolize? It implies that death spares nobody, howsoever great he is. While all the great warriors are preparing to fight with the hope of victory and its great rewards, none of them knows that death is awaiting him just round the corner on any of the 18 days of war. No moment of precious human life is too early to stand on the side of Dharm and fight for it, not against it, because death is lurking in the shadow of life all the time to hit us at any moment.*

Lyricist Santosh Anand writes in film *Roti Kapadaa Aur Makaan*:

'समय की धारा में, उमर बह जानी है ।
जो घड़ी जी लेंगे, वही रह जानी है ॥'

(Life is flowing in the strong current of time. Only that moment, which we have lived properly, is truly ours)

---

3   *Out of 18 Akshauhinee (equal to 40 million approximately) persons engaged in the Great War, only ten namely Krishn, 5 Paandavs and Saatyaki on Paandav side, and Ashwatthaamaa, Krupaacharya and Krut Vermaa on Kaurav side could survive.*

Note that, even in his upset condition, Arjun gives two beautiful similes, one of rivers and the other of insects as explained here.

ॐ

Arjun requests God to tell him the purpose of
His so fearful appearance.

(11/31)

आख्याहि मे को भवानुग्ररूपो नमोऽस्तु ते देववर प्रसीद ।
विज्ञातुमिच्छामि भवन्तमाद्यं न हि प्रजानामि तव प्रवृत्तिम् ॥ ११/३१॥

Aakhyaahi me ko bhavaanugraroopo
namoʃstu te Devavar praseed I
Vijnaatumichchhaami bhavantamaadyam
n hi prajaanaami tav pravruttim II (11/31)

Aakhyaaahi (describe) me (to me) k: (who) bhavaan (you) ugra (terrible) roop: (form) nam: (bowing in obeisance) astu (be) te (to you) Devavar (Krishn) praseed (be gracious, kind, pleased)I Vijnaatum (to know in detail) Ichchhaami (wish) bhavantam (to you) aadyam (Krishn) n (not) hi (because) prajaanaami (be fully aware of) tav (your) pravruttim (characteristic disposition, mission)II (11/31)

Please describe to me who You are in this most frightening appearance. O Devavar (Krishn, the noblest of Devs)! Salutations to You! Please be kind & graceful to me. I wish to know all about You O Aadyam (Krishn, the Primeval One)! Because I neither know why You have appeared in this fierce form nor do I know what Your mission is, and how You wish to accomplish it." (11/31)

Stupefied by His magnanimous appearance and spell bound by His devastating energy, Arjun submits his request to Krishn to tell him who He really is, and what He intends to do now. If He is forecasting the result of the war by demonstrating annihilation of everybody, how He is going to implement it, especially when he is aware of His vow of not wielding any weapon in ensuing Mahaabhaarat war.

It appears that Arjun's request here, to let him know who He is, is twofold. Firstly, he wants to know all about the unborn unmanifested Supreme Soul existing since time immemorial; and secondly as Krishn, manifested before his eyes as a fierce person like a cyclone, a Tsunami, a devastating fire impatient to swallow & devour everything in its way and cause great destruction, ruin, pain & mass annihilation. The first One about whom Gita talked so far is the provider of eternal peace, whereas the second One whom Arjun is seeing now is the incarnation of death & mass destruction.

৶৶

Krishn describes His mission; and instruct Arjun to be instrumental in implementing it.

(11/32, 33 & 34)

श्रीभगवानुवाच

कालोऽस्मि लोकक्षयकृत्प्रवृद्धो लोकान्समाहर्तुमिह प्रवृत्तः ।
ऋतेऽपि त्वां न भविष्यन्ति सर्वे येऽवस्थिताः प्रत्यनीकेषु योधाः ॥११/३२॥
तस्मात्त्वमुत्तिष्ठ यशो लभस्व जित्वा शत्रून् भुङ्क्ष्व राज्यं समृद्धम् ।
मयैवैते निहताः पूर्वमेव निमित्तमात्रं भव सव्यसाचिन् ॥११/३३॥
द्रोणं च भीष्मं च जयद्रथं च कर्णं तथान्यानपि योधवीरान् ।
मया हतांस्त्वं जहि मा व्यथिष्ठा युध्यस्व जेतासि रणे सपत्नान् ॥११/३४॥

Shree Bhagawaan Uvaach
Kaalo∫smi lokakshayakrutpravruddho
lokaansamaahartumih pravrutt: I
Rute∫pi twaam n bhavishyanti sarve
ye∫vasthitaa: pratyaneekeshu yodhaa: II (11/32)
Tasmaattwamuttishth yasho labhaswa
jitwaa shatroon bhunkshwa raajyam samruddham I
Mayaivaite nihataa: poorvamev
nimittamaatram bhav Savyasaachin II (11/33)
Dronam ch Bheeshmam ch Jayadratham ch
Karnam tathaanyaanapi yodhaveeraan I

Mayaa hataanstwam jahi maa vyathishthaa
yudyasva jetaasi rane sapatnaan II (11/34)

Kaal: (Lord of death) asmi (am) lok kshay krut (destroyer of worlds) pravruddh: (grown) lokaan (of people, worlds) samaahartum (in destroying) Ih (this) pravrutt: (engaged, occupied, inclined) I Rite (without, except) api (even, certainly) twaam (you) n (not) bhavishanti (will be there in future) sarve (all) ye (those) avasthitaa: (arrayed) pratyaneekeshu (in opposite army) yodhaa: (warriors)II (11/32)

Tasmaat (refore) twaam (you) uttishth (get up) yash: (glory) labhaswa (gain) jitwaa (conquer) shatroon (enemies) bhunkshwa (consume) raajyam (kingdom) samruddham (prosperous)I Mayaa (by Me) ev (only) ete (all those) nihataa: (slain) poorvam (beforehand) ev (already) nimitt (instrumental; also means, cause) maatram (just) bhava (become) Savyasaachin (Arjun)II (11/33)

Dronam (Dron) ch (and) Bheeshmam (Bheesham) ch (and) Jayadratham (Jayadrath) ch (and) Karnam (Karn) tathaa (and) anyaan (others) api (also) yodh veeraan (warriors)I Mayaa (by Me) hataan (killed) twaam (you) jahi (vanquish) maa (do not) vyathishthaa: (be anguished) yudyasva (resolve to fight) jetaasi (shall win) rane (in battle) sapatnaan (to foes)II (11/34)

God said:

"I am the Lord of death, the destroyer of the worlds, grown (in this form) to undertake full destruction of all these people. All those warriors, arrayed in the army on the opposite side (as well as on this side), shall not be there certainly in near future even if you do not fight with them. (11/32)

Therefore, you must stand up, conquer your enemies, earn glory and enjoy this prosperous kingdom. O Savyasaachin (Arjun)! Since all of them are pre-destined by Me to be slain, you have to now become mere instrumental in implementing it. (11/33)

You must kill Dron, Bheeshm, Jayadrath, Karn as well as other warrior heroes who are already killed by Me. Do not

be anguished. Resolve to fight because you shall certainly vanquish your opponents in the battle." (11/34)

Raajyam Samruddham denotes not only the kingdom on earth but also *'The kingdom of God'* because the person who performs his duties merely as an instrument in carrying out work of God can never err, fail or fall. All works done in this spirit are guaranteed to be successful, perfect, and blissful.

Arjun had expressed a great doubt in 2/6 that it was not even certain who shall emerge victorious at the end of war. Krishn is allays his concern and builds up his confidence by assuring that his victory is a foregone conclusion since his opponents are already killed as witnessed by him in His **Vishw Roop** just now. With this assurance, He motivates him to take up the fight and savour the taste of victory, earn glory and enjoy the prosperous kindom of Hastinaapur on earth in his remaining life; and the eternal bliss of kingdom of God in afterlife for he fought in favor of **Dharm**. He addresses him as **Savyasaachin** to encourage him to rise up and demonstrate his extr-ordinary capability of shooting arrows with left hand also, a quality that none else possessed in Mahaabhaarat.

Kaal Asmi Lok Kshay Krut Pravruddh: God is the Lord who decides the time and cause of death of all the people in the world. He declares that He has appeared in the form of **Kaal** to destroy everybody present in the war. However, should God, who pronounced Himself as **Suhrud Sarv Bhootaanaam**, the benefactor of all beings in 5/29, do such dreadful thing to anybody? No! He simply appoints the time, means, place and a person (or cause) to implement an event predecided by His divine justice for every individual according to his **Karm** and **Karm Phal**. A **Nimitt** is therefore only an executive appointed to carry out His divine judgment. The act of a **Nimitt** is equivqlent to that of **Jallaad**, the executioner of capital punishment as per the order issued by the judge. In the war of Mahaabhaarat, God appoints Arjun (and people on his side) to be His **Nimitt** and carry out envisaged devastation of **Pratyaneekeshu** i.e. everyone in the opposite army. God orders Arjun to kill opposite army here because Arjun would not kill people on his own side. We should infer here that His divine will simultaneously motivates the warriors in Kaurav army also to annihilate Paandav army.

Clarification: *God normally appoints a Nimitt indirectly, but here He has to instruct Arjun directly to be His Nimitt and undertake fighting since he is the only person not willing to fight in the war. It is like a father ordering his unwilling son to do something. All others present there are already charged enough to work indirectly as God's Nimitt.*

I have tried to express this thought in three lines written by me as below:

माचिस की तीली जले किसी का घर जलाने के लिए ।
या फिर अंधकार में कोई दीप जगमगाने के लिए ॥
तीली! तेरी सार्थकता केवल जलने में है, जलती रह ॥॥

{A matchstick can burn to set someone's house on fire, or to light a lamp. O matchstick! Your only purpose of existence is in burning. Continue burning therefore, as long as you can (in the hands of the igniter)}

Two soldiers of opposite armies meet at the end of the day and talk to each other thus. First: Do you know why our kings are fighting? Second: Frankly speaking, I do not know. However, I know this much that it is our duty to follow the command of our kings and fight for them; and leave the worry of victory or defeat for them. The second soldier unknowingly revealed the reality of life that all of us are **Nimitt** in the hands of our Supreme Master. We have come to this world as actors to play roles in the grand theatre of God. It should not make any difference to an actor whether the director of the play assigns him the role of Lakshman or Meghnaad. We are like clay in the hands of God, the master potter. It is up to Him whether to carry his clay on head, or to pound it with feet, or put on wheel, or strike and mould with His hands, bake His clay pots in fire, give any pot to anybody free or for a price, break it raw & throw away; or select another lot of clay.

Moral: *We have to do the job allotted by God to us to the best of our ability and sincerity; and the result to His supreme desire.*

A pertinent question that arises here is:

QUESTION: WHY GOOD PEOPLE LIKE BHEESHM, DRON ETC. ON KAURAV SIDE, AND OTHERS ON PAANDAV SIDE SHOULD ALSO BE KILLED IN THE WAR?

It is because they too had come to fight not for the sake of **Dharm** but to serve their ego and self-interests like reward and protection from victor; or to settle their personal, political scores with opponents; or as relatives and friends to show their solidarity with them; or out of fear or an obligation. They are like proverbial *Ghun*, the weevil pests, thriving on wheat, and therefore destined to crushing & grinding to death along with wheat in the flourmill of battle between two sides. Only Krishn and Paandavs served the ideal of fighting against **Adharm**, and protecting **Dharm**.

Krishn mentions here only those whom Arjun likes very much namely Dron, his teacher, Bheeshm, his grand sire, and Jayadrath, the husband of his cousin sister Dushalaa; and Karn, who considers Arjun as his bitterest enemy and rival. This seems to be a deliberate attempt to withdraw him from **Raag**, the emotional relationships of attachment and **Dwesh**, the envy. Note that in actual war also, Arjun would not be able to fell Bheeshm and kill Jayadrath and Karn on his own without the guidance of Krishn.

"A person tells a Saadhu, standing on the bank of a river, to look at the speed with which the water of the river was flowing towards the sea. He then, also points towards the people moving rapidly towards their destination on the bridge above. Saadhu ponderously replies, 'If you observe minutely, you would see that not only water but the river itself is also flowing rapidly towards its end; similarly the bridge along with the men on it is also moving rapidly towards its ultimate destination".

Morals*:*

1. *God grants us premature success by declaring that when we are out to perform our duty in the most righteous & meritorious manner, the job is accomplished by God's divine will and power already. We have to just avail the occasion with good intention and become the means to execute it in the eyes of the world.*

It is neither our nature nor the capability which determines the action and reaction but the inspiration given to us by the will of Supreme Being. Gita tells us here to join ourselves in a work that His sheer will and nature has already accomplished. Men have to act simply as a bow & arrow in the hands of the Divine Archer who has preset the target.

2. *In order to qualify to carry out God's will we have to first condition ourselves by freeing from personal desire, attachment and will, enmity, hatred, antagonism and ego like a tool in the hands of a craftsman which is devoid of all these passions and feelings. We have to contribute simply our might as per the wish of Supreme Artist in creating the artifact for Lok Sangrah.*

Destruction is the preamble of any meaningful progress. We know that the great devastation caused by the earthquake in Gujarat in 2001 paved the way for the tremendous progress and transformation of affected areas like Kuchch, its most backward region earlier.

ज़माने का दस्तूर है ये पुराना ।
बना कर मिटाना मिटा कर बनाना ॥

(It is the age-old custom of the world to make and break; and destroy to remake)

Moral*: Everything in the universe is moving rapidly towards its ultimate end. However, one is free to choose his destination in two ways: physical death of his body at the hands of Kaal and be born again; or attain eternal, blissful abode of God through Yog.*

Creation and destruction are two sides of the same coin called universe. Let me explain it with the following legend from Matsya Puraan:

"God appears in the form of Matsya, a great fish before a devout king named Satya Vrat and informs him that Pralay, the Great Deluge would devastate everything on earth after seven days from now. He instructs him further to collect male and female specimen of every living entity and seeds of each kind of vegetation in a large boat and

wait for Him with patience. The king assiduously works for seven days to comply with God's will exactly as told and calmly waits in the boat for Him amidst threatening waters of deluge. When the Great Deluge swallows everything else except the king's boat, God appears as Matsya and rescues him with other inmates in the boat until the water recedes to its normal level again. In this way, Satya Vrat works simply as an agent of God to implement His supreme will to destroy and resurrect universe, without any ifs and buts from his side as a faithful king".

CAUTION: *If someone chooses abstention and behaves like an observer by ignoring God's will, it shall be implemented in any case without him but the inaction of such absconder shall be regarded as Anaaryam, ignoble, Aswargyam, leading to hell, Akeertikaram, the dishonor and klaibyam, the unmanliness, as Krishn cautioned Arjun in 2/2 & 3.*

Let us pause here for a while to recall that Gita is primarily a dialogue between Dhrutraashtr and Sanjay, in which latter narrates to former of what transpired in the battle of Kurukshetr. Normally speaking, Dhrutraashtr should have violently reacted on hearing such supposedly preposterous statement of Krishn that He has already killed all the warriors on Kaurav side, but he remained speechless. Why? It seems that on hearing this statement of Krishn, Dhrutraashtr loses his senses for he is a guilt ridden, morally weak person struck with profound grief due to fall of Bheeshm. He does not accept Krishn as God but is afraid of Him within his heart due to His mystic powers. It is due to this fear that he continues to listen to Sanjay without any reaction, holding the thin thread of hope of Arjun abandoning the battle and running away.

Moral: *A man with thousand lies & scheming mind may sometimes become worldly powerful but he is always weaker from inside than those who are on the righteous path of truth & duty.*

Sanjay describes condition of Arjun; and
how he prepares to respond to God.

(11/35)

सञ्जय उवाच

एतच्छ्रुत्वा वचनं केशवस्य कृताञ्जलिर्वेपमानः किरीटी ।
नमस्कृत्वा भूय एवाह कृष्णं सगद्गदं भीतभीतः प्रणम्य ॥११/३५॥

Sanjay Uvaach
Etachchhrutwaa vachanam Keshavasya
krutaanjalirvepamaan: Kireetee I
Namaskrutwaa bhooy evaah Krishnam
sagadgadam bheetabheet: pranamya II (11/35)

Etat (these) shrutwaa (on hearing) vachanam (speech) Keshavasya (of Krishn) krutaanjali: (with folded hands) vepamaan: (trembling) Kireetee (Arjun- who was crowned by Indr in recognition of services rendered to him)I Namaskrutwaa (bowed with obeisance) Bhoy: (again) ev (still) aah: (spoke) Krishnam (to Krishn) sagadgadam (in a faltering voice choked with emotion) bheetabheet: (frightened) pranamya (prostrated)II (11/35)

Sanjay said:

"On hearing these words of Krishn, Kireetee (Arjun), still trembling and frightened, prostrated and bowed before Krishn with hands folded in reverence and spoke thus to Him in a faltering voice choked with emotion." (11/35)

Sanjay calls Arjun as **Kireetee** to remind Dhrutraashtr of the honor he received from Indr, the lord of demigods, who crowned him with his divine crown in recognition of his victory over the enemies of **Devs**. **Vepamaan** is same as **Vepathu** in 1/29 and **Vikampitum** in 2/31, all of which mean trembling, quivering, shivering. Arjun told God in 11/24 also that his innermost faculties were extremely distressed and tormented on seeing His fearsome form. Sanjay confirms that the same Kireetee Arjun, whom Indr honored once for his extra ordinary valor, is trembling with fear and awe now.

Voice of Arjun is choked due to mixed emotions of fear of seeing His frightening form, by amazement, and by his reverence for Krishn as God.

☙❧

Arjun praises God in universal form.

(11/36)

अर्जुन उवाच
स्थाने हृषीकेश तव प्रकीर्त्या जगत्प्रहृष्यत्यनुरज्यते च ।
रक्षांसि भीतानि दिशो द्रवन्ति सर्वे नमस्यन्ति च सिद्धसंघाः ॥ ११/३६॥

Arjun Uvaach
Sthaane Hrusheekesh tav prakeertyaa
Jagatprahrushyatyanurajyate ch I
Rakshaansi bheetaani disho dravanti
Sarve namasyanti ch siddhsanghaa: II (11/36)

Sthaane (befittingly) Hrusheekesh (Krishn) tav (your) prakeertyaa (by fame) jagat (universe) prahrushyati (feel happy and joyous) anurajyate (loving, devoted) ch (and)I Rakshaansi (Raakshas, the fiendish, wicked people) bheetaani (frightened) dish: (directions) dravanti (running away helter-skelter) sarve (all) namasyanti (bowing with obeisance) ch (and) Siddh sanghaa: (groups of siddhs) II (11/36)

Arjun said:

"O Hrusheekesh (Krishn)! It is highly befitting of You that whole world becomes happy and joyous by devotion to Your name & fame; the groups of great accomplishers in spiritual realm are bowing before You in obeisance; and the fiendish, wicked persons are fleeing helter-skelter in all directions with fear. (11/36)

God informed Arjun in 11/32 that He has appeared as **Kaal** to annihilate all the wicked people. Because of His declaration, he sees demons & devils running here and there thinking that their death has appeared before them in personified form. He simultaneously feels happy to observe that groups of righteous people and great accomplishers of Yog are bowing before God with joy appreciating His initiative to relieve them from the tyranny of evil doers. Arjun calls Krishn Hrusheekesh, the Lord of sensory and functional organs as if requesting to calm down his internal and external faculties.

৯৵৶৶

Arjun sees the great expanse and supremacy
of God, and salutes Him repeatedly.

(11/37, 38, 39 & 40)

कस्माच्च ते न नमेरन्महात्मन् गरीयसे ब्रह्मणोऽप्यादिकर्त्रे ।
अनन्त देवेश जगन्निवास त्वमक्षरं सदसत्तत्परं यत् ॥ १ १ /३ ७॥
त्वमादिदेवः पुरुषः पुराणस्त्वमस्य विश्वस्य परं निधानम् ।
वेत्तासि वेद्यं च परं च धाम त्वया ततं विश्वमनन्तरूप ॥ १ १ /३ ८॥
वायुर्यमोऽग्निर्वरुणः शशाङ्कः प्रजापतिस्त्वं प्रपितामहश्च ।
नमो नमस्तेऽस्तु सहस्रकृत्वः पुनश्च भूयोऽपि नमो नमस्ते ॥ १ १ /३ ९॥
नमः पुरस्तादथ पृष्ठतस्ते नमोऽस्तु ते सर्वत एव सर्व ।
अनन्तवीर्यामितविक्रमस्त्वं सर्वं समाप्नोषि ततोऽसि सर्वः ॥ १ १ /४ ०॥

Kasmaachch te n nameranMahaatman
gareeyase brahmano∫pyaadikartre I
Anant Devesh Jaganniwaas
twamaksharam sadasattatparam yat II (11/37)
Twamaadidev: purush: Puraanastwam-
asya Vishwsya param nidhaanam I
Vettaasi vedyam ch param ch dhaam
twayaa tatam Vishwmanantaroop II (11/38)
Vaayuryamo∫gnirvarun: shashaank:
Prajaapatistwam prapitaamahashch I
Namo namaste∫stu sahastrakrutw:
punashch bhooyo∫pi namo namaste II (11/39)
Nam: purastaadath prushthataste

namoʃstu te sarvat ev sarv I
Anantaveeryaamitvikramastwam
sarvam samaapnoshi tatoʃsi sarv: II (11/40)

Kasmaat (why) ch (and) te (to you) n (not) nameran (bow in reverence) Mahaatman (Krishn) gareeyase (the greatest) Brahman: (of Brahmaa) api (even) aadi (origin, beginning) kartre (creator, doer)I Anant (Krishn) Devesh (Krishn) Jaganniwaas (Krishn) twam (you) aksharam (imperishable) sat (absolute truth) asat (unreal) tatparam (ultimate perfect one beyond them)II (11/37)

Twam (you) aadi dev: (the origin of all gods) Purush: (the primary person) puraan: (primeval, ancient) twam (you) asya (of this) Vishwsya (of the world) param (Ultimate) nidhaanam (repository, resting place)I Vettaa (expert knower) asi (you are) vedyam (knowable) ch (and) param (ultimate) ch (and) dhaam (abode) twayaa (by you) tatam (pervades in) Vishwm (world) anant roop (Krishn)II (11/38)

Vaayu: (wind) yam: (Lord of death) agni: (fire) varun: (Lord of water & aquatic creatures) shashaank: (moon) Prajaapati: (Brahmaa) twaam (you) prapitaamah: (great grandfather) ch (and) I Nam: nam: (bowing, saluting with obeisance) te (to you) astu (be) sahastrakrutw: (thousands of times) pun: (again) ch (and) Bhooy: (again) api (still) nam: nam: (bowing with reverence) te (to you)II (11/39)

Nam: (bowing with reverence, obeisance) purastaat (from the front) ath (now) prushthat: (from rear) te (to you) nam: (bowing with reverence) astu (be) te (to you) sarvat: (on all sides) ev (also) sarvaa (everything)I Anant veerya (Krishn) amit (immeasurable) vikram: (valor) twam (you) sarvam (all) samaapnoshi; (bring to an end) tat: (by which) asi (you are) sarv (everything)II (11/40)

O Mahaatman (Krishn, the greatest of all souls)! Why should they not bow in reverence to You, the Greatest One and the origin and creator even of Brahmaa, the lord of creation? O Anant (Krishn, the Endless One)! O Devesh (Krishn, Supreme Lord of Devs, the Demigods)! O Jaganniwaas (Krishn, the ultimate abode and refuge of universe)! You are Akshar, the imperishable Supreme Being and Sat as well as Asat i.e. all the

existential & non-existential things, and also the one beyond them. (11/37)

You are the origin of all Devs, the primeval person, and ultimate repository of entire world. You are the most knowledgeable one as well as the only One to know really. O Anant Roop (Krishn, in infinite forms)! Whole universe is pervaded by You and you are the ultimate home (of every soul). (11/38)

You are Vaayu, the Lord of wind, Yam, the Lord of death & divine judgment, Agni, the Lord of fire & brilliance, Varun, the Lord of water, and Shashaank, the moon. You are also Prajaapati Brahmaa, the Lord of all generations. You are also the Great grandfather of everyone (as father of Brahmaa) . I salute to You thousands of times. I salute, salute and repeatedly salute to You again and again. (11/39)

O Anant veerya (Krishn, the extremely vigorous One)! Salutations to You from front side and salutations to You from the back side, I bow to You from all sides in obeisance. Your valor is immeasurable; you are everything and everything is in You i.e. You are the beginning and end of each & everything. (11/40)

Earlier Arjun saw the trinity of Brahmaa, Shiv and Vishnu along with other gods and great sages in attendance of God singing in His praise. Now, he witnesses that all of them are actually different manifestations of God in various, endless forms. He realizes His greatness, enormous energy, boundless effulgence, eternal existence, omnipresence spread all over, and beyond, for the first time. He understands it well now that all kinds of knowledge are incomplete until one knows God in His full perfect form.

What does it symbolize? God had explained the fate of **Sakaam Bhakt**, the devotee, who wants to fulfill his material desires quickly through devotion of lesser gods. He added further that the result achieved by such devotee of low intelligence is bound to perish but He who devotes exclusively to Him shall reach His imperishable place. Arjun realizes it now, as he is flabbergasted to see all gods physically within a part of the indivisible Supreme Being.

Sat and **Asat** were explained earlier in 2/16 as the existential real substance, the Absolute Truth, and the non existential illusion visible anywhere respectively. Then, in 9/19, God proclaimed that He is **Sat**, the existent, real thing; and **Asat**, the non-existent, unreal thing. Now, when Arjun sees His **Vishw Roop**, he realizes that God is not only in every **Sat**, the existent thing and **Asat**, the non-existent imaginary thing; He is also there where **Sat** and **Asat** can never reach. For example, though the sky and earth appear to meet each other in the horizon, it does exist at a point far beyond their reach. While **Sat** and **Asat** can be realized by comparing each other, God cannot be realized without proper insight and detachment from both. We shall see God confirming this observation of Arjun in 13/12 as below:

"Brahm, the Ultimate Perfect Being, is neither Sat - the absolute existence, nor Asat - the illusory non-existence."

We understood explanations of **Aksharam** under *'What is that which is called Brahm'* in 8/3-4, and again in 8/21 as imperishable, immortal Supreme Being, the ultimate destination of a soul. Chapter 16 shall describe **Akshar** as **Kshetrajn**, the soul dwelling in a **Kshetr**, the body.

৵৽

Arjun asks pardon of Krishn for treating Him
earlier as an ordinary person.

(11/41, 42, 43 & 44)

सखेति मत्वा प्रसभं यदुक्तं हे कृष्ण हे यादव हे सखेति ।
अजानता महिमानं तवेदं मया प्रमादात्प्रणयेन वापि ॥११/४१॥
यच्चावहासार्थमसत्कृतोऽसि विहारशय्यासनभोजनेषु ।
एकोऽथवाप्यच्युत तत्समक्षं तत्क्षामये त्वामहमप्रमेयम् ॥११/४२॥
पितासि लोकस्य चराचरस्य त्वमस्य पूज्यश्च गुरुर्गरीयान् ।
न त्वत्समोऽस्त्यभ्यधिकः कुतोऽन्यो लोकत्रयेऽप्यप्रतिमप्रभाव ॥११/४३॥
तस्मात्प्रणम्य प्रणिधाय कायं प्रसादये त्वामहमीशमीड्यम् ।
पितेव पुत्रस्य सखेव सख्युः प्रियः प्रियायार्हसि देव सोढुम् ॥११/४४॥

Sakheti matwaa prasabham yaduktam
hey Krishn hey Yaadav hey sakheti I
Ajaanataa mahimaanam tavedam
mayaa pramaadaatprayayen vaapi II (11/41)
Yachchaavahaasaarthamasatkrutoʃsi
vihaarashayyaasanabhojaneshu I
Ekoʃthawaapyʃchyut tatsamaksham
tatkshaamaye twaamahamaprameyam II (11/42)
Pitaasi lokasya charaacharasya
twamasya poojyashch gururgareeyaan I
N twatsamoʃstyabhyadhik: kutoʃnyo
loktrayeʃpyapratimaprabhaav II (11/43)
Tasmaatpranamya pranidhaay kaayam
prasaadaye twaamahameeshameedyam I
Pitev putrasya sakhev sakhyu: priy:
priyaayaarhasi dev sodhum II (11/44)

Sakhaa (a dear friend) Iti (thus) matwaa (thinking) prasabham (impetuously, presumptuously) yat (in that) uktam (addressed) hey (O) Krishn (Krishn, as an ordinary person, colloquially, Kaaliyaa, Kaalu) hey (O) Yaadav (Krishn, descendent of Yadu) hey (O) sakhe (dear friend) Iti (like this)I Ajaanataa (out of ignorance) mahimaanam (of glory) tav (your) Idam (this) mayaa (by me) pramaadaat (due to negligence) pranayen (out of emotional love) vaa (or) api (also)II (11/41)

Yat (whichever) ch (and) avahaasaartham (for pastime merriments) asatkrut: (insulted) asi (is) vihaar (recreational activities) shayyaa (lying on bed) aasan (sitting) bhojaneshu (eating) I Ek: (one) athawaa (or) api (even) Achyut (Krishn) tatsamaksham (in presence of others) tat (those) kshaamaye (beg pardon) twaam (you) aham (I) aprameyam (Krishn, the incomparable One)II (11/42)

Pitaa (father) Asi (you are) lokasya (of the world) charaacharasya (of moving or stationary entities) twam (you) asya (of this) poojya: (most venerable) ch (and) guru: (teacher) gareeyaan (most superior) I N (no) twatasam: (equal to you) asti (is there) abhyadhik: (more) kut: (how) any: (any other) lok traye (in all three worlds) api (even) apratim prabhaav (Krishn)II (11/43)

Tasmaat (therefore) pranamya (prostrate with full body on ground) pranidhaay (laying at your feet) kaayam (with whole body) prasaadaye (beg to bestow Your gracious mercy) twaam (you) aham (I) eesham (unto the Supreme Lord) eedyam (most praiseworthy)I Pitaa (father) Iv (like) putrasya (of son, child) sakhaa (close friend) Iv (like) sakhyu: (of close friend) priy: (lover) priyaayaa: (beloved) arhasi (befitting) dev (Krishn) sodhum (to endure)II (11/44)

Thinking of You just as my good friend (among other humans), I used to impetuously call You Hey Krishn, Hey Yaadav, Hey dear friend. It was all due to my ignorance about Your greatness and grandeur, and also out of my emotional affection & love for You (as the best friend). (11/41)

O Achyut (Krishn, the imperturbable One)! In whatsoever manner I ill treated and mocked at You whether alone or in presence of others, during our pastime merriments, recreational activities, lying down on bed, sitting and dining together, or at any other time; I beg Your pardon for all those offences O Immeasurable, Incomparable One. (11/42)

You are the father of this universe with all its moving & unmoving, animate & inanimate entities. You are the seniormost Guru, the teacher & guide and the most solemn One for worship. O Apratim Prabhaav (Krishn, the incomparably powerful & influential One)! There is no one in all the three worlds, that can equal You, how can then there be anyone greater than You? (11/43)

Therefore, I prostrate with my whole body at Your feet and pray to You, the most praiseworthy Supreme Lord and beg to bestow Your gracious mercy on me. O Dev (Krishn, the God)! It is befitting of You to endure (and excuse) my inadvertent mistakes just as a father tolerates an impertinent, mischievous son; or a true friend to a frolicsome friend; or a lover to the negligence of his beloved one. (11/44)

Speaking in singular grammatical number like *'Tu'* (तू) or *'Tum'* (तुम) Instead of plural number Aap (आप) to a respected person is considered uncouth in India. Arjun, as an intimate pal and cousin of Krishn, used to talk to Him often in singular number like any other commoner. Sometimes, he might have even ridiculed, insulted and ignored Him in private or in public. Now, on seeing His **Vishw Roop**, he realizes that Krishn is not an ordinary being but the incarnation of God on earth. He feels guilty for behaving with Him as an ordinary human being all along his life, and begs pardon for his ignorance and folly. Repenting for such impolite, sometimes disrespectful, treatment he bows to Him by circumambulating on all sides and virtually *eats humble pie* with deep regret and apology. He bows before Him in full prostration repeatedly to seek His mercy. Arjun had bowed with head & shoulders and folded hands before God earlier in 11/14 out of fear and amazement, but now he lies before Him in **Saashtaang Dandawat** i.e. stretches on the ground like a stick with eight vital body parts namely forehead, breast, shoulders, hands and feet touching it. With great modesty, he requests Him to forgive him as a father tolerates mischiefs of his child; a friend overlooks faults of his dearest friend.

Moral: *God is that father, friend, and lover of every soul. If someone begs His pardon for his mistakes with a heart free from pretence and deciet, He benevolently converts his sins into great opportunities to turnaround in life.*

Guru: Gareeyaan means the supreme teacher, mentor & spiritual guide. God is the first Guru of the universe who gave first lessons in the form of **Veds** to Brahmaa before he could disburse that knowledge to others.

৵৽৽৶

(11/45 & 46)

अदृष्टपूर्वं हृषितोऽस्मि दृष्ट्वा भयेन च प्रव्यथितं मनो मे ।
तदेव मे दर्शय देवरूपं प्रसीद देवेश जगन्निवास ॥ ११/४५॥
किरीटिनं गदिनं चक्रहस्तमिच्छामि त्वां द्रष्टुमहं तथैव ।
तेनैव रूपेण चतुर्भुजेन सहस्रबाहो भव विश्वमूर्ते ॥ ११/४६॥

Adrushtapoorvam hrushitoʃsmi drushtwaa
bhayen ch pravyathitam mano me I
Tadev me darshay devaroopam
praseed Devesh Jaganniwaas II (11/45)
Kireetinam gadinam chakrahastam-
ichchhaami twaam drashtumaham tathaiv I
Tenaiv roopen Chaturbhujen
Sahasatrabaaho bhav Vishwamoorte II (11/46)

Adrusht poorvam (never seen earlier) hrushit: (delighted) asmi
(am) Drushtwaa (by seeing at) bhayen (in fear) ch (and) pravyathitam
(are extremely distressed) man: (mind) me (my)I tat (that) ev (only)
me (me) darshay (appear) dev roopam (divine appearance) praseed
(be gracious, kind, pleased) Devesh (Krishn) Jaganniwaas (Krishn)
II (11/45)

Kireetinam ((crowned) gadinam (holding a mace) chakr hastam
(having a discus in hand) Ichchhaami (wish) twaam (you) drashtum
(see) aham (I) tathaa (same) ev (only)I Ten (that) ev (only) roopen
(in the form) chaturbhujen (four-armed) Sahastr baaho (with
thousands of arms) bhav (become) Vishw moorte (in universal form)
II (11/46)

**I am highly delighted and simultaneously terribly upset due
to fear by seeing You in the form never seen earlier. Therefore,
O Devesh (Krishn, Lord of Demigods)! O Jaganniwaas (Krishn,
the ultimate abode & refuge of the universe)! Please be kind and
appear before me in Your (pleasant) divine form only. (11/45)**

**I wish to see You only in the same crowned form wielding
a mace in one hand and a discus in the other hand. Therefore
O Vishw Moorte (Krishn, in universal form)! O Sahastr Baaho
(Krishn, with thousands of arms)! Please appear in Your
Chaturbhuj, the four-armed form." (11/46)**

Arjun was very much frightened to see universal form of God
wearing crowns on many heads, holding maces and discus in many
hands in 11/14 earlier. But now, he prays to Him to show His
Shaantaakaar, the calm, pleasant divine form of Chaturbhuj, the

four armed form in which also He holds discus, mace, conch and lotus but only one in each hand. Note that Arjun is in a state of fearful delight but he is intelligent enough to take the benefit of the situation and requests Krishn to show to him His Chaturbhuj form of Lord Vishnu before He resumes His normal human form as Krishn with two hands. In Mahaabhaarat, Krishn often becomes Chaturbhuj to display His unanimity with God, and punish the guilty.

৯৹৶

God consoles Arjun.

(11/47, 48 & 49)

श्रीभगवानुवाच
मया प्रसन्नेन तवार्जुनेदं रूपं परं दर्शितमात्मयोगात् ।
तेजोमयं विश्वमनन्तमाद्यं यन्मे त्वदन्येन न दृष्टपूर्वम् ॥ १ १/४७॥
न वेदयज्ञाध्ययनैर्न दानैर्न च क्रियाभिर्न तपोभिरुग्रैः ।
एवंरूपः शक्य अहं नृलोके द्रष्टुं त्वदन्येन कुरुप्रवीर ॥ १ १/४८॥
मा ते व्यथा मा च विमूढभावो दृष्ट्वा रूपं घोरमीदृङ्ममेदम् ।
व्यपेतभीः प्रीतमनाः पुनस्त्वं तदेव मे रूपमिदं प्रपश्य ॥ १ १/४९॥

Shree Bhagawaan Uvaach
Mayaa prasannen tawaArjunedam
roopam param darshitamaatmayogaat I
Tejomayam Vishwamanantamaadyam
yanme tvadanyen n drushtapoorvam II (11/47)
n vedayajnaadhyayanairn daanairn
ch kriyaabhirn tapobhirugrai: I
Evamaroopam shakya aham nruloke
drashtum twadanyen Kurupraveer II (11/48)
Maa te vyathaa maa ch vimoodhabhaavo
drustwaa roopam ghorameedrunmamedam I
Vyapetabhee: preetamanaa: punastwam
tadev me roopamidam prapashya II (11/49)

Mayaa (by Me) prasannen (by propitious grace) tav (to you) Arjun (Arjun) Idam (this) roopam (appearance) param (ultimate) darshitam (shown) aatm yogaat (by My mystic power of yog)I Tejomayam (full of Tej) Vishwam (universal) anantam (with oy end) aadyam (origin of everything) yat (that) me (My, Mine) tvadanyen (no one except you) n (not) drusht (seen) poorvam (in the past)II (11/47)

n (not) vedyajn (by performing sacrificial Yajns) adyayanai: (by study) n (nor) daanai: (by donations) n (nor) ch (and) kriyaabhi: (by any other activity) n (nor) tapobhi: (by penances) ugrai: (severe)I Evam (in this way) roop: (appearance) shakya: (possible) aham (I) nruloke (in human world) drashtum (see) twadanyen (anybody else except you) Kurupraveer (Arjun)II (11/48)

Maa (do not) te (you) vyathaa (anguish) maa (do not) ch (and) Vimoodh bhaav: (bewildered disposition) drashtwaa (seeing) roopam (form) ghoram (awesome, terrible) eedruk (as it is) mam (My) Idam (this)I Vyapetabhee: (give up fear) preet manaa: (mentally happy & composed) pun: (again) twam (you) tat (same) ev (only) me (My) roopam (appearance) Idam (this) prapashya (see)II (11/49)

God said:

"O Arjun! By My mystic power of Yog and My propitious grace, I have shown to you My universal form, which is full of energy and brilliance, the ultimate origin of everything and without any end. It has been not seen by anybody else except you earlier. (11/47)

O Kuru Praveer (Arjun)! It is not possible for anyone in the human world other than you to see Me in this form, neither by study of Veds, nor by performing sacrificial Yajns, nor by donations & charity, nor by severe penances, nor by any other activity. (11/48)

Do not be anguished and bewildered to see this terrific form of Mine here. Shed off your fear, have happy and peaceful mind again, and see My Chaturbhuj form that you wish to see." (11/49)

Krishn compliments Arjun that he is extremely lucky to see Him in a form which none else has seen before. Then, He comforts him with soothing words and restores him to his normally calm state of mind by showing His **Chaturbhuj** form. Arjun fully realizes now that Krishn, standing before him, is simultaneously the fearful God for **Dushkrutaam**, the wicked, evil doers; and the benevolent God deliverer of **Saadhoos**, the righteous, virtuous people. His inner faculties, greatly perturbed earlier, are restored to normal condition completely at this very moment. He is now in de-stressed from:

1. Fear generated by seeing God's fearsome form,
2. Unfounded anxiety about the outcome of war,
3. Grief, which gripped him in the beginning of Gita due to misplaced compassion towards friends and relatives.

Clarification: *Some people try to equate Vishw Roop Darshan of Gita with some parallels in other scriptures. It should be clear to us absolutely by this statement of God that the universal form shown by Krishn to Arjun is unique and only one among all scriptures of Hinduism. No one other than Arjun has seen it so far, and nor would anyone be able to see it ever in future.*

Moral: *Full realization of the potential of God's Yogam Aishwaram (9/5 & 11/8) cannot be attained simply by studying Veds and, or other scriptures, or by performing sacrificial works, or by resorting to severe asceticism, or by helping the needy with charities, or by other activities carried out in isolation. A determined practiser can definitely attain this ultimate realization by patiently pursuing Samagr Yog of Gita in entirety.*

꧁꧂

Sanjay concludes the description of God's universal form.

(11/50)

सञ्जय उवाच

इत्यर्जुनं वासुदेवस्तथोक्त्वा स्वकं रूपं दर्शयामास भूयः ।
आश्वासयामास च भीतमेनं भूत्वा पुनः सौम्यवपुर्महात्मा ॥१ १/५०॥

Sanjay Uvaach

ItyArjunam VaasuDevstathoktwaa
swakam roopam darshayaamaas bhooy: I

Aashwaasayaamaas ch bheetamenam bhootwaa
pun: saumyavapurMahaatmaa II (11/50)

Iti (in this way) Arjunam (to Arjun) Vaasudev: (Krishn) tathaa
(like this) uktwaa (having said so) swakam (his own) roopam
(appearance) darshayaamaas (appeared before) bhooy: (then)
I Aashwaasayaamaas (reassured, comforted) ch (and) bheetam
(frightened) enam (that, this) bhootwaa (by becoming) pun: (again)
saumya (placid, charming) vapu: (body) Mahaatmaa (Krishn)II
(11/50)

Sanjay said:

**"Having spoken to Arjun in this way, Vaasudev Krishn, the son
of Vasudev then appeared again in His own Chaturbhuj form
before him. Krishn, the greatest & most venerable soul then
again adopted His always cheerful normal human form and
reassured frightened Arjun." (11/50)**

Sanjay informs Dhrutraashtr here that Krishn appears
consecutively in two forms before Arjun in quick succession. Being
an avatar of Lord Vishnu, He first appears in eternally blissful
Chaturbhuj (four-armed) form of Lord Vishnu as desired by
Arjun and then He resumes His normal form of Krishn, the son
of Vasudev, with two hands like other human beings. Description
of manifestation of Krishn in the great universal form of God by
Sanjay ends here. Sanjay is the only fortunate person, besides
Arjun, in whole world who could see Krishn in Vishw Roop. He shall
acknowledge it gratefully in 18/77.

৵৽

Arjun admits regaining his normal status.

(11/51)

अर्जुन उवाच
दृष्ट्वेदं मानुषं रूपं तव सौम्यं जनार्दन ।
इदानीमस्मि संवृत्तः सचेताः प्रकृतिं गतः ॥ ११/५१॥

Arjun Uvaach
Drushtavedam maanusham roopam tav saumya Janaardan I
Idaaneemasmi samvrutt: sachetaa: prakrutim gat: II (11/51)

Drushtwaa (by looking at) Idam (this) maanusham (human) roopam (form, shape, appearance) tav (yours) saumyam (placid, blissful) Janaardan (Krishn)I Idaaneem (now) asmi (am) samvrutt: (settled, restored) sachetaa: (with composed & tranquil conscience) prakrutim (natural state) gat: (obtained, returned)II (11/51)

Arjun said:

"O Janaardan (Krishn)! I have now returned to my natural state of composed, tranquil conscience on seeing this very compassionate and blissful form of Yours as a normal human being". (11/51)

All fears and awe of Arjun are vanished as soon as he looks at the normal human form of Krishn. He calls Him Janaardan, the sustainer & well-wisher of his devotees in recognition of His kind act of restoring him to normal healthy state, thus signifying that He has accepted him as His devotee.

☙❦

God says that though it is impossible for anybody to see Him in this form, a dedicated devotee can achieve Him.

(11/52 & 53)

श्रीभगवानुवाच
सुदुर्दर्शमिदं रूपं दृष्टवानसि यन्मम ।
देवा अप्यस्य रूपस्य नित्यं दर्शनकाङ्क्षिणः ॥ ११/५२॥
नाहं वेदैर्न तपसा न दानेन न चेज्यया ।
शक्य एवंविधो द्रष्टुं दृष्टवानसि मां यथा ॥ ११/५३॥
भक्त्या त्वनन्यया शक्य अहमेवंविधोऽर्जुन ।
ज्ञातुं द्रष्टुं च तत्त्वेन प्रवेष्टुं च परंतप ॥ ११/५४॥

Shree Bhagawaan Uvaach

Sudurdarshamidam roopam drushtawaanasi yanmam I

Devaa apyasya roopasya nityam darshanakaankshin: II

(11/52)

Naaham vedairn tapasaa n daanen n chejyayaa I

Shakya evamvidho drashtum drushtawaanasi maam yathaa

II (11/53)

Bhaktyaa twananyayaa shakya ahamevamvidho∫rjun I

Jnaatum drashtum ch tattven praveshtum ch Parantap II

(11/54)

Sudurdarsham (extremely rare to see) Idam (this) roopam (form) drushtawaan (just seen) asi (you have) yat (which) mam (My)I Devaa: (Demigods) api (even) asya (this) roopasya (of form) nityam (always) darshanakaankshin: (eagerly desirous, aspiring to see)II (11/52)

N (not) aham (Me) vedai: (by Veds) n (nor) tapasaa (by penances ascetic practices) n (nor) daanen (by donations, charity) n (nor) ch (and) Ijyayaa (by Sacrificial Yajns) I Shaky: (possible) evamvidh: (in this way) drashtum (to see) drushtawaan (seen) asi (you have) maam (to Me) yathaa (like)II (11/53)

Bhaktyaa (with wholehearted devotion) tu (but) ananyayaa (by undivided, singly devoted) shaky: (possible) aham (I) evamvidh: (in this way) Arjun (Arjun)I Jnaatum (to know) drashtum (see) ch (and) tattven (by the fundamentals) praveshtum (to enter, merge) ch (and) Parantap (Arjun) II (11/54)

God said:

"This form of Mine, which you have just seen, is extremely rare to see. Even Devs, the Demigods are always eagerly desirous to have a glimpse of this form of Mine. (11/52)

It is not possible (for anyone) to see Me in the form as you could see Me, neither by study of Veds, nor by penance and ascetic practices, nor by donations and nor by sacrificial Yajns. (11/53)

O Arjun! Even then, it is definitely possible to see Me in this form and truly realize Me with basic fundamentals and merge into Me only by remaining exclusively devoted to Me in an undeviating manner O Parantap (Arjun)! (11/54)

Krishn calls Arjun as Parantap, the one who chastises his enemies, probably to remind of his power by which he should subdue his greatest spiritual enemy, **Aasakti**, the emotional attachment with his relatives; and others like **Kaam**, **Krodh**, **Lobh** etc. Some scholars think that by **Idam** i.e. this, Krishn is referring to His Chaturbhuj form here that He showed just before resuming His human form, whereas others think that the reference is made to the universal form. Since God tells that it is not easy for anyone (including Devs) to see Him in this form, He must be referring to His universal form only in my opinion because He as well as Arjun and Sanjay are repeatedly telling that His universal form was never seen before by anyone. Besides, it is not mentioned anywhere that **Chaturbhuj** form is extremely difficult to see. In fact, almost in all scriptures, God frequently appears in Chaturbhuj form before his devotees like Dhruv, Pralhaad, Kaushalyaa, and even animals like Kaag Bhushundi, Gajendr etc. He frequently obliges Devs also by appearing in Chaturbhuj form whenever they call upon His divine help. However, if some devotees prefer to think of Chaturbhuj form here, I see no reason to discourage them either.

৵৽৽

God tells the method to attain Him.

(11/55)

मत्कर्मकृन्मत्परमो मद्भक्तः सङ्गवर्जितः ।
निर्वैरः सर्वभूतेषु यः स मामेति पाण्डव ॥ ११/५५॥

Matkarmakrunmatparamo madbhakt: sangavarjit: I
Nirvair: sarvabhooteshu y: s maameti Paandav II (11/55)

Matkarm krut (engaged to work on My behalf & in My service) matparam: (thinks of Me as the ultimate refuge) madbhakt: (my devotee) sang varjit: (free from attachment & mental speculation for material world) I Nirvair: (without animosity) Sarv Bhooteshu (in all living beings) y: (who) s: (he) maam (to Me) eti (attains) Paandav (Arjun) II (11/55)

O Paandav (Arjun)! He, who is engaged in performing all of his actions on My behalf and in My service, thinks of Me as the ultimate refuge, is devoted to Me without any attachment with worldly things, and who is peaceable towards all the living beings, that person attains Me." (11/55)

Nirvair Sarv Bhooteshu: It means without any trace of envy and enmity towards all beings. God told Arjun to be instrumental by resorting to fighting the war to kill his opponents and partake in his role in implementing His will. Thus, the work that Arjun was asked to do is not his own but of God, which he should simply carry out as a faithful general carries out orders of his king. Krishn repeats the same instruction to practisers of Yog by using the phrase **Matkarm Krut** to perform all of their works with a resolve and commitment considering each one of them as instructions of God. He shall elaborate this idea further in 12/10 for those who find it difficult to work in this way.

Matparam was explained earlier in 2/61 and again as **Matparaayan** in 9/34 as depending entirely & exclusively on God and thinking of Him as the ultimate refuge. **Sang Varjit** is same as **Asakt** or **Anaasakt** (5/14) i.e. free from all kinds of attachments, expectations and mental speculation for material world.

Moral: *A practiser should do his duties considering them as opportunities given by God to serve His mission of uprooting evil and establishing rule of righteousness in the world. Such participation and contribution must also be free from self-interest totally. Success achieved must be dedicated to God, and failure, if any, should be reviewed in the light of introspection.*

CONCLUSION OF CHAPTER 11

God disclosed His **Vibhooti**, the majesty and magnificence in a vivid spectrum of some most outstanding entities in **Sagun Niraakaar** i.e. the invisible manifestation in chapter 10. Chapter 11 described God in His **Sagun Saakaar** i.e. visible manifestation. In simple words, if chapter 10 is the audio narrative of God's divinity, chapter 10 is His audiovisual version. As far as I know, this is the only complete description of God in His different flamboyant forms depicting all other gods, good and bad human and super human beings positioned in their respective places; time and death spitting flames and devouring all irreligious people; His calm and most pleasant Chaturbhuj form; and finally the human form of Krishn. This chapter should therefore, set at rest all the doubts about **Krishn** being God Himself.

Clarification: *Some sceptical people vainfully try to mock Vishw Roop Darshan as an act of hypnotism by Krishn in order to frighten and goad Arjun to undertake fighting. However, in their ill-conceived zeal, they forget that not only this topic but entire Gita is being narrated by Sanjay to Dhrutraashtr sitting about 175 km away in Hastinaapur, much beyond the range of the strongest kind of hypnotism. This may be one reason for Vyaas also to make Sanjay speak three times in this chapter. Besides, as explained earlier, Krishn has no personal motive to achieve by inciting Arjun for war, except to serve His divine mission of destroying Adharm and restoring Dharm.*

There are 4 Shree Bhagawaan Uvaach, 4 Arjun Uvaach and 3 Sanjay Uvaach and two beautiful similes in this chapter. It should also be delightfully noted that Arjun and Sanjay addressed Krishn with highest number of adjectives and names of God in this chapter.

ॐ तत्सदिति श्रीमद्भगवद्गीतासूपनिषत्सु ब्रह्मविद्यायां योगशास्त्रे श्रीकृष्णार्जुनसंवादे विश्वरूपदर्शनयोगो नामैकादशोऽध्यायः ॥ ११

(In the name of God, the ultimate truth thus ends the eleventh chapter named 'Vishw Roop Darshan Yog' of Shreemad Bhagwad Gita, the best Upanishad, Brahm Vidyaa & Yog Shaastr, a dialogue between Shree Krishn and Arjun)

CHAPTER 12

BHAKTI YOG

(Devotion tends to degenerate soon into routinely performed rituals whereas its ultimate goal is to transcend us constantly from lower to higher.)

PREAMBLE & CONTEXT

We have completed studying 469 (67%) shloks of Gita until chapter 11. This qualifies us with first class marks to continue our journey through remaining chapters and climb to the highest realm of the Himalaya of knowledge called Gita. Vyaas had fixed the plain canvas of Gita on the easel of chapter 1 on which Krishn, the great artist, started painting long and short strokes in vivid colors from chapter 2 to 10. As He starts painting the finest strokes beginning with Bhakti in this chapter, it shall be our great delight and good fortune to see the final picture of **Samagr Yog** emerging on the canvas of Gita from now onwards.

I had mentioned in the *Conclusion of chapter 9* that it could have been also named as part one of **Bhakti Yog** instead of **Raaj Vidyaa Raaj Guhya Yog** for it introduced us to the fundamental knowledge of **Bhakti**, the devotion of God. Krishn might have continued it but He had to interject chapters 10 and 11 in between in order to satisfy the curiosity of Arjun to learn about His divine **Vibhooti,** and then to see Him in His universal form respectively. Highly satisfied and happy Arjun now requests Krishn in the beginning of this chapter to complete His talk on **Bhakti**, one of the high ideals of Yog.

WHY CHAPTER 12 IS NAMED BHAKTI YOG?

Arjun would not talk, from here onwards, of his fears or delusion as his mind shall concentrate mainly on exploring deeper insights of the subjects grossly talked so far. In this way, Gita has by now successfully moved us, the normal human beings, away from all that was of much lower quality but normal for most of us so far like our value systems, standards, ego, motives, outlook, prejudices, inhibitions, ignorance, desires, selfishness etc. Now, it leads us gradually from that lower level, where we were positioned wrongly earlier, to new, higher level that would eventually become spiritual, impersonal, and universal. By dealing with **Bhakti**, the devotional service of God from this chapter, Gita in its finale starts fortifying the level where we have already reached so that there is no scope or fear of falling or deviating from our final destination. If chapter 9 was part 1 of **Bhakti Yog**, chapter 12 is its part 2 as God would dedicate as many as 8 shloks in 12/13-20 to explain the qualities that shall entitle a devotee to become His dearest devotee. From now onwards, until we reach its pinnacle in 18/66, He shall frequently mention **Bhakti** as a very important means to attain His blissful Yog.

People often confuse with what devotion of God is. This chapter is dedicated to clearing this confusion as it explains to us what **Bhakti** really means and who the ideal **Bhakt** of Gita is. This chapter starts with Arjun asking the same question in 12/1, which tickles in our minds too. Hence, this chapter is named as **Bhakti Yog**.

Arjun expresses desire to know who the best devotee of God is.

(12/1)

अर्जुन उवाच
एवं सततयुक्ता ये भक्तास्त्वां पर्युपासते ।
ये चाप्यक्षरमव्यक्तं तेषां के योगवित्तमाः ॥१२/१॥

Arjun Uvaach

Evam satatayuktaa ye bhaktaastwaam paryupaasate I
Ye chaapyaksharamavyaktam teshaam ke yogavittamaa: II
(12/1)

Evam (in this way) Satat (perpetually, constantly) Yuktaa: (united) Ye (who) Bhaktaa: (devotees) Twaam (to you) Pari upaasate (worship) I Ye (who) ch (and) Api (or, only) Aksharam (imperishable Supreme Being) Avyaktam (unmanifested) Teshaam (of them) Ke (who) Yog Vittamaa: (perfect knowers of Yog) II (12/1)

Arjun said:

"Which of the two categories of Your devotees, is the most outstanding knower of Yog: they who worship in the aforesaid way by remaining perpetually united with You in Your Saakaar i.e. manifested personified form; or they who devote to Akshar Brahm, the Niraakaar i.e. formless, unmanifested, immutable form of Supreme Being?" (12/1)

In this shlok, Arjun uses **Twaam** for Krishn as God manifested in personified form explained mainly in chapter 9; and **Aksharam Avyaktam** to denote **Brahm**, the unmanifested, imperishable impersonal form of God explained mainly in 7th and 8th chapters. **Yog Vittamaa** are people who have acquired perfect knowledge about connecting themselves with God. They are same as **Yog Yukt Aatmaa** described in 5/21, 6/29, 7/18, and 9/28 earlier. **Satat Yuktaa** means those devotees who adore God with their entire being i.e. conscience, thought, action, and emotion all the time everywhere. Arjun had earlier asked a very similar question about **Jnaan** and **Karm** in 5/1:

"You are commending Sannyaas, the path of knowledge on one hand and Karm Yog, the path of action on the other hand. Please tell me clearly which one of the two is the most meritorious for me".

In the same way, he wants to know now who out of two kinds of devotees perfectly realizes God's divine Yog; he who constantly worships Him in **Saakaar**, the manifested, personified form; or he who devotes to Him in **Niraakaar**, unmanifested, impersonal, eternal form of **Brahm**.

৵৽৹

God replies in the same way as He did in 5/2 to 6.

(12/2, 3, 4 & 5)

श्रीभगवानुवाच

मय्यावेश्य मनो ये मां नित्ययुक्ता उपासते ।

श्रद्धया परयोपेतास्ते मे युक्ततमा मताः ॥ १२/२॥

ये त्वक्षरमनिर्देश्यमव्यक्तं पर्युपासते ।

सर्वत्रगमचिन्त्यं च कूटस्थमचलं ध्रुवम् ॥ १२/३॥

संनियम्येन्द्रियग्रामं सर्वत्र समबुद्धयः ।

ते प्राप्नुवन्ति मामेव सर्वभूतहिते रताः ॥ १२/४॥

क्लेशोऽधिकतरस्तेषामव्यक्तासक्तचेतसाम् ।

अव्यक्ता हि गतिर्दुःखं देहवद्भिरवाप्यते ॥ १२/५॥

Shree Bhagawaan Uvaach

Mayyaaveshya mano ye maam nityayuktaa upaasate I

Shraddhayaa parayopetaaste me yuktatamaa mataa: II (12/2)

Ye twaksharamanirdeshyamavyaktam paryupaasate I

Sarvatragamachintyam ch kootasthamachalam dhruvam II (12/3)

Sanniyamyendriyagraamam sarvatr samabuddhay: I

Te praapnuvanti maamev sarvabhootahite rataa: II (12/4)
klesho∫dhiktarasteshaamavyaktaasaktchetasaam I
avyaktaa hi gatirdu:kham dehavadbhiravaapyate II (12/5)

Mayi (unto Me) Aaveshya (possessed) Man: (mind & heart) Ye (who) Maam (to Me) Nitya (always) Yuktaa: (united) Upaasate (worship) I Shraddhayaa (with faith) Parayaa: (unflinching, perfect) Upetaa: (endowed, obtained) Te (they) Me (by Me) Yukt Tamaa: (the best among Yogees) Mataa: (are considered) II (12/2)

Ye (who) Tu (but) Aksharam (immutable Supreme Being) Anirdeshyam (indefinable, imperceptible) Avyaktam (unmanifested, impersonal) Pari upaasate (properly devote) I Sarvatr Gam (Omnipresent) Achintyam (inconceivable) Ch (and) Kootastham (uppermost) Achalam (stable) Dhruvam (constant) II (12/3)

Sanniyamya (regulating) Indriy Graamam (group of Indriys) Sarvatr (everywhere) Sam Buddhay: (with equally disposed intelligence) I Te (they) Praapnuvanti (get) Maam (to Me) Ev (also) Sarv Bhoot Hite Rataa: (engaged with commitment to work towards the well being of all entities) II (12/4)

klesh: (tribulation, trouble, affliction, anguish, tedium, strenuous) Adhik tar: (very much) Teshaam (they) Avyakt (invisible) Aasakt (attached with) Chetasaam (conscience) I Avyaktaa (imperceptible) hi (certainly) Gati: (destination) du:kham (distressful) Dehavadbhi: (by embodied persons) Avaapyate (is attained) II (12/5)

God said:

"The devotees who, endowed with unflinching faith, worship My manifested form with mind & heart engrossed in Me and always remain engaged in Me; they are the best Yogees **in My opinion. (12/2)**

But those who properly worship that imperishable, indefinable, impersonal, Omnipresent, inconceivable, steady, constant and the uppermost and mysterious Supreme Being; control the group of their sensory and functionary organs in all situations; and engage themselves in the well being of every

entity with intelligence of equanimity everywhere; they too surely attain Me. (12/3 & 4)

However the path of those who choose to engage their conscience, mind and heart in the impersonal Brahm, is fraught with great tribulations and troubles because it is definitely very painful for embodied persons to pursue and achieve an imperceptible, invisible goal. (12/5)

Krishn tells in 12/2 that the worshippers of God in **Saakaar**, the personified, perceptible form must be:

1. **Mayi Aaveshya Man: Man**, the mind with the help of Buddhi, intelligence classifies the information received through **Jnaanendriys**, into *'Things to do or not do'* and orders **Karmendriys** to execute the *'to do'* things according to its instructions. Thus, since **Man** is the master of all **Indriys**, this phrase tells us to engage all our internal and external faculties in the devotion of God.

2. **Nitya Yuktaa**: are the people constantly engaged, permanently connected with God as explained earlier in 7/17 & 8/14. And,

3. **Shraddhayaa Parayaa**: were explained in 3/31 as devotees possessing reverential belief and undulating, unflinching, perfect faith in God. Gita refers to same people as **Shraddhaa May, Shraddhaa Vaan, Shraddadhaanaa, Shraddhaa vant, Shraddhayaa Anvitaa** etc. at other places. Arjun is such a person in Mahaabhaarat. We witnessed his unwavering faith in Krishn in 2/7 when he fell in the deep ditch of delusion and requested Him to teach what is best for him. Even after he is relieved of bewilderment and acquires perfect knowledge at the end of Gita, he shall demonstrate the same faith saying, **Karishye Vachanam tav** i.e. *'I shall do as decided & instructed by you, not by me'*.

He calls such devotees **Yukt Tamaa,** the best, the cream of all Yogees who engage with Supreme Soul most intimately and appropriately as explained in 6/47 earlier. This relationship can be of master & servant, father & son, husband & wife, lover & beloved, devoted & devotee, or just friendship like between Krishn & Arjun. He also describes following qualities essential for worshippers of God in **Niraakaar**, the impersonal, imperceptible form in 12/4:

1. **Sanniyamya Indriy Graamam** was dealt in 6/24 earlier for people who are able to exercise effective control on entire group of sensory and functionary organs.

2. **Sarvatr Sam Buddhay**: It refers to people endowed with the quality of **Samatv**, the equipoise explained under 'Some additional thoughts on Samatv' in 2/48.

3. **Sarv Bhoot Hite Rataa**: It was explained from 5/24 to 26 under 'Some additional thoughts on Sarv Bhoot Hite Rataa' as persons engaged with commitment to work towards the well being of all living as well as inert entities. Galileo Galilee equates such person with:

'The sun, with all those planets revolving around it and dependent on it, can still ripen a bunch of grapes as if it had nothing else in this universe to do'.

In Mahaabhaarat 12/261/9, a grosser named Tulaadhaar teaches **Dharm** to a **Braahman** named Jaajali thus:

सर्वेषाम् य: सुहृन्नित्यम् सर्वेषाम् च हिते रत: ।
कर्मणा मनसा वाचा स धर्मम् वेद जाजले ॥

(O Jaajali! He only has really understood Dharm who engages himself in the service of all beings with his Man, the mind & heart, speech & works; and who perpetually remains the most affectionate, good-hearted friend of all beings)

Vivekaanand exhorts us to engage in the welfare of others in strong words:

'This life is short, vanities of the world are transient, but they alone live who work for others, the rest are more dead than alive'.

Clarification: Above-mentioned six qualities however, are applicable to both types of devotees. A devotee of Saakaar gets the latter three *qualities automatically by the abundant grace of God; and similarly, a devotee of Niraakaar is endowed with first three qualities. It is because of different paths people may choose to devote to God; God however, never discriminates between His true devotees. What He expects from them is sincerity in their approach.*

Arjun raised query in 5/1 about difference between **Jnaan** and **Karm** that Krishn replied in 5/4-6 saying that both paths lead to the same destination of Yog, but with a rider that **Karm** is easier and more practical to follow. In the same way, He tells Arjun now in 12/2 that the worshippers of **Saakaar,** the manifested, personified form of God are the best achievers of Yog**,** the permanent connection with God; and then states in 12/3 and 4 that the same Yog is also achievable through the worship of **Niraakaar,** the unmanifested, impersonal **Brahm,** the Supreme Being. Krishn is well aware of the question that if the same destination is achievable by devotees of **Saakaar** as well as **Niraakaar**, why He considers the devotee of **Saakaar** as best Yogee. Therefore, without waiting for a question from Arjun after 12/4, He immediately qualifies His statement saying in 12/5 that the latter path of worship of **Niraakaar** God is tedium, laden with great troubles, afflictions as well as risks of falling down.

QUESTION: WHY DEVOTION OF NIRAAKAAR BRAHM IS MORE DIFFICULT THAN OF SAAKAAR GOD?

Note that Krishn speaks in first person for God's **Saakaar** i.e. personified form but He uses following eight adjectives for **Niraakaar** impersonal God:

1. **Aksharam**: It denotes imperishable, immutable, eternal God. It is also the sacred syllable ॐ (Om) representing God. We understood **Akshar** in 8/3-4. **Jnaan**, His true knowledge is **Akshar**.

2. **Anirdeshyam**: **Nirdesh** means pointing, guiding or directing to something. **Anirdeshya** therefore, indicates indefinable, indescribable, inexpressible, imperceptible God. One can realize and experience Him only by his own effort. All

external aids like scriptures, teachers, implements etc. are mere means to help him in his journey towards Him. **Aakaash**, the space is an example of **Anirdeshya** among material things since no one can point out where it exists.

3. **Avyaktam**: Explained in 8/20-21, it stands for unmanifested, imperceptible, invisible, impersonal form of God. Vaayu, the wind is **Avyakt** i.e. invisible among material things.

4. **Sarvatr Gam**: It is same as **Sarvatrag** in 9/6 meaning pervading in everything and available everywhere. Aakaash is **Sarvatr Gam** as it pervades in all materials of universe.

5. **Achintyam**: It was explained in 2/25 & 8/9 as something inconceivable, unimaginable, and this cannot be analyzed by intelligence and is beyond the reach of thought power. Future of anything in the world is **Achintya** i.e. unpredictable.

6. **Kootastham**: It means something situated at the uppermost, top position; and is secret, hidden, enigmatic, and mysterious. God being the Supreme Master of the universe and the most mysterious one to know, is called here as **Kootasth**. Incidentally, I may mention that **Kootasth** appeared in 6/8 also for equipoise Yogee, and explained there. Readers may refer there for full understanding of this word. Mount Everest is **Koot** of the world since it is its highest point.

7. **Achalam**: It means steady, immovable, firm, fixed, stable, constant, and imperturbable i.e. God. Mountains are called **Achal** in Sanskrit because of their immovability.

8. **Dhruvam**: It is something eternal, certain, sure, and definite. God is **Dhruvam**. North Star is named **Dhruv** in Sanskrit because of its fixed position in the sky. Great Bear, the constellation of seven stars, named as Saptarshi in Hinduism after its seven most revered sages, circumambulates daily around this star.

Above adjectives used to indicate **Brahm** are abstract in nature, prove that **Brahm** is incomprehensible. Men need a base, a foundation, on which they can build up the temple of their devotion and faith. And this base can be in any form like an idol, a photo, a Holy Scripture, a holy symbol, a holy relic, a holy place, a holy man, a holy object, a holy shrine etc. For example, no numerical value can be derived from zero alone, unless a numeral (from 1 to 9) precedes it. **Saakaar** provides that base to the faith of every practiser on which he can easily conceive and worship His God. The path of **Niraakaar Brahm** is indirect, highly specialized, and arduous for him to conceptualize and practice. For a common person, the exercise to comprehend **Niraakaar Brahm** is futile like a monkey trying to feel the sharpness of a razor's edge. Take few more examples to understand the difficulty:

1. Two persons travel from Ahmedabad to Delhi, one by Air Conditioned class and the other by general coach. Though both shall reach Delhi, the journey of the second person is certainly very cumbersome in comparison to the first one.

2. An infant happily accepts foods that he can easily drink or swallow in one gulp without chewing because he does not have teeth. It takes 5-7 years for him to take all kinds of foods as teeth grow in his mouth.

3. A common person cannot afford to eat in utensils made of silver but he can certainly relish the same food in easily affordable earthenware and stoneware.

4. Though a much safer and well known, traditionally followed land route between Europe and Indian sub-continent existed, two European sailors, Columbus and Vasco Da Gama, set sails and ventured to find a sea route to reach India. Columbus could never realize his dream though, until his end, he remained under the illusion that he had journeyed along the east coast of Asia. Vasco, the second voyager also had no knowledge of the route, the distance, and the difficulties that lay ahead in his expedition, but he wisely selected another

sea route. Albeit he successfully landed on the Indian coast at Kappadu, Calicut (Kozhikode), his journey was full of hazards and it cost him very dearly. Besides taking almost two years for his back and forth journey far longer than a full voyage around the world along the Equator and the longest distance of about 10,000 kilometers in open sea without the sight of land, he too suffered the loss of 2 ships, 115 men, and his brother among them.

Moral: *Devotion of Saakaar is like travelling in air-conditioned class; like drinking milk; like eating in earthen pots and like the land route in above examples. the worship of Niraakaar Brahm, on the other hand, is as Klesh Adhik tar i.e. extremely difficult as travelling in general coach; eating nuts from a silver bowl; and undertaking voyages like Columbus (he could never reach his destination) and Vasco Da Gama in above examples.*

QUESTION: WHAT ARE THE REAL KLESH FOR A PRACTISER OF YOG?

Klesh means tribulations, troubles and suffering. Krishn regards worship of imperceptible God as **Klesh Adhik tar** i.e. more painful and difficult. Sage Patanjali cautions a practiser of **Yog,** in his **Paatanjal Yog Darshan** 2/3, to beware of five types of **Klesh** that can afflict him and block his progress:

अविध्यास्मिता राग द्वेषाभिनिवेशा: क्लेशा ।

(Avidyaa, the wrong kind of education which leads to ignorance; Asmitaa, the egoistic self; Raag, the passionate infatuation and desires; Dwesh, the hateful aversion, dislike and envy, and Abhinivesh, gross indulgence in life's pleasures and fear of death)

Clarification: *These spiritual Klesh, the afflictions await every practiser of Yog in the path of practice whether he takes the route of Jnaan, or Karm, or Bhakti of Saakaar or Niraakaar.*

Patanjali says further that ignorance is the root cause of all afflictions among the five mentioned above. It is for this reason that Gita lays primary stress on removal of ignorance and acquisition of knowledge throughout its teachings. It therefore assumes utmost importance that having understood the difference between **Saakaar** and **Niraakaar Bhakti** as above; we should not infer that **Saakaar** is superior to **Niraakaar**. In fact, **Saakaar Bhakti** must ultimately culminate and merge into **Niraakaar** as God said in 4/33:

"All sacred activities must ultimately culminate into Jnaan, the knowledge of Brahm".

A true devotee of **Saakaar** however, need not worry about the difficulty in acquiring **Jnaan** since God undertakes the responsibility to bless him with everything including **Jnaan,** as a father takes care of the welfare of his obedient young child fully dependent on him. However, God treats a devotee of **Niraakaar** as His grown up, independent son who must earn what he wants by his own efforts.

☙❧

God promises to devotee of Saakaar to
relieve him from Punarjanm.

(12/6 & 7)

ये तु सर्वाणि कर्माणि मयि संन्यस्य मत्पराः ।
अनन्येनैव योगेन मां ध्यायन्त उपासते ॥ १२/६॥
तेषामहं समुद्धर्ता मृत्युसंसारसागरात् ।
भवामि नचिरात्पार्थ मय्यावेशितचेतसाम् ॥ १२/७॥

Ye tu sarvaani karmaani mayi sannyasya matparaa: I
Ananyenaiv yogen maam dhyaayant upaasate II (12/6)
Teshaamaham samuddhartaa mrutyusansaarsaagaraat I
Bhawaami nachiraatPaarth mayyaaveshitachetasaam II (12/7)

Ye (those) Tu (but) Sarvaani (all) Karmaani (in doing Karm) Mayi (unto Me) Sannyasya (by properly surrendering) Matparaa: (who come to my refuge; remain dedicated to me) I Ananyen

(wholeheartedly, with no deviation) Ev (and) Yogen (in Yog) Maam (to Me) Dhyaayant: (meditating) Upaasate (worship) II (12/6)

Teshaam (their) Aham (I) Samuddhartaa (savior, deliverer, rescuer) Mrutyu (death) Samsaar (mortal world) Saagaraat (in the ocean of) I Bhawaami (become) Nachiraat (promptly) Paarth (Arjun) Mayi (unto Me) Aaveshit (is engrossed) Chetasaam (Inner faculty like conscience, mind & heart) II (12/7)

But O Paarth (Arjun)! For those who surrender all of their activities unto Me, come to My refuge, meditate, worship Me in manifested form by uniting wholeheartedly with My Yog, and whose conscience is fully engrossed in Me; I promptly become their savior in the ocean of death & rebirth in mortal world. (12/6 & 7)

Samuddhartaa refers to someone who delivers a person from his sufferings, troubles and agony properly and completely leaving no trace behind. Christianity also reveres God as the ultimate **Samuddhartaa,** the savior and deliverer of His followers. Krishn extended an assurance to His devotees in 11/55 saying:

"He, who is engaged in performing all of his actions on My behalf and in My service, thinks of Me as the ultimate refuge, is devoted to Me without any attachment with worldly things, and who is peaceable with all the living beings, he attains Me."

Since Krishn talked there in first person while showing His universal form, then Chaturbhuj form and finally the normal human form, He obviously referred to a devotee who worships Him in any of His **Saakaar** forms. Now, in these two shloks, He reiterates His commitment to be His deliverer almost in the same words. He showed the same enthusiasm and loving care for such devotees in 9/34 earlier and shall continue to do so repeatedly in Gita; and end His teaching with the same promise in 18/65-66.

QUESTION: WHAT IS MEANT BY MRUTYU SAMSAAR SAAGAR?

Scriptures define **Samsaar** as *'Y: Samsarati Iti Samsaaram'* meaning that is called **Samsaar**, which keeps continuously changing its position like a snake crawling in zigzag manner in unpredictable directions. **Samsaar** is same as **Jagat** or **Vishw,** the universe where all materials appear and disappear; where souls take birth, pass through various physical, emotional stages, meet an end, transmigrate, and where souls, born as humans, make efforts to liberate themselves from its tangles; and where God manifests His prowess in various inhabitants. Lao Tse says:

'Life & death are one thread, the same line viewed
from different sides'.

Gita as well as other scriptures give it the simile of **Saagar,** the ocean because the souls are drifting up and down in its never ending fearful waves of **Mrutyu,** the death and **Punarjanm,** the rebirth. Shankaraachaarya describes the agony of **Samsaar Saagar** in his prayer *Bhaj Govindam* and seeks God's help in crossing it over as below:

पुनरपि जननम् पुनरपि मरणम् पुनरपि जननी जठरे शयनम् ।
इह संसारे खलु दुस्तारे कृपया पारे पाहि मुरारे ॥

{It is very difficult to cross over this dreadful ocean of world in which one has to again and again pass through (the menacing waves of) birth, death and lying in the womb of mother. O Muraaree (Krishn, the killer of demon Mur)! Please be merciful and help me to cross it}

Chetasaam was explained in 10/22 as **Ant:karan,** the inner faculty of conscience, mind and heart; collectively called the conscience. By using **Mayi Aaveshit Chetasaam,** Krishn directs a devotee to engross his conscience unto Him. **Matpar** was discussed in 9/34 as **Matparaayan** that means a devotee should depend solely on God by raising his soul from lower, mundane world to the supreme abode of God. **Mayi Aaveshit Chetasaam** is same as **Mayi Arpit Man: Buddhi** used in 8/7 on complete dedication of mind, heart and intelligence unto God. God shall repeat it verbatim very soon in 12/14 while enumerating qualities of a devotee most liked by Him.

SOME ADDITIONAL THOUGHTS ON SAGUN SAAKAAR & NIRGUN NIRAAKAAR BHAKTI

Hindu philosophy conceives God broadly in two categories:

1. **Nirgun Niraakaar** i.e. the formless, unmanifested, impersonal **Brahm** devoid of qualities, attributes and modes of nature, and,

2. **Sagun Saakaar** i.e. incarnated and manifested in a personified form and shape like Krishn, and appearing to possess qualities, attributes and modes of nature.

Both these categories are equally acceptable to Gita, as it makes no distinction between them as stated from 12/2 to 4. Nevertheless, in the next shlok 12/5 Gita did say that the first path of **Nirgun Niraakaar** is very troublesome for a beginner to pursue because he would find it an imperceptible, invisible goal. It therefore recommended in 12/6-7 to a practiser to tread on the easier, not superior, path of devotion of **Sagun Saakaar.** As stated earlier also, Krishn is indisputably the **Sagun Saakaar** God of Gita as He talks in first person as God wherever **Sagun Saakaar** is the topic of discussion. Besides it, He shall also identify Himself in 14/26-27 with **Nirgun Niraakaar Brahm,** the immortal, immutable, eternal, ultimate, blissful abode of **Dharm** and resting place of a **Gunaateet** Yogee. In this way, Gita establishes oneness of both paths of devotion beyond doubt and teaches us that the proper path to transcend three modes of material nature is to perpetually engage in His **Avyabhichaarinee Bhakti**, the incorruptible devotion and render selfless service unto Him; it is immaterial whether one devotes to Him as **Sagun Saakaar** or **Nirgun Niraakaar**. We shall understand **Avyabhichaarinee Bhakti** in 13/10, 14/26 & 18/33 later. I recommend to go to 9/22, 26, 27 & 34; and explanations under *'Why does Krishn calls himself as God'* after 2/61.

QUESTION: WHY DOES GITA REGARD DEVOTION OF SAAKAAR EASIER THAN THAT OF NIRAAKAAR?

This question is a supplement to 'Why devotion of Niraakaar Brahm is more difficult than of Saakaar God' discussed under 12/2-5. A common man tries to approach infinite God through his finite intelligence and perception; and by combining both, he carves out a form, gives it a name and attributes certain qualities to that which, in fact, is formless, nameless and quality less. But if he is told in the beginning itself that God is unimaginable, invisible, ineffable, immutable, inconceivable, abstract, and beyond any contemplation by senses; and yet he has to strive to reach Him, he faces a wall studded with precious stones of lofty adjectives of negation 'Neti Neti' i.e. not this, not this, he is bound to be totally confused. In all probability, he may either give up his effort or call it utter nonsense, and become atheist. Let me explain it with a simile below:

'A person is sitting restlessly in a closed dark room. He gets up and opens a window to feel the fresh air and look at the outside world through that window. On seeing the beauty spread outside, he realizes the limits imposed on his sight by the frame of the window, and decides to go out of the room, wander in wilderness outside and experience its vividness. It gradually dawns on him that the room was full of darkness of Ajnaan, the ignorance about outside world; his act of opening the window was his first right step to move out of that dark room. And, the moment he moves out of that dreadful room, the light of Jnaan relieves him from the darkness of ignorance. We can imagine his fate if he had not taken the first right step of opening the window in time. The narrow window here is symbolic of the concept of Sagun Saakaar God with name and form for a devotee to begin with his practice. When he opens it, it should motivate him to explore and experience the vastness of Nirgun Niraakaar Brahm; and cultivate a desire to reach there. Nonetheless, if the yearning of such Sagun Saakaar devotee is so intense and acute as of Dhruv, Prahlaad, Meeraa, Tulasidaas, Narasee etc., the vastness of Brahm shall one day come searching him as sunrays, cool breeze, raindrops, rustling sound of the woods, twinkle of the stars come to *a person standing in a window. Then, he sees the same Aakaash, the space inside his room as well as outside it, and within himself. He achieves oneness with Brahm as He descends to him in the form he worshipped Him. He appears as Vishnu for Dhruv, Nrusimh for Prahlaad, Girdhar Gopaal for Meeraa, Raam for Tulasidaas and Saanwaliyaa seth for Narasee'.*

Tulasidaas sees Raam & Seetaa in whole world in the same spirit:

सिया राम मय सब जग जानी । करहुँ प्रणाम जोरि जुग पानी ॥

(I know that Lord Raam and Lady Seetaa pervade whole world. I therefore bow to everybody with both hands folded in reverence)

It is said that Raam appeared before Tulasidaas as described in the couplet below:

चित्रकूट के घाट पर भई सन्तन की भीर ।
तुलसिदास चंदन घिसे तिलक करे रघुबीर ॥

(A large crowd of saints has gathered on the banks of Chitr Koot. While Raam appears before him and applies Tilak, the auspicious mark on His forehead, Tulasidaas is busy in grinding sandalwood.)

A prisoner in a dark cell does not know what light is unless he makes a hole in the wall to let a beam of sunrays in. Worship of God in **Sagun Saakaar** form is like opening that hole in the wall of ignorance, which separates light, beauty and joy of Supreme Soul from a soul imprisoned in the cell of body of a man.

Clarification: *However, it must, be understood that worship of Sagun Saakaar is only a means and not an end in itself for a common person. If someone were stuck up in its ritual ties, he would be deprived from the experience of eternal bliss, as his further progress would be blocked. He must develop a vision to see the same God in others' Gods, realize His presence in every being and strive to ascend the steps of equality, kindness, tolerance, love etc. with this broadened vision and perform his duties selflessly.*

Yog Vaashishth says:

अक्षरावगमलब्धये यथा स्थूलवर्तुलदृषत्परिग्रह: ।
शुद्धबुद्धपरिलब्धये तथा दारुमृण्मयशिलामयार्चनम् ॥

(The way we teach alphabets to children by placing pebbles in the form of a particular alphabet, the same way we deploy idols made of wood, stone, clay or metal to let someone attain the knowledge of the ever pure, ever enlightened Brahm)

This much about **Sagun Saakaar**. Nevertheless, we are also aware of many **Rishis** and sages who isolate themselves in unapproachable caves to do penance, austerities, follow regimentation of ascetic practices and thereby realize **Nirgun Niraakaar Brahm** without passing through the devotion of **Sagun Saakaar**. As seen in 12/2-7 above, Gita accepts both devotional practices as equally effective in reaching God, but also strikes a gentle note of differentiation at the same time, saying that Nirgun Niraakaar is more difficult than **Sagun Saakaar**. Tukaaraam says in Gaathaa 38/7:

रहता है वह् सर्वत्र ही व्यापक एक समान ।
पर निज भक्तों के लिये छोटा है भगवान ॥

(That great Brahm pervades equally everywhere. Still He becomes a little being (like an idol) to please His Sagun Saakaar devotees}

CAUTION: *People engaging in Sagun Saakaar practice of devotion often tend to be misled to ask favors from God, which is a kind of bartering, the practice of giving something and getting something in return. Such devotees do not want to do anything as per Gods will; on the contrary, they command God to act as per their will. We must remember that devotion means giving ourselves completely with no Ifs and Buts; and without expecting anything in return.*

Mrutyu Samsaar Saagar is the 34th simile of Gita.

ॐ

God tells various methods from 12/8 to 11
to attain Him through devotion.

(12/8)

मय्येव मन आधत्स्व मयि बुद्धिं निवेशय ।
निवसिष्यसि मय्येव अत ऊर्ध्वं न संशयः ॥१२/८॥

Mayyev man aadhatswa mayi buddhim niveshay I
Nivasishyasi mayyev at oordhwam n sanshay: II (12/8)

Mayi (to Me) Ev (only) Man: (mind) Aadhatswa (fixing) Mayi (unto Me) Buddhim (intelligence) Niveshay (settle down) I Nivasishyasi (shall dwell) Mayi (unto Me) Ev (only) At: (then) Oordhwam (sublimate) N Sanshay: (no doubt)II (12/8)

Fix your mind in Me alone and settle down your intelligence also in Me alone. Thereafter you shall sublimate to dwell in Me only. There is absolutely no doubt in it. (12/8)

Krishn instructed us in 12/7 **Mayi Aaveshit Chetasaam** i.e. to engross our conscience unto Him. Now onwards, He starts explaining various easy techniques to achieve it. In this shlok, He tells us that we can merge our individual identity into Him by stabilizing our intelligence i.e. becoming **Sthit Prajn** (2/55 to 72) and concentrating our mind only on Him.

Moral: *Even a student cannot learn anything without concentrating on what the teacher teaches him; or a housewife cannot cook a good meal if her mind drifts on something else. Then, how can one achieve God without concentration?*

৵৽৻৵

If one is unable to concentrate his mind on God,
he should try with Abhyaas Yog.

(12/9)

अथ चित्तं समाधातुं न शक्नोषि मयि स्थिरम् ।
अभ्यासयोगेन ततो मामिच्छातुं धनंजय ॥१२/९॥

Ath chittam samaadhaatum n shaknoshi mayi sthiram I
Abhyaasayogen tato maamichchhaaptum Dhananjay II (12/9)

Ath (if) Chittam (inner faculty of conscience, mind & heart)
Samaadhaatum (to properly fix, establish) N (not) Shaknoshi
(capable) Mayi (unto Me) Sthiram (stable, firm) I Abhyaas Yogen
(regular practice of Yog) Tat: (then) Maam (to Me) ichchh (cultivate
desire) Aaptum (obtain) Dhananjay (Arjun) II (12/9)

**O Dhananjay (Arjun)! If you are not able to properly
concentrate and steady your Chitt, the mind and intelligence
on Me, then cultivate strong desire to obtain Me by constantly
practising Yog (and gradually move your soul towards Me).
(12/9)**

Concentration of **Man** or **Chitt**, the mind, heart and intelligence
is a precondition for meditation but since most beginners are
entrenched in worldly matters, they find it very difficult to
concentrate and fix it on God. Arjun expressed the same difficulty
earlier in 6/33-34, and Krishn suggested a simple remedy for it
there in 6/35 saying:

'Though Man is undoubtedly fickle and difficult to control, it can
be controlled by regular practice'.

He confirmed it again in 8/8 saying:

"A person, endowed with regular practice of Yog, concentrates
his inner faculties on Supreme Soul, attains Him".

He prescribes the same remedy here. **Abhyaas** is repetitive
constant practice. Practice makes a man perfect if done assiduously
as Yog. If a learner casually strums the wires of a sitar now and
then, he should not aspire to be a maestro someday. It requires
constant practice with devoted labor spread over long years to
become like Pandit Ravi Shankar. We discussed **Abhyaas** in 6/35
earlier as repetitive practice to achieve something. It reappears in
8/8, 12/10 & 18/36 with the same meaning.

Moral: A big mountain range, covered with thick jungles of Kaam, the
desire, Krodh, the anger, Matsar, the jealousy etc., is very difficult to

cross because it has been seldom treaded upon. However, if one can find a jungle trail, he can easily cross it because not even a blade of grass grows in a trail constantly pounded by the feet of tribes living there. Abhyaas is such a jungle trail that leads us to our destination.

Krishn addresses Arjun as Dhananjay, the one who collected wealth by repetitive expeditions, as if to point out the importance of repetitive actions for achieving ultimate success.

৵৽৻

However, some others may find it difficult even to pursue the path of constant practice. Gita offers them the alternative of rendering selfless service to God.

(12/10)

अभ्यासेऽप्यसमर्थोऽसि मत्कर्मपरमो भव ।
मदर्थमपि कर्माणि कुर्वन्सिद्धिमवाप्स्यसि ॥ १२/१ ०॥

Abhyaaseʃpyasamarthoʃsi matkarmaparamo bhav I
Madarthamapi karmaani kurvansiddhimavaapsyasi II (12/10)

Abhyaase (in practice) Api (if) Asamarth: (unable) Asi (you are) Matkarm Param: (resolved to perform all actions on My behalf and in My service) Bhav (be) I Madartham (for my sake) Api (still) Karmaani (all works) Kurvan (doing) Siddhim (accomplishment in spiritual realm) Avaapsyasi (will accomplish) II (12/10)

If you are unable to practice regularly, then just resolve to perform all actions on My behalf and in My service. You shall still accomplish the same success by performing all works only for My sake. (12/10)

This is the third alternate method offered by Gita to achieve God by devotional path. If a practiser is unable to achieve concentration of **Chitt,** or finds it difficult to practice it constantly, Gita suggests him to perform his duties as per God's will and assign results to Him in the spirit of **Shree Krishnaarpanamastu** i.e. *'I dedicate everything to Krishn'.* This method conforms to 9/27-28 where God said:

"Whatever you do, whatever you consume and enjoy, whatever you offer as oblations in Yajn, whatever you donate and whatever penance and austerities you perform; you must offer all of it unto Me. In this way, you shall be delivered from the bonds of auspicious & inauspicious results of your actions, and thereby attain Me".

Please refer to explanations under 9/27 also. Tulasidaas submits everything he does, to God:

'सेवा पूजा बंदगी सबहि तुम्हारे हाथ ।
मैं तो कछु जानू नहीं तुम जानो रघुनाथ ॥'

(The result of all my services, devotional activities and prayers are in your hands O Raghunaath! I know only one thing that You know everything but I know nothing)

❧

Will there be no divine grace for the poorly equipped, hapless, pathetic persons who cannot follow any of the aforesaid practices? God's universal compassion is available for them also.

(12/11)

अथैतदप्यशक्तोऽसि कर्तुं मद्योगमाश्रितः ।
सर्वकर्मफलत्यागं ततः कुरु यतात्मवान् ॥१२/११॥

Athaitadapyashakto∫si kartum madyogamaashrit: I
Sarvakarmaphalatyaagam tat: kuru yataatmavaan II (12/11)

Ath (if) Etat (this) Api (still) Ashakt: (unable) Asi (you are) Kartum (to do) Madyogam (My Yog) Aashrit: (rely on) I Sarv karm Phal Tyaagam (giving up desire of fruition of all actions) Tat: (then) Kuru (act) Yataatm Vaan (contentedly situated in self by conquering Indriys, mind and intelligence) II (12/11)

And if you are still unable even to perform your works (as told in 12/10 above) relying only on attaining Yog, the union

with Me, then just give up the desire of results of all your actions, and do your duties while remaining situated in Self (not in results) with contentment. (12/11)

Sarv Karm Phal Tyaag means giving up interest in the fruits of all actions. This is the fourth alternate method of devoting to God if a practiser is unable to practise according to the three methods mentioned from 12/8 until now. Though this method is the last one in this topic, it is the most important of all since it is the dearest theme of Gita, as Krishn shall repeat it in 18/2 also. Let us understand it in more detail:

SOME ADDITIONAL THOUGHTS ON SARV KARM PHAL TYAAG

Karm means action, work or deed and **Phal** means fruit, produce, yield or result. If **Karm** is considered as a plant sown by its doer, it is bound to yield some kind of **Phal**, the fruit in due course; and if we consider **Karm** as an action, that too would bounce back as a reaction in the life of its doer. As this plant grows into a tree with many branches, it yields more fruits; similarly, as we continue to indulge in more activities, it generates more and more reactions akin to the sparks generated by igniting a firecracker. As a seed is inlaid in every fruit; and every spark is capable of initiating more fireworks, similarly every **Karm** also spreads tentacles of its sinister network in multitudinous directions burdening our very existence with bundles of Karm Phal in our current life as well as afterlife. We had understood **Karm Phal** earlier in 2/47 as fruition and/or reaction of an action performed by a person into some result eventually. **Karm Phal** is not in the hands of the doer. Doing works is akin to playing in share market where, howsoever hard one may buy or sell, the dynamics of the market ultimately control the profit or loss. Dynamism of theory of **Karm** similarly controls results of our works.

Clarification: *We are often told that no one can carry anything from this world after death, but, in my opinion, it is true only with respect to material things like wealth, fame etc. Every soul is otherwise bound to carry the burden of two suitcases: the first one contains the ego of being the doer of some good works, and the other is full* *of the guilt of performing bad works in his lifetime. Only a Yogee, a Mahatma, a saint is free from this burden, because he endeavored to keep these suitcases empty and leave them behind upon death.*

Gopaldaas Neeraj stresses the need to shed as much load as we can before marching on our last journey:

जितना कम सामान रहेगा, उतना सफ़र आसान रहेगा ।

जितनी गठरी भारी होगी, उतना तू हैरान रहेगा ॥

उससे मिलना नामुमकिन है, जब तक खुद का ध्यान रहेगा ॥।

{The less you carry luggage, the more your journey shall be comfortable. The heavier your baggage is the more uncomfortable you would be. It is impossible to meet Him (God) as long as your attention is centered on you (and your belongings)}.

Sarv Karm Phal Tyaag, total absence of interest and attachment in the fruits of all of our actions is the way out. **Tyaag** is a consciously performed act of abandonment, giving up, renouncing, dismissing, leaving, relinquishing, discarding, disregarding or getting rid of someone or something. Applied to spirituality it means **Tyaag** of self-interest and expectation in the result of our works. Gita teaches us to nip every plant of Karm in its budding stage by giving up our belongingness for it and expectation of getting some fruits. By doing all of our works in this fashion, our every **Karm** shall automatically wither away fruitless like a plant abandoned in a deserted place; or like a firecracker soaked with water. Once we start practising this principle, **Sarv Karm Phal Tyaag** becomes an inseparable part of our **Swabhaav**, the characteristic nature. Gita shall deal with **Tyaag** in detail in chapter 18. How can we achieve **Sarv Karm Phal Tyaag**? Krishn showed us the way in previous shlok 12/10 saying:

'Perform all actions on My behalf, only in My service and only for My sake'.

QUESTION: HOW TO REGULATE CHITT AND ENGAGE IT IN GOD?

Chitt, derived from the root **Chit**, is the subconscious mind, the storehouse of all kinds of good or bad, useless or useful memories. In Yog, **Chitt** is often called as a synonym of **Ant:karan**, the internal faculty consisting of **Buddhi**, the intellect, **Ahamkaar**, the ego and **Indriys**, the senses. Gita attaches great importance on regulating **Chitt** (the subconscious mind or **Man**) throughout its text, more specifically here from 12/2 to 11. Let us therefore discuss how we can achieve it. As mentioned under 6/20 to 23, **Paatanjal Yog Darshan** 1/2 defines **Yog** as 'योगश्चित्तवृत्तिनिरोध' i.e. *'Restraining Vrutti, the natural tendency of Chitt, the inner faculty of conscience comprising of mind, intelligence & heart from swaying, is Yog.* **Chitt** of a person can be in one of the five stages:

1. **Kshipt**, the fickle, restless, distracted **Chitt** is overpowered by **Rajas,** the quality of passion. It is therefore extremely unsteady, unable to concentrate on anything, and is the source of pleasure or pain. Gita calls it **Chanchal** in 6/35.

2. **Moodh**, the stupid, infatuated **Chitt** is overpowered by **Tamas,** the quality of ignorance. Influenced by violent emotions, it succumbs to commit unrighteous acts. Gita called people with **Moodh** or **Vimoodh Chitt** as **Nashtaan Achetas,** the self-destructive stupid people in 6/32.

3. **Vikshipt**, the crazy, agitated, scattered, or occasionally steady **Chitt** remains unsteady or indecisive at most of the time as it is influenced by **Sattv**, the quality of goodness. It withdraws itself from painful situations and engages in pleasurable things. He is a *'Kim Kartavya Vimoodh'* person not able to decide his duty properly like Arjun in Gita. It is evident from 2/33 where Krishn warned him thus:

   'If you fail to decide your sacred duty to fight, you would not only be fallen from your duty, but also lose your fame and incur sin'.

   Then, in 2/37, He encouraged him to be **Krut Nischay** i.e. to take a positive decision with determination.

4. **Ekaagr: Chitt** is focused on single point, influenced by superior **Sattv**, the quality of the best. Since it remains focused on one single object, it tends to withdraw from all objects and become totally introvert. Krishn advised a meditator in 6/12 to sit for meditation with **Ekaagr Man**.

5. **Niruddh,** The restrained, regulated **Chitt** is also influenced by **Sattv** but in an alert, awakened state. Though it dwells in the righteous mode in normal times, it is also capable of completely suspending all mental modes and sub-conscious dispositions while pursuing spirituality. Krishn advised a meditator in 6/20 to meditate with **Niruddh Chitt**.

Though some scriptures disqualify first two stages **Kshipt** and **Moodh** of **Chitt**, and some others even the third **Vikshipt,** from attaining **Yog** for they are inflicted by lower mental modes, Gita very kindly opens its doors for every willing and determined person including those with **Kshipt** or **Chanchal**, the flirtatious, fickle mind, as stated in 6/35 & 36. Krishn considered **Vikshipt** Arjun as the most deserving person for redemption in Gita. Liberation achieved by devotees like Vaalmeeki, Ajaamil, Soordaas, Kaalidaas, Ganikaa, the prostitute etc., who spent their initial life in first three stages, are some good examples of eligibility of everybody for **Yog**. Regulation of **Chitt** and thereby achieving self-control is given great importance by Gita as it has dedicated entire chapter 6 **Aatm Samyam Yog** to teach it. Readers may like to read it again with specific attention on shloks from 6/19 & 20, and again from 6/25 to 27. However, Gita would prohibit us, in 18/67-71, from imparting its knowledge to certain types of undeserving people.

Moral: *A plain mirror reflect true image of an object before it till it remains there but retains no trace of it thereafter. We should make our Chitt (or Man) like a plain mirror and reflect on thoughts crossing it only for the limited period until that particular subject matter is there before us. We should neither let it become crooked and distort every object as convex or convex mirrors do; nor should it be allowed to work like a CCTV camera that promptly catches and stores images of every object passing before it. Like an expert Kshetrajn[4], the farmer, we too should not let the weeds and cacti of undesirable, negative thoughts take roots in Kshetr[4], the field of our Chitt and total existence.*

౸౨౬

---

4   *Refer to chapter 13 named as Kshetr Kshetrajn Vibhaag Yog for full understanding of Kshetr and Kshetrajn.*

God establishes superiority of Karm Phal Tyaag.

(12/12)

श्रेयो हि ज्ञानमभ्यासाज्ज्ञानाद्ध्यानं विशिष्यते ।
ध्यानात्कर्मफलत्यागस्त्यागाच्छान्तिरनन्तरम् ॥१२/१२॥

Shreyo hi jnaanamabhyaasaajjnaanaaddhyaanam
vishishyate I
Dhyaanaatkarmaphalatyaagastyaagaachchhaantiranantaram
II (12/12)

Shrey: (meritorious, better) hi (certainly) Jnaanam (knowledge) Abhyaasaat (than practice) Jnaanaat (than Jnaan) Dhyaanam (meditation) Vishishyate (distinctively better) I Dhyaanaat (than meditation) Karm Phal Tyaag: (giving up fruits of actions) Tyaagaat (by Tyaag) Shaanti: (peace) Anantaram (immediately) II (12/12)

Jnaan, the knowledge is better than Abhyaas, the regular practice; and Dhyaan, the meditation is distinctively superior to Jnaan, but renunciation of fruits of actions is the best among them as one can immediately attain eternal peace by this renunciation. (12/12)

Gita beautifully described following four alternative routes, one after the other in 12/6-11, which are also successively easier to practise Yog:

1. **Jnaan,** the knowledge of concentration of mind and intelligence (12/8),

2. **Abhyaas,** the regular practice as mentioned (12/9),

3. **Dhyaan,** the meditation (12/6), and, finally

4. **Sarv Karm Phal Tyaag** as explained in 12/11 i.e. doing all works for the sake of God as instructed in 12/10.

It concludes, in 12/12, that **Sarv Karm Phal Tyaag,** the renunciation of the results of works performed by individuals is the best and quickest way to attain eternal peace i.e. freedom from stress and distress in life.

Clarification: *Gita established the superiority of Jnaan in 4/33, and again in 6/46 and 47, but it seems that Jnaan is given the lowest status here in comparison to other three alternative paths for attaining Yog. It is therefore, clarified that what Gita actually means by Jnaan here is the bookish knowledge of methods and practices, which one can professionally possess but does not put it into practice. Raavan was a great scholar of scriptures; but he failed to translate his knowledge into positive, righteous actions miserably.*

Dhyaan was explained in detail from 6/10 to 28.

☙◦৶

Next eight shloks from 12/13 to 20 describe the qualities of the devotee most liked by God. Since He calls it Amrut of Dharm, let us read it with rapt attention.

(12/13 & 14)

अद्वेष्टा सर्वभूतानां मैत्र: करुण एव च ।

निर्ममो निरहंकार: समदु:खसुख: क्षमी ॥१२/१३॥

संतुष्ट: सततं योगी यतात्मा दृढनिश्चय: ।

मय्यर्पितमनोबुद्धियों मद्भक्त: स मे प्रिय: ॥१२/१४॥

Adweshtaa sarvabhootaanaam maitr: karun ev ch I
Nirmamo nirahamkaar: samadu:khsukh: kshamee II (12/13)
Santusht: satatam yogee yataatmaa drudhanishchay: I
Mayyarpitamanobuddhiryo madbhakt: s me priy: II (12/14)

Adweshtaa (free from envy) Sarv Bhootaanaam (all beings) Maitr: (friendly) Karun (compassionate) Ev (also) Ch (and) I Nirmam: (free from proprietorship, personal interest) Nirahamkaar: (not having ego) Sam Dukh Sukh: (equipoise in distress and happiness) Kshamee (person with forgiving nature) II (12/13)

Santusht: (contented) Satatam (constantly) Yogee (who has achieved Yog) Yataatmaa (temperate with self-control) Drudh (firm) Nishchay: (determination) I Mayi (unto Me) Arpit (dedicated) Man: (mind & heart) Buddhi: (intelligence) Y: (who) Madbhakt: (my devotee) S: (he) Me (to Me) Priy: (very dear) II (12/14)

That devotee is very dear to Me, who is not envious but friendly and compassionate towards all beings (whether living or inanimate) free from proprietary, personal interest in anything; free from ego; equipoise in happiness and distress; a forgiving, fully contented person perpetually united with Me with firm resolve and self-control. He assigns his mind, heart and intelligence unto Me. (12/13 & 14)

Sarv Bhootaanaam, explained under 5/29, encompasses all living beings, humans and other species, and other moving, non-moving, animate, inanimate objects in whatsoever form and state they exist. It also covers **Panch Mahaa Bhoot**, the basic five grand elements namely **Aakaash**, the space, **Vaayu**, the wind, **Agni**, the fire, **Jal**, the water and **Pruthivee**, the earth. Gita uses **Sarv Bhootaanaam** many times with the same meaning. Krishn lists 12 outstanding qualities of the devotee He loves the most in these shloks. They are:

Adweshtaa is used here for **Anasooyant** person explained in 3/17-18 under question 'What is meant by Anasooyant and Abhyasooyant'. **Adweshtaa** devotee is free from the evil of finding faults in others. He is like a person who appreciates beauty of the clothes worn by other people rather than looking for holes, defects and patches in them. **Adweshtaa** is also **Vimatsar**, free from jealousy, as mentioned in 4/22.

Maitr is same as **Suhrud** or **Suhrut** or **Mitr** appearing in 5/29, 6/9 & 9/18. He is an extremely affectionate, good-hearted, well-wisher, and benefactor friend of everyone. Refer to 'What is the difference between Mitr and Suhrud' in 6/9; and 'Some additional thoughts on Suhrud Sarv Bhootaanaam' in 5/29 for full understanding. A common person goes out in search of a good person so that he can befriend him but seldom finds one, whereas a devotee (or a Yogee) outreaches everyone to become his good friend without any self-interest. If we want to be a friend, we should become a giver and not taker. God told in 5/29 that He is **Suhrud Sarv Bhootaanaam**, the best friend of everybody, and expects His devotees to be like Him.

Karun, a derivative of **Karunaa**, the quality of compassion with charity for all without any discrimination, is the person who abounds with unlimited compassion towards every living or inanimate entity from the bottom of his heart. Arjun also was taken over by **Karunaa** in 1/31 but his misplaced **Karunaa** was wrapped in his attachment for own relatives, not for **Sarv Bhootaanaam** i.e. everybody. **Karunaa** is one of the greatest virtues required for a practiser treading the path of spiritual attainment in all religions of Indian origin like Hinduism, Buddhism and Jainism; and in some other religions of the world. In Buddhism, **Karunaa** is one of the four divine conducts along with **Mett**, the friendship (**Maitr** in 12/13), **Muditaa**, the bliss (**Sukh** or **Prasannataa** in Gita) and **Upekkhaa**, the indifference (**Anapekshaa** in 12/16). It recommends cultivating these 4 virtuous mental states to every householder as well as ascetic. When one develops **Karunaa**, the awareness imbued with abundant, expansive, immeasurable compassion, free from hostility and ill will for anybody, it starts purifying his own mind and pervading in all directions including above, below and all around, and in every respect. Albert Schweitzer says:

'The purpose of human life is to serve and to show compassion and will to help others'.

Nelson Mandela opines:

'Our human compassion binds us one to other, not in pity or patronizingly, but as human beings who have learnt how to turn our common suffering into hope for future.'

Cruelty is the enemy of **Karunaa**. We shall reflect on this great virtue more in 16/2 where Gita shall call it **Dayaa** and count it as a divine quality.

Nirmam derived from **Mam**, the mine, defines a person detached from proprietary ownership, interest and/or affection for persons or things he considers his own. It is said that migratory birds become **Nirmam** i.e. detach themselves completely from their weak offspring who cannot fly with them, and leave them behind during remigration. In Gita, Krishn abandoned His **Mamatv** while killing His uncle Kans, cousin Shishupaal, and later even whole Yaadav family was annihilated at His instance. But, Arjun is struck with **Mamataa** for cruel, irreligious Kauravs whom he regards as his own. **Nirmam** was explained in 2/71 under the topic of **Sthit Prajn**. Tulasidaas describes this state in Raamcharit Maanas in 7/117 (क) as:

'ममता मल जरि जाइ'

*(Mal, the dirt, impurity, and waste matter of Mamataa,
the belongingness burns off)*

Nirahamkaar denotes a person free from **Ahamkaar**, the falsified misplaced ego about self. We have understood it in detail in 2/71 as an important quality of **Sthit Prajn**.

Sam Sukh Dukh: **Sam** is the same as **Samatv**, the quality of equanimity. We understood it very well at various shloks like 2/48, 5/17-19, 6/8 and lastly 6/29-32 in the light of teachings in those places. **Sukh** means happiness, pleasure, comfort, joy, convenience and bliss; and **Dukh**, its opposite, means misery, sorrow, distress, unhappiness, grief, pain, dejection, chagrin, sufferance, misfortune, trouble etc. we have discussed **Sukh** and **Dukh** in detail in shloks like 2/14, 38, 56 & 66 earlier. **Sam Sukh Dukh** therefore means to remain equipoise in **Sukh** and **Dukh** as repeated in some other places like in 2/38, 12/18, 14/24 and from 18/36 to 38 later. As **Samatv** is a very important trait of a Yogee, Gita repeatedly talks of equanimity in dualities like **Sukh** & **Dukh**; **Laabh** & **Alaabh; Jay** & **Ajay; Siddhi** & **Asiddhi**; **Sheet** & **Ushn; Mitr** & **Shatru**; **Harsh** & **Amarsh; Maan** & **Apamaan; Keerti** & **Akeerti; Nindaa** & **Stuti**; **Yash** & **Apayash** etc.

Kshamee derived from **Kshamaa**, the virtue of forgiveness, pardon, and absolution as explained in 10/4 & 34 earlier. We shall discuss more about **Kshamaa** in 16/3 later. **Kshamee** is the person who has cultivated the virtue of **Kshamaa** in his **Swabhaav**, the characteristic nature. Forgiveness is like the flower, which clings fast to the heel of the person who willfully crushed it, so that it can continue to give its fragrance to him. *'To err is human'* but forgiving a defaulter person is a noble, divine act. When Ashwatthaamaa is captured and produced before Draupadee to punish him for killing her five sons in sleep after the war had ended, she forgives him saying:

'I do not want his mother also to cry for her son like me'.

We should learn to forgive even the unpardonable ones because God has very kindly forgiven the inexcusable in us. Legends describe how Maharshi Vashishth forgives Vishwaamitr, the killer of his one hundred sons, and decorates him with the title of **Brahmarshi**. Holding a grudge never makes anyone strong; on the contrary, it does make him weak. Forgiveness sets him free from that weakness, and the bitterness, which he may otherwise nurture in his heart. Martin Luther King Jr. observes:

'Forgiveness is not an occasional act, it is a constant attitude'.

Most people think that they love someone because of matching chemistry, or due to some acts of kindnesses, or sometimes by sheer coincidence. It seldom occurs to them that the attitude of *'Forgive & forget'* towards each other is the main force that forges loving, lasting relationships.

Caution: *We are sometimes compelled to let go a powerful wrong doer because of our own weakness. We should never take it as forgiveness. In fact we must rise, gather courage and strength to set it right at the earliest. For example, Yudhishthir counseled Draupadee to forgive Dushaashan for dragging her by hair to the court of Hastinaapur and trying to denude her, because Paandavs were in a very weak position at that time. They wisely waited for thirteen years, gathered strength in that period and avenged the unjust, immoral treatment meted out to them by Kauravs.*

Guru Gobind Singh advises:

'Forgive a weak person if he humiliates you, because it is the duty of the strong to pardon weak; but if a strong person dares to humiliate you, you must punish him'.

Santusht: It was discussed as **Tusht** in 2/55 and as **Santusht** in 3/17. Being the derivative of **Santosh**, the contentment, it denotes a person fully satisfied and contented from whatever he gets in life. Contentment comes not from increasing our possessions, but by decreasing our wants. Devotees no longer look upon material objects as the source of pleasure, and thus are content with whatever they get. We shall discuss it more in 12/19.

Satatam Yogee is one who has accomplished perfection in Yog, the union of the Soul with God, the Supreme Being and remains perpetually 24/7 connected with Him because God fulfills all his needs, and all his deeds are in the service of God.

Yataatmaa: Since Yat means restrained, moderate and temperate, **Yataatmaa** literally translates into a temperate person with full control on self. **Drudh Nischay** is the resolve to finish the work we are in. he is equivalent of **Drudh Vrataa,** the people who do meritorious works unyieldingly with firm resolve and determination, explained earlier in 7/28 & 9/14. His conviction is so firm in that even if whole world tries to convince him otherwise, he never budges from his resolve.

Mayi Arpit Man: Buddhi: is the stage where one's mind, heart and intellect are in the refuge of God, the giver of Man and Buddhi to differentiate the right from wrong. He does not indulge in false pretensions of devotion and lip service because his mind, heart and intelligence dedicate to God. He knows none other than God. God used this phrase verbatim in 8/7 earlier; and we discussed it there. God declares with great delight, after describing above 12 qualities, that the person possessing them is His most loved **Bhakt**. Ashw Ghosh writes about such person:

'He is the soul of all conscious creatures who constitute all things in this world, those which fall within the range of his senses, and those which are beyond his senses'.

ॐ‌ॐ

God describes four more qualities of His dear Bhakt.

(12/15)

यस्मान्नोद्विजते लोको लोकान्नोद्विजते च यः ।
हर्षामर्षभयोद्वेगैर्मुक्तो यः स च मे प्रियः ॥१२/१५॥

Yasmaannodwijate loko lokaannodwijate ch y: I
Harshaamarshbhayodvegairmukto y: s ch me priy: II (12/15)

Yasmaat (by whom) N (neither) Udwijate (be anxious, perturbed) Lok: (people) Lokaat (from people) N (nor) Udwijate (be perturbed, agitated) Ch (and) Y: (who) I Harsh (delight, joy) Amarsh (jealousy, envy, spite) Bhay (fear, threat) Udwegai: (from anxiety, unease, agitated feelings, dejection, temper) Mukt: (liberated) Y: (who) S: (he, that) Ch (and) Me (to Me) Priy: (very dear)II (12/15)

He, who neither perturbs other people nor is he himself agitated by other people; and who is free from joy and jealousy, fear and perturbations, he is very dear to Me. (12/15)

Krishn lists 4 more outstanding qualities of the devotee He likes the most. They are:

Yasmaat N Udwijate Lok and **Lokaat N Udwijate y:** First phrase points to person who does not upset and bother others by forcing his thought and action on them; and the **second phrase Lokaat N Udwijate y** means that he is not provoked and perturbed by actions and/or reactions of others. **Udwijate** is derived from **Udweg,** which we shall discuss under 16th quality below. Meeraa pursued the path of her devotion to Krishn relentlessly in spite of intolerable cruelties by the king and her in laws and criticism by few others:

म्हे तो गुण गोबिंद रा गास्यां ए माय,

राणाजी रूठे तो म्हांरो कांई करसी ।

राणाजी रूठे तो वांरो देस राखसी,

म्हांरा हरिजी रूठे तो कठे जास्यां ए माय ।।

लोक लाज री काण न मानां,

म्हे तो निरभै निसाण घुमास्यां ए माय ।।

राम नाम री जाज चलास्यां,

म्हे तो भौ सागर तर जास्यां ए माय ।।

{O my mother! I shall surely continue to sing in the praise of Govind (God) what can Raanaaji (Vikramjeet Singh, her brother in law and king of Chittaud) do to me if he is displeased. Displeased Raanaaji, at the most, can banish me from his

country, but where would I take refuge if my Hariji (God) becomes angry on me. I shall also disregard low opinion of some people about me and continue to wave the flag (of God) fearlessly. I am determined to row the boat of Raam Naam (the name of God) and cross the ocean of world by it}

God's beloved devotee is like **Aakaash**, the space that remains unperturbed whether it is winter, summer or rain.

Harsh Amarsh Mukt: Harsh means delight, joy, rapture, cheer, happiness, pleasure and ecstasy. All kinds of happiness derived from material things, provided by others, is short lived and replaced soon by distress as spiritual realization only can provide real permanent **Aanand**, the bliss. We have seen how ecstatic Duryodhan was in 1/12 when Bheeshm blew his conch shell, and how it transformed soon into fear in 1/19 after hearing the deafening clarion call of Paandav side. **Harsh** is interpreted sometimes as **Sukh** also, which was explained earlier in 2/14, 56, 66 etc.

Amarsh is the feeling of anger, jealousy and/or intolerance especially aroused, either due to someone else possessing the thing one wants to have for himself, or due to inability to effectively counteract an enemy or competitor. Since all these emotions lead ultimately to **Shok**, the worry and distress, **Harsh** is often paired along with its first cousin **Shok** to form **Dwandw** called **Harsh & Shok** as appearing in 18/27 in Gita also. If we analyze the situations of Harsh– the delight and **Amarsh (Shok)**, the sorrow in our life we shall find that the very person or thing, that once delighted us often becomes the cause of our sorrow later. The same thing holds true conversely also. Baiju was very happy in the company of his love Gauree in the film *Baiju Baawaraa*, but her death made him Baawaraa, i.e. insane; and the pain of separation ultimately proved a boon for him, as he became one of the best singers of his time. I have written in one of my poems:

हर्ष-शोक की लहरों ऊपर डगमग बहती जीवन् कश्ती,
मझधारे में फँसी तब लगा महँगा जीवन मौत है सस्ती,
जब टूटे हिम्मत का चप्पू, तब दिखला देना साहिल को।

{The boat of my life is rocking unsteadily on the waves of happiness and unhappiness (in the ocean of world). Whenever it is caught in the strong currents I feel life is priceless compared to death. O Navigator of my boat! Please be merciful to show me the shores when the oar of my courage is about to break}

Tulasidaas prays to Raam in Raamcharit Maanas 2/2 for remaining calm and serene in two extreme situations of **Harsh** and **Amarsh** that took place on the same day in His life:

प्रसन्नतां या न गताभिषेकतस्तथा न मम्ले वनवासदुःखतः।
मुखाम्बुजश्री रघुनन्दनस्य मे सदास्तु सा मञ्जुलमंगलप्रदा॥

(The splendid grace of the lotus[5] like face of Raghu Nandan Raam neither exhibited happiness on hearing the news of His coronation nor was it stained with sorrow for living in the forests (for fourteen years). I pray His charming face to bless me always with its charm and auspiciousness.)

God describes **Harsh & Amarsh** caused to a practiser by others. He shall talk about obtaining Harsh & Dwesh by a practiser in 12/17 but there it would be in relation to his own material achievements. **Bhay Mukt**: He is a person free from **Bhay**, the fear. God's instruction to His every devotee in almost every religion is, *'Love Me; Fear Me not'*. W B Yeats clearly states:

'The God that frightens is no god, God that loves, lives in heavenly abode'.

A poet writes:

'ख़ौफ़ से ख़ुदा ख़ुश नहीं होता,
मुहब्बत पहली शर्त है अक़ीदे की'

(God cannot be pleased by being afraid of Him; love is the first & foremost condition to show faith & belief in Him)

Sometimes we hear someone proclaiming him *'God fearing'* but, in my opinion, it amounts to having no faith in God, because fear

---

5   *The beauty, Charm and fragrance of a lotus remain the same whether it is in mud or in a vase.*

and faith cannot co-exist. In fact, if someone's faith is founded on fear, it is standing in the marshy, murky land of fear, not on the firm ground of love. **Buddh** says:

'Fear closes all doors (of reason) and makes a believer undesirably meek and submissive. We mostly live in the constantly lurking penumbra of fear and apprehension'.

Moral: *Punarjanm is the greatest fear that stalks a person as the agony he suffered during his dreadfully confined stay in the den of mother's womb haunts him all the time. Gita teaches us that we can get rid of the fear of Punarjanm by doing our works dutifully and selflessly as per the will of God, and leave their outcome on His supreme judgment.*

Udweg Mukt: Freedom from **Udweg**, the restlessness is repeated here after its derivative **Dwijate** appeared two times in the first line of this shlok. It is therefore, clarified here that God's dearest **Bhakt**, apart from not being agitated by others or agitating others, does obtain to any kind of restlessness as other common beings do due to impatience, weakness, annoyance or some other **Vikaar**, the disorder like **Kaam, Krodh, Lobh** etc. within them.

SOME ADDITIONAL THOUGHTS ON UDWEG AND UDWIGN

We had understood **Udweg** as the uneasy emotional feeling of perturbation, anxiety, agitation, provocation, perplexity, and dejection while discussing **Anudwign Manaa** in 2/56. God told us there that he, whose **Man**, the mind and heart is free from **Udweg**, the anxiety, is called **Sthit Prajn**. Note that the phrase **Lokaat N Udwijate ch y** i.e. he does not get provoked and perturbed by others in 12/15 here is in line with **Anudwign Manaa** in 2/56. God now makes a great value addition and tells here that His most loved devotee remains calm and placid not only within himself, and unperturbed by others, but he also ensures that others also are not upset and vexed by his thoughts and actions. Besides this, we can also interpret it that a true devotee neither bothers other people by his behavior, nor does he bother how they would react to his thoughts and actions; he simply moves ahead steadily on the path of devotion. He leads his life like an elephant in the forest that normally neither harms other animals nor can be harmed by them easily. Epicurus describes the state of such person as:

'His state is tranquil, undisturbed, innocuous, non-competitive fruition, approaching nearly to the perfect happiness of gods; as, like them, he too neither suffers vexation in himself nor causes vexation to others'.

☙❧

God describes six more qualities of His dear Bhakt.

(12/16)

अनपेक्षः शुचिर्दक्ष उदासीनो गतव्यथः ।
सर्वारम्भपरित्यागी यो मद्भक्तः स मे प्रियः ॥१२/१६॥

Anapeksh: shuchirdaksh udaaseeno gatvyath: I
Sarvaaarambhparutyaagee yo madbhakt: s me priy: II (12/16)

Anapeksh: (who does not expect, anticipate anything from anyone) Shuchi: (clean, pure) Daksh (proficient, dexterous, deft) Udaaseen: (stoically indifferent, uninvolved) Gat Vyath: (whose distress has departed) I Sarv Aarambh Pari Tyaagee (who completely gives up starting any endeavor for achieving some result) Y: (who) Madbhakt: (my devotee) S: (he) Me (to Me) Priy: (very dear) II (12/16)

That devotee of Mine is very dear to Me who does not expect and anticipate anything from anyone; is bodily clean and pure at heart; is highly proficient in whatever he does; is stoically indifferent in all situations; is completely relieved from distress; and who does not get involved in an activity to achieve some result. (12/16)

Krishn lists 6 more outstanding qualities of the devotee He likes the most. They are:

Anapeksh is derived from **Apekshaa** meaning expectation, or looking towards someone in expectation of fulfilling our wish or need. Thus, **Anapeksh** is a person who does not expect anything from anybody. He is self sufficient and fully satisfied by himself for he has limited his needs by his highly regulated and controlled way of living. As a result, he remains indifferent, impartial and neutral with everybody under all situations. It is truly said that if we nurture some expectations from someone, his expectations from us shall be doubled and, if our expectation from him is fulfilled, we shall be obliged to repay his debt by hook or crook, sometimes even by resorting to evil and unjust actions. Duryodhan favored Karn with the crown of Ang Desh and, because of this one favor, Karn had to lifelong repay his debt by supporting his immoral acts. **Anapeksh** is equivalent to **Niraashee** discussed in 4/21 & 6/10 earlier as a person who nurtures not any hope from others to do some favor or service to him. An accomplished **Nirapeksh** or **Niraashee** devotee does not desire anything from God also because he knows that God knows his needs and provides, without asking, what is best for him.

A person sometimes expects from himself also like success of an action, achievement of a target, fulfillment of a vow etc. A common man normally nurture such expectations for progress in life, but a devotee (and a Yogee) keeps him away from it by submitting his every work to God and leaving its result to His supreme will. Another form of expectation is that of others from us like parents expecting from their children, or a friend from his friend. A devotee should try to meet such expectations only as long as they serve the purpose of **Lok Sangrah** (3/20 & 25), but ensure simultaneously that they do not become hurdles in the path of devotion.

Shuchi means clean, pure, faultless, pious and virtuous. Its derivative Shauch, the virtue of maintaining inside and outside cleanliness, shall appear in 13/7, 16/3 & 7, 17/14 and 18/42, and discussed there as appropriate. Its opposite word **Ashuch** i.e. unclean, impure shall appear in 16/16 & 18/27.

Daksh denotes an expert person proficient, dexterous, competent, skilled and deft in doing his duties. God tells that the devotee most loved by Him must be **Daksh** in His devotion. Gita advised us in 2/50 **Yog: Karmasu Kaushalam** i.e. performing works with dexterity, proficiency, competence, and expertise is Yog.

As the dearest devotee of God is also a perfect Yogee, this advice hold true for him also. J. R. D. Tata says:

'Making steel is comparable to making chapatti. To make a good chapatti, even a golden pin will not work unless the dough is good'.

Udaaseen, explained in 6/9, is a person who remains stoically indifferent, uninvolved, non-participant and neutral under all circumstances since he has no self-interest in anything. He is like the sky that witnesses everything in the world but never gets involved in any of its affairs. It shall appear in 9/9 & 14/23 also.

Gat Vyath is the person for whom personal pain, anguish, and distress have ceased to exist. A devotee remains always calm and blissful even in most trying situations like death of a close relative, some disease, loss in business, insult by others for he considers them as acts of God to strengthen his devotion by removing obstructions in his path.

Sarv Aarambh Pari Tyaagee: He is the practiser of Sarv Karm Phal Tyaag that we understood in 12/11 as the virtue of total abandonment of interest and attachment in the fruits of all of our actions. A **Sarv Aarambh Pari Tyaagee** voluntarily abandons involvement of own self by restricting his mind, heart, intelligence, speech and body from commencing any endeavor for own sake or to achieve some result, as he directs his entire being to work only as per Supreme Will of God. Proverbially speaking, he *'rests on his laurels'* i.e. sits fully contented with what he has, and makes no further effort to achieve more things for self. The quality of **Sarv Aarambh Pari Tyaag** is a step further of **Sarv Karm Phal Tyaag as** stops generating fresh **Karm Phal** by not initiating any fresh action for him to fulfill a desire, or for others. Such devotee may physically seem to involve in some righteous works, but his conscience remains free from those works. On many difficult occasions in Mahaabhaarat, Vyaas comes to advise Dhrutraashtr, Kauravs and Paandavs to follow the righteous path of **Dharm** but never involves personally in their affairs. Though he is capable of forcing his wishes on them, he, as an accomplished **Sarv Aarambh**

Pari Tyaagee, lets the will of God prevail upon his counsels and decide its own course.

Clarification: *The phrase 'Madbhakt s me Priy' meaning 'My that devotee is dear to me' does not reflect God's partisan attitude in any way towards His Bhakt compared to His other worshippers. It only confirms what God said about His various worshippers in 4/11, 'People take refuge in Me in whatsoever manner they like; and I too take care of them by rewarding in the same manner'. In fact, God also used similar phrase 'S Mam Priy' for Jnaanee also in 7/17.*

๛

God adds five more qualities of His dear Bhakt.

(12/17)

यो न हृष्यति न द्वेष्टि न शोचति न काङ्क्षति ।
शुभाशुभपरित्यागी भक्तिमान्यः स मे प्रियः ॥१२/१७॥

Yo n hrushyati n dweshti n shochati n kaankshati I
Shubhaashubhparityaagee bhaktimaany: s me priy: II (12/17)

Y: (who) N (neither) hrushyati (rejoices, delights, cheers) N (nor) Dweshti (envies, hates, dislikes) N (neither) Shochati (laments) N (nor) Kaankshati (aspires) I Shubh Ashubh (good & bad, auspicious & inauspicious, favorable & unfavorable) Pari Tyaagee (who voluntarily gives up, abandons something) Bhaktimaan: (person endowed with devotion) Y: (who) S: (he) Me (to Me) Priy: (very dear) II (12/17)

He who neither takes delight nor envies; neither grieves nor aspires; and voluntarily renounces the auspicious and the inauspicious from his life; that person, endowed with great devotion, is dear to Me. (12/17)

Krishn lists 5 more qualities of the devotee He likes the best:

N Hrushyati: He does not rejoice, takes delight and rapture on achieving good results of his works like birth of a child, an award of a senior position in royal court, a bumper profit in business or a victory in a battle. Though freedom from **Harsh** (and **Amarsh**) was mentioned under **Harsh Amarsh Mukt,** the 14th virtue above in 12/15, it applied there for delight caused by behaviour of others with him, but God says here that his beloved devotee is not delighted by personal achievements and successes in material field.

N Dweshti: God's dearest devotee never envies, hates, dislikes anybody for his virtues or vices because he sees his God in everybody and loves him even if he opposes his thoughts and actions. Abraham Lincoln might have never read Gita but his following words surely reflect his clear understanding of how a devout man must do the task he is supposed to do:

'With malice towards none, with charity for all, firmness in the right as God gives us to see the right, let us finish the work we are in'.

Clarification: *God spoke of Adweshtaa earlier in 12/13 but it was for the virtue of not looking for faults in others as explained there. He uses similar word N Dweshti here, but it is to convey that His dear Bhakt does not envy and hate anyone.*

N Shochati: It means that a devotee does not lament, grieve for any personal loss caused to him by others or by destiny as he takes every situation of his life as the will of God. As far as a loss suffered by others due to him inadvertently or due to own **Karm Phal** is concerned, he always tries his best to alleviate them from that loss with utmost compassion. It is highly noteworthy that when Krishn started teaching Gita to Arjun from 2/11 the first word He spoke was **Ashoch**; and He shall also end His teaching in 18/66 with **Maa Shuch**; and both these utterances are opposite of **Shoch** literally meaning *'Do not grieve'*. This shows that the purpose of Gita is to teach how to remain free from grief and stress in life as explained earlier also in 2/11.

N Kaankshati: Derived from **Aakaankshaa**, the wish, ambition, desire, **N Kaankshati** means not cherishing **Aakaankshaa** for self or for others. The mission of the life of a true devotee of God should be to work for own spiritual development, and well-being of every soul, but leave results on His Supreme Will.

Moral: *Success achieved is Prasaad, the propitious blessings of God; and a failure as a signal to redouble our effort.*

Shubh Ashubh Pari Tyaagee: Shubh and **Ashubh,** as understood in 2/57 and 9/28 earlier, are the reactions of our good and bad actions respectively. They consist of **Shubh**, the auspicious, materially pleasant, agreeable, weal and desirable ones; and **Ashubh**, the inauspicious, materially unpleasant, disagreeable, woeful and undesirable ones. One has to consume results of all of them by going through numerous cycles of birth and death in **Oordhw,** the upper worlds for good works, and **Adh:,** the lower worlds for evil works; but he cannot attain the eternal world of no return until he gives up his desire for both, the auspicious and the inauspicious results. Once done, he becomes the dearest devotee of God.

QUESTION: WHY IS IT NECESSARY TO GIVE UP SHUBH, THE AUSPICIOUS ALSO, WHICH BRINGS HAPPINESS?

Gita says all works, whether good or bad, result in bondage if performed with the desire to achieve certain result. One cannot liberate from the cycles of birth & death since **Shubh** binds him to return to the world in order to consume **Punya**, the favorable results. For example, it is immaterial and irrelevant for a prisoner whether his shackles are made of gold (auspicious one) or iron (inauspicious one) as long as he remains fettered by thcm. If a person makes a fixed deposit (auspicious) in a bank, it will call him upon maturity to take back the money or renew it. Conversely, if he borrows a loan (inauspicious) from the bank it will not leave him until it recovers the loan. The bank shall not close his account in either case and add interest until the account squares up. The bank of **Punarjanm**, the birth & death also acts in similar fashion.

Clarification: *No one ever wants to suffer an inauspicious result of any of his works. Does it mean that such a person has succeeded half way in giving up attachment with results? Not at all! He would have to suffer for his every good or bad work, done whether he likes it or not. A thief never wants the police to catch him but it shall* *eventually catch and punish him one day. A person must suffer for both Shubh & Ashubh works like judgments of civil and criminal courts delivered separately.*

However, if a person were able to give up expectations of auspicious results of good deeds done by him voluntarily, he would have automatically detached himself from the inauspicious also. How can one achieve it practically in life? The simplest way, that Gita shows, is to think that whatever good works he is able to perform, actually they are due to the energy & resources provided by God to him. Simultaneously, he must owe entire responsibility of his bad works. Consequently, God becomes the beneficiary of the result of his good deeds and guides him to rectify his evil deeds. He should consider himself just as an instrument the hands of God.

৵৵৽

God describes nine more qualities of His dear Bhakt.

(12/18 & 19)

समः शत्रौ च मित्रे च तथा मानापमानयोः ।
शीतोष्णसुखदुःखेषु समः सङ्गविवर्जितः ॥१२/१८॥
तुल्यनिन्दास्तुतिर्मौनी सन्तुष्टो येन केनचित् ।
अनिकेतः स्थिरमतिर्भक्तिमान्मे प्रियो नरः ॥१२/१९॥

Sam: shatrau ch mitre ch tathaa maanaapamaanayo: I
Sheetoshnsukhdu:kheshu sam: sangvivarjit II (12/18)
Tulyanindaastutirmaunee santushto yen kenchit I
Aniket: sthirmatirbhaktimaanme priyo nar: II (12/19)

Sam: (equipoise) Shatrau (in enemy) Ch (and) Mitre (in friends) Ch (and) Tathaa (similarly) Maan (respect, honor, prestige) Apamaan (disrespect, insult) Y: (who) I Sheet: ushn Sukh du:kheshu Sam: (equipoise in heat & cold, happiness & distress) Sang: (attachment, association) Vivarjit: (devoid of) II (12/18)

Tulya (equal, balanced) Nindaa (harsh criticism) Stuti: (praise) Maunee (vowed to silence to think with deep introspection and reflection) Santusht: (contented) Yen ken chit (in whatever circumstance) I Aniket: (who has no belongingness to the place he resides) Sthir Mati: (person with stable intelligence) Bhaktimaan (person endowed with devotion) Me (to Me) Priy: (very dear) Nar: (person) II (12/19)

He, who is equipoise with friends & foes, in honor & dishonor; and equipoise in heat & cold and happiness & distress; and is devoid of attachment; (12/18)

Who is equal in criticism & praise; is vowed to silence in order to think with deep introspection and reflection; remains satisfied under all circumstances with whatever he gets; has no belongingness and attachment in the place of residence; and whose intelligence is stable; such person endowed with devotion is very dear to Me. (12/19)

Krishn adds 9 more virtues to the list of outstanding qualities of the devotee He likes the best:

Sam Shatrau Mitre: He is a person who remains equipoise with his enemies as well as friends. In 12/13, God said that His most loved devotee is always **Maitr** i.e. friendly and **Karun** i.e. compassionate with everybody because he sees no fault in him. God now adds that such devotee does not differentiate between a person who regards him as his enemy or he who regards him as his friend, and treats both of them with same equanimity. He is like a tree that gives its shade and fruits equally to the gardener who sowed its seed, watered and nurtured it to grow; and to a wood cutter who cuts it. In fact, it gives its wood also to the latter. As Sugarcane gives its sweet juice equally to the farmer who grows it, and also gives the same happily to the cane crusher, so does a true devotee treat everybody, whether a friend or foe, with same equanimity. Readers may refer to 6/9 also for further understanding. Following quartet written by me should explain meaning of friendship for a devotee of God:

'Be friendly to everyone riding in the same boat with you,
In waters supple, calm, placid, and breeze cool, fragrant;
But choose only the best ones from them who shall not
Desert you in stormy winds and waters highly turbulent'.

Sam Maan Apamaan Y: Maan means respect, honor, prestige, pride, regard and reputation; and **Apamaan,** its opposite, means disrespect, dishonor, slander, contempt, insult and humiliation. God tells us here that He loves His devotee most if he remains equipoise in all situations that normally cause **Maan** and **Apamaan** for a common person. We had discussed **Maan Apamaan** in 6/7. It will appear again in 14/25.

Sheet Ushn Sukh Dukheshu Sam: The most liked devotee of God remains equipoise in dualities like **Sheet** & **Ushn** i.e. cold and hot, and **Sukh** & **Dukh** i.e. pleasure and pain. It was discussed in 6/7. The virtue of **Sam Sukh Dukh** will also appear in 14/25.

Sang Vivarjit: He is same as **Asang** person in 15/3, **Sang Rahitam** in 18/23. It means that he is forbidden from any kind of attachment, association, connection with persons, things and situations that do not support or promote **Dharm** in the society. His conscience remains free from attachment, attraction, infatuation, disenchantment with material things. A devotee is situated always in the company of God.

Tulya Nindaa Stuti: A devotee remains equipoise in **Nindaa**, harsh criticism, and **Stuti**, the praise. Since **Nindaa** & **Stuti** appear here for the first time in Gita, let us understand them well here:

SOME ADDITIONAL THOUGHTS ON TULYA NINDAA STUTI

Nindaa is defined as vilification, blame, harsh criticism, reproach, scorn, abuse, defamation and slander hurled scornfully on a person in his presence or behind his back; and **Stuti** is the praise and eulogy showered devoutly and lavishly on someone either publicly or in private in his presence or in absence by his followers and admirers. Arjun used the word **Stutibhi** earlier in 11/21 but it was to describe how great men and demigods were singing in praise of Universal form of God before Him.

Freedom of speech, guaranteed in liberal, democratic societies, confers right on its every member to comment, criticize or praise anybody for his good or bad works. Ignorant persons therefore, indulge in **Nindaa** or **Stuti** of almost every person who gains some prominence in society. It has become so fashionable now a days that many of them do not desist from inflicting reckless criticism and insults not only on great men living in their times but also on deceased great souls. A normal person takes **Nindaa** in bad taste, gets agitated and tries his best to retort and repay his harsh critic in the same coin if he is strong; and, if he is weak, he is dejected and becomes gloomy. A perfect devotee of God should never pay any heed to his unfounded, unwarranted criticism because of his **Aatm Rati** (3/39) but a practiser must carefully take his criticism as a positive feedback and improve himself wherever lacking. Kabeer rightly advises a practiser as follows:

'निंदक नियरे राखिए आँगन कुटी छवाय ।
बिन पानी साबुन बिना निर्मल करे सुभाय ।।'

(Keep your critic close to you by constructing a room for his stay in your premises for he is the one who would cleanse your character without demanding soap and water)

Sheikh Saadi warns us to beware of him, who vilifies someone, particularly in his absence:

'He, who vilifies someone in his absence before you, is sure to criticize you also before others in your absence.'

Moral: *Baseless vilification can retract a practiser from spiritual pursuit if he is not Drudh Nishchay, a determined person; and it can enrage him to react and take revenge. A devotee should therefore, remain unaffected by Nindaa just as a pitcher with smooth, oily surface does not let a drop of water stick on it.*

Stuti, the praise, the accolades showered on a person often turns into flattery. A devotee never feels elated even if he is worthy of it because firstly he believes that any virtue achieved by him is not due to his efforts but it is the propitious blessing and compassion of God, and secondly he may become swollen head by flattery and fall from his graceful place.

Moral: *Stuti, the praise is like a strong magnet that attracts an elegant piece of furniture towards it only to dismember it by extracting nails from its joints. One must immediately hide under cover of humility to save himself.*

Let us take the example of Hanumaan in Raamcharit Maanas. Hanumaan, the greatest devotee of Raam, is beyond the effects of **Nindaa-Stuti**. First, when tied by a noose and brought to the court of Raavan, he remains undisturbed by **Nindaa**, the scorn and insult hurled by Raavan and his subjects on him, and calmly advises Raavan to return Seetaa to Raam. Secondly, when he returns to Raam after accomplishing the arduous task of crossing the sea, burning Lankaa and bringing the information of Seetaa, Raam showers **Stuti**, the praise on him for his extra ordinary fete. See how Hanumaan responds to it in 5/32/6 to 9:

प्रभु प्रसन्न जाना हनुमाना। बोला बचन बिगत अभिमाना॥
साखामृग के बड़ि मनुसाई। साखा तें साखा पर जाई॥
नाघि सिंधु हाटकपुर जारा। निसिचर गन बिधि बिपिन उजारा।
सो सब तव प्रताप रघुराई। नाथ न कछू मोरि प्रभुताई॥

(When Hanumaan saw His Lord happy, he spoke these words with no trace of pride, 'A monkey's greatest ability is that it can jump from one branch of a tree to another branch. I could cross over the sea, burn the golden city of Lankaa, kill hordes of demons and ruin their garden only due to the vigour provided by You O my Lord Raghunaath! It was none of my own greatness.')

Sheikh Saadi cautions us also to beware of a flatterer:

'Take care how you listen to the voice of the flatterer, who, in return for his little stock, expects to derive from you considerable advantage. If one day you do not comply with his wishes, he imputes to you two hundred defects instead of perfections'.

Look at the following amusing but inspiring anecdote below:

"A donkey fell in a deep, dry well and could not come out. When all efforts to pull it out failed, the villagers decided to bury it in the well and started pouring dust in the well. Some of them praised the beauty of the donkey and took pity for its fate whereas others abused it for its carelessness. The donkey was an astute, wise animal. Not scared of his almost certain death due to burial under the dust, it started jumping violently in order to shake it off from its body and rise about it. as the villagers continued to pour more and more dust

into the well and the donkey also continued to shake it off and rise above it until the dust reached a level from which it managed to jump out of the well and walk away happily".

The message of the donkey to us humans, the most intelligent species on earth, is clear.

Moral: *Let us not be steered by our own fear, nor by the praise and insult by others. After all, it is our own life; and we should handle it with utmost ease and wisdom.*

We shall have some more discussions on **Tulya Nindaa Stuti** in 14/24 where it would appear as a similar phrase **Tulya Nindaa Aaatm Sanstuti**.

Maunee: He is one who is vowed to think with deep introspection & reflection about spirituality. Even for an ignorant man, nothing is better than silence because, if he is sensible enough to observe silence at appropriate time & place, he shall not be ignorant anymore. He becomes a **Muni** explained in 2/56.

Santusht Yen Ken Chit: God described **Santusht** in 8th quality of His devotee earlier in 12/14 as a person fully contented, satisfied with whatsoever he gets from others. Nevertheless, He repeats here the same virtue with the addition of **Yen Ken Chit** meaning that he remains contented under all situations irrespective of whether he gets something desirable or not. He is a person satisfied within own self, a step ahead of **Santusht** in 12/14. Gita described him also as **Aatmani ev Aatmanaa Tusht** in 2/55 under the topic of **Sthit Prajn**. We had understood it in 3/17 & 18 under *'Some additional thoughts on Aatm Santusht'*. The shlok given below from scriptures describes such person well:

अकृत्वा पर सन्तापम् अगत्वा नम्रतां ।
अक्लेशयित्वा निर्जात्मानम् यत् स्वल्पमपि तद्वहु ॥

(Without causing anguish to others, without going to and bowing before undeserving people, and without troubling his own self much, whatever one gets or doesn't get, he is always satisfied)

Socrates says:

'He is the richest who is content with the least, for content is the wealth of nature'.

See the example below:

"A Saadhu lived in an Aashram by begging alms in nearby village. A poor farmer living next door used to often wonder why everyone visits Saadhu with lot of gifts and offer voluntary services to him though a Saadhu has renounced everything; and nobody comes to him who really needs their help. Saadhu, however, politely declined to accept anything saying that he is self-sufficient. Unable to restrain himself, one day the farmer asked Saadhu to explain the reason for it. Saadhu explained to him thus, 'Answer of your question lies within itself. People offer help to me knowing well that I don't need anything; and they do not go to you because they know that you shall not only accept their help but also ask more things from them. The day I start accepting their things, they will stop coming to me also".

'Ichigyo-zammai' is a Japanese way of living by fully concentrating, involving with the activity we are in at this moment (as per will of God), and enjoying it. The tourist, who trains his mind to resist the frenzy of do-it-all itineraries, and visits just one place, enjoys his tour to its full potential.

Moral: *Learn to live and enjoy in the present moment. Relish Daal Rotee, the bread and lentils cooked by the house lady rather than think of sumptuous, candle light dinner in a star hotel; wear the best clothes you have than storing them for some grand occasion that may never turn up; de-congest your home from excessive furnishing to grant freedom of movements to yourself in your own house.*

Abraham Lincoln describes an ever-dissatisfied person for his insatiable wish in typical witty way:

'If this is coffee, give me tea; and if this is tea, I want coffee'.

Aniket: He is the one who has no belongingness and attachment with the place he resides. **Mahaabhaarat** describes him in 3/12/11, as **Yatr Saayam Gruh** meaning a wandering ascetic considers the place where night falls, as his temporary home, the place to rest for just that night. Though he roams here and there like wind but is not a destitute, since he believes in **Vasudhaiv Kutumbakam** i.e. whole world is one family and, therefore, considers entire earth his home. Lyricist Pradeep writes in film *Sambandh*:

बिछौना धरती का कर ले । अरे! आकाश ओढ़ ले ॥

(Make the ground your bed; and cover yourself with the quilt of sky.[6])

We are often scared on seeing lizards crawling in our houses. One day I heard a conversation between a baby lizard and its mother:

"Baby lizard: 'Mama! I feel very happy when these persons leave our home every morning, but I am damn scared when they return every evening'.

Wise mom then explained thus to her child:

'My child! This house is home not only to us. It houses many other creatures like rats, cockroaches, ants, flies etc. also. The people, who go out every day for work and return for rest in night, have built this house. Be a good lizard! Learn to live in this house with all of its inhabitants".

Moral: *Total land area of Earth after subtracting uninhabitable areas covered by water, deserts, mountains etc., is 15.77 billion acres. It means God has provided 36,000 sq. meters of land for a family of four to live happily on it. it is a great travesty of life that, though a Saadhu considers 2 sq. meters[7] of land enough for him, people wage wars to own more than their equitable share of 9,000 sq. meters each to snatch others' share.*

Tad Williams suggests:

'Make a home for yourself inside your own head. You'll find what you need to furnish it, memory, friends you can trust, love of learning, and other such things. That way it will go with you wherever you journey'.

---

6   *The size of a quilt is limited, it consists of two, three layers; but the quilt of sky is limitless, and it has seven layers of stratosphere, exosphere, mesosphere, thermosphere, troposphere, ozone and ionosphere.*

7   *Legends mention that even God, in His Vaaman Avatar, begged for just three steps (2 Sq. meters approx.) of land from Bali for His sustenance.*

Moral: *Birds make only one nest for laying eggs and rearing their offspring; once that purpose is over, they abandon it. Human beings are the only foolish species on this planet who treat God given land as property. They acquire it and build houses on it in which they may never live.*

In Raamaayan, when Raam asks Vaalmeeki to show Him a suitable place where He could build a hut and live for some time in the forest, Vaalmeeki counter-questions Him, the omnipresent God:

'Tell me the place O Raam where You do not reside, and I will recommend that place to You to build Your hut'.

It is therefore, natural and befitting for God's devotee also to regard whole world his home for he finds his God everywhere.

Sthir Mati is a person with stable, firm, undulating intelligence. He is same as **Sthit Prajn** of Gita described in detail from 2/55 to 2/72. His intelligence is like a lantern whose flame remains stable because it is secure in the glass bulb that surrounds it. When placed at the doorstep of a house, it illuminates the house of its owner as well as that of his neighborhood, and even lights up the path for passerby wayfarers without any discrimination.

❧᪐

God describes two final qualities of His dear Bhakt.

(12/20)

ये तु धर्म्यामृतमिदं यथोक्तं पर्युपासते ।
श्रद्दधाना मत्परमा भक्तास्तेऽतीव मे प्रियाः ॥१२/२०॥

Ye tu dharmyaamrutamidam yathokt paryupaasate I
Shraddadhaanaa matparamaa bhaktaaste∫teev me priyaa: II
(12/20)

Ye (who) Tu (and) Dharmyaamrutam (nectar of Dharm conferring immortality) Idam (this) Yathoktam (aforesaid) Pari Upaasate (assiduously engaged in devotional service) I Shraddadhaanaa:

(who possess undulating faith and reverential belief) Matparamaa: (depend entirely and exclusively on Me) Bhaktaa: (devotees) Te (they) Ateev (extremely) Me (to Me) Priyaa: (dear) II (12/20)

Devotees who possess undulating faith and reverential belief in Me, depend exclusively on Me, and engage assiduously in My devotional service as per aforesaid Dharmyaamrut, the nectar of Dharm that confers immortality; those devotees are extremely dear to Me." (12/20)

Krishn finally adds 2 virtues to the list of qualities of God's most loved devotees:

Shraddadhaanaa are the devotees who possess undulating faith and reverential belief in God. Gita describes them also as **Shraddhaa may, Shraddhaa Vaan, Shraddadhaanaa, Shraddhaa vant, Shraddhayaa Anvitaa,** and **Shraddhayaa Parayaa** at different places. Please refer to 3/31-32.

Matparamaa are the devotees who depend entirely on God. It is same as **Matpar** or **Matparaayan** appearing in 2/61, 6/14, 9/34, 12/6, 18/57 etc.

Dharmyaamrut consists of two words **Dharmya + Amrut** meaning the **Amrut**, the nectar of **Dharm**. God states here that whatever He has told from 12/13 to 20 is **Amrut**, the essence of **Dharm** because, like the nectar of gods, it is pure and infallible and capable to cure all kinds of physical, mental and spiritual ailments of its practiser without any side effect or after effect on him. Once perfected, it confers immortality on him by liberating from the cycles of birth, sufferance and death. His immortality exceeds that of demigods because he is remembered until eternity for his virtuous deeds and exemplary life dedicated completely in the service of God and His creation. The idea of **Amrut** first appeared in 2/15 and explained there. Besides, it also repeats in more than 9 shloks in Gita.

SOME ADDITIONAL THOUGHTS ON BHAKT, THE DEVOTEE OF GITA

A **Bhakt** chooses the path of **Bhakti** to attain Gita's **Samagr Yog**, the ultimate union with God in **Saakaar** or **Niraakaar** form. **Bhakti** is founded on the theme of love, adoration and devotion of Supreme Being among other major themes of Gita like **Jnaan**, the knowledge, and **Karm**, the action; and all are independently capable to lead their practisers to ultimate union with God. Though Gita does not discriminate between these three main paths, let us recall here what God told us, from 5/2 to 6, to understand importance of **Bhakti** in Gita:

> "Sannyaas (or Jnaan), the knowledge and Karm, the action both lead to liberation but Karm is distinctively superior; ..... but Sannyaas without Karm is afflicted with great distress while the practiser of Karm Yog achieves Brahm quickly with ease".

Gita does not make any comparison between **Jnaan** & **Bhakti** or **Karm** & **Bhakti** in its entire text. On the contrary, highly appreciative, positive, favorable statements invariably accompany **Bhakti** in 9/34, 11/55, 14/26-27, and many other shloks besides here. **Bhakti** is the heart of Gita while **Jnaan** is her head, and **Karm** her **Karmendriys**. When thoughts of head and actions of **Karmendriys** unite and harmonize with heart, the grand fusion of the highest order, called **Samagr Yog** of Gita, takes place. The fact that Krishn consciously concludes His teachings in Gita with 18/65-66, dedicated exclusively to **Bhakti,** amply demonstrates its importance in attaining Yog. **Bhakti** is the easiest thing that everyone can adopt, as it requires him only to attach his heart with God, while lot of preparations and practice are required in **Jnaan** and **Karm**.

Raamcharit Maanas praises **Bhakti** in 7/45/1 in these words:

'कहहु भगति पथ कवन प्रयासा। जोग न मख जप तप उपवासा॥'

(The path of Bhakti does not need one to undertake arduous efforts required in other practices like Hath Yog, Yajn, penance and fasting)

Who is a **Bhakt**? Tukaaraam defines him as:

जिसका नहीं हो कोई हृदय से उसे लगाये।
प्राणिमात्र के लिए प्रेम की ज्योति जगाये॥

सब में प्रभु को व्याप्त जान सबको अपनाये ।
है जो ऐसा वही जगत में भक्त कहाये ॥

(The world knows him as a true Bhakt who embraces those who have none to support them; who lights the lamp of love for all living beings and who treats others like his own self because he sees the same God pervading also in them.)

A devotee loved by God is like an expert gardener who sows the seeds of **Bhakti** in the garden of his heart, irrigates them daily with the water of love, nurtures it with the fertilizer of faith and patiently waits for it to sprout, grow and bear fruits for him, as well as others. Hindus believe that bathing in Gangaa cleanses their sins and relieves them from physical, mental and spiritual sufferings, but there always looms the fear of drowning in its depths or be swept away in its strong currents. Nevertheless, he who drowns his egoistic self in the river of devotion is sure to attain immortality. A devotee is like the calf of a cow that suckles milk (Dharmyaamrut) from his mother's udders effortlessly because the mother knows that he depends on solely her. However, the case of a common person wanting to milk the same cow is different. He has to put in lot of efforts like tying her with a rope, initiate her teats to release the milk and be cautious of her kicks because he regards her as his *'milch cow'*, the source of profit. Shreemad Bhaagawat, the greatest devotional Scripture, states in 3/29/12:

'अहैतुक्य व्यवहिता या भक्ति: पुरुषोत्तमे'

(Bhakti, the devotion, practised without wanting anything in return for self, is the real devotion of Purushottam, the Supreme Soul)

The faith and dependence of a true devotee of God is unwavering and unflinching. Recall the promise **Yog Kshemam Vahaami Aham** made by God to His devotees in 9/22 in this regard. A blind devotee used to visit a temple daily. One day a person asked him why he goes to the temple daily when he is not able to have *Darshan* of God. His reply is an eye-opener for everybody:

'It is true that I am not able to see God; but I come here daily to ensure that God does not forget me'.

Leonardo da Vinci correctly says:

'I love those who can smile in trouble, who can gather strength from distress, and grow brave by reflection. It is the business of little minds to shrink, but they, whose heart is firm, and whose conscience approves their conduct, will pursue their principles unto death'.

God loves His devotees certainly more than Leonardo da Vinci does. It is recommended to revisit question & additional thoughts after 4/42 and 12/6-7 for better understanding of **Bhakti**. We shall conclude our thoughts on **Bhakti** after 18/65-66.

CONCLUSION OF CHAPTER 12

Krishn described four kinds of devotees in 7/16: **Aart**, the one in extreme distress, **Arthaarthee**, the seeker of material wealth, **Jijnaasu**, the inquisitive one and **Jnaanee,** the matured knower; and said in 7/17 that **Jnaanee** is most eminent among them; and therefore **S ch Mam Priy:** i.e. he is dear to Me. Nevertheless, He did not think it appropriate there to elaborate what kind of **Jnaan** qualifies a **Jnaanee** to be His dearest devotee. He first taught us the fundamentals of **Bhakti** in chapter 9 and then waited until Arjun fully accepted Him as Almighty God after seeing His universal and Chaturbhuj forms in chapter 11. Now, in chapter 12, Krishn finds the best opportunity to describe the qualities that His dearest devotees must possess.

The point I wish to make by above analysis is that though chapter 12 is titled **Bhakti Yog**, it does not even touch the commonly understood forms and methodology of Bhakti like Shrawan, Keertan, Smaran, Poojaa, Aaratee, visiting temple etc. (as those preliminary steps were already discussed in chapter 9). Instead, it very boldly prescribes the greatest qualities and traits that the best human being must know, cultivate, possess and practise in his life and become God's most liked person. It is of little or no consequence for God whether such outstanding person reaches Him through **Jnaan**, or **Karm** or **Bhakti**, or **Dhyaan**, or any other.

A beginner in the path of devotion should not feel discouraged by the long list of 38 qualities for the simple reason that even if he starts practising only one of them with utmost sincerity, the rest shall automatically come in his life like all streams eagerly rush to merge in Gangaa. God speaking **Me Priy** i.e. My Darling 6 times in a short span of 8 shloks from 12/13 to 20 also proves His continuous reassurance to such beginner at practising stage. Yog Vaashishth mentions some of aforesaid qualities of a devotee:

'His life is illustrious who is free from attachment and hatred, looks upon this world like a mere spectator, has understood how to abandon all ideas of acceptance and rejection, and who has realized the conscience within the innermost chamber of his heart'.

Caution: *I had cautioned readers about some people, who tend to divide Gita into three parts, Karm Yog from chapter 1 to 6; Bhakti Yog from 7 to 12; and Jnaan Yog from 12 to 18 but it is not wise to divide Gita in this way and inadvertently cause great harm to its universal message. It is like tearing a Dhotee, a whole loincloth to make few handkerchiefs out of it.*

Chapter 12 offers the perfect amalgamation and conjunction of **Sthit Prajnaa** (2/55-72), the resolute intelligence and **Bhakti**, the wholehearted devotion of God explained earlier in chapter 9. It is also interesting and educating to note that this is the smallest chapter of Gita consisting of just 20 shloks, besides chapter 15 later, which also comprises of 20 shloks. It seems to me that Gita has dealt with both these chapters in the spirit of **Sootr**, an ancient Indian technique of imparting knowledge in short phrases. Chapter 12 teaches **Bhakti** as the best way to connect with God and chapter 15 to realize **Purushottam**, the Supreme Soul. There are only 1 **Shree Bhagawaan Uvaach** and 1 **Arjun Uvaach** in this chapter.

ॐ तत्सदिति श्रीमद्भगवद्गीतासूपनिषत्सु ब्रह्मविद्यायां योगशास्त्रे श्रीकृष्णार्जुनसंवादे
भक्तियोगो नाम द्वादशोऽध्यायः ॥ १२ ॥

(In the name of God, the ultimate truth thus ends the twelfth
chapter named Bhakti Yog of Shreemad Bhagwad Gita, the
best Upanishad, Brahm Vidyaa & Yog Shaastr, a dialogue
between Shree Krishn and Arjun)

CHAPTER 13

KSHETR KSHETRAJN VIBHAAG YOG

(Know yourself. Your existence, potential & sovereignty extend much beyond the body & world.)

PREAMBLE & CONTEXT

As we founded our faith on the solid base of **Bhakti** while passing through chapter 12, which assured further progress of our spiritual journey toward the highest realm of the Himalaya of Gita's knowledge without any fear because our Sherpa, the expert guide Krishn is in full command now. Vyaas beautified the sketchy canvas of Gita with fine strokes of brilliant colors of **Bhakti** in chapter 12; and in this chapter, he continues to do so with subtler strokes to reveal the seemingly complicated relationship between soul, a part of Supreme Soul and His creation, the world. Gita calls them **Kshetrajn** and **Kshetr** respectively.

God briefly stated in 12/3-4 in previous chapter that those, who worship Him as **Niraakaar**, unmanifested, omnipresent, imperishable God, surely attain Him but did not explain the spiritual knowledge required for it in detail. He undertakes to explain it now in this chapter.

WHY CHAPTER 13 IS NAMED KSHETR KSHETRAJN VIBHAAG YOG?

Six shloks after God began His teachings, He told us in 2/17:

"You must know that Sat, the indestructible and imperishable one which pervades entire universe; and also Asat, the non-existent".

Then in 9/4, He said, **Mayaa Tatam Idam Sarvam Jagat Avyakt Moortinaa** i.e. *'This entire universe is pervaded by Me in My Avyakt, the unmanifested form'* but did not elaborate till now who that unmanifested **Sat** and manifested **Asat** are because of many complex situations and questions raised by Arjun. Now, in this chapter, He identifies the soul as **Sat** and **Samsaar**, the material world (including the body) as **Asat**; and names them as **Kshetrajn** and **Kshetr** respectively. This chapter decisively draws the distinction between **Kshetrajn**, the pure soul, a part of Supreme Soul that dwells within everyone and remains aloof from the works of nature on one side; and **Kshetr**, the lower nature of material world that embodies it on the other side. It conclusively states in the end that the soul, that realizes the difference between **Kshetrajn** and **Kshetr**, is delivered from the binds of material world and attains Yog i.e. connects permanently with his origin, the Supreme Soul. Hence, the name of this chapter **Kshetr Kshetrajn Vibhaag Yog** is justified. Gita dealt with immortality of soul in detail in 2/11-30 though words like **Aatmaa, Dehee, Shareerin** etc. were used there for **Kshetrajn;** and **Shareer, Deh, Kalevar** etc. for **Kshetr**. I recommend reading *'Some additional thoughts on Aatm Jnaan'* after 2/30 before proceeding further.

৺

God defines Kshetr and Kshetrajn.

(13/1)

श्रीभगवानुवाच
इदं शरीरं कौन्तेय क्षेत्रमित्यभिधीयते ।
एतद्यो वेत्ति तं प्राहुः क्षेत्रज्ञ इति तद्विदः ॥१३/१॥
क्षेत्रज्ञं चापि मां विद्धि सर्वक्षेत्रेषु भारत ।
क्षेत्रक्षेत्रज्ञयोर्ज्ञानं यत्तज्ज्ञानं मतं मम ॥१३/२॥

Shree Bhagawaan Uvaach

Idam shareeram Kauntey kshetramityabhidheeyate I
Etadyo vetti tam praahu: kshetrajn iti tadvid: II (13/1)
Kshetrajnam chaapi maam viddhi sarvakshetreshu Bhaarat I
KshetraKshetrajnayorjnaanam yattajjnaanam matam mam II
(13/2)

Idam (this) Shareeram (body) Kauntey (Arjun) Kshetram (field)
iti (in this way) Abhidheeyate (is called) I Etat (this) Y: (who) Vetti
(knows) Tam (to him) Praahu: (is said) Kshetrajn: (knower of field)
iti (thus) Tat Vid: (its knower) II (13/1)

Kshetrajnam (knower of field) Ch (and) Api (also) Maam (to Me)
Viddhi; (know well) Sarv (all) Kshetreshu (in fields, bodies) Bhaarat
(Arjun) I Kshetr (field) Kshetrajn (knower of field) Y: (he who)
Jnaanam (perfect spiritual knowledge) Yat (whichever) Tat (that)
Jnaanam (Jnaan) Matam (opinion) Mam (My) II (13/2)

God said:

**"O Kauntey (Arjun)! This body matter of a person is named
as Kshetr, the field, and the one who knows it in this way, is
Kshetrajn, the knower of the field. (13/1)**

**And, O Bhaarat (Arjun)! Know Me well as Kshetrajn, the soul
in the bodies of all the persons also. In My opinion, the proper
knowledge of this Kshetr, the body and its knower, master
& owner called Kshetrajn, the soul, is the ultimate perfect
knowledge. (13/2)**

Gita started with **'Dharm Kshetre Kuru Kshetre'** spoken by
Dhrutraashtr in 1/1. There, I had explained **Kshetr** as a farm
(degenerated into खेत in Hindi) in which an activity like agriculture
is undertaken, and **Kshetrajn** as its owner farmer. Applying this
symbolically to spirituality, the body of a person, with all materials
that surround it, is **Kshetr**, the field, and the soul, which owns and
situates in it, is **Kshetrajn,** the farmer. Rigved states:

*'Body is the field; farmer is its owner who sows two types of
seeds in it, the good & the bad'.*

He is an expert farmer who knows well his field and cultivates it in such a way that he reaps the best possible harvest from it. **Kshetrajn** also should similarly use his **Kshetr** in the best possible manner to attain **Jnaan**, the perfect spiritual knowledge that provides eternal bliss and **Yog**, the reunion with God. Krishn tells us further to know **Kshetrajn** as God, since He is its origin, as would declare later in 15/7:

"Soul of every embodied living being in the world is certainly an eternal, indivisible part of Me".

Thus, God is ultimately the Supreme ancestor of all **Kshetrajn** since they descend from Him in the material world as per their **Karm Bandhan**. A farmer is at liberty to sow good or bad seeds in his farm but he is sure to get good or bad harvest accordingly. Similarly, **Kshetrajn** also deploys his body and available resources in performing right or wrong deeds as per his will, and is destined to get auspicious or inauspicious results from them.

Kshetrajn is like a District Magistrate (DM) in charge of a district i.e. **Kshetr**. If DM has all round good knowledge of his area, exercises good control on people and resources at his command, and deploys them properly, the area prospers under him. However, if he becomes a puppet in the hands of subjects and utilizes available means carelessly, his seniors punish him, and the district is also impoverished.

Moral: *If a soul loses control on its passionate emotions, senses, body and the material environment surrounding it, it cannot escape punishment according to the theory of Karm & Karm Phal. It must fall in the vicious circle of Punarjanm, and be born either as an inferior human being, or even in sub-human species.*

ॐ

God undertakes to describe Kshetr briefly with its Vikaars and Kshetrajn.

(13/3 & 4)

तत्क्षेत्रं यच्च यादृक्च यद्विकारि यतश्च यत् ।
स च यो यत्प्रभावश्च तत्समासेन मे शृणु ॥ १ ३/३॥
ऋषिभिर्बहुधा गीतं छन्दोभिर्विविधैः पृथक् ।
ब्रह्मसूत्रपदैश्चैव हेतुमद्भिर्विनिश्चितैः ॥ १ ३/४॥

Tatkshetram yachch yaadrukch yadvikaari yatashch yat I
S ch yo yatprabhaavashch tatsamaasen me shrunu II (13/3)
Rushibirbahudhaa geetam chhandobhirvividhe: pruthak I
Brahm Sootrpadaishchaiv hetumadbhirvinishchitai: II (13/4)

tat (that) Kshetram (field) Yat (which) Ch (and) Yaadruk (as it is) Ch (and) Yat (which) Vikaari (undergo changes, disorders) Yat: (from which) Ch (and) Yat (that which) I s (he) Ch (and) Y: (who) Yat (which) Prabhaav: (influence) Ch (and) Tat (that, then) Samaasen (in brief) Me (My) Shrunu (listen) II (13/3)

Rishibhi: (by great sages) Bahudhaa (in many ways) Geetam (sung in poetic language) Chhandobhi: (by Vedic hymns) Vividhai: (of different sorts) Pruthak (classified) I Brahm Sootr padai: (in verses of Brahm Sootr) Ch (and) Ev (also) Hetumadbhi: (with logic & rationale) Vinishchitai: (well ascertained) II (13/4)

Listen from Me in brief about that Kshetr, the body as it is with its Vikaars, the mutations which it undergoes, and of which it is also constituted. Know also about him (Kshetrajn, the soul) and its influence and power on it (Kshetr). (13/3)

Many great sages have frequently explained and classified it in poetic language in various Vedic hymns; and by pithy maxims of Brahm Sootr with appropriate reasoning & well-ascertained rationale. (13/4)

Vikaars relate with the body in two ways as would be described in next shlok. It is important to remember here that the word **Kshetr** also includes its field of action i.e. the entire life of a person. Krishn tells Arjun to listen attentively to Him because He wants to give only the summary explanation of **Kshetr** and its **Vikaars**, and of **Kshetrajn**. He informs Arjun that great Rishis have explained them earlier in poetic maxims of the grand scripture called **Brahm Sootr**. Krishn cuts short this topic (probably due to the call of urgent task on hand to fight for **Dharm** in the battlefield) expecting that Arjun had studied **Brahm Sootr** earlier, or he may refer to them later. However, since we are not hard pressed for time in our study of Gita, let us gather some introductory knowledge about **Brahm Sootr** as given below:

QUESTION: WHAT IS BRAHM SOOTR AND WHAT IS ITS RELEVANCE WITH RESPECT TO GITA AND PRASTHAAN TRAYEE?

We understood **Sootr** as thread or string in 7/7 earlier but in present context, it means a short pithy aphoristic statement condensed into a maxim to state an eternal truth. For example, *'Samatvam Yog Uchyate'* (2/48) in Gita and *'Satyamev Jayate'* in Mundak Upanishad 3/1/6 are such **Sootr**. Political Pandits regard the astute observation *'Power tends to corrupt, and absolute power corrupts absolutely'*, of Lord Acton, as a **Sootr**. In a way, we can also infer that **Brahm Sootr**, as a thread, literally threads together the flowers of spiritual knowledge of **Vedaant** into a logical, self-consistent & beautiful garland with no loose ends.

Brahm Sootr, also known as **Shaareerak Sootr** or **Vedaant Sootr,** is one of the three canonical texts of **Vedaant** school of Hindu philosophy. **Shankaraachaarya** therefore appropriately describes **Brahm Sootr** in his **Bhaashya** on it as a collection of Sootrs, the short phrases of Veds & Upanishads to expound **Brahm**. Some scriptures also refer to it as **Yukti Prasthaan** since **Yukti** is the logical approach to attain **Brahm** and some call it **Uttar Meemaansaa**, the investigation of Veds. Thus, **Brahm Sootr** is a summary exposition of **Vedaantik** interpretation Upanishads and an attempt to systematize various loose strands left by them about various ancient schools of thoughts[8] about universe, soul, Supreme Soul and their inter-relationships.

Sage Baadaraayan, identified by many with Krishn Dwaipaayan popularly called Ved Vyaas, the author of the Mahaabhaarat and Gita, is attributed for composition of **Brahm Sootr**. It seems that

---

8   *Jnaaneshwar beautifully describes different Indian schools of thoughts about Kshetr and Kshetrajn in his treatise Jnaaneshwaree.*

Vyaas was called as Baadaraayan also when he lived in Badreenath region of the Himalayas for some time and composed **Brahm Sootr**. **Brahm Sootr** contains 555 **Sootrs** in four chapters, and each chapter is divided into four quartets each having several topics. Let us learn about four chapters of **Brahm Sootr** briefly:

1. Chapter 1, named **Samanvay** i.e. harmony, contains 134 **Sootr** in 39 **Adhikaran**. It tells that all that **Vedaant** talks about is **Brahm**, the ultimate real goal of life. The very first **Sootr** 1/1/1 provokes our curiosity to investigate Brahm, "अथातो ब्रह्म जिज्ञासा" i.e. *'Now, therefore the inquiry of Brahm'.* It is of greatest importance for a practiser of Yog of Gita to have a clear and correct knowledge of **Brahm**, which alone can lead him to **Moksh**, the liberation from transmigration. This chapter explains **Brahm** as the source from where the universe came into existence, in whom it inheres and to whom it returns at the end of each cycle of creation. It states that the only source to know this **Brahm** is **Shruti**, the Upanishads.

2. Chapter 2 is **Avirodh**, the non-conflict. It refutes all possible objections to **Vedaant** philosophy. It critically examines and dismisses the refutations raised by other schools of thoughts one by one and establishes oneness among them.

3. Chapter 3 deals with **Saadhan**, the means and process that lead to ultimate emancipation. This is the longest chapter with 186 **Sootr** spread in 67 **Adhikaran**.

4. Chapter 4 talks of **Phal**, the result, achieved in final emancipation. This is the shortest chapter with 78 Sootr in 38 **Adhikaran**. It mainly describes the journey of **Jeevaatmaa**, the individual soul after death to **Brahm Lok**, the God's abode of no return through **Archiraadi Maarg** or **Dev Yaan** (refer to 8/24-26 in Gita) i.e. the path of light and of gods.

Prasthaan Trayee is the triad of most important scriptures of **Vedaant** philosophy of Hinduism namely Upanishads also known as **Shruti Prasthaan** i.e. the knowledge acquired by listening to teacher; **Brahm Sootr** also known as **Nyaay Prasthaan.** It set forth the teachings of **Vedaant** in a systematic and logical order; and Gita, also known as **Smruti Prasthaan** i.e. the knowledge to be remembered forever. This serializing however, does not reflect or establish superiority of any one over the rest, neither in chronology nor in knowledge. In fact, a close study of these scriptures reveals that they refer to each other at many places. The fact that Vyaas is the original composer of all three of them strengthens this observation.

Above explanation of **Brahm Sootr** should be sufficient to explain why Krishn wants to describe **Jnaan** of **Kshetrajn** and **Kshetr** in brief here and refers us to **Brahm Sootr** for its detailed knowledge. The aim of Gita is not to dig deep into the intricate knowledge of **Vedaant**, but to present only its essence in a very simple, practical way to every human being. Gita interweaves the weft of **Jnaan** contained in **Prasthaan Trayee** with the warp of different activities in the metaphoric fabric of our day-to-day life, whether the activity is as terrible as the war of Mahaabhaarat at one time or as subtle as devotion, love and compassion at another time.

⊱⊰

God briefly describes Kshetr in two shloks.

(13/5 & 6)

महाभूतान्यहंकारो बुद्धिरव्यक्तमेव च ।
इन्द्रियाणि दशैकं च पञ्च चेन्द्रियगोचराः ॥१३/५॥
इच्छा द्वेषः सुखं दुःखं संघातश्चेतना धृतिः ।
एतत्क्षेत्रं समासेन सविकारमुदाहृतम् ॥१३/६॥

Mahaabhootaanyahamkaaro buddhiravyaktamev ch I
Indriyaani dashaikam ch Panch chendriyagocharaa: II (13/5)
Ichchhaa Dwesh: Sukham du:kham sanghaatashchetanaa
Dhruti: I
Etatkshetram samaasen savikaaramudaahrutam II (13/6)

Mahaa Bhootaani (five basic elements: space, wind, fire, water and earth) Ahamkaar: (ego) Buddhi: (intelligence) Avyaktam (invisible nature) Ev (also) Ch (and) I Indriyaani (Indriys) Dash (ten) Ekam (mind, the only one) Ch (and) Panch (five) Ch (and) Indriy gocharaa: (sensory passions of Indriy) II (13/5)

Ichchhaa (desire) Dwesh: (envy) Sukham (happiness) Du:kham (unhappiness) Sanghaat: (collection of) Chetanaa (consciousness) Dhruti: (steadfastness) I Etat (this) Kshetram (field) Samaasen (in brief) Savikaaram (with its Vikaars) Udaahrutam (is cited) II (13/6)

The collective group of Panch Mahaa Bhoot, the five great basic elements of nature (Aakaash, the space, Vaayu, the wind, Agni, the fire, Jal, the water, and Bhoomi, the earth), Ahamkaar, the ego, Buddhi, the intelligence, Avyakt, the invisible causal nature, ten Indriys (5 sensory & 5 action organs) with five subjects of their sensory passions (scene, smell, sound, taste & touch), and also the one (Man, the mind) is Kshetr. (13/5)

And, the collective group of desire, envy, happiness, distress, consciousness and resoluteness are briefly cited as its Vikaars, the mutations & interactions. (13/6)

These shloks describe **Kshetr** in brief as the body of a person and the material field of environment that surrounds it, and in which it carries out all of its activities. **Kshetr** comprises of 24 constituents, classified into following two sub groups:

1. The first sub group consists of 8 elements: **Avyakt** or **Samashti Prakruti**, the invisible causal nature in purest form, its 5 basic elements called **Panch Mahaa Bhoot** enjoined and the duo of **Samashti Ahamkaar**, the pure, basic ego or existence and **Samashti Buddhi**, the uncorrupted, pure, basic intelligence. Gita described this sub group earlier as **Ashtadhaa** or **Aparaa Prakruti** in 7/4-5. Readers may refer there to refresh their learning about it.

2. The second sub group consists of 16 elements: 5 **Jnaanendriys**, the sensory organs, 5 **Karmendriys**, the functionary organs, 5 **Vishays**, the passions of sensory organs, and **Man**, the mind.

Vikaars are the mutations, changes, transformations that often result in disorder, deterioration and abnormality in the purity of a thing or situation. We had learnt birth, death, growth, reduction (in size), existence and change as **Vikaars** of physical body and **Kaam, Krodh, Lobh, Moh, Mad** and **Matsar** as **Vikaars** of mind in 2/25 earlier while discussing **Avikaarya** nature of soul. Gita describes in 13/6 here one more set of six **Vikaars** namely **Ichchhaa**, the desire, **Dwesh**, the envy, **Sukh**, the pleasure, **Dukh**, the pain & misery, **Chetanaa**, the consciousness and **Dhruti**, the resolution to do something which take place in **Kshetr**.

It is now easy for us to understand that the first sub group of 8 elements is the purest, uncorrupted form of nature like the water from Himalayan glaciers. It remains homogenous and in perfect equilibrium, and therefore, **Jad** i.e. inactive. It is the second sub group of **Indriys, Vishays** and their gang leader **Man** that renders it impure, heterogeneous and unbalanced by joining with **Vikaars**, which destroy purity of **Kshetr** and involve it in good or bad affairs of material world. The job of our sensory organs is to collect information as per their respective subject, put it before their leader **Man** to evaluate it with the help of intelligence. If we are not alert like **Sthit Prajn** (2/55-72), flirtatious **Man** takes undue advantage of wavering intelligence and decides future course of action as per its passion towards the subject. **Vikaars** then generate in our **Prakruti**, the characteristic and emotional behavior in the form of attachment, self-interest, anger, lust etc. and, together with **Man,** they compel **Karmendriys** to act accordingly.

Ichchhaa, Dwesh, Sukh and **Dukh** were explained earlier in relevant places, **Chetanaa** in 10/22, and **Dhruti** in 6/25. **Sanghaat** is the collective group of the 24 constituents of **Kshetr** and these **Vikaars** which manifests as **Kshetr** in the form of the physical body of a person but it is not the whole of our being; there is something more called **Kshetrajn** here (**Jneyam** in 13/12) which needs to be known through Jnaan. **Kshetr** is **Jad** i.e. inert without **Kshetrajn** just as a farm is useless if there is no farmer to till, plough and cultivate it to get a harvest. An action is still unborn until **Kshetrajn**, the knower and owner of **Kshetr,** the embodied soul, enjoined with the lower nature of **Vikaars,** acts in the field of **Kshetr.**

Chapter 15 shall give the simile of a **Peepal** tree for world, the largest manifestation of **Kshetr.** As a tree cannot sprout without sunlight, similarly **Kshetr,** the body becomes a live person when it receives light of **Jnaan,** the perfect knowledge of **Kshetrajn,** the soul. A person is not just his body; the soul provides him his complete identity and activates his body. Whole world is **Kshetr** for an accomplished Yogee as he lives in it by **Dharm** and serves others by his **Karm.**

Clarification: *Chetanaa and Dhruti are regarded generally as good, auspicious traits, not as Vikaar, an abnormality. However, it is important for a practiser of Yog to train and control them during practising stage and rise above them to attain liberation from distress in life and Punarjanm after death ultimately. He must always remember that both good and bad works bind him with Karm Bandhan. The way shown by Gita in 2/45 is to become Nirdwandw (same as Dwandwaateet in 4/22) and Nistraigunya (same as Gunaateet in 14/25).*

Ahamkaar was explained along with **Nirahamkaar,** the egoless, in 2/71 as ego in 7/4-5. We shall further deal with it in 17/5-6.

৵৹৵

We now climb another peak of the Himalayan knowledge of Gita, as it starts explaining Jnaan & Ajnaan in 13/7-11.

(13/7)

अमानित्वमदम्भित्वमहिंसा क्षान्तिरार्जवम् ।
आचार्योपासनं शौचं स्थैर्यमात्मविनिग्रहः ॥१३/७॥

Amaanitvamadambhitvamahimsaa kshaantiraarjavam I
Aachaaryopaasanam shaucham sthairyamaatmavinigrah: II
(13/7)

Amaanitvam (absence of pride, conceit) Adambhitvam (modesty, absence of hypocrisy) Ahimsaa (non-violence) Kshaanti: (endurance)

Aarjavam (simplicity, candidness) I Aachaarya Upaasanam (reverent service of teacher) Shaucham (cleanliness) Sthairyam (constancy) Aatm Vinigrah: (self-control) II (13/7)

Absence of pride and hypocrisy; non-violence, endurance, simplicity and candidness, reverent service of Guru, the teacher; purity and cleanliness, constancy, self-control; (13/7)

Logically, Krishn ought to explain **Kshetrajn** after explaining **Kshetr** in 13/5-6 but instead of it He now starts describing **Jnaan** from 13/7 to 11, and then **Jney** in 13/12-17 before returning to **Kshetr** and **Kshetrajn** in 13/18. Why does He take this detour? This is because unlike **Kshetr, Kshetrajn** is not a physical entity like a piece of furniture that a salesperson can showcase and a customer can understand easily. **Kshetrajn** is soul, the indivisible part of **Paramaatmaa**, the Supreme Soul that one can realize only by acquiring **Jnaan**, the perfect spiritual knowledge. Once a person comes to know **Jney**, the Only Knowable One, God the next step to know His **Ansh** (10/41 & 15/7), the soul (called **Kshetrajn** here) automatically follows. It is utmost necessary for a practiser to develop the qualities mentioned in 13/7-11, light the lamp of **Jnaan** and remove the darkness of **Ajnaan**. Krishn takes this detour for this reason in order to describe the qualities required to realize **Brahm** and **Kshetrajn**. We shall try to understand these very important qualities one by one so that we can emulate them in our life. Let us first take 9 qualities mentioned in this shlok:

Amaanitvam: It is the quality of humility and absence of pride and/or conceit. He, who possesses it, is never moved by false pride. Take the example of Abraham Lincoln:

"On the first day of his presidency, when Abraham Lincoln was about to deliver his inaugural address, a rich aristocrat man stood up and said with scorn, 'Mr. Lincoln, you should not forget that your father used to make shoes for my family'. Whole Senate laughed with him at Lincoln.

But people like Lincoln are made of a totally different mettle. He looked straight into the eyes of the man and coolly said, 'Sir, I know that my father used to make shoes for your family, and there will be many others like you here. He was a creator because he made shoes the way nobody else can. His shoes were not just shoes; he poured his whole soul into them. I want to ask you, if have you any complaint because I know how to make shoes myself. If you have any complaint, I can make you another pair of shoes. But, as far as I know, nobody has ever complained about my father's shoes. He was a genius, a great creator and I am proud of him'.

The Senate was struck dumb. They could not understand what kind of man Lincoln was. He was proud because his father did his job so well that not even a single complaint was ever heard".

Moral: *No one can hurt us without our consent. Our response to a particular situation hurts us, not what the situation we are in. Let us be excellent at our work and ignore those who are not.*

Caution: *Amaanitvam is not giving up Swaabhimaan, the self-respect.*

Adambhitvam: It means lack of **Dambh** (16/4), the hypocrisy, pretence, boasting, arrogance and ostentation. A **Jnaanee** hides his knowledge and good works as a rich man hides his wealth underground and lives like a poor man; he normally lives like a cloud that does not mind wind sweeping it here and there; and is capable of raising hailstorms also at appropriate time. It will be useful to read explanation under **Mithyaachaar** also in 3/6. Hanumaan is the embodiment of **Amaanitvam** and **Adambhitvam**. After finding whereabouts of Seetaa and burning Lankaa when he returned to Raam He asked him how he could accomplish such a formidable task single handedly. The reply of Hanumaan with folded hands in Vaalmeeki Raamaayan sets the best example of modesty for all of us until eternity:

'O Lord! It was not I but my father (Pawan, the Lord of wind) who burnt it; the curses of the sages & saints burnt it; the sorrow of mother Jaanakee burnt it. It was your valor that burnt it; and above all it was sins of Raavan that burnt it; I could have been able to do nothing if Raavan was not a sinful person'.

Ahimsaa: It is derived from Sanskrit root *'Hims'* meaning to strike or injure. Thus, **Himsaa** is injury or harm, and its opposite **Ahimsaa** is one of the cardinal virtues of Hinduism (and other religions of Indian origin) of not harming or injuring or nonviolence in general. In its limited sense, it implies not killing others. Nevertheless, in wider context, it is based on the premise that all living beings have the same spark of divine spiritual energy in them; and humans, the most sensible and intelligent among them, must bear the responsibility to protect, not hurt or injure or violate, their right to life. If he does not do so, in effect, he is hurting himself. **Ahimsaa** prohibits violence of any kind, whether mental, verbal or physical, towards anyone or anything. In its finest application, the principle of **Ahimsaa** expects us to avoid reckless exploitation even of natural resources and supposedly inert materials like water, air, oceans, hills, forests, deserts, rivers, greenery etc. Mahatma Gandhi is regarded as the strongest exponent of **Ahimsaa** in modern times. Even Geneva Convention prescribes **Ahimsaa** for a soldier, expected to kill or be killed in a combat, by forbidding shooting of an unarmed person, and/or torturing someone. Gita and Mahaabhaarat, however, take a very practical view of this highly praised virtue. Readers are likely to be confused because Krishn preaches non-violence as one of the important qualities of a **Jnaanee** to Arjun here, but simultaneously also wants him to rise and start fighting in Gita. It may sound as double standard on His part. A clarification as below is therefore, warranted here.

Supporters of **Ahimsaa** often quote a half shlok from Mahaabhaarat *'Ahimsaa Paramo Dharm'* literally translated as *'Non-violence is the ultimate Dharm'*, but they ignore quoting its second part. The complete shlok spoken by Dharm Vyaadh, a meat seller, to a Braahman named Kaushik in Mahaabhaarat Van Parv while teaching **Dharm** states:

'अहिंसा परमो धर्मः धर्म हिंसा तथैव च: l'

(Non-violence is the ultimate Dharm. But so is violence done in the service of Dharm.)

If Arjun adopts **Ahimsaa** by not killing **Aatataayee** Kauravs, they would kill him immediately resulting in the rule of **Adharm** that would cause unimaginable harm to people of Hastinaapur for a long time. Such act is comparable only to dismantling the fort to build wall around it; or cutting fruity trees to install fence in the field; or burning own clothes to get relief from cold. A truly non-violent person should be like a loving mother who is ready to give up her life to protect her child but does not hesitate to scold and slap to discipline him when necessary.

Ahimsaa is declared as one of the primary virtues prohibiting killing or harming any life but scriptures like Upanishads, Mahaabhaarat etc. also deal with questions like *'Whether there is a way for a human being to live without harming animal and plant life. If yes, under what conditions and to what extent, should he be allowed to commit Himsaa on other humans, animals, plants or other entities of nature; and what are the likely effects of Himsaa or Ahimsaa on his own life or on the society in different situations like saving own or others' life, protecting and supporting Dharm, performing his duties'.*

Finally, they also prescribe **Praayashchit**, the penitential actions to remedy and atone to an act of **Himsaa** committed voluntarily or involuntarily under certain constraints of life and complex human needs in overall universal interest. We shall learn more about **Ahimsaa** in 16/2 as divine wealth.

Morals*:*

1. *Non-violence is not the ultimate Dharm in every situation. It becomes sometimes necessary to be violent in order to ensure non-violence for others.*

2. *Gita teaches us to test every virtue it teaches, ultimately on the Kasautee (touchstone to test purity of gold) of Dharm in every situation, and adopt it only if approved by Dharm; or it protects Dharm.*

3. *In my opinion we should perceive and practise Ahimsaa in its universal application to 'Live and let live' without causing physical, mental, sentimental or emotional injury to anyone by our thought, speech and action as long as it is conforms to eternal, universal Dharm.*

Caution*: Some enthusiasts of Ahimsaa drag this great virtue into debates on eating habits of different societies like vegetarianism, Non-*

vegetarianism, and veganism. Though I am a vegetarian personally, I feel such debates are meaningless.

Kshaanti: It is the virtue of patience, endurance, forbearance and forgiveness. As an elephant walks in majesty without bothering about dogs barking around him, a **Jnaanee** takes no notice or offence of his critics. Gita shall describe it again in 18/42 as the quality of a Braahman.

Aarjavam: It is the quality of simplicity, candidness, directness, straightforwardness and uprightness. This quality is imbibed in Arjun by birth as his name itself suggests. We shall understand it in 16/1, 17/14 & 18/42. Look at the utmost simplicity of Socrates when he says, *'I know one thing; and that is that I know nothing'.*

Aachaaryopaasanam is formed by coalescence of **Aachaarya** (the teacher) + **Upaasanam** (sitting on a lower seat in modesty and reverence). It is therefore, defined as always being in attendance and reverent service of **Guru**. A student of Jnaan must always serve and revere his teacher and exercise patience for learning from him. Great, accomplished souls have always showered praise on their Guru. Kabeer reveres his Guru thus:

गुरू गोविन्द दोऊ खड़े, काके लागूं पांय।
बलिहारी गुरू अपने गोविन्द दियो बताय।।

(Whose feet should I touch first: Guru or God as both have appeared before me simultaneously? O my Guru! I must devote to you first because you revealed God to me).

Scriptures advise students to hold their teachers in great esteem like God:

गुरुर्ब्रह्मा गुरुर्विष्णुः गुरुर्देवो महेश्वरः।
गुरुः साक्षात्परं ब्रह्म तस्मै श्री गुरवे नमः ॥१॥
अज्ञानतिमिरान्धस्य ज्ञानाञ्जनशलाकया।
चक्षुरुन्मीलितं येन तस्मै श्री गुरवे नमः॥२॥

{Guru is Brahmaa, the god of creation, Guru is Vishnu, the god of maintenance and Guru is Maheshwar Shiv, the god

of destruction. I bow to Guru because Brahm, the Supreme God manifests completely in Guru.

I was blinded by the darkness of Ajnaan; it is Guru, who opened the eyes of my heart by applying Anjan, the kohl. I, therefore, must bow to such great Guru}.

Krishn also advised Arjun in 4/34:

"You must approach Tattv Darshee Jnaanee to learn Jnaan; prostrate before them; and render selfless services; and then ask your questions with modesty and obeisance. Then only will they initiate & instruct you with Jnaan".

Guru holds the key to unlock the lock of **Ajnaan** fastened on our intelligence.

Cautions:

1. *Beware of hordes of imposters proclaiming themselves as Guru. A true Guru reveals his identity and imparts knowledge only to a deserving student.*

2. *Some people think that it is impossible to acquire Jnaan without adopting a Guru; they search for a good Guru for whole life and ultimately land into the hands of some fraudster out of frustration. I recommend to them strongly to take shelter in great scriptures like Gita; or divine personalities.*

When sage Dattaatrey could not find a perfect Guru as per his expectations, he adopted as many as 24 Gurus out of the most ordinary things and common beings. They are:

'Earth, wind, space, water, fire, moon, sun, pigeon, python, ocean, fire insects, honeybee, elephant, honey collector, deer, fish, a prostitute, a bird, a child, a virgin, maker of arrows, snake, spider, and a typical worm'.

Moral: *If we have inclination and aptitude to learn, we can learn from everything around us.*

Shauch means cleanliness, purity, piety in every stage of life.

SOME ADDITIONAL THOUGHTS ON SHAUCH

Shauch is of three types; purity of inner faculties like heart, mind & conscience; of speech, and cleanliness of external physical objects like body, the household, work & surrounding public places and the environment. All of them are necessary to attain **Jnaan**.

"An iron scoop approached an alchemist with a request to make it golden. The alchemist carefully observed it and then advised, 'If you sincerely want to become golden, you must first clean off the dirt, rust, oil, foods, the odor, color etc., imbibed and deposited on you".

J R D Tata says:

'Cleanliness is the Hallmark of perfect standards; and conscience is the best quality inspector'.

Moral*: Purity of mind, body, speech and soul is the most important condition to advance, ameliorate and elevate ourselves to a higher divine status from a lower mundane one.*

Ten golden rules to achieve complete **Shauch** are stated below:

1. Body purifies by following simple rules of maintaining good health, hygiene and fitness. Clean water, **Saattvik** food, walking, exercise and **Praanaayaam** are important healthy practices. Remember, *'A Healthy mind dwells in a healthy body.'*

2. Wealth purifies by sharing, donating and deploying in global well being.

3. Environment purifies by living in simplicity, and practising three 'R's, Repair, Reuse and Recycle. We should learn to live as close to nature as possible, and protect and maintain purity of all natural resources like water, air, earth, space and vegetation and lower species. It is truly said since ages, *'Cleanliness is the virtue next only to Godliness'.*

4. Society remains clean if members maintain cleanliness & hygiene in utilities & public places.

5. Ego purifies by rendering selfless service to others.

6. Mind purifies by meditation; intellect by learning; memory by repetitive practice and heart by selfless love and compassion.

7. Character purifies by positive attitude, and good company. It is well said, *'A person is known by the company he keeps'*.

8. Soul purifies by undulating faith.

9. Speech purifies by observing silence and reflective thinking.

10. Knowledge purifies by striding unscathed through adversities of life by adopting only righteous & meritorious means.

Moral*: We should always remember, 'The more the gold is subjected to fire, the purer it becomes'.*

Caution*: Maintaining external cleanliness only without cleaning internal faculties is not of much value. It is equivalent to beautifying a dead body with cosmetics, flowers & ornaments.*

Following anecdote should explain the implication of above caution:

"A Bhishtee⁹, the water carrier used to move around carrying a Mashak¹⁰ on his back to fetch water to needy villagers. Everybody was very much satisfied with his service. One day, a Saadhu, suffering badly due to thirst passed by him and inquired from the Bhishtee thus, 'Though I am in dire need of water, you must first satisfy me about the cleanliness & purity of your Mashak before I accept water from it'. With a wry smile on his face, the Bhishtee counter questioned Saadhu, 'Rest assured O Swami! I always maintain cleanliness & purity of my Mashak inside and outside but I do not know whether your Mashak, the body, is also as clean and pure as mine to receive its water. Now, kindly tell me quickly whether I should pour water for you because I have to serve those who have full faith in the quality of my Mashak and its water."

Sthairyam is the quality of fixity, stability, constancy, calmness, and equability even in the most difficult and trying situations. God

---

9   *In casteist India in ancient times, a Bhishtee was considered a low caste person.*

10   *Mashak is a traditional water container made of sheep or buffalo hide, to fetch water. In symbolism, it means that Ant:karan, the internal faculties of a person must be clean & pure rather than only his body.*

had mentioned Himalaya as His **Vibhooti** among **Sthaavaraanaam**, all the immovable objects. A **Jnaanee** remains emotionally and spiritually unmoved and unperturbed by **Dwandws**, the dualities of the world and **Triguns**, the three modes of nature.

Aatm Vinigrah means self-control, restraint. Gita deals with it by **Aatm Samyam** or **Indriy Samyam** etc. A **Jnaanee** must exercise full restraint on his sensory and functionary organs as well as **Man**, **Buddhi** and self under all disturbing situations.

Aarjavam is the quality of simplicity, directness, candidness, uprightness, and straightforwardness. It frees us from the vices of deceit, trickery, dissembling, hypocrisy, fraud, pretence, stratagem and faultfinding. We shall learn more about it in 16/1 where it is counted as one of the divine qualities, and in shloks like 17/14 & 18/42 also.

ॐ

God describes six more qualities of a Jnaanee in two shloks.

(13/8 & 9)

इन्द्रियार्थेषु वैराग्यमनहंकार एव च ।
जन्ममृत्युजराव्याधिदुःखदोषानुदर्शनम् ॥१३/८॥
असक्तिरनभिष्वङ्गः पुत्रदारगृहादिषु ।
नित्यं च समचित्तत्वमिष्टानिष्टोपपत्तिषु ॥१३/९॥

Indriyaartheshu vairaagyamanahamkaar ev ch I
Janmamrutyujaraavyaadhidu:khadoshaanudarshanam II
(13/8)
Asaktiranabhishvang: putradaaragruhaadishu I
Nityam ch samachittatvamishtaanishtopapattishu II (13/9)

Indriyaa Artheshu (passions of Indriys) Vairaagyam (detachment) Anahamkaar (absence of ego) Ev (also) Ch (and) I Janm (birth) Mrutyu (death) Jaraa (old age) Vyaadhi (disease) Dukh (misery) Dosh (fault, evil, vice, sin) Anudarshanam (keen observation, thought) II (13/8)

Asakti: (absence of attachment) Anabhishvang: (dissociation) Putr (son) Daar (wife) Gruh Aadishu (in household etc.) I Nityam (perpetual) Ch (and) Sam Chittatwam (with equipoise conscience) Isht (desirable) Anisht (undesirable) Upapattishu (on getting) II (13/9)

Freedom from attachment with the passions of sensory and organs, and results of actions performed by functionary organs; total absence of ego; and also a keen, clear perception of the evils of birth, death, decrepitude, disease and other miseries; (13/8)

Absence of attachment & belongingness in children, wife, household & other related things; with conscience perpetually equipoise upon getting the desirables & undesirables in life; (13/9)

Indriyaartheshu Vairaagya: We had understood Vairaagya in 6/35-36 as the freedom from **Raag**, the attachment. **Indriyaartheshu Vairaagya** therefore means complete detachment and dissociation from attraction, infatuation towards mundane objects of passion like wealth, relations, self interests, name & fame; or with forbidden activities like drinking, gambling, womanizing, cheating, overpowering etc. in order to get some material gains in physical, mental and emotional fields. Vairaagya is qualified with **Indriyaartheshu** to stress that the detachment of a **Jnaanee** must be not only from the passions of **Jnaanendriys**, the 5 sensory organs, but also from the results of actions performed by **Karmendriys**, the 5 functionary organs. **Jnaanee** distastes passions of all ten **Indriys** as one distastes vomited food.

Anahamkaar is total freedom from onslaughts of egoistic sense, idea, motive, and thought; and from consideration of being the doer of something. A **Jnaanee** becomes egoless in his action, talk and mind like the sun, which does not harbour any egoistic pride in removing darkness, and giving warmth & light to entire world.

Janm Mrutyu Jaraa Vyaadhi Dukh Doshaanudarshanam: **Vyaadhi** is a type of misery related to the physical health of a person's body. It includes, in this context, other kind of misery also known as **Aadhi**, the misery caused by the mental and emotional health of a person that can be in the form of insanity, worry, fear, anxiety etc. Birth & death are the miseries related directly to **Punarjanm**, whereas **Jaraa**, the old age, ill health etc., are the painful subjections of a person in his current life due to **Karm Phal**, the results of works done in current or previous births. A **Jnaanee** examines and analyzes the causes of his sufferings critically and works to eliminate them from his life.

Asakti, commonly known as **Anaasakti** also, is absence of attachment, attraction, infatuation; and disenchantment and indifference towards all living beings and/or things of material world. Though the shadow of a man is always attached with him, he is seldom aware of it. Similarly, a **Jnaanee** lives in the world but is free from attachment of its shadowy things like children, wife, household or any other material things. Buddh calls it **Upekshaa**, the neglect. **Aasakti** in things is like chasing a prostitute who runs away from us as long as we chase her, but the moment we turn away from her, she comes in search of us. Akbar Ilaahaabaadee beautifully expresses **Asakti** i.e. **Anaasakti** in these two couplets:

'दुनिया में हूँ दुनिया का तलबगार नहीं हूँ,
बाज़ार से निकला हूँ ख़रीदार नहीं हूँ ।
इस ख़ाना-ए-हस्त से गुज़र जाऊँगा बेलौस
साया हूँ फ़क़्त, नक़्श बेदीवार नहीं हूँ ॥'

(I am in this world I have but have no desire from the world. I am just a passerby, not a customer in this bazaar. I will pass untainted through this life for I am only a shadow, not a photo frame put on the wall).

Janak, the king of Mithilaa, says in Mahaabhaarat Shaanti Parv:

'मिथिलायाम् प्रदीप्तायाम् न मे दह्यति किंचन'

(Even if whole Mithilaa is in flames, nothing of mine is burnt)

"Kumbh Melaa, the biggest religious congregation on earth, is visited by two types of pilgrims. Though both of them go there to take dips daily in holy Sangam, perform various religious ceremonies and

live in the company of saints, their characteristics are very different. The first one meticulously plans for his travel, stay, food, health etc.; and at the end of Melaa, he carefully collects all of his belongings, and if something is left behind by chance, he rushes back to collect it. The second kind of pilgrim consigns his worries of stay, food, health etc. to God and travels with barest minimum things; and in the end he leaves everything there for other pilgrims. The first person is Aasakt and the second one is Asakt or Anaasakt".

Anabhishvang: Putr Daar Gruh Aadishu: Such person is emotionally and mentally dissociated from involvement in familial affairs of his children, wife and in laws, and any other thing related to household & family matters. He regards whole world as his family.

Nityam Sam Chittatwam Isht Anisht Upapattishu: He is a person whose conscience is perpetually equipoise in all situations whether they are likable and favorable or undesirable, unfavorable. As sun remains the equipoise during sunrise, sunset and noon, similarly a **Jnaanee** remains equipoise in all situations. This half shlok echoes the virtue of **Yadruchchhaa Laabh Santusht** dealt with in 4/22. Please refer to some additional thoughts expressed on Samatv, the equality and related matters in 2/48, 5/18-20, 6/8 & 29-32.

☙❦

God describes final five qualities of a Jnaanee in these two shloks.

(13/10 & 11)

मयि चानन्ययोगेन भक्तिरव्यभिचारिणी ।
विविक्तदेशसेवित्वमरतिर्जनसंसदि ॥१३/१०॥
अध्यात्मज्ञाननित्यत्वं तत्त्वज्ञानार्थदर्शनम् ।
एतज्ज्ञानमिति प्रोक्तमज्ञानं यदतोऽन्यथा ॥१३/११॥

Mayi chaananyayogen bhaktiravyabhichaarinee I
Viviktadeshasevitvamaratirjansansadi II (13/10)
Adhyaatmajnaananityatvam tattvajnaanaarthadarshanam I
Etajjnaanamiti proktamajnaanam yadatoɾnyathaa II (13/11)

Mayi (unto Me) Ch (and) Ananya (exclusively) Yogen (in Yog) Bhakti: (devotion) Avyabhichaarinee (incorruptible) I Vivikt Desh Sevitvam (aspiring to live in solitude) Arati: (uninterested) Jan Sansadi (society) II (13/10)

Adhyaatm Jnaan (spiritual knowledge of Adhyaatm) Nitya (always, forever) Twam (you) Tattv Jnaanaarth (in quest of Tattv, the fundamental truth) Darshanam (seeing) I Etat (all this) Jnaanam (perfect knowledge) iti (thus) Proktam (is said) Ajnaanam (ignorance) Yat (whatever) At: (than that) Anyathaa (other) II (13/11)

Remaining singularly devoted and exclusively united with Me; living in solitary places; without taking keen interest in the affairs of human establishments around him; and being constantly in quest of acquiring spiritual knowledge and learning the basic fundamentals of truth; all of it is known as Jnaan, the perfect knowledge. And, anything other than mentioned here (13/7-11) is said to be Ajnaan, the ignorance. (13/10 & 11)

God adds 5 more qualities of a **Jnaanee** in these shloks. They are:

Mayi Ananya Yogen Bhakti Avyabhichaarinee: We had discussed under '*Some additional thoughts on Ananya Chintayant Janaa*' in 9/22 that **Ananya** devotees see their Lord only in everything with undeviating faith in Him. Their every moment, action, thought, and desire is fully connected with the supreme will of Lord. **Bhakti**, the devotion of a **Jnaanee,** is **Avyabhichaarinee** i.e. unadulterated, incorruptible, inviolable, and unpolluted like the water of Gangaa. His devotion is as flawless and uncompromising as the loyalty and honesty of Munshee Vansheedhar, the Salt Inspector hero of the famous short story '*Namak kaa Daarogaa*' by Munshi Prem Chand. Devotion of Tulasidaas for Raam is a good example of **Avyabhichaarinee Bhakti**.

Vivikt Desh Sevitvam: A **Jnaanee** lives in secluded, lonely places uninhabited by humans and remains aloof from the affairs of nearby human settlements until his duties call on him to intervene when irreligious situations arise there. **Arati Jan Sansadi: Rati,** explained earlier in 3/17, is intense passionate liking and consequent engagement with something. **Arati**, the opposite of **Rati,** is the quality of not being attracted and engaged in passionate activities. For example, Arjun remains **Arati** and declines the advances made by Urvashee, the dancer in the court of Indr during his stay in heaven. A **Jnaanee** does not harbour **Rati** either by nurturing infatuation or by delight from a fulfilled desire.

Adhyaatm Jnaan Nityatvam: We understood **Adhyaatm** as the spiritual study and knowledge of **Jeevaatmaa**, the soul embodied in an individual and its eternal relationship with **Brahm**, the Supreme Soul in 3/30; and later under, *'What is Adhyaatm'* in 8/3 as **Swabhaav,** the existence of one's self as his spirit, the embodied soul. Both these explanations imply the same in spiritual context.

Tattv Jnaanaarth Darshanam means seeking knowledge from its basics and fundamentals. A **Jnaanee** always remains a seeker of the knowledge of **Adhyaatm** as the ever-inquisitive Rishis and their pupils were in the Upanishad era. The final qualification of a **Jnaanee** is that he must seek and turn towards spiritual knowledge within him with undeviating, incorruptible devotion, and detach from all external things.

Krishn listed 20 symptoms of **Jnaan** in above 5 shloks and states in corollary that the opposite of these qualities should be understood as **Ajnaan.** Absence of knowledge is ignorance just as the absence of light is darkness; of heat is cold, and of strength is weakness. By stating *'it has been described'*, Krishn implies that other scriptures, besides Gita, also describe **Jnaan** and **Ajnaan** in similar way.

Socrates defines a **Jnaanee** and an **Ajnaanee** as:

'A fool who knows that he is a fool is actually a knowledgeable person (Jnaanee) but the knowledgeable person who does not even know that he knows nothing is actually the greatest fool (Ajnaanee).

The topic describing symptoms of a **Jnaanee** started from 13/7 ends here. Readers may also refer to some additional thoughts under 7/27-28 in this respect.

જ⊶ઈ

God starts describing inexplicable form of
Brahm from 13/12 to 17.

(13/12)

ज्ञेयं यत्तत्प्रवक्ष्यामि यज्ज्ञात्वामृतमश्नुते ।
अनादिमत्परं ब्रह्म न सत्तन्नासदुच्यते ॥१३/१२॥

Jneyam yattatpravakshyaami yajjnaatvaamrutamashnute I
Anaadimatparam Brahm n sattannaasaduchyate II (13/12)

Jneyam (knowable) Yat (which) Tat (that) Pravakshyaami (shall
explain) Yat (which) Jnaatwaa (knowing well) Amrutam (divine
nectar conferring immortality) Ashnute (attains) I Anaadimat
(without beginning) Param Brahm (Supreme God) N (not) Sat
(absolute truth) Tat (that) N (nor) Asat (false) Uchyate (is said) II
(13/12)

**I shall now explain to you that which only is worth knowing;
and by knowing which a person achieves immortality. That
Param Brahm, the Ultimate, Perfect Being is said to be without
any beginning (nor any end) and He is neither existential nor
the non-existential i.e. beyond the limited scope of Sat and
Asat. (13/12)**

Krishn described 20 qualities of **Jnaan**, the knowledge and
Jnaanee, its knower from 13/7 to 11; and the last two were
Adhyaatm Jnaan Nityatvam and **Tattv Jnaanaarth Darshanam**
i.e. to learn and know **Adhyaatm**, the spiritual knowledge of soul and
Supreme Soul. He starts describing **Jney**, the ultimate knowable
object now in 13/12-17, which a **Jnaanee** ought to know because
this final destination alone can make him immortal (refer to *'Why
does Gita talk of Amrut....'* in 2/15). This description of God as **Jney**
is highly poetic and literary as it resorts to extreme metaphysical
positions an object can take like *'Neither this nor that'*, or *'This as
well as that'*. Here, in 13/12, Krishn says that God is **Anaadimat**
i.e. with no beginning; and neither **Sat** i.e. something that has
material existence, nor **Asat** i.e. the thing that does not exist. What
does it mean? It simply means that God exists in entire transient,

limited mutable, ephemeral & mortal world; simultaneously He is also absent and uninvolved in it. God's relationship with the world is like that of the sun with the earth. Sun is the primeval cause of days and nights, of darkness and light, of heat and cold in the world though there are no such mutations like days or nights in the sun per se. People on earth are accustomed to attribute their days and nights to sun wrongly, whereas the fact is that they are created by the earth's own rotation. Similarly, people blame God for the vicissitudes in their lives, though they are the results of rotation of their souls in the cycles of **Punarjanm**, and the shadows of their actions. Sun is an ever-shining stationary celestial object but the clouds of **Ajnaan** i.e. lack of knowledge appear to hide it from us. God said in 9/19:

"I am immortality as well as death. I am Sat, every existent, real thing; and also Asat, the non-existent, unreal thing".

Sat Asat Vivek was introduced by Krishn in Gita in 2/16-18 while dealing with immortality of **Aatmaa**, the soul. There, He applied this concept to soul because a soul is an indivisible part of **Paramaatmaa**, the Supreme Soul. Arjun described God in 11/37 while viewing His universal form:

"You are the imperishable Supreme Being O Supreme Lord of Demigods! You are Sat and Asat O Ultimate Abode and Refuge of universe! And You are also beyond them".

We shall have some more insight about **Sat** and **Asat** in 17/26-27.

༺✿༻

Krishn continues to describe Brahm.

(13/13, 14 & 15)

सर्वतः पाणिपादं तत्सर्वतोऽक्षिशिरोमुखम् ।
सर्वतः श्रुतिमल्लोके सर्वमावृत्य तिष्ठति ॥१३/१३॥
सर्वेन्द्रियगुणाभासं सर्वेन्द्रियविवर्जितम् ।

असक्तं सर्वभृच्चैव निर्गुणं गुणभोक्तृ च ॥१ ३/१४॥
बहिरन्तश्च भूतानामचरं चरमेव च ।
सूक्ष्मत्वात्तदविज्ञेयं दूरस्थं चान्तिके च तत् ॥१ ३/१५॥

Sarvat: paanipaadam tatsarvato∫kshishiromukham I
Sarvat: shrutimalloke sarvamaavrutya tishthati II (13/13)
Sarvendriyagunaabhaasam sarvendriyavivarjitam I
Asaktam sarvabhruchchaiv nirgunam gunabhoktru ch II
(13/14)
Bahirantashch bhootaanaamacharam charamev ch I
Sookshmatwattadavijneyam doorasth chaantike ch tat II
(13/15)

Sarvat: (on all sides) Paani (hands) Paadam (feet) Tat (that) Sarvat: (on all sides) Akshi (eyes) Shir: (heads) Mukham (mouths) I Sarvat: (on all sides) Shrutimat (having ears) Loke (in universe) Sarvam (all) Aavrutya (covering) Tishthati (remains situated) II (13/13)

Sarvendriy (all Indriys) Gun (qualities) Aabhaasam (provides light) Sarvendriy (all Indriys) Vivarjitam (devoid of) I Asaktam (detached) Sarv bhrut (sustainer of everyone) Ch (and) Ev (still) Nirgunam (beyond Guns) Gun Bhoktru (beneficiary of Guns) Ch (and) II (13/14)

Bahi: (outer side) Ant: (inner side) Ch (and) Bhootaanaam (all living and animate entities) Acharam (all inanimate stationary objects) Charam (all moving, animated beings) Ev (and) Ch (and) I Sookshmatwaat (smaller than the smallest) Tat (that) Avijneyam (unknowable) Doorastham (located faraway) Ch (and) Antike (closely situated) Ch (and) Tat (he) II (13/15)

That Brahm with His hands & feet on all sides; His eyes, heads & mouths everywhere and His ears on all sides, is situated in whole universe and encompasses everything with His existence. (13/13)

He is the one who empowers all Indriys, the sensory organs to sense the objects of their respective passions but does not have any Indriy Himself. He sustains everyone in spite of not

having attachment with anybody. He is the sole beneficiary of all Guns, the qualities of nature though He Himself does not possess any Gun. (13/14)

He exists in the inner as well as outer sides of every entity whether animated and moving, or inanimate and stationary. He is incomprehensible because He is infinitesimally small (as well as inconceivably big). He is farther than the farthest possible place, and nearer than the nearest one. (13/15)

Arjun was highly surprised in 11/16 and 23 on seeing God with multiple arms, bellies, mouths, eyes, and legs in His universal form. Shlok 13/13 echoes almost the same description of God and adds further that His numerous hands, feet, eyes, ears, heads and mouths, in fact His entire existence, is spread all over covering everything in whole universe.

Nirgun denotes that God is never subjected to **Sattv**, **Raj** and **Tam**, three modes of nature because nature itself is subservient to Him. Let me explain it with an incident from the life of Tulasidaas:

'When followers of a particular sect told Tulasidaas that his Lord Raam possesses only 12 out of the 16 noble qualities of God, he was greatly delighted to know that his Lord has as many as 12 divine virtues whereas he had been regarding Raam as Nirgun i.e. quality less until then. He thanked them profusely for making such great revelation on him'.

Sookshm is something infinitesimally small, thin, subtle, and fine. **Brahm** is **Sookshmaatisookshm** i.e. smaller than the smallest (He is also bigger than the biggest). He situates nearest to everyone in his heart as soul but is also far away from those who cannot realize Him e.g. water always exists around us in the form of miniscule particles floating in the air but we are unable to see it unless sunrays fall on it just as the light of **Jnaan** removes **Ajnaan**.

Antik means neighbor. **Antike** therefore, literally refers to someone located in immediate vicinity like a neighbor. Nevertheless, God is situated closer than a neighbor is as He lives within the heart and conscience of all living beings as proclaimed **Hrudi Sarvasya Vishthitam** in 13/17. The proverb 'बगल में छोरा, शहर में ढिंढोरा' i.e. *"Missing something right under one's nose"* holds well here also.

Bahi: It denotes something external; and **Ant**: is the thing situated within. I have come across an interpretation of **Bahirant** by some commentators that **Bahi** stands for the material world, which lies outside the body of a person, but he regards it as his own self due to ignorance; and **Ant**: i.e. within stands for **Aatmaa**, the soul inside the body. This interpretation seems to be based on the argument that if **Brahm** is situated only without and within something, it implies that He is not present in between the external and internal. It is probably to prevent this misunderstanding that God subsequently adds He is also **Achar**, the unmoving as well as **Char**, the moving beings. Learned readers need not see any controversy here because **Brahm**, the ultimate Knowable One physically manifests as the bodies of all moving and unmoving entities of the external world; and dwells within them as souls. Ishaavaasya Upanishad explains Nirgun Brahm in verse 5 thus:

तदेजति तन्नेजति तद् दूरे तद्वन्तिके ।
तदन्तरस्य सर्वस्य तद् सर्वस्यास्य बाह्यत: ॥

(He walks, He does not walk; He is away, He is near. He is inside everything; He is outside everything.)

❧❦❧

Krishn concludes description of Brahm.

(13/16 & 17)

अविभक्तं च भूतेषु विभक्तमिव च स्थितम् ।
भूतभर्तृ च तज्ज्ञेयं ग्रसिष्णु प्रभविष्णु च ॥१३/१६॥
ज्योतिषामपि तज्ज्योतिस्तमस: परमुच्यते ।
ज्ञानं ज्ञेयं ज्ञानगम्यं हृदि सर्वस्य विष्ठितम् ॥१३/१७॥

Avibhaktam ch bhooteshu vibhaktamiv ch sthitam I
Bhootbhartru ch tajjneyam grasishnu prabhavishnu ch II
(13/16)
Jyotishaamapi tajjyotistamas: paramuchyate I
Jnaanam jneyam jnaanagamyam hrudi sarvasya vishthitam
II 13/17)

Avibhaktam (indivisible) Ch (and) Bhooteshu (in all entities) Vibhaktam (divided) iv (as if) Ch (and) Sthitam (situated) I Bhoot bhartru (Lord Vishnu, the sustainer of all entities) Ch (and) Tat (that) Jneyam (knowable) Grasishnu (Shiv, the devourer) Prabh Vishnu (Lord Brahmaa, the creator) Ch (and) II (13/16)

Jyotishaam (objects of light) Api (even) Tat (that) Jyoti: (light) Tamas (darkness of ignorance) Param (supreme) Uchyate (is said) I Jnaanam (the perfect spiritual knowledge) Jneyam (knowable) Jnaan Gamyam (approachable by knowledge) Hrudi (in heart) Sarvasya (of everything) Vishthitam (well situated) II (13/17)

He is indivisible though appears to be situated as if divided in all entities individually. He must be known as the Supreme Trinity of Lord Vishnu, the sustainer & Providence, Lord Shiv, the devourer, and Lord Brahma, the creator of all beings. (13/16)

That Brahm is described also as the ultimate light that illuminates every other source of light and is totally beyond the darkness of ignorance and illusion. He is simultaneously Jnaan, the perfect knowledge; Jney, the only One Knowable who already situates well in the heart of everyone; and He can be reached by practising this Jnaan. (13/17)

Avibhaktam: It means indivisible. God is One and only One since He is Apramey, the incomparable and immeasurable One (refer 11/16 & 17) but that **Avibhakt** God also appears as **Vibhakt** i.e. divided into 'नाना नाम रूपात्मक जगत्' i.e. many names and forms of material world. Bruhadaaranyak Upanishad says in 5/1/1:

ॐ पूर्णमदः पूर्णमिदं पूर्णात्पूर्णमुदच्यते ।
पूर्णस्य पूर्णमादाय पूर्णमेवावशिष्यते ॥

{Om! That (Brahm) is complete in itself, and this (universe, His creation) also is infinite because the infinite remains infinite if something is added to it; and f something is taken out from the infinite, the remainder is still infinite}.

My mathematics teacher was also a spiritually awakened person. He used to express this verse to us mathematically as follows:

$$\infty + u = \infty; \infty, u = \infty; \infty \times u = \infty; \infty \div u = \infty; \infty^n = \infty; \sqrt[n]{\infty} = \infty$$

The symbol '∞' stands for infinity, and 'u' represents universe in above equations.

Moral*: Let us not waste our energy and time in cutting that Whole Being into parts and pieces to suit sectarian leanings in our heads; it would result only in blunting our tools. Ignorant are they who try to divide Him into theirs and others' God and fight to establish supremacy of their own God over others'.*

9/18 explained **Bhartaa** as maintainer, protector, sustainer, nourisher and nurturer. **Bhoot Bhartru** is the Providence that bears and supports all beings invisibly in its all-pervading self-existence like earth, the ultimate base of all material things though they may individually appear to be supported, rooted, seated, resting, standing, sleeping, running, jumping on different things. For example, if a pen is placed on a book kept on a table resting on the ground, all of them are supported by the ground only. Raamkrishn Paramhans never worried for his sustenance. He used to narrate following inspiring anecdote to his followers:

"A student was sent first time by his Guru to get alms from nearby village. When he called for alms at a house, a young woman, in advanced stage of pregnancy, appeared with some food. The student had never seen a pregnant woman before. On seeing her swollen abdomen and breasts wet with milk, he thought that she was suffering with some disease. Greatly concerned, he offered to call his Guru who would surely cure her. On hearing this, her mother in law came out and informed him that she was about to give birth to a baby, and it would be very auspicious for her and the baby if she gives you some food with her hands. Please bless her for a safe delivery, and the baby for good health.

The student, surprised to learn how a baby is born, continued with his concern for her, 'But Mother! What about those two large tumors on her chest with some liquid oozing from them? This must certainly be very painful for her.'

The mother in law replied smilingly, 'My dear child! These are not tumors but two pots brimming with milk kept by God to feed the baby who is about to take birth.' The student happily collected the alms, profusely blessed the young woman, her forthcoming child and entire household. On reaching his Aashram, he spoke thus to his Guru, 'Guruji! Henceforth I shall not waste my time any more on collecting alms because I have realized today that God's great providence keeps not one but two pots full of pure milk ready for a child who is not yet born. Won't He make some arrangement to feed me too without asking?"

Shlok 13/16 clearly states that people call Him by different names like **Bhoot Bhartru** i.e. Lord **Vishnu**, the sustainer form of God, **Prabh Vishnu** i.e. Lord **Brahmaa**, the creative form of God, and **Grasishnu** i.e. Lord **Shiv,** the God of destruction. Nevertheless, He is actually the only one Supreme Lord appearing as the divine trinity of **Brahmaa, Vishnu & Shiv**. God is the ultimate source of light that even pitch-black darkness cannot put out. He is the sum total of the trio of **Jnaan**, the supreme knowledge, **Jney**, the supreme knowable and **Jnaan Gamyam**, that supreme destiny of **Jnaan**. Bruhadaaranyak Upanishad says:

'How can anyone know Him who is the ultimate knower of everything?'

As explained earlier also, God is like **Aakaash**, the space that is a great void and non-entity but still is the source as well as holder and sustainer of other four basic elements namely wind, fire, water & earth and the multitudinous physical entities produced by them. **Aakaash** does not have hands, feet, eyes, ears, heads and mouths but even then it touches, walks, feels, sees, listens, eats, talks and supervises everything; though it is dimensionless, its spread covers all entities of the world. **Aakaash** is vast yet intangible, near but beyond the reach of anybody, and it pervades within and without all beings. It provides shelter to everyone, sustains and maintains him with full care, and also destroys everything but remains aloof and detached from all beings. **Aakaash** is one indivisible entity, and yet it appears divided into a pitcher, a tumbler, a room, a cage.

છ∞ઉ

God returns to the topic of Kshetr & Kshetrajn.

(13/18)

इति क्षेत्रं तथा ज्ञानं ज्ञेयं चोक्तं समासतः ।
मद्भक्त एतद्विज्ञाय मद्भावायोपपद्यते ॥१३/१८॥

Iti kshetram tathaa jnaanam choktam samaasat: I
Madbhakt etadvijnaay madbhaavaayopapadyate II (13/18)

Iti (thus) Kshetram (body & the field of activities) Tathaa (and) Jnaanam (perfect knowledge) Jneyam (knowable, worth knowing) Ch (and) Uktam (is said) Samaasat: (briefly) I Madbhakt: (my devotee) Etat (in this) Vijnaay (by knowing) Madbhaavaay (to My eternal form, being) Upapadyate (attains, obtains) II (13/18)

Kshetr, the body, Jnaan, the perfect knowledge and Jney, the ultimate knowable Brahm are explained thus to you briefly. My devotee avails My eternal existence by knowing Me like this. (13/18)

Krishn first explained **Kshetr** in 13/5-6 briefly, and took a detour without explaining **Kshetrajn** thereafter. Instead, He described symptoms of **Jnaan**, the knowledge in 13/7-11, and then **Jney** i.e. God, the only one knowable in 13/12-17 before returning to **Kshetr** and **Kshetrajn** here in 13/18. He did it purposefully to stress the importance of **Jnaan** of **Jney** before knowing **Kshetr** and **Kshetrajn**. Once a practising devotee attains knowledge of God's eternally existent nature, and His different manifestations, and thereby realizes the difference between Kshetr and Kshetrajn, he merges immediately into God.

Clarification: *Though Kshetrajn is not mentioned here specifically, it is implied that once knowledge of Brahm is perfected, understanding of Kshetr and Kshetrajn follows automatically.*

৵৹৻৶

Relationships between Prakruti or Kshetr, and Purush or Kshetrajn are explained.

(13/19)

प्रकृतिं पुरुषं चैव विद्ध्यनादी उभावपि ।
विकारांश्च गुणांश्चैव विद्धि प्रकृतिसंभवान् ॥१३/१९॥

Prakrutim Purusham chaiv viddhyanaadee ubhaavapi I
Vikaaraanshch gunaanshchaiv viddhi prakrutisambhavaan II
(13/19)

Prakrutim (nature) Purusham (individual soul) Ch (and) Ev (indeed) Viddhi; (know well) Anaadee (without beginning) Ubhau (both) Api (also) I Vikaaraan (mutations) Ch (and) Gunaan (Sattv, Raj and Tam) Ch (and) Ev (certainly) Viddhi; (understand well) Prakruti (nature) Sambhavaan (are born of) II (13/19)

Understand it well that Prakruti, the causal nature, and Purush, the individual soul, both have no beginning i.e. they co-exist since time immemorial. And know this also that Vikaars, the mutations and Guns, the three modes of nature also are the products only of causal nature (not of individual soul). (13/19)

Readers should bear in mind that **Purush** (or **Aatmaa**) and **Prakruti** mentioned from here onwards in this chapter denote **Kshetrajn** and **Kshetr** respectively as individual soul embodied in a body, surrounded by material nature and its products namely **Vikaars**, the infinite mutations and **Guns** of **Sattv**, the righteousness, **Raj**, the passions and **Tam**, the darkness of ignorance. Though **Prakruti** and **Purush** i.e. **Kshetr** and **Kshetrajn** both are creations of God, the first one is as ephemeral as a bubble and the other is as permanent as God is. This statement almost conforms to the doctrine called **Saamkhya** propagated by sage **Kapil**. Please refer to chapter 2 under *'Why this chapter is named Saamkhya Yog'* and also *'Some additional thoughts on Aparaa and Paraa natures'* in 7/4-5 for better understanding. God shall later speak about **Kshar**

& **Akshar,** the equivalent words of **Prakruti** & **Purush** or **Kshetr** & **Kshetrajn** in chapter 15. Nature, with its three modes, was also described as **Maayaa** in 7/14.

҂

God explains how and why Purush and Prakruti interact with each other.

(13/20 & 21)

कार्यकरणकर्तृत्वे हेतुः प्रकृतिरुच्यते ।
पुरुषः सुखदुःखानां भोक्तृत्वे हेतुरुच्यते ॥१३/२०॥
पुरुषः प्रकृतिस्थो हि भुङ्क्ते प्रकृतिजान्गुणान् ।
कारणं गुणसङ्गोऽस्य सदसद्योनिजन्मसु ॥१३/२१॥

Kaaryakaranakartrutve hetu: prakrutiruchyate I
Purush: sukhdu:khaanaam bhoktrutve heturuchyate II (13/20)
Purush: prakrutistho hi bhunkte prakrutijaangunaan I
Kaaranam gunsangolsya sadasadyonijanmasu II (13/21)

Kaarya (action) Karan (instruments) Kartrutve (doer) Hetu: (cause) Prakruti: (nature) Uchyate (is said) I Purush: (soul) Sukh Dukhaanaam (joy & distress) Bhoktrutve (experience) Hetu: (cause) Uchyate (is said) II (13/20)

Purush: (person) Prakrutisth: (situated in material nature) Hi (certainly) Bhunkte (consumes) Prakrutijaan (produced by nature) Gunaan (modes of nature, Sattv, Raj and Tam) I Kaaranam (basic cause) Gun (modes of nature) Sang: (association) Asya (with it) Sat Asat (good and bad) Yoni (species) Janmasu (of births) II (13/21)

The causal nature is said to be the cause and power behind all actions, the effects of five basic elements and the means of carrying them out. However, the consciousness of an individual person is said to be the real cause of experiencing happiness & distress from effects of causal nature. (13/20)

When an individual person situates his self in aforesaid material nature he must certainly consume (suffer or enjoy) the material products of nature according to its three modes of Sattv, Raj & Tam. His association with these modes is the primary cause of his births in superior and inferior species of living beings. (13/21)

A person's body, called **Kartaa**, the doer of all **Kaarya**, the action, is created by nature; and the nature forces it to do works by lodging its **Guns**, the modes and **Vikaars**, the mutations in it. An action also is therefore inert and neutral i.e. neither good nor bad like nature, its creator. By itself, **Kaarya** or **Karm** neither catches hold of anyone nor leaves him but it is his **Chetanaa**, the consciousness (combination of intelligence, mind and heart) that creates the feelings of happiness or distress in him as per the degree of his association with the action and its result. **Karan** are the material implements, the means and resources made available by nature to **Kartaa**, the doer. If **Kartaa** chooses good **Karan**, the output of his work shall also be good as a farmer uses good seeds to get a good crop. Mahatma Gandhi placed a goal of independence before India but he was very careful in choosing the means that based on principles of truth, purity of thought, honesty of purpose, and physical & mental non-violence. Gita shall throw more light on **Kartaa**, the doer, **Kaarya**, the action & **Karan**, the instruments required for it in 18/13-15. I may, however, briefly explain here that a group of ten things namely five basic elements, the space, wind, water, fire & earth with five passions of seeing, hearing, tasting, feeling touching & smelling constitutes an action. In addition, a group of thirteen: ten **Indriys**, mind, intelligence & ego, forms **Karan**, the implements or means of doing a work. Thus, **Kaarya**, **Karan** and **Prakruti**, the nature itself with its 24 constituents, carry out the whole gambit of works of nature (or body). **Purush**, the soul should remain detached from it; and unaffected by its results because it is a part of ever-blissful Supreme Soul. **Sat** and **Asat** are used here respectively for the superior species like **Dev, Pitr** etc. and for inferior species like animals, birds, reptiles, insects, ghosts, demons etc. Thus, the ultimate cause of the greatest distress of passing through cycles of

Punarjanm, the painful rigmarole of repetitive births and deaths in lower and upper species, for a person is he remaining engrossed in the works of nature and their results. The soul appears to be consuming the results of the works of body i.e. nature just as a parent emotionally attached with his child, suffers or enjoys due to happy or unhappy situations in his life.

Moral: *Water transforms into ice, snow, steam, vapor, hailstone, raindrop etc. due to climatic changes. It becomes hot, chilled or cool depending on variation in temperatures; muddy, clean or salty by contact with external things; it flows downwards as liquid, upwards as steam or remains stationary as ice; it appears to cause comfort or discomfort to people around it; but nonetheless, water retains its originality as water. Soul is like water.*

࿐

What in reality is all this about? And what happens when one realizes it?

(13/22 & 23)

उपद्रष्टानुमन्ता च भर्ता भोक्ता महेश्वरः ।
परमात्मेति चाप्युक्तो देहेऽस्मिन्पुरुषः परः ॥१३/२२॥
य एवं वेत्ति पुरुषं प्रकृतिं च गुणैः सह ।
सर्वथा वर्तमानोऽपि न स भूयोऽभिजायते ॥१३/२३॥

Upadrashtaanumantaa ch Bhartaa Bhoktaa Maheshwar: I
Paramaatmeti chaapyukto deheſsminpurush: par: II (13/22)
Y evam vetti purusham prakrutim ch gunai: sah I
Sarvathaa vartamaanoſpi n s bhooyoſbhijaayate II (13/23)

Upadrashtaa (overseer, witness, onlooker) Anumantaa (adviser, decider) Ch (and) Bhartaa (provider, sustainer, protector) Bhoktaa (consumer) Maheshwar: (Supreme Lord) I Paramaatmaa (Supreme Soul) Iti (thus) Ch (and) Api (also) Ukt: (is said) Dehe (in body) Asmin (in it) Purush: (soul) Par: (ultimate) II (13/22)

Y: (the one who) Evam (in this way) Vetti (knows well) Purusham (individual soul) Prakrutim (causal nature) Ch (and) Gunai: (of three modes of nature, Sattv, Raj & Tam) Sah (along with) I Sarvathaa (in all respects) Vartamaan: (acts, deals) Api (regardless) N (never) S: (he) Bhooy: (again) Abhijaayate (is born) II (13/23)

It has been said that the soul is simultaneously the onlooker, the adviser & decision maker, the consumer as well as the provider of all activities of the body & nature and also Supreme Lord of his life. In this way, the soul in a body is said to be the Supreme Soul also (because of its ultimate relation with Him). (13/22)

He, who realizes well that the soul and the causal nature, along with of its three modes, Sattv, Raj and Tam, interact with each other in all respects, he is never born again regardless of his current position in life. (13/23)

Upadrashtaa is the onlooker and/or witness. 14/19 shall mention it as **Drushtaa**, the seer. **Anumantaa** means adviser, counselor. **Bhartaa** was understood in 9/18 & 13/16 as provider, maintainer, sustainer and protector. **Bhoktaa,** explained in 9/24, is one who enjoys, suffers, or endures. He is ultimate consumer and beneficiary of the result of an action.

Maheshwar: We had understood Him as the Supreme Lord & Master of all other Lords in 5/29, 9/11, 10/3 earlier. **Paramaatmaa** is Supreme Soul i.e. God as explained in 6/7. **Dehe Asmin Purush:** It refers to an individual soul embedded in the body. Gita also describes it as **Dehee, Dehin** or **Dehinam** in 2/13, 22, 30, 59; 3/40, 5/13, 14/5, 7; and 14/20; **Shareerin** in 2/18 and **Aatmaa** in 4/21 & 10/20. It is same as **Kshetrajn**, the knower, owner and master of **Kshetr** or **Deh**, the body and dwells in it. We had learnt about it as **Aatm Jnaan** in 2/30.

In this shlok, Gita agrees with the idea of **Saamkhya** propagated by sage Kapil that the embodied soul is **Updrashtaa,** the witness, and **Anumantaa**, the advisor for every work done by body & nature, but it immediately adds that the individual soul is also the lord of nature since it is an indivisible part of Supreme Soul. A spoonful of milk, taken from a bucket, has the same qualities as the milk in bucket. It must however be noted that the spoonful milk separated from the bucket can start losing its qualities when it comes in contact with impurities created by **Guns** and **Vikaars**, the forces of nature. A weak soul lets loose its power to exercise control on the body and gets involved in the acts of nature at the bidding of Man and Indriys like a king playing in the hands of his queen. On the other hand, a Yogee does only those works, which are approved and certified as righteous by his soul i.e. in accordance with **Dharm**. A strong soul is like an obedient son who dutifully carries out the instructions of his righteous father, Paramaatmaa i.e. God.

Moral: *No one else but the person himself is the sole in-charge of his life. Krishn can only teach Arjun the philosophy of life, but ultimately it is Arjun who must decide whether to fight or not.*

Soul as **Upadrashtaa**, an onlooker, exists normally in calm self-existence and is not an active participant or intervener in the workings of a man as per nature but it still has a relation, a connection with him as it witnesses, supports and silently & impersonally approves and even enjoys what he does. This apparently double identity of soul can be explained thus that when it is weak and connects with nature, it is forced into the works of nature; but on the other side, a strong soul that knows of its lineage from God, remains uninvolved and keeps itself away from the works of nature. Soul is like a newlywed girl whose dispositions and likings change when she is with her in-laws; and when with her parents at another time. Once a person realizes the fact that all works are the creation of nature by interactions of its materials in three modes **Sattv**, **Raj** and **Tam** as stated earlier **Gunaa Guneshu Vartant in** 3/28; and that **Purush**, the soul in him just witnesses their play like a spectator, he is freed from rebirth. Saahir Ludhiyaanavee reflects this sentiment very well by in film *'Dil Hi to Hai'*:

कोरी चुनरिया आत्मा मोरी मैल है माया जाल,
वो दुनिया मेरे बाबुल का घर ये दुनिया ससुराल ।
जा के बाबुल से नज़रे मिलाऊँ कैसे, घर जाऊँ कैसे,
लागा चुनरी में दाग़ छुपाऊँ कैसे ॥

{My soul was as pure as an undyed grey Chunaree (the long cloth worn by Hindu girls to cover breasts and loin) but the cobwebs of Maayaa, the illusive nature, have dirtied it. My Chunaree is blemished with stains since I departed from my parental home, that other world of God, and came to this world of my in-laws. Is there a way by which I can hide the stains on my Chunaree, return to my parent (God), and look into His eyes once again?}

Moral: *As long as the world of passions and material pleasures attracts a soul, it would continue to become dirtier, and shuttle in the cycles of Punarjanm.*

Gita, through its teachings of three main paths of practice: **Jnaan**, the knowledge, **Karm**, the works, and **Bhakti**, the devotion, for liberation from distress of **Punarjanm**, provides us with a harmonious synthesis of the philosophies of **Vedaant, Saamkhya & Yog** which is almost impossible to achieve if a practiser opts for only one or two of them. Gita irons out the differences between them, and triumphs over them by offering a simple, practical solution of its **Samagr**, the all-inclusive Yog (2/39-40).

৯৽৩

Gita explains four methods of understanding soul and nature with three modes.

(13/24 & 25)

ध्यानेनात्मनि पश्यन्ति केचिदात्मानमात्मना ।
अन्ये सांख्येन योगेन कर्मयोगेन चापरे ॥१३/२४॥
अन्ये त्वेवमजानन्तः श्रुत्वान्येभ्य उपासते ।
तेऽपि चातितरन्त्येव मृत्युं श्रुतिपरायणाः ॥१३/२५॥

Dhyaanenaatmani pashyanti kechidaatmaanamaatmanaa I
Anye saankhyen yogen karmyogen chapare II (13/24)
Anye twevamajaanant: shrutwaanyebhya upaasate I
Te∫pi chaatitarantyev mrutyum shrutiparaayanaa: II (13/25)

Dhyaanen (by meditation) Aatmani (within own self) Pashyanti (see, perceive) Kechit (some of them) Aatmaanam (Supreme Soul) Aatmanaa (by own self) I Anye (others) Saamkhyen (by Saamkhya) Yogen (by Yog) Karm Yogen (by performing duties without any desire of fruition) Ch (and) Apare (many others) II (13/24)

Anye (others) Tu (but) Evam (in this way) Ajaanant: (not conversant) Shrutwaa (by listening) Anyebhy: (from others) Upaasate (render service with modesty) I Te (they) Api (also) Ch (and) Ati Taranti (easily swim across) Ev (undoubtedly) Mrutyum (death) Shruti Paraayanaa: (dedicated, intent listeners) II (13/25)

Some people see God, the Supreme Soul situated within them through conscious meditation; others by uniting with Him through the path of perfect knowledge whereas still others by performing their duties without any desire of their fruition. (13/24)

However others, who do not know these three paths in this way, but listen, with modesty, to the teachings of other accomplished knowers with complete devotion, such intently devoted listeners also cross over (the sea of) death (and rebirth) easily. (13/25)

God describes four methods commonly followed by practisers to transgress **Punarjanm**, the cycles of death and rebirth, 3 in 13/24, and the one in 13/25. They are:

1. **Dhyaan Yog**, the meditation: We learnt it from 6/11 to 32 earlier as based largely on Paatanjal Yog. Please also refer specifically to *'Some Additional thoughts on Dhyaan....'* under 6/28. God shall also talk about **Dhyaan** as an important symptom of a Yogee in 18/52.

2. **Jnaan Yog**, the path of acquiring spiritual knowledge based principally on Saamkhya Yog of Kapil. We have learnt about it at many places in Gita besides some additional thoughts on **Jnaan Deep** in 10/10-11; **Jnaanee** or **Jnaan Vaan** under 3/38-39; and **Jnaan** & **Ajnaan** under 4/42; and shall learn more later in 18/18-22.

3. **Karm Yog:** It is the path of doing own duty (3/29) sincerely according to **Dharm** with the spirit of **Lok Sangrah** without

nurturing any attachment with desired result. God shall also describe three modes of **Karm** later in 18/8-9. Like **Jnaan Yog**, Gita teaches **Nishkaam Karm Yog** also extensively throughout its text but especially in chapters 2, 3, 4 & 18.

4. By being **Shruti Paraayanaa,** an ardent listener of knowledge taught by knowledgeable people or by scriptures. Recall that Krishn advised Arjun in 4/34 earlier to go to learned people and acquire perfect knowledge from them. God shall also advise Arjun later in 16/23-24 to find his way by referring to Shaastr, the Scripture and work accordingly. However, note that this is not an independent path per se, but only a direction, by which a knowledgeable Guru guides him towards any of the three paths mentioned above.

꩜

God reaffirms existence of soul in every moving or stationary entity of the world.

(13/26)

यावत्संजायते किंचित्सत्त्वं स्थावरजङ्गमम् ।
क्षेत्रक्षेत्रज्ञसंयोगात्तद्विद्धि भरतर्षभ ॥१३/२६॥

Yaavatsanjaayate kinchitsattvam sthaavarjangamam I
KshetraKshetrajnasanyogaattadviddhi Bharatarshabh II
(13/26)

Yaavat (as long as) Sanjaayate (are produced) Kinchit (all of them) Sattvam (being) Sthaavar (stationary & Inert) Jangamam (moving & living) I Kshetr (body, the field of activities) Kshetrajn (knower of field) Sanyogaat (by meeting, uniting) Tat (those) Viddhi; (understand well) Bharatarshabh (Arjun) II (13/26)

O Bharatarshabh (Arjun)! Know all the moving & living, or non-moving & inanimate entities existing (in this universe) as produced by the union of Kshetr, the field of activities and Kshetrajn, its knower. (13/26)

God classifies all entities in the universe into two categories of **Sthaawar**, the stationary & inanimate things like hills, forests, deserts, trees etc. and **Jangam**, all species of living beings that are able to move. Some people think that soul, a part of Supreme Soul, exists only in **Jangam**. Gita clarifies here that the same soul that exists in **Jangam** also exists in **Sthaawar** since nothing can exist without soul. Our environmentalist friends should surely be encouraged by this confirmation of Gita and propagate the idea of existence of soul (and therefore God) in all materials and resources in nature besides humans and other living beings; and the humans must deal with them with the same compassion and respect as towards other humans and lesser beings. The only difference between the two classes of **Sthaawar** and **Jangam** is that the degree of their consciousness and power to react varies; it is highest in humans, less in animals and least in inanimate ones although all of them feel the impact of an action. **Sthaawar** & **Jangam** were described as **Achar** & **Char** in 10/39 & 11/43.

Moral: *A Sthaawar material or resource of nature is akin to a Jangam infant child. They both feel happy when caressed, kissed and loved by a person; and they too feel sad when someone ill-treats them, although unable to express their feelings and react. This is the underlying thought of the principle of Karunaa (same as Dayaa in 16/2), the compassion towards all entities, preached by all religions of Indian origin.*

God alerts Arjun to be aware of this fact and work accordingly as he is **Bharatarshabh**, the greatest descendent of Great Bharat.

❧❦

God urges us to see the same God situated in all entities in order to attain Him.

(13/27 & 28)

समं सर्वेषु भूतेषु तिष्ठन्तं परमेश्वरम् ।
विनश्यत्स्वविनश्यन्तं यः पश्यति स पश्यति ॥१३/२७॥
समं पश्यन्हि सर्वत्र समवस्थितमीश्वरम् ।
न हिनस्त्यात्मनात्मानं ततो याति परां गतिम् ॥१३/२८॥

Samam Sarveshu Bhooteshu tishthantam Parameshwaram I
Vinashyatsvavinashyantam y: pashyati s pashyati II (13/27)
Samam pashyanhi Sarvatr samavasthitameeshwaram I
N hinastyaatmanaatmaanam tato yaati Paraam Gatim II
(13/28)

Samam (Samatv) Sarveshu (in all) Bhooteshu (in all beings)
Tishthantam (situated) Parameshwaram (Supreme Lord) I
Vinashyatsu (destructible) Avinashyantam (indestructible) Y: (who)
Pashyati (sees) S: (he) Pashyati (knows) II (13/27)

Samam (equanimity) Pashyan (seeing) Hi (because) Sarvatr
(everywhere) Sam Avasthitam (well situated, stationed) Ishwaram
(Supreme Lords) I n (not) Hinasti (does not think as dead) Aatmanaa
(own Self) Aatmaanam (to self, Soul) Tat: (by that) Yaati (goes to)
Paraam (supreme) Gatim (destination) II (13/28)

**He, who sees the same indestructible Supreme Lord of
all lords pervading equally in all beings, he only has really
understood (the truth). Because, by seeing the same Supreme
Lord situated equally in all beings and everywhere, he never
thinks of destroying his own soul by himself i.e. he realizes
that the soul does not die when its body dies. Knowing this,
he attains ultimate destination (eternal blissful abode of God).
(13/27 & 28)**

God declared indestructibility of soul in 2/20 when Arjun was
bewildered with the thought of killing his relatives, or meeting own
death at their hands:

*"It (the soul) does not die even if its body is killed, nor does it kill
anybody else (or own self)".*

Now, He elaborates the same declaration adding deep spiritual
perspective to it as He says that if one can realize omnipresence of
same eternal immortal soul (a part of God) in every entity including
himself and others, it becomes impossible for him to kill someone,
or be killed by someone else. Killing, or being killed, symbolically
implies harming also. A wise farmer (**Kshetrajn**) never thinks of
harming another good farmer. The practiser, who has known this
fact, shall harm neither others, nor himself, physically, mentally,

emotionally or spiritually. He becomes **Sarv Bhoot Hite Rataa** as told in 5/25 & 12/4 with no grudge towards none, and compassion for all. Let us understand it with the help of following inspiring story:

"A Saadhu, after staying in a village for about a week, was moving to next village to carry on his mission of teaching morality. On reaching the village, he saw two gangs fighting violently in the darkness of predawn hours. As he was trying to stop them, the police arrived. The gangsters jointly blamed Saadhu for the fight and ran away. As he was a stranger, police also accused him for fomenting trouble, locked him up and used its standard methods while questioning him.

Next morning, the headman of previous village came to police station for some work. He was taken aback to see the holy man in the lock up. He vouched for his righteousness, got him released immediately, called a doctor to treat the wounds inflicted by the gangsters and police.

Then the headman suggested Saadhu to lodge a complaint against the gangsters, but Saadhu replied with a serene smile on his face:

'Yes, I know who the real culprit is behind this entire incident. He is the same person, called Natawar, the great juggler, actor & mimic. He first met me as gangsters, hit me hard, then handed over to police and disappeared. The next moment, he donned the robe of a policeman, and handled me roughly in the lock up. In the morning, he arrived again as the village headman and got me released. Then, He appeared as a doctor and applied ointment on my wounds; and now, He asks me to complain against His various manifestations. Should I ask Him, a policeman now, to register an FIR on Himself when He was in the role of gangsters? No! I have recognized well that great actor who is playing tricks on me to test my endurance. I have decided to enjoy His entire play, not fall a victim of His trickery any more".

Clarification: *Krishn prods Arjun frequently to fight and kill his enemies in the war but here He talks of not killing or harming anyone.*

It is because a man is duty bound to uphold the rule of Dharm over Adharm; and if it needs destroying immoral, irreligious, Aatataayee people in the process of protecting and reestablishing Dharm, he must fulfill his duty. No sin or blame accrues to such person. In this case, a soul is not killing another soul, but a body is eliminating wicked bodies from the scene of fight and providing a chance to those souls to reform in next birth.

க்ஷ

God tells that Prakruti, not the soul, is the doer of works.

(13/29)

प्रकृत्यैव च कर्माणि क्रियमाणानि सर्वशः ।
यः पश्यति तथात्मानमकर्तारं स पश्यति ॥१३/२९॥

Prakrutyaiv ch karmaani kriyamaanaani sarvash: I
Y: pashyati tathaatmaanamakartaaram s pashyati II (13/29)

Prakrutyaa (by nature) Ev (only) Ch (and) Karmaani (in activities) Sarvash: Kriymaanaani (entirely done) I Y: pashyati (who sees) Tathaa (and) Aatmaanam (by soul) Akartaaram (non-doer) S: pashyati (he knows) II (13/29)

And, he who sees all kinds of activities entirely as the works of nature only, and considers his soul as a non-doer; he only truly knows. (13/29)

Akartaaram: **Kartaa** was explained as the doer of a work and **Akartaa**, being its opposite denotes he who non-doer of a work. God said earlier in 4/13 that He Himself is **Akartaa** though He is the creator of everything in the world. In 3/37, He said:

"All the activities in this world take place entirely due to three modes of nature. But a person, bewildered by ego, thinks his own self as the doer of those activities".

God reaffirms above statement here saying that he, who realizes that **Prakruti**, the nature as a body with its resources carries out all the works in the world; and that the soul in him is **Akartaa** i.e.

it has nothing to do with any of the works, has known everything worth knowing to liberate his soul. We had discussed this aspect of soul under 2/19-21 earlier.

❧ ☙

God tells to see all entities situated in Brahm
and as His expansion.

(13/30)

यदा भूतपृथग्भावमेकस्थमनुपश्यति ।
तत एव च विस्तारं ब्रह्म संपद्यते तदा ॥ १ ३/ ३ ०॥

Yadaa bhootapruthagbhaavamekasthamanupashyati I
Tat ev ch vistaaram Brahm sampadyate tadaa II (13/30)

Yadaa (when) Bhoot Pruthak Bhaavam (existence of different living & inanimate entities) Ekastham (situated in one God) Anupashyati (visualizes) I tat: (of that) Ev (only) Ch (and) Vistaaram (spread, expanse) Brahm (the all pervading Ultimate Being) Sampadyate (attains) Tadaa (then) II (13/30)

The moment he visualizes the existence of various kinds of entities situated in the one and only being God, and sees them only as His expansion, he attains Brahm then & there. (13/30)

As all entities are merely an expansion of earth because they are born and evolved on earth, live on earth and perish on earth, similarly every living being and material thing in the world is an extension of God's eternal existence. When a person sees entire world this way, he immediately realizes God. Kathopanishad says in 4/11 'नेह नानास्ति किंचन' i.e. *'there is nothing else at all'* and Chhaandogya Upanishad also states in 6/2/2 'एकमेवाद्वितीयम्' i.e. *'He only is there, none other.*

❧ ☙

That all-pervading Brahm never involves in the works of nature.

(13/31)

अनादित्वान्निर्गुणत्वात्परमात्मायमव्ययः ।
शरीरस्थोऽपि कौन्तेय न करोति न लिप्यते ॥१३/३१॥

Anaaditwaannirgunatwaatparamaatmaayamavyay: I
Shareerasthoʃpi Kauntey n karoti n Lipyate II (13/31)

Anaaditwaat (due to having no beginning) Nirgunatwaat (due to being transcendent of three modes of nature) Paramaatmaa (Supreme Soul) Ayam (this) Avyay: (inexhaustible) I Shareerasth: (situated in body) Api (although) Kauntey (Arjun) N (neither) Karoti (does) N (nor) Lipyate (implicated) II (13/31)

O Kauntey (Arjun)! This inexhaustible Supreme Soul is without any beginning; it transcends the modes of nature. Although He is situated in a body (as a soul), He neither does anything nor is entangled in it. (13/31)

Anaadi means without a beginning. God is beyond the measure & reach of any dimension including time, as His existence is **Apramey** i.e. immeasurable, unlimited, and incomparable; and **Shaashwat** i.e. eternal, everlasting, and immortal. This shlok also implies that God does not interfere in the works of **Prakruti** or **Kshetr** and lets it do what it should as per theory of **Karm**, except when He incarnates to fulfill His pledge given in 4/7-8.

৵৽৽

Two examples explain the relationship between
Kshetr & Kshetrajn.

(13/32 & 33)

यथा सर्वगतं सौक्ष्म्यादाकाशं नोपलिप्यते ।
सर्वत्रावस्थितो देहे तथात्मा नोपलिप्यते ॥१३/३२॥
यथा प्रकाशयत्येकः कृत्स्नं लोकमिमं रविः ।
क्षेत्रं क्षेत्री तथा कृत्स्नं प्रकाशयति भारत ॥१३/३३॥

Yathaa sarvagatam saukshmyaadaakaasham nopalipyate I
Sarvatraavasthito dehe tathaatmaa nopalipyate II (13/32)
Yathaa prakaashayatyek: Krutsnam lokamimam Ravi: I
Kshetram kshetree Tathaa Krutsnam prakaashayati Bhaarat
II (13/33)

Yathaa (as) Sarv Gatam (all pervading) Saukshmyaat (due to being infinitesimally small, finest) Aakaasham (space, sky) N (not) Up Lipyate (gets entangled) I Sarvatr (everywhere) Avasthit: (situated, stationed) Dehe (in body) Tathaa (similarly) Aatmaa (soul) N (not) Up Lipyate (get implicated) II (13/32)

Yathaa (as) Prakaashayati (illuminate) Ek: (only one) Krutsnam (entire) Lokam (universe, cosmos) imam (this) Ravi: (sun) I Kshetram (field) Kshetree (same as Kshetrajn) Tathaa (similarly) Prakaashayati (illuminates) Bhaarat (Arjun) II (13/33)

As Aakaash, the space pervades everywhere due to its infinitesimal fineness but does not entangle in anything; similarly, the soul, situated in body, does not entangle in its affairs. O Bhaarat (Arjun)! As sun illuminates entire universe alone; similarly, soul, the knower & owner of the field, illuminates entire field (the body with its consciousness). (13/32 & 33)

Sarv Gatam: It indicates to that which occupies and pervades everything and everywhere. God first described soul as **Sarv Gat** in 2/24, and then **Brahm**, Supreme Being as **Sarv Gat** in 3/15. He reiterates the same here in 13/32 and explains it with the example of **Aakaash**, the space. **Saukshmyaat:** It is the quality of something existing in a form finer than the finest. For example, electrons and positrons are finer than atom, the finest form of matter known earlier. God described **Param Purush**, the Ultimate Soul as **Ano Aneeyaansam** i.e. a fraction of atom in 8/9. **Kshetree** is same as **Kshetrajn** the soul in an individual body, the subject of this chapter.

N Up Lipyate: Lipyate was explained earlier in 5/7 & 10 that which is attached, involved, implicated, engrossed, and entangled with something; and *'Up'* prefix stresses this quality. The phrase **N Up**

Lipyate therefore means that the soul remains aloof and unaffected by the works of the body and nature. Soul is like a **Karachhee** (the long Indian spoon with deep bowl used for preparing and serving curries) that does not even know the taste of the curry in which it is always immersed. Compare it with the tongue of a person fond of food. Though his tongue is exposed to the curry momentarily, it promptly acquires its taste and asks for more.

Ek: It means one, and denotes God, the only One. An amusing episode from the life of Meeraa is worth quoting here:

"It is said that once when a Sannyaasee was camping in Vrundaavan. When Meeraa wanted to meet him, he spurned her request saying that no woman is allowed in his audience. To this, Meeraa modestly replied, 'I believed till now, that Krishn is the only Purush, a male in entire Vraj and all others are Gopees, His female devotees. I am delighted to know that another Purush (man) has now come in Vrundaavan?' The Sannyaasee walked down to the hut of Meeraa and met her".

Shloks 13/35-36 give two beautiful similes of space and sun to explain the subject matter taught in 13/26-31. Unmanifested **Brahm** is like space and sun. These are the closest examples given to understand indescribable, inconceivable **Brahm**.

SOME ADDITIONAL THOUGHTS ON THE SIMILE OF AAKAASH, THE SPACE

All things are contained in space; and space dwells within them. It is similar to space occupying the inner as well as outer side of an earthen pot. Readers may also note that the same space also fills the voids between earth particles in the body of pot. Likewise, space is pervading insides and outside of each entity of entire universe and in the material, that constitutes the entity. In the cosmos, it is between various celestial bodies whereas it also exists in its infinitesimal form in an atom between electrons, positrons and neutrons. While space holds together everything from the celestial bodies to the atoms in their individual identities & shapes, it has no shape or identity of its own. Soul and Supreme Soul are akin to **Aakaash**. Simile of **Aakaash** was discussed in detail earlier in 2/23, 9/4-6, and 12/2-5.

SOME ADDITIONAL THOUGHTS ON THE SIMILE OF RAVI, THE SUN

We cannot see anything in the absence of light, of which sun is the primary source. When sun rises in the morning, its rays illuminate everything in the universe; and when they reflect from it, they enable us to see the true shape, size, color and identity of every object on earth. We are able to see even the celestial bodies like moon, stars, constellations, nebulas etc. only because of the light of sun falling on them. It is noteworthy that though the sun reveals the identity of everything in the world, its rays are formless, colorless and have no identity of their own. We never need another source of light to search sun, as a person does not need a lighted lamp to search a lighted lamp. Soul of a person is **Swayam Prakaashit** i.e. self-illuminated like sun and lighted lamp; what he needs is **Jnaan Chakshu**, the eyes of knowledge to see the divine light, as would be recommended in next shlok 13/34. Bharat Vyaas prays thus in film *'Do Aankhen Baarah Haath'* on behalf of souls who lost their way in the darkness of **Ajnaan**:

ये अँधेरा घना छा रहा, तेरा इंसान घबरा रहा ।
हो रहा बेखबर, कुछ न आता नज़र, सुख का सूरज छिपा जा रहा ॥
है तेरी रोशनी में वो दम, जो अमावस को कर दे पूनम ।
नेकी पर चलें और बदी से टलें, ताकि हँसते हुये निकले दम ॥
ऐ मालिक तेरे बंदे हम .....

(Man, Your creation, is flustered as pitch darkness spreads around him. He has lost his bearings and is not able to see anything as the sun of bliss is hidden from him. Your light has so much power that it can transform a dark moon night into full moon night. O Master! We are at Your service; please bless us to tread on the path of goodness so that we can meet our death with a smile).

Bruhadaaranyak Upanishad invokes God's blessings to lead us from darkness to light in 1/3/28:

ॐ असतो मा सद्गमय: ।
तमसो मा ज्योतिर्गमय: ॥

मृत्योर्मा अमृतम् गमय: ।।।
ॐ शांति: । शांति: ।। शांति: ।।।

{Aum! Lead us from unreal (falsity) to real (truth), from darkness to light, and from death to immortality! Aum! Let there be Peace (in physical world), Peace (in mental world) and Peace (in spiritual world)}.

Moral: *We have only two choices in life, to move towards the light or to move away from it.*

৵৽ঌ৾

Knowers of difference between Kshetr & Kshetrajn attain ultimate liberation.

(13/34)

क्षेत्रक्षेत्रज्ञयोरेवमन्तरं ज्ञानचक्षुषा ।
भूतप्रकृतिमोक्षं च ये विदुर्यान्ति ते परम् ॥१३/३४॥

KshetraKshetrajnayorevamantaram jnaanachakshushaa I
Bhootaprakrutimoksham ch ye viduryaanti te Param II (13/34)

Kshetr Kshetrajnayo: (of field & its knower) Evam (in this way) Antaram (difference) Jnaan Chakshushaa (with eyes of Jnaan) I Bhoot Prakruti Moksham (liberation of all beings from nature & its works) Ch (and) Ye (who) Vidu: (know) Yaanti (reach) Te (they) Param (ultimate) II (13/34)

Those who see this fundamental difference between Kshetr (the body & material nature) & Kshetrajn (its owner, the embodied individual soul and its parent Supreme Soul) in this way with the eyes of perfect spiritual knowledge, and understand it as the way of liberation from the bondage of causal nature and its works; they reach the Ultimate Being". (13/34)

Antar means difference between two things. The power of discernment enables living beings to differentiate between good

& bad, right & wrong, just & unjust, favorable & unfavorable, auspicious & inauspicious. **Bhoot Prakruti Moksh** is finding the way of liberation from the bonds of works of nature and the entities (and Guns) created by it including own body.

SOME ADDITIONAL THOUGHTS ON JNAAN CHAKSHUSH

Jnaan Chakshush literally means eyes of Jnaan. A **Jnaanee** keeps his eyes of **Jnaan** always open and alert; therefore, he is capable of spontaneous discernment when he comes across something or some situation in life. **Jnaan Chakshush** shall appear in 15/10 also.

Gita shall proclaim **Man**, the mind as the sixth sensory organ in 15/7. It implies that though other 5 sensory organs eyes, ears, tongue, nose and skin perform their respective functions of seeing, hearing, tasting, smelling and touching all the time and transmit them to **Man**, none of their functions are registered unless **Man** attaches to them. A person is unable to notice something happening before his eyes if his is absent from the scene. A 3 to 4 month old infant cannot recognize different objects though his eyes see them for his **Man** has not yet attached with them, as he grows his Man learns to recognize objects by eliminating and ignoring certain types of differences in varied scenarios that it feels irrelevant. A color blind cannot distinguish green from red; and a myopic patient can see only close objects clearly, but distant objects look blurred and distorted in shape size and location to him.

What does it all mean? It means that we require a sixth sense when we deal with basic five senses in the physical world. Shlok 13/34 clearly states that **Jnaan**, the perfect spiritual knowledge of **Kshetr** and **Kshetrajn** is the sixth sense a Yogee must develop to understand, analyze and properly deal in spiritual matters.

৯৽৻৶

CONCLUSION OF CHAPTER 13

This chapter beautifully imparted spiritual knowledge about **Kshetr**, inert, mutable, momentary, ever changing, mortal world of nature, and **Kshetrajn**, the live, conscious, immutable, eternal, immortal individual soul called **Purush.**

God explained **Aatm Jnaan**, the basics of Soul and body in 2/12-30, with particular stress on immortality of the former and unavoidable death of the latter. Then, in chapter 3, He dealt with **Prakruti**, the causal nature, divine force, that evolves entire material world and is the doer of all works. He introduced us to **Aparaa** and **Paraa**, the kinds of **Prakruti** in chapter 7 and stated in chapter 9 that great saintly people depend only on divine **Prakruti** and come to know Him as the primeval source of all entities whereas those relying on demonic **Prakruti** lead a worthless life. In this chapter, He proceeded further to explain how **Kshetrajn**, the soul and **Kshetr**, the nature, interact in this world. He also touched upon the relationship of **Kshetrajn** and **Kshetr** with God, but we shall see it culminating into the complete triangle of supreme spiritual knowledge when the third angle of **Purushottam** i.e. God, the Supreme Soul will close it in chapter 15. Bhrugu describes **Kshetr, Kshetrajn & Paramaatmaa** to Bhardwaaj in Mahaabhaarat thus:

आत्मा क्षेत्रज्ञ इत्युक्त: संयुक्त: प्राकृतैर्गुणै: ।
तैरेव तु विनिर्मुक्त: परमात्मेत्युदाहृत: ॥

(As long as a soul is tied up with Kshetr, the body and nature it is known as Kshetrajn or Jeevaatmaa, the embodied soul. And when it is freed from the Guns of nature and body, it is said to become Paramaatmaa, the Supreme Soul)

Chapter 13 has 2 similes in 13/32-33; 1 **Shree Bhagawaan Uvaach,** but no **Arjun Uvaach**.

ॐ तत्सदिति श्रीमद्भगवद्गीतासूपनिषत्सु ब्रह्मविद्यायां योगशास्त्रे श्रीकृष्णार्जुनसंवादे क्षेत्रक्षेत्रज्ञविभागयोगो नाम त्रयोदशोऽध्यायः ॥ १३ ॥

(In the name of God, the ultimate truth thus ends thirteenth chapter named Kshetr Kshetrajn Vibhaag Yog of Shreemad Bhagwad Gita, the best Upanishad, Brahm Vidyaa & Yog Shaastr, a dialogue between Shree Krishn and Arjun)

CHAPTER 14

GUN TRAY VIBHAAG YOG

(Live in Sattv, the quality of righteousness, with the vision to attain Him who is quality less)

PREAMBLE & CONTEXT

Though Gita sowed the seed of **Gun** as early as in 2/45 when Krishn stated **Traigunya Vishayaa Vedaa** i.e. the ritualistic portions of Veds deal with **Triguns,** the three basic modes **Sattv, Raj** and **Tam** of nature; and went on to tell Arjun to become **Nistraigunya** i.e. unaffected by three **Guns.** Nevertheless, Arjun, bewildered by his emotional attachment with his family and relatives, was in no position to understand and immediately follow His instruction at that time. Thereafter, Krishn mentioned **Guns** frequently, particularly in chapters 3 & 7, but He did not clarify what **Guns** are and how they affect a person. In chapter 13, He clearly brought out the distinction between **Kshetr** the **Prakruti** i.e. nature and **Kshetrajn** the **Purush** i.e. individual soul; and their characteristic powers to interact with each other. **Prakruti** exerts its power and influence on individual souls through its three **Guns**, the qualities or modes called **Sattv, Raj** & **Tam.** He further told that the soul must ultimately rise above the effects of these three **Guns** in order to liberate from miseries of life and blissfully unite with Supreme Soul. God finds it the most appropriate time to explain **Guns** in continuity of chapter 13.

WHY CHAPTER 14 IS NAMED GUN TRAY VIBHAAG YOG?

Gita casts the infinitely intricate, complex actions of nature in this chapter in the mould of **Triguns,** the three broad modes of quality namely **Sattv, Raj** & **Tam** that inextricably intertwine with every action of men and nature. It tells us what these modes are & how to identify them; how they act singly or in combination with each other; how they affect our lives; how we can benefit from them; and where they take us after death. Arjun too would pick up in 14/21, the thread of **Nistraigunya** which he left loose in 2/45 due to his mind preoccupied with personal considerations, and request Krishn to teach the symptoms of **Nistraigunya** or **Gunaateet** or **Trigunaateet** person. Krishn would explain it gladly in 14/22-27. Since this chapter deals with classification of **Triguns** in detail and shows us the way to use this knowledge as a stepping-stone to achieve Yog, the liberation from distress in life, it is named as **Gun Tray Vibhaag Yog**.

ॐ

God promises to explain knowledge once again saying he who becomes one with Him is freed from Punarjanm.

(14/1 & 2)

श्रीभगवानुवाच
परं भूयः प्रवक्ष्यामि ज्ञानानां ज्ञानमुत्तमम् ।
यज्ज्ञात्वा मुनयः सर्वे परां सिद्धिमितो गताः ॥१४/१॥
इदं ज्ञानमुपाश्रित्य मम साधर्म्यमागताः ।
सर्गेऽपि नोपजायन्ते प्रलये न व्यथन्ति च ॥१४/२॥

Shree Bhagawaan Uvaach
Param bhooy: pravakshyaami jnaanaanaam
jnaanamuttamam I
Yajjnaatwaa munay: sarve paraam siddhimito gataa: II (14/1)
Idam jnaanamupaashritya Mam saadharmyamaagataa: I
Sarge∫pi nopajaayante pralaye n vyathanti ch II (14/2)

Param (ultimate) Bhooy: (again) Pravakshyaami (shall explain) Jnaanaanaam (in all types of knowledge) Jnaanam (knowledge) Uttamam (most superior) I Yat (which) Jnaatwaa (by knowing) Munay: (introspective sages of high order) Sarve (all) Paraam (supreme) Siddhim (accomplishment in spiritual realm) it: (from this world) Gataa: (went) II (14/1)

Idam (this) Jnaanam (knowledge) Upaashritya (adheres to) Mam (My) Saadharmyam Aagataa: (attains oneness with God) I Sarge (in beginning of world) Api (even) N (neither) Upajaayante (be reborn) Pralaye (in end of world) N (nor) Vyathayanti (anguished) Ch (and) II (14/2)

God said:

"I shall now explain to you again the ultimate of all kinds of knowledge by knowing which, all the great sages were liberated from this world (Punarjanm) and attained the ultimate accomplishment in spiritual realm. (14/1)

They, who attain oneness with My transcendental nature i.e. eternal form, quality etc. by adhering wholeheartedly to this perfect knowledge, shall neither be reborn even in the creation of the world, nor shall be anguished at the time of its dissolution. (14/2)

Jnaanaanaam Uttamam is the most superior of all kinds of knowledge like languages & grammar, scriptures, material & social sciences, arts, commerce & finance, law & justice, management, and above all the spiritual knowledge, that are available in the world. It is the ultimate knowledge that only can lead a person to lead a blissful, stress free life, and which only a most competent Guru like Krishn can teach to a deserving disciple like Arjun. Please also refer to *'Why did Krishn select Arjun .... not Yudhishthir?'* under 2/11 in this regard.

God revealed **Rahasyam Uttamam,** the top secret of ancient mystical knowledge, to Arjun in 4/3 for the first time saying God exhibits his energy through **Prakruti**, the nature in-charge of creation, and **Maayaa**, the force of illusion, but He remains uninvolved in them. In 6/27, He told further that a Yogee, with calm Man and pacified thoughts & activities, definitely attains the ultimate bliss. Moreover, in 9/2, He described realization of perfect knowledge as the king of all learning, and of most mysterious esoteric secrets of the purest, perfect knowledge. Now, in the very first shlok of this chapter, He undertakes to explain that topmost knowledge once again. Krishn would ask Arjun to listen to the same supreme knowledge once again in 18/64 also before finally summing up the essence of His teaching. Why does He repeat the same thing repeatedly? It is because of His immense love for Arjun who submitted unconditionally to Him as His pupil in 2/7, besides being His dearest friend and cousin. A good teacher always repeats the core of his teachings to his pupil until the latter grasps it fully, and acts accordingly.

SOME ADDITIONAL THOUGHTS ON SIDDHI, ACCOMPLISHMENT OF SUCCESS

Siddhi is commonly understood as some supernatural extra ordinary power supposedly achieved by a person by following some kind of ascetic and sacrificial practices like penance, **Tantr Saadhanaa,** the sorcery etc. Sometimes such **Siddhs** claim capability of walking on fire or water, hanging bodily in air, remaining underwater for long periods, become invisible, produce articles from nowhere, bestow children to childless, cure incurable diseases etc. Scriptures mention **Asht,** eight types of **Siddhi** as:

अणिमा महिमा चैव लघिमा गरिमा तथा
प्राप्ति: प्राकाम्यमीशित्वम वशित्वम चाष्टसिद्धया:

(Eight types of Siddhi, the supernatural powers, are: to minimize body size to Anu, the molecule; to grow the body to biggest size; to make the body light and weightless; to become very heavy; to become invisible, to reach desired destination in no time without any difficulty; to obtain desired material things; to dominate, overlord everyone; and to subjugate & control others).

Patanjali, the founder of **Ashtaang Raaj Yog,** also mentions that a practiser of **Raaj Yog** can achieve such **Siddhi** in due course. Simple common people are easily impressed and often carried away by the miracles due to blind faith in 'चमत्कार को नमस्कार' i.e. *'The world bows to miracle'* though most of them are trickery performed by unscrupulous cheats claiming to possess some kind of supernatural power. It is my firm opinion that if, at all, such supernatural powers exist; they belong to the realm of superhuman, supernatural beings beyond our mortal world. Nevertheless, life histories of almost all gods, saints, great people mentioned in books of all religions are full of their supernatural powers. But in their case a **Siddhi**, at best, should be perceived as a symbol of divine potential and power deployed to ensure well being of others in the spirit of **Lok Sangrah** (3/25-26). As far as common beings like us are concerned, we should not be swayed from the path of leading a righteous, dutiful life and misled by display or claim of some tricks by anybody. Hanumaan, the greatest devotee and servant of Raam in Raamaayan, possesses all the eight types of **Siddhi** but never uses them for any purpose other than a work in the service of Raam. He is the **Siddh** of Gita in true sense. None of these **Siddhi**, even if possible to achieve, is the target prescribed for the practiser of its Yog by Gita as it attaches no importance to achieving powers to perform miracles. **Siddhi** of Gita is the successful accomplishment of perfect knowledge of the Ultimate. It is in the realm of spiritual realization for self; and gradual progress of society from **Tamas** & **Rajas** to **Sattv** i.e. from darkness of ignorance & passions to righteousness as told in **'Tamaso Maa Jyotirgamay'**.

Siddhi also means achieving success in some endeavor like passing an examination, getting a desired employment etc. Though Gita accepts this kind of **Siddhi**, it considers it as an achievement of lower quality for it satisfies material wants and serves self-interests only of **Sakaam** devotees who worship demigods for such success as told in 4/12. Gita preaches us to be calm and equipoise in **Siddhi** & **Asiddhi** i.e. success & failure in the material world and rise above their effects in 2/48, 4/22, 18/26 besides many other places.

Saadharmyam is one of the five forms of liberation described in Hindu scriptures explained earlier under *'Some additional thoughts on Nirvaan, Mukti & Moksh'* in 2/72 as **Saayujya** i.e. uniting completely and attaining oneness with unmanifested form of God. Gita shall also use the phrase **Brahm Bhooyaay** in 14/26 for this kind of liberation meaning that the practiser becomes **Brahm** itself. In this way, he liberates from the rigors of **Punarjanm**.

Clarification: *The souls of such persons do acquire all the qualities of Brahm, the Supreme Soul like purity, detachment, truth, eternal existence, bliss, steady intelligence etc. due to merger with Him. They wish to neither acquire nor possess His opulence and other divine powers of creation, sustenance and annihilation; delivering judgment on actions performed by individual souls.*

કૈૂ

God imparts the knowledge He promised in 14/1.

(14/3 & 4)

मम योनिर्महद्ब्रह्म तस्मिन्गर्भं दधाम्यहम् ।
संभवः सर्वभूतानां ततो भवति भारत ॥१४/३॥
सर्वयोनिषु कौन्तेय मूर्तयः संभवन्ति याः ।
तासां ब्रह्म महद्योनिरहं बीजप्रदः पिता ॥१४/४॥

Mam yonirmahadBrahm tasmingarbham dadhaamyaham I
Sambhav: sarvabhootaanaam tato bhavati Bhaarat II (14/3)
Sarvayoneshu Kauntey moortay: sambhavanti yaa: I
Taasaam Brahm mahadyoniraham beejaprad: pitaa II (14/4)

Mam (My) Yoni: (womb) Mahat Brahm (the great principal nature of Brahm) Tasmin (in that) Garbham Dadhaami (impregnate embryo) Aham (I)I Sambhav: (birth, origin, production) Sarv Bhootaanaam (all entities in the universe) Tat: (thereby) Bhavati (takes place) Bhaarat (Arjun)II (14/3)

Sarv Yonishu (for all species) Kauntey (Arjun) Moortay: (embodied) Sambhavanti (are born) Yaa: (who)I Taasaam (of all those) Brahm Mahat (great nature of Brahm) Yoni: (mother) Aham (I) Beej Prad: Pitaa (father, provider of seed)II (14/4)

O Bhaarat (Arjun)! Prakruti, the great principal nature of Brahm, is My great womb which I impregnate (with My consciousness). All living beings are thereby born in this world. (14/3)

O Kauntey (Arjun)! That principal nature of Brahm is the mother of all embodied species that are born, and I am their father, who puts the seed in it for fertilizing into an embryo. (14/4)

God said in 7/6:

'All species of living and inanimate beings are born from the womb of nature; and I am the ultimate source of creation as well as dissolution of entire universe'.

He adds further here that He is the only one parent of all beings because He as father impregnates the womb of Prakruti, their mother, in His female form. It is interesting to note that modern science has also found out that a single cell, the basic unit of creation, undergoes the process of mitosis and produces two genetically identical cells. Only a few special cells out of them are capable of becoming eggs in females and sperm in males. We all grow from a single embryonic cell to the person we are now through mitosis because even after full growth of body, mitosis replaces cells lost through everyday wear & tear. Spiritually speaking, the origin of whole creation is just one, its parent God. He multiplies and manifests into many by His own creative energy, called Prakruti as told in Chhaandogya Upanishad in 6/2/3: 'सदैक्षत् बहु स्याम् प्रजायेयेति' i.e. *'Sat, the eternal existence wished to be many'.*

Moral: *Irrespective of our creed, caste, complexion, place of birth, geographical location, nationality, religion, sect, society or any other classification that defines our identity in the world, we all are ultimately the children of the same one and only God whom we call by different names due to ignorance.*

The famous verse below from scriptures reflects this sentiment very well:

त्वमेव माता च पिता त्वमेव त्वमेव बन्धुश्च सखा त्वमेव ।
त्वमेव विद्या द्रविणं त्वमेव त्वमेव सर्वं मम देव देव ॥

(You truly are my mother and You truly are my father. You truly are my relative and You truly are my friend. You truly are my knowledge and You truly are my wealth. You truly are everything for me, my God of gods.)

Following Parable of twin embryos, talking in their mother's womb written by Dr. Wayne Dyer in *'Your Sacred Self'* is very thought provoking:

"First: Do you believe in life after delivery?

Second: Of course! There has to be something after delivery. May be we are here to prepare ourselves for what we will be later.

First: Nonsense! There is no life after delivery. What kind of life you think that would be?

Second: I do not know, but can imagine there would be more light there than here. May be we will walk on our legs and eat from our mouths. May be we will have other senses that we can't understand now.

First: That is absurd. Walking on our legs is impossible. And eating with our mouths? Ridiculous! The umbilical cord supplies nutrition and everything that we need but it is too short. Life after delivery is logically excluded.

Second: Well, I think there is something and maybe it is totally different than it is here. May be we won't need this physical cord anymore.

First: Nonsense! Moreover, if there is life why no one has ever come back from there? Delivery is the end of life, and after delivery, there is nothing but darkness, silence and oblivion. It takes us nowhere.

Second: I don't know. Nevertheless, we will meet our Mother certainly and She will take care of us there.

First: Mother? Where is She? You really believe in Mother? That's laughable. If Mother exists, where is She now?

Second: She is all around us. We are surrounded by Her. It is in Her that we live. Without Her, this world would not and could not exist.

First: Well I don't see Her, so it is only logical that She does not exist.

Second: Sometimes when you are in silence and focus, and listen, you can perceive Her presence, and you can hear Her loving voice, calling down from above."

Above parable illustrates very well God's existence; and our ignorance about Him. Bheeshm speaks of the glory of mother in Mahaabhaarat Shaanti Parv:

'A teacher who imparts genuine knowledge is more important than ten tutors; a father is more important than ten teachers having genuine knowledge; and a mother is greater than ten such fathers. There is no greater guru than mother'.

Majrooh Sultanpuri penned children's devotion for mother in film *Daadi Ma*:

उसको नहीं देखा हमने कभी, पर इसकी जरुरत क्या होगी।
ए माँ तेरी सूरत से अलग, भगवान की सूरत क्या होगी॥

(We have never seen God, nor is it necessary because O Mother! His appearance won't be anything different from your appearance)

❧

God names three modes of nature and tells that Sattv is the best among them.

(14/5 & 6)

सत्त्वं रजस्तम इति गुणाः प्रकृतिसंभवाः।
निबध्नन्ति महाबाहो देहे देहिनमव्ययम्॥ १४/५॥
तत्र सत्त्वं निर्मलत्वात्प्रकाशकमनामयम्।
सुखसङ्गेन बध्नाति ज्ञानसङ्गेन चानघ॥ १४/६॥

Sattvam Rajastam Iti gunaa: prakrutisambhavaa: I
Nibaadhnanti Mahaabaaho dehe dehinamavyayam II (14/5)
Tatr Sattvam nirmalatvaatprakaashakamanaamayam I
Sukhasangen badhnaati jnaanasangen chaAnagh II (14/6)

Sattvam (most superior mode of righteousness of nature) Raj: (medium mode of passion of nature) Tam: (lowest mode of ignorance of nature) Iti (this much) Gunaa: (Sattv, Raj and Tam) Prakruti (causal, material nature) Sambhavaa: (are born)I Nibadhnanti (bind) Mahaabaaho (Arjun) Dehe (in body) Dehinam (soul, owner of body) Avyayam (imperishable, eternal, inexhaustible)II (14/5)

Tatr (of those) Sattvam (Sattv) Nirmalatvaat (being purest) Prakaashakam (which illuminates) Anaamayam (free from disorders, diseases)I Sukh (happiness, comfort) Sangen (due to attachment) Badhnaati (binds, tethers) Jnaan (knowledge) Sangen (due to association) Ch (and) Anagh (Arjun, sinless)II (14/6)

O Mahaabaaho (Arjun)! Sattv, the righteousness, Raj, the passion and Tam, the darkness of ignorance, are three modes originated from causal nature that bind the imperishable soul with the body (created by nature). (14/5)

O Anagh (Arjun)! Out of those three modes of nature, Sattv, being the purest & faultless one, illuminates and frees the soul from the tethers of its association with pleasures & comforts, and pride of knowledge. (14/6)

Sattv is the first & most superior mode of nature, of righteousness in which a man lives with virtues like truth, poise, purity, knowledge, contentment, goodness, merit, compassion etc. **Raj** is the second & medium mode of nature in which he lives and acts with passion, struggle, emotion, desire, likes and dislikes, anger, jealousy, frenzy, revenge etc. **Tam** is the lowest mode of nature in which he lives in darkness, ignorance, and evils like conceit, false pride, harming, torturing and even killing others for pleasure, or serve self-interest. Gita shall explain in detail in chapters 17 and 18 how these three modes of nature affect different traits and actions like **Shraddhaa** i.e. faith, **Tap** i.e. penance, **Aahaar** i.e. food habits, **Yajn**, **Daan**

i.e. charity, **Karm** i.e. works, **Jnaan** i.e. knowledge, **Buddhi** i.e. intelligence, **Dhruti** i.e. perseverance etc.

God mentioned three modes of nature, **Sattv Raj** & **Tam** for the first time in 7/12 but He did not elaborate on them further. He deals with them from here onwards in this chapter as suggested by its name **Gun Tray Vibhaag Yog**. Three **Guns** exist in every matter and person in mixed and compounded forms in different proportions as they cannot exist individually in pure, isolated forms. Also, note that the person opts for a particular **Gun** or a combination at any time in his life and attaches with it, not **Gun** per se. It is similar to a householder selecting a place of residence and developing belongingness towards it. The house never attaches itself with its occupant or binds him with it.

Anaamay is an adjective used for something pure, faultless, sound, healthy, untainted, and is unaffected by miseries, disorders, diseases. Krishn talked of **Padam Anaamayam** earlier in 2/51 to denote purity and immortality of that ultimate status and goal a practiser wants to achieve. Here He says that **Sattv**, the most virtuous mode of nature illuminates the path leading him to that ultimate goal. By addressing Arjun as **Anagh** i.e. sinless & pure, He confirms that he can easily achieve **Anaamay Pad**.

❧

God explains how Raj & Tam generate.

(14/7 & 8)

रजो रागात्मकं विद्धि तृष्णासङ्गसमुद्भवम् ।
तन्निबध्नाति कौन्तेय कर्मसङ्गेन देहिनम् ॥१४/७॥
तमस्त्वज्ञानजं विद्धि मोहनं सर्वदेहिनाम् ।
प्रमादालस्यनिद्राभिस्तन्निबध्नाति भारत ॥१४/८॥

Rajo raagaatmakam viddhi trushnaasangasamudbhavam I
Tannibadhnaati Kauntey karmasangen Dehinam II (14/7)
Tamastvajnaanajam viddhi mohanam sarvadehinaam I
Pramaadaalasyanidraabhistannibadhnaati Bhaarat II (14/8)

Raj: (mode of passion) Raagaatmakam (inherent with passion, emotional desire, infatuation): Viddhi (understand) Trushnaa (thirst, longing) Sang (attachment, association): Samudbhavam (produced by)I tat (that) Nibadhnaati (binds) Kauntey (Arjun) Karm (action) Sangen (due to association) Dehinam (soul)II (14/7)

Tam: (Tam) Tu (but) Ajnaanajam (born of ignorance) Viddhi (know) Mohanam (delusion) Sarv (all) Dehinaam (of embodied souls) I Pramaad Aalasya Nidraabhi: (by frenzy, indolence & drowsiness) Tat (that) Nibadhnaati (captivates) Bhaarat (Arjun)II (14/8)

O Kauntey (Arjun)! Know Raj as the quality inherent with passionate, emotional desire and infatuation, produced by Trushnaa, the longing and Sang, the attachment. It entangles the soul due to its association with Karm, the actions (with desire of fruition). (14/7)

But O Bhaarat (Arjun)! Understand Tam, the quality of darkness & evil, which deludes all the embodied entities, as born of ignorance. It captivates the soul by frenzy, indolence & drowsiness. (14/8)

Raagaatmakam means inherent with passionate, emotional desires, attachment, attraction and infatuation. **Trushnaa** is the thirst and passionate longing for something. **Mohanam,** explained earlier in 2/62-63 as **Sammoh,** is extreme delusion and bewilderment caused by ignorance, error of judgment, infatuation, allurement or enticement. **Pramaad** is deliberate negligence, mistake and frenzy. Krishn says that **Raj**, the quality of passion essentially consists of passionate desires; it is born out of intense longing for material things; and it binds a soul when it associates with the works of body and nature. On the other hand, **Tam**, the quality if darkness deludes everybody due to lack of knowledge to differentiate between right & wrong; and it enslaves a soul due to its willful attitude of negligence in life. If **Sattv** is the light of morality that illuminates a man's path as told in 14/6, and **Tam** is the darkness of **Ajnaan** that hides his path, **Raj** is the smog (abbreviated word for smoke+fog) which obscures his vision from seeing the path. The burning fire of passion person generates smoke of desires, and when fog, an external phenomenon of nature, envelops smoke, it becomes smog and assumes illusory form of **Maayaa**. Thus, **Raj** exists primarily in our life only until passionate desires continue to burn in the hearth of **Man**, the mind & heart.

SOME ADDITIONAL THOUGHTS ON TRUSHNAA, THE PASSIONATE LONGING

Trushnaa (*Pyaas* in Hindi) is the state of acute deprivation of body from water for a long time resulting in dehydration. We have heard many thrilling accounts of desert travellers how acute thirst afflicted them when they wanted nothing else but water. When applied to spirituality, **Trushnaa** is acute **Kaamanaa**, the desire and longing for a worldly pleasure without which a person feels his life is worthless. Learned people and scriptures warn practisers of Yog to desist from nurturing such **Trushnaa** because, if fulfilled, it would lead to lust for desiring for more; and if unfulfilled, it shall result in anger or depression. Vaishampaayan raises a caution in Mahaabhaarat:

'As fire within wood burns and completely consumes it, similarly a person is completely destroyed by thirst and desire within him'.

Kabeer knew the fatality of pursuing Trushnaa in life, and said:

धन गया जोबन गया मर मर गया सरीर ।
आसा तृष्णा ना मरी कह गये दास कबीर ॥

(Kabeer says it for posterity that a man's expectations and desires never die even though his wealth goes away, his youth departs; and his body dies many deaths.)

An inspiring story from Mahaabhaarat is worth quoting here:

"A king named Somak had only one son. One day he saw his son crying due to an ant bite. He started worrying that he may lose his only son someday if a poisonous creature bites him. Shall he die childless? His worry soon evoked Trushnaa in him to get more sons, and it gradually grew so much that he sacrificed his only son in a

Yajn expecting that gods would be pleased and bless him with many sons. As a result, he suffered for the rest of his life in this world, and went to hell in afterlife.

Compare this with Abraham (or Ibrahim) offering his son for sacrifice, not for some personal benefit, but for his community. He is held in very high esteem by three world religions: Judaism, Christianity and Islam for his selfless sacrifice whereas Somak is condemned for his heinous act of sacrifice."

Moral: *It is the motive behind an act, not the act itself, which decides whether the latter is good or bad.*

ༀ

God explains how Guns bind a person.

(14/9)

सत्त्वं सुखे संजयति रजः कर्मणि भारत ।
ज्ञानमावृत्य तु तमः प्रमादे संजयत्युत ॥ १ ४/९॥

Sattvam sukhe sanjayati raj: karmani Bhaarat I
Jnaanamaavrutya tu tam: pramaade sanjayatyut II (14/9)

Sattvam (Sattv) Sukhe (in pleasure, comfort) Sanjayati (appoint) Raj: (Raj) Karmani (in doing Karm) Bhaarat (Arjun)I Jnaanam (knowledge) Aavrutya (covering) Tu (but) Tam: (Tam) Pramaade (in frenzy) Sanjayati (fasten) Ut (it is said)II (14/9)

O Bhaarat (Arjun)! Sattv, the righteous mode of nature, fastens in pleasure and Raj, the mode of passion, fastens in fruitive activity. But, it is said that Tam, the darkness of ignorance, conceals the knowledge and appoints him in frenzy and negligence. (14/9)

Gita reveals how three modes of nature bind a person in their tentacles. **Tam**, the lack of true knowledge, obscures his judgment and drives him into frenzied works or just inaction; whereas **Raj**, the mode of passion, inducts him into pursuance of such works which shall satisfy his passions. It says further that even the apparently innocuous, virtuous mode of **Sattv** is also powerful enough to taint its practiser as he derives **Ras**, the joy (2/59) from his righteous works. Most of the world religions accord highest status to leading life in the mode of **Sattv** but Gita takes us a step further by teaching us to be above all the three modes of nature because each one of them binds us in its fold. It states that even **Sattv** cannot be an exception in this regard because virtuous deeds do result in name & fame in the society, and bring in a sense of false pride in the doer. A crowd of followers gathers around him and influences his deeds. Some of them also take undue advantage of being close to him. Meanwhile, his ego continues to inflate by others' praise; his power to discern between right & wrong gradually dilutes, and is substituted ultimately by desire for more praise. Such practiser falls from his aim of attaining high pedestal of Yogee who must engage in works solely for **Lok Sangrah** (3/20 & 3/25), not to earn fame.

৵৽ঌ৵

Sattv, Raj & Tam constantly change their hold on a person.

(14/10)

रजस्तमश्चाभिभूय सत्त्वं भवति भारत ।
रजः सत्त्वं तमश्चैव तमः सत्त्वं रजस्तथा ॥ १४/१० ॥

RajasTamashchaabhibhooy Sattvam bhavati Bhaarat I
Raj: Sattvam Tamashchaiv Sattvam Rajastathaa II (14/10)

Raj: (Raj) Tam: (Tam) Ch (and) Abhibhooy (suppressing) Sattvam (Sattv) Bhavati (becomes) Bhaarat (Arjun)I Raj: (Raj) Sattvam (Sattv) Tam: (Tam) Ch (and) Ev (also, indeed) Tam: (Tam) Sattvam (Sattv) Raj: (Raj) Tathaa (similarly)II (14/10)

O Bhaarat (Arjun)! Sometimes Sattv, the mode of righteousness becomes prominent by suppressing Raj & Tam; sometimes Raj, the mode of passion surpasses Sattv & Tam; and similarly Tam, the mode of ignorance takes over Sattv & Raj at other times. (14/10)

God states one more reason why a practiser must overcome modes of righteousness, passion and ignorance. He says that the same person sometimes lives in **Sattv** when it overpowers **Raj** & **Tam**; in **Raj** when it takes over **Sattv** and **Tam**; and in **Tam** when it takes over **Sattv** and **Raj**. It is because all the three modes of nature are constantly in competition with each other to gain supremacy in a one's life; and he cannot attain true peace and tranquility till this competition continues in his life. It is noteworthy that this competition is at its worst when driven by lust & self-interest; and the least when he works for **Lok Sangrah** i.e. for the well-being of others.

Moral: *It is foolish for us to expect peace and bliss in life by pursuing qualitative modes which themselves constantly quarrel with each other. The best strategy for a practiser is to take help of superior mode of Sattv, wherever required to overcome an obstacle, and move forward without looking back at it.*

❧

How should a practiser know which quality
prevails over others?

(14/11, 12 & 13)

सर्वद्वारेषु देहेऽस्मिन्प्रकाश उपजायते ।
ज्ञानं यदा तदा विद्याद्विवृद्धं सत्त्वमित्युत ॥१४/११॥
लोभः प्रवृत्तिरारम्भः कर्मणामशमः स्पृहा ।
रजस्येतानि जायन्ते विवृद्धे भरतर्षभ ॥१४/१२॥
अप्रकाशोऽप्रवृत्तिश्च प्रमादो मोह एव च ।
तमस्येतानि जायन्ते विवृद्धे कुरुनन्दन ॥१४/१३॥

Sarvadwaareshu dehe∫sminprakaash upjaayate I
Jnaanam yadaa tadaa vidyaadvivruddham Sattvamityut II
(14/11)
Lobh: pravruttiraarambh: karmanaamasham: spruhaa I
Rajasyetaani jaayante vivruddhe Bharatarshabh II (14/12)
Aprakaasho∫pravruttishch pramaado moh ev ch I
Tamasyetaani jaayante vivruddhe Kurunanadan II (14/13)

Sarv Dwaareshu (in all gates) Dehe (of body) Asmin (in this) Prakaash: (illumination) Upajaayate (is born)I Jnaanam (wisdom) Yadaa (when) Tadaa (then) Vidyaat (know) Vivruddham (grows) Sattvam (Sattv) Iti Ut (it is said)II (14/11)

Lobh: (greed) Pravrutti: (intense inclination to indulge in something) Aarambh: (start a work to achieve certain result) Karmanaam (of actions) Asham: (restlessness) Spruhaa (eager desire)I Rajasi (of Raj) Etaani (all these) Jaayante (are born) Vivruddhe (increasing) Bharatarshabh (Arjun)II (14/12)

Aprakaash: (darkness) Apravrutti: (disinclination to do anything) Ch (and) Pramaad: (frenzy) Moh: (delusion) Ev (certainly) Ch (and)I Tamasi (of Tam) Etaani (all) Jaayante (are born) Vivruddhe (growing) Kuru Nandan (Arjun)II (14/13)

It is said that when prudent wisdom illuminates all the gates of one's body, he should then understand that Sattv is growing in him. (14/11)

O Bharatarshabh (Arjun)! Greed, restlessness, eager craving and intense inclination to initiate some activities to gain fruits; all these are produced when Raj, the mode of passion rises. (14/12)

O Kuru Nandan (Arjun)! Darkness, inertia in doing anything, frenzy and bewilderment; all these are certainly born upon growth of Tam, the mode of ignorance & evil. (14/13)

Asham is opposite of **Sham**, the restraint of senses, passions and mind, as explained earlier in 6/3. **Asham** therefore means to gratify every demand of restless, unrestrained **Indriys**, **Man** for their **Vishays**, the passionate desires. **Pravrutti** is strong, intense tendency and inclination to indulge in works to achieve certain results. **Apravrutti**, on the other hand, means disinclination, unwillingness, inertia, shirking from any activity, and/or the feeling of boredom. **Spruhaa** (2/56) is intense longing, craving and elation in material pleasures. **Lobh** was explained as characteristic of greed, avarice, temptation and covetousness in 1/38-39.

Sarv Dwaareshu refers to the nine holes of two eyes, two ears, two nostrils, mouth, anus and the genital in a human body, explained in 5/13. They symbolize nine gates through which **Jnaanendriys**, the sensory organs along with **Man**, go out in search of **Vishays**, the passions of outside world. This is the 37th simile of Gita. 14/11 states that whenever the light of positivity and optimism illuminates these gates with the light of virtue and morality, a practiser should understand that he is currently situated in the mode of **Sattv**. He should immediately catch hold of that moment as the best opportunity and consciously align all of his **Indriys**, the sensory and functionary organs, **Man**, the mind and heart, and also **Buddhi**, the intelligence on the unidirectional path of merit and stretch, as far as he can, his experience of bliss due to growth of **Sattv** within him. Wise men define right time to do something as:

'**T**: Today, **I**: Is, **M**: My, **E**: Everything'.

A Chinese Proverb teaches us:

'The best time to plant a tree was 20 years ago. The second best time is now.'

Albert Einstein found it out with his own experience that:

'The best opportunity lies in the midst of worst difficulties'.

Moral: Let us not commit the mistake of looking for the next opportunity because the one we have in hand is the right opportunity. Trying to perfect something before doing, invariably results in losing the opportunity to do it. Most of us fail to recognize an opportunity because it is masked usually in dirty overalls indicating very hard labour ahead.

And, if a practiser finds that **Lobh**, the greed, **Pravrutti Aarambh:**, tendency to involve in every wayside attraction, **Karmanaam Asham** i.e. unrestrained indulgence in works, and **Spruhaa**, the longing for material happiness have grown more in his life, he should realize that the fog of Raj has obscured his vision from finding proper path that shall lead him to liberation. He must act immediately to remove the fog of **Raj** and let the light of **Sattv** shine again. However, when **Tam** overlords **Sattv** and **Raj**, it casts the cover of pitch darkness of **Ajnaan**, the absence of true knowledge in the life of a practiser and completely hides the light of Sattv. **Tam** drags him into **Apravrutti**, the inertia, **Pramaad**, the frenzy and **Moh**, the delusion. Raamcharit Maanas 5/6/3 describes him:

तामस तनु कछु साधन नाहीं। प्रीति न पद सरोज मन माहीं॥

(Embodied by Taamas, I neither know any means to get rid of it, nor developed faith in the lotus feet of God.)

Moral: *A person, under the influence of Tam, cannot redeem him by his own effort. He must immediately seek help and guidance from a knowledgeable person as Arjun did in 2/7 when captured by the three generals of Tam mentioned above namely Apravrutti, the shirking from the war, Pramaad, the idea of living as a mendicant, and Moh, the attachment with his kinsmen and family. His innate conscience counseled him to request Krishn for rescue from sinking in the mire of Tam.*

Krishn reminds Arjun of his great lineage of Bharat and Kuru by addressing him as Bharatarshabh, the greatest among the descendents of great Bharat, and Kuru Nandan, the descendent of noble Kuru respectively.

☙❦

Where do people, entrenched in Sattv, Raj or
Tam reach after death?

(14/14 & 15)

यदा सत्त्वे प्रवृद्धे तु प्रलयं याति देहभृत् ।
तदोत्तमविदां लोकानमलान्प्रतिपद्यते ॥१४/१४॥
रजसि प्रलयं गत्वा कर्मसङ्गिषु जायते ।
तथा प्रलीनस्तमसि मूढयोनिषु जायते ॥१४/१५॥

Yadaa sattve pravruddhe tu pralayam yaati dehabhrut I
Tadottamavidaam lokaanamalaanpratipadyate II (14/14)
Rajasi pralayam gatvaa karmasangishu jaayate I
Tathaa praleenastamasi moodhayonishu jaayate II (14/15)

Yadaa (when) Sattve (in Sattv) Pravruddhe (is grown) Tu (but) Pralayam (end) Yaati (goes) Deh Bhrut (embodied person)I Tadaa (then) Uttam Vidaam (persons of good thoughts & deeds) Lokaan (superior worlds of) Amalaan (pure, spotless) Pratipadyate (attains) II (14/14)

Rajasi (of Raj) Pralayam (dissolution) Gatvaa (having reached) Karm Sangishu (amidst persons engaged in fruitive works) Jaayate (is born)I Tathaa (and) Praleen: (upon Pralay) Tamasi (of Tam) Moodh Yonishu (ignorant, lower species) Jaayate (takes birth)II (14/15)

When a person dies in the state of developed righteousness, he attains pure, superior worlds attainable by persons of good thoughts, deeds and knowledge. If he dies when the mode of passion is strong, he is reborn among persons engaged in fruitive works; and the person dying in the mode of increased ignorance is reborn in the lower species of living beings. (14/14 & 15)

Pralay normally denotes great or total devastation of life on earth but here it is used for the death of the body of a person in line with the popular saying 'आप मुए तो जग मुआ' i.e. *'The moment you die, the world is also dead for you'*. Body, the physical matter identified by the soul as its own due to ignorance, disintegrates and dissolves into **Panch Mahaa Bhoot**, the basic 5 elements of nature, from where it came into existence. The immortal soul continues to exist and it resumes its works with nature in a newly acquired body as per **Karm Phal**, the results of earlier works. We discussed it in 2/30.

14/14 says that persons dying in **Sattv** mode shall attain **Oordhw Lok** (8/16) i.e. worlds superior to those of humans like heaven etc. Shlok 14/15 adds further that persons in **Raj** mode shall be reborn in the human world among persons engaged in fulfilling their material desires, but the worst kind of persons who live in **Tam** are sure to be reborn among the species inferior to human beings like animals, birds, fishes, insects, worms, reptiles etc. Since 14/14 talks of being righteous at the time of death, it implies that we must be in the righteous mode all the time, until achieving the state of Gunaateet, for none of us knows when his death would arrive. It should however be carefully noted that the destination attainable through Sattv is not the ultimate one as it also is fraught with return to the cycle of death and birth. Gita shall clarify in the end of this chapter that only he who frees himself from the effects of all three modes including **Sattv**, gets the abode of permanent peace. It is therefore necessary for a practiser desirous to attain that goal to become **Gunaateet** (14/25) or **Nistraigunya** (2/45). **Sattv** is only a stepping-stone for him towards that goal.

Most of the worldly people live in the mixed modes of **Sattv, Raj & Tam**. In a way, God assures us here, as He did earlier in 2/40 also, that if we steadily enrich our life with right thought, attitude, deed and knowledge even in small, insignificant increments, we shall surely reach ultimate destination of eternal peace.

ॐ

Fruits of Saattvik, Raajasik and Taamasik
works are now described.

(14/16 & 17)

कर्मणः सुकृतस्याहुः सात्त्विकं निर्मलं फलम् ।
रजसस्तु फलं दुःखमज्ञानं तमसः फलम् ॥१४/१६॥
सत्त्वात्संजायते ज्ञानं रजसो लोभ एव च ।
प्रमादमोहौ तमसो भवतोऽज्ञानमेव च ॥१४/१७॥

Karman: sukrutasyaahu: saattvikam nirmalam phalam I
Rajasastu phalam du:khamajnaanam Tamas: phalam II
(14/16)
Sattvatsanjaayate jnaanam Rajaso lobh ev ch I
Pramaadmohau Tamaso bhavato[jnaanamev ch II (14/17)

Karman: (of Karm) Sukrutasya (of virtuous, noble deeds) Aahu: (is said to be) Saattvikam (endowed with Sattv) Nirmalam (pure, sinless) Phalam (fruit)I Rajas (the mode of Raj) Tu (but) Phalam (result) Du:kham (misery, distress) Ajnaanam (lack of Jnaan, the knowledge) Tamas (mode of Tam) Phalam (fruit)II (14/16)

Sattvaat (from Sattv) Sanjaayate (produces) Jnaanam (true knowledge) Rajas (mode of Raj) Lobh: (covetousness, greed) Ev (only, indeed) Ch (and)I Pramaad (frenzy, negligence) Mohau (bewilderment) Tamas (mode of Tam) Bhavat: (are given rise) Ajnaanam (lack of Jnaan, stupidity) Ev (certainly) Ch (and)II (14/17)

The result accrued to noble, meritorious deeds is said to be pure and endowed with excellent qualities of Sattv. The result of being in the mode of passion is misery and distress; and lack of true knowledge is the result of acting in mode of ignorance. (14/16)

True knowledge develops from the mode of goodness; the mode of passion produces greed; and the mode of ignorance certainly gives rise to frenzy, bewilderment & stupidity. (14/17)

Sukrut was explained earlier in 2/50 & 5/16 as good, virtuous, meritorious, noble act with auspicious result, and it is synonym of **Punya**. It is called **Saattvik** because it is enjoined with excellent qualities of **Sattv** like truth, purity, goodness, merit, virtue, nobility etc. **Saattvik** work always fructifies in **Nirmal** i.e. pure, clean, spotless, and sinless **Jnaan**. **Sukrut** are like good quality seeds which if a farmer sows in the fertile land of life and carefully nurtures by providing water, good manure, protection from weeds and animals at the right time, shall yield a bountiful harvest of happiness and pleasure. **Raajasik** work is like eating sweets; we are tempted to eat more of it due to taste but it results in ailments in the body. And the result of living in **Tamas** is the worst comparable to addiction to alcoholic drinks that leads to inebriation, incoherent behavior, loss of memory & wisdom to differentiate between right and wrong, bewilderment and darkness of false knowledge. Gita shall classify **Karm**, the actions of a person in **Saattvik**, **Raajasik** and **Taamasik,** and explain their qualities in 18/23-25.

QUESTION: WHAT IS THE DIFFERENCE BETWEEN AJNAANEE AND MOODH (VIMOODH, SAMMOODH) PERSON?

Ajnaan means lack of knowledge. An **Ajnaanee** is therefore an ignorant person who lacks proper knowledge of a subject but deserves attention of knowledgeable persons, whereas a **Moodh** is an insane, stupid and foolish person not ready to listen to anybody. **Vimoodh** is the superlative of **Moodh** and **Sammoodh** is he who is firmly entrenched in insanity & stupidity. Good teachers like Krishn would take pity on an **Ajnaanee** for his deficient knowledge and put in all efforts to remove the darkness of **Ajnaan** from his life but the situation of a **Moodh** is irretrievable in most cases because of his egoistic refusal to learn true knowledge from anyone and correct himself. **Arjun** in Gita is the perfect example of an **Ajnaanee**, and Duryodhan of a **Moodh, Vimoodh** & **Sammoodh** person in Mahaabhaarat.

In the opinion of Albert Einstein:

'Insanity is doing the same thing over & over again and expecting different results.'

৵৵৵

God describes destinations of Saattvik, Raajasik & Taamasik people afterlife.

(14/18)

ऊर्ध्वं गच्छन्ति सत्त्वस्था मध्ये तिष्ठन्ति राजसाः ।
जघन्यगुणवृत्तिस्था अधो गच्छन्ति तामसाः ॥१४/१८॥

Oordhwam gachchhanti Sattvasthaa madhye tishthanti raajasaa: I

Jaghanyagunvruttisthaa adho gachchhanti taamasaa: II
(14/18)

Oordhwam (ascend, sublimate upwards) Gachchhanti (go, reach) Sattvasthaa: (situated in Sattv) Madhye (in the middle) Tishthanti (remain situated) Raajasaa: (persons with qualities of Raj) I Jaghanya (extremely abominable, vile) Gun (mode, quality, virtue) Vruttisthaa (occupied in) Adh: (lower, downward) Gachchhanti (go, attain) Taamasaa: (persons with qualities of Tam)II (14/18)

Those situated in the mode of goodness ascend upwards i.e. towards superior worlds like heaven etc.; those in the mode of passion remain in the middle i.e. in the human world; and those occupied with the extremely abominable mode of ignorance go to the lower worlds of animals, birds, insects etc. or to hell (14/18)

God reconfirms what he just told in 14/14-15 that the soul of a person situated in **Sattv** keeps rotating between human and upper worlds; that situated in **Raj** keeps rotating in human world; and the one that is situated in **Tam** continues to be consigned to animal worlds and hell. He would pronounce the same again in 16/19. Souls of persons living in mixed modes shall have to pass through all the three routes likewise.

Besides the straight and clear meaning as stated above this shlok also has a deeper thought. It directs a practiser of Yog to give up his thoughts and actions arising out of modes of passion and ignorance, get a foothold only in Sattv, the mode of goodness, and use it as a stepping-stone to move from the lower level to the higher level. He should understand it clearly that movement from **Tam** to **Raj** is still in the lower level like moving from darkness to fog. He must simultaneously quit **Tam** & **Raj** and move directly to **Sattv** that should dominate both most of the time. However, remember he must that ultimately **Sattv** also is a mode of nature, and transgress it to reach his goal of liberation. This would be explained in detail after 14/20 *'Why are we required to give up & surpass the quality of Sattv also which is described as the most superior quality of every entity in nature?'*

ॐ

Krishn motivates us to become Gunaateet in next two shloks.

(14/19 & 20)

नान्यं गुणेभ्यः कर्तारं यदा द्रष्टानुपश्यति ।
गुणेभ्यश्च परं वेत्ति मद्भावं सोऽधिगच्छति ॥१४/१९॥
गुणानेतानतीत्य त्रीन्देही देहसमुद्भवान् ।
जन्ममृत्युजरादुःखैर्विमुक्तोऽमृतमश्नुते ॥१४/२०॥

Naanyam gunebhy: kartaaram yadaa drashtaanupashyati I
Gunebhyashch param madbhaavam soɟdhigachchhati II
(14/19)
Gunaanetaanateetya treendehee dehsamudbhavaan I
Janmmrutujaraadu:khairvimuktoɟmrutamashnute II (14/20)

N (not) Anyam (other) Gunebhy: (than Guns, Sattv, Raj and Tam) Kartaaram (performer, doer) Yadaa (when) Drushtaa (overseer, witness, onlooker) Anupashyati (sees properly)I Gunebhy: (than Guns, Sattv, Raj and Tam) Ch (and) Param (ultimate, beyond) Vetti (experiences well) Madbhaavam (My eternal, spiritual existence) S: (he) Adhigachchhati (reaches, transcends)II (14/19)

Gunaan (modes of nature) Etaan (all these) Ateetya (transcend) Treen (three) Dehee (embodied soul) Deh (body) Samudbhavaan (originated, produced by)I Janm Mrutyu Jaraa du:khai: (from miseries, distress of birth, death & old age) Vimukt: (liberated, freed) Amrutam (Nectar of gods) Ashnute (eats)II (14/20)

When one properly understands as an onlooker, that there is no other doer of any activity except these three modes of nature, and experiences his self to be well beyond those three modes; he immediately transcends into My eternal, spiritual existence. And when he transcends all these three modes of nature, the real causes of embodiment of his soul, he is liberated from the miseries of birth, death and old age; because he has taken Amrut, the nectar of immortality. (14/19 & 20)

God lays two conditions to attain bliss of His eternal existence:

1. To realize that all activities are the results of three modes of nature interacting with each other and he himself is not the doer of those works; and,

2. To realize that his soul being part of the supreme authority of God is also beyond the reach and effects of these modes. In fact the modes are of nature (not self) which itself is controlled by God.

Once a practiser fulfills them, he attains God's eternal bliss without any delay.

Kartaar is the same as **Kartaa** the performer, doer of some work. As said in 3/27, all people think themselves as the doer of an activity under the influence of ego, but it is not true. Actually, **Sattv**, **Raj**, and **Tam** enjoin **Panch Mahaa Bhoot** of nature, and force his ego to do certain work.

Drushtaa, explained in 2/59, is a person whose vision has broadened so much that he sees the ultimate truth of nature & its agents, three guns as the doer of all activities. He simply witnesses their play as an onlooker. Following incident explains **Drushtaa**:

"Swami Raam Teerth, clad in saffron robe with clean shaven head, was once roaming in the streets of an American city as a Sannyaasee. Some mischievous children mocked, abused and even manhandled him, but he remained totally calm and continued to chant God's name. Upon return to his camp, when his followers became perturbed on seeing him in such pitiable state he laughed and spoke with utmost serenity in his voice:

'You know what an interesting thing happened today! I was greatly delighted to witness how this Raam (pointing index finger to himself), who thinks of him as a great Sannyaasee, was abused, mocked and beaten by innocent children of God. He deserves it very much so that his ego is punctured and flattened to dust."

Madbhaav was understood in 4/10, 8/5, 10/6 etc. as My i.e. God's eternal, spiritual existence as **Paramaatmaa**, the Supreme Soul.

The phrase **Janm Mrutyu Jaraa Dukh** symbolizes the distress and miseries an embodied soul has to pass through right from the time of conception of its body in the womb of mother, to the time of its death intervened by dreadful periods of **Jaraa**, the infirmity and old age, and **Dukh**, other pains of life. We had discussed it in detail in 12/6-7 under *'What is meant by Mrutyu Samsaar Saagar?'* In fact, soul suffers even in afterlife due to **Karm Bandhan**. Thus, it is a never-ending phenomenon until it perfects in Yog by realizing and restoring its permanent connection with God. Miseries of birth, death and old age are universal for all living and inanimate entities, even for atheists. The teachings of Gita therefore also address this greatest concern of humanity with its universally applicable message. Prince Siddhaarth was shocked when he faced these miseries for the first time. He recognized them as the real enemies of a person, found almost the same ultimate solution that Gita preaches, and became Buddh.

As discussed in 2/15 & 10/27, **Amrut** is a legendary concept of some powerful divine potion capable of conferring immortality to whosoever drinks it. It symbolizes that he, who understands and practises the message of Gita, becomes immortal i.e. freed from painful cycles of birth and death.

QUESTION: WHY ARE WE REQUIRED TO GIVE UP & SURPASS THE QUALITY OF SATTV ALSO WHICH IS DESCRIBED AS THE MOST SUPERIOR QUALITY OF EVERY ENTITY IN NATURE?

From 14/5 to 18, Gita is all praise for a person situated in the **Sattv** mode of nature. **Sattv** may therefore appear to some readers as the best stage and they may never like to give it up. Practically also, we find people using the word **Saattvik** to differentiate the best and virtuous from other inferior, virtue less things. There is no doubt that **Sattv** is the mediator, the catalyst for our transformation from the lower planes of **Tam** & **Raj** but Gita advises us in 14/19-20 to transcend beyond **Sattv** also and be just an onlooker. This ascent is comparable to a satellite that first drops two stages of its rocket to reach outer space with the help of its final stage, and then detaches the third one also, when it is able to move with own power.

Gita replied to this question already in 14/18, saying ऊर्ध्वं गच्छन्ति सत्त्वस्थाः: i.e. those situated in **Sattv** can ascend upwards to superior world of heaven but cannot be liberated from the miseries of birth, death, disease and old age, as they must return to these cycles repeatedly after enjoying their sojourn there. In simple words, I can say that as **Raj** implicates us in passionate selfishness and **Tam** in ignorance and darkness, so does **Sattv** entangle us with a false sense of pride, ego, self-praise, elation and achievement of success. A **Gunaateet** himself remains an onlooker, a witness of what his mind and body do; and his natural instincts continue to exercise control on them so that they remain constantly engaged in **Saattvik** works effortlessly.

Now, let us also look into the finer side of it. Even when we think that we are now able to perform **Saattvik** works without any attachment, there will always be some remnants of ego, capability, power concealed within us and they may escape from the eye of even most careful introspection since they appear with the sugary coating of piety. We then feel elated and delighted of our accomplishment. Nevertheless, so long as they are there they hold us in their captivity. A chain is a chain whether it is made of gold, copper, iron, or silk thread. Liberation, the highest mastery of inner self on the external self, reveals only when even the finest muslin veil of **Sattv** lifts off i.e. when we see our soul merged with Supreme Soul, and act in unison with His will & directions. We have then united **Purush,** the soul with **Purushottam,** the whole being. When it is accomplished, soul is no more a slave of nature but its master as it is able to mould its workings into fulfillment of divine actions with nature as a means. Let us try to understand this concept with the example below:

'A pole-vaulter uses a pole to lift himself up higher than the height of a horizontal bar in order to cross over it to the other side. In doing so, he hinges his entire energy on the pole while swinging up with its support. It is the pole, which enables him to achieve a height greater than that required to cross the bar. But, what does he do once he attains his desired height and position? He lets his hold on the pole go and concentrates his energy now on crossing the bar and landing on the other side. A Gunaateet must likewise, learn from a pole-vaulter the technique of taking requisite support from Sattv, and leaving it at an appropriate moment to attain his ultimate goal of crossing over the bar of the world and unite integrally with Brahm, Supreme, Ultimate Being on the other side of world. The quality of Sattv is his pole, not the goal. He should cultivate and develop Sattv in his characteristic nature by practice & effort, elevate himself to the height required to cross the bar of ego and attachment and abandon the support of Sattv for his further journey in attaining eternal bliss. Remember, if the pole-vaulter does not leave the pole at the right time

he shall not be able to cross the bar. He has to choose between the two, the pole or his quest to cross the bar. His goal of liberation shall be unachieved if he does not leave the pole.'

Aurobindo describes this final state of existence after giving up **Sattv** thus:

'.... *We are drawn towards it by the highest, most passionate, most stupendous and ecstatic of all desires; but we can securely live in it only when all desires drop away from us. We have, at a certain stage, to liberate ourselves even from the desire of our liberation.'*

Moral*: All ethical actions are ultimately the means required for purification of soul so that it can reach the goal of attaining divine delight.*

☙❧

Krishn first explained Sattv, Raj & Tam and said Sattv is the superior most. Then in 14/19-20 he prodded Arjun to transgress three modes to attain liberation. Thereupon Arjun could not resist knowing the qualities & symptoms of Gita's Gunaateet.

(14/21)

अर्जुन उवाच
कैर्लिङ्गैस्त्रीन्गुणानेतानतीतो भवति प्रभो ।
किमाचारः कथं चैतांस्त्रीन्गुणानतिवर्तते ॥१४/२१॥

Arjun Uvaach

Kairlingaistreengunaanetaanateeto bhavati Prabho I

Kimaachaar: katham chaitaanstreengunaanativartate II
(14/21)

Kai: (which) Lingai: (symptoms) Treen (three) Gunaan (modes of nature) Etaan (all these) Ateet: (past, transcended) Bhavati (becomes) Prabho (Krishn)I Kim (what) Aachaar: (character) Katham (how) Ch (and) Etaan (all these) Treen (three) Gunaan (of Guns) Ativartate (transgresses, leaps over,) II (14/21)

Arjun said:

"O Prabho (Krishn)! What are the symptoms by which a person, who has transcended three modes of nature, can be distinguished? Please tell me how he behaves and how he surpasses these three modes". (14/21)

Lingai is used for symptoms and distinctive marks to identify a **Gunaateet** person. Sanskrit grammar describes three lings i.e. genders namely, **Pulling**, the masculine, **Streeling**, the feminine and **Napunsak ling**, the impotent to know the gender group of an object. Arjun is greatly impressed with the knowledge of **Guns** imparted by Krishn. At the mention of **Gunaateet** person, he asks three very important questions to learn more about him:

1. What are his symptoms? It shall be replied in 14/22 & 23.
2. How does he behave? It shall be replied in 14/24 & 25.
3. How does he surpass three modes of nature? It shall be replied in 14/26.

Above questions are similar to those asked by Arjun in 2/54 to know the symptoms of **Sthit Prajn** but he was in the initial stage of learning there. By now, he is transformed from **Vishaadee**, a highly distressed person, into **Jijnaasu**, an inquisitive seeker of knowledge, to liberate from stress and become a serious learner. I am sure that the same transformation has taken place in all of us also after our study of Gita until now. He had addressed Krishn as **Prabhu**, the Master in 11/4 earlier to show His Vishw Roop, and now he calls Him again as **Prabho**, the Supreme Master of entire universe to reconfirm his faith in Him as his teacher and master, and teach him the symptoms of **Gunaateet**.

৯৽৽৶

If Gita is the vast range of Himalayas in which we are roaming, we are now face to face with its another great summits, the topic of Gunaateet from 14/22 to 26. Readers are advised to summon all of their faculties to understand it.

(14/22)

श्रीभगवानुवाच
प्रकाशं च प्रवृत्तिं च मोहमेव च पाण्डव ।
न द्वेष्टि संप्रवृत्तानि न निवृत्तानि काङ्क्षति ॥१४/२२॥

Shree Bhagawaan Uvaach
Prakaasham ch pravruttim ch mohamev ch Paandav I
n dweshti n sampravruttani n nivruttani kaankshati II (14/22)

Prakaasham (light) Ch (and) Pravruttim (inclination to do something to achieve certain result) Ch (and) Moham (delusion) Ev (even) Ch (and) Paandav (Arjun)I n (neither) Dweshti (dislikes) Sampravruttani (on proper involvement in an activity) N (nor) Nivruttani (relieved of an activity) Kaankshati (aspires)II (14/22)

God said:

"O Paandav (Arjun)! He (Gunaateet person) neither dislikes getting selflessly involved in an activity, whether for enlightenment or for achieving some result or even due to ignorance; nor he aspires for anything on detaching (from an activity). (14/22)

God said in 14/20:

'When a practiser transcends all the three modes of nature, he is liberated from the miseries of birth, death and old age; because he has taken Amrut.'

Now, He proceeds to explain how a practiser can become **Gunaateet** and obtain **Amrut**, the nectar of immortality. **Prakaash** i.e. the light of knowledge represents **Sattv; Pravrutti** i.e. starting or getting involved in an activity is **Raj** whereas **Moh** is bewilderment, confusion and ignorance in one's life; and an activity takes place due to anyone of them or a mixture thereof. A **Gunaateet** neither dislikes nor like an activity per se. He is free from the delusion of achieving something for himself by starting an activity because his enlightened soul directs him to leave the decision of involving or not involving in an activity to God's supreme will. We have heard God forecasting in 11/32 & 34 that, under His overall plan, He has already destined the opponents of Arjun to death in the war; Arjun should simply involve himself as the means to execute His plan. God assured him, that by acting in this way, no sin should accrue to him even by engaging in war and slaughtering opponents of **Dharm**.

SOME ADDITIONAL THOUGHTS ON PRAVRUTTI & NIVRUTTI

The word **Pravrutti** is formed by the prefix *'Pra'*, lending weight to **Vrutti** that was explained in 6/20-23 as natural tendency, instinct. **Pravrutti** therefore is the strong urge to indulge and involve in an endeavor or situation. **Pravrutti** of normal worldly people is with a motive to achieve some material gain and/or fame or to fulfill some familial and social responsibilities, whereas **Pravrutti** of a Yogee becomes **Sampravrutti** meaning balanced **Pravrutti** because he directs it toward **Lok Sangrah**, the welfare of external world. If practised properly, it is the path of **Karm Yog**.

Nivrutti is the opposite of **Pravrutti**. It is freeing, detaching, abstaining, and refraining from undesirable works, things oriented on worldly things such as possessions, career, money, fame, appreciation, concern for relatives and friends. **Nivrutti** is the path of turning inward to spiritual contemplation with focus on God. If properly practised, it leads a practiser to the path of **Jnaan Yog**. When a Yogee is in a state of **Pravrutti**, he constantly seeks perfection in his actions and tries to improve his spiritual status. **Nivrutti**, on the other hand, is the existence in the state of perfection, and acceptance of God's will to indulge in some action.

Cautions:

1. *Practisers of Yog should be cautiously indulge in some work because Pravrutti, wearing the mask of Paropakaar, the beneficence of others, can distract him from his practice and lead on the path of earning name and fame. His Pravrutti should follow the will of God, not own.*

2. *Nivrutti should not result in Akarmanyataa i.e. inaction, idling or shirking from own duty and responsibility. It is only a means, not the end, in attaining Yog. A Yogee must always work for Lok Sangrah as directed by God in 3/20 & 25.*

Clarification*: It is proper and necessary for every householder to fulfill his responsibilities and duties towards his own health, his family and society; and be comfortable and prosperous in life. Nevertheless, if he lives exclusively in such Pravrutti, totally wrapped up in Maayaa, he misses the boat to cross Samsaar Saagar, the ocean of world and attain the bliss of liberation from Punarjanm.*

Moral*: Both, Nivrutti misdirected towards inaction as well as unrestrained Pravrutti, result in constant suffering, misfortune and pain. Maintaining an appropriate balance between the two only can bring spiritual development, contentment and peace.*

Ashtaavakr says:

'Nivrutti of a fool is equivalent to Pravrutti; but Pravrutti of a Jnaanee bears the same fruit as of Nivrutti (because his Pravrutti is Sampravrutti)'.

৵৯৬

More qualities of Gunaateet are described.

(14/23)

उदासीनवदासीनो गुणैर्यो न विचाल्यते ।
गुणा वर्तन्त इत्येव योऽवतिष्ठति नेङ्गते ॥१४/२३॥

Udaaseenavadaaseeno gunairyo n vichaalyate I
Gunaa vartant ityev yoʃvatishthati nengate II (14/23)

Udaaseen vat (like a stoically neutral, uninvolved observer) Aaseen: (situated, seated) Gunai: (by Guns) Y: (who) N (not) Vichaalyate (strayed, deviated)I Gunaa (Guns) Vartante (deal with) iti (like thi) Ev (only) Y: (who) Avatishthati (remains situated, steady) N (not) ingate (waver, tremble, quiver, flicker)II (14/23)

He who is situated (in all actions and reactions) like an uninvolved stoic observer; is not strayed by the modes of nature knowing it full well that it is these modes only (not he) which deal with each other; and who remains steady and does not waver; (14/23)

The phrase **Gunaa Vartant Ityev** is same as **Gunaa Guneshu Vartant** in 3/28. It explains that a **Gunaateet** aware of the fact that all actions and reactions are commenced and ended by three **Guns** of **Sattv, Raj & Tam** of nature as they interact with each other in varying proportions; and such activities and creations do not last for forever because **Guns** themselves are very transient by nature.

Udaaseen vat means like a stoically neutral, uninvolved observer. A **Gunaateet** simply observes all actions and things in the world without attaching himself with them physically or emotionally as if he is watching a film show. **N Vichaalyate** and **N Ingate** indicate that he is never strayed, deviated, or agitated by reacting to pleasure or pain in life for he knows it well that all favorable or unfavorable effects are results of constant interactions of **Guns**. He is like a plain sheet of glass that does not absorb water or honey poured on it; or a black cloth, which retains its black color even if dipped in other colors; or an electric bulb illuminates its surroundings regardless of the onslaughts of wind, rain or dust storm on it. Tulasidaas beautifully describes in Kavitaawalee the **Udaaseen** state of Raam when He proceeds to the forests after banishment from Ayodhyaa for fourteen years:

कीर के कागर ज्यों नृप चीर विभूषण उप्पम अंगनि पाई,
औध तजी मग़वास के रूख़ ज्यों पन्थ के लोग ज्यों लोग लुगाई ।
संग सुबंधु पुनीत प्रिया मनु धर्म क्रिया धरी देह सुहाई,
राजिवलोचन राम चले तजि बाप को राज बटाऊ की नाई ॥

{Lotus-eyed Raam gave up the kingdom of his father (in spite of being its heir apparent) and walked away (to the forest) like a nomadic wayfarer on foot. His half-naked body glowed (with natural beauty) as He removed His royal clothing and ornaments just as a parrot discards its feathers (to let new ones grow). He abandoned Ayodhyaa with the same ease with which

a traveller leaves the tree of his night halt. He left men and women of Ayodhyaa behind as a traveller departs from other travellers (who meet and depart from him in his journey). Now, His beloved wife Seetaa and pure hearted brother Lakshman are accompanying Him as if Kriyaa (activity, the feminine form of Karm) and Dharm, the duty have come embodied themselves.}

Ashtaavakr asserts a soul's stoical nature in these words:

'Righteousness and unrighteousness, pleasure and pain are purely of the mind and are no concerns of yours. You are neither the doer nor the reaper of the consequences; you are always free.'

Moral*: He is an expert boatman who navigates his boat skillfully in deep water, without letting it enter the boat.*

ॐ

A Gunaateet can acquire above-mentioned
qualities by being equipoise.

(14/24 & 25)

समदुःखसुखः स्वस्थः समलोष्टाश्मकाञ्चनः ।
तुल्यप्रियाप्रियो धीरस्तुल्यनिन्दात्मसंस्तुतिः ॥१४/२४॥
मानापमानयोस्तुल्यस्तुल्यो मित्रारिपक्षयोः ।
सर्वारम्भपरित्यागी गुणातीतः स उच्यते ॥१४/२५॥

Samsukhdu:kh: swasth: samloshtaashmkaanchan: I
Tulyapriyaapriyo dheerastulyanindaatmsanstuti: II (14/24)
Maanaapamaanayostulyastulyo mitraaripakshayo: I
Sarvaarambhparityaagee gunaateet: s uchyate II (14/25)

Sam du:kh: Sukh ((equipoise in distress and happiness) Swasth: (situated in self) Sam Losht Ashm Kaanchan: (equipoise in clay, stone & gold)I Tulya (equally disposed in) Priy (agreeable, pleasant) Apriy: (not agreeable, unpleasant) Dheer: (steadfast, patient) Tulya (equally disposed in) Nindaa (vilification, defamation) Aatm Sanstuti: (lavish praise of self done by others; also self praise) II (14/24)

Maan Apamaan (in honor & dishonor, prestige & humiliation) Y: (who) Tulya: (equally disposed in) Tulya: (equally disposed in) Mitr (friend) Ari (enemy) Paksh y: (sides)I Sarv Aarambh Pari Tyaagee (who voluntarily abandons involvement in commencing any endeavor, especially to achieve some result) Gunaateet: (who has overstepped three modes of nature) S: (he) Uchyate (is said)II (14/25)

A Gunaateet is equipoise in distress & happiness; blissfully situated in own self; equipoise in a lump of clay, stone & gold; equally disposed in pleasant & unpleasant situations; steadfast & balanced-minded in vilification & praise by others; disposed equally in honor & dishonor. He treats factions of friends & enemies alike; and voluntarily abandons involvement of self in commencing any work (especially to achieve some favorable result). (14/24 & 25)

These two shloks should immediately remind us of God's unequivocal declaration **Samatvam Yog Uchyate** i.e. *'Equanimity is called Yog'* in 2/48. We had reflected on this very important quality of a Yogee also in 5/18-20; 6/8 and in 6/29-32. However, since this is the finale of **Samatv** in Gita, let us take some more time to understand it as much as possible:

SOME ADDITIONAL THOUGHTS ON SAMATV IN THE LIGHT OF GUNAATEET

Samatv, the equanimity of Gita is like the observation deck on 102nd floor of the United States' most iconic skyscraper Empire State building. As a visitor, standing there enjoys the panoramic view of the skyline of tall buildings, streets, gardens etc. in Manhattan, and observes the minute details with a binocular; similarly, a student practiser of Gita can grasp its beauty and absorb its knowledge in his soul if he positions him on its highest platform of practice called **Samatv**.

The quality of **Sam Dukh Sukh** is to remain calm and composed with balanced mind, and equanimity of heart in distress and happiness. This phrase first appeared in 2/15, and later in 12/13.

It symbolically also covers other dualities like profit & loss, victory & defeat, success & failure, cold & hot, respect & disrespect, favorable & unfavorable, likes & dislikes, desirable & undesirable etc. Note that incidence of **Sukh**, the happiness or **Dukh**, the distress in one's life is the results of anyone or more of these, or any other, dualities. J R D Tata, a down to earth visionary, observed:

'Most of our troubles are due to poor implementation, wrong priorities and unattainable targets'. He wished, *'I do not want India to be an economic superpower. I want India to be a happy country'.*

Moral: *Happiness is not a measure of economical and material prosperity, but a state of contentment. It lies in giving, not getting; sharing, not looting; empathizing, not antagonizing; producing, not consuming; and in providing, not depriving.*

Sam Losht Ashm Kaanchan is person equipoise in clay, stone and gold. This phrase had earlier appeared verbatim in 6/8 and discussed there.

Caution: *Sam Losht Ashm Kaanchan should not be construed as a license to rob someone's gold and claim that I have done nothing more than taking away some of his clay and stones.*

Tulya Priy Apriy is equanimity in **Priy**, the dear, agreeable, pleasant, favorable, and liked; and **Apriy**, the disagreeable, unpleasant, unfavorable, and disliked things, persons and situations. The message here is the same as conveyed in 5/20:

'He, who neither rejoices on getting something agreeable nor is upset upon coming across an unpleasant thing, has known Brahm'.

Examples to undertand **Tulya Priy Apriy**:

1. When Arjun and Duryodhan approach Krishn before Mahaabhaarat war began to seek His support on their side, He receives them with the same respect and ease; in fact, He gives first preference to Duryodhan to put up his request though He disliked him due to his irreligiosity.

2. When Amitabh Bachchan was very much depressed for not getting a job, he very much aspired for in his young age, his father Harivanshrai Bachchan told him:

    'It is good if something happens the way you like, but it is better if what you like does not materialize for it is according to the will of God'.

Tulya Nindaa Aatm Sanstuti: It is same as **Tulya Nindaa Stuti** that we had discussed under 12/18-19. A **Gunaateet** is neither perturbed by criticism and vilification by others, nor elated when someone praises him. On the contrary, criticism offers him an opportunity to know and correct his weaknesses, and emerge stronger; and praise alerts him by raising his antenna to be extra cautious lest its strong current fells him into the gorge of ego. He not only remains equipoise in his own **Nindaa** & **Stuti** by others, but also desists from indulging in **Nindaa** and **Stuti** of others. Nevertheless, he does not miss an opportunity to appreciate meritorious acts of others to encourage them; as well as to point out the mistakes of his loved ones so that they can correct them well in time.

'A king, with an ambition to expand his kingdom, plans to attack neighboring kingdom. Everybody, except the wise prime minister, appreciates his move and wishes him victory. When the king wants to know the reason for his silence, the P. M. replies, 'Excuse me for my frank opinion O king. Waging a war on the neighbouring king would eventually result in transforming a good friend into a bitter enemy forever. We shall be actually weakening our own defenses in this way whereas extending a hand of friendship shall ensure peaceful co-existence and prosperity of both kingdoms. In Raamaayan, Vibheeshan warns Raavan of dire consequences for antagonizing Raam by abducting Seetaa while other courtiers felicitated him for his misdeed'.

Maan Apamaan: It also was discussed first in 6/7 and then in 12/18 & 19 as **Sam Maan Apamaan Y.** a **Gunaateet** does not take any delight of respect and honor by others, nor does he take any offence of disrespect, dishonor and slight meted out to him by someone. **Maan**, the respect and **Apamaan**, the disrespect are like the shadows of the tree of a man's character; the denser the tree is, the more comfortable its shadow will be. Abraham Lincoln set an example of equipoise on his first day of Presidency of USA:

'On his first day in office as President, when Abraham Lincoln entered to give his inaugural address, one man stood up. He was a rich Aristocrat. He said, "Mr. Lincoln, you should not forget that your father used to make shoes for my family." And the whole Senate laughed; they thought they had made a fool of Lincoln.

But certain people are made of a totally different mettle. Lincoln looked at the man directly in the eye and said, "Sir, I know that my father used to make shoes for your family, and there will be many others here. Because he made shoes the way nobody else can, he was a creator. His shoes were not just shoes; he poured his whole soul into them. I want to ask you, have you any complaint? Because I know how to make shoes myself. If you have any complaint, I can make you another pair of shoes. But as far as I know, nobody has ever complained about my father's shoes. He was a genius, a great creator and I am proud of my father".

The whole Senate was struck dumb. They could not understand what kind of man Abraham Lincoln was. He was proud because his father did his job so well that not even a single complaint had ever been heard.'

Lincoln believed:

'Character is the tree and honor & reputation are its shadow.'

Excessive **Maan**, the respect & honor is also dangerous as explained below:

"The baby calf of a cow felt very sad when he saw his master taking very good care of an ugly lamb by bathing him with own hands and feeding sumptuous foods, whereas some grass was carelessly thrown before him and his mother to eat every day. His wise mother consoled him saying that too much care & love is dangerous.

Few days passed by in the same way. The lamb became fat in this period. One day the calf was very much annoyed to see the master decorating the lamb with flowers, vermilion, henna etc. and offering him good food, and not even looking at him. The cow asked him to be calm and watch for some more time. After few minutes, the calf was horrified to see the master pulling out his sword, beheading the lamb in single deadly stroke and cutting his body into pieces. The cow reminded her son of the lesson she gave him earlier and advised him to be happy with what he gets in life."

Tulya Mitr Ari Paksh y: This phrase conveys the same message as **Sam: Shatrau ch Mitre ch** did in 12/18; also explained earlier in *'Some additional thoughts on Mitr and Ari'* under 6/9. It seems Krishn is telling Arjun to start fighting for the sake of his duty to protect **Dharm** without any regard for his friendly or unfriendly relationship with those have assembled here to perpetuate **Adharm**. A **Gunaateet** knows it very well that in case of a conflict between a knife and a watermelon, the latter is cut into pieces. Conflict always inflicts injury on its initiator.

Swasth: This word normally denotes a healthy person. Extending this meaning a bit further, it is interpreted spiritually as a person situated in himself i.e. his eternally blissful soul. The well known saying, *'A healthy mind dwells in a healthy body'* holds true as it ensures good health of one's mind, the leader of **Jnaanendriys**, the sensory organs responsible for sensing pain and pleasure of life. Shreemad Bhaagawat describes the story of Jad Bharat who was **Swasth** physically as well as spiritually.

Dheeram: It was explained earlier in 2/13 to mean a sedate, calm, steadfast, patient person who possesses the quality of **Dhruti** or **Dhairya**, the patience. Gita would mention **Dhruti** as an important **Daivee Sampadaa** (divine wealth) in 16/3. Michelangelo says:

'Genius is eternal patience'

And, Sheikh Saadi advises the impatient:

'Have patience. All things are difficult before they become easy'.

Let us therefore always remember, *'No one can hurt us without our consent'*; and *'It is not what happens to us but our response that hurts us'*. When we drive on the busy road of life, we are bound to come across hurdles of traffic signals. A patient person does not frown or horn but waits for the traffic light to become green.

Sarv Aarambh Pari Tyaagee: He is a person who voluntarily abandons involvement of self in commencing any endeavor, especially to achieve some desired result. A **Gunaateet** person initiates no action to fulfill his wishes, as he knows that all works are the results of interactions of three **Guns** of nature as already explained in 3/28 under **Gunaa: Guneshu Vartant.** He directs his entire energy and effort towards fulfilling God's Supreme Will.

SOME ADDITIONAL THOUGHTS ON GUNAATEET

As early as in 2/45, Krishn asked Arjun to become **Nistraigunya** i.e. beyond the effects of **Sattv, Raj** & **Tam,** the three modes of nature but He did not talk further about it until now because Arjun was under the spell of great emotional agony and mental disturbance. He now devotes entire chapter 14 to elaborate His idea of one of the ideal persons of Gita, and calls him **Gunaateet.** We have seen in our study so far how Arjun gradually regains his composure and tranquility of mind due to gracious teachings of Krishn in Gita that transformed him from a **Dharm Sammoodh Chetaa** (2/7) person into **Jijnaasu**, a spiritually awakened inquisitive person asking Krishn in 14/21 to describe symptoms of **Gunaateet.** Krishn, the ocean of compassion replies to his query in 14/22-27.

A **Gunaateet** takes delight neither when **Sattv** brings him enlightenment, nor abhors **Raj** for inducing him in impulsive action nor **Tam** dragging him in inaction. He is like a tree that stands firmly in its place and strides, with the same calm and quietude, through the stages of denuding in autumn, flowering and fructifying in spring, and flourishing in rains. As a tree lets the nature do its works but does not tire from doing his own duties of giving leaves, fruits, shade & shelter to passersby, nests to birds, wood to woodcutter; and medicines to doctors, a **Gunaateet** similarly directs all his works only towards **Lok Sangrah**. He is always equipoise like a sandalwood tree that never discriminates between a serpent and the axe of a woodcutter, or a passerby hermit in giving its fragrance. A **Gunaateet** is a liberated soul neither situated in the nature nor entangled by its modes and dualities. He is a complete, self-sustained **Purush**, eternally integrated with **Purushottam**. He is free from all kinds of personal limitations and tethers of qualitative differentiation. Maithilee Sharan Gupt writes in Saaket:

'जितने प्रवाह हैं, बहें अवश्य बहें वे ।
निज मर्यादा में किंतु सदैव रहें वे ॥'

(All streams may surely flow in natural way, but they must also realize their limit and remain in it)

Let me explain how **Guns** spoil us with proverbial निन्यानवे का चक्कर:

'We normally use this phrase meaning the whirlpool of ninety nine for a person engrossed in pursuit of money and materials. However, I wish to view it from a different angle here. If we divide Rs. 99 equally in three persons, each one of them is equally happy to get 33. Nevertheless, the moment we add 1 Rupee to 99, the available kitty becomes 100. Thus, one Rupee virtually reduces all of 99 to 00; and occupies the prime position. Now, when we try to divide Rs. 100 among same three persons, each one still gets 33, but longs passionately to get the balance 1 (Ahamkaar, the false ego) and thus establish his supremacy over other two persons; the peace and equilibrium among them goes haywire. The whirlpool of world also assumes ferocious proportions in the same way when our ego enjoins one of the three modes of nature, which were in balance hitherto, and disturbs their calm state of equilibrium. The Chakkar is actually the creation of 1, the ego that cleverly manipulates 99 into 100 through temptation of value addition, not of 99. A Gunaateet eliminates 1, his ego from the figure 100 by standing aloof as Udaaseen & Drushtaa and watching the play of Guns. The vicious Chakkar of Punarjanm disappears from his life forever because he reduces the material value of 100 to 00 i.e. Shoonya, the cipher, the non-existence reality of Asat in his life'.*

Readers must have observed by now, the striking similarity between the traits of **Gunaateet** mentioned here in 14/22-25;

of a **Bhakt** dear to God in 12/13-20; and of a **Jnaanee** in 13/7-11; especially in respect of **Samatv**, the attitude of equilibrium. It shows that **Samatv** is the most important trait that a practiser must develop whether he chooses the path of **Karm Yog, Jnaan Yog** or **Bhakti Yog**. These three paths must converge at the tri-junction of **Samatv**, which alone can lead him onto the singularly unified path of **Vijnaan**, the **Samagr Yog** of Gita.

Trigunaateet, Nistraigunya and **Gunaateet** appearing in Gita or various other books at various places are synonyms of a person unaffected by three Guns, the modes of **Prakruti**, the nature.

౸౷

God equates Gunaateet with Brahm.

(14/26 & 27)

मां च योऽव्यभिचारेण भक्तियोगेन सेवते ।
स गुणान्समतीत्यैतान्ब्रह्मभूयाय कल्पते ॥१४/२६॥
ब्रह्मणो हि प्रतिष्ठाहममृतस्याव्ययस्य च ।
शाश्वतस्य च धर्मस्य सुखस्यैकान्तिकस्य च ॥१४/२७॥

Maam ch yo∫vyabhichaaren bhaktiyogen sevate I
S gunaansamateetyaitaanBrahmabhooyaay kalpate II (14/26)
Brahmano hi pratishthaahamamrutsyaavyayasya ch I
Shaashwatasya ch dharmasya sukhasyaikaantikasya ch II
(14/27)

Maam (to Me) Ch (and) Y: (who) Avyabhichaaren (incorruptible) Bhakti Yogen (by uniting with devotion) Sevate (renders service)I s; (he) Gunaan (by Guns) Samteetya (transcends, oversteps) Etaan (them) Brahm (Supreme Ultimate Being) Bhooyaay (integrally united with) Kalpate (is eligible, entitled)II (14/26)

Brahman: (of Brahm) Hi (certainly) Pratishthaa (the resting place) Aham (I) Amrutasya (of immortality) Avyayasya (of immutability, imperishability) Ch (and)I Shaashwatasya (of eternal) Ch (and)

Dharmasya (of Dharm) Sukhasya (of bliss, happiness) Ekaantikasya (of the only one & constant) Ch (and)II (14/27)

He, united with incorruptible devotion, renders selfless service unto Me, properly transcends all three modes of material nature and is entitled to be integrally united with Brahm, the Supreme Ultimate Being because I am immutable Brahm, the ultimate place of refuge of immortality; of everlasting Dharm; and also of constant ultimate bliss, the only one of its kind. (14/26 & 27)

We learned **Avyabhichaarinee Bhakti** in 13/10 as the unadulterated, incorruptible, inviolable, unpolluted, flawless, uncompromising devotion. It is as pure as the snow of Mount Kailash, the abode of Lord Shiv. God shall use **Avyabhichaarinee** for **Saattvikee Dhruti** also in 18/33. **Brahm Bhooyaay Kalpate:** Such **Gunaateet** person, endowed with **Avyabhichaarinee Bhakti**, is regarded as **Brahm** i.e. God. This phrase shall repeat in 18/53 in the same sense as here for **Jnaanee**. **Shaashwatasya** is something eternal; and **Dharmasya** means that which belongs to **Dharm**. Manu Smruti mentions ten symptoms of **Dharm** in 6/92 thus:

'धृति: क्षमा दमोऽस्तेयम् शौचमिन्द्रियनिग्रह: ।
धीर्विद्या सत्यमक्रोधो दशकं धर्मलक्षणम् ।।'

(Steadfastness, forgiveness, self-control, not stealing, inward and outward cleanliness, restraining Indriys from their Vishays, stable intelligence, spiritual education, truth, and freedom from anger are ten symptoms of Dharm.)

Holding on to anyone of them ensures inculcating other virtues also in our life and leads us to **Dharm**.

Sukhasya Ekaantikasya: Everyone wants happiness in his quest to overcome distress and sorrow in life, but he unfortunately looks for it in materials and persons that are the very causes and givers of distress. Thus, his search never ends as it is like searching dryness in water, or relief from burns in fire. Once he relinquishes his thirst for materials, he achieves **Ekaantik Sukh**, the only real extreme bliss. Let us recall what Gita said as early as in 2/46:

'Such a person shall have no use of a small water body after
he finds a vast reservoir overflowing with water from all sides'.

His thirst for happiness is satisfied forever since he has found a pond brimming with **Amrut** of **Dharm**. **Ekaantik Sukh** is exclusive bliss that remains eternally perfect in quality like a Himalayan stream of pure, unpolluted, cool, and ever fresh, clean water jumping, singing, splashing in joy in its course at every step. Nevertheless, once it descends in the plains of material world, it becomes polluted, dirty, impure, and even unfit for human consumption by greedy, self-centered people living on its banks. A soul is similarly pure and blissful at the time of its birth but its bliss becomes polluted and impure as it meets **Trigunaatmak Vishays** of **Prakruti** in the journey of its life. The soul must move up towards God from the plains of mundane, material world to regain its original, everlasting bliss.

We have learnt all about **Triguns**; and the symptoms of **Gunaateet** so far but the very important question *'How to become Gunaateet'* is still tickling in our minds. **Krishn,** as God and the most benevolent and compassionate teacher, answered this question in 14/26-27 above without waiting for Arjun to ask. Note that the *'Modus operandi'* prescribed here is similar to what He suggested earlier in 12/2-4.

QUESTION: IS IT NECESSARY TO BE A DEVOTEE OF GOD FOR A PERSON TO BECOME GUNAATEET?

As far as atheists are concerned, my straight answer is *'No'*. But I certainly wish to qualify this *'No'* by adding that if a person is a true devotee of God, as elaborated by Gita in chapters 9 and 12, he need not make any special effort to become **Gunaateet** because such qualities flow automatically into his personality. It simply means that the path of devotion is the easiest way to become Gunaateet; and Krishn shall endorse it in 18/66. Look into the life of devotees like Meeraa, Narasee, Tulasidaas etc. Their devout adoration and unflinching faith in God paved the easiest, surest and sweetest path for them to attain Him.

The qualities covered in the most shining topics of Gita namely **Sthit Prajn** in 2/55-72; **Sam Darshee** in 5/18-20; **Yogaaroodh** in 6/3-9; Yogee in 6/2-32; **Jnaanee** in 13/7-11; **Gunaateet** in 14/22-27; and **Daivee Sampadaa** in 16/1 to 4 are very similar. They seem repetitive on first glance; though I see no harm in repeating such outstanding qualities as *'Repetitive practice makes a man perfect'*, we would realize, on minute observation, that there is a gradual yet steady and very distinct up gradation from first to last.

CONCLUSION OF CHAPTER 14

This chapter explicitly and emphatically says that **Triguns** are inextricably embedded in all the material things that exist in the world; and they interact with each other under the influence of **Triguns** in varying proportions under the directives of the force of nature. Three modes of **Sattv**, **Raj** and **Tam** are somewhat akin to good, medium and bad, or knowledge, confusion and ignorance. **Guns** are like seasons of spring, summer and winter of nature, which give cheer, fear, pain etc. to us. If we can be insensitive to them, we become **Nistraigunya** (2/45). Universe is like a big jail in which every living being is a prisoner tied with the shackles of **Guns** of nature. A person desirous of liberation must realize that shackles, whether made of gold, silver or iron, are ultimately meant to keep him a slave of nature; he must make all efforts to cut them off and become **Gunaateet. Purush**, the individual soul is part of God and therefore **Nirgun** i.e. quality less, like a transparent mirror.

By looking at the life stories of saints & great souls, we can understand the rest about **Gunaateet** that I have not been able to explain due to my limited knowledge & vocabulary. Standing atop the cliff of **Gunaateet,** one can have the delight of seeing the panoramic view of other summits like **Sthit Prajn** (2/55-72), **Bhakt** (12/13-20), and **Jnaanee** (13/7-11 & 18/49-54) of the Himalaya of knowledge exhibited by Gita.

There are 2 **Shree Bhagawaan Uvaach,** 1 **Arjun Uvaach** and one beautiful simile in this chapter.

৵৵৵

ॐ तत्सदिति श्रीमद्भगवद्गीतासूपनिषत्सु ब्रह्मविद्यायां योगशास्त्रे श्रीकृष्णार्जुनसंवादे गुणत्रयविभागयोगो नाम चतुर्दशोऽध्यायः ॥१४॥

(In the name of God, the ultimate truth thus ends the fourteenth chapter named Gun Tray Vibhaag Yog of Shreemad Bhagwad Gita, the best Upanishad, Brahm Vidyaa & Yog Shaastr, a dialogue between Shree Krishn & Arjun)

CHAPTER 15

PURUSHOTTAM YOG

(We are never alone in the journey of life. The Supreme Master of everyone & everything in this world is there with us all the time. Let us recognize Him as our most reliable friend & guide and seek shelter in His benevolence.)

PREAMBLE & CONTEXT

Krishn told us in 13/26-27:

> *"All moving & non-moving entities are produced by the union of Kshetr, the field of activities and Kshetrajn, its knower; and he, who sees the same God pervading in all beings, has known the reality".*

Thus, Gita first subscribed to the doctrine of **Saamkhya** of Kapil that multitudinous combinations of inert **Prakruti**, the divine creative energy and conscious **Purush** or **Jeevaatmaa**, the individual soul, create all things in the universe. It then expanded the scope of doctrine of **Saamkhya** by adding in quick succession that unless one realizes the presence of **Parameshwar**, the supreme lord in everything constituted by union of **Prakruti** and **Purush**, he cannot attain the ultimate position of bliss. Krishn now picks up the same thread, as He equates **Prakruti** with a **Peepal** tree, and advises us to cut it with the weapon of detachment to attain God.

WHY CHAPTER 15 IS NAMED PURUSHOTTAM YOG?

This chapter is dedicated to establishing undoubted superiority and overall control of **Purushottam,** the Supreme Lord of all **Purush** i.e. every individual soul and the material environment created by **Prakruti** around it. As it describes **Purushottam** in detail and shows the way to connect with Him, it is called **Purushottam Yog** appropriately.

৵৽৶

God describes Samsaar, the world with the simile
of a Peepal tree.

(15/1 & 2)

श्रीभगवानुवाच
ऊर्ध्वमूलमधःशाखमश्वत्थं प्राहुरव्ययम् ।
छन्दांसि यस्य पर्णानि यस्तं वेद स वेदवित् ॥१५/१॥
अधश्चोर्ध्वं प्रसृतास्तस्य शाखा गुणप्रवृद्धा विषयप्रवालाः ।
अधश्च मूलान्यनुसंततानि कर्मानुबन्धीनि मनुष्यलोके ॥१५/२॥

Shree Bhagawaan Uvaach
Oordhwamoolamadh:shaakham
ashwattham praahuravyayam I
Chhandaansi yasya parnaani yastam ved s vedvit II (15/1)
Adhashchordhvam prasrutaastasya
shaakhaa gunpravruddhaa vishaypravaalaa: I
Adhashch moolaanyanusantataani
karmaanubandheeni manushyaloke II (15/2)

Oordhw (upwards, above) Moolam (origin, root) Adh: (downwards, below) Shaakham (branches) Ashwattham (Peepal tree) Praahu: (is said) Avyayam (inexhaustible)I chhandaansi (hymns of Veds) Yasya (whose) Parnaani (leaves) Y: (who) Tam (to him) Ved (know) S: (he) Ved vit (scholars of Veds)II (15/1)

Adh: (downwards) Ch (and) Oordhwam (upwards, above) Prasrutaa: (spread, extended, expanded) Tasya (its, of that) Shaakhaa: (branches) Gun Pravruddhaa: (grown by Guns) Vishay Pravaalaa: (having sprouts of Vishays, the objects of passions)I Adh: (downwards, below) Ch (and) Moolaani (roots) Anusantataani (spread) Karm Anubandheeni (entangled, bonded due to reactions of actions) Manushya Loke (in the human world)II (15/2)

God said:

"It has been said that there is an eternal Peepal tree with its roots upwards and branches downwards; and its leaves are hymns of Veds. He, who knows this tree well, is the true knower of Veds. (15/1)

Its branches developed by three modes (Sattv, Raj & Tam) of nature, spread downwards as well as upwards and continuously sprout with objects of passions. Its roots seem to extend downwards also and entangle due to reactions of fruitive actions in the human world. (15/2)

These shloks beautifully explain the material world with the simile of an inverted Peepal tree, said to originate from the uppermost realm of God and spread gradually all over in **Samsaar**, the world of human beings, below. In **Vedaant,** it is the tree of cosmic existence which has neither a beginning nor an end, whether in space or in time. The adjective **Avyay**, the imperishable, used by Gita for **Aatmaa**, the soul and **Paramaatmaa**, the Supreme Soul, has been used for the tree of material world also here in order to denote its origin from **Avyay** God as told categorically by God in 10/26, *'I am Peepal among all kinds of trees'*. Nevertheless, even if we look at it from the angle of rationality, Gita says that this **Ashwatth** tree of world as **Avyay**, the imperishable one because it does exist in all of its enormous reality before us. Carlyle gives a picturesque description of the tree of existence in his work *Heroes*:

"Its boughs with their buddings and disleafings—events, things suffered, things done, catastrophes—stretch through all lands and times. Is not every leaf of it a biography, every fibre there an act or word? Its boughs are histories of nations. The rustle of

it is the noise of human existence, onwards from of old. It grows there, the breath of human passion rustling through it.... It is Igdrasil[11], the Tree of Existence. It is the past, the present and the future; what was done, what is doing, what will be done: the infinite conjugation of the verb 'to do".

In a way, Carlyle recognizes bondage of **Karm**, because if a man does not do any work, there won't be any past, present or future i.e. the tree of life would cease to exist; and we can easily derive from it that by performing good works in selfless manner, one can step over recurring deaths and births, and achieve deathlessness.

Clarification: *Universe, a manifested form of Prakruti, is Avyay as per the doctrine of Saamkhya propagated by Kapil. Nevertheless, according to Gita and most other scriptures, universe is neither Avyay i.e. never-ending nor eternal like God in the absolute sense of the word because they also call it Kshan Bhangur i.e. ephemeral, which can become extinct in a moment. It is Avyay only until Prakruti and Maayaa, the two deputies of God, maintain it. It vanishes when God's supreme will decides to wind it up. A theatrical play continues to play only until its organizer pulls the curtain down.*

It is worth observing that initially many stems sprout from earth when a seed of **Peepal** germinates and with time, they integrate into single strong trunk. Similarly, the seed of a person's **Karm Phal** gives birth to multiple sprouts with several knots of actions and reactions in the soil of **Vishays**, the objects of passion, which gradually consolidate themselves into one single stem called his **Swabhaav,** the characteristic behavior. Three modes of **Sattv, Raj & Tam** act like sunshine, water and carbon dioxide to nurture and grow the tree of his life to its full potential. The sprouts feed on the fertilizer of desire, ignorance and imprudent wisdom, and become stronger. Though the tree of **Samsaar** has its origin in the world of God above (as a result of divine law of **Karm** & **Karm Phal**),

---

11 *Also called Yggdrasil in Norse myth, it is the ash tree that was thought to overshadow whole world, binding earth, heaven and hell together with its roots and branches.*

its roots start spreading downwards i.e. away from God and get ensnared with fresh actions and reactions performed by him in his current life. This entanglement in the materialistic world and its affairs finally becomes so strong that even its origin becomes obscure. Kabeer, a weaver saint, laments for such people who remain willfully entangled in this reverse phenomenon:

मैं कहता सुलझावन हारी तू राखे उरझाइ रे ।
तेरा मेरा मनवा कैसे इक होई रे ॥

(I keep telling you to unravel yourself but you entangle more & more. How can it be then possible for yours and my Man, the mind & heart to become one?)

The words upwards & downwards are used here in symbolism since men always talk of God being situated in a world above their own. Actually, God is **Anirdeshyam** i.e. directionless as told in 12/3. All directions, like any other measurements, are creations of humanity to define materials & their positions in relativity. God is beyond any definition by man. Raidaas says:

'बतक बीज जैसा आकार, पसरयो तीन लोक पसार'

(Though His shape is like the egg of a duck, He actually spreads all over the universe.)

Hymns of Veds are akin to the leaves of the tree of **Samsaar** because almost 80% of them invoke men in **Karm Kaand**, the rituals to achieve material benefits in this world and afterlife. Nevertheless, the pleasures derived from such rituals wither away in course of time as the leaves of any tree fall down on earth in autumn. The practiser who realizes this fact has truly understood Veds. Readers may like to refer to *'Some additional thoughts on Veds & their treatment in Gita'* after 2/45.

Our body is like a tree that consists of many elements like roots, trunk, main & small branches, leaves, fruits, seeds, buds, sprouts, stalks, twigs etc. It houses many **Vikaars** like **Kaam, Krodh, Lobh, Moh, Mad** and **Matsar** just as a tree contains water, air, chlorophyll, gum, fiber, seeds etc. in it. Many creatures and other living beings like bacteria, germs, insects, ants, birds etc. thrive in a human body as they do in a tree. Krishn mentioned **Peepal** earlier in 10/26 by identifying Himself with it as His **Vibhooti** among all types of trees. Please see notes there also to know more about the superiority of **Peepal** over other trees.

Karm Anubandheeni is the process of getting more and more entangled in the worldly affairs due to attachments in them and actions performed in current as well as previous lives. It points towards the doctrine of **Karm** and **Karm Bandhan** dealt in *Introduction* briefly, and discussed later after 2/47, and 9/28 besides many other places. Note that **Bandhan** is not any act of God, but due to the net of reactions cast by our own actions. It is the labyrinth laid down by fruitive works in the path of liberation of soul.

❧❦❧

How can one get rid of the trappings of this tree of world?

(15/3 & 4)

न रूपमस्येह तथोपलभ्यते नान्तो न चादिर्न च संप्रतिष्ठा ।
अश्वत्थमेनं सुविरूढमूलमसङ्गशस्त्रेण दृढेन छित्त्वा ॥१५/३॥
ततः पदं तत्परिमार्गितव्यं यस्मिन्गता न निवर्तन्ति भूयः ।
तमेव चाद्यं पुरुषं प्रपद्ये यतः प्रवृत्तिः प्रसृता पुराणी ॥१५/४॥

n roopamasyeh tathopalabhyate
naanto n chaadirn ch sampratishthaa I
Ashwatthamenam suviroodhmoolam-
asangshastren drudhen chhittvaa II (15/3)
Tat: padam tatparimaargitavyam
yasimngataa n nivartanti bhooy: I
Tamev chaadyam purusham prapadye
yat: pravrutti: prasrutaa puraanee II (15/4)

n (not) Roopam (form, shape) Asya (its) ih (this) Tathaa (similarly) Upalabhyate (is found) N (neither) Ant: (end) N (nor) Ch (and)

246 • GITA for GEN A to Z - Vol III

Aadi: (beginning, start) N (nor) Ch (and) Sampratishthaa (firmly established)I Ashwattham (Peepal tree) Enam (this) Suviroodh (firm, strong) Moolam (roots) Asang (detachment, dissociation) Shastren (by the weapon of) Drudhen (with firm) Chhitvaa (by cutting off)II (15/3)

tat: (thereafter) Padam (destination, status) Tat (that) Parimaargitavyam (search properly) Yasmin (in which) Gataa: (go) N (not) Nivartanti (return) Bhooy: (again)I tam (to him) Ev (only) Ch (and) Aadyam (primeval) Purusham (Supreme Being) Prapadye (surrender, take shelter) Yat: (by that) Pravrutti: (get activated, started) Prasrutaa (spread, extend) Puraanee (since time immemorial)II (15/4)

But in reality, this tree is not found in the form and shape described above because it has neither a beginning nor an end nor does it have any firm existence i.e. it is illusionary. Therefore, by cutting off this apparently strong rooted Peepal tree with the firm weapon of detachment, one must set out in search of that Ultimate Destination from where no one ever returns after reaching there. Then he should seek shelter in that primeval Supreme Being from whom this tree of world sprouts, grows and exists since time immemorial. (15/3 & 4)

Pravrutti, the urge to act & react is the underlying principle of the unchecked growth of this tree of life. It inducts a person to do more and more fruitive actions and be tied up to suffer or enjoy their reactions.

SOME ADDITIONAL THOUGHTS ON THE SIMILE OF ASHWATTH TREE

Scriptures define **Ashwatth** as श्व: पर्यन्तम् न तिष्ठातीति अश्वत्थ: meaning *'That which will not remain the same till tomorrow'.* This is the harsh reality of **Samsaar,** the ephemeral world we live in, for it is not stable even for a moment for it undergoes continuous transformation. Yam describes **Ashwatth** tree to Nachiketaa in Kathopanishad 2/3/1 thus:

ऊर्ध्वमूलोऽवाक्शाख एषोऽश्वत्थ: सनातन: ।
तदेव शुक्रं तद् ब्रह्म तदेवामृतमुच्यते ॥
तस्मिँल्लोका: श्रिता: सर्वे तद् नात्येति कश्चन ॥ एतद्वै तत् ॥।

{The eternal Peepal tree (of this world) has its root upwards and branches downwards. That immortal (Brahm) is the purest, strongest base on which all worlds rest. Nothing can ever overstep Him}

These verses describe **Brahm**, the immortal, purest Supreme Being as the principal root of **Samsaar Vruksh**, the tree of creation. It spreads its branches in the phenomena of heat and cold, pleasure and pain, birth and death, and all other changing conditions of the mortal realm of world. Gita adds that ordinary mortal beings engrossed in worldly affairs regard, due to their ignorance, this **Ashwatth** tree rooted endlessly in the material world, and remain entangled in them without ever realizing **Brahm**, its true source. In symbolism, **Ashwatth** is the tree of ever changing universe, and an individual's Life is only a small part of it like a sprout or leaf or fruit or seed of a tree. Nourished by three **Guns,** the initiators of all its phenomena, its branches spread in all directions because of past deeds; and the freshly committed actions throw down secondary rootlets that generate more actions and reactions leading to ceaseless cycles of Punarjanm. One must mercilessly trample upon secondary roots and branches to unite him with its main root, the God. Gita advises further the practiser of its **Yog** to cut off the tangles of branches and downward flowing roots with the forceful weapon of detachment of sense objects. He who frees himself from the mire of sense life can win that place from which there is no return, for he has taken refuge in the Primeval Source wherefrom flows the never-ending stream of bliss. Raamaanujaachaarya says:

'One must search for that place of no return from which whole universe has sprouted; and submerge his individual entity into it'.

Mention of **Ashwatth** as the tree of Samsaar is found in many scriptures like Rigved 1/24/7, 10/135/1, 1/164/22 and 5/54/12; Taittireey Braahman 3/8/12/2 etc. besides Kathopanishad. Gita uses it for **Naam Drushya Roopaatmak Jagat**, the universe and its entities that we define by name, and which have some form we can see and sense.

Clarification: *Most of the commentaries on Gita have interpreted Ashwatth as Peepal tree. However, I feel equally comfortable with them who replace Peepal with banyan (Vat) tree for Ashwatth because the virtuous qualities of a banyan tree like having longest life among trees; its vast and massive expanse; its roots coming downwards from branches above and transforming into new trunks in due course; match very closely to the qualities of Ashwatth of Gita. In any case, this fine distinction should not matter much for our study of Gita.*

God describes the qualities required to attain
His eternal abode.

(15/5 & 6)

निर्मानमोहा जितसङ्गदोषा अध्यात्मनित्या विनिवृत्तकामाः ।
द्वन्द्वैर्विमुक्ताः सुखदुःखसंज्ञैर् गच्छन्त्यमूढाः पदमव्ययं तत् ॥१५/५॥
न तद्भासयते सूर्यो न शशाङ्को न पावकः ।
यद्गत्वा न निवर्तन्ते तद्धाम परमं मम ॥१५/६॥

Nirmaanamohaa jitasangadoshaa
adhyaatmanityaa vinivruttakaamaa: I
Dwandwairvimuktaa: sukhdu:khasanjnair
gachchhantyamoodhaa: padamavyayam tat II (15/5)
n tadbhaasayate sooryo n shashaanko n paavak: I
Yadgatwaa n nivartante taddhaam paramam mam II (15/6)

Nirmaan Mohaa: (beyond considerations of respect and infatuation) Jit sang Doshaa: (conquered the evil of attachment, association) Adhyaatm Nitya: (perpetually situated in spirituality) Vinivrutt kaamaa: (dissociated from desire)I Dwandwai: (from dualities) Vimuktaa: (liberated) Sukh du:kh ((happiness & sorrow) Sanjnai: (named as) Gachchhanti: (go) Amoodhaa: (not deluded) Padam (status) Avyayam (eternal) Tat (that)II (15/5)

n (no) Tat (that) Bhaasayate (Illuminates) Soory: (sun) N (nor) Shashaank: (moon) N (nor) Paavak: (fire)I Yat (to which) Gatwaa (after reaching) N (not) Nivartante (return) Tat (that) Dhaam (abode) Paramam (supreme) Mam (my)II (15/6)

Those who are beyond considerations of respect & infatuation; have conquered the evil of attachment; are perpetually situated in spirituality; dissociated from all kinds of desires; free from dualities like happiness & unhappiness and from delusion; they attain that eternal destination which neither sun nor moon nor fire can illuminate i.e. it is self-illuminated. That ultimate place is My abode from where no one returns to the material world once he reaches there. (15/5 & 6)

A practiser must cast away considerations of respect and disrespect, be indifferent to attractions of world of passions, be equipoise in comfort and discomfort and other dualities and remain situated continuously in the spiritual knowledge of soul and Supreme Soul in order to enter into the kingdom of God. Otherwise, he is doomed to remain trapped in the tentacles of the world. Friedrich Nietzsche says:

'The snake which cannot cast its skin has to die'.

Yadgatwaa n Nivartante Taddhaam Paramam Mam points to the place of God from where one never returns to the mortal world once he attains it. Gita reflects the same thought in many places like 4/9, 5/17, 8/21, and 15/4 & 6. Shlok 15/6 resembles very much with similar shloks appearing in Upanishads like Kath 2/2/15, Mundak 2/2/10 and Shwetaashwatar 6/14.

ॐ

God explains why an embodied soul is attracted towards the play of nature.

(15/7)

ममैवांशो जीवलोके जीवभूतः सनातनः ।
मनःषष्ठानीन्द्रियाणि प्रकृतिस्थानि कर्षति ॥१५/७॥

Mamaivaansho jeevloke jeevbhoot: sanaatan: I
Man:shashthaaneendriyaani prakrutisthaani karshati II
(15/7)

Mam (my) Ev (certainly) Ansh: (indivisible part) Jeev (living being) Loke (in the world) Jeev Bhoot: (soul) Sanaatan: (eternal)I Man: (mind) Shashthaani (sixth) Indriyaani (Indriy) Prakrutisthaani (situated in nature) Karshati (pulls)II (15/7)

The soul of every embodied living being in the world is certainly My eternal indivisible part. Nevertheless, his five sensory organs along with the sixth one, Man, the mind & heart, situated in the material nature, attract and condition it into the world. (15/7)

God clearly and loudly states that an embodied soul is an indivisible part of His eternal existence, called **Sachchidaanand**. Hence soul also is **Sat** (2/16) as much as God is, since time immemorial. However, separated from Him, it has fallen prey to the creations of **Prakruti** and its modes of **Sattv, Raj** & **Tam**, and lost its real identity. It is similar to a prince becoming a beggar or sinner when separated from his father, the king. **Vedaant Sookt** asserts in 2/2/43 that **Jeev**, the individual embodied soul is a minuscule yet indivisible part of eternal **Brahm**. Tulasidaas says in Raamcharit Maanas 7/116 (ख)/2:

ईस्वर अंस जीव अबिनासी। चेतन अमल सहज सुख रासी॥

(The embodied soul is an indivisible part of God. Hence, like God, it also is indestructible & everlasting, conscious, spotlessly clean & pure by nature and the treasury of bliss.)

Consider the life of a person as a **Rath**, the chariot pulled by the horses of sensory organs; whose **Rathee**, the owner is his soul and **Saarathee**, the driver is **Man**, the mind. A **Rath** can run on a proper course only if its **Saarathee** is under full control of **Rathee** and drives the **Rath** properly to his desired destination. On the contrary, if **Rathee** permits the driver to take all decisions, the driver may let the horses run amuck to take the path of **Vishays** of their liking; or still verse, the driver may drive **Rath** to a destination not favorable to **Rathee**. It is unfortunate that this process of control is reverse in the lives of most of us as we hand over ownership of our lives to **Man,** the mind & heart that decides, in collusion with **Indriys**, the course of our entire life. Shlok 15/7 empowers us by directing to take charge of our lives into our hands by exercising full control on **Man**. Readers may like to refer to discussions held in 3/42, 6/26 & 34 earlier to realize how unchecked **Man** drags the chariot of our lives into the gorge of complete destruction. God identified **Man** among **Indriys** as His **Vibhooti** in 10/22 due to its power over them.

Though sensory organs viz. eyes, ears, nose, tongue and skin are constantly engaged in sensing objects of their respective passions, a person does not register their feedback unless his **Man,** the mind joins them. For example, his eyes may see something physically but he himself remains unattached with the scene until his mind pays attention to it. Senses alone are unable to translate any perception into an action unless directed by mind. It is for this reason that Gita advises us in 2/67 and at many other places to control **Man** from wandering unnecessarily after objects of passion of every sensory organ. Mind must act as an effective filter, and reject unnecessary from the necessary in our life.

ॐ

(15/8)

शरीरं यदवाप्नोति यच्चाप्युत्क्रामतीश्वरः ।
गृहित्वैतानि संयाति वायुर्गन्धानिवाशयात् ॥१५/८॥

Shareeram yadavaapnoti yachchaapyutkraamateeshwar: I
Gruheetvaitaani sanyaati vaayurgandhaanivaashayaat II
(15/8)

Shareeram (body) Yat (which) Avaapnoti (possesses, takes) Yat (which) Ch (and) Api (also) Utkraamati (gives up) ishwar: (soul, the master of body)I Gruheetvaa (taking, holding, seizing) Etaani (all of them) Sanyaati (proceeds) Vaayu: (wind) Gandhaan (smell, odor) iv (like) Aashayaat (from place of origin, source)II (15/8)

As wind carries odors from their source to another place, similarly soul, the master of a body, also takes possession of all of them (the senses & mind) at the time of giving up a body and lodges them in new body it acquires. (15/8)

Krishn gives 38th simile in Gita. Though scriptures describe smell as the principal characteristic trait of earth, actually the wind carries the smell emanated by earth to various places along with it regardless of it being good or bad, foul or fair, or pleasant or unpleasant. Similarly, though the body of a man performs certain good, bad, or mixed actions in conjunction with **Man** and **Indriys** during his life, his soul has to carry the burden of those works and suffer or enjoy their fruits in its journey after death of current body. It is noteworthy that as all kinds of good or bad smells dilute and vanish into thin air of nothingness in due course of time, similarly the ties of old **Karms** also vanish upon fruition, but new bonds are created by fresh works. Krishn uses **Ishwar** here to imply that the individual soul is a part of Supreme Soul.

৽৽৽

God explains how the soul is bonded with its body.

(15/9 & 10)

श्रोत्रं चक्षुः स्पर्शनं च रसनं घ्राणमेव च ।
अधिष्ठाय मनश्चायं विषयानुपसेवते ॥१५/९॥
उत्क्रामन्तं स्थितं वापि भुञ्जानं वा गुणान्वितम् ।
विमूढा नानुपश्यन्ति पश्यन्ति ज्ञानचक्षुषः ॥१५/१०॥

Shrotram chakshu: sparshanam ch rasanam ghraanamev ch I
Adhishthaay manashchaayam vishayaanupsevate II (15/9)
Utkraamantam stitham vaapi bhunjaanam vaa gunaanvitam I
Vimoodha naanupashyanti pashyanti jnaanchakshush: II
(15/10)

Shrotram (ears) Chakshu: (eyes) Sparshanam (skin) Ch (and) Rasanam (tongue) Ghraanam (nose) Ev (also) Ch (and)I Adhishthaay (taking support, dwelling within) Man: (of mind) Ch (and) Ayam (this) Vishayaan (of objects of passions) Upasevate (partakes with pleasure, enjoys)II (15/9)

Utkraamantam (giving up, quitting) Sthitam (situated) Vaa (or) Api (even) Bhunjaanam (consuming, experiencing) Vaa (or) Gunaan Anvitam (fraught with Sattv, raj and tam)I Vimoodhaa: (deluded) N (not) Anupashyanti (see properly) Pashyanti (sees) Jnaan Chakshush: (eyes of perfect spiritual knowledge)II (15/10)

This soul takes support of mind, the leader of the group of 5 sensory organs viz. ears, eyes, skin, tongue & nose; and partakes with the pleasures of their respective objects of passion. (15/9)

Persons bewildered with ignorance are unable to see it (soul) when it leaves the body upon death, or when it is situated in the body, or when it enjoys (or suffers) the objects of passion (of Indriys) because it is fraught with three modes of nature. Only those, whose eyes focus on perfect spiritual knowledge, can see that (soul) properly. (15/10)

Krishn mentions three stages of an embodied soul in 15/10 with respect to the body with which it attaches. It leaves the body when a person dies; it resides in it as long as he is alive, and it experiences all the pleasant as well as distressful situations of life due to its involvement with three modes of nature and the body. These illusory stages of soul last only till it is trapped in **Trigunaatmak**, the three fold **Vishays**, the passions of **Indriys** and **Man** of its body, for basically, by nature, a soul is beyond the effects of **Guns** and **Maayaa**, the illusion. Such person, engrossed in the works of nature of body, never realizes true identity of soul as a part of God's eternal bliss; and its potential to achieve His status. He is happy with his spiritual blindness like Dhrutraashtr, who even refuses to accept the gift of **Jnaan Chakshu**, the eyes of **Jnaan** from a great sage like Vyaas, saying he does not need them. We had discussed **Jnaan Chakshu** earlier in 13/34 also.

❧❦

Who is able to see the soul residing within him?

(15/11)

यतन्तो योगिनश्चैनं पश्यन्त्यात्मन्यवस्थितम् ।
यतन्तोऽप्यकृतात्मानो नैनं पश्यन्त्यचेतसः ॥१५/११॥

Yatanto yoginshchainam pashyantyaatmanyavasthitam I
Yatantoʃpyakrutaatmaano nainam pashyantyachetas: II
(15/11)

Yatant: (assiduous, attempting) Yogin: (practitioners of Yog) Ch (and) Enam (this) Pashyanti (sees) Aatmani (in self) Avasthitam (placed) I Yatant: (attempting, endeavoring) Api (also) Akrut Aatmaan: (who has not accomplished perfection in purifying, realizing self) N (not) Enam (this) Pashyanti (see) Achetas: (not discerning, ignorant persons)II (15/11)

Only the assiduous practitioners of Yog can see this soul stationed in their self. Persons, not discerning to accomplish realization of self, cannot know this soul even if they attempt for it. (15/11)

Gita expressed this idea of knowing self by self and remaining satisfied with it earlier as **Aatmani ev Aatmanaa Tusht** in 2/55, as **Aatmani ev ch Santusht** in 3/17 and as **Aatmanaatmaanam Pashyannaatmani Tushyati** in 6/20 also.

Moral: *Once a person recognizes the soul within him it radiates its light within and all around him like a lamp placed in a house of glass. All that Gita wants us to do is to remove the opaqueness created by the cover of Ajnaan, the ignorance on our real self.*

৵৹৶

Gita describes 6 of God's Vibhootis from 15/12 to 14 to establish His supremacy.

(15/12, 13 & 14)

यदादित्यगतं तेजो जगद्भासयतेऽखिलम् ।
यच्चन्द्रमसि यच्चाग्नौ तत्तेजो विद्धि मामकम् ॥१५/१२॥

गामाविश्य च भूतानि धारयाम्यहमोजसा ।
पुष्णामि चौषधी: सर्वा: सोमो भूत्वा रसात्मक: ॥१५/१३॥
अहं वैश्वानरो भूत्वा प्राणिनां देहमाश्रित: ।
प्राणापानसमायुक्त: पचाम्यन्नं चतुर्विधम् ॥१५/१४॥

Yadaadityagatam tejo jagadbhaasayate[khilam I
Yachchandramasi yachchaajnau tattejo viddhi maamakam II
(15/12)
Gaamaavishya ch bhootaani dhaarayaamyahamojasaa I
Pushnaami chaushadhee: sarvaa: somo bhootvaa rasaatmak:
II (15/13)
Aham vaishwaanaro bhootvaa praaninaam dehamaashrit: I
Praanaapaansamaayukt: pachaamyannam chaturvidham II
(15/14)

Yat (which) Aaditya Gatam (located in sun) Tej: (energy, brilliance, splendor) Jagat (universe) Bhaasayate (illuminates, radiates) Khilam (entire)I Yat (which) Chandramasi (is there in moon) Yat (which) Ch (and) Agnau (in fire) Tat (that) Tej: (energy, heat, brilliance) Viddhi; (understand well) Maamakam (My)II (15/12)

Gaam (earth) Aavishya (entering) Ch (and) Bhootaani (all beings) Dhaarayaami (hold, preserve) Aham (I) Ojasaa (splendor, lustre)I Pushnaami (nourish, nurture) Ch (and) Aushadhee: (sacred herbs & other vegetation) Sarvaa: (all) Som: (moon) Bhootvaa (by becoming) Rasaatmak: (formant of juice, sap to refresh)II (15/13)

aham (I) Vaishwaanar: (a kind of fire in the stomach which digests food taken by living beings) Bhootvaa (by becoming) Praaninaam (of all living beings) Deham (in the body) Aashrit: (situated)I Praan (the exhaling breath vital for sustenance of life which acts upwards) Apaan (the inhaling breath vital for sustenance of life which acts downwards) Samaayukt: (along with, united with) Pachaami (digest) Annam (food, grains) Chaturvidham (of four kinds)II (15/14)

Understand it well that the energy located in the sun that radiates whole universe; the brilliance in the moon; and the heat in the fire are really Mine. I permeate My energy into the earth to sustain all the living and inanimate entities; I

nurture all herbs and entire vegetation as moon, the formant of nourishing juices & sappy substances. I am Vaishwaanar, a kind of fire, situated in the bodies of all living beings that digests four kinds of foods in conjunction with Praan, the exhaling breathe and Apaan, the inhaling breathe. (15/12, 13 & 14)

Gita described 14 divine **Vibhootis** in 7/8-12 earlier, then 37 again in 9/16-19, and 127 in chapter 10. It now describes last six **Vibhootis** here in 15/12-14. Let us ponder on it.

QUESTION: WHY GOD'S VIBHOOTIS ARE SCATTERED IN DIFFERENT PLACES IN GITA?

The central idea behind the theism of Gita is that God is **Sarvatr**, the omnipresent i.e. present everywhere, **Sarvajn**, the omniscient i.e. knows everything and **Sarv Shaktimaan**, omnipotent i.e. possessor of ultimate power and energy. Omnipresence is described as **Sarv Bhootastham** in 6/29, as **Sarv Bhoot Sthitam** in 6/31, as **Sarvatrag** in 9/6 & 12/3 and **Sarv Gat** in 2/24, 3/15 & 13/32; Omniscience is described as **Sarv Vid** in 15/19; and Omnipotence is vividly described in chapter 11, particularly in 11/19, 30, 32 & 40. It seems that Gita has scattered the shloks exhibiting various **Vibhootis** of God in its text in different places with an intention to reveal His divinity in a kaleidoscopic manner so that the beauty of this idea gradually percolates and ensconces well in the minds and hearts of its students. Readers must have observed that some of these Vibhootis are abstract, some are humans and super humans, some are other live creatures, some others are inert entities and still others are part of the cosmos. This divine revelation, however, ends with shloks 15/12-14 here. Please also refer to explanations in chapter 10 in this regard.

Bruhadaaranyak Upanishad describes **Vaishwaanar** thus in 5/9/9:

अयमग्निर्वैश्वानरो यो{यमंतः पुरुषे येनेदमन्नम् पच्यते यदिदमध्यते

(The fire inside a person is called Vaishwaanar by which the food, he consumes, is digested.)

Scriptures classify foods into four kinds as **Bhakshya**, those which are to be chewed with teeth like bread, meat etc.; **Bhojya**, which are to be swallowed & gulped down like milk, juices etc.; **Lehya**, which need to be licked and lapped by tongue like sauces, pickles etc.; and **Choshya**, which need to be squeezed by teeth & sucked like sugarcane, pulps etc. **Vaishwaanar** is the fire in the belly of a living being which processes all kinds of food further into the digestible and refuge. The body absorbs the digested part and rejects undigested through anus and urethra. The power of digesting all kinds of foods in **Vaishwaanar** is of God. We must therefore ensure that our food is pure, earned rightfully by own hard work and consumed with happiness and satisfaction after offering it to God as His **Prasaad**. See *'Some additional thoughts on Aahaar'* after 17/10. **Praan** & **Apaan,** the breathing in and out of our respiratory system energized by God, help **Vaishwaanar** to do its work properly.

❦◈

God tells in which form He resides in the heart of everybody.

(15/15)

सर्वस्य चाहं हृदि संनिविष्टो मत्तः स्मृतिर्ज्ञानमपोहनं च ।
वेदैश्च सर्वैरहमेव वेद्यो वेदान्तकृद्वेदविदेव चाहम् ॥१५/१५॥

Sarvasya chaaham hrudi sannivishto matt: smrutirjnaanamapohanam ch I

Vedaishch sarvairahamev vedyo vedaantkrudvedvidev chaaham II (15/15)

Sarvasya (of everyone) Ch (and) Aham (I) Hrudi (in the heart) Sannivisht: (well seated) Matt: (by me) Smruti: (memory, remembrance, recollection) Jnaanam (knowledge) Apohanam (the wisdom of clarification and analysis)I vedai: (by Veds) Ch (and) Sarvai: (all) Aham (I) Ev (only) Vedya: (knowable) Vedaant Krut (author of Vedaant) Ved Vit (scholar of Veds) Ev (also) Ch (and) Aham (I)II (15/15)

I am well seated in the heart of all beings. Smruti, the power of remembrance & knowledge, and Apohan, the wisdom of clarification & analysis in them, is due to Me. I am the only one worth knowing by study of Veds. Indeed, I am the author of Vedaant and the supreme knower of Veds. (15/15)

God asserts that He resides in the heart of everybody in the form of remembrance, knowledge and wisdom of discerning and choosing between right and wrong. In 18/61, we shall see God proclaiming again that though He is situated in the heart of everybody, he is gyrated by His power of **Maayaa**, the divine energy that creates confusion, as if mounted on a rotating machine. Reading these shloks together would immediately relieve us from all doubts, apprehensions and fear of the unknown in life by leading us on the path of knowing God, the Supreme Source of entire knowledge worth knowing including that contained in **Veds** because **Veds** also are His creation. If someone develops intimate contact with the prime minister of the country, he need not bother any more about likely hurdles created by bureaucracy in his well-intentioned work.

Apohan is the quality of logical analysis and discernment by which one can clarify and wash away his doubts and **Aviparyay**, the freedom from false knowledge formed about a thing other than what it really is. Hanumaan displayed this rare quality in Lankaa and decided to take the initiative of establishing friendship with Vibheeshan, the brother of his lord's enemy, Raavan. He could invoke this distinct quality because he had firmly placed Raam in his heart all the time.

ॐ

God describes two kinds of entities in the world
as Kshar & Akshar.

(15/16)

द्वाविमौ पुरुषौ लोके क्षरश्चाक्षर एव च ।
क्षरः सर्वाणि भूतानि कूटस्थोऽक्षर उच्यते ॥१५/१६॥

Dwaavimau purushau loke ksharashchaakshar ev ch I
Kshar: sarvaani bhootaani kootastho∫kshar uchyate II (15/16)

Dwau (two types) Imau (these) Purushau (beings) Loke (in the world) Kshar: (perishable, mutable) Ch (and) Akshar: (imperishable one) Ev (only) Ch (and)I Kshar: (impermanent entity) Sarvaani (in all) Bhootaani (all beings) Kootasth: (immutable soul) Akshar: (unchangeable entity) Uchyate (is said)II (15/16)

There are only two types of entities in this world known as Kshar, the perishable one & Akshar the imperishable one. It is said that the body of every being is Kshar, the perishable one, and the immutable soul well placed inside them is Akshar, the imperishable one. (15/16)

We had learnt about **Akshar** as something imperishable, immutable and eternal; and **Kshar** as something impermanent, perishable and mutable in 8/3-4. Krishn divides all things existing in the world into two categories, some as **Kshar,** the perishable and others as **Akshar,** the imperishable. Prashn Upanishad calls them Rayi and Praan in 1/4. Since this shlok talks of **Purush**, the people, it also conveys that there are two kinds of people in the world. The first kind are **Kshar** i.e. who spend their lives clinging to pleasures (and sorrows) of mortal body; and the others are **Akshar** i.e. those whose aim of life is to know the immortal soul that resides in their bodies.

Clarification: *God described Akshar as Paramam Brahm in 8/3. We need not confuse when God describes Akshar as imperishable, immutable soul here in 15/16. 'Shaatee Sootr Nyaay' says that a Saaree and the thread, of which it is made, are of the same material. He shall pronounce later in 18/61 that God lives in everybody's heart (in the form of soul).*

Kootasth: It was explained in 6/8 as something lodged deep within; and it spiritually implies to **Akshar**, immutable, immovable, indestructible soul. It is noteworthy that Koot was also explained to denote an anvil or **Ookhal**, the mortar, an implement used for pounding grains, spices etc.; or to increase the potency of **Aayurvedic** medicines by repeatedly grinding them in a mortar with a pestle. A practiser should likewise lay his ego on an anvil or in an **Ookhal** and be ready to receive the pounding and grinding strokes of world. The harder the strokes are, the finer he becomes. I am inclined to believe that besides pointing towards the soul residing within the deepest part of the body, Krishn uses the word **Kootasth** here in this sense also.

Moral: *Those who dedicate themselves to the temporary, transient pleasures of life are wasting the precious opportunity of being born as human. No doubt, they should do their duties towards everyone in the world according to Dharm, but they should not forget the main objective of achieving eternal happiness attainable only by realizing soul as a part of Supreme Soul, striving to reunite with Him.*

ॐ

Concept of eternal existence of Paramaatmaa, the Supreme Soul besides Prakruti and soul, is introduced and explained now.

(15/17 & 18)

उत्तमः पुरुषस्त्वन्यः परमात्मेत्युदाहृतः ।
यो लोकत्रयमाविश्य बिभर्त्यव्यय ईश्वरः ॥१५/१७॥
यस्मात्क्षरमतीतोऽहमक्षरादपि चोत्तमः ।
अतोऽस्मि लोके वेदे च प्रथितः पुरुषोत्तमः ॥१५/१८॥

Uttam: purushastvanya: Paramaatmetyudaahrut: I
Yo lokatrayamaavishya vibhartyavyay Ishwar: II (15/17)
Yasmaatksharamateetoʃhamaksharaadapi chottam: I
Atoʃsmi loke vede ch prathit: Purushottam: II (15/18)

Uttam: (perfect) Purush: (person, being) Tu (but) Any: (other) Paramaatmaa (Supreme Soul) Iti (thus) Udaahrut: (is cited, exemplified)I y: (who) Lok Trayam (three worlds) Aavishya (permeating) Bibharti (maintains) Avyay (inexhaustible, immutable) Ishwar: (God)II (15/17)

Yasmaat (for this reason) Ksharam (mutable, impermanent entity) Ateet: (beyond) Ishwar (God, Lord of Lords) Aham (I)

Aksharaat (than the imperishable, unchangeable) Api (also) Ch (and) Uttam: (greater, superior)I at: (therefore) Asmi (am) Loke (in the world) Vede (in Veds) Ch (and) Prathit: (famous, acknowledged) Purushottam: (Krishn, Supreme Being)II (15/18)

Nevertheless, the Supreme Soul, besides the two described above, is someone else who permeates in all the three (upper, middle and lower) worlds and maintains them. He is cited as the immutable, imperishable Ishwar, Supreme Lord of all Lords because I am beyond the reach of Kshar, the perishable one, and also superior to Akshar, the imperishable soul as I am acknowledged by Veds as Purushottam, the superior most of all Purush i.e. the embodied individual souls, and by entire world also. (15/17 & 18)

Gita is in agreement with **Saamkhya** doctrine of Kapil so far as existence of two independent entities, **Prakruti** i.e. **Kshar**, and **Akshar**, the embodied soul is concerned, and it extends it further by saying that there is yet another entity called **Parameshwar**, the ultimate Lord of all lords, or **Purushottam**, the supreme master of all souls.

SOME ADDITIONAL THOUGHTS ON PURUSHOTTAM

Though the word **Purushottam** appeared earlier also in shloks like 8/1, 10/15 and 11/3 in Gita, it was uttered there by Arjun for Krishn in acknowledgement of His divinity. Now, in 15/18 & 15/19, Krishn explains the real and complete meaning of **Purushottam**. Let us understand it:

Purush commonly connotes a person as used by Gita in 2/15 & 3/4, but in spirituality, Gita also applies it to an individual soul in shloks like 8/4, 10 & 22, 11/18, 13/19 & 13/20 and 15/4. Since **Uttam** means the best, **Purushottam** (**Purush+Uttam**) literally means the very best, most superior, perfect, noblest, and supreme among all persons, and the supreme, ultimate master of all **Purush**, the individual souls. According to Mahaabhaarat 5/70/11 'पूर्णात् सदनाञ्चापि ततोऽसौ पुरुषोत्तमः:' i.e. *'Because He, as Purush, is complete in all respects, abode of every being; and since Krishn is the best among all Purush, He is called Purushottam.'*

Saamkhya says that **Prakruti** and **Purush** are the only two things that exist in the world since time immortal, and there is nothing before or after them. This is akin to atheism. Gita takes the apparent atheism of **Saamkhya** to the highest & perfect plane of theism by saying that God alone is the real, eternal being because He is the originator, creator, maintainer and destroyer of all works of **Prakruti** (and its Guns) And is also the primeval source of all **Purush**, the individual souls. Gita establishes God as the Ultimate, Supreme and Absolute Existence called **Sat**, that existed even before the world came into existence; that exists within the world as long as it exists, and that which shall also continue to exist forever even after the world is destroyed. All individual souls emerge from that Supreme Soul at the beginning of creation, and submerge into Him upon extinction. Yaajnavalkya tells to his wife and disciple Maitreyee in Bruhadaaranyak Upanishad:

'As ocean is the refuge of water, skin is the refuge of touch,
nose is the refuge of smell, tongue is the refuge of taste, eyes
is the refuge of scenes, ears are the refuge of sound, Man, the
mind is the refuge of all propositions, heart is the refuge of all
kinds of learning, hands are the refuge of all works, penis is
the refuge of sexual pleasure, anus is the refuge of discharge,
legs are the refuge of all paths, and speech is the refuge of all
Veds; similarly, Paramaatmaa, the Supreme Soul is the ultimate
refuge of all souls.'

Kabeer sees **Param Purush** as:

नाद बिंदु ते अगम अगोचर, पाँच तत्त्व से न्यारा ।
तीन गुणन ते भिन्न है, पुरुष अलक्ख हमारा ॥

{My Purush (God) is invisible, different than five basic elements
(which constitute the world). He is inaccessible to any sensory
organ like Naad, the divine song of God (which cannot be heard
by normal ears), and dimensionless like Bindu, a point (which
cannot be seen by normal eyes)}

Moral: *Every soul is bound to live restlessly in the world called Dukhaalay, the house of sorrow until it raises itself to avail the eternal bliss of tryst with God, its lover & master.*

જે⚬ન્ડ

What is the benefit of knowing Purushottam God?

(15/19)

यो मामेवमसंमूढो जानाति पुरुषोत्तमम् ।
स सर्वविद्भजति मां सर्वभावेन भारत ॥१५/१९॥

Yo maamevamasammoodho jaanaati Purushottamam I
S sarvavidbhajati maam sarvabhaaven Bhaarat II (15/19)

y: (who) Maam (to me) Evam (thus) Asammoodh: (without delusion, doubt, bewilderment) Jaanaati (knows) Purushottamam (Krishn)I s: (he) Sarv vid (one who knows everything) Bhajati (worships, adores) Maam (to me) Sarv Bhaaven (whole heartedly, in all respects) Bhaarat (Arjun)II (15/19)

O Bhaarat (Arjun)! He who knows Me as Purushottam, the greatest of all souls, the Supreme Being without any delusion or doubt in this way, he has known everything; and he devotes unto Me whole heartedly in all respects. (15/19)

Krishn calls upon us to shed all ignorance and foolishness, and know Him as **Purushottam** (as explained above), and devote, by all means, to Him with the spirit of **Bhaav Samanvitaa** i.e. who has integrated his body and soul, with all emotions and sentiments, with God as told by Him in 10/8 & 18/26.

જે⚬ન્ડ

Scriptures proclaim this knowledge as the most esoteric,
ultimate knowable one.

(15/20)

इति गुह्यतमं शास्त्रमिदमुक्तं मयानघ ।
एतद्बुद्ध्वा बुद्धिमान्स्यात्कृतकृत्यश्च भारत ॥१५/२०॥

Iti guhyatamam shaastramidamuktam mayaAnagh I

Etadbuddhwaa buddhimaansyaatkrutkrutyashch Bhaarat II

(15/20)

Iti (thus) Guhya tamam (the most esoteric secret) Shaastram (Holy Scripture) Idam (this) Uktam (is told) Maayaa (by me) Anagh (Arjun)I Etat (this) Buddhwaa (by understanding) Buddhi Maan (the most intelligent, wisest) Syaat (become) Krut Krutya: (who has perfectly accomplished the work/s he is supposed to do) Ch (and) Bhaarat (Arjun)II (15/20)

O Anagh (sinless, pure hearted Arjun)! The Doctrine, that has been revealed to you by Me now, is the most esoteric secret of Holy Scriptures. O Bhaarat (Arjun)! He, who has understood it perfectly, becomes the most intelligent & wisest person, and the purpose of his endeavors and existence in the world is perfectly accomplished. (15/20)

Krishn proceeded to teach **Guhya Tam**, the pinnacle of secret and deepest esoteric knowledge called **Jnaan** & **Vijnaan** in 9/1. Now, in 15/20, He concludes His teaching of that deepest and highly specialized spiritual knowledge. It implies that knowing **Paramaatmaa** perfectly is the ultimate culmination of entire learning and education. Once a person comes to know Him, he is the wisest person on earth; and he becomes **Krut Krutya** i.e. he who has successfully accomplished the purpose of his life. It is worth noting here that Krishn shall speak of His entire teaching of Gita as **Guhyaat Guhya Taram**, the top most of all esoteric secrets in 18/63, **Sarv Guhya Tam**, the top most of all secrets in 18/64, and **Paramam Guhya**, the ultimate secret in 18/68. By 'Iti', He means this is the end of all knowledge.

The question that arises here is that if this is the ultimate end of His teachings why Gita continues for three more chapters. We will understand it in the preamble of next chapter.

CONCLUSION OF CHAPTER 15

Chapter 15 first described world with the simile of a **Peepal** tree that spreads its roots and branches all over and hold us in them like the tentacles of an octopus. It then talked of God's **Vibhootis** in 15/12-15 as a specimen of His Divine, Absolute & Supreme Existence, and said that he, who knows Him in this fundamental way, has known everything. Finally, it elevated us in a high-speed elevator to the highest level of spiritual knowledge of **Adwait**, the utmost undivided form of Monism where normal beings like us have never set foot so far. Standing atop observation platform at this level, we could see the mysterious multiplicity, supra-cosmic reality and absolute existence of **Purushottam**, the Supreme Soul. We saw Him, manifested or unmanifested, in every inanimate & living, moving & stationary entity; in five basic elements & their mutations; in senses, emotions & feelings, thoughts & imagination; in action & inaction; in energy, power & force; creation & destruction, birth & death, in consciousness & sleepiness, in celestial bodies, in laws, rules and their administration, in all the dimensions & the dimensionless, in past, present and future & timeless. We realized that He is inside & outside, and in between all beings & non-beings.

We learned here that though **Bhakti**, the devotion of God, **Jnaan**, the perfect spiritual knowledge, and **Karm**, the action are very important steps in achieving **Yog,** but knowing right kind of works, doing them dutifully and dedicating them to God with whole hearted devotion is the most important to attain **Samagr Yog** of Gita. By unification of **Jnaan**, **Bhakti** and **Karm** in his current life, a practiser can elevate himself to the highest blissful status of **Purushottam**, who, at once is, the Supreme Master of spiritual calm of **Purush**, the individual soul, as well as of **Prakruti**, the creator of material world and cosmic activity. Until and unless he does it, his practice is incomplete and imperfect. Harivanshrai Bachchan feels God's presence (and necessity) in life in these words:

'कि हम तुम एक दूजे को नहीं पर्याप्त,
कोई तीसरा ही हाथ मेरा औ' तुम्हारा गहे ।'

(You and I alone are not sufficient to support each other; there is also the unknown third one who is holding the hands of us both)

I had talked about this synthesis of Gita at the beginning of chapter 2 **Saamkhya Yog,** and elsewhere.

Mundak Upanishad 3/1/1-3[12] describes the triad of Samsaar, Jeevaatmaa and Paramaatmaa in a highly ornamental and poetic simile of two birds sitting on a tree, in following three verses:

द्वा सुपर्णा सयुजा सखाया समानं वृक्षं परिषस्वजाते।
तयोरन्यः पिप्पलं स्वाद्वत्त्यनश्नन्नन्यो अभिचाकशीति॥ १ ॥

(Two golden plumaged birds (soul & Supreme Soul) live together as fast friends on the same Peepal tree. The first one is constantly engaged in consuming its supposedly delicious (but often bitter) fruits whereas the other simply looks on (pitying his friend eating those bitter fruits) but does not eat them himself (because He is eternally satisfied)}.

समाने वृक्षे पुरुषो निमग्नोऽनिशया शोचति मुह्यमानः।
जुष्टं यदा पश्यत्यन्यमीशमस्य महिमानमिति वीतशोकः॥ २ ॥

{Similarly, Purush, the individual soul, deluded by his own weakness (the attraction of fruits of his works), is sitting remorsefully (on the tree) but whenever he looks at the grandeur and bliss of contentment of the other bird, the Supreme Master also seated on the same tree, he is (partially) relieved from his grief.}

यदा पश्यः पश्यते रुक्मवर्णं कर्तारमीशं पुरुषं ब्रह्मयोनिम्।
तदा विद्वान् पुण्यपापे विधूय निरञ्जनः परमं साम्यमुपैति॥ ३ ॥

{That seer is wise who constantly beholds (in this way) Param Purush, the Creator, Lord, and progenitor of Brahmaa, radiating His golden brilliance all over. And he only is able to shake off the shackles of the results of his good and evil deeds; and attain complete oneness (Yog) with that impeccably perfect, Supreme Lord}

---

12 *Verses 1 & 2 appear in Shwetashwatar Upanishad 4/6 & 7; and verse 1 in Rigved 1/164/20 & Atharv Ved 9/14/20 also.*

This is the essence of **Vedaant** Philosophy. The first bird is **Purush**, the embodied individual soul of Gita, the wielder of own will, and the second is **Purushottam** or **Paramaatmaa**, the Supreme Soul. Both of them are dwelling on the same tree of **Prakruti** (or human body), described as **Peepal** by Gita from 15/1 to 4 but the first is attracted towards the fruits of the tree and enjoys the sweet fruits but is anguished on finding some of them bitter. Whenever the fruit is bitter, he moves closer to his friend, the second bird perched on a bough up on the same tree with great serenity, tranquility and glory as he is not attracted by the tree and its fruits; but his temptation forces him to resume eating the fruits once again. This cycle repeats umpteen times until, at last, the first bird decides to give up its futile search of fruits and approach the second bird to learn the secret of his bliss. Then, he finds at once that actually there never were two birds as he is merely a reflection, a mirage image of the second. Once he realizes this eternal truth, he attains the same serenity, tranquility and glory as of the second bird. He is like a solo chess player who plays the black piece in one move; and rotates the chess board 180 degrees in the next move to play with white piece with the same skill and expertise.

Moral: *Dropping our embodied soul's identity with the tree of Prakruti i.e. the body and mind, and identifying ourselves as a part separated from God due to own Karm resulting in cycles of birth and death; and reuniting ourselves with our origin is the path prescribed by Gita for liberation from distress of current and future lives. In the words of Vivekaanand, we need to 'Arise (from the sleep of delusion), and Awake (to Absolute Reality)'.*

Let us divide this chapter into three parts for the sake of understanding. Shloks 15/1-6 give a universal setting; shloks 15/7-15 place the individual person in his interior and exterior environment in the universe; and 15/16-20 finally instruct him to convert his individual effort into collaborative effort as per the supreme will of God to ensure universal good and welfare. This is the real unification of **Purush** with **Purushottam** seated within him. Neither **Karm,** the action with vehemently active & dynamic **Man** that seeks fruitive results, nor **Jnaan**, the light of the indifferent, impersonal, inactive ascetic who seeks own liberation, is the ideal of Gita for, one is immersed totally in **Kshar**, and the other dwells entirely in **Akshar.** Gita tells us to go beyond these two conflicting standards of humanity and seek reunion with **Purushottam** in order to transgress this conflict and resolve it into divine bliss. Aurobindo says:

'God is not only in silence but in action also. Neither of it is a reality or a falsehood in perpetual conflict & hostility to each other. They are the double terms of the divine manifestation'.

There is 1 simile, and 1 **Shree Bhagawaan Uvaach** in this chapter but no **Arjun Uvaach**.

ॐ तत्सदिति श्रीमद्भगवद्गीतासूपनिषत्सु ब्रह्मविद्यायां योगशास्त्रे श्रीकृष्णार्जुन संवादे पुरुषोत्तमयोगो नाम पञ्चदशोऽध्यायः ॥ १५ ॥

(In the name of God, the ultimate truth thus ends the fifteenth chapter named Purushottam Yog of Shreemad Bhagwad Gita, the best Upanishad, Brahm Vidyaa & Yog Shaastr, a dialogue between Shree Krishn and Arjun)

CHAPTER 16

DAIVAASUR SAMPAD VIBHAAG YOG

(We are mixtures of divine and devilish qualities. Let us purge out the devilish ones from our life and fill it with the divine.)

PREAMBLE & CONTEXT

God used *'Iti'* in 15/20 to convey, *'This is the end of revelation of the most esoteric secret knowledge of all Holy Scriptures to you by Me'*. why did He say so when there are still three more chapters containing 130 shloks balance for us to study in Gita? Let us try to get an answer as below:

When Arjun conveyed his final decision of not fighting to Krishn in 2/9, Krishn started preaching him from 2/11 onwards and promised in 4/3 to reveal **Rahasyam Uttamam**, the greatest secret to him. He stated in 4/33, *'All sacred actions finally culminate into Jnaan'*; ordered Arjun in 4/42 to, *'Use the sword of Jnaan to cut off the bondage of doubt and ignorance; and be situated in Yog'*; promised in 7/2 to, *'Tell Jnaan with Vijnaan without any omission after knowing which nothing else worth knowing shall remain'*. After explaining *'The distinction between Kshetrajn, the pure soul, and Kshetr, the lower nature of material world'* in chapter 13, He told in 14/1 to once again explain *'The ultimate of all kinds of knowledge by knowing which, great sages got liberated from this world and attained the ultimate spiritual realm'*. In the finale of His teaching,

He ultimately imparted top-secret knowledge of **Kshar** and **Akshar**, and established **Paramaatmaa** or **Purushottam** as the Supreme Master and lord in chapter 15. Hence, chapter 15 is truly *'Iti'* i.e. the end of **Jnaan** and **Vijnaan** taught by Krishn to Arjun in Gita.

Chapters 16, 17 & 18 now teach us to apply Gita's teachings in the most practical way so that we can transform our strife-torn lives into blissful existence. It is worth noting that, though *'Iti'* appeared in more than 60 shloks earlier, God shall use *'Iti'* hereafter only in 18/64 & 70 to reiterate what He taught earlier, with occasional references and reminders of the same. God stated in 9/12-13:

> *"People having vain hopes of fruition of useless activities, imprudent conscience and worthless knowledge, resort to demonic, fiendish characteristic nature; but great souls resort to My divine nature".*

Thus, He briefly mentioned two types of **Prakruti** or **Swabhaav** of people viz. **Aasuree** & **Daivee** there but He postponed explanation of this statement due to one or the other reason. He picks it up now and dedicates this chapter to elaborate what He meant by **Aasuree** and **Daivee Prakruti** there.

WHY CHAPTER 16 IS NAMED DAIVAASUR SAMPAD VIBHAAG YOG?

Legends of **Daivaasur Sangraam**[13], the conflicts and wars between two groups of people, **Devs**, the demigods and **Asurs**, the Titans & Demons, appear as one of the founding ideas of Rigved, the first Holy Book of humanity. In symbolism, we should understand them at society level as the endless strife that goes on in the world between two classes of people, **Devs**, the good ones who believe in giving, sharing and co-existence; and **Asurs**, the bad ones whose credo is *'Might is right'*. At an individual's mental and emotional levels, **Daivaasur Sangraam** depict clashes in thoughts, emotions, behavior, and at spiritual level, they represent conflicts between **Dharm** & **Adharm, Swaarth,** the self-interest and **Paramaarth**, the

---

13 *Avesta, the Holy book of Zoroastrianism, the religion of Paarasees, also narrates similar conflicts between right and wrong people.*

well-being of others as explained in *'Introduction'*. Gita dedicates this entire chapter to describe in detail the qualities treasured by **Devs**, the good, righteous people as **Daivee Sampadaa**, the divine wealth in 16/1-3; and of **Asurs**, the demonic, wicked, rascal people as **Aasuree Sampadaa**, the wealth dear to people of demonic nature from 16/4 to 18. The suffering and loss accrued to an individual possessing **Aasuree Sampadaa,** are described in 16/19-23 with an advice to do works prescribed and approved by Scriptures. Hence, the title **Daivaasur Sampad Vibhaag Yog** of this chapter is fully justified.

౭౿౨

God describes 26 divine qualities.

(16/1, 2 & 3)

श्रीभगवानुवाच
अभयं सत्त्वसंशुद्धिर्ज्ञानयोगव्यवस्थितिः ।
दानं दमश्च यज्ञश्च स्वाध्यायस्तप आर्जवम् ॥१६/१॥
अहिंसा सत्यमक्रोधस्त्यागः शान्तिरपैशुनम् ।
दया भूतेष्वलोलुप्त्वं मार्दवं ह्रीरचापलम् ॥१६/२॥
तेजः क्षमा धृतिः शौचमद्रोहो नातिमानिता ।
भवन्ति संपदं दैवीमभिजातस्य भारत ॥१६/३॥

Shree Bhagawaan Uvaach
Abhayam sattvasanshuddhirjnaanayogavyavasthiti: I
Daanam damashch yajnashch swaadhyaayastap aarjavam II
(16/1)
Ahimsaa satyamakrodhastyaag: shaantirapaishunam I
Dayaa bhooteshvaloluptvam maardavam hreerachaapalam II
(16/2)
Tej: kshamaa dhruti: shauchamadroho naatimaanitaa I
Bhavanti sampadam daiveemabhijaatasya Bhaarat II (16/3)

Abhayam (fearlessness) Sattv Sanshuddhi: (purification of self with Sattv) Jnaan Yog Vyavasthiti: (positioning self in pursuance of

Jnaan Yog)I Daanam (donating, giving in charity) Dam: (subduing, restraining Indriys from their Vishays) Ch (and) Yajn: (sacrificial rites & actions as per Dharm) Ch (and) Swaadhyaay: (study of self & own conduct, study of scriptures) Tap: (purification of self by penance & ascetic practices) Aarjavam (simplicity, uprightness)II (16/1)

Ahimsaa (non-violence) Satyam (truthfulness) Akrodh: (total absence of anger) Tyaag: (renunciation of material things & self-interest) Shaanti: (tranquility, peace) Apaishunam (aversion to slandering, tale bearing)I Dayaa (compassion, kindness) Bhooteshu (in all beings) Aloluptvam (freedom from greed, avarice) Maardavam (tenderness, gentleness, flexibility) Hree: (modesty, decency) Achaapalam (steadfastness, determination)II (16/2)

Tej: (vigor, energy) Kshamaa (forgiveness, pardon) Dhruti (fortitude, steadfastness, resoluteness, perseverance): Shaucham (cleanliness, purity) Adroh: (absence of rancor, ill-will, hostility, enmity) N Atimaanitaa (freedom from unjustifiable pride, conceit; modest, humble)I Bhavanti (are) Sampadam (wealth, property) Daiveem (divine, transcendental) Abhijaatasya (innate, inborn) Bhaarat (Arjun, descendent of king Bharat)II (16/3)

God said:

"Fearlessness, purification of self by righteousness, positioning self in pursuance of perfect knowledge, donating for charity, subduing & control of Indriys & their Vishays, engaging in sacrificial & selfless activities, study & introspection of self & own conduct, and of scriptures like Veds, purification of self by penance & ascetic practices and simplicity, (16/1)

Nonviolence, truthfulness, absence of anger, renunciation of material things & self-interest; tranquility, aversion to slandering, compassion for all beings, freedom from avarice, tenderness & flexibility, modesty and steadfastness, (16/2)

Vigor, forgiveness, fortitude, cleanliness & purity, absence of rancor & hostility, and freedom from conceit are innate qualities of a person endowed with Daivee Sampadaa, the divine wealth O Bhaarat (Arjun)! (16/3)

Towards the end of chapter 15, God instructed us to know Him in entirety as **Purushottam**. Now, He starts describing 26 virtuous qualities in three shloks that a practiser must develop to know Him.

Abhay, the freedom from fear, is the first divine virtue. Once a practiser consigns all his worries to God's will and relies totally on Him, he treats **Abhay** and **Bhay** as two sides of the same coin. We are always free to interpret FEAR as *'Face Everything And Rise'* or *'Forget Everything And Run'*. Swami Vivekaanand gave a clarion call to Indian youth:

'Awake, Arise and Charge'.

About **Bhay** & **Abhay,** he says:

'It is fear that is the greatest cause of misery in the world. It is fear that is the greatest of all superstitions. It is fear that is the cause of our woes, and it is fearlessness that brings heaven even in a moment'.

The choice is ours. Jay, the hero, of film Sholay kept a coin in his pocket with heads on both sides. Though he used to toss it before his friend Veeru for deciding on crucial matters, he always chose head so that the toss concurred with what he wished to do. Jalaaluddin Rumi says:

'Move within, but not the way fear makes you move'.

Fearlessness is the key to move blissfully in the world.

Root cause of fear is **Jijeevishaa**, the basic instinct of survival, the desire to continue living and emerging victorious in every situation. Non-acceptance of uncertainty is fear. The moment we accept and decide to face that uncertainty, the fear transforms into a fearless adventure. Our superstitions and blind faith are founded always on fear when we feel weak; but if the same fear can lead us to cruelty if it is enjoined by might and false pride. We can develop **Abhay** by boldly staring right in the face of Bhay and stride through the precarious situation we are in with courage. We can then joyfully say to others and ourselves:

'I have lived through this horrific situation; and I can definitely take on the next uglier thing that may come along in my life'.

Saahir empowers such fearless persons in film *Sone ki Chidiya*:

रात भर का है मेहमाँ अँधेरा, किसके रोके रुका है सवेरा ।
रात जितनी ही संगीन होगी, सुबह उतनी ही रंगीन होगी,
ग़म न कर गर है बादल घनेरा, किसके रोके रुका है सवेरा ॥

(Darkness is a nocturnal visitor who shall flee away soon because no one can stop dawn from breaking. Don't be stricken with grief if the cloud is dense & dark now, for the morning that arrives after a stony dark night is always the most colorful. Can anyone stop that morning from happening?)

In a storm in the sea, that man is the wisest who prays to God not for the safety from the danger of drowning but for the strength to brave it. A lion is neither as big as an elephant, nor tall like a giraffe, nor fast like a cheetah, nor clever like a fox, nor is he agile as a monkey, but it is the king of the jungle because of fearlessness, self-confidence, and prowess. T S Eliot says:

'Only those who risk going too far can possibly find out how far one can go'.

A devotee, who entrusts his entire **Yog Kshem** to God (refer to 9/22), need not be afraid of something or someone because omnipotent God has taken the responsibility of looking after his safety, security and well-being. A Yogee knows that creation, destruction re-creation are temporary as parts of God's will & overall plan for greater happiness of righteous people; and even if he has to suffer for sometime in that process, he is actually contributing to fulfill His mission pronounced in 4/7-8. History teaches us that London, Hiroshima and Bhuj emerged as better cities out of disastrous ruin. A practiser may choose to move from **Bhay** to **Nirbhay** first but his ultimate goal is **Abhay** as **Nirbhay** smacks of **Dussaahas**, an act of proud, immature defiance of imminent danger, or overpowering others. Bertrand Russell says:

'Neither a man nor a group nor a nation can be trusted to act humanely or to think sanely under the influence of a great fear'.

Refer to 2/39-40, and 4/10 for '*Some additional thoughts on Bhay, the fear*' besides explanations in 2/56, 3/35, 5/28, 10/4, 12/15, 18/8, 30 & 35.

Sattv Sanshuddhi, the cleansing, purification of self by situating in the mode of righteousness, truth, goodness and morality, is the second gem in the treasure of divine virtues. God cautioned a practiser in chapter 14 to not remain stuck up in **Sattv** (or any other **Gun**, the mode of nature), but to move further to the state of **Gunaateet**. Sattv is a means, not an end, like a cake of soap. We use it to clean our body, but wash it off from the body once it is clean. It is like the intermediate landing of a staircase where we can stop only for a respite before climbing further to our destination.

We can interpret **Jnaan Yog Vyavasthiti** in two ways. The obvious one means well situated in **Jnaan Yog**, the path of knowledge; and it matches with the declaration in 4/33, '*All sacred actions culminate into Jnaan*'. However, the words **Jnaan** and **Yog** read separately, also denote **Jnaan Yog** and **Karm Yog** respectively (Recall that Arjun used **Yog** for **Karm Yog** in 5/1). In 3/3, we have heard God declaring two kinds of **Nishthaa**, the reverential faiths and allegiances namely **Jnaan Yog,** the path of perfect knowledge, and **Karm Yog,** the path of selfless activities. Then, He went on meticulously to explain them and suggested various methods like going to a **Tattv Darshee** & **Jnaanee** (4/34), meditation (chapter 6), **Abhyaas Yog** (6/35 & 8/8), being in the company of right people, **Aachaaryopaasanam** (13/7), study of scriptures (16/23 & 24), **Swaadhyaay**, learning by introspection and reflection (here & 17/15) etc. to practise them. Keeping this background in mind, we can now understand **Jnaan Yog Vyavasthiti** as the virtue of positioning self in pursuance of anyone of the two prescribed paths of **Jnaan** or **Karm,** without envying the other, to attain ultimate knowledge & unite with **Purushottam**, the Supreme Soul.

Cautions:

1. *A Jnaan Yogee should never envy or criticize a Karm Yogee; and similarly a Karm Yogee should never be envious or critic of Jnaan Yogee*

276 • GITA for GEN A to Z - Vol III

2. *A practiser of Yog as well as an accomplished Yogee should never stop learning. He must always be Jnaan Yog Vyavasthit. The moment he thinks he has known everything, he becomes like a deadwood, fit only for burning.*

Daan: It is the virtue of donating, granting, giving, providing, and supporting the needy and deprived people. All world religions attach great importance to this quality because their founders found vast majority of people dying due to hunger, thirst, and disease, and suffering due to lack of clothing and shelter. It is a great tragedy and imbalance created ironically by men themselves in modern world that, though the resources are available in plenty, the scenario of deprivation of the masses has not changed much.

Shelley valued charity above faith as she wrote:

"Ah! What a divine religion might be found out if charity were really made the principle of it instead of faith."

Mahaabhaarat narrates the story of four princes who wished to attain heaven because of their acts of outstanding charity:

"Four princes, famous for charity, once set forth for heaven. They met Naarad on the way and asked him who, among them, would be lucky to reach heaven. Naarad said, 'I accompanied the first prince once in his chariot. When we came across some cows grazing in the pastures, he boastfully told me that all those cows actually belonged to him, and he had donated them to a Braahman. I disqualify for his boast and wrong claim on donated cows'. Naarad narrated his experience with second prince saying, 'I travelled with him also once in his chariot. On the way, we met a Braahman who insisted on him to give a horse immediately. Since the prince, well known for charity, could not refuse, he reluctantly gave him the only horse yoked in the chariot, commenting it was highly deplorable for a Braahman to take away his only horse and force him to pull the chariot himself. His reluctance and sarcasm disqualify him for heaven'. Then, he talked about third price, 'Once, when I visited his court, he promised me to give all of his cows in charity, but did not fulfill it immediately. Thereafter, every time I reminded him of his promise his cunning reply was that the cows were already mine and he was only their

caretaker. His cunningness and pretense disqualify him for heaven'. Naarad turned to fourth prince now and declared him as the only one fit to enter heaven. He explained it thus, 'Once when I visited him, I asked him to keep food ready for me by the time I return after bathing in the nearby river. I also imposed the condition that he must cook the food with his own hands; and must not attend to any other work before feeding me. The prince gladly did as told and waited for me but when his gasping servants reported that I was setting his palace on fire, he immediately rushed to me carrying the food in his hands, and requested me to first accept the food prepared by him and satisfy my hunger; and then resume burning his palace. He merits entering heaven due to his whole hearted undivided, selfless charity'. The charity of first three princes was shadowed with their Raajasik & Taamasik natures."

We shall learn more about **Daan** in 17/20-22.

Dam: We had understood it in 10/4 as the act of restraint and control of self by subduing **Indriys** & their **Vishays** from behaving as they like. We can achieve it by cessation of mental thoughts, intentions and propositions; and dropping physical activities that lead to gratification of demands and desires of **Indriys**.

Yajn: It is defined as pious, meritorious and righteous activities performed selflessly while remaining situated in **Dharm**. Though it literally also means sacrificial rites & rituals performed as per procedures laid down in Smaartaa or other scriptures, this meaning is of little significance in the context of our study of Gita albeit, some benefits like purifying environment and pleasing some demigods are likely to accrue. Refer to *'Some additional thoughts on Yajn'* in 3/14-15, and 4/42.

Swaadhyaay: Swa means self. We learnt about it in 4/28 as a method of acquiring perfect spiritual knowledge contained in **Veds** and other scriptures, and developing own self & conduct by introspection.

Tap: It is purification of self by penance & ascetic practices. We shall learn more about Tap in *'What is Tap.....'* after 17/19.

278 • GITA for GEN A to Z - Vol III

Aarjav: It was explained in 13/7 as the quality of simplicity, clarity, straightforwardness, uprightness, uprightness, directness & candour that relieves us from the evils of deceit, trickery, dissembling, hypocrisy, fraud, pretence, stratagem and faultfinding. God included **Aarjav** as an important quality of **Jnaanee** there. He includes it now in the divine wealth; then in **Shaareerik Tap**, the physical penance in 17/14; and finally describes it as **Swabhaav**, the characteristic nature of a **Braahman** in 18/42. We shall learn more about it in those places as well. A person possessing the quality of **Aarjav**, the rectitude never abandons morally correct behaviour even if subjected to the most severe situations because he believes in *'Plain living and high thinking'*.

SOME ADDITIONAL THOUGHTS ON AARJAVAM, THE SIMPLICITY

It is the virtue which liberates and declutters us from complications, confusions and doubts arising out of evils like deceit, fraud, dissembling. It is the quality of rectitude, simplicity, directness, candidness, uprightness, straightforwardness that allows us to admit what we are and to enjoy what we have as it frees us from the entanglement of what we conceal & hide from others, and what we possess in excess of our need. The picture of Mahatma Gandhi that always comes to our mind is not the one in the sophisticated attire of a barrister, but clad simply with a half loincloth holding a staff in hand. Leonardo da Vinci says:

'Simplicity is the ultimate sophistication'.

Mahatma Gandhi was undoubtedly the most sophisticated man among all participants in the Round Table Conference held in London in September, December 1931. **Aparigrah** (4/21 & 6/10) is the key to enter the house of simplicity. The biggest impediment we face in practising **Aarjavam** is lack of awareness about purpose and priorities in life. What we really need is to live a fulfilled, complete, value based life. Let us drop imaginary threats posed by not having something and insecurity from unknown future and our own created enemies.

Moral: *We should begin with removal of the mess from our worktable, wardrobe, kitchen, bathroom, office, home, car, and above all from mind. A kinked arrow can never hit the target; a cacophony cannot provide the melody of a symphony; and running desperately in maize leads us nowhere.*

Ahimsaa: It means observance and practice by a person of non-violence in all phases of life including physical, mental, psychic and spiritual. Mahatma Gandhi attached highest importance to **Ahimsaa** in his personal as well as public life. A reporter once asked him what would be his choice if he had to choose between freedom of India and Ahimsaa; his immediate response was, **Ahimsaa**. He did not hesitate to withdraw his non-cooperation movement against the wish of other congress leaders on hearing about a violent incident committed by **Satyaagrahees** in Chauri chaura, Bihar. Unlike contemporary revolutionaries, he did not see the British as enemies but questioned their right to rule India. He believed:

'Non-violence is the greatest force at the disposal of mankind. It is mightier than the mightiest weapon of destruction devised by the ingenuity of man'.

Mahaaveer places **Ahimsaa** at the top of all virtues when he says:

'If you kill someone it is yourself you kill; if you overpower someone it is yourself you overpower; if you torment someone it is yourself you torment; and if you harm someone it is yourself you harm'.

Shreemad Raaj Chandr establishes supremacy of **Ahimsaa** over **Himsaa** with following simple example:

'As a cloth soaked in blood can be cleaned only with water, not with blood, similarly violence can be wiped out only by non-violence, not by violence'.

It is unfortunate in today's world that *'Kill or be killed'* is displacing the principle of *'Live and let live'* taught by almost all religions of the world. We discussed **Ahimsaa** in detail in 13/7 also earlier as an important virtue of a **Jnaanee**.

Satya: Gita talked of **Satya** for the first time in 10/4 as the meritorious virtue of a **Jnaanee**. **Asatya**, the lie, falsehood and untruth is opposite of **Satya**. We resort to telling lies when afraid, afraid of what we don't know, afraid of what others will think about us, and afraid of the truth that would surely be found out one day, but every time we tell a lie, our fear grows stronger. Nevertheless, let us understood it well that Satya is not just the opposite of **Asatya**, but the ultimate, absolute, immutable truth of **Sat**, the eternal existence. Gita applies it at spiritual level to its valued concepts of **Aatmaa**, the soul, **Paramaatmaa**, the Supreme Soul, and **Jnaan**, the perfect knowledge of their relationship; and at the social level of human behavior, it shall teach us in 17/15 to speak the truth. Truth is the greatest verifier and purifier of existence of everything. Manu Smruti says:

सत्यपूताम् वदेद्वाचम् मन:पूतम् समाचरेत् ।

(Speak only that which has been purified by truth and do only that which is purified by conscience.)

My father often quoted a couplet, which reminds us of two great kings, Harishchandr and Vikramaaditya, the icons of **Satya** in personified form:

सत मत छोड़ो हे नरा सत छोड़ियाँ पत जाय,
सत की बाँधी लक्ष्मी फेर मिलेगी आय.

(O men! Do not abandon truth because, if you do, your honor shall abandon you. And if you are firm in truth, Lakshmee, the goddess of all wealth shall return to you as it is bonded with truth.)

Kabeer considers truth as the best form of penance:

सांच बराबर तप नहीं झूठ बराबर पाप ।
जाके हिरदे सांच है ता हिरदै हरि आप ॥

(There is no penance greater than truth, and no evil greater than falsehood. God dwells in those hearts, which are full of truth)

Maithilee Sharan Gupt writes in Saaket:

सत्य से ही स्थित है संसार, सत्य है सब धर्मों का सार ।

(Whole world rests on truth; truth is the essence of all religions.)

Absolute truth can be never hidden by false principles of untruth. It is like expecting flowers made of paper to emit fragrance. A lie needs hundred more lies but only one truth exposes the farce behind all of them in the end. Take the example of a centuries old dispute between Muslims and Hindus about the existence of a temple of Lord Raam at the site of Baabaree structure in Ayodhyaa. The dispute was put to rest once for all after The Archeological Survey of India discovered, among many other things, an 11th century stone tableau inside a thick masonry wall. The inscription on it confirmed beyond any doubt:

'A magnificent temple of Lord Raam did exist there before, and its glory has been restored now (in 11th century)'.

Thus, the ultimate truth emerged from the long buried foundation walls of the structure as if God Himself appeared once again to reveal the truth as Nrusingh did by tearing a stone pillar apart to reveal truth and re-establish its eternal rule.

Clarification: *Asatya, a lie, if spoken for a good cause, is Satya in reality. Though Asatya is the antonym of Satya, it becomes 'A Satya' if spoken for a meritorious & virtuous cause.*

I am reminded of film *Bawarchi*[14] here:

'Rajesh Khanna works as a cook named Raghu in a joint family whose every member was quarrelsome, squabbling, and self-centered. He skillfully fabricates and speaks lies to each member so that he/she believe how other members loved and praised him/her. This way, he succeeds in uniting them into a happy family. In the climax, when he learns that the young Krishnaa cannot marry her lover because of the prejudice of stubborn family elders against him, he even fakes a drama. He steals a box of jewelry, gives it

---

14 *Film Bawarchi was a Hindi remake of Bengali film 'Galpa Holeo Satyi' literally meaning 'The gossip becomes the truth'.*

to her lover. As instructed by Raghu, the boy appears before the family with the box claiming that he recovered it from fleeing Raghu. Stunned by this turn of events, the family members agree for the marriage of the boy with Krishnaa. Meanwhile, Krishnaa sees Raghu standing outside the house and asks him why he did all this. An emotional Raghu then tells the truth that he was professor Prabhakar, but when he saw many families like theirs' on the brink of breaking up, he assumed the false name of Raghu, and decided to work as a household servant with a mission to bring happiness in those families.'

SOME ADDITIONAL THOUGHTS ON AHIMSAA AND SATYA

Non-violence and truth are complimentary to each other. One practised without the other is as useless as wearing ornaments without clothes. Mahatma Gandhi says, *'My religion is based on truth & non-violence. Truth is my God. Non-violence is the means to realize Him'.* Dharm Vyaadh, a meat seller, preaches **Braahman** Kaushik thus in Mahaabhaarat 3/207/74:

अहिंसा सत्यवचनम् सर्वभूतहितम् परम् ।
अहिंसा परमो धर्मः स च सत्ये प्रतिष्ठितः ॥
सत्ये कृत्वा प्रतिष्ठाम् तु प्रवर्तन्ते प्रवृत्तयः॥।

(Non-violence and speaking truth ensure ultimate well-being of all living beings. Non-violence is the greatest Dharm only if situated in truth. Noble people consider truth only before initiating any work)

Akrodh: It means total absence of **Krodh**, the anger, rage, wrath, and resentment. We had discussed **Krodh** in 2/62 & 63, and 4/10 earlier. Krodh is like champagne filled with pressure in a corked bottle. The moment someone presses its cork open, it gushes and spills out all around; Akrodh, on the other hand, is like mineral water in a bottle that we can open and use as per our need and discretion, and close it again. Elizabeth Kenny says:

'He, who angers you, conquers you'.

No one can shake hands with someone with a clenched fist. An inspiring anecdote from the life of Eknaath is worth quoting here to explain **Akrodh**:

"An adversary of Eknaath decided to teach him a lesson. His house was located on the street through which Eknaath used to go to take daily bath in the holy river Godavari. Burning with jealousy, one day he sat in the balcony of his house and spitted on Eknaath returning after bath. Eknaath did not even look above, and went back to the river for a re-bath. The adversary again spat on him on his return, and Eknaath went again to the river for bath. This went on for a number of times until the fellow felt exhausted and ashamed. At last, he went down, asked pardon from Eknaath, and wanted to know why he was not angry with him. Eknaath replied serenely, 'Brother, I have no reason to be angry on you. In fact, I am very much indebted to you for giving me an opportunity of taking bath 108 times in sacred Godavari on this auspicious day of Ekaadashee, the eleventh moon. You are my true well wisher and friend".

Tyaag: It is a consciously performed act of abandoning, giving up, renouncing, dismissing, leaving, relinquishing, discarding, disregarding or getting rid of someone or something. Applying it to spirituality and the doctrine of Karm, we learnt it as total absence of interest and belongingness in the fruits of our actions in 12/11. Though God spoke of **Tyaag** at numerous places in Gita till now, He shall deal with it in detail in chapter 18 when Arjun would pose his last question in 18/1 to know:

'The fundamental difference between Sannyaas, the asceticism and Tyaag, the order of leading life by giving up'.

Shaanti: It means tranquility, calmness, quiet, peace of mind and soul. We must have understood it by now that the main objective of Gita is to let a person attain imperturbable **Shaanti** in his life. We had dealt with it in 2/66, and many shloks like 2/70, 2/71, 4/39, 5/12, 5/29 etc.

Apaishun: It is the divine quality of not indulging in slandering, tale bearing, and/or passing on secrets, faults and weaknesses of someone to others, particularly in his absence. As a derivative of

Pashu, an animal, we can understand it also as not behaving in a treacherous, villainous, wicked manner like an animal. Implicating someone in false, concocted complaints to harm him, to extract undue benefits for self, to satisfy own ego, or to blab secrets by indiscrete talk are some other forms of **Paishun** a practiser must avoid. Read following amusing anecdote to understand **Apaishun**:

"A king had two horn shaped growths in his head. His barber knew this secret and felt very uneasy due to Paishun, the habit of disclosing others' secrets to someone. When he could not control him any longer, one day he went into deep forest and shouted, 'The king has two horns on his head, but don't tell anybody' and returned fully relieved now to his house. After few months, when a musician was trying to play on a newly acquired Saarangee, a kind of violin in the royal court, the sound it emitted was, 'The king has two horns on his head, but don't tell anybody'. Hearing this, the Tabalaa player, who accompanied the violinist, immediately responded on his Tabalaa, 'Who told you, who told you'? The Saarangee replied promptly, 'King's barber told me but don't tell anybody'. On inquiry, it turned out that the Saarangee was made out of the wood, cut by a woodcutter from a tree in the same forest where the barber had blabbed the king's secret. The wood absorbed the sound in it and was impatient to reveal it at the first opportunity."

A practiser should never waste his time and effort in such activities and concentrate only on introspection and spiritual reflection like a **Muni** besides rendering selfless service to benefit others.

Dayaa Bhooteshu: It means compassion, kindness and mercy towards all living beings. We had discussed in 1/31 that though Arjun was overwhelmed with compassion but his compassion was not global as it was based on his infatuation and concern limited to his relatives and friends only. God described his dearest devotee as **Karun,** a compassionate person in 12/13. **Karunaa** or **Dayaa** is an essential virtue of a **Bhakt**.

SOME ADDITIONAL THOUGHTS ON DAYAA BHOOTESHU, THE COMPASSION FOR ALL

Dayaa, and its synonym **Karunaa,** is one of the topmost virtues in Indic tradition and form an undisputed founding principle of all religions of Indian origin like Hinduism, Jainism, Buddhism, and Sikhism. It has been held in very high esteem by all schools of thought including **Sufism** which flourished well in India and acted as a catalyst in forging mutual understanding & co-existence among followers of different faiths. **Dayaa** or **Karunaa** is heartfelt compassion and genuine concern for the sufferings and misfortunes of others, and making sincere, selfless efforts to alleviate them. A similar word often used to define **Dayaa** or **Karunaa** is pity but, in my opinion, it evokes a passive and sympathetic state of mind where one wants to remove suffering of others but for self-aggrandizement. On the other hand, compassion calls for an active empathy, participation and sharing of pain in the process of emancipation of suffering of others. Kindness is a bit nearer to compassion than pity. In Buddhism, **Karunaa** is the principal virtue among its four virtues; the remaining three are **Muditaa,** the bliss, **Maitree**, the friendship and **Upekshaa**, the indifference.

Vedic principle, *'I am Brahm, and so are you'* i.e. seeing the Supreme Being in everybody, elevates compassion to a higher plane where a compassionate person becomes totally free from ego by not differentiating between his own existence and that of others. He regards both, his own self and of others as **Brahm**. Duality of a sufferer and a deliverer is completely vanished at this plane, as there is no one delivering or obliging the other. An act of compassion then becomes a spontaneous, natural act for him, not of mere self-satisfaction. Compassion is a necessity for someone wanting to elevate his soul, not a luxury to adorn. Shankaraachaarya says, *'Even gods offer their salutations to the one whose main virtue is Dayaa'*. He elaborated **Dayaa** as kindness towards the miserable and friendship with the good people. Dalai Lama advises:

'If you want others to be happy, practice compassion. If you want to be happy yourself practice compassion'.

In **Bhakti Maarg**, the path of devotion of Hinduism, God is named **Dayaa Saagar, Karunaa Saagar, Dayaa Nidhi, Karunaa Nidhi, Dayaa Nidhaan, Karunaa Nidhaan** etc. all of which point towards God as the ocean, the inexhaustible store, the abode of compassion. Arthur Schopenhauer extends compassion to the animal world too:

'The assumption that animals are without rights and the
illusion, that our treatment of them has no moral significance,
is a positively outrageous example of crudity and barbarity.
Universal compassion is the only guarantee of morality'.

Shakespeare sees mercy as an attribute to God in his play *'The Merchant of Venice'*.

"The quality of mercy"

(Part of celebrated speech by Portia in Venetian court of justice)

The quality of mercy is not strain'd,

It droppeth as the gentle rain from heaven

Upon the place beneath: it is twice blest;

It blesseth him that gives and him that takes:

Tis mightiest in the mightiest:

But mercy is above this sceptred sway;

It is enthroned in the hearts of kings,

It is an attribute to God himself;

We do pray for mercy;

And that same prayer doth teach us all to render

The deeds of mercy.

Peace alludes them whose hearts are devoid of compassionate emotions. They are like volcanoes spitting lava everywhere.

Aloluptv: It means total absence of **Lobh**, the lust, greed, avarice, temptation and covetousness. Let us recall 1/38 where **Arjun** labeled **Kauravs** as **Lobh Upahat Chetas** i.e. people whose conscience was struck with **Lobh**, the intense desire to acquire, by hook or crook, what was not theirs. Please see explanations under 1/38-39. Ishaavaasya Upanishad tells in Mantr 1, *'Maa Grudh: Kasya Swid Dhanam'* i.e. *'Don't be rapacious ever because wealth belongs to nobody forever'*. All of us must have heard the Greek Mythological story of a greedy king named Midas and his golden touch. Once God was pleased with him and blessed him, upon his request, with the power of converting anything he touches into gold. The result was that he could not attend to his daily routine like eating, drinking, bathing, putting on clothes etc. because as soon as he touched something it turned into gold. In the climax, when he tried to embrace his daughter who he loved very much, she also became a statue of gold. He cried, repented for his avarice and asked God to withdraw his power, and restore all things to normal state. God took mercy on him and fulfilled his request. Midas hugged his daughter in full happiness and decided to share his great fortune with his people from then onwards.

Maardav: It is the quality of suppleness, affability, adjustability, tenderness, flexibility, softness and gentleness. Its closest equivalent word is लोच in Hindi. For example, wheat flour, when kneaded with water, acquires the quality of लोच making it easy for us to roll Chapaatee, Pooree etc. from it; लोच in clay enables a potter to make beautiful earthenware from it. As gentleness, it resembles the virtue of **Nirahamkaar**, the lack of **Ahamkaar**, the false egoism and pride as explained in 2/71 & 12/13. *'Gently does it'* is the motto. Refer to 7/4 & 5 to recapitulate what **Ahamkaar** is. **Maardav** is similar to **Vinay**, the modesty, humility and gentleness (5/18). **Maardav,** as flexibility, is very close to the doctrine of **Anekaant Vaad** or **Syaad Vaad,** the acceptance of many-sidedness of a thing or thought or situation. It is religious pluralism & inclusiveness without insisting on own point of view. It teaches a practiser to develop intellectual tolerance and respect towards another's point of view, and to reject fanaticism, even if his point of view is correct. When Voltaire came to know that, his followers condemned and burnt on streets a book he did not like, his immediate reaction was:

'I disapprove of what you (the writer) say, but I will defend to the death your right to say it'.

Such person knows that absolute truth can be never realized by sticking to a single point of view because an individual, an object, or a situation is multidimensional; and it should be explored from innumerable angles, some of which may reveal the absolute truth. A Yogee may appear to be rough and hard like the crust of earth but the quality of **Maardav**, the tenderness within him lets a small seed sprout through its crust. Remember age-old sayings:

'Strong, stormy wind uproots big trees, but causes no harm to a tender blade of grass that bows to it'.

'Tough metals like steel have to be heated and melted to mould them into desired shape; but flexible metals like silver and copper can be easily formed into desired shapes without any heat treatment'.

'That man is the wisest who admits that he knows nothing'.

Moral: We should not start flying in air and hopping from one flower to other like a butterfly as soon as we get wings forgetting that we were a caterpillar earlier that crawled out of its shell with great difficulty.

Hree: Also called लज्जा (**Lajjaa**) in Hindi, it is the virtue of modesty, decency, sense of honor, and the feeling of shame or repentance for some wrong done knowingly or unknowingly. Legends describe **Hree** as the wife of **Dharm**, symbolizing that practising **Dharm** is incomplete if not accompanied by his consort **Hree**, the modesty. 'Penance and Reconciliation' (commonly called Confession) is one of the seven sacraments of Catholic Church, in which the faithful obtain absolution for the sins committed by them. Gods revere Mother Goddess thus in Durgaa Sapt Shatee from 5/44 to 46:

'या देवी सर्वभूतेषु लज्जारूपेण संस्थिता
नमस्तस्यै ॥ नमस्तस्यै ॥ नमस्तस्यै ॥ नमो नम: ॥'

(We bow to the Mother Goddess who situates appropriately as Lajjaa, the modesty in every living being. We bow to thee, we bow to thee, and we bow to thee again and again.)

Achaapalam: It is the opposite of **Chapalataa** (explained as **Chanchalataa** in 6/26, 33 & 34 as fickle, volatile, flirtatious nature of **Man** because of inconstancy, unsteadiness, and lack of firmness in its behaviour. Scriptures describe **Lakshmee**, the goddess of wealth, and the lightning as **Chapalaa**, that are always inconstant and flirtatious. **Achaapalam** therefore is the virtue of constancy, firmness, steadfastness, and resoluteness, and of not being fickle, flirtatious and moody.

Tej: we have already understood **Tej** as vigor, energy, brilliance, splendor, and effulgence i.e. extremely dazzling, stunning brightness. Common people are awe-struck and stunned when they observe this divine virtue in a person. Wicked people also are found to give up their wickedness sometimes on coming in contact with a **Tejaswee**, an extremely effulgent person as Vaalmeeki did on meeting Naarad. Gita attributes this quality to saints, **Mahatma**, and to sun and God.

Kshamaa: It was explained as forgiveness, pardon, absolution in 10/4 & 34, and 12/13. In a broader sense, it encompasses overlooking, absolving, condoning, excusing someone for his mistake. Please refer to explanations under 12/13-14 along with some additional thoughts given below:

SOME ADDITIONAL THOUGHTS ON KSHAMAA, THE FORGIVENESS

Kshamaa, the divine virtue of forgiveness means letting go of hard feelings like anger, sadness, frustration, annoyance caused by someone else's mistake either knowingly or unknowingly by overlooking or pardoning them. Recognizing that no one is perfect, and *'To err is human'* is the basic step of not getting upset initially, or not staying upset any longer for the wrong behaviour meted to us by others. Saying *'That's okay'* when someone apologizes for his behaviour helps us in two ways: it relieves him of guilt feeling for his misbehavior, and us from the hurt. Thus, both are poised immediately to move ahead and do more important, constructive things jointly once again. He who cannot forgive someone destroys the bridge of relationship that was very important and valuable for him earlier. By forgiving someone, we not only wipe out the scar of some unpleasant past incident with him, we also build a strong future for both of us. God rewards with peace of mind to him who forgives and forgets past things. Philosophically speaking, we are not doing any favor to someone by exonerating him for his guilt, but to ourselves so that we can move forward in life. **Kshamaa** helps us in two ways to move forward: first, it wins back the friendship with the offender, and second, it teaches us to be cautious in future while dealing with him. Refusing to forgive someone is equivalent to taking poison ourselves and expecting him to die. Vidur Neeti says:

'Kshamaa acts like enchantment. What can't be achieved by Kshamaa? Even wicked persons cannot harm him who wields the sword of Peace (or Kshamaa).'

Kshamaa is a great virtue and strength, not weakness of the pardoner. In fact, a weak person has no *locus standi* to pardon a strong offender. Mahatma Gandhi says:

'The weak can never forgive. Forgiveness is the attribute of the strong'.

Scriptures glorify the greatness of **Kshamaa** of sandalwood which imparts its fragrance even to the blade of the axe that cuts it; and of flowers like **Champaa** (plumeria) that leave their fragrance on the feet that trample upon them. Raheem refers to a legend to prove this point in his couplet:

क्षमा बड़न को चाहिए, छोटन को उत्पात ।
का रहीम हरि को घट्यो, जो भृगु मारी लात ॥

(Kshamaa is a virtue that befits great people because they always pardon the mischief of lesser ones. Raheem says the greatness of Lord Vishnu was not at all diminished when Bhrugu kicked[15] Him).

---

15 *Lord Vishnu was lying with eyes closed in divine bliss and did not notice arrival of Bhrugu, but Bhrugu took it as an insult because He did not get up in his welcome. Enraged with anger, he kicked Him very hard on His chest. Alarmed Vishnu immediately got up, pressed the foot of Bhrugu*

Let me illustrate **Kshamaa** with the example of a **Saadhu** and a trader:

"A Saadhu lived in his Aashram by begging alms and a trader lived nearby. Many people used to visit Aashram with gifts and to offer voluntary service, which Saadhu politely declined to accept saying that he is self-sufficient. The trader wondered why nobody offers gifts to him though he supplied them grains and other provisions they needed; and go to Saadhu with gifts though he doesn't need anything. His jealousy with Saadhu grew so much that he set his Aashram on fire one night; but while returning he noticed that Saadhu had seen him doing it. Villagers rushed immediately to the scene, extinguished the fire and asked Saadhu whether he had seen the culprit but his reply was, 'No'. When the farmer came to know of the forgiveness of Saadhu, he went and fell to his feet repenting for his misdeed. Saadhu however, assured him lovingly, 'Don't worry! No harm can come to you till I am here. Forget the incident and be calm. The Aashram anyway needed urgent repairs, and your act accelerated it."

The other aspect related to **Kshamaa** is the virtue of asking pardon when we ourselves hurt someone's feelings. All of us know that it needs great courage to admit our fault and sincerely ask pardon for it with purity of heart because our false ego comes in between. We are afraid that the ego of that person shall inflate further and he shall score a point on us. Tendering an apology for a misdeed without fear or favor is a virtue far greater and courageous than forgiving someone for his misdeed. Sometimes, it becomes necessary to ask pardon from a person for entering into an interminable argument with him though our stand is right. Thus, asking to forgive may not always prove our weakness, but it does reveal docility in our nature and shows that we value the feelings and relationships with others more than our ego. Asking to forgive for a wrong deed benefits us in two ways; first, we remain friendly with him, and second, we use utmost caution in dealing with him

---

to comfort him and asked pardon apologizing that his tender foot was injured due to the kick on His very hard chest.

in future lest we have to ask for a pardon again. Nevertheless, as is true with all good things, there is a limit beyond which asking pardon for self is taken as weakness by the offender, particularly if latter is a strong person. Guru Gobindsingh advises:

'Forgive a weak person if he insults you for it is the duty of the brave to protect him; but if a powerful person insults you (for no reason) punish him by all means'.

When Bali the grandson of Prahlaad, a great devotee of Lord Vishnu, asked him which divine wealth out of valor and forgiveness is greater valuable, he replied that both are equally great values and must be applied as appropriate according to the situation then prevailing.

Dhruti: As explained under 6/23 to 26 earlier, it is the quality of fortitude, steadfastness, resoluteness, and perseverance, also called **Dhairya**. Since the practiser of **Dhruti** is called **Dheer**, it will be useful to also refer to *'What is meant by 'Dheer: ...'* under 2/12-13. Ho Chi Minh counsels us:

'Remember, a storm is a good opportunity for the pine and the cypress to show their strength and stability'.

The story of an ant trying to climb a wall is a good example of **Dhruti**. Orison Swett Marden says:

'The world makes way for the determined man. Everybody believes in the man who persists, sticks, hangs on, when others let go. Tenacity of purpose gives confidence'.

Moral: *Try, try again. You will succeed at last.*

Shauch: It was explained in 13/7 as virtue of maintaining cleanliness, purity, piety and tidiness of our body and inner faculties, and our surroundings & environment.

Adroh: It means absence of **Droh**, the rancour, ill will, hostility, and malice. **Droh** is the nearest cousin of **Dwesh** discussed after 2/64 & 65 in detail. An **Adrohee** is same as **Adweshtaa** described in 12/13 as the first symptom of God's dearest devotee. A practiser should desist from thoughts and deeds, which are injurious and rancorous for self as well as others.

N Atimaanitaa: It is the quality of freedom from unjustifiable pride, conceit, immodesty, and haughtiness. We discussed it earlier as **Amaanitvam** in 13/7 while dealing with the virtues of a **Jnaanee**. This virtue was covered amply as remaining equipoise in **Maan** & **Apamaan** in 12/18 & 14/25 also. Veteran film actor Dilip Kumar narrates an interesting experience in this regard as below:

"At the peak of my career, I was once travelling by plane. The passenger next to me was elderly. Dressed in a simple shirt and pant, he appeared middle class but well educated. Other passengers kept glancing at me. But this gentleman appeared unconcerned. He read his newspaper, looked out of the window, and when tea came, he sipped it quietly. Trying to strike a conversation, I smiled. The man courteously smiled back and said hello.

We got talking and I brought the subject to cinema and asked, 'Do you watch films?'

The man replied, 'Oh, very few. I did see one many years ago.'

I mentioned that I worked in films myself.

The man said, 'Oh, that's nice. What do you do?'

I replied, 'I am an actor.'

The man nodded, 'Oh, wonderful.' That was it.

When we landed, I held out my hand and said, 'It was good to travel with you. By the way, my name is Dilip Kumar.'

The man shook my hand and smiled, 'Thank you. I am J R D Tata.'

It must however, be noted that **N Atimaanitaa** should never substitute **Swaabhimaan**, the self-respect. God asserts in the end of 16/3 that the aforesaid are the innate qualities of a person endowed with **Daivee Sampadaa**, the divine wealth.

SOME ADDITIONAL THOUGHTS ON DAIVEE SAMPADAA

He, who is a liberal benefactor, kindhearted giver, is called **Devataa**, or **Dev**, and **Sur** i.e. the one who makes others' lives melodious. Most of the 26 divine qualities, virtues & habits described in these shloks were earlier described by Gita under topics of **Sthit Prajn** in chapter 2, of God's **Priy Bhakt** in chapter 12, of **Jnaanee** in chapter 13 and **Gunaateet** in chapter 14 in detail. These three shloks conclude that when these virtues become an inseparable, permanent part of a person's **Swabhaav**, the characteristic nature, they culminate into a precious treasure of Divine Wealth, the plenitude of moral and spiritual energy. His temperament is tuned to his desired destination now as his will follows divine will. The vehicle of his life starts moving in the auto-drive mode towards the goal of eternal peace.

All religions and societies shower praise and accord highest importance to the virtues listed in these three shloks because they are actually the humanitarian virtues though Gita calls them divine qualities implying that the person who possesses them is equal to gods. Every sane individual in the world, whether theist or atheist, believer or non-believer, religious or not religious, living in east or west, black or white or wheatish in complexion, literate or illiterate, certainly values these qualities and wants to develop them in his life. Gita's message about divine and demonic traits is universal and eternal in application.

Which one of them is the most superior and worth practising? The simplest suggestion to resolve this dilemma is to catch hold of anyone of them, which they find most suitable and practical for them. Once they start practicing that single virtue firmly, the balance 25 virtues shall automatically come running into their lives. It is like a person setting his boat sail in one of the numerous tributaries of **Gangaa** with an aim to join its main stream. Once he arrives in the main course, he shall be please to find that the waters of other tributaries have already merged into **Gangaa**. Harishchandr practised the path of **Satya**; Buddh of **Karunaa (Dayaa)** Mahaaveer of **Tap**; Mahatma Gandhi of **Ahimsaa**; Nelson Mandela of **Abhay**; Raamkrishn Paramhans of **Sattv Sanshuddhi**; Christ of **Kshamaa**; Yudhishthir of **Dhruti**; Arjun of **Aarjav**; and other virtues developed automatically in them.

Description of 26 virtues, that constitute divine wealth, ends here.

❧❦

Aasuree Sampadaa, the demonic wealth is
now described briefly.

(16/4)

दम्भो दर्पोऽभिमानश्च क्रोधः पारुष्यमेव च ।
अज्ञानं चाभिजातस्य पार्थ संपदमासुरीम् ॥१६/४॥

Dambho darpoʃbhimaanashch krodh: paarushyamev ch I
Ajnaanam chaabhijaatyasya Paarth sampadamaasureem II
(16/4)

Dambh: (hypocrisy, ostentation) Darp: (conceit, boastfulness) Abhimaan: (unjustifiable pride, arrogance) Ch (and) Krodh: (anger, rage) Paarushyam (harshness, abusiveness, especially in speech & behavior) Ev (only, certainly, also) Ch (and)I Ajnaanam (idiosyncrasy, lack of knowledge) Ch (and) Abhijaatyasya (innate) Paarth (Arjun) Sampadam (wealth) Aasureem (demoniacal)II (16/4)

O Paarth (Arjun)! Ostentation, conceit, arrogant pride, anger, harshness in behavior, abusive speech and idiosyncrasy are certainly the inborn qualities of a person possessing Aasuree Sampadaa, the demoniacal wealth. (16/4)

God lists six main evils that constitute **Aasuree Sampadaa**, the riches of demonic people. They are:

Dambh: It means the vice of hypocrisy, pretence, boasting, arrogance and ostentation. God mentioned **Adambhitvam**, the lack of **Dambh** in 13/7 as an important virtue of a **Jnaanee**. Gita shall repeatedly remind us to become free from **Dambh** while elaborating **Aasuree Sampadaa** in 16/10 & 17; and as an evil of **Taamasik** mode in 17/5, 12 & 18. Dambh was explained as **Mithyaachaar** also earlier in 3/6. Ancient Greek aphorism 'Gnothi Seauton' i.e. 'Know Thyself' warns boastful persons in this way:

"Those whose boasts exceed what they are, 'Know Thyself' is a warning to them".

A poet laments for betrayal of his faith by an ostentatious person thus:

ज़िंदगी भर जिन्हें पूजा जिन्हें चाहा हमने,

ख़ुद वही टूटे हुए निकले है बुतखाने से ।

आज अपने भी नज़र आते हैं बेगाने से ॥

(They, whom we adored and worshipped for whole life, are coming out of the temple broken into pieces; our own people have become aliens today.)

Kabeer advises hypocrites in his typical way:

'माला फेरत जुग गया गया न मन का फेर ।

कर का मन का डारि दे मन का मनका फेर ॥'

(Aeons have passed in telling beads of a string, but the twist has not gone from your heart. Drop the bead in your hand and rotate the bead of your heart.)

Darp: It is the evil of conceit, insolence and vanity. **Darp** is like the dust that soils a mirror to the extent that one cannot recognize his own self in it. **Abhimaan,** also known as **Ghamand** in Hindi, is the feeling of false pride. Raamcharit Maanas says in 7/73 (ख)/6:

संसृति मूल सूलप्रद नाना। सकल सोक दायक अभिमाना॥

(Abhimaan is the root cause of all kinds of troubles in the world, and also the giver of all sorrows.)

Paarushyam: It is roughness, harshness, abusiveness, especially in speech and behavior. We shall learn about speech as Tap in 17/15. **Krodh** & **Ajnaan** were already explained many times as anger and lack of knowledge respectively.

ॐ

God tells the results of possessing divine or demonic wealth.

(16/5)

दैवी संपद्विमोक्षाय निबन्धायासुरी मता ।
मा शुचः संपदं दैवीमभिजातोऽसि पाण्डव ॥१६/५॥

Daivee sampadvimokshaay nibandhaayaasuree mataa I
Maa shuch: sampadam daiveemabhijaayato[si Paandav II
(16/5)

Daivee (divine) Sampat (wealth) Vimokshaay (frees) Nibandhaay
(binds) Aasuree (demoniacal) Mataa (is believed)I Maa (do not)
Shuch: (grieve) Sampadam (wealth) Daiveem (divine) Abhijaat:
(born with) Asi (are) Paandav (Arjun)II (16/5)

**It is believed that the Divine wealth is for liberation while
the demoniacal one binds. O Paandav (Arjun)! Do not grieve
because you have been already born with the divine wealth.
(16/5)**

Krishn asserts that those who possess divine wealth are sure
to liberate from the painful rigmarole of Punarjanm and the ones
who chase demonic qualities shall definitely remain tied up with
Karm Bandhan. He also assures Arjun that he is endowed with
Daivee Sampadaa, the wealth of divine virtues since birth, and
developed them further to a very high standard of morality in his
life. He therefore need not be disturbed with the thought that he
is yielding to **Aasuree** impulses by agreeing to fight in the war. In
fact, by undertaking to fight at His bidding and counsel, he would
be credited in fulfilling His mission of *'Protection of the righteous,
annihilating the wicked and re-establishing Dharm'* stated in 4/7-8.
Maa Shuch is His assurance to him to grieve not, for unjustified
bewilderment. Krishn shall repeat this assurance to Arjun by
uttering **Maa Shuch** i.e. *'Don't worry'* in 18/66 in the end of His
teaching.

৵৽

God proceeds to elaborate Asurs from here till 16/19.

(16/6)

द्वौ भूतसर्गौ लोकेऽस्मिन्दैव आसुर एव च ।
दैवो विस्तरशः प्रोक्त आसुरं पार्थ मे शृणु ॥ १ ६/६॥

Dwau bhootsargau lokeʃsmindaiv aasur ev ch I
Daivo vistarash: prokt aasuram Paarth me shruNu II (16/6)

Dwau (two types) Bhoot Sargau (of created beings) Loke (in the world) Asmin (this) Daiv: (of Devs) Aasur: (of demoniac) Ev (only) Ch (and)I Daiv: (divine) Vistarash: (in detail) Prokt: (is told) Aasuram (demoniacal) Paarth (Arjun) Me (from Me) Shrunu (listen)II (16/6)

O Paarth (Arjun)! Only two types of people have been created in this world, the divine ones and the demoniac ones. I have already told about the divine ones in detail so far. Listen now from Me about the demoniac people also in detail. (16/6)

After describing **Daivee Sampadaa** in 16/1-3, Krishn now explain Aasuree Sampadaa also in 13 shloks from here till 16/19. Superficially looking it seems unjustified to allot 13 shloks to demonic qualities whereas He spoke of divine wealth in three shloks only. Since Arjun is already bestowed with divine virtues, it seems to me that the sole purpose of Krishn in describing demonic wealth in detail is to make common people like us fully aware of the dangerous pitfalls of demonic vices that await us in the journey of our lives. He shall draw a fearful picture of the fall of those lowly, base and egoist people who deliberately choose to walk into these pitfalls.

Clarifications:

1. *Actually, God does create two types of persons, Devs & Asurs in the world. Gita has explained well earlier that every soul takes rebirth after death of its last body because of works performed by it in its previous births, and develops itself into category of Devs or Asurs by its own deeds & character.*

2. *Though there are three Guns of Prakruti, Sattv, Raj and Tam which force people to involve in different works, people themselves*

can be of two types only, the good and bad. However, the same person can be Dev i.e. righteous now, and Asur, a demon next moment according to his self-interest and inclination towards the result of work.

ॐ

Krishn continues to describe characteristics of Asurs till 6/19.

(16/7, 8, 9 & 10)

प्रवृत्तिं च निवृत्तिं च जना न विदुरासुराः ।
न शौचं नापि चाचारो न सत्यं तेषु विद्यते ॥१६/७॥
असत्यमप्रतिष्ठं ते जगदाहुरनीश्वरम् ।
अपरस्परसंभूतं किमन्यत्कामहैतुकम् ॥१६/८॥
एतां दृष्टिमवष्टभ्य नष्टात्मानोऽल्पबुद्धयः ।
प्रभवन्त्युग्रकर्माणः क्षयाय जगतोऽहिताः ॥१६/९॥
काममाश्रित्य दुष्पूरं दम्भमानमदान्विताः ।
मोहाद्गृहीत्वासद्ग्राहान्प्रवर्तन्तेऽशुचिव्रताः ॥१६/१०॥

Pravruttim ch nivruttim ch janaa viduraasuraa: I
N shaucham naapi chaachaaro n satyam teshu vidyate II
(16/7)
Asatyamapratishtham te jagadaahuraneeshwaram I
Aparasparsambhootam kimanyatkaamhaitukam II (16/8)
Etaam drushtimavashtabhya nashtaatmaanoʃlpabuddhay: I
Prabhavantyugrakarmaan: kshayaay jagatoʃhitaa: II (16/9)
Kaamamaashritya dushpooram dambhamaanamadaanvitaa: I
Mohaadgruheetvaasadgraahaanpravartanteʃshuchivrataa: II
16/10

Pravruttim (proper involvement & indulgence in doing own duties) Ch (and) Nivruttim (refraining from undesirable works, things) Ch (and) Janaa: (persons) Vidu: (know) Aasuraa: (demoniac) I n (neither) Shaucham (cleanliness, purity) N (nor) Api (even) Ch (and) Aachaar: (behavior, character) N (nor) Satyam (truthfulness; also in truth) Teshu (in those) Vidyate (is, exists)II (16/7)

Asatyam (falsehood) Apratishtham (unfounded, dishonored, obscure) Te (they) Jagat (universe) Aahu: (say) Aneeshwaram (without any God, also atheism)I Aparaspar Sambhootam (automatically produced by mutual contact) Kim (what) Anyat (else) Kaam (sexual desire; longing) Haitukam (cause)II (16/8)

Etaam (this) Drushtim (vision, viewpoint) Avashtabhya (assenting, subjected to) Nasht Aatmaan: (having ruined, devastated own self) Alp Buddhay: (persons with very low wisdom)I Prabhavanti ((become capable) Ugr Karmaan: (doers of horrific activities) Kshayaay (for destruction) Jagat: (world) Ahitaa: (harmful)II (16/9)

Kaamam (desire) Aashritya (enslaved by) Dushpooram (insatiable) Dambh (hypocrisy) Maan (respect) Mad Anvitaa: (fraught with frenzy)I Mohaat (due to infatuation) Gruheetvaa (accepting) Asadgraahaan (false principles, doctrines, things) Pravartante (indulge) Ashuchivrataa: (vowed to impure conduct)II (16/10)

Those demoniac people do not know how to get properly involved in performing their duties, nor do they know how to remain aloof from undesirable works. Neither purity & cleanliness, nor good character, nor even truthfulness exists in them. (16/7)

They brag that universe is something false, ungodly, and unfounded, and not created any god, but produced automatically (through union of male & female species). They think that sexual infatuation (in living beings) in the world is the only reason of creation of universe, none else. (16/8)

Such persons, subjected to false vision and very low intelligence, become very powerful and indulge in horrible activities. They devastate their own self besides inflicting immense harm and ruin to whole world. (16/9)

Enslaved by numerous insatiable desires, possessed of pretence, undeserving honor and frenzy, accepting false principles due to bewilderment, and vowed to disgraceful conduct, they engage themselves in this world. (16/10)

We have already understood **Pravrutti** & **Nivrutti** in 14/22; and **Shauch**, **Satya** & **Asatya** in 16/1-3. **Aachaar** is the righteous behaviour and conduct in conformity with **Dharm**. Buddh says:

'Physical charms attract the eyes, goodness attracts the mind'.

Good looks may be a good material asset, but a good character is an identity. It is wrong to judge someone only by his looks and not by character. Abraham Lincoln thinks:

'Character is the tree; and honor and reputation are its shadow'.

Aneeshwaram are non-believers, atheists who do not accept existence of God. They believe in nihilism, that rejects religious and moral principle, and the need of righteousness in the society. They consider all actions & transactions in this world as phantasmagoric i.e. a sequence of irrelevant, irregular happenings which keep shifting swiftly on their own from one scene to another as the projection of many separate scenes in quick succession gives the impression of a continuous movie on the screen.

Kaam Haitukam points to sex as the primary cause of creation and reproduction of all species in the world. **Aparaspar Sambhootam** therefore is the false notion that sexual indulgence between male and female species is the only cause of producing everything. Some of them even go to the extent of calling themselves as accidental products of sexual lust of their parents. They switch over their belief from **Brahm Satyam jaganmithyaa** i.e. *'God is truth and world a myth'*, as proclaimed by scriptures, to **Jagat Satyam Brahm Mithyaa** i.e. *'This world is the only real truth, not Brahm, the God*. Atheists may feel elated by 16/8 if they read it in isolation without knowing its context in preceding and succeeding shloks. However, those who have faithfully continued with our study of Gita know it well that Gita rejects this thought outright for God proclaimed in 14/3 & 4:

"All living beings are born in this world when His consciousness impregnates the great womb of Prakruti, the nature. Thus Prakruti is the mother of all species born, and God is their father".

Nothing, not even a blade of grass, can be born unless God infuses His consciousness in its primordial source of nature. Krishn uses few derogatory adjectives as mentioned below for people of demonic nature in these shloks:

Alp Buddhay: They are persons with very low, trivial, vain, frivolous, absurd, mean, and base wisdom and intelligence. They are not capable even to know what is good for them. They behave like a woodcutter who cuts the very branch on which he is sitting.

Ugr Karmaan: They are habituated to indulge in fierce, horrific, terrible activities. They derive pleasure out of torturing innocent, weak people without any reason. God also called them **Aghaayu** in 3/6, **Paapmaanam** in 3/41, **Dushkrutaam** in 4/8, **Paap kruttam** in 4/36, and **Paapeshu** in 6/9.

Ahitaa: They were explained in 2/36 as harmful, inimical, depraving and hostile persons who never wish well for anyone. They are always busy in devising ways and means to harm others.

Kaamam Aashritya Dushpooram: People of **Aasuree** nature are always in the grip of innumerable, insatiable desires. Refer to explanations in 3/39.

Asadgraahaan: They accept false principles and doctrines and seek shelter in them; and provide outright support to falsehood. Their sole objective is to achieve what they like by hook or crook.

Ashuchi Vrataa: They behave in a villainous manner as if vowed and committed to do nothing but immoral, impure, disrespectful acts.

Madaanvita: Such people are highly possessed and intoxicated with false pride, insatiable lust, frenzy and passion. **Mad** shall also appear in 16/17 & 18/35. **Dambh** was explained earlier in 16/4, **Maan** in 6/7, and **Moh** in 2/62 & 63 as **Sammoh** respectively.

Nasht Aatmaan: Krishn foretells the destiny of such people who relish **Aasuree** wealth mentioned above and succeeding shloks. He says that they not only harm others but also devastate and ruin their own self. He shall elaborate it in 16/19-20 also.

ॐ

(16/11 & 12)

चिन्तामपरिमेयां च प्रलयान्तामुपाश्रिताः ।
कामोपभोगपरमा एतावदिति निश्चिताः ॥१६/११॥
आशापाशशतैर्बद्धाः कामक्रोधपरायणाः ।
ईहन्ते कामभोगार्थमन्यायेनार्थसञ्चयान् ॥१६/१२॥

Chintaamaparimeyaam ch pralayaantaamupaashritaa: I
Kaamopabhogaparamaa etaavaditi nishchitaa: II (16/11)
Aashaapaashashatairbaddhaa: kaamakrodhaparaayanaa: I
Eehante   kaamabhogaarthamanyaayenaarthasanchayaan   II
(16/12)

Chintaam (anxiety, worry) Aparimeyaam (immeasurable, countless) Ch (and) Pralay Antaam (until death, end) Upaashritaa: (situated in, swamped by)I Kaam: Up Bhog Paramaa: (grossly absorbed in gratifying desire, lust) Etaavat (as much as this) Iti (thus) Nishchitaa: (having firm belief, ascertained)II (16/11)

Aashaa (hope) Paash (noose, snare) Shatai: (hundreds of) Baddhaa: (bound, fastened) Kaam (desire, longing) Krodh (anger, rage) Paraayanaa: (assiduously engaged, occupied)I Eehante (endeavor, aspire) Kaam Bhogaa Artham (for satisfying their desire for sensory pleasures) Anyaayen (by unjustified, wrong means) Arth (wealth, assets) Sanchayaan (amass, accumulate)II (16/12)

Swamped by countless anxieties till death, and grossly absorbed in gratifying passionate desires, they firmly believe that this much only is the happiness; (16/11)

Fastened with hundreds of nooses of expectations, and gripped by passionate desires and anger, they labor hard to amass wealth by this or that unjustified means to satisfy their lust for more pleasures. (16/12)

Chintaa is anxiety, apprehension, worry, concern and fear of the known or unknown not in our control. It is like sitting in a rocking chair. Though we are apparently engaged in the activity of rocking with the chair, it actually doesn't get us anywhere. Vivekaanand advises us:

'Give up the habit of worrying for the future, for nothing can be achieved by it. if worry you must, do it to develop character'.

The only thing one can ever accomplish by worrying is to raise his level of stress and blood pressure and land in depression. Christ says in Bible, Matthew 6/25 to 34:

'I tell you not to worry about everyday life, whether you have enough food and drink, or enough clothes to wear. Isn't life more than food and your body more than clothing? Look at the birds. They don't plant or harvest or store food in barns, for your heavenly Father feeds them. And aren't you far more valuable to him than they are? Can all your worries add a single moment to your life?

And why worry about your clothing? Look at the lilies of the field and how they grow. They don't work or make their clothing, yet Solomon in all his glory was not dressed as beautifully as they are.

And if God cares so wonderfully for wildflowers which are here today and thrown into the fire tomorrow, he will certainly care for you. Why do you have so little faith?'

See what difference a half 'N' can make to our worries. If we nurture **Chintaa** the 'N' that conveys 'Don't worry' (Maa Shuch, 16/5 & 18/66) in it would soon disappear leaving **Chitaa**, the funeral pyre for us. Raheem says:

रहिमन कठिन चितान तै चिन्ता को चित चैत ।
चिता दहति निर्जीव को चिन्ता जीव समेत ॥

(Raheem says, 'Beware of Chintaa, the worry O my heart, for it is harsher than Chitaa, the funeral pyre. Chittaa burns a person after he is dead but Chintaa burns him alive.)

Moreover, if we suffix **Chintaa** with a single 'N' it transforms into **Chintan**, the reflective thinking and/or meditating. If we were nimble enough to move away quickly from **Chintaa** to **Chintan** by facing it with courage and positive attitude, a worrisome situation would surely turn into a great opportunity for us to prove our mettle.

"Mahatma Gandhi took Suharavardi, the Muslim leader of undivided Bengal with him, to Calcutta in a car with a determination to quench the fire of riots between Hindus & Muslims as fallout of partition of India. A violent mob, highly charged with rage, gathered around them threatening their lives. Suharavardi started shivering with fear and cursing the moment he decided to accompany Gandhi, and did not dare to come out of car. But what did Gandhi do? He reflected for while on the grave situation and decided to step out of the car and face and pacify the mob. His spontaneous courage ultimately resulted in both factions giving up violence towards each other; and not a single life was lost. Lord Mountbatten mentioned it as a miracle carried out single handedly by unarmed, unclad Gandhi that his army 30,000 strong could not do in Punjab".

Moral: *Let us recognize the power of Chintan over Chintaa. Shadows of obstacles in our path look large or small depending upon the angle from which we look at them and how the light of our reflection falls upon them.*

Arthur Somers Rache says:

'*Worry is a thin stream of fear trickling through the mind. If encouraged, it cuts a channel into which all other thoughts are drained*'.

Swett Marden observes:

'*Worry is a hammer that breaks the minute, delicate nerves of our mind and destroys its power to think rationally.... Worry clogs the brain and paralyzes the thought. A troubled brain cannot think clearly, vigorously, locally*'.

Kaam Up Bhog Paramaa: They are people grossly absorbed in gratifying passionate desires as they think this is the only purpose of life. It is similar to a dog chewing a bone, relishing the taste of own blood as his mouth bleeds; nevertheless, he does not give up the bone.

Aashaa: It is expecting some work to fructify according to the desire with which it was performed. Persons of **Aasuree** nature inflict cruelties on righteous people and expect that they respect them.

They perpetrate sins and anarchy in this world and still expect to go to heaven after death. **Paash**, the strings of such vain hopes keep them mercilessly tied up to demonic nature just as a noose on the neck of a monkey tightens more as he tries to free himself from it. Maithilee Sharan Gupt writes in Saaket:

'वह आप क्यों न नाता तोड़े, पर कौन है कि उसको छोड़े'

'{No one gives it (Aashaa) up until it itself leaves him (upon death)}'.

Arth Sanchayaan: They are the people who are always after money. Money is their mother, master, moral and mission. An amusing anecdote explains the point:

'A man was travelling to a place called Rupayaa Nagar for the first time. When the train stopped at a station, he inquired from a person standing outside his window whether it was Rupayaa Nagar but when the man demanded one rupee before answering; he understood that it was Rupayaa Nagar'.

Sitting on a pile of money, they think they are the most powerful as they can buy everything they desire with the money. Alas! It is not the truth. They forget that Alexander the Great also could not add even a day to his life in exchange of all the money he collected in his expeditions.

Moral: *Money can't buy everything. It is just an easy means of exchanging merchandise, not the merchandise itself. A thirsty traveller cannot buy a drop of water in Sahara even with a sachet of gold coins.*

I am tempted to quote Maithilee Sharan Gupt again from Saaket about such greedy collectors of wealth:

हाँ, तब अनर्थ के बीज अर्थ बोता है,
जब एक वर्ग में मुष्टि बद्ध होता है।
जो संग्रह करके त्याग नहीं करता है,
वह दस्यु लोक धन लूट लूट धरता है॥

{Yes, Arth, the wealth sows the seeds of Anarth, the senseless futility (of its purpose) when it is confined in the fists of a small group of people. He, who collects wealth but does not release it for (the welfare of) others, is a bandit who amasses wealth by robbing people.}

ॐ

What kinds of thoughts occupy the minds of Aasuree people?

(16/13, 14 & 15)

इदमद्य मया लब्धमिमं प्राप्स्ये मनोरथम् ।
इदमस्तीदमपि मे भविष्यति पुनर्धनम् ॥१६/१३॥
असौ मया हतः शत्रुर्हनिष्ये चापरानपि ।
ईश्वरोऽहमहं भोगी सिद्धोऽहं बलवान्सुखी ॥१६/१४॥
आढ्योऽभिजनवानस्मि कोऽन्योऽस्ति सदृशो मया ।
यक्ष्ये दास्यामि मोदिष्य इत्यज्ञानविमोहिताः ॥१६/१५॥

Idamadya mayaa labdhamimam praapsye manoratham I
Idamasteedamapi me bhavishyati punardhanam II (16/13)
Asau mayaa hat: shatrurhanishye chaaparaanapi I
Ishwaroʃhamaham bhogee siddhoʃham balwaansukhee II (16/14)
Aadhyoʃbhijanavaanasmi koʃnyoʃsti sadrushu mayaa I
Yakshye daasyaami modishya ityajnaanavimohitaa: II (16/15)

Idam (this) Adya (today) Mayaa (by me) Labdham (achieve, acquire) Imam (this) Praapsye (shall achieve) Manoratham (aspiration, earnest ambition of mind)I Idam (this) Asti (is there) Idam (this) Api (also) Me (mine) Bhavishyati (increase in future) Pun: (again) Dhanam (wealth)II (16/13)

Asau (that) Mayaa (by me) Hat: (slain) Shatru: (enemy) Hanishye (shall kill) Ch (and) Aparaan (others) Api (also)I Ishwar: (God) Aham (I) Aham (I) Bhogee (voluptuous person) Siddh: (most accomplished one) Aham (I) Bal Vaan (powerful) Sukhee (happy)II (16/14)

Aadhya: (wealthy) Abhijanavaan (having large family & followers) Asmi (am) K: (who) Any: (other) Asti (is) Sadrush: (like) Mayaa (to me)I Yakshye (shall perform Yajns) Daasyaami (shall give in charity) Modishye (capriciously make merry without any restraint for own delight) Iti (thus) Ajnaan Vimohitaa: (deluded due to ignorance)II (16/15)

Bewildered and intoxicated by their ignorance, they (People of Aasuree nature) are always preoccupied with thoughts like: "I have achieved this much today; I shall also materialize my remaining aspirations shortly; I already possess this much wealth, and I shall multiply it further in future; I have slain that enemy, and shall certainly kill the remaining ones also. I am the God and therefore, the sole enjoyer (of every joy)I am the most accomplished one with mystic powers; and I am the most powerful and the happiest person (in the world). Who else is there like me for I am born in a great, prosperous family and have a large following; I shall perform many sacrificial & fruitive activities, give enormous donations so that I can capriciously make merry without any restraint on my own delight. (16/13, 14 & 15)

These shloks describe the kind of hundreds of nooses, which tie them in their network endlessly. The journey of the life of Aasuree people is like a rat race, everybody competing with other without any purpose and sight on the ultimate goal of human life. They live like animals that focus their every activity only on material pleasures like good food, joy, sex and survival by overpowering the weak based on jungle rule of 'Survival of the fittest'.

Dhan: It means money, wealth, property and riches. New Testament of Bible mentions a mythological figure called *Mammon* (Hebrew word for money) as the god that promises worldly riches, and promotes greediness to acquire more. The real wealth of a man is his character. It is truly said:

'If money is lost we lose nothing; if health is lost we lose something; but if character is lost, we lose everything'.

J R D Tata says:

'Money is like manure. It stinks when you pile it; it grows when you spread it'.

❦

Description of Aasuree Sampadaa is continued.

(16/16, 17 & 18)

अनेकचित्तविभ्रान्ता मोहजालसमावृताः ।
प्रसक्ताः कामभोगेषु पतन्ति नरकेऽशुचौ ॥१६/१६॥
आत्मसंभाविताः स्तब्धा धनमानमदान्विताः ।
यजन्ते नामयज्ञैस्ते दम्भेनाविधिपूर्वकम् ॥१६/१७॥
अहंकारं बलं दर्पं कामं क्रोधं च संश्रिताः ।
मामात्मपरदेहेषु प्रद्विषन्तोऽभ्यसूयकाः ॥१६/१८॥

Anekachittavibhraantaa mohajaalasamaavrutaa: I
Prasaktaa: kaamabhogeshu patanti narake∫shuchau II
(16/16)
Aatmasambhaavitaa: stabdhaa dhanamaanamadaanvitaa: I
Yajante naamyaajnaiste dambhenaavidhipoorvakam II
(16/17)
Ahankaaram balam darpam kaamam krodham ch
sanshritaa: I
Maamaatmapardeheshu pradwishanto∫bhyasooyakaa: II
(16/18)

Anek Chitt Vibhraantaa: (conscience perplexed in several ways) Moh Jaal Samaavrutaa: (fully wrapped/covered with network of bewilderment)I Prasaktaa: (deeply engrossed in) Kaam (desire) Bhogeshu (in sensory enjoyments) Patanti (fall down, disgrace) Narake (into hell) Ashuchau (dirty, impure)II (16/16)

Aatm Sambhaavitaa: (think great, esteemed of self) Stabdhaa: (impudent, impertinent) Dhan Maan Mad Anvitaa: (possessed of wealth, false prestige & passion)I Yajante (perform sacrifices, austerities) Naam Yajnai: (for namesake of Yajn) Te (they) Dambhen (out of hypocrisy, ostentation) Avidhi Poorvakam (with disregard to procedures & regulations laid down by scriptures)II (16/17)

Ahamkaaram (misplaced ego) Balam (strength, power) Darpam (arrogance, pride) Kaamam (lust) Krodham (ange) Ch (and) Sanshritaa: (adhering to)I Maam (of me) Aatm par Deheshu (in the bodies of self and others) Pradwishant: (person filled with blasphemy, envy) Abhyasooyakaa: (persons malicious of others)II (16/18)

Highly deluded by ignorance, with conscience perplexed in several ways, fully wrapped and trapped in the networks of allurement, and deeply absorbed in passionate desires and sensory pleasures; they fall down into the dirtiest hell. (16/16)

Impertinently possessed of their wealth, false prestige & passion, they think of themselves to be the greatest. They perform many sacrificial activities out of ostentation in the name of Yajn with blatant disregard to laid down procedures & regulations. (16/17)

Foolishly ensconced in their falsified ego, power, arrogant pride, lustful longings and anger, these blasphemous persons are filled with envy, malice and unwarranted criticism even toward Me, the one who is equally situated deep inside their bodies, and of others. (16/18)

Egoistic **Aasuree** people are like balloons which float high in the sky when inflated by the air of their arrogant pride; but fall in the dust when punctured and deflated. They boast of them as second to none. Scriptures describe their ego as:

'एकोऽहम द्वितीयोनास्ति । न भूतो न भविष्यति' ॥

(I am the only one, none other. Neither there was anyone like me in the past, nor shall be in future)

They fancy that they know everything though they know nothing worth knowing whereas learned saints modestly admit they know nothing. Socrates compares himself with a boastful man thus:

'Neither of us appears to know anything great and good. But he fancies he knows something, although he knows nothing; whereas because I do not know anything, I do not fancy that I do. In this trifling matter, then, I appear to be wiser than he, because I do not fancy I know what I do not know'.

Aatm Sambhaavitaa: Totally lacking in modesty, such people nurture false pride of very high opinion about them. They think that there is no one greater, wiser, more resourceful and influential than them. They even fool themselves into conjecturing that people regard them well and hold in very high esteem whereas the fact invariably is that people flatter them to serve self-interest, or out of fear and coercion. For example, most of the contemporary kings used to praise Jaraasandh, the mighty king of Magadh, in Mahaabhaarat until Krishn managed to get him killed by Bheem in a duel. An inspiring story explains the hollowness of such people:

"A highly ambitious king became Chakravartee, the supreme emperor after conquering other kings. After long celebrations, he thought of erecting a monument to commemorate his glory till eternity and approached his Guru for suitable advice. When the Guru saw the fire of vanity burning in his eyes, he quietly asked him to follow him to locate a suitable place for the proposed memorial. He led him to a cave in a deep forest thitherto unknown to anyone, and told that it was the cave of Chakravartee emperors. Handing over a lighted a torch and a piece of charcoal, he asked him to enter the cave and write his name as a Chakravartee in a vacant space on any wall. The king roamed about in the cave for a long time to write his name as instructed by the Guru, but, to his utter dismay, he found innumerous names written very closely wherever he went. At last, when he could not find any vacant space to write his name, he picked up a stone to erase one name and write his name in the newly created space. As he was about to do so, the Guru appeared suddenly, held his hand and told, 'O king! The way you are trying to erase the name of a Chakravartee who was far greater than you to create space for you; know it well that one day someone greater than you shall also come

here and erase your name likewise'. The king realized the folly of his haughtiness, and fell to the feet of Guru."

Moral: *We should neither blame nor praise ourselves because blaming self for a sin not committed degrades our soul; and indulging in self-praise, even if true, makes us immodest and egoistic. Instead, we must sincerely carry out introspection on such occasions, and take corrective steps.*

Stabdhaa: Though it literally means standstill, motionless and numb like a statue, it also applies to impudent, impertinent people fixed in oppressive activities not ready to heed to anybody's advice. For example, stubborn Raavan turned deaf ears to wise counsels of his principal queen Mandodaree, uncles Maareech and Maalyavaan, brother Vibheeshan, and detective Shuk, besides Hanumaan and Angad, the emissaries of Raam, and ridiculed them. Krishn shall describe a **Taamasik** doer as **Stabdh** in 18/28.

We already understood **Dhan** as riches in 16/13, **Maan** as respect & reputation in 6/7, **Mad** as frenzy in 16/10, **Dambh** as hypocrisy & ostentation in 16/4, **Ahamkaar** as ego in 2/71 (under **Nirahamkaar**), **Bal** as strength & power in 7/11, and **Darp** as conceit & vanity in 16/4. **Yajn** as a sacrificial activity, **Kaam** as a passionate desire and **Krodh** as anger, were explained earlier many times. Demonic people are charged with these evils all the time. They carry out even a sacred activity like Yajn in an ostentatious way, not as a sacrifice of self-interest.

Pradwishant: Stemming from **Dwesh**, it means persons filled with envy, hate, contempt and blasphemy, towards God, and godliness in holy persons and sacred violate things. God told us to be **Adweshtaa Sarv Bhootaanaam** i.e. not envious but friendly and compassionate towards all beings in 12/13.

Abhyasooyakaa: They are people engaging in unwarranted criticism and spreading malice and slander towards others. We discussed them as **Abhyasooyant** in 3/31-32. Proverbially speaking, they look for holes, defects and patches in the robes of others without bothering about the quality of their own robes. **Abhyasooyakaa** are like the small sized, underdeveloped grains that move around in a sieve counting the holes in its bottom, and eventually fall down through the holes of the sieve. Unfortunately, they still accuse the sieve for their downfall but never realize their own smallness as its real cause. Lying low in the rejected stuff & dirt, they envy larger grains that remain undisturbed above sieve.

Moral: *Let us not blow off another's lamp for it would never make ours shine better. Rather, we should learn from his lamp how to radiate light all around us for a long time.*

৵৹৵

God describes the ultimate destiny of Aasuree people.

(16/19)

तानहं द्विषतः क्रूरान्संसारेषु नराधमान् ।
क्षिपाम्यजस्रमशुभानासुरीष्वेव योनिषु ॥ १६/१९॥

Taanaham dwishat: krooraansamsaareshu naraadhamaan I
Kshipaamyajastramashubhaanaasureeshvev yonishu II
(16/19)

Taan (those) Aham (I) Dwishat: (envious) Krooraan (cruel) Samsaareshu (in corporeal world) Naraadhamaan (lowest, vilest persons)I Kshipaami (throw down) Ajastram (perpetually, continually) Ashubhaan (inauspicious) Aasureeshu (of demoniacal) Ev (certainly) Yonishu (in species of living beings)II (16/19)

I certainly throw down such envious, cruel and vile persons perpetually into the inauspicious demoniacal species of living beings in this corporeal world. (16/19)

This statement seems to contradict God's declaration in 5/29 *'I am Suhrudam Sarv Bhootaanaam i.e. the greatest well wisher of all beings'*. In clarification, we should understand well that actually, not God, but the quality of **Karm** of a person decides his destiny in every rebirth. Since the doctrine of **Karm** and **Karm Phal** is God's divine law, God is indirectly the enforcer of His law. In fact, by assigning them to the lower level of life, He favors them with another chance to rectify their past follies in new birth.

God's purpose in making this statement may also be to threaten miscreants, and stop them from living like demons repeatedly. Description of **Aasuree Sampadaa** ends here.

ॐ

God reveals the destiny of Aasuree people.
(16/20)

आसुरीं योनिमापन्ना मूढा जन्मनि जन्मनि ।
मामप्राप्यैव कौन्तेय ततो यान्त्यधमां गतिम् ॥१६/२०॥
त्रिविधं नरकस्येदं द्वारं नाशनमात्मनः ।
कामः क्रोधस्तथा लोभस्तस्मादेतत्त्रयं त्यजेत् ॥१६/२१॥

Aasureem yonimaapanna moodhaa janmani janmani I
Maamapraapyaiv Kauntey tato yaantyadhamaam gatim II
(16/20)
trividham narakasyedam dwaaram naashamaatman: I
Kaam: krodhastathaa lobhastasmaadetattrayam tyajet II
(16/21)

aasureem (of demoniacal) Yonim (species of living beings) Aapannaa: (get, obtain) Moodhaa: (stupid, ignorant persons) Janmani janmani (in birth after birth)I maam (to me) Apraapya (not achieve) Ev (only) Kauntey (Arjun, son of Kuntee) Tat: (than that) Yaanti (reach) Adhamaam (lowest, vilest) Gatim (destination) II (16/20)

trividham (of three kinds) Narakasya (of hell) Idam (this) Dwaaram (gates) Naashanam (which lead to destruction, ruin) Aatman: (of soul)I Kaam: (desire, ambition) Krodh: (anger) Tathaa (and) Lobh: (covetousness, greed) Tasmaat (therefore) Etat (all these) Trayam (three) Tyajet (should be given up)II (16/21)

O Kauntey (Arjun)! The stupid persons cannot attain Me because they are born birth after birth in the demoniacal

species of living beings. There, they continue sliding down further to the lowest of the lowly destinies. (16/20)

Desire, anger and covetousness are the three gates of hell that lead this soul to its ruin. Give up therefore, all three of them (immediately). (16/21)

Aasuree people who do not give up their demonic character, are bound to pass through the vicious circle of death, and rebirth; and every time they are degraded to more worse species like animals, creatures, insects, worms, bacteria etc. This process continues until they realize the futility of their life style and resolve to change the course of their life on to positive, righteous path. By saying **Naashanam Aatman** i.e. ruin their souls, God clarifies here that they themselves, not He, are responsible for their predicament.

Out of all the evils and demonic vices mentioned from 16/4 to 19, Krishn identifies **Kaam**, the passionate desire, **Krodh**, the anger and **Lobh**, the greed as the three main gates through which a soul enters hell after the death of its body. Tulasidaas adds **Mad** also to them in Raamcharit Maanas 5/37:

काम क्रोध मद लोभ सब नाथ नरक के पंथ।
सब परिहरि रघुबीरहि भजहु भजहिं जेहि संत॥

(O Master! Desire, anger, frenzy and avarice are the roads to hell. Give up all of them and devote to Raam as saints do)

Lobh is the opposite of **Aloluptv**, a divine wealth mentioned in 16/2. **Lobh** was explained earlier in 1/38-39 as lust to acquire more to gratify the demands of insatiable passionate desires. When our eyes and nose sense the beauty and fragrance of a flower, we often pluck it from its stem. However, once we learn to love a flower bloomed on its branch, we start caring and watering the plant daily so to let it blossom longer. This is the difference between lust and love. In lust, we try to satisfy our physical needs only, but in love, we nurture a lasting relationship.

SOME ADDITIONAL THOUGHTS ON AASUREE SAMPADAA

He is an **Asur** who is not Sur i.e. Devataa or Dev, the giver. They treasure qualities opposite to those of Devs, described from 16/1 to 3. Thus, **Asur** is not a clan by itself like Daitya, the wicked sons of Diti, or Daanav, the sons of Danu. God divides entire human race into two classes of Devs, the moral, righteous & virtuous, and Asurs, the immoral, evil doers, devoid of good virtues, according to their Swabhaav, the character, irrespective of their dynasty or caste. For example, there are Dev kinds of persons like Prahlaad, Virochan, Bali etc. in Daitya clan whereas **Asurs** like Raavan among Braahamans, Duryodhan, Shishupaal, Jaraasandh, Dantavakr, Kans etc. among Kshatriys. Note that God shall also classify people according to their **Gun**, the traits, in three categories of **Saattvik, Raajasik** & **Taamasik** people in chapter 18. God described from 16/4 to 18, the bad qualities, habits and traits of humans, which are primarily the results of **Raajasik** & **Taamasik** modes of nature. If a person continues to practise the cult of ego and desire, it hardens his **Swabhaav** into **Aasuree** characteristic nature. **Aasuree Sampadaa** drags his soul into ignorance, the slavery of lower nature through any or all of the three gates of **Kaam, Krodh** and **Lobh**.

Their world is a own, limited version, akin to hell on earth, as they have no place in it for anybody else except for themselves, and whom they consider as theirs. It is a weird world devoid of virtue, justice, truth, love, compassion, respect, service and all that is good, virtuous and positive. Their lives are full of lies, cheating, pretence, injustice, cruelty, wrath, envy, violence, arrogance and delusion. They not only shame God within their hearts but also despise and look down on God situated in others. Sometimes, they may appear performing sacred deeds like sacrifices, donations, penance, welfare of others, but their entire activities center essentially on serving self-interest. Their nihilistic approach towards life is like a deluge that drowns everything it comes in contact, without sparing them. It is as worthless as a eucalyptus tree which sucks water and other nutrients from earth, grows tall, but neither bears fruits nor spreads its branches to provide shade to a traveller. **Asurs** are also called **Nishaachar**, the nocturnal creatures like owls, bats, cats, rodents, wasps, preying animals in jungle, and thieves, burglars and arsonists in human societies who become active in darkness due to their **Taamasik** nature and animal-like behaviour. They carry out nefarious, anti social, demonic activities in the dark hours of night thinking that there is no one watching them in night; but they forget that the same God, who witnesses conduct of everyone with just one eye of sun during daytime, is watching them with billions of eyes of stars in the night as well. Nothing can escape from His watchful eyes, be it situated in dazzling light or pitch dark, in a cave or in ocean, on a mountain cliff or deep underground, in desert or in forest, in the heart or in mind of a person. Demonic persons, like nocturnal creatures, are not only afraid of light but also shut their eyes from seeing the light of goodness.

Bad company and/or bad rearing, bewilderment and ignorance are the root causes of **Aasuree** nature. Plato observes:

'We can easily forgive a child who is afraid of darkness; the real tragedy of life is when men are afraid of light'.

Normally speaking a person willfully situated in **Tam** can never ascend to **Sattv** by himself unless guided by a teacher as happened with Vaalmeeki, Angulimaal, Ajaamil etc.

ॐ

God shows the way to get rid of Aasuree nature.

(16/22)

एतैर्विमुक्तः कौन्तेय तमोद्वारैस्त्रिभिर्नरः ।
आचरत्यात्मनः श्रेयस्ततो याति परां गतिम् ॥१६/२२॥

Etairvimukt: Kauntey tamodwaaraistribhirnar: I
Aacharatyaatman: shreyastato yaati paraam gatim II (16/22)

etai: (from these) Vimukt: (liberated) Kauntey (Arjun) Tam: dwaarai: (the gates of darkness) Tribhi: (three kinds of) Nar: (person)I Aacharati (conducts himself) Aatman: (of own self) Shrey:

(acts conducive to virtuous acts) Tat: (by that) Yaati (goes) Paraam (supreme) Gatim (destination)II (16/22)

O Kauntey (Arjun)! The person, who frees himself from these three gates that lead to darkness of hell, and performs meritorious acts conducive to salvation of own self, he only reaches the ultimate destination. (16/22)

A practiser must gradually build his character in such a way that there is no place for **Kaam**, **Krodh** and **Lobh** in his life; and simultaneously display divine virtues in his conduct & behaviour for the liberation of his soul and betterment of the society. Such practiser ultimately attains supreme destination of God.

ॐ

How can we build our character? God shows the simplest way.

(16/23 & 24)

यः शास्त्रविधिमुत्सृज्य वर्तते कामकारतः ।
न स सिद्धिमवाप्नोति न सुखं न परां गतिम् ॥१६/२३॥
तस्माच्छास्त्रं प्रमाणं ते कार्याकार्यव्यवस्थितौ ।
ज्ञात्वा शास्त्रविधानोक्तं कर्म कर्तुमिहार्हसि ॥१६/२४॥

Y: shaastravidhimutsrujya vartate kaamakaarat: I
N s siddhimavaapnoti n sukham n paraam gatim II (16/23)
Tasmaachchhaastram pramaanam te
kaaryaakaaryavyavasthitau I
Jnaatwaa shaastravidhaanoktam karm kartumihaarhasi II
(16/24)

y: (one who) Shaastr vidhim (procedures & regulations laid down by scriptures) Utsrujya (discarding) Vartate (deals) Kaam Kaarat: (whimsical acts in desire)I n (neither) S: (he) Siddhim (success in spiritual realm) Avaapnoti (attain) N (nor) Sukham (bliss, happiness) N (nor) Paraam (ultimate) Gatim (destination)II (16/23)

Tasmaat (therefore) Shaastram (scriptures) Pramaanam (standard, authority) Te (for you) Kaarya Akaarya vyavasthitau (in deciding works which must be performed as duty or which are forbidden works)I jnaatwaa (knowing well) Shaastr vidhaan uktam (rules & regulations proclaimed by scriptures) Karm (work) Kartum (to perform, practice) ih (this) Arhasi (most qualified, capable)II (16/24)

He who engages in whimsical acts misdirected by passionate desires discarding the rules & regulations laid down by scriptures; he neither attains spiritual accomplishment nor eternal bliss nor ultimate destination. (16/23)

Therefore, whenever you are in this dilemma of determining whether a work is your duty that must be performed, or is forbidden to perform; take the scriptures as the final authority (in this respect). You shall be most capable to perform your duty well only after properly knowing the rules & regulations authenticated by the scriptures. (16/24)

Gita prescribes a good formula here to determine one's proper duty whenever he is in a dilemma of doing, or not doing it.

Kaarya Akaarya Vyavasthitau: Kaarya is an activity worth performing, which a person must regard as a sacred duty to perform. **Akaarya** is the opposite of **Kaarya**; it is a forbidden work, which a righteous man should never do, or inaction. This phrase therefore, means to properly differentiate between the two and situate own self to do tight things properly and avoid indulging in wrong activities. Rabindranath Tagore penned,

'I slept & dreamt that life was beauty; I woke and then found life was duty'.

Akaarya, as inaction, is like taking life wishfully as a beautiful dream; **Kaarya** is realizing own responsibility and duty in real life.

Moral: *Any work is not an end in itself; it is only a means of self-purification; and of rendering selfless service to others.*

Kaam Kaarat: The trio of insatiable desire, anger and lust drives his all activities whimsically. Fancied by attractive, passionate and stimulating objects and persons, he chases them to obtain with scant regard to laws and regulations of the society. A **Kaam Kaarat**

person loses his ability to differentiate between **Kaarya** & **Akaarya** i.e. what is best for him to do and what he must never do. In action, he is a rebellion of the rule of **Dharm** and in thought, a nihilist. Scriptures are just gossips for him.

QUESTION: WHAT IS MEANT BY SHAASTR IN GITA? IS IT A REFERENCE TO SOME HOLY BOOK OF A PARTICULAR RELIGION?

No! Though **Shaastr** literally means the Holy Scripture, doctrine, book, authoritative treatise of a religion, Gita attaches a much wider scientific meaning to it. Gita's **Shaastr** is a document of authenticated right knowledge of right works & the code of conduct, the right way of living, developed over long periods through introduction, collection and refinement of wisdom, experiences, and practices of learned men & women, who also institutionalized them. **Shaastr** should not be confused with rigid framework of rules, customs, traditions and rituals prescribed by someone or a group long time ago. A **Shaastr** becomes dead, and deserves burial, unless it embraces continuous amendments and improvements, and sets the best standards for betterment of its society concurrent with its time. A true **Shaastr** binds the members of a society with the mortar of morality consistent with modernity. *'To Change not is the rule of the animal world, not of humans'.*

Caution: *A practiser does not have liberty to bend Shaastr as per his immature thinking and self-interest; nor he should follow it blindly. He should adopt Shaastr as a diving board to plunge into the depths of eternal spiritual laws of Dharm.*

Like **Sattv**, the mode of righteousness, **Shaastr** is a means to reach the ultimate end, not an end in itself. **Shaastr** & **Sattv** are inter-dependent and inseparable because **Shaastr** teaches us to live in **Sattv** until it (**Sattv**) starts enhancing our ability to fathom the depth of the knowledge of Scripture. Referring to **Shaastr** by a practiser is akin to a troubled person seeking advice from friends & well wishers but doing ultimately as per judgment & decision of his soul as per the dictum 'सुनना सब की, करना मन की' i.e. listen to everybody but do as per the bidding of your heart. Krishn is the teacher and guide of Arjun but he lets him take the final decision to fight or not in the war without imposing His intent on him. The objective of **Shaastr** is to direct a person to ascend from **Taamasik** & **Raajasik** modes to **Saattvik** mode by giving up the demonic qualities, especially desire, anger and lust, and following ethical rules prescribed by it in his personal and social life. Shreemad Bhaagawat says:

> *'Like the bee gathering honey from different flowers, the wise man accepts the essence of different scriptures and sees only the good in all religions'.*

Kaalidaas writes in *Abhijnaan Shaakuntalam* 1/20:

> 'सतां हि सन्देहपदेसु वस्तुषु प्रमाणमन्त:करणप्रवृत्तय:'

> *(Whenever good people are in doubt in any matter they accept only that which their conscience certifies.)*

Shaastr, as a reference, is like a water body of shallow water in which an accomplished Yogee just washes his hands & feet, and does not purify his whole being. Following blindly or misinterpreting Shaastr for own convenience results in total ruin of a man as illustrated by this anecdote:

> *"A Guru taught* 'महाजनो येन गत: स पंथा:' *a famous phrase from Mahaabhaarat that means 'Follow the path traversed by Mahaa Jan, the great people', as the last lesson to his two students before they left him to return to their homes. The students met a convoy of wealthy merchants on their way. Attracted by the pomp and luxury of the merchants, the first student willfully misinterpreted the last lesson of his Guru as, 'Follow the path of wealthy merchants', since Mahaa Jan also means eminent merchants & traders, and decided to join the convoy. However, the conviction and morale of the second student was high. He departed from his colleague saying what Guru meant by Mahaa Jan was great persons possessing noble character, not great wealth. He took a detour of the convoy and reached his home in a few days. Meanwhile, the first one was happily enjoying luxury and pleasures of life with the merchants; he became fat and*

looked like a merchant himself. One night, when entire convoy was sleeping, a gang of bandits attacked it. They looted and killed all the merchants, but when the student could not give them anything, they took him hostage, and demanded ransom from his family in the village for his release. Hearing this sad news, the second student came forward to save his friend's life. He established contact with the dacoits through a wandering sage, told them entire story and convinced them that their captive was the only son of his poor parents who found it difficult to meet both ends in his absence. The bandits believed him and released the boy. The first boy thanked his friend profusely for his love and kindness for him and swore to follow the path of knowledge and character only in life, never of pleasures and wealth."

A **Shaastr** of the highest order acts in three ways in our life. First, it cleans our physical self, then our social self and finally takes up cleansing of our **Ant:Karan**, the innermost faculty consisting of **Man**, the mind & heart, **Buddhi**, the intelligence, **Chitt**, the conscience, and Soul. **Shaastr** is thus instrumental in the realization of eternal existence of **Aatmaa** & **Paramaatmaa;** as, at its pinnacle, it transforms into **Adhyaatm** (3/30 & 8/3) after which nothing remains to be learnt. Discussion on **Shaastr** shall continue in 17/1 in next chapter.

Clarification: *God advised us to approach a Tattv Darshee in 4/34, but here he tells us to refer to Shaastr. Why? I wish to clarify that the best way to get rid of confusion, delusion and dilemma is to go to a Tattv Darshee, prostrate before him with utmost humility and submission; render selfless service to him; and then ask our questions after he is pleased with our obeisance. He would then initiate and instruct us in Jnaan, the perfect knowledge, as told in 4/34. Since it is very difficult to find a Tattv Darshee, and if someone is lucky to find, he shall not be available to guide him at every step and all the time; Shaastr comes to his rescue in those times and shows the path forward.*

Moral: *We should try to remain in the good company of great learned people all the time to seek guidance from them; and also keep sacred* *scriptures like Gita, Mahaabhaarat and Raamaayan etc. in the house and study and refer to them frequently.*

CONCLUSION OF CHAPTER 16

Krishn spoke in chapter 14 that every action of men and nature is self-generated according to three modes of nature, **Sattv**, **Raj** and **Tam**. He talked of Guns as the forces of nature (**Prakruti** as well as **Swabhaav**) and the quality of our every work depends on them (it would become clear in chapters 17 & 18). Now, in chapter 16, Krishn divides entire mankind into two categories: **Daivee**, the divine and **Aasuree**, the demonic according to their attitudes, thoughts, character and works which can be either positive or negative, appropriate or inappropriate, worthy or unworthy, moral or immoral and religious or irreligious depending on individual's choice and inclination. Chapter 16 describes them as divine and demonic riches, which a man is free to acquire and possess in his current life. In short, **Guns** thrust themselves upon us, but we are responsible for opting for divine or demonic qualities and conducting our lives accordingly. It is like a father asking his two sons to choose between his wealth and knowledge; the wiser son takes the knowledge and the foolish one feels is delighted to get wealth. God, the father of all embodied souls, similarly has kept open his treasure box of divine and demonic wealth before us; it is up to us to wisely pick the golden ornaments of divine virtues, or be lured by the glitter of fake ornaments made of brass. Choice is ours.

Though termed as **Daivee** and **Aasuree Sampadaa**, these are actually the traits of human and inhuman persons dwelling in this very world. To be divine is to be **Saadhu** i.e. human, and to be demonic is to be **Dushkrutaam**, the inhuman. Rationally speaking, both these categories exist in this very world before us. God declared in 4/8 that He appears in this world whenever wicked demonic people threaten the existence & survival of divine people.

It is worth noting that only 3 shloks are allotted by Krishn to define divine qualities but description of demonic qualities took as many as 16 shloks. It symbolizes that fistful righteousness is more than enough to counter a pail of wrongness. In Mahaabhaarat, 5 Paandavs with 7 Akshauhinee army emerge victorious against 100 Kauravs having 11 Akshauhinee. This almost impossible could happen only because Paandavs relied on divine wealth & guidance of Krishn, whereas Kauravs remained glued until end to demonic wealth of immoral, dubious stratagems of Shakuni and Karn.

Moral: *Let us remember, 'All that glitters is not gold' and make right choices to lead a blissful, purposeful life. Being born as human, we must respect and tread on the path of humanity.*

There is only 1 **Shree Bhagawaan Uvaach** and no other **Uvaach** in this chapter.

॰ॐॐ

ॐ तत्सदिति श्रीमद्भगवद्गीतासूपनिषत्सु ब्रह्मविद्यायां योगशास्त्रे श्रीकृष्णार्जुनसंवादे दैवासुरसंपद्विभागयोगो नाम षोडशोऽध्यायः ॥ १६ ॥

(In the name of God, the ultimate truth thus ends sixteenth chapter named Daivaasur Sampad Vibhaag Yog of Shreemad BhagwadGita, the best Upanishad, Brahm Vidyaa & Yog Shaastr, a dialogue between Shree Krishn & Arjun)

CHAPTER 17

SHRADDHAA TRAY VIBHAAG YOG

(Keep right kind of faith alive within you, and live happily by it.)

PREAMBLE & CONTEXT

Shraddhaa is undulating, unflinching, reverential faith and belief that leads to **Jnaan**. God talked about **Shraddhaa** for the first time in Gita in 3/31 saying, *'They who follow this eternal doctrine of Mine (Karm Yog), faithfully, are liberated forever from Karm Bandhan'*. He said in 4/39, *'The faithful acquires Jnaan'* and in 6/47, *'He is the greatest Yogee who is faithful and transcended into Me with devotion'*. He opined again in 12/2 *'Devotees endowed with unflinching faith are the best Yogees'*.

Eloquent praise of **Shraddhaa** showered frequently by God in these and other shloks, made Arjun curious to learn more about it but he could not ask about it because of other more important questions in his mind. At last, when God directed him in 16/23-24 to refer to **Shaastr**, the Holy Scriptures whenever in doubt or dilemma in order to firm up his faith, he found it as the best opportunity to raise the question in the opening shlok 17/1 of this chapter about **Shraddhaa** that was pending till now in his mind.

WHY CHAPTER 17 IS NAMED SHRADDHAA TRAY VIBHAAG YOG?

Shraddhaa of a man is his faith & belief, which he consciously cultivates in his life and accepts that only as the truth and purpose of his life. It is the driving force of conviction behind whatsoever a man does in his life, whether he worships, or observes ascetic practices & penance, or performs sacrificial works & duties, or donates, or what he eats, speaks, thinks. It is the backbone of his character and way of life. **Ashraddhaa**, dealt with in 4/40 & 9/3 earlier, on the other hand, is complete absence of faith in God, Scripture, Guru, saints, or whatsoever can bring a wrong doer back on the right path. God dedicates complete chapter 17 to explain three kinds of **Shraddhaa** and other related aspects while replying to the inquiry made by Arjun to know how one can evaluate his **Shraddhaa** on the scale of three modes of nature, **Sattv, Raj** & **Tam**. God shall speak of **Shraddhaa** in 17/2, 3, 13, 17 & 28 in this chapter, and proclaim in 18/71:

"Even if a person faithfully listens to it i.e. Gita without envy & criticism, he is liberated from all sins and attains the superior world that one can achieved otherwise only by performing sacred acts".

This is why chapter 17 is named as **Shraddhaa Tray Vibhaag Yog**.

৯৮৫

Arjun wants to know more about Shraddhaa.

(17/1)

अर्जुन उवाच
ये शास्त्रविधिमुत्सृज्य यजन्ते श्रद्धयान्विताः ।
तेषां निष्ठा तु का कृष्ण सत्त्वमाहो रजस्तमः ॥ १७/१॥

Arjun Uvaach
Ye shaastravidhimutsrujya yajante shraddhayaanvitaa: I
Teshaam nishthaa tu kaa Krishn Sattvmaaho rajastam: II
(17/1)

Ye (who) Shaastr Vidhim (rules & regulations proclaimed by Scriptures) Utsrujya (discard) Yajante (worship by performing sacrifices) Shraddhayaa Anvitaa: (endowed with undulating faith)

I Teshaam (their) Nishthaa (reverential allegiance) Tu (but) Kaa (what, which) Krishn (Krishn) Sattvam (the mode of righteousness, goodness) Aaho (or, otherwise) Raj: (the mode of passion & fruitive works) Tam: (the mode of darkness, ignorance, inertia) II (17/1)

Arjun said:

"O Krishn! The reverential allegiance of those, who are fully possessed of faith in God and worship Him though they do not follow the rules and regulations proclaimed by Scriptures, is of which category? Is it of Sattv, the goodness, of Raj, the passion or of Tam, the darkness of ignorance?" (17/1)

Ye Shaastr Vidhim Utsrujya refers to those who do not practice as directed by the Scriptures. A practiser faithfully pursuing his goal to become a Yogee may not follow the Scripture due any of the following reasons:

1. Scripture becomes outdated and irrelevant in due course of time.
2. It degenerates into a bundle of customs, rituals and orthodoxy.
3. The same or some other Scripture gives conflicting and confusing statements and directions.
4. Modern knowledge has already surpassed the original knowledge contained in the Scripture.
5. The knowledge contained in the Scripture needs to probe and discover further.
6. With the passage of time, somebody might have played with it and twisted the contents of a Scripture to suit his thinking or interest.
7. His teacher or mentor forbids him to follow the Scripture.
8. He is atheist and does not attach any importance to the Scripture.

It is not bad to challenge or question Scriptures if done with a **Saattvik** frame of mind. Buddh, in his quest for knowledge, studied Veds & Upanishads first before propagating his Ashtaangik Maarg, the eightfold path (refer 5/22). It gave birth to a great religion like Buddhism; and whole world reveres Siddhaarth, once a prince, as Lord Buddh, the enlightened soul.

Caution: *A practiser must have the quest, patience, preparation & clarity of thought like Buddh before challenging the authority of Scripture.*

Gita spoke very high of **Shraddhaa** earlier in 3/31, 4/39, 6/47 etc., as stated in the context above. Arjun therefore wants to clarify here which out of the three, **Saattvik, Raajasik** or **Taamasik** kinds of **Shraddhaa** is good for a practiser who does not give due importance to Scripture, and why.

Whatever may be the reason for disregarding the bidding of **Shaastr** the most important part of Arjun's query is that if such a practiser is faithful in his quest for liberation, whether his faith is situated in **Sattv,** or **Raj** or **Tam**? The underlying query is that if his faith is **Raajasik** or **Taamasik**, will it still lead him towards his goal of liberation or not?

Though **Nishthaa** generally denotes faith, it is the concentrated will of devotion, the reverential, firm allegiance towards a person or deity or God. When differentiated, we can say that **Nishthaa** is superlative form of **Shraddhaa**. Robinson Crusoe's man Friday was **Nishthaa Vaan**, the most faithful to him, to the core of his heart. Please refer to 3/31-32 for more thoughts on **Nishthaa**.

ॐ

God prepares to describe three kinds of Shraddhaa.

(17/2)

श्रीभगवानुवाच
त्रिविधा भवति श्रद्धा देहिनां सा स्वभावजा ।
सात्त्विकी राजसी चैव तामसी चेति तां शृणु ॥१७/२॥

Shree Bhagawaan Uvaach
Trividhaa bhavati shraddhaa dehinaam saa swabhaavajaa I
Saattvikee raajasee chaiv taamasee cheti taam Shrunu II
(17/2)

Trividhaa (of three kinds) Bhavati (is) Shraddhaa (faith) Dehinaam (embodied living beings) Saa (that) Swabhaavajaa (born of nature, character)I Saattvikee (endowed with Sattv) Raajasee (with Raj) Ch (and) Ev (also) Taamasee (with Tam) Ch (and) iti (about them) Taam (those) Shrunu (listen)II (17/2)

God said:

"The faith of all embodied living beings born out of their characteristic nature is of three kinds. They are Saattvikee, of goodness, Raajasee, of passions and Taamasee, of ignorance. Listen about them now. (17/2)

Krishn tells Arjun indirectly in this shlok that he framed his question in 17/1 wrongly because actually **Shraddhaa,** not **Nishthaa,** the allegiance, is of three types: **Saattvik, Raajasik & Taamasik. Shraddhaa** it is born out of the nature of all beings. Indirectly He reminds him of His earlier statement in 3/3 where He had proclaimed only two kinds of **Nishthaa** in this world, the first one as **Jnaan Yog** practised by believers in **Saamkhya (Jnaan)** And the second one as **Karm Yog** practised by believers in **Karm.** The fine difference between **Shraddhaa** and **Nishthaa** therefore is that **Shraddhaa** is the real cause of success or failure of one's work since it is the spark, the motive force that ignites and engages him in an activity; whereas **Nishthaa** is the means employed by him to transform his **Shraddhaa** into an activity and arrive at his goal. **Shraddhaa** is the motive force that drives a practiser to become Yogee; and he can adopt **Nishthaa** in **Jnaan, Karm** or **Bhakti** or any other path to attain it.

৯৩৯

Shraddhaa of all people is according to his nature.

(17/3)

सत्त्वानुरूपा सर्वस्य श्रद्धा भवति भारत ।
श्रद्धामयोऽयं पुरुषो यो यच्छ्रद्धः स एव सः ॥१७/३॥

Sattvaanuroopaa sarvasya shraddhaa bhavati Bhaarat I
Shraddhaamayoʃyam purusho yo yachchhraddh: s ev s: II
(17/3)

Sattv Anuroopaa (according to his existing characteristic nature)
Sarvasya (of everyone) Shraddhaa (faith) Bhavati (is) Bhaarat
(Arjun)I Shraddhaa may: (endowed with faith) Ayam (this) Purush:
(the individual person) Y: (the one who) Yat (which) Shraddh: (faith)
S: (he) Ev (also) S: (he)II (17/3)

**O Bhaarat (Arjun)! Quality of faith of every being is according
to his existing characteristic nature. Every person is endowed
with faith; and therefore he himself becomes of the same
quality as of his faith. (17/3)**

The quality of faith differs as per the characteristic nature,
temperament, the stuff that constitutes the whole existence of a
person. It is thus made clear here that a man builds up the quality
of his faith in things and persons according to the way chosen
consciously or unconsciously by him to lead his life. In order to
make his faith **Saattvikee,** he must first build up his character on
the strong foundations of sound morality, principles and **Dharm**
as directed by **Shaastr.** As we persistently try to live in accordance
with the Scripture and do our duties our **Shraddhaa** firms up in
Sattv; and from there, it gradually culminates into divine **Nishthaa.**
Shraddhaa May Ayam Purush: y: Yat Shraddh: s: ev s: This
phrase proclaims that soul embodied in a person, his existence, is
a reflection of his faith, will & belief. It is said further explicitly that
a person becomes of the same quality as of his faith.

৵৵৹

What type of people worship which type of beings?

(17/4)

यजन्ते सात्त्विका देवान्यक्षरक्षांसि राजसाः ।
प्रेतान्भूतगणांश्चान्ये यजन्ते तामसा जनाः ॥ १७/४ ॥

Yajante saattvikaa devaanyaksharakshaansi raajasaa: I
PretaanbhootgaNaanshchaanye yajante taamasaa janaa: II
(17/4)

Yajante (worship by Yajn) Saattvikaa (persons endowed
with Sattv) Devaan (to demigods) Yaksh (Yaksh, descendents &
attendants of Kuber) Rakshaansi (the guarding powers) Raajasaa:
(persons with qualities of Raj)I pretaan (spirits of the dead persons)
Bhoot ganaan (ghosts) Ch (and) Anye (others) Yajante (worship)
Taamasaa: (persons with qualities of Tam) Janaa: (people, devotees)
II (17/4)

**Persons in the mode of righteousness worship gods; persons
in the mode of passion worship Yaksh & Raksh; and others in
the mode of ignorance & darkness worship spirits of the dead,
like ghosts. (17/4)**

People with **Raajasik** or **Taamasik** faith are motivated to perform
sacrificial works due to ostentation, pride, ego, lust, revenge, anger
and jealousy because they driven by the desire of quick, favorable
fruition of their works. For this, **Raajasik** men worship lesser gods
like **Yaksh, Gandharv, Pitr** and other superhuman powers, which
protect them; and the **Taamasik** men worship perverse souls like
the ghosts, devils, genii etc. who have limited powers to act as
guardians of their worldly desires. But the person with **Saattvik
Shraddhaa** worships **Devs**, the Demigods, the manifested forms
of God who, besides meeting his worldly needs (whether prayed
for by him or not), also facilitate, help and guide him to achieve
his ultimate goal of liberation. **Shankaraachaarya** probably had
persons of **Saattvik** faith in his mind when he prescribed to worship
any of **Panch Dev** viz. **Shiv, Naaraayan, Ravi, Ganesh** and **Devee**,
(abbreviated as शंनारगदे as explained in 4/25). Worship of God in any
form reaches Him directly or indirectly depending on the quality of
faith, and objective of worship.

If performed with perseverance, such devotional works gradually
transcend a person having **Saattvik** faith to the state of **Gunaateet**
(chapter 14) as he becomes beyond the effects and compulsions of
Guns & **Shaastr**. In fact, his works & words become standards of

Guns and **Shaastr** for others to follow as a group of people follows a torchbearer in darkness, their life becomes like a lighthouse in the sea. He attains his ultimate goal of uniting with **Sat-Chitt-Aanand** i.e. the eternal existence, consciousness & bliss of the Supreme Soul, in his current life itself. He becomes **Jeevan Mukt**, a liberated soul in this world as all of his personal will, desire, action, worry, stress and need dissolve into Supreme will of God.

जाहि विधि राखे राम ताहि विधि रहिये ।
प्रेम से सीताराम सीताराम कहिये ॥

(Live only as per the will of God; faithfully continue to chant His name.)

৵৽৽

God describes the kind of Tap performed by people of Aasuree nature.

(17/5 & 6)

अशास्त्रविहितं घोरं तप्यन्ते ये तपो जनाः ।
दम्भाहंकारसंयुक्ताः कामरागबलान्विताः ॥ १७/५॥
कर्षयन्तः शरीरस्थं भूतग्राममचेतसः ।
मां चैवान्तःशरीरस्थं तान्विद्ध्यासुरनिश्चयान् ॥ १७/६॥

Ashaastravihitam ghoram tapyante tapo janaa: I
Dambhaahankaarasamyuktaa: kaamaraagabalaanvitaa: II
(17/5)
Karshayant: shareerastham bhootgraamachetas: I
Maam chaivaant:shareerastham
taanvidhyaasuranishchayaan II (17/6)

Ashaastr vihitam (not approved by Scriptures) Ghoram (terrible) Tapyante (perform ascetic practices) Tap: (penance, austerities) Janaa: (people)I Dambh Ahamkaar samyuktaa: (fully engaged in hypocrisy, pretence & falsified ego) Kaam Raag Bal Anvitaa: (impelled by ambition, attachment & power)II (17/5) karshayant: (tormenting) Shareerastham (situated with body) Bhoot graamam (group of five basic elements, space, wind, water, fire & earth of body)) Achetas: (conscienceless)I maam (to me) Ch (and) Ev (also) Ant:shareerastham (situated in the innermost chamber of body) Taan (those) Viddhi; (know well) Aasur (of demoniac) Nishchayaan (persons having resolve)II (17/6)

People, who do penance by undertaking severe ascetic practices not approved by Scriptures, fully engage in false ego and hypocrisy; and are solely impelled by ambition, attachment and power; they firstly weaken their own body consisting of five basic constituents by tormenting it; and then even Me, the Supreme Soul dwelling in the innermost chamber of their body. You should know them as conscienceless persons, possessed of Aasuree, the demoniac resolve & characteristic nature. (17/5 & 6)

Since the meaning of above shloks is self-explanatory and Gita is going to discuss three Kinds of **Tap** & their three modes in this chapter later in 17/14-19, I limit our discussions about **Tap** for the time being as follows:

Note from these two shloks that Gita rejects severe ascetic practices as **Aasuree,** the demoniac though many sects, religions and communities consider it as a prime condition to attain liberation. Gita thinks of it as a self-inflicted violence on own soul as well as on God residing within his body. It is in fact a self-erected impediment in the path of his liberation. Readers must have noticed by now that Gita does not preach extremities of any kind and presents **Dharm** in its simplest and most practical form. If we can think a little deeper, we shall find that this thought of Gita is near to its oft-repeated supremacy of **Karm Phal Tyaag**, the giving up of all expectations of favorable fruition of works over **Karm Sannyaas** i.e. physically renouncing all kinds of works, to attain liberation. We shall visit the pinnacle of this last proposition of Gita in chapter 18.

Dambh Ahamkaar Samyuktaa: They are people fully engaged in hypocrisy, pretence and false ego. Very ugly scenes of heads of some big religious sects quarreling for their right to take the first dip in

Sangam (the confluence of Gangaa, Yamunaa & Saraswatee) during the auspicious dates of Kumbh (the biggest religious congregation on earth) have been often reported in India. Someone has well said:

"If we can replace 'I' with 'We', our illness transforms into wellness".

SOME ADDITIONAL THOUGHTS ON KAAM RAAG BAL ANVITAA

Kaam Raag Bal Anvitaa They people possessed by **Kaam**, the intense, passionate desires, **Raag**, the infatuation and attachment with material objects and matters, and unrestricted **Bal**, the physical power of body, wealth and position. Overpowered by these vices they develop **Ashraddhaa**, the lack of faith in Scriptures and totally disregard their directions and strictures. Their every activity is motivated by self-interest. Gita deplores such people at every step of its teachings. Duryodhan is a **Kaam Raag Bal Anvit** person.

Caution: *Kaam, the desire to attain Jnaan and/or to connect with God through Yog; Raag, the attachment with God; and Bal, the strength to work as per the will of God are virtues, not vices. Kaam, Raag & Bal are forbidden by Shaastr only for impermanent worldly things, not for pursuance of spiritual goals. Maanasik, the mental Bal is greater than Shaareerik, the physical Bal, and Aadhyaatmik, the spiritual Bal is the greatest of all. Chaanakya, a simple teacher, could bring down the mighty empire of Dhaananand due to his spiritual Bal.*

God stated in 7/11:

"I am Bal, the power of the powerful people who are free from ambition and attachment; I am Kaam, the sexual (and other desires) that are consistent with Dharm in all living beings".

Clarification: *A Kaam Raag Bal Anvit person is asur, not Dev because these traits are Aasuree, forbidden by Gita.*

ॐ ॐ

Which ingredients contribute in firming up a person's
Shraddhaa?

(17/7)

आहारस्त्वपि सर्वस्य त्रिविधो भवति प्रियः ।
यज्ञस्तपस्तथा दानं तेषां भेदमिमं शृणु ॥ १ ७/७॥

Aahaarstwapi sarvsya trividho bhavati priy: I
Yajnstapastathaa daanam teshaam bhedamimam Shrinu II II
(17/7)

Aahaar: (food) Tu (even) Api (also) Sarvasya (of everyone) Trividh:
(of three kinds) Bhavati (is) Priy: (liked)I Yajn: tap: (penance) Tathaa
(similarly) Daanam (charity) Teshaam (their) Bhedam (classification)
imam (this) Shrinu (listen)II (17/7)

**Even the foodstuffs that everyone takes as per his liking
are classified into three kinds (Triguns, three modes of nature).
Then listen also to the similar distinctive qualities of Yajn
(sacrificial as well as other actions), tap (ascetic practices for
penance) and Daan (donation) also. (17/7)**

Gita first talked about three types of faiths and then directed
us to cultivate our life in **Saattvik Shraddhaa** with the help
of Scripture. Since the faith of a person depends on the food he
takes, the sacrifices and works he does, the austerity & penance
he performs & the charity he gives, Gita now describes their
qualitative modes so that a person desirous to develop **Saattvik
Shraddhaa** can improve himself in these fields. This is in short
how Scriptures also describe them. It was said earlier that the three
modes of nature are pervading in all entities of universe. Hence,
we shall now deal with **Aahaar**, the food, in 17/8, 9 & 10; **Yajn** in
17/11-13; **Tap** in 17/14-19; and **Daan** in 17/20-22 with respect
to their three qualities of **Sattv, Raj** & **Tam**. Thus, Gita introduces
teachings of **Shaastr** in 17/8-22 to build the character of a man,
and simultaneously develop his faith.

This introduction of **Triguns**, three qualitative modes of nature
is brief, conventional and symbolic and we must expand and apply

it in all situations of life. In chapter 18, Gita also would dwell upon **Triguns** of more things like **Tyaag**, the renunciation, **Jnaan**, the knowledge, **Karm**, the work, **Kartaa**, the doer of work, **Buddhi,** the intelligence, **Dhruti**, the steadfastness and **Sukh**, the happiness. This exposure to three modes enables us to mould our life style & live blissfully.

ॐ

God takes up Aahaar, the food as the first
and foremost cause of Shraddhaa.

(17/8, 9 & 10)

आयुःसत्त्वबलारोग्यसुखप्रीतिविवर्धनाः ।
रस्याः स्निग्धाः स्थिरा हृद्या आहाराः सात्त्विकप्रियाः ॥१७/८॥
कट्वम्ललवणात्युष्णतीक्ष्णरूक्षविदाहिनः ।
आहारा राजसस्येष्टा दुःखशोकामयप्रदाः ॥१७/९॥
यातयामं गतरसं पूति पर्युषितं च यत् ।
उच्छिष्टमपि चामेध्यं भोजनं तामसप्रियम् ॥१७/१०॥

Aayu:sattvabalaarogyasukhapreetivivardhanaa: I
Rasyaa: snigdhaa: sthiraa hridyaa aahaaraa: saattvikapriyaa:
II (17/8)
Katvamlalavanaatyushnateekshnarookshavidaahin: I
Aahaaraa raajasasyeshtaa du:khashokaamayapradaa: II
(17/9)
Yaatayaamam gatarasam pooti paryushitam ch yat I
Uchchhishtamapi chaamedhyam bhojanam taamasapriyam II
II (17/10)

Aayu: (span of life) Sattv (the quality of Sattv) Bal (strength, energy) Aarogya (freedom from disease) Sukh (Happiness) Preeti (liking, gladness) Vivardhanaa: (enriching)I Rasyaa: (succulent, juicy, tasty) Snigdhaa: (reasonably oily) Sthiraa: (long lasting) Hridyaa (easily digestible) Aahaaraa: (food) Saattvik (endowed with Sattv) Priyaa: (loved)II (17/8)

Katw (bitter) Aml (acid, sour) Lavan (salty) Ati (too much) Ushn (hot) Teekshn (pungent, spicy) Rooksh (dry, crusty) Vidaahin: (inflammatory)I Aahaaraa (food) Raajasasya (of Raajasee persons with the quality of Raj) Ishtaa: (cherished, favorite) Du:kh Shok Aamay Pradaa: (result in pain, regret & disease)II (17/9)

Yaat Yaamam (expired, partially cooked, raw) Gat Rasam (tasteless, unpalatable) Pooti (emanating foul smell) Paryushitam (stale, decomposed) Ch (and) Yat (which)I Uchchhishtam (food remnant after someone else ate partially) Api (also) Ch (and) Amedhyam (impious) Bhojanam (meals) Taamas (persons with qualities of Tam) Priyam (agreeable)II (17/10)

The foodstuffs, which prolong life; promote good conduct; provide strength, freedom from disease, happiness and satiation; and are succulent, palatable, effective for long time, easily digestible & pleasing to heart and not dry & crusty; such foods are loved by a Saattvik person i.e. who is endowed with qualities like righteousness, virtues, purity of heart, truth etc. (17/8)

The foodstuffs that are too bitter, acidic, salty, hot (also implies too cold) Pungent & spicy, dry & crusty and inflammatory (to the digestive system), are the favorite foods of a Raajasik person i.e. who is endowed with the quality of passion & desire though such foods result in pain, regret & disease. (17/9)

A Taamasik person, endowed with Tam, the lowest qualities of darkness, ignorance, evil, malice, indolence etc., likes foodstuffs, semi-cooked, prepared long back (3 hours or more before consuming), or unripe; and which are unpalatable, stale, decomposed & spoiled, emanate foul smell, leftover as remnant by others after eating from the same, and are impious. (17/10)

Krishn defines qualities of food that alone can cultivate **Saattvik** qualities in a person, in 17/8. These are:

1. **Aayu: Sattv bal Aarogya Sukh Preeti Vivardhanaa**: **Saattvik** food enriches and increases life span; **Sattv**, the quality of righteousness, purity inner & outer vigour, positive attitude and creative mind; **Bal**, the physical, mental

and spiritual strength; **Aarogya**, the freedom from disease and ill-health; **Sukh**, the happiness of body and soul; and **Preeti**, the love for others & delight for self. Ripe fruits, dry fruits, fresh vegetables, salads, cow milk, honey, Ghee are some such foods.

2. **Rasyaa**: **Saattvik** food should be succulent, juicy, palatable and tasty. Most of the fruits bear this quality. Boiled foods like Daal, rice, whole grains like wheat, corn, Idalee, sweet potato, vegetables etc. and liquids like Sherbet, butter milk, milk, cane juice, orange juice etc., are **Rasya**.

3. **Snigdhaa**: **Saattvik** food should be soft, smooth, not dry, crusty or hard to chew, made tender and supple by applying Ghee, butter, honey etc. on it. Chapaatee, Halawaa, Khichadee, **Upamaa** etc. are Snigdh foods.

4. **Sthiraa**: **Saattvik** food should be nourishing & effective for a long time. Dry fruits, sprouted grains etc. are Sthir foods.

5. **Hridyaa**: **Saattvik** food should be pleasing to heart and stomach i.e. tasty and easily digestible and satisfying the soul.

In short, **Saattvik** foodstuffs are those that improve the life of a person by providing good health and longevity, and develop **Saattvik Shraddhaa** in him. A practiser desirous of **Saattvik Shraddhaa** must avoid foods lacking in above five qualities, but rich in qualities mentioned as **Raajasik** in 17/9 and **Taamasik** in 17/10. Though taste is mentioned as a quality of **Saattvik** diet, it implies satisfying the soul of a person, not his taste buds. The sense of taste is not inborn but acquired from outside world; an infant dislikes unnaturally sweetened or salted food. Gita stated in 3/14:

"All living beings are born from food and subsist on it"

Aahaar, in its wider sense, includes foods and other basic needs of body like air and water. On a still higher plane, it is also the food for mental thoughts, conscience and soul. Thus, **Aahaar** is the basic intake of every living being, including humans, as it nourishes his physical, mental, emotional and spiritual needs. **Aahaar** is the first and foremost thing to develop right kind of faith. Lot of literature on foods is available, but I feel it appropriate to discuss it here with reference to these and other shloks of Gita. It would help us to develop a holistic understanding about what and how we should eat, how we should earn our food so that our body, mind and soul are always fit, blissful and recharged to do our duties properly.

SOME ADDITIONAL THOUGHTS ON AAHAAR, THE FOOD

Krishn dealt with material aspects of **Aahaar** in **Yajn Shishtaasin** (3/13) and **Yajnashisht Amrut Bhuj** (4/31) which mean the foodstuffs and materials leftover as **Prasaad**, the propitious blessings of God after performing a **Yajn** i.e. an auspicious and sacred activity. **Yajnashisht** food is always of the highest quality since no one would offer **Raajasik** and **Taamasik** food to guests or as oblations to God. In order to reconnect with current discussion properly, I recommended re-reading *'Some additional thoughts on Yajnashishtaashin'* under 3/13; and recapitulating the warning given by God in 3/12:

> *"He, who ignores His instruction to discharge his duties properly to feed lower and upper species of His creation, shall be treated as a thief by Him".*

The word **Niraahaar** was used in 2/59 while discussing the nature of **Indriys,** always hungry for **Vishays**, the passionate objects as their **Aahaar** on which they feed and grow. Gita cautioned such people there who may outwardly seem to succeed in forcing their **Indriys** to abstain from **Vishays** but remain mentally famished of material pleasures since their infatuation towards them remains active. The **Aahaar** mentioned there is for mental faculties, the important kind of **Aahaar** that a Yogee must control. On the other hand, **Niyataahaaraa** mentioned in 4/30 is for those practisers who offer oblations by regulating and controlling their **Aahaar** (including all kinds of intakes like food, water, air for body and **Vishays** for senses, mind and conscience). **Niyataahaaraa** are therefore superior to **Niraahaar** of 2/59. Abstinence by using force while remaining mentally desirous and involved in any activity including eating is condemned by Gita. A great devotee expresses **Niyataahaar** very nicely as:

'If I eat too much, my God's stomach would pain; and if I eat too less my God shall die of hunger.'

Phrases **Naatyashnatastu Yogoʃsti n chaikaantamashnat** (6/16) and **Yuktaahaaravihaar** (6/17) strike a balance in line of **Niyataahaaraa.** They define them as persons who neither eat too much nor abstain from eating because **Yog,** the union of the Soul with the Supreme Soul, which mitigates all sorrows, is possible only for persons who appropriately regulate their **Aahaar** and recreational activities (of **Vishays**). Gita talks of two kinds of leftover food. The first one is **Yajnashisht** in 3/13 & 4/41 is of the highest quality as explained above, and the second one, **Uchchhisht** described here in 17/10 is जूठन i.e. food leftover after someone else ate from it partially, is of lowest quality fit only for animals. **Yajnashisht** is as sacred and pious as **Prasaad** of God for it is bestowed with the human quality of sharing and giving; it is **Amrut,** while **Uchchhisht** is poison because if contaminated with virus, it spreads communicative diseases.

Like everything in the world, the lowest (**Taamasik**) part of food is mostly rejected as stool, the medium (**Raajasik**) partly nourishes the body and the finest (**Saattvik**) part nurtures inner faculties of **Man,** the mind & heart, **Buddhi,** the intelligence, **Chitt,** the conscience, and **Aatmaa,** the soul. Although our body is able to segregate them automatically by quality, are we, as a person, able to do it for the things we physically accept as Aahaar from outside world for our mental, emotional and spiritual nourishment? Pathetically, in most cases, the answer would be 'No' because our intake habits are mostly impelled by **Raajasik** and **Taamasik** traits, we accept only what **Vishay Lolup Indriys** and **Man,** always eager for sensual pleasures, like.

People bog down often in controversies of vegetarianism & non-vegetarianism; and start defining them as per their convenience and traditional belief. Some people think eating fish & other seafood, eggs etc., as vegetarian whereas others consider dairy products, honey also as non-vegetarian. Some religions preach that God created everything in this world primarily for human consumption only whereas some other religions prohibit vegetables like onions, garlic, potatoes, carrots, leafy vegetables etc. from the list of eatables. Almost all Tibetans including **Dalai Lama** eat meat. Nevertheless, I will be a great hypocrite if I claim to be more **Saattvik** than him simply because I am vegetarian. Once, a non-vegetarian person asked me why Gita prohibits non-vegetarianism but when I politely asked him to tell me the shlok number, he could not tell me. Gita, true to its graceful style, skillfully circumvents all such controversies unless it becomes necessary to propagate its core teaching. Therefore, it does not name any food item that one should or should not eat but describes only the qualities in a very subtle, rational manner that one should consider before taking any food. It neither preaches vegetarianism nor prohibits one from eating certain other things but leaves it to individual's judgement. Nevertheless, my person opinion in this regard is that the *'first fundamental right of living'* granted to every human being in a civilized society, is also the fundamental right of every animal in the world, and we have no right to infringe its right to satisfy our taste buds. Nevertheless, Gita lays great emphasis on the essential qualities of food for the overall, physical, mental and spiritual growth of a person, not on things or objects per se. Importance of choosing a diet that enhances **Aayu, Sattv, Bal, Aarogya, Sukh** and **Preeti** should be never overlooked. **Sattv,** among them, is the most important since all other qualities are bound to follow **Sattv** automatically. J R D Tata says:

'Common people have an appetite for food; uncommon people have an appetite for service.'

This is perhaps also the under lying idea in the Christian daily prayer, *'Give us our daily bread.'* Common people can occasionally take **Raajasik** foods (17/9), but a practiser should avoid them as far as possible. **Taamasik** foods (17/10) are prohibited for every human being completely.

Some other considerations, which I feel are important while taking food:

1. Always try to sit in a clean, pious and relatively quiet place preferably facing east or north for eating. Avoid eating while standing, lying down, working, exercising or doing some strenuous work.

2. Thank God, for providing you the food you are going to take. I recommend offering the food to God first by chanting shlok 9/6 of Gita.

3. Do not divide your attention on things other than the meal like TV, reading, talking etc. Concentrate all thoughts on food, enjoy each morsel and think that it is providing full nourishment to your body, conscience and soul.

4. Do not rush through your food. You are performing a pious act.

5. Anger, ambition, emotion, envy, lust etc. must be avoided. Even a **Saattvik** food would effectually become inferior if taken with disturbed state of mind. Milk consumed by a snake turns into poison due to its Taamasik nature whereas a bitter medicine serves as Amrut for a patient. It is rightly said 'जैसा खाए अन्न वैसा हो जाये मन' i.e. *'your mind and heart adopt the quality of food you take'.*

6. Take only that much food in your dish which you can comfortably consume. Do not let anything go waste. Wasting food is a social crime perpetrated by those who have plenty, on the starving millions.

7. Eating together in a group with light, cheerful chatting is O. K. but over indulgence in any matter is sure to spoil your meal.

8. Clean well your hands before and immediately after eating. Remove footwear if possible.

9. It is advisable to avoid drinking water at least 30 minutes before and after eating.

10. Help yourself as well as others particularly the elders, women and children by serving them first and assisting them in eating.

A septuagenarian friend of mine once invited me to lunch at his house. When we were about to finish, he wiped his dishes and bowls clean with his finger and licked the finger. I felt it ill mannered, grossly out of etiquette. He then quietly explained why he does it daily in his house. He said if he leaves some food in his dish, it would tantamount to:

1. Disrespect to my daughter in law who cooks healthy, tasty food for me with love and care.

2. She would have to cook more for the waste.

3. Disrespect to my son who earns, through hard, honest work, to feed me.

4. Rats, cockroaches, flies, insects, mosquitoes will thrive on leftover food and infest my house.

5. Its stale odour shall make the air impure.

6. Its disposal becomes a social and environmental problem.

7. Someone less fortunate than me can have some morsels to satisfy his hunger if I do not overeat or leave unconsumed in my dish.

8. My grandchildren keenly watch my habits. Children usually pick up bad habits faster than good ones.

9. More consumption or waste shall need more production of ingredients.

10. Insult of farmer who labored to produce it, of trader who stocked it and made available.

Clarification: *Above expressed thoughts are mine without any insistence on readers to follow them. They may disregard or modify them, as they feel fit.*

Three types of Yajn are described.

(17/11, 12 & 13)

अफलाकाङ्क्षिभिर्यज्ञो विधिदृष्टो य इज्यते ।
यष्टव्यमेवेति मनः समाधाय स सात्त्विकः ॥ १७/११ ॥
अभिसंधाय तु फलं दम्भार्थमपि चैव यत् ।
इज्यते भरतश्रेष्ठ तं यज्ञं विद्धि राजसम् ॥ १७/१२ ॥
विधिहीनमसृष्टान्नं मन्त्रहीनमदक्षिणम् ।
श्रद्धाविरहितं यज्ञं तामसं परिचक्षते ॥ १७/१३ ॥

Aphalaakaankshibhiryajno vidhidrushto y ijyate I
Yashtavyamevevti man: samaadhaay s saattvik: II (17/11)
Abhisandhaay tu phalam dambhaarthamapi chaiv yat I
Ijyate Bharatashreshth tam Yajnam viddhi raajasam II (17/12)
Vidhiheenamashrushtaannam mantraheenamadakshinam I
Shraddhaavirahitam Yajnam taamasam parichakshate II
(17/13)

Aphal Aakaankshibhi: (persons not desirous of fruits) Yajn: (sacrificial action) Vidhi Drusht: (according to rules & regulations of Scriptures) Y: (which) ijyate (is done)I yashtavyam (must be performed as sacred duty) Ev (only) Iti (thus) man: (mind) Samaadhaay (resolved) S: (he) Saattvik: (endowed with Sattv)II (17/11)

Abhisandhaay (allied with) Tu (but) Phalam (fruit) Dambh (hypocrisy) Artham (for the sake of) Api (only) Ch (and) Ev (even) Yat (that which)I ijyate (is performed, done) Bharat Shreshth (Arjun) Tam (to that) Yajnam (sacrificial or any other action) Viddhi (know) Raajasam (with quality of Raj)II (17/12)

Vidhi Heenam (deficient in rules & regulations) Ashrushtaannam (without offering oblations to gods & invitees) Mantr Heenam (without chants of sacred hymns) Adakshinam (without paying gratuity to priests)I Shraddhaa Virahitam (devoid of faith) Yajnam (sacrificial action) Taamasam (with qualities of Tam) Parichakshate (is seen as)II (17/13)

When a person desireless of any reward, performs **Yajn** i.e. a sacrificial or any other work in accordance with rules & regulations prescribed by Scriptures fully convinced that it is his sacred duty, that Yajn becomes Saattvik i.e. of righteous & meritorious quality. (17/11)

But, O Bharat Shreshth (Arjun)! Yajn that is performed only for the sake of hypocrisy or even with an eye on some benefit, know such Yajn as Raajas i.e. of quality of passion. (17/12)

Yajn, performed faithlessly with total disregard to prescribed rules & regulations of Scriptures, without offering oblations to Gods and food to invitees, without chanting Holy Hymns, without paying gratuity to priests for their services, and without giving appropriate donations to others; such Yajn is Taamas i.e. lowest in merit due to qualities of ignorance and darkness. (17/13)

Gita earlier talked about **Yajn** in 3/10-12 and then again described their twelve types from 4/24 to 30. It shall be useful to read there for proper understanding of these shloks. Besides traditional & ritualistic meaning of **Yajn** to please gods by lighting fire and offering sacrifice as prescribed in Scriptures, it also encompasses sacred works done for the well-being of others by sacrificing self-interest as directed by most of the Holy Scriptures including Gita. Note that great importance is attached to charity and paying the due gratuity and share of **Yajn** to every participant. Such act is symbolic of the sacrifice, help, and expressing solidarity & concern for others. These shloks set standards by which one can gauge whether the supposedly pious work done by him is sacred (17/11), mediocre (17/12), or sacrilegious (17/13). A good work done with the spirit of **Saattvik Yajn** strengthens **Shraddhaa**, the faith of its doer.

Aphal Aakaankshibhi: Gita preaches repeatedly to not nurture any desire of favorable result for the work done even if it is sacred and pious because its result is in the domain of divine law of **Karm** & **Karm Phal.** Please refer to explanations under shlok 2/47.

Man: Samaadhaay is the sacrificial work that is convincing and pleasant for the mind and heart of its doer. If not done in a **Saattvik**

manner, we remain burdened with the feeling of guilt and regret like a person suffering from diabetes repents after taking sweets.

Let us also understand what kind of **Yajn** is **Adakshinam. Dakshinaa** is not just donation or an obligation to pay a priest conduct a holy ceremony as commonly understood these days. The spirit behind **Dakshinaa** is a win-win situation where the priest is whole-heartedly committed to perform **Yajn** or any other ceremony without any material expectation in return, and **Yajn Kartaa**, the doer of **Yajn** pays him abundantly, more than his capacity. The well known Mahaabhaarat story of Dron demanding thumb of innocent Ekalavya as **Guru Dakshinaa**, the fee for being his teacher (though he refused to teach him) is a blot on cunning Braahmans who cheat a faithful person in the name of **Dakshinaa**; and it simultaneously also sets the best example of what the beneficiary of his services should do. A **Yajn** in which its doer does not take proper care of his priest's needs or pays him unwillingly with scorn and disrespect is termed as **Adakshinam. Shraddhaa Virahit** is same as **Ashraddadhaan** in 4/40, an ostentatious person or faithless act.

☙◦❧

God describes Shaareerik, Vaangamay and Maanasik, three kinds of Tap.

(17/14, 15 & 16)

देवद्विजगुरुप्राज्ञपूजनं शौचमार्जवम् ।
ब्रह्मचर्यमहिंसा च शारीरं तप उच्यते ॥१७/१४॥
अनुद्वेगकरं वाक्यं सत्यं प्रियहितं च यत् ।
स्वाध्यायाभ्यसनं चैव वाङ्मयं तप उच्यते ॥१७/१५॥
मनः प्रसादः सौम्यत्वं मौनमात्मविनिग्रहः ।
भावसंशुद्धिरित्येतत्तपो मानसमुच्यते ॥१७/१६॥

Devadwijaguruapraajnapoojanam shauchamaarjavam I
Brahmacharyamahimsaa shaareeram tap uchyate II (17/14)
Anudwegakaram vaakyam satyam priyahitam ch yat I

Swaadhyaayaabhyasanam chaiv vaangmayam tap uchyate II
(17/15)
Man:prasaad: saumyatvam maunamaatmavinigrah: I
Bhaavasamshuddhirityetattapo maanasamuchyate II (17/16)

dev (gods) Dwij (Braahman) Guru (spiritual guide, teacher, elderly person) Praajn (wise, learned) Poojanam (worship) Shaucham (cleanliness) Aarjavam (simplicity, uprightness)I Brahmacharyam (chastity, celibacy) Ahimsaa (non-violence) Shaareeram (of body) Tap: (Tap) Uchyate (is said)II (17/14)

Anudweg Karam (which does not cause anxiety, agitation) Vaakyam (words) Satyam (truthfulness) Priy (pleasant) Hitam (beneficial) Ch (and) Yat (which)I Swaadhyaay (study of self) Abhyasanam (by repetitive practice) Ch (and) Ev (certainly) Vaangmayam (of speech) Tap: (penance) Uchyate (is said)II (17/15)

Man: Prasaad: (cheerfulness of mind & heart) Saumyatwam (charm) Maunam (spiritual & reflective thinking with a calm mind) Aatm Vinigrah: (effective self-control)I Bhaav Samshuddhi: (purity of natural & emotional instincts) Iti (thus) Etat (these) Tap: (penance) Manasam (mind, heart) Uchyate (are said)II (17/16)

Devoted worship of Devs, Braahmans, spiritual teachers & elderly and wise persons; and qualities of cleanliness, uprightness, chastity and non violence; all these are said to be Tap, the austerities to be performed for purification of the body. (17/14)

The austerity with respect to speech is said to be of that speech which certainly does not cause anxiety & agitated feelings, is pleasant & benevolent; truthful with objectivity and is spoken for self-study & practice of spirituality. (17/15)

Contentment of mind & heart; mildness & charm in character; spiritual & reflective thinking with a calm mind; effective self-control; purity of natural & emotional instincts; all these are said to be the austerity of mind & heart. (17/16)

Tap enables a person to purify his whole being, as it develops the power of tolerance of dualities in life. A practiser should be like gold in the hands of a goldsmith who subjects it to various processes of heating, melting, moulding, forming, fitting etc. to make an ornament. All practisers as well as accomplished Yogees must therefore observe all the three kinds of **Taps** in their life. Purification is the single most powerful tool to prevent ill health of body, mind and heart. When the impure, unusable water of the sea evaporates by the power of its **Tap** in hot sun it forms clouds, and rains to quench the thirst of people, fills up various water bodies on land and thus becomes useful and indispensible. Similarly, an embodied soul can purify its body and elevate above worldly considerations by austerities and serving people in the society. Such person merges into its origin, the Supreme Soul just as water merges back into the sea. Gita mentions here three kinds of **Tap** necessary for a person to cultivate **Saattvik** faith. They are **Shaareerik** or **Kaayik** which are performed by the body; **Vaangamay** or **Vaachik** which are performed by the speech; and **Maanasik**, the **Tap** performed by the mind, conscience & heart. Let us understand them one by one in more detail:

SOME ADDITIONAL THOUGHTS ON SHAAREERIK OR KAAYIK TAP

This kind of **Tap** is called Shaareerik because it is primarily performed by one's body through physical actions, which purify the body and physical self so that all of our anatomical parts can perform their physiological functions in perfect harmony without excessive physical strain. We need to purify our body first in order to balance and tune it for sound mind, heart and soul because the way we treat our body has a profound impact on our physical, mental and spiritual health. Virtues like worship of **Devs**, the gods; and reverence to **Dwij**, the learned **Braahmans**, **Guru** and **Praajn**, the wise, knowledgeable people are **Tap** performed externally by the body. **Shauch**, the cleanliness & purity, **Aarjavam**, the simplicity & uprightness, **Brahmacharya**, the chastity & celibacy, and **Ahimsaa**, the non-violence have been listed as austerities performed by body for itself, and ultimately for the soul in it. Very important steps like regulation of breathing were first discussed in 4/30 under *'Some additional thoughts on Praanaayaam'*, then about regulation of food, sleep, work, and entertainment, in 6/16-17 under '*Some additional thoughts on too much or too low indulgence in activities*' in order to keep our body fit and healthy. Lastly, we learned about regulation of food under '*Some additional thoughts on Aahaar– the food*' in this chapter in 17/8-10. We should apply **Shaareerik Tap** to all the activities that we do with our body. Some practical hints are:

1. Keep the body fit and healthy so that we can properly discharge our duties, works and obligations. Scriptures describe a human body as the ladder to reach abode of God. Kaalidaas says in Kumaar Sambhav 5/33 'शरीरमाध्यम् खलु धर्मसाधनम्' i.e. *body is the basic means of practising and accomplishing Dharm.*

2. Earn our livelihood by honest, ethical, righteous means, and hard work.

3. Physically serve the weak, old, ill, infirm & poor people. George Washington, the Commander General, did not hesitate for a moment to help some laborers who were struggling to lift a log while their captain stood just watching and supervising them because he felt it below dignity to join the labor.

4. Maintain cleanliness in own and surrounding premises.

5. Save environment, plant trees, do not waste resources. Live with nature.

6. Cultivate good habits. Avoid bad habits like drinking, gambling, smoking, extra marital relationships, tobacco & drugs addiction, lottery etc.

7. Use money & resources for the causes we consider good & worth. Avoid being spendthrift.

SOME ADDITIONAL THOUGHTS ON VAANGAMAY OR VAACHIK TAP

This kind of **Tap** is performed primarily by speech or any other means of communication like writing, preaching, teaching, commenting, mailing, talking on phone, singing, reciting, public speech etc. **Vaangamay** or **Vaachik Tap** should be **Anudweg**

Karam i.e. not causing anxiety and disturbance; and **Satyam Priyam** and **Hitam** i.e. truthful, dear & lovable and beneficial to the listener. **Abhyasanam**, the practice of **Swaadhyaay** i.e. the study of Scriptures, achieves such control on speech. When Raam meets Hanumaan for the first time and listens to his noblest style of speech, He appreciates it to Lakshman in these words in Vaalmeeki Raamaayan 4/3/28-32:

> *'He, who is not learned in Rik, Yaju & Saam Veds, cannot talk in such a beautiful language. He has thoroughly studied grammar because he has not uttered even one wrong or slang word. His face, eyes, eyebrows, forehead or any other part of body did not convey anything other than what he said. His speech is neither too long nor too short; neither doubtful nor secretive; neither too slow nor too fast. Whatever is in his heart, it comes through his throat in a nobly modulated tone. He speaks a highly cultured & auspicious speech the tone of which is neither too feeble nor too loud but pleasant to heart.'*

When a Yogee talks his body language conveys the coolness of a waterfall, the calm of a placid lake, the compassion of a Guru, the love of a parent. Very soothing and comforting words pour thereafter from his mouth. Sanatkumar teaches Naarad in Mahaabhaarat 1n 12/319/13:

सत्यस्य वचनम् श्रेय: सत्यादपि हितम् वदेत ।

यद्भूतहितमत्यन्तम् एतातसत्यम् मतम् मम ॥

(Speaking truth is good; but speaking that which is beneficial is better because the truth, in my opinion, is that which is good for everybody)

Speech reveals the character of a person:

इंसान एक दुकान है और उसकी ज़ुबान उस पर जड़ा हुआ ताला है ।

दुकान हीरे की है या कोयले की, ये ताला खुलने पर ही पता चलता है ॥

(A person is a shop, closed by the lock of his tongue. We come to know whether the shop is of diamonds or of coal only when the lock opens.)

SOME ADDITIONAL THOUGHTS ON MAANASIK TAP

Maanas is primarily the same as **Man**, the mind and heart of a person as explained in 6/35-36 earlier. It is the seat of perception, reflection, contemplation and emotional feeling. **Maanasik Tap** therefore, is the austerity observed for purification of **Man** the mind and heart. The qualities like **Man Prasaad**, the cheerfulness of **Man**; **Saumyatwam**, the charms & coolness; **Maunam**, reflecting well before speaking; **Aatm Vinigrah**, the effective restraint & control; and **Bhaav Samshuddhi**, the purity of natural & emotional instincts mentioned here are therefore, austerities related not only to optimal functioning of mind alone but also of heart. **Maanasik Tap** leads to achieve mental, moral, psychological, emotional & spiritual purification & perfection. It influences how we feel, behave and react in day-to-day life, and enables us to overcome challenges without mental stress.

Clarification: *Maun is understood normally as observing silence of speech in a highly regulated manner. But since speech is already covered in 17/15 as Vaangamay or Vaachik Tap, I have interpreted it in the context of Man. It therefore means thinking calmly and withdrawing mind from outside world.*

Some ways to practise **Maanasik Tap** are suggested below:

1. Meditation.
2. Praying.
3. Being in good company.
4. Having a purpose of life and setting goals and targets to achieve.
5. Reading good literature.
6. Feeling more confident, hopeful, positive and energetic.
7. Purging negativity from life.
8. Striking a pleasant balance between inner and outer worlds.
9. Not reacting immediately, and letting the passion cool down.

10. Being always busy in some useful and productive activity. It is said that *'An empty mind is truly said to be the devils workshop'*.

11. Cultivating a good hobby besides normal professional work.

Maithilee Sharan Gupt warns us in Saaket:

> मानव मन दुर्बल और सहज चंचल है,
>
> इस जगती तल में लोभ अतीव प्रबल है ।
>
> देवत्व कठिन, दनुजत्व सुलभ है नर को,
>
> नीचे से उठना सहज कहाँ ऊपर को?

{Human mind is weak and unsteady by nature because greed (the attraction towards Vishays) is very powerful in this world. It is easy for a common person to acquire demonical nature but very difficult to attain godliness as his normal instinct makes it difficult to rise from lower to higher level.}

Nevertheless, it is also true that perseverant humans can achieve godliness if they practice austerity in physical, social, mental lifestyles as explained above. These austerities develop right kind of faith in them.

☙❦❧

Tap is categorized on the scale of three qualities.

(17/17, 18 & 19)

> श्रद्धया परया तसं तपस्तत्त्रिविधं नरै: ।
>
> अफलाकाङ्क्षिभिर्युक्तैः सात्त्विकं परिचक्षते ॥१७/१७॥
>
> सत्कारमानपूजार्थं तपो दम्भेन चैव यत् ।
>
> क्रियते तदिह प्रोक्तं राजसं चलमध्रुवम् ॥१७/१८॥
>
> मूढग्राहेणात्मनो यत्पीडया क्रियते तप: ।
>
> परस्योत्सादनार्थं वा तत्तामसमुदाहृतम् ॥१७/१९॥

Shraddhayaa parayaa taptam tapastattrividham narai: I
Aphalaakaankshibhiryuktai: saattvikam parichakshate II
(17/17)
Satkaaramaanpoojaartham tapo dambhen chaiv yat I
Kriyate tadih proktam raajasam chalamadhruvam II (17/18)
Moodhagraahenaatmano yatpeedayaa kriyate tap: I
Parasyotsaadanaartham vaa tattaamasamudaahrutam II
(17/19)

Shraddhayaa Parayaa (with extreme, unflinching faith) Taptam (ardently performed) Tap: (Tap) Tat (that) Trividham (threefold) Narai: (by persons)I Aphal Aakaankshibhi: (persons not desirous of fruits) Yuktai: (united with Supreme Being) Saattvikam (of quality of Sattv) Parichakshate (is seen as)II (17/17)

Satkaar Maan Poojaa Artham (for felicitation, honor) Tap: (Tap) Dambhen (out of hypocrisy) Ch (and) Ev (also) Yat (that which)I Kriyate (is done) Tat (that) ih (this) Proktam (is called) Raajasam (with quality of passion) Chalam (inconstant) Aadhruvam (temporary)II (17/18)

Moodh Graahen (foolishly undertaken) Aatman: (of self) Yat (which) Peedayaa (to torture) Kriyate (is done) Tap: (Tap)I Parasya (to others) Utsaadan (eliminate, cause harm) Artham (for the sake of) Vaa (or) Tat (that) Taamasam (of Tam) Udaahrutam (is cited as) II (17/19)

This (aforesaid) threefold austerity, when ardently practiced by persons having unflinching faith without desiring any result but engaging only with the Supreme Being, is looked upon as Saattvik, the noblest quality. (17/17)

And the penance which is done with the purpose of gaining felicitation, honor and worship and also out of ostentation, that penance is called Raajas, the quality of passion that is inconstant and impermanent. (17/18)

The penance which is undertaken foolishly by torturing own self or to harm or eliminate others is cited as Taamas i.e., with quality of darkness and ignorance. (17/19)

God described three kinds of **Tap** as **Shaareerik, Vaangamay** and **Maanasik** in previous shlok as an important means to achieve **Saattvik Shraddhaa**. He now tells that all three of them should be faithfully performed in **Saattvik** mode as a duty without expectations of **Satkaar Maan Poojaa Artham**, the appreciation & felicitation, respect & honor, reverence & following, and any other social recognition because such expectations drag him in the world of mushrooming of passionate desires. **Tap** is often mistaken as severe painful vows like fasting for long durations, standing on one leg, or in water, burying up to neck in sand, lying on bed of thorns or steel spikes, sitting with fire around him, swallowing glass or iron bits, walking on a bed of ignited coal etc. Some religious sects also believe and preach that the body is an obstacle between soul and its liberation. Others popularize it as a means of achieving some **Siddhi**, the power of miracles, some others try to cheat innocent public to profit from their blind faith, and the worst of them do penance to acquire powers to harm & oppress the weak. Krishn calls such people **Moodh Graahen** i.e. possessed with stupidity for they not only torture their own body but also kill their soul by exploiting simple faithful people, and/or to impose rule of their might on others. Such **Tap** is **Taamasik** i.e. of the worst kind. We often come across sights of some self proclaimed **Saadhoos** performing apparently impossible & amazing tricks in places of pilgrimage and religious congregations like Kumbh but we should never regard such activities as **Tap** for they are nothing more than tricks and jugglery performed by imposters, tricksters who tarnish the image of real **Saadhoos**.

QUESTION: WHAT IS TAP & WHY ONE SHOULD PERFORM IT?

Tap (or **Tapasyaa**) is an ascetic practice, done with great fervor, religious austerity & penance. An individual undertakes it at his personal level as none else is involved in it except those trying to disturb or distract him or the aim of the doer is to attract others.

The main objective of **Saattvik Tap** is purification of complete self, bodily, mentally and spiritually. It is also undertaken sometimes for atonement and repentance of sins committed earlier; or at other times to help and relieve someone from pain & distress; but the best form of **Tap** is to acquire power, courage and material resources to fight against **Adharm** and protect **Dharm**. Mahatma Gandhi used to undertake fasts unto death for **Satyaagrah**, the pertinacity to insist for a right, just cause. **Tap** is carried out to please God (or demigods) also to facilitate liberation. Highest principle of goodness, virtue & faith without desiring personal gratification guide its doer towards realizing his ethical, social and spiritual duty and responsibility. Such an ascetic develops his temperament, behavior and character by imposing self-discipline on his body, speech, mind and heart as mentioned in 17/14-16 above. Arjun performed this kind of **Tap** many times throughout his life and succeeded in acquiring many divine weapons and powers besides purifying his soul.

Raajasik persons indulge in **Tap** in order to gain favor of gods to either obtain some material objects, or seek honor, name & fame, or satisfaction of his passionate desires and ego. Though this kind of **Tap** may give pleasures to them in this world, and after death in heaven for some time, they prove to be worthless ultimately in the purification and perfection of their souls. Even a **Tap** done for a right cause but with arrogance, pride and self-elation falls in **Raajasik** category.

A **Taamasik** person, due to deluded state of his mind, carries out **Tap** in pursuit of fulfilling his very low, narrow and mean ambitions like gaining power & control on others or destroying natural resources or taking revenge. Perverted demons like Hiranyakashipu, Raavan etc. gained some supernatural boons by performing **Taamasik Tap**. Gita has already described this **Tap** as **Aasuree Tap** in 17/5-6.

All **Raajasik** or **Taamasik Taps** are in violation of the correct way of life. Therefore, they are in contradiction of the Scripture and against the underlying spirit of **Tap**. **Saattvik** way of doing **Tap** is the only way acceptable to **Shaastr**, and therefore, is the proper preparatory to achieve purification of body, mind & heart and soul, and also attain **Jnaan Vijnaan**, the ultimate perfect knowledge (chapter 7). **Tap** was the greatest means to attain liberation in **Sat Yug**, the ancient aeon of Indian culture when people led their lives in truth & **Dharm**. Buddh practiced severe **Tap** for six years in his first step in search of perfect **Dharm**. It is mentioned that when he was about to die of weakness caused by **Tap,** he heard some passerby girls singing a song:

'Tighten not the strings of your Veenaa, the Indian Sitar, too much lest they break and stop producing music; nor leave them so loose that your fingers cannot play on them.'

He grasped the message in right perspective and decided to stretch not his body by extremely troublesome **Tap**. After attaining enlightenment, he forbade his followers from indulging in severe penance saying:

"Tap, the austerities only confuse the mind. In the exhaustion and mental stupor to which they lead, one can no longer understand the ordinary things of life, still less the truth that lies beyond the senses. I have given up extremes of luxury as well as asceticism. I have discovered the Middle Way."

Then he showed **Ashtaangik Maarg** (6/16-17) to attain **Nirwaan**, the liberation from distress discussed after 2/72. The striking commonality & similarity between what Krishn teaches about **Tap** here and what Buddh preached about 3000 years later is not just a matter of coincidence; the middle path preached by both to do everything in a regulated, modulated manner is the principle followed by Indian people until date. In this context, we should not miss to remember Mahaaveer (599, 527 BC)[16], a contemporary of Buddh (563/480 or 483/400 BC)[13]. Mahaaveer attached greatest importance to penance and arduous ascetic practices for attaining **Kaiwalya**, the liberation in Jainism. However, in my humble opinion, he too must have prescribed **Tap** to detach the soul from

---

16 *Periods are mentioned just to show contemporariness, not to claim any reliability.*

the worldly matters and purify it; and if my supposition is true, it matches with Gita's teachings if followed with moderation. A person who sincerely performs **Saattvik Tap** culminates into a perfectly calm, pure and equipoise soul with a clear, generous and compassionate will for the well-being of everybody.

Let me illustrate how **Tap** purifies a person with the example of milk. Fresh milk without heating spoils in 1-2 hours but hot milk remains good for few hours. Milk, seeded with **Jaaman**, the rennet, coagulates into curd that can last for 2-3 days; if curd rejects buttermilk on churning and yields butter, which remains fit for eating for few days. When butter is heated, melted and boiled for a long time on slow fire, it separates remaining impurities and becomes pure Ghee, which stays good for many years. The processes like heating and churning of milk in this example are **Tap** in a practiser's life that goes on refining and purifying him. Raamcharit Maanas eulogizes the power of **Tap** in 1/72/2-5:

तपु सुखप्रद दुख दोष नसावा॥
तपबल रचइ प्रपंच बिधाता। तपबल बिष्नु सकल जग त्राता॥
तपबल संभु करहिं संघारा। तपबल सेषु धरइ महिभारा॥
तप अधार सब सृष्टि भवानी।

(Lord Shiv tells mother goddess Bhawaanee: Tap brings happiness and destroys evils. Brahmaa creates universe with the power of Tap, Vishnu maintains it, Shiv destroys it, and Shesh bears the load of earth. Whole creation rests on Tap.)

God has talked at length about **Tap** in this chapter. He first explained its demonic and divine forms in 17/5-6, and then applied them to our physical body, speech, and mind & heart in 17/14-16. He categorized them into three qualitative modes of **Sattv, Raj** & **Tam** in 17/17-19, and would tell us in 17/27-28 finally to direct all ascetic practices faithfully towards God only.

॰॰

God describes three qualitative modes of Daan, the charity.

(17/20, 21 & 22)

दातव्यमिति यद्दानं दीयतेऽनुपकारिणे ।
देशे काले च पात्रे च तद्दानं सात्त्विकं स्मृतम् ॥१७/२०॥
यत्तु प्रत्युपकारार्थं फलमुद्दिश्य वा पुनः ।
दीयते च परिक्लिष्टं तद्दानं राजसं स्मृतम् ॥१७/२१॥
अदेशकाले यद्दानमपात्रेभ्यश्च दीयते ।
असत्कृतमवज्ञातं तत्तामसमुदाहृतम् ॥१७/२२॥

Daatavyamiti yaddaanam deeyateAnupkaarine I
Deshe kaale ch paatre ch taddaanam saattvikam smrutam II
(17/20)
Yattu pratyupkaaraatham phalamuddishya yaa pun: I
Deeyate ch pariklishtam taddaanam raajasam smrutam II
(17/21)
Adeshkaale yaddaanamapaatrebhyashch deeyate I
Asatkrutamavajnaatam tattaamasamudaahritam II (17/22)

Daatavyam (donation which is given considering it as sacred duty) Iti (thus) Yat (which) Daanam (donation, charity) Deeyate (is given) Anupkaarine (without expecting something in return)I deshe (at a suitable place) Kaale (appropriate time) Ch (and) Paatre (to eligible, deserving person) Ch (and) Tat (that) Daanam (Daan) Saattvikam (of quality of Sattv) Smrutam (is remembered as)II (17/20)

Yat (in which) Tu (but) Pratyupkaar Artham (for the sake of getting something in return) Phalam (fruit) Uddishya (with purpose of) Vaa (or) Pun: (then)I Deeyate (is given) Ch (and) Pariklishtam (grudgingly, unwillingly) Tat (that) Daanam (Daan) Raajasam (with quality of passion) Smrutam (is remembered)II (17/21)

Adesh Kaale (at a wrong place & inappropriate time) Yat (which) Daanam (Daan) Apaatrebhy: (to undeserving person) Ch (and) Deeyate (is given)I Asatkrutam (ill treatment, disrespect) Avajnaatam (contempt, scorn) Tat (that) Taamasam (with qualities of Tam) Udaahrutam (is cited, quoted, told as)II (17/22)

The donation given, considering it as one's sacred duty to give in charity, to the most deserving person at the most suitable place, at the most appropriate time without expecting something in return; that donation is remembered as Saattvik, the highest quality of righteousness. (17/20)

However, donation given grudgingly or for the sake of getting something in return or with an intention of gaining some fruit is considered Raajas i.e. with quality of passion. (17/21)

And, the donation given at a wrong place and inappropriate time to an unworthy person with disrespect and scorn is told as Taamas i.e. with qualities of ignorance & darkness. (17/22)

Daan is considered as one of the most pious and sacred activity in all religions. God directed us in 9/27 to offer unto him whatever we donate. He also included Daan as a very important symptom of a Jnaanee in 10/5, and again as a divine wealth in 16/1. Like Shraddhaa (17/2-3), Aahaar (17/8-10), Yajn (17/11-13) and Tap (17/17-19), He now categorizes Daan also into three quality modes of Sattv, Raj and Tam.

SOME ADDITIONAL THOUGHTS ON DAAN

Daan is an act of giving, bestowing, endowing, granting, donating, gifting, making offerings & charities or giving alms to the needy person/s as help or as contribution to social or religious establishments. It is the act of being generous in giving back to them from whom we benefit directly or indirectly in kind or cash or service, or sometimes even through a long untraceable chain of actions. Daan can be in the form of money, materials like food and clothes, providing comfort & relief, rendering selfless services, and offering pleasure, emotional happiness etc. Girdhar Kaviraya advises rich people:

जो जल बाढे नाव में घर में बाढे दाम ।
दोनों हाथ उलीचिए यही सयानो काम ॥

(If money grows in the house, think of it as if water in your boat is rising. It is therefore the wisest thing to empty both of them with both hands.)

That **Daan** is **Saattvik,** which is given whole heartedly, happily, with modesty & humility, and concern & empathy to the right person at the right time for a right cause with the sole aim of benefitting, helping him in mitigating his troubles, and empowering him for future to the extent possible. The donor must consider himself as a trustee of social wealth, not its owner and giver. He should endeavor to stretch his Daan a little bit beyond his capacity, means & resources. **Daan** given without criticizing, passing judgment on the recipient and without any discrimination of caste, creed, color, faith etc., and not trying to trace its end use is **Saattvik**. Some examples of **Saattvik Daan** are:

1. Raheem kept his eyes always downwards while giving charity to the needy people every day. When someone wanted to know reason, he replied him with utmost humility:

'देनहार कोइ और है देवत है दिन रैन ।
लोग भरम हम पर धरें ताते नीचे नैन ॥'

(I keep my eyes down in shame because people mistake me as the giver of these things whereas the fact is that Providence is the true giver and I am just a humble servant of Him)

2. A young boy asked for two paise in alms from Ishwar Chandr Vidyaa Saagar for food. He gave him one Rupee with the advice to do some business with it. The boy felt so empowered with his kindness that he became a big businessman in due course.

3. Mahatma Gandhi visited lepers & scavengers' colonies often, and rendered physical service.

4. Dadheechi donated bones to Indr to make Vajr, the divine weapon to kill demon Vrutraasur.

5. Demon king Bali did not hesitate for a moment before donating his empire, even against the caution raised by his Guru, to God who appeared in the form of Vaaman, a dwarf.

6. Karn donated his divine Kavach, the armour and Kundal, the ear rings to Indr knowing that he is depriving him from invincibility. Scriptures teach us to give, give and give.

Atharv Ved tells:

'May you earn by hundred hands and disburse by a thousand! When you are involved in benevolent work, your capacity to earn multiplies... God surely blesses those who give for a good cause.'

Kabeer says:

चिड़ी चोंच भर ले गयी नदी न घटियो नीर।
दान दिये धन ना घटे कह गये दास कबीर॥

(Kabeer says that wealth never shrinks by donating. The water of a river does not diminish if a bird drinks dips its beak in it and drinks some water.)

Moral: *If a rich person shares the water of his well with needy villagers, nature refills it with fresh water; a cow starts yielding more milk on seeing its owner giving some milk to a hungry child. In fact, entire nature and divine powers come forward to replenish and increase the resources of a true donor.*

Caution: *Scriptures and legends accord great importance to Daan; and preach us often to donate to a Braahman, Saadhu, Rishi etc., in ancient times. Charity and by giving and sharing was justifiable in those times when available means and resources were very limited. However, today, the world is aplenty with them. Hence, in modern times, the criterion of choosing a recipient of our charity should not be based on his caste or costume but whether he is a wise, learned man; an astute, austere practiser of Yog and a righteous, moralistic person deserving our help.*

It is the imperative sacred duty of a recipient of **Saattvik Daan** also to repay abundantly to the donor or to other needy persons as soon as his financial condition improves so that the chain of such sacred work continues. He, who does not give back to society more than he gets from it, is like a person eating from the reserve, the bank balance of good works. He and his society cannot progress and flourish. It is a *'Win, Win'* situation for the donor and the recipient.

Raajasik Daan constitutes of acts of charity done unwillingly, regretfully to fulfill personal or egoistic aims like name & fame, or reserving a seat in heaven, or to escape from social criticism, ostentation, and pride. The eyes of such donors are on receiving back from the recipient later in a much larger proportion. People desirous of heaven or profit in their profession are seen donating large amounts to some Math, Aashram, Dargaah, temple, Church, Gurudwaaraa etc. though they are already flush with funds. Such misguided donations result in breeding corruption, misappropriations and embezzlement in holy places of worship. Political leaders utilize social or Government grants like for hospitals, schools, R & D etc. to impress their vote bank for the impending elections, and derive undue advantage, wield authority and exploit them later. This is a *'Win, Lose'* situation for both, the donor and the recipient.

Taamasik Daan is given under duress or some compulsion or in a contemptuous, ungenerous, ignoble, inconsiderate manner completely devoid of compassion, sympathy and concern for the recipient. Even the recipient may despise and refuse to accept such charity. This is a *'Lose, Lose'* situation for the donor & the recipient.

Moral*: The best form of charity is to empower the recipient with money, resources, and opportunities so that he can stand on his own legs and achieve his full potential to lead a respectable life with self-esteem. Charity done with the intention of earning Punya, the good fortune, without empowering the recipient, actually results in making him more dependent on others. Such unproductive activity proves to be detrimental and injurious to his growth as well as of social structure. This however should not deter us from providing immediate relief to a deserving person in dire need of physical or monetary help. Helping someone with money and resources just for his sustenance is like helping a cocoon of grasshopper to come out of its shell, it actually kills it. What the "Have Not's" need from the "Haves" today is an opportunity to live with dignity, not charity.*

Krishn describes God as Aum Tat Sat

(17/23, 24, 25 & 26)

ॐतत्सदिति निर्देशो ब्रह्मणस्त्रिविधः स्मृतः ।
ब्राह्मणास्तेन वेदाश्च यज्ञाश्च विहिताः पुरा ॥१७/२३॥
तस्मादोमित्युदाहृत्य यज्ञदानतपःक्रियाः ।
प्रवर्तन्ते विधानोक्ताः सततं ब्रह्मवादिनाम् ॥१७/२४॥
तदित्यनभिसन्धाय फलं यज्ञतपःक्रियाः ।
दानक्रियाश्च विविधाः क्रियन्ते मोक्षकाङ्क्षिभिः ॥१७/२५॥
सद्भावे साधुभावे च सदित्येतत्प्रयुज्यते ।
प्रशस्ते कर्मणि तथा सच्छब्दः पार्थ युज्यते ॥१७/२६॥

ॐ tatsaditi nirdesho Braahmanastrividh: smrut: I
Braahmanaasten vedaashch Yajnaashch vihitaa: puraa II
(17/23)
Tasmaadomityudaahrutya Yajnadaanatap:kriyaa: I
Pravartante vidhaanoktaa: satatam Brahmavaadinaam II
(17/24)
Tadityanabhisandhaay phalam Yajnatap:kriyaa: I
Daanakriyaashch vividhaa: kriyante mokshakaankshibhi: II
(17/25)
Sadbhaave saadhubhaave ch sadityetatprayujyate I
Prashaste karmani tathaa sachchhabd: Paarth yujyate II
(17/26)

ॐ (Aum, the sacred syllable symbolizing Brahm) Tat (that Brahm) Sat (is the eternally existential, real, absolute, ultimate truth) Iti (thus) Nirdesh: (pointing out, instruction) Braahman: (of Brahm) Trividh: (of three kinds) Smrut: (is told as)I Braahmanaa: (a kind of Scriptures) Ten (by him) Vedaa: (Veds) Ch (and) Yajnaa: (sacrificial & other acts) Ch (and) Vihitaa: (appointed) Puraa (earlier)II (17/23)

Tasmaat (therefore) Aum (Aum) Iti (thus) Udaahrutya (by pronouncing, quoting) Yajn (Yajn) Daan (Daan) Tap: (Tap) Kriyaa: (activities)I Pravartante (engages, initiates with action, works) Vidhaan uktaa: (as per rules & regulations prescribed by Veds)

Satatam (regularly) Brahm Vaadinaam (true knowers of Brahm)II (17/24)

tat (that) Iti (thus) Anabhisandhaay (not connected with) Phalam (fruit) Yajn (Yajn) Tap: (Tap) Kriyaa: (activities)I Daan (Daan) Kriyaa: (activities) Ch (and) Vividhaa: (various) Kriyante (are done) Moksh kaankshibhi: (by persons desirous of liberation)II (17/25)

Sadbhaave (characteristic nature of Supreme Being) Saadhu Bhaave (characteristic of Saadhu) Ch (and) Sat (eternal existence, absolute truth) Iti (thus) Etat (this) Prayujyate (is used)I prashaste (commendable, laudable, admirable) Karmani (in doing Karm) Tathaa (similarly) Sat (eternal existence, absolute truth) Shabd: (word) Paarth (Arjun) Yujyate (is used, applied)II (17/26)

Aum Tat Sat is the triune name of Brahm by which He is referred. He, in the very beginning of the creation, ordained Veds, other Scriptures like Braahmans, and Yajn etc. (17/23)

Therefore, the true knowers of Brahm always initiate the sacred activities of Yajn, Daan, the donation & Tap, the penance as per rules and regulations prescribed by Veds (and other Scriptures) by first pronouncing ॐ (Aum). (17/24)

Various activities of Yajn, Daan & Tap must be performed by persons aspiring for liberation without any alliance with material results, with the thought that "Every activity is done for Tat (that Brahm) only". (17/25)

His name Sat is used to indicate the characteristic nature of Supreme Being as the eternal existence, absolute truth and the ultimate reality, and the quality of righteousness. O Paarth (Arjun)! This is why 'Sat' is used (as a prefix or adjective) while doing a commendable, noble work. (17/26)

These four shloks define Brahm with just three words: ॐ **Tat Sat**.

QUESTION: WHAT IS MEANT BY ॐ तत्सत् (AUM, TAT & SAT)? IT SEEMS VERY INTRIGUING.

Yes, intriguing it is since it is the phrase of last three words to know and realize **Brahm**, the Supreme Being. It is the ultimate, best attempt by **Rishis, Veds** and all other Scriptures like Gita, Upanishads**, Braahmans, Smruti, Puraans** and **Yajns** to describe the indescribable **Brahm**. Nothing better has been devised since those ancient times to define Him. Some similar **Mahaa Vaakya**, the Grand Statements in Scriptures about identifying **Brahm** are:

1. तत्त्वमसि: Rishi Uddaalak teaches his son Shwetaketu in Chhaandogya Upanishad (6/8-16, each stanza ending with **Tattwamasi**) with beautiful examples. It is translated in various ways as *"That art thou," "That thou art"; "Thou art that"; "You are that";* or *"That you are"*. Simply stated, it means that **Aatmaa**, the soul, in its original, pure, primordial state, is wholly identical with **Brahm**, the Ultimate Reality who is the ground and origin of all phenomena, actions and knowledge, or partially identifiable with Him (as **Jeevaatmaa**, embodied soul).

2. Bruhadaaranyak Upanishad (2/3/6) states the futility in trying to define Brahm. It pronounces 'नेति नेति एतस्मादन्यत्परमस्ति' i.e. *'Not this, not this. Real Brahm is beyond whatever has been said about Him.'*

3. Some other Upanishad describes it thus 'सदेव सौम्येदमग्रम् आसीत्' i.e. *'It was Sat in placid state which only existed before everything.'*

4. Avadhoot Gita (1/25) says 'नेति नेति श्रुतिर्ब्रूयादनृतं पाञ्चभौतिकम्' i.e. *'Scripture says, Not this, not this. Whatsoever is made of five elements is false.'*

Moreover, there are many others: some confusing, others contradictory due to our limited power of understanding them. Gita also acknowledged in 13/4 the efforts of many **Rishis** to describe **Brahm** as illustrated by me with four examples above. Now it gives it final decision to clear all confusions, contradictions and misunderstandings by proclaiming **Brahm** as ॐ तत्सत् (**Aum Tat Sat**), and explaining each of these three words in 17/24, 25 and 26 respectively. It directs us to start every sacred activity, whether **Yajn** (the sacrificial duty), or **Daan** (giving in charity), or **Tap** (practising asceticism) or any other, with the pronunciation of

ॐ; and to dedicate the activity to **Tat** i.e. Him, who is **Sat**, the only eternal, real and absolute existence, and the primeval source of all other ephemeral existences of the world.

In fact, words, actions, directions, or anything else cannot explain **Brahm**; an ardent practiser can only experience and realize Him upon culmination of his practice. However, the ancient sages of **Vedic** times designated Him with the unique syllable ॐ **(Aum)** and associated it with each **Mantr,** the sacred hymns and prayers. At best, this explanation is like **Shaakhaa Chandr Nyaay,** a method to show almost invisible crescent new moon to someone who is not able to see it, by telling to take reference of a particular branch of a tree and then expand his vision around it to locate the moon. Though both of them want to see the moon he, who has seen it, can point to it with reference to the branch only knowing well that the branch is not the moon. Different Rishis apply similar techniques while explaining **Brahm**. Let us look deeper into each syllable of the triune of unfathomable ॐ **Tat Tat:**

Let us first understand ॐ (Aum)

ॐ **(Aum)** constitutes of three vowels, A, U & M, in which M is **Anuswaar,** the **Chandr Bindu** as appearing in अँधेरा, but it is also a complete vowel as in **Man** and **Tam**. The first word that an infant child is able to utter is **Maa** or Mother or its equivalent in other languages; and most of them contain A, U & M in some form or the other. ॐ exists even before universe is created, and after it is dissolved, and therefore in between also. ॐ is the primeval sound and syllable that produces all other sounds, letters, words and language. Its three vowels A, U & M are the three stages of **Tripad Gaayatree,** the mother of three **Veds**, **Rik, Yaju** & **Saam**. In spiritualism, each of these letters also explain **Brahm** in triple stages: that which is visible outwards, situated inside every being, and is simultaneously Omniscient & causal **Param Purush,** the Supreme Soul. The significance of the order, in which these letters appear in succession for a practiser trying to know **Brahm,** is noteworthy as 'A' is the first step to devote to Him as **Sagun**

Saakaar, 'U' the next step of **Sagun Niraakaar** and 'M' the final third step of realizing Him as **Nirgun Niraakaar**.

God said in 10/22, **Bhootaanaam Asmi Chetanaa** i.e. *'I am the consciousness in all beings'*. Maandookya Upanishad therefore appropriately links ॐ (**Aum**) with four states of consciousness as follows:

1. **A:** It represents **Jaagrat**, the waking state of consciousness, also described as **Bahishprajnaa** i.e. the knowledge of the outer consisting of own body and entire physical world.

2. **U:** It symbolizes **Swapn**, the dreaming state, also described as **Antarprajnaa** i.e. the knowledge of the subtle body and universe as seen by mind during sleeping.

3. **M:** It stands for **Suṣhupti**, the state of deep sleep in which the base of consciousness remains undisturbed and undistracted.

4. All three together form ॐ, the fourth stage called **Tureeya**, the pure consciousness of **Brahm** as it transcends above-mentioned three states of consciousness. It is the true ultimate state of experiencing of **Anant**, the infinite, the limit of the expanse of universe, **Adwait**, the only one, **Anaadi**, the one without an origin, called ॐ the primeval syllable representing the Absolute & Ultimate Supreme Soul. In this stage, a Yogee achieves oneness with **Brahm**.

It is mandatory to pronounce ॐ before chanting sacred Hymns of Hinduism in order to invoke **Brahm** and obtain His sanction and benediction in all pious acts of sacrifice like charity, austerity, penance etc. or other holy works. Performing such works faithfully with total detachment from the results in an egoless, impersonal way for universal well being at once establishes oneness of the doer with God. All schools of thoughts, philosophies, and numerous sects of Hinduism are unanimous in this act of oblation.

Let us now understand what is meant by Tat

Tat literally means that or this, the pronoun of third person in grammar used for someone or something in singular number.

Thus, it first points out to **Tat** i.e. that God towards ॐ **(Aum)** and then towards **Sat**, the absolute truth. The singular number is used because **Brahm** is the only one and real that exists in all times, all entities, and beyond them. Use of third person indicates that He is **Purushottam**, the Supreme Soul who exists eternally and is different from **Prakruti**, the nature and **Purush**, the individual soul. In fact, He is the Master of both of them as the Prime Minister is the master of other ministers, and the bureaucracy though in case of **Brahm** He is the only one as all others are simply His reflections and appearances.

Let us now understand what is meant by Sat.

Sat means Eternal Existence and also the truth since only God, the Absolute & Eternal Truth can really exist permanently. In the ethos of Hinduism, **Sat** or **Satya** and **Dharm** are inseparable. Mundak Upanishad states in 3/1/6:

सत्यमेव जयते नानृतं सत्येन पन्था विततो देवयानः ।
येनाक्रमन्त्यृषयो ह्याप्तकामा यत्र तत् सत्यस्य परमं निधानम् ॥

(Truth alone triumphs; not falsehood. Truth spreads out the divine path by which the sages, who have relinquished their desires completely, reach there where that supreme treasure of Truth is.)

Pandit Madan Mohan Malaviya brought this slogan into the national lexicon first in 1918. Independent India later adopted it as national motto on 26 January 1950.

Many scholars tried to explain **Aum Tat Sat** in different ways but its simplest meaning to my mind is:

'That Brahm symbolized by the sacred syllable ॐ is the eternally existential, real, absolute & ultimate truth.

Indrajeet Singh Tulsi gives the simile of water in the song of film *Shor:*

पानी रे पानी तेरा रंग कैसा, जिसमें मिला दो उसके जैसा ।
गंगा से जब मिले तो बनता गंगाजल तू पावन ॥

बादल से तू मिले तो रिम झिम बरसे जैसे सावन ।
पानी रे पानी तेरा रंग कैसा, दुनिया बनाने वाले रब जैसा ॥

*(O water! What is your true color? When you mix with something,
you become of the same color. By assimilating with Gangaa,
you become sacred Gangaa Jal, and by mixing with the cloud,
you start raining like Saawan, the month of rain. O water! What
is your true color? It is like God, the creator of universe.)*

It is noteworthy that the phrase ॐ **Tatsaditi** appears in
Pushpikaa, the closing statement of every chapter of Gita implying
that whatever is said in that particular chapter is in the name of
Aum, that eternally existential, real, absolute & ultimate truth.

ॐ

God links Sat with Yajn, Tap and Daan.

(17/27 & 28)

यज्ञे तपसि दाने च स्थिति: सदिति चोच्यते ।
कर्म चैव तदर्थीयं सदित्येवाभिधीयते ॥१७/२७॥
अश्रद्धया हुतं दत्तं तपस्तसं कृतं च यत् ।
असदित्युच्यते पार्थ न च तत्प्रेत्य नो इह ॥१७/२८॥

Yajne tapasi daane ch sthiti: saditi chochyate I
Karm chaiv tadartheeyam sadityevaabhidheeyate II (17/27)
Ashraddhayaa hutam dattam tapastaptam krutam ch yat I
Asadityuchyate Paarth n ch tatpretya no ih II (17/28)

Yajne (in Yajn) Tapasi (in Tap) Daane (in Daan) Ch (and) Sthiti:
(situation, condition) Sat (eternal existence) Iti (thus) Ch (and)
Uchyate (is said)I Karm (action) Ch (and) Ev (also) Tadartheeyam
(for that Supreme Being) Sat (eternal existence, truth) Iti (this
much) Ev (certainly) Abhidheeyate (is called)II (17/27)

Ashraddhayaa (without of faith) Hutam (offering, sacrifice
made in Yajn) Dattam (things given in donation) Tap: (Tap) Taptam

(executed reluctantly, painfully) Krutam (done) Ch (and) Yat (that which)I Asat (as good as not done) Iti (thus) Uchyate (is said) Paarth (Arjun) N (neither) Ch (and) Tat (that) Pretya (after death) No (nor) ih (in this life)II (17/28)

And it is said thus that being situated in Yajn, a sacrificial work, donation and penance is also called Sat; and a work performed for that Supreme Being is certainly Sat. O Paarth (Arjun)! Oblations offered, donations given and austerities or any other noble activity performed reluctantly without faith; all of them are called Asat i.e. not done, and are beneficial neither in this life nor after death. (17/27 & 28)

Gita explains further **Sat** & **Asat** in these two concluding shloks of this chapter as interpreted above. **Sat** is always good, morally strong and righteous. Hence, all acts performed in the right earnest with good intention of sacrificing self-interest, doing penance, and giving in charity; and all other similar works in **Saattvik** mode, are included in the ambit of **Sat.** Nevertheless, if these works are performed in **Raajasik** or **Taamasik** modes, willingly or unwillingly as a burden due to some personal interest or social compulsion, they fall in the category of **Asat.** It is highly relevant to recall some phrases from earlier shloks where Gita mentioned **Sat** & **Asat** as:

1. *'Neither Asat, the non existential illusion exists anywhere nor Sat, the existential real substance, the Absolute Truth is ever absent'* as stated by Krishn in 2/16.

2. *'I am indeed Sat, every existent, real thing; and Asat, the nonexistent, unreal thing'* as stated by God in 9/19.

3. *'You are Akshar, the imperishable Supreme Being and Sat as well as Asat i.e. all the existential & non-existential things, and also the one beyond them'* as stated by Arjun in 11/37.

4. *'That Param Brahm is neither Sat, the existent nor Asat, the nonexistent i.e. beyond the limited scope of Sat and Asat'* as stated by Krishn in 13/12.

Wandering in the realm of highly spiritual explanations above, let us not disconnect ourselves from **Shraddhaa**, the faith with which this chapter started. **Shraddhaa** is the central key stone supporting the entire arch of everybody's life; the backbone of his physical, emotional and spiritual existence, the sure way to lead a blissful life in this strife torn world. Even highly qualitative & virtuous works done without faith prove to be useless and bad in the end. A person walking on his own legs may or may not succeed in reaching his destination but he, who walks on the legs of faith and belief, is sure to find his destiny. Faith is the string with which his destiny pulls him towards itself. Mahatma Gandhi says:

'I have not the shadow of doubt that any man or woman can achieve what I have, if he or she would make the same effort and cultivate the same hope and faith.'

CONCLUSION OF CHAPTER 17

In this chapter, God explained three modes, **Saattvik**, **Raajasik** and **Taamasik** of **Shraddhaa**, the faith, and all related aspects like sacrificial works in 17/4; food in 17/7-9; body in 17/14; speech in 17/15; mind & heart in 17/16; asceticism in 17/14-19; and charity in 17/20-22. All of them play very important role in developing and firming up one's **Shraddhaa**. Then, He pronounced **Mahaa Vaakya**, the Grand statement ॐ **Tat Sat** in 17/23 and ordered Arjun to cultivate right kind of faith in performing all sacred activities like, **Yajn**, **Daan**, **Tap** etc., with right intent, purpose and in right manner as prescribed by scriptures, as per God's supreme will and directions, and offer them to Him. Right kind of faith shall deliver him from **Punarjanm**, and the wrong type shall keep him tied up with it.

There is one each of **Shree Bhagawaan Uvaach** and **Arjun Uvaach** in this chapter.

ॐ तत्सदिति श्रीमद्भगवद्गीतासूपनिषत्सु ब्रह्मविद्यायां योगशास्त्रे श्रीकृष्णार्जुनसंवादे
श्रद्धात्रयविभागयोगो नाम सप्तदशोऽध्यायः ॥ १७॥

(In the name of that ultimate truth called God, thus ends
the 17th chapter named Shraddhaa Tray Vibhaag Yog of
Shreemad BhagwadGita, the best Upanishad, Brahm Vidyaa
& Yog Shaastr, a dialogue between Shree Krishn & Arjun)

CHAPTER 18

MOKSH SANNYAAS YOG

(Giving up the non-essentials immediately and detaching gradually from the essentials also is the sure way to attain bliss in life.)

PREAMBLE & CONTEXT

Vyaas had fixed the plain canvas of Gita on the easel of **Vishaad** of Arjun in chapter 1. Krishn, the great artist, started painting long and short strokes in vivid colors of **Aatm Jnaan, Sat & Asat, Saamkhya, Karm, Samatv, Sthit Prajnaa, Dwandws, Brahm, Nirwaan, Yajn, Swadharm, Prakruti &** its three modes, **Bhakti,** secret of God's Avatars, **Jnaan** etc., from 2/11 until the end of chapter 4. Then He painted moderate strokes in chapters 5 to 10 like the concepts of **Nishkaam Karm & Sannyaas**, achieving self-control through meditation, learning **Jnaan & Vijnaan**, knowing the secrets of the king of spiritual knowledge, and description of some of His important **Vibhootis**. Then, till the end of chapter 17, He completed the grand picture of Gita with finest strokes of manifestation of His **Vishw Roop;** attributes of His dearest **Bhakt;** the intricate relationship between the body, nature, individual soul and Supreme Soul; modes of nature; divine and demonic wealth; and finally, with the importance of right faith. In this chapter, He gives the final touches to the great painting of Gita, and presents to us an overall view of its beauty, colors, scenes and themes. It would be a great delight for us to see the magnificent picture of **Samagr**

Yog emerging from the blank canvas of Gita after Krishn painted it laboriously with **Karm, Jnaan, Dhyaan, Bhakti** etc. through 17 chapters. Chapter 18 is the summation & conclusion of God's teachings. Bharat Vyaas wonders in film *Boond Jo Ban Gai Moti* ये कौन चित्रकार है' i.e. who that painter is who painted such a beautiful, picture in unforeseen vivid, bright colors.

If Gita is a movie with an intricate story plot, chapter 18 unfolds all the intricacies and offers the best solutions of all complications in its happy end.

WHY CHAPTER 18 IS NAMED MOKSH SANNYAAS YOG?

This chapter begins with Arjun wanting to the fine difference between **Sannyaas**, traditionally meaning renouncing household and adopting asceticism, and **Tyaag**, the real spirit of giving up attachment, not the things by themselves. Krishn clarifies the difference between the two. Then, He explains how liberation can be achieved by detaching own self from **Saattvik, Raajasik** & **Taamasik** kinds of **Jnaan** in 18/18-22, **Karm** in 18/23-25, **Kartaa** in 18/26-28, **Buddhi** in 18/29-32, **Dhruti** in 18/33-35, and **Sukh** in 18/37-39. He finally asks us to elevate self to the highest plane of total surrender to His will. Since this chapter lays the surest path of achieving **Moksh**, the liberation in unequivocal words by practising real **Sannyaas** from the bonds of **Karm Bandhan**, it has been named **Moksh Sannyaas Yog**.

☙◦❧

Arjun wants to know the basic difference between Sannyaas
and Tyaag.

(18/1)

अर्जुन उवाच
संन्यासस्य महाबाहो तत्त्वमिच्छामि वेदितुम् ।
त्यागस्य च हृषीकेश पृथक्केशिनिषूदन ॥१८/१॥

Arjun Uvaach

Sannyaasasya Mahaabaaho tattvamichchhaami veditum I

Tyaagasya ch Hrusheekesh pruthakKeshinishoodan II (18/1)

Sannyaasasya (about the path, order of leading life by renunciation) Mahaabaaho (Krishn) Tattvam (fundamentals of) Ichchhaami (I wish) Veditum (to know)I Tyaagasya (about Tyaag) Ch (and) Hrusheekesh (Krishn) Pruthak (separate, different) Keshi Nishoodan (Krishn)II (18/1)

Arjun said:

"O Mahaabaaho (Krishn)! O Hrusheekesh (Krishn)! I want to understand the fundamental difference between Sannyaas, the order of leading life by way of renunciation, and Tyaag, the order of leading life by way of giving up, O Keshi Nishoodan (Krishn)!" (18/1)

God defined a **Sannyaasee** in 6/1 as:

'He is a true Sannyaasee who carries out his works as his obligatory duties without seeking favorable fruition of his actions; not he, who has stopped performing sacred works like Yajn etc. with fire; nor he, who remains inactive in discharging his duties.'

Then, in 12/11, He instructed Arjun to:

'Do duties while remaining situated in the spirit of Sarv Karm Phal Tyaag i.e. totally giving up the consideration of results of all of his actions.'

Later, He spoke of **Sannyaas** and **Tyaag** many times but Arjun, flabbergasted by delusion, could not understand His message properly. Now, when the teaching of spiritual knowledge is almost over, he politely expresses his desire to know the difference between **Sannyaas** and **Tyaag** in his last question here in Gita. In it, he seeks clarification between two similar sounding words, **Sannyaas** & **Tyaag.** As told above, Gita frequently uses both of them in its text in their principal & derivative forms.

Readers may recall how Arjun asked questions to Krishn earlier in somewhat rude, blunt manner, especially in 3/1-2, 4/4 and 5/1, but his tone and body language started gradually improving from 6/33 onwards. in 18/1 here it is very pleasing to see his arrogance transforming into humility and humbleness completely after listening to teachings of Krishn in 17 chapters of Gita. I pray God to help us also in bringing about such change in our attitude and understanding after we complete our study of Gita.

Conventionally speaking, **Tyaag** refers to an activity of giving up, abandoning, renouncing, dismissing, leaving, discarding, relinquishing and/or disregarding something or someone, either willingly or unwillingly; Whereas **Sannyaas** is generally understood as renunciation of householder's life & worldly matters, and living in isolation in hermitage, forests, mountains, caves etc. away from human settlements, or as an ascetic wanderer. However, Arjun is not a common person. He is a **Jignaasu Bhakt**, the highly inquisitive devotee (6/44 & 7/16) in the quest to learn how to practically apply the spiritual knowledge taught by Krishn in complicated situations of life, in other words what to leave and what to retain. Let us not forget that it was Arjun's express, explicit request in 2/7 that made Krishn to teach Gita. Besides this, Krishn also spoke of two kinds of **Nishthaa**, **Jnaan** (the path of **Sannyaas**) & **Karm** (the path of action) in 3/3 and explained both of them as per context in various chapters. Arjun was a beginner student of primary level in 2/7, but as he is about to clear Post Graduation level of learning Gita in 18/73, he finally wants to get the best tips about Gita's Yog from Krishn, as a student seeks from his teacher before leaving the school to enter the battle of life.

Krishn makes a very different, unique distinction between **Tyaag** and **Sannyaas** from conventional understanding. How? He would reveal it to us in next few shloks. Let us attentively listen to His sweet voice.

ॐ

God states the opinions of scholars about Sannyaas & Tyaag in two shloks below.

(18/2 & 3)

श्रीभगवानुवाच
काम्यानां कर्मणां न्यासं संन्यासं कवयो विदुः ।
सर्वकर्मफलत्यागं प्राहुस्त्यागं विचक्षणाः ॥१८/२॥
त्याज्यं दोषवदित्येके कर्म प्राहुर्मनीषिणः ।
यज्ञदानतपःकर्म न त्याज्यमिति चापरे ॥१८/३॥

Shree Bhagawaan Uvaach
Kaamyaanaam karmanaam nyaasam sannyaasam kavayo vidu: I
Sarvakarmaphalatyaagam praahustyaagam vichakshanaa: II
(18/2)
Tyaajyam doshavadityeke karm praahurmaneeshin: I
Yajnadaanatap:karm n tyaajyamiti chaapare II (18/3)

Kaamyaanaam (Kaamya or Sakaam Karm performed with the desire of some result) Karmanaam (of Karm) Nyaasam (renunciation) Sannyaasam (the path of renunciation) Kavay: (scholars of scriptures) Vidu: (know)I Sarv Karm Phal Tyaagam (renunciation of fruits of all actions) Praahu: (is said) Tyaagam (leading life by way of Tyaag) Vichakshanaa: (discerning, sagacious seers)II (18/2)

Tyaajyam (worth giving up) Dosh vat (fraught with fault, evil) Iti (thus) Eke (few others) Karm (work) Praahu: (is said) Maneeshin: (great introspective & reflective thinkers)I Yajn (Yajn) Daan (Daan) Tap: (Tap) Karm (work) N (no) Tyaajyam (worth giving up) Iti (thus) Ch (and) Apare (other)II (18/3)

God said:

"Some learned scholars of Scriptures understand Sannyaas as renunciation of Kaamya Karm, the actions performed with a desire to achieve a desired result whereas some other discerning seers talk of it as abandonment of results of all actions. (18/2)

Some other introspective & reflective thinkers say that since all actions are fraught with some fault, they are worth giving up totally. Still others tell in this way that Yajn, the sacrificial rites & other pious, righteous works, Daan, the donation for charity; and Tap, the austerities for self-purification are the activities, which a person should never abandon. (18/3)

We have now reached 28th, the last **Shree Bhagawaan Uvaach**, the speech of God in Gita. God started speaking from 2/2 and He shall continue to speak uninterruptedly from here until 18/72 in order to sum up His teachings in the most practical and simple and explicit manner. He first sets out, in these two shloks, to explain viewpoints of four kinds of **Maneeshee**, the scholars and thinkers, revered and followed by the common people, about their understanding of **Sannyaas**. He classifies their viewpoints into four categories:

1. Renunciation of actions performed with a desire to achieve some result,

2. Abandonment of results of all actions,

3. Totally giving up all actions since every action is fraught with some fault or the other, and,

4. Giving up all other works except **Yajn, Daan** and **Tap**

Superficially, they all seem to conform to Gita's ideals on a cursory look at them, but on a deeper analysis we shall find that they propagate those ideals partially as explained below in the same order of different views expressed above:

1. Gita shall advise us in 18/23 not to give up **Saattvik Karm**, the righteous works at all even if performed with the desire of some fruit. Similarly, **Swadharm** also must be done at any cost as said in 2/31 & 3/35.

2. In 18/9, Gita would tell us to give up attachment with the desire of a fruit, not the result or the target of work per se. We must perform a work as a matter of duty to achieve the targeted result (but not lament upon facing failure).

3. Gita disapproves the viewpoint of totally giving up all actions since it is impossible to give up all the works and still carry on the journey of life as explained in 3/8. It also denounces giving up all works due to the fear that they may result in some fault while doing them. It would teach us in 18/48 to never giving up naturally obtained works & duties just because they are fraught with some minor fault. Lighting a fire is essential to perform a **Yajn** but no one can ignite a fire without generating some smoke initially, and ash in the end.

4. Gita shall tell in 18/5 to give up sacred works like **Yajn**, **Daan** and **Tap** never, as it would add more noble deeds in 18/6. However, the most important modification it makes is that we should perform them as a matter of duty with an attitude of complete dissociation from their fruits. Krishn gave His own example in support this aspect in 3/22-24. Also refer to *'Some additional thoughts on Lok Sangrah'* expressed after 3/26. Doing useful work is everyone's social responsibility.

We understood **Sarv Karm Phal Tyaag** as giving up interest and attachment in the fruits of all actions in 12/11 earlier. Different viewpoints of individual thinkers are akin to offering only **Daal**, or only **Bhaat**, or only **Chapattis**, or only curry as a meal to someone whereas Gita offers a wholesome spiritual meal to our souls in next shloks.

⌘

After different opinions about Sannyaas & Tyaag, God pronounces His decision.

(18/4, 5 & 6)

निश्चयं शृणु मे तत्र त्यागे भरतसत्तम ।
त्यागो हि पुरुषव्याघ्र त्रिविधः संप्रकीर्तितः ॥१८/४॥
यज्ञदानतपःकर्म न त्याज्यं कार्यमेव तत् ।
यज्ञो दानं तपश्चैव पावनानि मनीषिणाम् ॥१८/५॥

एतान्यपि तु कर्माणि सङ्गं त्यक्त्वा फलानि च ।
कर्तव्यानीति मे पार्थ निश्चितं मतमुत्तमम् ॥१८/६॥

Nishchayam shrunu me tatr tyaage Bharatasattam I
Tyaago hi Purushavyaaghr trividh: samprakeertit: II (18/4)
Yajnadaanatap:karm n tyaajyam kaaryamev tat I
Yajno daanam tapashchaiv paavanaani maneeshinaam II
(18/5)
Etaanyapi tu karmaani sangam tyaktvaa phalaani ch I
Kartavyaaneeti me Paarth nishchitam matamuttamam II
(18/6)

Nishchayam (ascertained decision) Shrunu (listen) Me (My) Tatr (of those) Tyaage (of Tyaag) Bharat Sattam (Arjun)I Tyaag: (path of Tyaag) Hi (certainly) Purushvyaaghr (Arjun) Trividh: (of three kinds) Samprakeertit: (declared)II (18/4)

Yajn (Yajn) Daan (Daan) Tap: (Tap) Karm (work) N (not) Tyaajyam (worth giving up) Kaaryam (duty to perform) Ev (undoubtedly) Tat (that)I Yajn: (Yajn) Daanam (Daan) Tap: (Tap) Ch (and) Ev (even) Paavanaani (purifying) Maneeshinaam (wise, introspective thinkers) II (18/5)

Etaani (all these) Api (also) Tu (but) Karmaani (other noble deeds) Sangam (attachment, association) Tyaktvaa (give up) Phalaani (to fruits) Ch (and)I Kartavyaani (to be done as a matter of duty) Iti (this much) Me (my) Paarth (Arjun) Nishchitam (ascertained) Matam (opinion) Uttamam (the best)II (18/6)

O Bharat Sattam (Arjun)! Now listen to My well ascertained decision about Tyaag, the order of leading life by way of giving up. O Purush Vyaaghr (Arjun)! Tyaag too is proclaimed of three kinds. (18/4)

The activities that one should never give up at all are Yajn i.e. the sacrificial, pious and righteous activities, Daan i.e. giving in charity, and Tap i.e. the austerities for self-purification. Rather, they are duties that he must undoubtedly perform. Even the wisest reflective thinkers keep purifying themselves by performing Yajn, Daan and Tap. (18/5)

Nevertheless, he should perform all these and any other noble deeds also as a matter of duty by giving up association with their desired fruits. O Paarth (Arjun)! This is My very best & well ascertained opinion. (18/6)

Krishn sums up, from 18/4 to 12, the essence of **Nishkaam Karm Yog** preached by Him in Gita. Let us read it very carefully.

Arjun wished to know first about **Sannyaas** and then **Tyaag,** but **Krishn** prefers to explain **Tyaag** first since He feels it would be much easier to understand **Sannyaas** once he understands **Tyaag** properly. After giving the opinions of four kinds of **Sannyaasee** in 18/2 & 3, He gives His well ascertained, firm opinion saying that all noble acts like sacrificial and duty bound actions, giving donations in charity, and self-purification through certain ascetic practices like meditation, worship etc., should be never given up by anyone at any stage of life. All such acts must be performed as **Kartavya**, a must do duty, not guided by desire for some kind of fruition.

Moral: *The real 'Joie de vivre', the joy of life, lies in giving up attachment with material things, not in possessing and remaining glued with them.*

Krishn calls Arjun by three names here. He calls him **Bharat Sattam** probably to remind him of his noble lineage from Emperor Bharat after who India is named as Bhaarat until today. As narrated in Mahaabhaarat, he was born and brought up among an ascetic outfit in forests by his mother Shakuntalaa who later moved with him to the kingdom of his father king Dushyant. **Purush Vyaaghr** is another adjective that Krishn uses for Arjun to show that his might is like a tiger amongst all the men in both armies. By addressing him as **Paarth** He encourages him to come to a proper decision about his duty as his mother Pruthaa (Kuntee) always did.

There is an apparent mismatch between what Krishn told in 8/28 *'A Yogee should transgress ritualistic works like Yajn, Tap & Daan as soon as possible'*, and what He says here in 18/5 *'We should never give up Yajn, Tap & Daan'*. Let us clear this confusion.

Clarification: *Krishn stated as above in 8/28 to ensure that a practiser of Yog is not distracted from practising Yog by indulging in* *ritualistic activities like Yajn, Tap and Daan which are prescribed by Veds purely for those who are attracted by their perishable fruits to enjoy in this world as well as the worlds beyond. Nevertheless, He is talking of a desireless, accomplished Yogee here who must continue to perform all sacred works without any desire of result in order to set an example for practisers of Yog as well as commoners.*

It is noteworthy that Gita, in its typical style, has refrained from raising any controversy or commenting on the opinions of hard core ascetics described in 18/2-3, who considered it very important to leave everything except activities necessary for their minimal sustenance like begging, wandering, attending to nature calls etc. They engaged themselves only in severe ascetic practices like penance, total abstinence, complete silence, living in isolated places etc. Gita's **Sannyaas,** on the other hand, does not lie in its physical outward exhibition and demonstration; it is in its adoption in an inner mental disposition of detachment from desires of fruitful results. This is the judgment given by Krishn about diverse opinions of various thinkers about **Sannyaas.**

Let us also recall what Krishn said in 3/4:

'A person can neither attain freedom from reactions of fruitive actions without performing some activities nor can he accomplish success by mere renunciation of physical activities'.

Now, He very beautifully & rationally expands the concept of **Tyaag** & **Sannyaas** here by first giving opinions of other learned people in 18/2-3, and then giving His decision in 18/4-6 that voluntarily giving up attachment with fruits of works is the best way than forcibly renouncing work itself.

ॐ

Krishn proceeds to describe three qualities of Tyaag.

(18/7, 8 & 9)

नियतस्य तु संन्यासः कर्मणो नोपपद्यते ।
मोहात्तस्य परित्यागस्तामसः परिकीर्तितः ॥१८/७॥

दुःखमित्येव यत्कर्म कायक्लेशभयात्त्यजेत् ।
स कृत्वा राजसं त्यागं नैव त्यागफलं लभेत् ॥१८/८॥
कार्यमित्येव यत्कर्म नियतं क्रियतेऽर्जुन ।
सङ्गं त्यक्त्वा फलं चैव स त्यागः सात्त्विको मतः ॥१८/९॥

Niyatsya tu sannyaas: karmano nopapadyate I
Mohaattasya parityaagstaamas: parikeertit: II (18/7)
Du:khamityev yatkarm kaayakleshabhayaattyajet I
S krutvaa raajasam tyaagam naiv tyaagaphalam labhet II
(18/8)
Kaaryamityev yatkarm niyatam kriyateʃrjun I
Sangam tyaktvaa phalam chaiv s tyaag: saattviko mat: II (18/9)

niyatasya (of regulated, prescribed) Tu (but) Sannyaas: (renunciation) Karman: (of Karm) N (never) Upapadyate (is worth doing)I Mohaat (due to delusion) Tasya (of that) Pari Tyaag: (renunciation, abandonment) Taamas: (of quality of Tam) Parikeertit: (is proclaimed)II (18/7)

Du:kham (distressful) Iti (thus) Ev (only) Yat (which) Karm (duty, work) Kaay: Klesh Bhayaat (out of fear of trouble, affliction & strain to body) Tyajet (gives up)I s (he) Krutvaa (is doing) Raajasam (with quality of passion) Tyaagam (the path of Tyaag) N (not) Ev (certainly) Tyaag (Tyaag) Phalam (result) Labhet (gains)II (18/8)

Kaaryam (which must be done as a matter of duty) Iti (thus) Ev (only) Yat (which) Karm (work, duty) Niyatam (prescribed) Kriyate (is done) Arjun (Arjun)I Sangam (attachment, association) Tyaktvaa (give up) Phalam (result) ch (and) Ev (certainly) S: (he) Tyaag: (Tyaag) Saattvik: (of Sattv) Mat: (is opined)II (18/9)

Never renounce prescribed duty. Abandonment of that prescribed duty due to delusion & infatuation is declared as Taamas Tyaag i.e. of the lowest quality of ignorance & darkness. (18/7)

If a person gives up doing his duty thinking it as distressful and painful for his body, his Tyaag is Raajas i.e. of quality of passion; and he certainly does not gain any fruit from such Tyaag. (18/8)

O Arjun! When a person performs his prescribed duty considering it only as a matter of discharging own responsibility and gives up all material associations with its fruit, his Tyaag is certainly opined to be Saattvik i.e. of the noblest quality of righteousness. (18/9)

Niyat karm was explained earlier in 3/8 as a duty performed in compliance of **Dharm** as prescribed and regulated by Scriptures or by acknowledged institutions like **Varn** & **Aashram** in ancient India; or by the government & its constitution in modern times; or spiritual & religious leaders of a society for its people from time to time. **Niyat karm** would also appear in 18/23 & 47 we shall try to sum up our thoughts on it in 18/47. If a person gives up such prescribed duties due to delusion and infatuation, Gita denounces such renunciation as **Taamasik**, the lowest category of **Tyaag**. Besides, if those duties are abandoned due the fear of being troublesome and painful to his body or cause grief to him or due to coercion or own ego, such **Tyaag** is termed **Raajasik**, the medium quality of passion. Nothing of real spiritual worth is achievable by both these types of **Tyaag** as they are motivated by traits of low quality like delusion, ignorance and passion for personal comforts & pleasures in life.

Saattvik quality of **Tyaag** is carried out by situating the self in the light of pure knowledge, farther away from the darkness of ignorance without any kind of personal demand, interest, ego and impulsive pride. A **Saattvik Tyaagee** performs all of his works as a matter of duty in the light of Dharm, truth and righteousness, as per the laws of right living. His every work is a sacred mission to fulfill with complete dissociation from their results. He thinks about every work that comes before him:

'This work is my duty and I must do it regardless of its consequence. It is my Kartavya, an obligatory, compulsory and must do duty in which God has appointed me'.

Moral: *If we find it difficult to perform Niyat Karm, the allotted duties, or even Vihit Karm, the prescribed works, the least we can do is to desist from doing Nishiddh Karm, the prohibited works.*

Cautions:

1. *Possibilities of committing prohibited works increase exponentially in doing Sakaam Karm, the works that we do with attachment to desirable results. It is because once we become desirous of results, we start moulding our effort and energy to achieve those results instead of channelizing them in the right and just direction.*

2. *The type and quality of the result of our every work depends entirely on sincerity of our motive and effort in doing it. A fool only can expect to gain a good fruit without planting the best quality of sapling and nurturing it with utmost care.*

Chitralekhaa, a royal danseuse challenges **Sannyaasee** Kumaargiri, an absconder from the world, as follows in the film of same title:

संसार से भागे फिरते हो भगवान को तुम क्या पाओगे,

इस लोक को भी अपना न सके उस लोक को क्या अपनाओगे ।

तुम कहते हो ये जग सपना है हम कहते हैं सब कुछ अपना है,

अपमान रचेता का होगा रचना को अगर ठुकराओगे ॥

(How can you attain God by running away from the world? How can you achieve that superior world if you cannot adapt even to this world? You say that this world is a dream but I think that everything in it is our own. It would be a great insult of its Creator if you kick His beautiful creation.)

Where can anyone go beyond this world? Film Guide reflects the same thought and discourages an escapist **Sannyaasee** from abandoning this world for the sake of a world yet unknown to him:

वहाँ कौन है तेरा मुसाफिर जाएगा कहाँ?

दम ले ले घड़ी भर ये छैइयाँ पाएगा कहाँ?

(O traveller! Is there anybody waiting for you where you aspire to go? Rest here for a while in the cool shade that you won't find anywhere else.)

Raamkrishn Paramhans, the most revered **Sannyaasee** in recent times, did not give up householder's life but he did relinquish attachment in results of his activities. He often used to advise his followers:

'As it is prudent to fight enemies from within a fort, so is it convenient to practice Sannyaas with the comforts of getting food, water and maintaining good health in the household.'

Shankaraachaarya, a **Sannyaasee** himself, instructs every **Sanyaasee** in his **Bhaasya** on **Vedaant Sookt**:

'Perform works to uphold and establish Dharm as per your capabilities for the benefit of all living beings.'

Though the subject matter here is of **Tyaag**, the renunciation by common people who are normally good natured, other wicked people like miscreants, thieves, dacoits etc. also can benefit from this discussion by giving up their bad works as Vaalmeeki, Angilimaal etc. did.

Caution: Sometimes a person, particularly in old age, is compelled to give up pleasures of life either due to physical disability or due to consideration of what other people would think about him. This does not mean that he has become a Tyaagee because he still nurtures the lust in those pleasures. The Hindi film titled Shaukeens illustrated this point very well.

Klesh: It was explained as tribulations, troubles and suffering in 12/5. **Kaay Klesh** refers to the suffering of physical body. We should never give up a good work just because it may subject our body to some physical pain while doing it.

೭ఄళ

Krishn explains who a Tyaagee is.

(18/10)

न द्वेष्ट्यकुशलं कर्म कुशले नानुषज्जते ।
त्यागी सत्त्वसमाविष्टो मेधावी छिन्नसंशयः ॥ १८/१०॥

N dweshtyakushalam karm kushale naanushajjate I
Tyaagee sattvasamaavishto medhaavee chhinnasanshay: II
(18/10)

N (neither) Dweshti (averse) Akushalam (misfortune, inauspicious) Karm (work) Kushale (good fortune, auspicious) N (not) Anushajjate (is associated)I Tyaagee (who gives up something) Sattv (Sattv) Samaavisht: (well incorporated) Medhaavee (judicious, intelligent) Chhinn Sanshay: (free from doubt)II (18/10)

He is a true Tyaagee, the renouncer, who, in matters of doing duty, neither despises the unfavorable result nor rejoices on getting the favorable result; who is judicious and free from any doubt; and in whom the quality of righteousness and truth is in-built very well. (18/10)

Kushal means well being, happiness, prosperity, auspiciousness, favorable and fortune, I have interpreted **Kushal** in this sense, and its opposite **Akushal** as unhappiness, inauspicious, misfortune and unfavorable here in 18/10. However, **Kaushal**, a derivative of the same root as of **Kushal**, also means dexterity, proficiency, competence, expertise, and deftness; and I interpreted it for the phrase **Yog: Karmasu Kaushalam** in 2/50 as:

'Yog automatically bestows dexterity, proficiency, competence, deftness in doing works if done with resolute intelligence, balance of mind & heart, and without any self-interest'.

Nevertheless, if we take **Kushal** and **Akushal** to connote to skill and efficiency of a person here in 18/10, we can infer that a **Tyaagee** neither abhors an unskilled, inefficient person nor adores a skilled, efficient one because he has given up discrimination; he is just an onlooker, a seer, not a judge. Conversely, if we apply the meaning of **Kaushal** as well-being and prosperity in 2/50, it would mean that **Yog** ensures happiness, well-being and prosperity of its practiser in physical, mental and spiritual worlds.

Chhinn Sanshay is the opposite of **Sanshay Aatmaa** that was explained in 4/40 as a person seized by **Sanshay**, the doubt, mistrust, uncertainty, hesitation, apprehension, anxiety, fear and

388 • GITA for GEN A to Z - Vol III

skepticism. Such person can never develop faith in anything; and cannot have peace as a result. **Chhinn Sanshay** therefore, means a person who is free from all kinds of **Sanshay**. A **Tyaagee** has cut off all the doubts that surround and confuse an ordinary person about his goal & purpose in human life, the standards he must follow, and the duties he must perform.

We knew **Medhaa** in 10/34 as the clear, sharp wisdom to discern, judge, decide, and resolve between right and wrong applied with the purpose of continuous self-improvement and well-being of the society. It is a synonym of **Prajnaa**, **Buddhi**, **Dhee** and **Mati**. He who possesses such **Medhaa** is **Medhaavee**. A **Tyaagee** is a clear minded, highly intelligent, wise person, like **Sthit Prajn** (2/55-72).

৵৹৵

It is impossible for anyone to give up work altogether.

(18/11)

न हि देहभृता शक्यं त्यक्तुं कर्माण्यशेषतः ।
यस्तु कर्मफलत्यागी स त्यागीत्यभिधीयते ॥१८/११॥

N hi dehabhrutaa shakyam tyaktum karmaanyasheshat: I
Yastu karmaphalatyaagee s tyaageetyabhidheeyate II (18/11)

N (not) Hi (because) Deh Bhrutaa (embodied persons) Shakyam (practical) Tyaktum (to give up) Karmaani (all activities) Asheshat: (completely, altogether)I y: (who) Tu (but) Karm Phal Tyaagee (who renounces fruits of actions) S: (he) Tyaagee (true renouncer) Iti (thus) Abhidheeyate (is said)II (18/11)

Because it is practically not possible for any embodied person to give up all activities entirely but he is called true Tyaagee, the renouncer who relinquishes (attachment with) fruits of his actions. (18/11)

By saying, '*it is not practical for anybody to entirely give up activities*' in the first line of this shlok, Krishn reminds us of what He said earlier in 3/8:

"If you shirk from performing your duty you shall not succeed even in maintaining and continuing the journey of your body and life".

Everybody has to do bare minimum activities like breathing, eating, drinking, sleeping, thinking, resting and engaging in some professional activity necessary for continuance of life lest it becomes meaningless. A **Tyaagee** must therefore focus on detaching himself from the desire of achieving only an auspicious, favorable result as per his liking.

༄༅

Three types of results are bound to accrue to any action of a desirous person.

(18/12)

अनिष्टमिष्टं मिश्रं च त्रिविधं कर्मणः फलम् ।
भवत्यत्यागिनां प्रेत्य न तु संन्यासिनां क्वचित् ॥१८/१२॥

Anishtamishtam mishram ch trividham karman: phalam I
Bhavatyatyaaginaam pretya n tu sannyaasinaam kwachit II
(18/12)

Anishtam (undesirable) Ishtam (desirable) Mishram (mixed) Ch (and) Trividhim (of three kinds) Karman: (of works) Phalam (result) I bhavati (is) Atyaaginaam (who have not given up fruits of action) Pretya (after death) N (no) Tu (but) Sannyaasinaam (true practitioner of Sannyaas) Kwachit (at any time)II (18/12)

Three kinds of fruits, undesirable, desirable & mixed, of actions accrue even after death for persons who do not give up the fruits of action but there is no reaction whatsoever (good, bad or mixed) at any time (during or after life) for those who are true Tyaagee, the abandoners. (18/12)

The outcome of **Sakaam Karm**, a work done with some desire, can be of three types only, **Isht** i.e. pleasant and to our liking, **Anisht,** the unpleasant, disliked by us, and **Mishrit** i.e. a mixture of both in infinitely varying proportions. We see practically in our lives that results of almost all of our actions are neither purely **Isht**, nor **Anisht** but **Mishrit**. Though light & darkness exist together, they also define each other as per the variations in their proportions. When light is less it becomes darkness, and when darkness is less, it is light. A **Mishrit** result similarly appears **Isht** or **Anisht**. It is very important to note in this context that the result of an action depends entirely on the quality of intention of doer behind it, the means deployed by him, and the effort he puts in while doing it; not on his wishful thoughts. Next shloks shall clarify this point.

Albeit, there is one more category of **Karm Phal** designated as **Vishisht**, the most outstanding. In fact, Gita's entire effort is to guide us in achieving **Vishisht Phal** by performing our works with total detachment from results. Everlasting peace i.e. freedom from distress and miseries in current life, and liberation from the painful cycles of birth and death is that **Vishisht Phal** as assured by Gita when it said in 12/12:

"Renunciation of fruits of actions is the best way by which one can immediately attain eternal peace".

It is also relevant for us to know here that though we wish our work to bear certain desired fruit immediately, the fact is that it may or may not take place in whole of our current life, as divine theory of **Karm** & **Karm Phal** may postpone it to any of our countless future lives until liberation from **Punarjanm**. We have already learnt about the intricate theory of **Karm** & **Karm Phal** earlier at many places during our study of Gita. Example:

'When a patient takes a medicine, apparently there can be two kinds of results: Isht or Anisht i.e. either it cures him or does not cure. However, on extending our thoughts a little bit further, we would find a Mishrit result: i.e. either the medicine cures him partially, or some of its side effects occur. In either case, he has to go for another round of treatment; and this vicious cycle goes on indefinitely. He forgets totally that the basic cause of his ailment lies in disregarding the rules of a healthy living. The moment he realizes this fact and decides to live an abstemious way of life as advised by learned

people and/ or the doctor, he starts getting Vishisht result of by way of becoming Anaamay i.e. healthy, free from ailment. A practiser can similarly attain Padam Anaamayam, the most sought after, faultless, untainted and purest divine position, by strictly following the regime of controlling his body and mind, sincerely discharging his duties and giving up desire of results, as specified by Gita here and earlier also in 2/51'.

Krishn uses **Sannyaasinaam** here for **Tyaagee**, who relinquishes fruits of the works, not the work per se. he does not mean a **Sannyaasee** who absconds from his duty and action. In this way, He establishes that a **Tyaagee** is always a **Sannyaasee** in the true sense of the term; but the vice versa is seldom true.

The essence of **Nishkaam Karm Yog** that Krishn started from 18/4 ends here.

ॐ

How an action is accomplished in the first place? Gita gives five primary causes & prerequisites and three implements for it.

(18/13, 14 & 15)

पञ्चैतानि महाबाहो कारणानि निबोध मे ।
सांख्ये कृतान्ते प्रोक्तानि सिद्धये सर्वकर्मणाम् ॥१८/१३॥
अधिष्ठानं तथा कर्ता करणं च पृथग्विधम् ।
विविधाश्च पृथक्चेष्टा दैवं चैवात्र पञ्चमम् ॥१८/१४॥
शरीरवाङ्मनोभिर्यत्कर्म प्रारभते नरः ।
न्याय्यं वा विपरीतं वा पञ्चैते तस्य हेतवः ॥१८/१५॥

Panchaitaani Mahaabaaho kaaranaani nibodh me I
Saankhye krutaante proktaani siddhaye sarvkarmanaam II
(18/13)
Adhishthaanam tathaa kartaa karanam ch pruthagvidham I
Vividhaashch pruthakcheshta daivam chaivaatr panchamam
II 18/14

Shareervaangmanobhiryatkarm praarabhate nar: I
Nyaayyam vaa vipareetam vaa panchaite tasya hetav: II
(18/15)

Panch (five) Etaani (all these) Mahaabaaho (Arjun) Kaaranaani (causes, means) Nibodh (know well) Me (from Me)I Saamkhye (in Saamkhya) Krutaante (which explains how to terminate reactions of actions) Proktaani (is called) Siddhaye (of accomplishing) Sarv (all) Karmanaam (works)II (18/13)

Adhishthaanam (ground) Tathaa (as well as) Kartaa (doer) Karanam (group of thirteen instruments, sensory organs viz. ears, skin, eyes, tongue & nose, 5 functionary organs viz. hands, legs, tongue, genital & anus with mind, intelligence and ego) Ch (and) Pruthak (separate) Vidham (kinds)I Vividhaa: (various) Ch (and) Pruthak (different) Cheshtaa: (efforts) Daivam (fate, destiny) Ch (and) Ev (also) Atr (here) Panchamam (fifth)II (18/14)

Shareer (body) Vaang (speech) Manobhi: (and mind) Yat (whichever) Karm (work) Praarabhate (initiates) Nar: (person)I Nyaayyam (lawful) Vaa (or) Vipareetam (opposite) Vaa (or) Panch (five) Ete (all these) Tasya (of it) Hetav: (cause)II (18/15)

O Mahaabaaho (Arjun)! While explaining how to terminate reactions of actions, the doctrine of Saamkhya has described five causes necessary for accomplishing all works. Understand them well from Me. (18/13)

Here, the first one Adhishthaan, the basis of doing a work; second Kartaa, the doer of work; third Karan, the various means & implements deployed for work; fourth different kinds of Cheshtaa, the efforts put in by him; and Daiv the fate is the fifth one here. All these five, together with the body, speech and mind, are the causes for a person to initiate whatsoever work, whether just or unjust. (18/14 & 15)

After summarizing **Nishkaam Karm Yog** in 18/4-12, Krishn deals with the physical aspects of executing **Karm**, its causes, prerequisites and components in 18/13-17.

We had learnt about Kapil and his **Saamkhya** theory first in chapter 2 and then at other relevant places. Krishn very modestly accredits Kapil with the five primary causes and prerequisites, and performing any work in their absence is not possible. He describes these five basic, indispensible requirements as:

1. **Adhishthaan:** It is the base, the resting place, the ground to install something. No one can do any work without a basic reason to do it. It is just like trying to sow a seed without land. To gain spiritual knowledge is **Adhishthaan** of our **Karm** of studying Gita.

2. **Kartaa:** He is the doer of the work. He must wholeheartedly involve in the work. If anyone, like Arjun in chapter 1, wants to withdraw himself from the work, it remains incomplete.

3. **Karan:** These are different kinds of instruments & implements described by **Saamkhya** as a group of thirteen. They are five sensory organs namely ears, skin, eyes, tongue & nose; five functionary organs namely hands, legs, tongue, genital & anus; mind is the eleventh, intelligence is the twelfth and the existential ego is the thirteenth. We need at least one, or few, or all of them for performing any work. Duryodhan uses the cunningness of Shakuni as Karan in Mahaabhaarat whereas Arjun seeks refuge in the wisdom of Krishn (2/7).

4. **Cheshtaa:** It is the effort, however small or big, put in by the doer of work. The doer needs to put in some kind of effort to perform a work. Working with **Purushaarth**, the purpose of being a person is the ultimate form of **Cheshtaa**. Duryodhan did all what he could like poisoning, burning alive, gambling, denuding Draupadee to deprive Paandavs from their rightful share of empire. In Raamaayan also, Kaikeyee focused her entire **Cheshtaa** on sending Raam to forest.

5. **Daiv:** We had discussed it as **Praarabdh**, the fate, fortune, kismet or destiny in 9/28; and are shortly going to have '*Some additional thoughts on Daiv*' under these shloks.

All the five causes quoted above from **Saamkhya** are in the order of their importance for a person to initiate an activity. A person can perform a new work, independent of Daiv, the fate, on his own volition but Daiv plays an important role in implementing divine law of **Karm** & **Karm Bandhan**. Krishn now modestly adds following three means of doing a work:

1. **Shareer:** It is the body, in which the soul of a person is embodied. A **Shaareerik Karm** is an action executed physically by the body; and it directly invites retaliation in the form of a reaction.

2. **Vaang:** It is the power of speech or expression like advising, counseling, teaching, ordering, inciting, criticizing, scolding, spreading misinformation, gesturing etc. The works executed by **Vaang** are called **Vaachik** works. They too are reciprocated by way of a reaction in this or later life.

3. **Man:** It is composed of the mind and heart as explained earlier also. **Maanasik Karm** is a mental intention that may or may not transform into **Shaareerik** or **Vaachik Karm** because it depends on the decision of our intelligence according to prevailing situation, time, and other factors. Since **Man** is continuously engaged in **Sankalp**, the propositions and **Vikalp**, the dispositions (4/19) most of them remain mere mental thoughts and never translate into an action. Naturally, no reaction of a **Maanasik Karm** would take place unless it converts into a **Shaareerik** or **Vaachik Karm**. Nevertheless, since such mental intentions also cannot escape from the all seeing eye of divine judgment, the law of **Karm** & **Karm Phal** shall definitely punish a person even for nurturing negative thoughts. This explains why a negative person is always under terrible stress though he may sometimes be able to hide it.

The phrase **Nyaayyam vaa Vipareetam** means just or unjust, good or bad, right or wrong, lawful or unlawful, and approved or unapproved by scriptures or society. In short, whatever may be the quality of works; all of them originate from these five elements; and the doer executes them bodily, verbally or mentally. It is also relevant to know that the quality of every **Shaareerik, Vaachik** or **Maanasik Karm** can be **Saattvik, Raajasik**, or **Taamasik** according to the intention, means and method adopted by the doer. Let me illustrate it with the following example:

'A person, standing on the bank of a river, sees a boy struggling to save himself from drowning. He jumps immediately into the river, brings him to the bank, gives first aid and takes him to nearby hospital. In this way, he has done a Shaareerik Karm. Suppose, he did not know swimming and shouts for help, he is doing a Vaachik Karm. In the third case if he happens to be dumb and cannot shout for help, but prays whole-heartedly for the life of the drowning person, his action is a Maanasik Karm. The quality of his Karm is Saattvik in all these cases.

However, if the person knows swimming but is afraid of drowning himself along with the boy while trying to rescue him, and chooses to call others for help, he is performing a Raajasik Vaachik Karm. In the worst scenario, in spite of being a good swimmer, he neither risks his life to save the boy nor calls any one for help for he thinks the boy himself is responsible for his misadventure of jumping in the water, and leaves the boy to his ill-fated end. He is doing a Maanasik Karm of meanest quality of Taamas.'

God, as Krishn, had pre-decided to uproot **Adharm** by eliminating 18 **Akshauhinee** uncontrollable fighters in the war of Mahaabhaarat; we have seen Him inviting Arjun (in 11/32-34) to play his role in fulfilling God's mission of destroying **Adharm** and re-establishing **Dharm** (4/7-8). It is also significant to note in this context that, a little later, He also stage-managed the end of His own Yaadav clan in Prabhaas Kshetr for they too had become very unruly during His long absence from Dwaarikaa.

Morals:

1. *If we can eliminate ego and self-interest from Karan, the implements, our real impersonal soul starts rising up by sensing and visualizing the force and will of God behind our every work. It is then that an outwardly terrible looking work of massacre of millions turns into an assignment by the Master of entire universe and its multitudinous phenomena; and we act like an instrument, a weapon, or a tool in His hand.*

2. *A practiser should always remember that God's supreme will is to ensure that entire world community crosses over all the impediments in the path of its progress and well-being regardless of the price to pay for every step forward. His every action then immediately becomes a divine Karm automatically.*

3. *No one can perform any work without applying at least one of these three means but the quality of its result would depend on the degree of the propriety of his Man, the mind & heart, Vachan, his speech, and Cheshtaa, the physical involvement. It is noteworthy that besides physically executed works Gita also includes spoken words, expressions and even thoughts in the category of an action since all of them are bound to incur Karm Phal i.e. a reaction to the person in his current or next lives.*

4. *We should learn to act, not to react.*

God briefly explained **Kaarya** & **Karan** earlier also in 13/20 as two constituents of nature among others.

SOME ADDITIONAL THOUGHTS ON DAIV I.E. PRAARABDH, THE FATE

Daiv mentioned here is same as **Praarabdh, Kismet, Bhaagya, Naseeb** etc. all of which mean fate, fortune & destiny. **Daiv** is the collective force exerted by gods and nature on the result of a **Sakaam** work. Two gardeners may sow seeds at the same time and nurture them with equal care but the quality & quantity of fruits they would get is never the same since fate plays its decisive role according to the quality of seed and the soil chosen by them, and the works done by them in the past. Not only the gardeners, but the plants also, are subject to their **Sanskaar**, the inborn instinct & faculty, and **Paristhiti**, the circumstances or opportunities that are completely in the domain of **Daiv**. Scriptures say:

तुष्टोऽपि राजा यदि सेवकभ्यो: भाग्यात् परम् नैव ददाति किंचित् ।
अहर्निशम् वर्षति वारिवाह: तथापि पत्रत्रितय: पलास ॥

(Even if the king is completely satisfied with his servant, he cannot give him anything more than he is destined to receive.

Maybe the clouds rain day & night on a Palaas[17] but it still cannot have more than three leaves.)

लब तक आते आते हाथों से सागर छूट जाता है ।
हमको ये मालूम ना था, कोई साथ नहीं देता,
माझी छोड़ जाता है, साहिल छूट जाता है ॥

(The cup of wine slips away from the hands just before reaching the lips; the boatman abandons the boat at the nick of the moment; and the shore within one's reach submerges under water. I never realized that everyone deserts us in bad times.)

Those, who do not believe in the doctrine of **Karm** & **Karm Bandhan**, and therefore in **Punarjanm**, may interpret **Daiv** as chance happening. Every one has experienced it when something happens all of a sudden unexpectedly, or a stranger appears before him from nowhere, or some natural phenomenon takes place at certain time, and changes the flow & direction of his life. Let us learn from the following examples from Mahaabhaarat:

1. When Arjun fails to fulfill his vow of killing Jayadrath before sunset, and a jeering Jayadrath comes out from hiding to witness his self-immolation, everybody is aghast to see the sun re-appearing in the sky all of a sudden. This miracle enables Arjun to kill Jayadrath just before the sun could set again. Only Krishn could understand how **Daiv** scheduled a full solar eclipse that evening in Kurukshetr to save righteous Arjun from imminent death, and ensure death of wicked Jayadrath.

2. Duryodhan is on his way to appear fully naked before his mother Gaandhaaree so that his body becomes impenetrable ansd strong as steel armour by the power in her eyesight. Daiv chanced Krishn to intercept him and advise to observe some decency and not expose his genitals before his mother. It is common knowledge how Krishn later signaled Bheem to

---

17 *Palaas, also called Dhaak, is a species of foliage named as Curcuma.*

hit him hard on his weak loin, and kill. His loin proved to be Achchilles heel[18] for him.

Moral: *As long as we are persistent in our pursuit of a right goal, we would surely continue progressing towards it. Nevertheless, a flower cannot choose the day or time when it will fully bloom. It happens at a time predetermined by destiny because the result is finally in its hands. Daiv, the divine force, provides the invisible support when other things fail. Daiv ensures victory of Dharm, not of person.*

Daadaa Bhagawaan considers **Daiv** as a part of Divine justice:

> *'Whatever you suffer or enjoy in this life, accept it gladly as a verdict of divine justice (as the result of some works previously done). At the same time, you should not willfully indulge in similar works in current life again lest the divine justice is compelled to make you suffer repeatedly.'*

Daiv is the engine of the train of a person's life, pulling it with the coaches of his actions, to its ultimate destiny as per divine justice.

Clarification: *A sinner may try to justify his sin saying that the fate of his victim motivated him to commit that sin but actually, it is not so. Divine justice also books the person, who chooses to be instrumental in executing the victim's fate, for his new, willfully committed action.*

For example:

1. If a careless driver hits a blind person, it is latter's fate; but simultaneously the driver also willfully performs a new act of cruelty. While the blind person has suffered due to a **Karm Phal** accrued for some wrong work done earlier, the careless driver too will have to suffer later for his rash driving.

---

18 *Achilles is a great warrior in Greek mythology who survived many battles until an arrow pierced his heel. Legend says that when his mother was foretold of his early death, she dipped his whole body in a magical river to render it impenetrable when he was a baby. As she held him by his heel, his whole body became invulnerable except his heel because it remained out of the water of the river. Achilles died due to his weak heel.*

2. Sometimes, a person appears to take revenge on someone. However, he has a choice to be or not to be the executor of his fate, and earn an unfavorable fate for himself in future.

Daiv does not spare anybody from its clutches, neither the wrong doer, nor the sufferer. Tulasidaas says in Raamcharit Maanas 1/159(ख):

तुलसी जसि भवतब्यता तैसी मिलइ सहाइ।

आपुनु आवइ ताहि पहिं ताहि तहाँ लै जाइ॥

(The kind of assistance a person gets depends on his destiny. It either comes to him on its own, or takes him where it awaits him.)

Clarification: *If a glass piece breaks when dropped by someone, it is neither his Praarabdh, nor a fresh Karm; it is just a happening with no consequence except material loss. However, if the person hits another person with it, it is a fresh Karm of the hitter, and Praarabdh of the hit.*

Having understood the power and inevitability of **Daiv**, the divine judgment as explained above; let us explore further its importance and impact on our life by trying to answer following question:

QUESTION: WHY HAS GITA MENTIONED DAIV, THE FATE, AS THE LAST CAUSE FOR PERFORMING A WORK?

Readers must have noted that Krishn mentions **Daiv** as the last, not the first, among five causes for a work to take place. In my opinion, He does it purposefully to give the least importance to it in comparison to the first four causes, **Adhishthaan, Kartaa, Karan** and **Cheshtaa.** This way, he raises a caution for the fatalistic people who believe in the saying:

'Destiny guides a man's work and if it is true there is no use to struggle in life'.

Gita, on the contrary, believes that destiny actually helps committed people in achieving their goals. In my opinion, the ultimate meaning of **Daiv** is not really the fate but the Divine will & omnipotent wisdom, which guide all affairs of individuals, societies and whole universe to strive continuously for betterment. Experience shows that when natural calamities like earthquakes, floods, drought etc., take place, they leave devastating effects on us; but simultaneously they also throw open new opportunities for reconstruction of a better world and improving our standard of living.

Results of our actions are similar to valuables kept in a bank locker that requires two keys to open. The first key of **Purushaarth**, the committed effort is in the hands of customer and the second key of **Daiv** or **Praarabdh**, the fate is with the bank manager. If we want to open the locker of our fortune, we must first have and apply the right key of **Purushaarth** and patiently wait for fate, the bank manager, to arrive and apply its key. If the locker does not open even after the manager applies his key, it is evident that we have either applied the wrong key or not inserted it properly. Actually, the manger is ready to open locker, but we are not.

The fact of life is that there is no chance, no destiny, no fate, which can circumvent or hinder or control the firm resolve of a determined soul that enjoys a fundamental right to rise from its present state to better by overcoming the obstructions posed by any external power, even by gods. C V Raman says:

'We need a spirit of victory, a spirit that will carry us to our rightful place under the sun, a spirit that can recognize that we, as inheritors of a proud civilization, are entitled to our rightful place on this planet. If that indomitable spirit were to arise in us, nothing can hold us from achieving our rightful destiny'.

Moral: *Destiny is not a matter of chance but choice. It is a thing to achieve by perseverance, not to wait for. If we cannot control our destiny, someone else surely will. We are the ones who hold and shape our destiny by taking proper decisions in crucial moments, not the stars. Those, who work half-heartedly, or leave things to others, are actually absconding from their duty and responsibility so that they can easily find a scapegoat in case of failure.*

Henry Kissinger thinks this thought is especially incumbent on leaders:

'Blessed are the people whose leaders boldly stare destiny right in its eye without blinking; but without attempting to play God'.

Camus writes boldly:

'Until an individual rebels against the established notions of fatalism and creates his own destiny, his existence on earth is like that of a crawling worm, likely to be trampled over any moment'.

The amusing anecdote below exposes the hollowness of taking **Daiv** as *'Fate accompli'* that leaves us with no option than to accept it:

'The villagers of a village believed very much in Bhaagya Lakshmee, the goddess of fate. They always consulted their fortuneteller before undertaking some work. When the village headman saw them abandoning or postponing some developmental works of the village on the advice of the fortuneteller, he started following him closely. One day he noticed the fortuneteller of the neighboring village coming to this fortuneteller's house. He hid himself behind the wall to know the purpose of his visit, and was taken aback to see that his fortuneteller was showing his palm to the visitor and asking to predict his future. He immediately called the villagers to witness it. When the villagers saw it, they understood that if their fortuneteller cannot know his own fate, how he can predict their fate, and of the whole village. The headman then, explained to them:

'You think that your fate is concealed in the lines on your hand, but the symbolism behind this belief is that it is in your own hand to shape your future, not in the hands of the fortuneteller who does not know his own fortune.'

Vashishth counsels Raam in Yog Vaashishth on **Praarabdh** & **Purushaarth**, as stated briefly below:

'Praarabdh & Purushaarth are like two strong rams, facing each other on an extremely narrow hilly track, not ready to

give way to other. Praarabdh became strong due to its past whereas Purushaarth gains its strength on the ground realities of the present. In their ensuing fight, Purushaarth can defeat Praarabdh, and find its way ahead, only if has learnt some lessons from the past and become stronger in the present by practice, perseverance and commitment.'

We hear very often that everything in a person's life is *'Pre-written'* by the invisible hand of divine powers in an illegible language; but are seldom told by anyone that it can be *'Re-written'* with determined efforts and practice. Allaamaa Iqbaal writes:

खुदी को कर बुलंद इतना कि हर तक़दीर के पहले,
खुदा बन्दे से खुद पूछे बता तेरी रज़ा क्या है?

(Elevate your Self to such a height that God Himself asks you to tell Him what you wish before prescribing your destiny.)

Galileo Galilee says:

'I do not believe that the same God who has endowed us with sense, reason, and intellect has intended us to forgo their use'.

Fortune of a person is like the Milky Way in the sky. It consists of numerous tiny stars of his insignificantly small but noble deeds. Asunder, they are not visible, but together, they radiate the brightest heavenly path of light.

Nevertheless, I regard fortunetelling as a technique developed by its enthusiast followers by statistical study of its various branches like astrology, palmistry, horoscopy, numerology etc., and compilation of their findings in millennia. Professional fortunetellers usually refrain from creating fear psychosis in fortune seekers by instilling hope in them and suggesting methods to overcome impending misfortune. Besides, the fortune seekers should also be cautious enough to avoid depression, dejection, hopelessness, inevitability of fate in life.

Clarification*: Additional thoughts expressed by me here are purely my personal views not necessarily supported by Gita. Learned* *readers should read them in this light and decide, as they feel proper in matters concerning Daiv or fate in their life.*

❧

They who do not understand this fact are fools.

(18/16 & 17)

तत्रैवं सति कर्तारमात्मानं केवलं तु यः ।
पश्यत्यकृतबुद्धित्वान्न स पश्यति दुर्मतिः ॥१८/१६॥
यस्य नाहंकृतो भावो बुद्धिर्यस्य न लिप्यते ।
हत्वापि स इमाँल्लोकान्न हन्ति न निबध्यते ॥१८/१७॥

Yasya naahamkruto bhaavo buddhiryasya n lipyate I
Hatvaapi s imaanllokaann hanti n nibadhyate II (18/17)
Tatraivam sati kartaaramaatmaanam kewalam tu y: I
Pashyatyakrutabuddhitvaann s pashyati durmati: II (18/16)

Tatr (of that subject) Evam (in this way) Sati (being truth) Kartaaram (doer) Aatmaanam (to self) Kewalam (one & only) Tu (but) Y: (who)I pashyati (sees) Akrut Buddhitvaat (due to impure & incapable intelligence) N (not) S: (he) Pashyati (sees, knows) Durmati: (perverse person)II (18/16)

Yasya (whose) N (not) Ahamkrut: (born of falsified ego of being the doer) Bhaav: (disposition, temperament) Buddhi: (intelligence) Yasya (whose) N (not) Lipyate (is attached, engrossed)I hatvaa (by killing) Api (even) S: (he) Imaan (all these) Lokaan (people) N (neither) Hanti (kills) N (nor) Nibadhyate (is bound)II (18/17)

In spite of explaining this reality in this way, he, who sees himself only as the doer of all works because his unclean, unrefined intelligence cannot understand this subject, that foolish, pervert person does not know it properly. But, he who does not think himself as the doer of a work due to falsified ego, and whose intelligence is not coated with material objects; he neither kills anyone nor is bound by the reaction of his action of killing all these people. (18/16 & 17)

Krishn stopped talking about war after telling Arjun in 11/32-34 to be merely instrumental in executing His supreme will by killing his opponents. But now, towards the end of His teachings, He resumes the context of war and reinforces the same thought by telling him:

'You are not the killer if you play your role in implementing the overall plan of Supreme Saviour, of securing good people from wicked, cruel & evil people'.

He guarantees him that no sin, no bondage, no reaction shall accrue to him even of such a terrible, ghastly work of killing all the people present in the war. The only condition He imposes on him is that he must completely shed the ego of being their killer.

QUESTION: WHO IS RESPONSIBLE FOR THE DEATH OF MILLIONS IN MAHAABHAARAT IF NOT ARJUN?

Before I attempt to reply to this question, I wish readers to remember that the fight is between **Adharm** and **Dharm**, not Kauravs and Paandavs, as most people generally believe. God exonerates Arjun from the sin of killing in these shloks provided he does it as directed by Him. Who then, is responsible for this massacre? The unfaithful would immediately raise an accusing finger towards Krishn by quoting His declaration in 4/7-8:

'I come into this world whenever Dharm languishes and Adharm flourishes predominantly over Dharm; and to protect the righteous men and annihilate the miscreants'.

They shall also remind us of what He told in 11/32:

'I am the Lord of death, grown up to destroy all these people arrayed here for fight'.

Their arguments seem powerful enough to confuse even the faithful readers. However, let us not forget that, just after 4/7-8, Krishn also told us in 4/13 'मां विद्धि अकर्तारम्' i.e. *'Know me as a non-doer of any work'*. It is true that **Aatmaa**, the soul, in its pure form, and **Paramaatmaa**, the Supreme Soul, both are **Akartaa**, the non-doer of any work. However, a soul must perform some work or the other as long as it is embodied. Simultaneously, he is free to liberate from the ephemeral body and reunite with **Paramaatmaa**, its origin by doing **Nishkaam Karm** i.e. duties without desiring a favorable result; or he performs **Sakaam**, the wishful **Karm**, or **Nishiddh**, the prohibited **Karm** and continues to suffer the pangs of death and rebirth. God exonerates Arjun from the sin of killing people knowing well that he shall choose the first method of **Nishkaam Karm** to perform his duty as per His will. Arjun shall demonstrate his firm determination in 18/73 by promising to Krishn 'करिष्ये वचनं तव' i.e. *'I shall do as per Your bidding'*.

As said above, God too is not the doer of any work. This statement brings us back to square one from where we started this question. Albeit, God appears doing some works in His incarnations to fulfill His divine mission, like teaching Gita to Arjun just now, His births and works are divine (4/9), free from any aspiration for fruition of actions done to reset the standard of **Dharm** so that common people can follow Him, as told in 4/14. Thus, though God kills demons like Hiranyaaksh, Hiranyakashipu etc., or wicked people like Kans, Shishupaal, Raavan etc. in His incarnations, but since He is **Akartaa**, no sin of killing them accrues to Him. Simultaneously, He also sets highly virtuous examples for us to follow and destroy **Adharm**. Neither a doer of **Nishkaam Karm** like Arjun, nor God is responsible for their killing; it is the result of deeds performed by people in this or previous births as per law of **Karm** & **Karm Phal.**

৵৽ঌ

What stimulates a person for an action? And how Karm Phal accrues to him?

(18/18)

ज्ञानं ज्ञेयं परिज्ञाता त्रिविधा कर्मचोदना ।
करणं कर्म कर्तेति त्रिविधः कर्मसंग्रहः ॥१८/१८॥

Jnaanam jneyam Parijnaataa trividhaa karmchodanaa I
karanam karm karteti trividh: Karmangrah: II (18/18)

Jnaanam (knowledge) Jneyam (the thing to know) Parijnaataa (knower) Trividhaa (of three kinds) Karm Chodanaa (impetuous, stimulus, motivation of an action)I Karanam (cause, means) Karm (work) Kartaa (doer) Iti (this much, thus) Trividh: (of three kinds) Karm Sangrah: (collection, compilation of actions)II (18/18)

Knowledge, the object of knowledge, and the knower, these are the three types of stimuli of an action. Moreover, the means, the work itself and the doer, these are the three essential constituents for stockpiling of results (of activities). (18/18)

In order to perform any action there must be three stimuli:

1. **Jnaanam:** It is recognizing the need to do certain work and the knowing the method of doing it,

2. **Jneyam:** It is the object which the doer must identify for doing some work, and,

3. **Parijnaataa:** He is the person accomplished with proper kind of **Jnaan** and knows **Jney** before undertaking a work.

Note that since these three motivating factors are abstract. An action can therefore, take place only after they jointly stimulate a person to do it. As children, we must have experienced this triad of **Jnaan**, **Jney** & **Parijnaataa** while viewing a kaleidoscope in which myriad shapes and colors appeared and disappeared before our eyes. The multitudinous shapes and colors are different varieties of **Jnaan,** the child in us is **Parijnaataa**, and the joy of seeing is **Jney**. Nevertheless, three physical entities namely **Karm**, the work, **Kartaa**, its performer and **Karan**, the means to do that work, are still required to translate that pleasant experience into an action. The child, in this example, can convert the images he saw in kaleidoscope into colorful sketches only if he decides to be **Kartaa** of his desired **Karm**; and finds **Karan**, the implements like colors, brushes, paper etc. to do it. It is important to know that the person himself is the key component, common in both groups; as **Parijnaataa**, the accomplished knower in the first group, and in the second, he is **Kartaa**, the determined doer. No one can achieve anything in life unless he involves himself in his work as **Parijnaataa** and **Kartaa**.

Clarification: *Though Gita expects us here to be in full charge of our work as Parijnaataa, the mature knowledgeable and Kartaa, fully responsible for it, it forbade us earlier from being its egoistic doer, and desiring a favorable outcome.*

Let me explain this concept with the simile of a prism:

'*A prism consists of three sloped surfaces converging into an apex. It simultaneously needs a triangular base to stand on. An activity also is similar to a prism based on the triangle formed by three sides of Jnaan, Jney & Parijnaataa; and, as a material, physical object, it owes its existence to three faces of Karm, Karan and Kartaa. Like any other object in nature, this prism of activity also possesses certain Guns, the qualities like shape, mass, volume, reflection, refraction, transparency etc. These qualities are the stockpile of results of action performed. If any one of the base, say Parijnaataa is detached with one face, say the Kartaa from the prism of work would at once collapse with all its other sides and faces and qualities of mass, volume, shape etc., its total existence is lost. This is what happens when a person performs an activity without proper knowledge and bearing the responsibility of being its doer. The prism of his action becomes quality less i.e. with no reactions whatsoever if he becomes a good Parijnaataa, Kartaa, and remains detached from its consequences.*'

SOME ADDITIONAL THOUGHTS ON KARM CHODANAA & KARM SANGRAH

Karm Chodanaa (also called **Karm Preranaa**) is the impulse, the motivational factor that inspires us to do certain work. Before discussing it we must first clearly understand and accept that the considerations of **Punya** or **Paap**, of good or bad, auspicious or inauspicious, **Dharm** or **Adharm** are applicable only to humans, not to any other living species or to inanimate objects. As said by the scriptures, God gifted human beings with **Sadaasad Vivek,** the wisdom of differentiating good from evil 'धर्मो हि तेषामधिको विशेष:' i.e.

'Dharm is the additional extraordinary quality endowed in them', the humans. As such, if an animal hits someone, law does not punish him; or if a storm devastates life and property, no one drags the sea to court. However, if a human being causes similar harm to others, the society does not spare him. This means that the virtue or vice, the goodness or evil is not in the action per se but in the motivational wisdom of its doer for he acts in **Dharm** or **Adharm** as dictated by his **Karm Chodanaa**. Krishn teaches Arjun in Gita to widen the sphere of his motivation, from personal vendetta & regain the kingdom, into a noble mission to relieve people of Hastinaapur from the **Adharm** of wicked Kauravs. Raam as a person (not God), might not have succeeded in killing Raavan if He had the limited intention of freeing His beloved wife Seetaa from his captivity. Nevertheless, He could achieve what was impossible even for gods because of the much larger motivation & purpose of liberating the sages and righteous people from the tyrannical, demoniac rule of Raavan. Accomplishment of this noble mission elevated Him to the position of God in the eyes of the world.

Moral: *The more we widen our vision, the more the divine powers and world come forward to support and make it happen.*

Dhammpad says:

'मनो पुब्बंगमा धम्मा मनोसेट्ठा मनोमया ।
मनसा चे पदुट्ठेन भासति वा करोति वा ॥
ततो नं दुक्खमन्वेति चक्कम्व वहतो पदम् ॥।

(Mind is the forerunner. Noble action of Dharm is performed only if mind is fully involved in it. Men do, or do not do, them as guided by their mind; and get happiness or sorrow accordingly)

God also values the spirit, not the monetary value, behind offerings made by a devotee in 9/26:

'Whatever insignificant thing, whether a leaf or flower or fruit or even plain water My devotee offers to Me wholeheartedly, I accept it lovingly.'

Karm Sangrah: It is the accumulation and stockpiling of **Karm** done with the desire of some result. It yields good or bad results eventually in this or later lives depending upon divine judgment. Thus, the individual person as **Parijnaataa**, the knower among three causes of **Karm Chodanaa**; and as **Kartaa**, the doer of work is responsible for **Karm Sangrah**.

Scriptures and scholars have attempted to explain intricacies of the principle of **Karm** and **Karm Phal** in various ways by classifying them into various categories like **Kriyamaan, Sanchit & Praarabdh;** or **Nitya, Aagaamee, Sanchit & Praarabdh**; or **Anaarabdh & Praarabdh.** I have already touched these classifications briefly in 9/28. Interested readers may look there or read Jnaaneshwaree by Jnaaneshwar, Saadhak Sanjeevanee by Raamsukhdaas, and Karm Siddhaant by Heeraa bhai Thakkar or any other. However, I feel we should not get lost in the labyrinthine details once again and listen to God's final sermons with rapt attention.

ॐ

Krishn differentiates Jnaan, Karm & Kartaa based on three modes of nature.

(18/19)

ज्ञानं कर्म च कर्ता च त्रिधैव गुणभेदतः ।
प्रोच्यते गुणसंख्याने यथावच्छृणु तान्यपि ॥१८/१९॥

Jnaanam karm kartaa ch tridhaiv gunbhedat: I
Prochyate gunsankhyaane yathaavachchhrunu taanyapi II
(18/19)

Jnaanam (knowledge) Karm (work) Kartaa (doer) Ch (and) Tridhaa (of three kinds) Ev (also) Gun bhedat: (difference according to Sattv, Raj & Tam)I prochyate (is said) Gun samkhyaane; (scripture dealing with qualities of things) Yathaa vat (as they are) Shrunu (listen) Taani (about them) Api (also)II (18/19)

Knowledge, action and the doer are described of three kinds each according to the difference in their quality by the Scriptures dealing with qualitative differentiation of things.

Listen about them from Me as described previously (for other things). (18/19)

Gita had earlier described **Shraddhaa, Aahaar, Yajn, Tap** & **Daan** with respect to their qualities of **Sattv, Raj** & **Tam** in chapter 17. Now it starts describing qualitative differences of **Jnaan, Karm** & **Kartaa** in the same way. This knowledge is important for a person as **Parijnaataa**, the knower; and as **Kartaa**, the doer in order to perform **Karm**, the action properly with input of proper knowledge so that he himself becomes the right kind of doer of that action. God picks up **Jnaan** only out of the three stimuli **Parijnaataa, Jnaan** & **Jney** for **Karm Chodanaa**; and **Karm** & **Kartaa** from the three causes **Karm, Kartaa** & **Karan** of **Karm Sangrah** (18/18), to differentiate them into three modes of **Sattv, Raj** & **Tam**. It is because if a **Parijnaataa** possesses proper **Jnaan,** it naturally inspires him to identify proper **Jney** also; and if a righteous **Kartaa** wants to perform a righteous **Karm**, he would automatically deploy righteous **Karan** too.

꙳

Krishn describes three modes of Jnaan.
(18/20, 21 & 22)

सर्वभूतेषु येनैकं भावमव्ययमीक्षते ।
अविभक्तं विभक्तेषु तज्ज्ञानं विद्धि सात्त्विकम् ॥१८/२०॥
पृथक्त्वेन तु यज्ज्ञानं नानाभावान्पृथग्विधान् ।
वेत्ति सर्वेषु भूतेषु तज्ज्ञानं विद्धि राजसम् ॥१८/२१॥
यत्तु कृत्स्नवदेकस्मिन्कार्ये सक्तमहैतुकम् ।
अतत्त्वार्थवदल्पं च तत्तामसमुदाहृतम् ॥१८/२२॥

Sarvabhooteshu yenaikam bhaavamavyayameekshate I
Avibhaktam vibhakteshu tajjnaanam viddhi saattvikam II
(18/20)
Pruthaktwen tu yajjnaanam naanaabhaavaanpruthagvidhaan I
Vetti sarveshu bhooteshu tajjnaanam viddhi raajasam II
(18/21)

Yattu krutsnavadekasminkaarye saktamahaitukam I
Atattwaarthavadalpam ch tattaamasudaahrutam II (18/22)

Sarv Bhooteshu (in all beings) Yen (by which) Ekam (only one)
Bhaavam (existence, form) Avyayam (immutable) Eekshate (sees)I
Avibhaktam (indivisible) Vibhakteshu (divided) Tat (that) Jnaanam
(knowledge) Viddhi; (know) Saattvikam (of the noblest quality of
Sattv)II (18/20)

Pruthaktwen (separately) Tu (but) Yat (which) Jnaanam
(knowledge) Naanaa (many) Bhaavaan (existences, forms) Pruthak
vidhaan (individual creations)I Vetti (must be understood) Sarveshu
(all) Bhooteshu (in all beings) Tat (that) Jnaanam (knowledge)
Viddhi; (know) Raajasam (with quality of passion)II (18/21)

Yat (in which) Tu (but) Krutsn vat (in totality) Ek (one) Asmin (in
this) Kaarye (in work) Saktam (attached) Ahaitukam (unnecessarily)
I Atattwaarth vat (devoid of basic knowledge) Alpam (insignificant)
Ch (and) Tat (that) Taamasam (of quality of Tam) Udaahrutam (is
cited)II (18/22)

**Know that knowledge of the noblest quality of righteousness
by which a person sees the Only One immutable, indivisible
Supreme Existence in all beings, though they look separate due
to their innumerable forms and characteristic natures. (18/20)**

**However, the knowledge by which one sees all beings
existing in their different multifarious forms as separately and
individually created; know that knowledge of the quality of
passion. (18/21)**

**Besides, the knowledge by which a person remains
completely attached with (result of) work unnecessarily; which
lacks basic, fundamental principles, and is very insignificant
& mean; such knowledge is cited as the quality of ignorance &
darkness. (18/22)**

A person with **Saattvik** knowledge sees everything in totality
in the light of universal good and righteousness existing in every
entity as part of the indivisible & integral Supreme Existence. He
visualizes God's Vibhooti manifested in the best qualities of every

being. Each & every action carried out by him with this type of knowledge is a right step taken towards fulfillment of the process, purpose & will of Supreme Being. He views multitudes of things, persons and situations that appear before him on the stage of the world as indivisible parts of Whole Being, and playing their individual roles in His overall operation.

A person equipped with **Raajasik** knowledge fails to see the underlying universal existence of God as the fundamental principle that holds together the multifaceted, multidirectional world. He believes that each entity is separate, individual and unique by itself; and there is no power (like God) that interlinks or makes them interdependent. Thus, he evaluates and treats them as individual entities as it suits his ego, and does not recognize them as a group or part of the whole being or even the society. For him, an enemy is enemy and a friend is a friend. His attitude never lets him to become **Sarv Bhoot Hite Rataa**, a friend, well-wisher of everyone. He neglects the concern and interest of others while doing a work.

Knowledge of only one kind of work here means that the knower is concerned only with results of his works, which are favorable and provide pleasures to him. He thinks that it is the only real purpose of living in the world. Simply said, he is fully devoted to himself with no concern for anyone else. This kind of knowledge is of **Taamasik** nature that narrows down a person's attitude from the vast panorama of universal interest to the single, insignificant point of self-interest and own pleasure. Laziness, obstinacy, impulsiveness and ignorance become a part of his characteristic nature.

Avibhaktam, used earlier also in 13/16, refers to indivisible God because He is **Apramey**, the immeasurable One. An immeasurable thing is also indivisible, e.g. no one can cut Anant Aakaash, the endless sky into pieces.

Moral: *All embodied souls are Vibhakt i.e. divided and individually different in their qualities and identities by nature of their existence since they separated from their origin, the Supreme Soul. However, an embodied soul can regain the quality of Avibhakt by becoming Bhakt, a devotee of God, and see same Avibhakt God in everyone.*

Readers may refer to some additional thoughts on Jnaan & related matters expressed under 3/38 & 39, 4/42, 10/10 & 11 and 13/34.

࿊

Krishn describes three modes of Karm.

(18/23, 24 & 25)

नियतं सङ्गरहितमरागद्वेषतः कृतम् ।
अफलप्रेप्सुना कर्म यत्तत्सात्त्विकमुच्यते ॥१८/२३॥
यत्तु कामेप्सुना कर्म साहंकारेण वा पुनः ।
क्रियते बहुलायासं तद्राजसमुदाहृतम् ॥१८/२४॥
अनुबन्धं क्षयं हिंसामनवेक्ष्य च पौरुषम् ।
मोहादारभ्यते कर्म यत्तत्तामसमुच्यते ॥१८/२५॥

Niyatam sangarahitamaraagadweshat: krutam I
Aphalaprepsunaa karm yattatsaattvikamuchyate II (18/23)
Yattu kaamepsunaa karm saahamkaaren vaa pun: I
Kriyate bahulaayaasam tadraajasamudaahrutam II (18/24)
Anubandham kshayam himsaamanavekshya ch paurusham I
Mohaadaarabhyate karm yattattaamasamuchyate II (18/25)

Niyatam (prescribed by scripture) Sang Rahitam (detached) Araag dweshat: (without passionate infatuation and hatred) Krutam (done)I Aphal Prepsunaa (desiring no fruit) Karm (work) Yat (which) Tat (that) Saattvikam (of the noblest quality of Sattv) Uchyate (is said)II (18/23)

Yat(that) Tu (but) Kaam Eepsunaa (one who longs for fruitive works) Karm (work) Saahamkaaren (egoistic) Vaa (otherwise) Pun: (again)I Kriyate (is done) Bahul Aayaasam (with lot of effort, exertion, labor, fatigue) Tat (that) Raajasam (with quality of passion) Udaahrutam (is citedII (18/24)

Anubandham (sequel, result) Kshayam (loss, decay) Himsaam (violence) Anavekshya (not visualizing) Ch (and) Paurusham (ability, competence)I Mohaat (due to ignorance) Aarabhyate (is commenced)

Karm (work) Yat (which) Tat (that) Taamasam (of quality of Tam) Uchyate (is said)II (18/25)

That work is said to be of the quality of goodness, which is performed as duty prescribed by scripture, without any attachment; with no passionate desire or envy, and without intention of gaining any fruit from it. (18/23)

However, the work performed by a person longing for the fruits of that work and false ego, and with lot of laborious effort, that work is mentioned to be of the quality of passion. (18/24)

The work, begun under the spell of ignorance & bewilderment without considering its consequential loss, violence etc., and the ability of the doer also; it is said to be of the quality of ignorance & darkness. (18/25)

Niyat Karm: God instructed us frequently to do **Niyat Karm** in 3/8, 18/7 & 9 and 18/47 besides here, which was explained under question, *'What is meant by Niyat Karm'* in 3/8 as duty prescribed and regulated by Scriptures, society, government, constitution etc. or as guided by spiritual leaders from time to time. We shall finally sum up our thoughts in 18/47.

Sang Rahitam: It is same as Asang, the complete detachment, dissociation, and disconnection as dealt in 15/3. Raamkrishn Paramhans advises us:

'Live in the world unaffected by it, as the tongue lives in the mouth. It eats lot of Ghee and oil whole life but still remains rough'.

Saattvik actions are those, which a person does with right intention and reason in tranquil state of mind & heart as a matter of duty & not of right, without any personal consideration of like or dislike, gain or loss, victory or defeat; and without influences of impulse, frenzy, envy or favor. The doer carries out such jobs in the light of his self-illuminated contented spirit, by becoming instrumental in fulfilling demands of divine justice & will. This type of work sets standard for other right-minded people also. Aristotle says:

'The actions of the just & wise are the realization of much that what is noble.'

When a **Saattvik Karm** attains preeminent, paramount position, it becomes **Akarm (Naishkarmya** in 3/4 & 18/49), the topmost quality of work as explained in 4/16-18. We shall learn about Naishkarmya in 18/49 also.

The dominant force behind a **Raajasik** work is the passionate desire to gain something. A doer performs them with egoistic considerations of personal material gains like wealth, property, name & fame, and to establish that he is right and others are wrong. Such doer leaves no stone unturned for achieve his personal targets. This type of action is ultimately not good for the doer, or for anybody else. **Raajasik karm** is same as **Karm**, the work done with some desire as described in 4/16-18.

A doer performs **Taamasik** actions mindlessly at inopportune time and place under impulsive instincts & intents without accessing own capabilities, weaknesses with total disregard of consequent wastage of resources and effort. Such works are regressive, destructive and violent in nature, and everybody, including the doer himself, stands to lose due to such works. **Taamasik karm** is same as **Vikarm**, the prohibited work described in 4/16-18.

We have discussed different aspects of **Karm** earlier in 'Some additional thoughts on Karm, Akarm & Vikarm' from 4/16 to 18 besides many shloks like 2/47, 4/16 to 18, 9/28, 13/20, 16/24, and 18/13 to 15 etc.

෮෧෨

Krishn describes three modes of Kartaa - the doer of work.

(18/26, 27 & 28)

मुक्तसङ्गोऽनहंवादी धृत्युत्साहसमन्वितः ।
सिद्ध्यसिद्ध्योर्निर्विकारः कर्ता सात्त्विक उच्यते ॥१८/२६॥
रागी कर्मफलप्रेप्सुर्लुब्धो हिंसात्मकोऽशुचिः ।
हर्षशोकान्वितः कर्ता राजसः परिकीर्तितः ॥१८/२७॥
अयुक्तः प्राकृतः स्तब्धः शठो नैष्कृतिकोऽलसः ।
विषादी दीर्घसूत्री च कर्ता तामस उच्यते ॥१८/२८॥

Muktasangoʃnahamvaadee dhrutyutsaahasamanvit: I
Sidhyasidhyonirvikaar: kartaa saattvik uchyate II (18/26)
Raagee karmaphalaprepsurlubdho himsaatmakoʃshuchi: I
Harshashokaanvit: kartaa raajas: parikeertit: II (18/27)
Ayukt: praakrut: stabdh: shatho naishkrutikoʃlas I
Vishaadee deerghasootree ch kartaa taamas uchyate II (18/28)

Mukt sang: (freed from attachment) Anaham Vaadee (egoless) Dhruti Utsaah Samanvit: (person endowed with resoluteness, and enthusiasm)I Siddhi: Asiddhi (success & failure) Y: (who) Nirvikaar: (imperturbable) Kartaa (doer) Saattvik: (of the noblest quality of Sattv) Uchyate (is said)II (18/26)

Raagee (passionately, emotionally desirous) Karm Phal Prepsu: (longing for fruit of an action) Lubdh: (covetous) Himsaatmak: (violent) Ashuchi: (unclean)I Harsh Shok Anvit: (possessed of joy and grief) Kartaa (doer) Raajas (with quality of passion) Parikeertit: (is mentioned, proclaimed as)II (18/27)

Ayukt: ((incoherent, disconnected) Praakrut: (uncultivated) Stabdh: (impertinent, obstinate) Shath: (crafty) Naishkrutik: (spoiler of others' livelihood) Alas (lazy)I Vishaadee (lamenting) Deergh Sootree (procrastinator, spinner person) Ch (and) Kartaa (doer) Taamas (of quality of Tam) Uchyate (is said)II (18/28)

The doer of a work who is free from association, in an egoless mode; endowed with steadfastness & enthusiasm; and remains unperturbed in success or failure, he is said to be of the highest quality of goodness. (18/26)

The doer who is passionately & emotionally attached to desire of fruit of his work; who is covetous, violent, malevolent and impure, impelled by joy and grief; he is proclaimed to belong to the quality of passion. (18/27)

The doer who is incoherent & disconnected from work, uncultivated, impertinently obstinate, crafty & deceitful, spoiler of others livelihood, lamenting & procrastinating; he is said to be in the lowly mode of ignorance & darkness. (18/28)

Saattvik doer of a work is free from egoism and worldly attachments. He takes neither delight in success nor distress in failure of his attempted work. Though he deploys unlimited zeal, enthusiasm & firm resolve in the work on hand, he mentally remains situated in a calm, impersonal state. Dualities of any kind do not disturb him as water cannot deteriorate a diamond, or the boiling water cannot cook gold.

The **Raajasik** performer of an action is passionately eager to achieve desired results of his actions. He lacks patience, purity of mind & large heartedness. He is often greedy, intolerant and cannot bear the undesirable consequences of his work. He always grabs the credit of success for him but also ready to blame others for the slightest failure. Self-interest motivates his every work.

Ignorance drives **Taamasik** doer of works as electricity drives an electric motor. His actions are the results of prejudice, contempt, thoughtlessness, obstinacy, stupidity, and not based on proper judgment and justice. The means adopted by him are cunning & scheming, cruel & destructive, crafty & uncivilized. He has no regard and concern for others but only for himself and his cronies. Even if he intends to engage in some good action he would postpone it as far as possible, show inconsistent & unpredictable behavior such that the action would ultimately become evil, not the originally intended good work. Krishn purposefully uses some derogatory adjectives for a **Taamasik** doer to warn innocent people from adopting such habits. It is therefore useful for us to understand them well as explained below:

Ayukt: As explained in 2/66 & 5/12, he is an inconsistent, incoherent, disoriented person disconnected from his targeted work. A **Taamasik** doer has no interest, enthusiasm to do anything. If at all, he has any **Karm Chodanaa** (18/18) i.e. inspiration for it, it is towards victimizing others or spoiling their chances. A **Taamasik** doer is **Ayukt** like a reluctant general who forecasts defeat of his army before the war, and flees from the battlefield at the first sign of defeat.

Praakrut: Derived from **Prakruti**, it denotes natural state of something e.g. unprocessed iron ore is the **Praakrut** state of steel, or a newly born child is of a mature human being. A **Taamasik** doer undertakes a work in a highly uncultivated, uncultured, unrefined manner as if it a burden thrust on him as an unskilled carpenter always blames his tools for bad quality of his work.

Stabdh: Krishn used **Stabdhaa**, the plural of **Stabdh** earlier in 16/17 to describe the nature of demonic people. A **Taamasik** doer is impudent, impertinent, obstinate, vain, and insensible, dumbfounded and numb like a statue, which has no concern about people around it. **Stabdh** also connotes his stubborn nature of engaging in oppressive, immoral activities without listening or caring for anybody.

Shath: He is a wicked, vicious, deceitful, and unprincipled rogue person. A **Taamasik** doer does all of his works like a **Shath** without caring for any principle, moral or public opinion, as a woodcutter recklessly cuts a fruity mango tree in his courtyard just because a cuckoo nesting on it makes noise.

Naishkrutik: He is a **Taamasik** doer who either shirks or deliberately spoils the work he is supposed to do properly. A **Naishkrutik** even throws the proverbial spanner in to spoil good works undertaken by well-intended persons for the well-being of the society e.g. a wicked student, not good in studies, tries to disgrace the best student of the class.

Alas: A **Taamasik** doer is lazy, indolent, inactive and uninterested when asked to attend to some work, especially if does not serve self-interest. Gita uses its derivative **Aalasya** in 14/8 & 18/39 as a trait of laziness. A python may sometimes move in search of food when very hungry, but not an **Alas** person who expects others to feed him.

Vishaadee: Entire chapter 1, named **Arjun Vishaad Yog,** dealt with **Vishaad**, the lamentation, languor, depression, sadness, dejection, despair, stress, and grief of Arjun. A **Taamasik** doer laments remorsefully for the eventual possibility of an unfavorable result of work, or for the labor in doing it. Arjun in chapter 1 is the perfect example of **Vishaadee** except that he overcomes his **Vishaad** in the end due to teachings of Krishn. We are fortunate to study what Krishn taught Arjun to relieve his Vishaad.

Deergh Sootree: It means a procrastinator, dilatory person, a spinner of matters, things and situations. He is like a judge who prefers to give date after date without trying to solve the dispute and delivering judgment. He complicates simple matters by stretching them in wrong directions without any visible end. He makes an easy task hard, a hard one harder, or even impossible. A **Deergh Sootree** farmer postpones harvesting of his ripened crop for a day, only to wake up next morning to find that hailstorm destroyed his entire crop in the night. Whatsoever, we need to do; we must do it here and now. **Kabeer** warns us in this respect in following couplet:

'काल करे सो आज कर, आज करे सो अब ।
पल में परलय होयगी बहुरि करेगो कब ॥'

(What you plan to do tomorrow you should do it today; and what you plan to do today you must do it now because if whole universe dissolves in a moment, how would you do anything later?)

Understand it with the example below:

"*An exemplary king one day called his courtiers and instructed them to donate his entire personal property jewelry amongst the poor after his death. All of them vowed to carry out King's instructions.*

The king was an accomplished Hath Yogee. He possessed the ability to transcend into Samaadhi, and return at will. Two weeks later, he feigned a heart attack and went into Samaadhi. Though the doctor pronounced him dead as his body was not breathing overtly anymore, the king was inwardly alive with all his sensory organs functioning normally. When the courtiers began removing rings, necklaces, bracelets etc. from the supposed dead body to prepare it for funeral, one of them reminded them of the king's last wish to distribute jewelry to the poor. The Prime Minister laughed at him, suggesting distributing the jewelry amongst them and giving cheap imitations instead to the poor. As the king who woke up from Samaadhi, the courtiers froze in fright. He coolly said, 'Stop this undignified drama. Thank you all for teaching me an important lesson of life by what you said just now'.

On the same day, he distributed his entire personal property including precious jewelry to the poor & needy with his own hands. The king then wrote in his diary, 'Everything that we spend on pleasure and feasting is lost. Only that, which we do for others with our own hands, is really ours. No one can create or earn anything after death. Therefore, let us do everything we intend to do now, for we don't know which of our breath will be the last one'."

Morals:

1. *People easily go astray from the path of Dharm due to their lust for power and possessions. Therefore, whatsoever you wish to accomplish, do it yourself without relying on others.*

2. *Do not put off your good intentions; carry them out immediately because opportunity and means shall not remain with you always. You need not always wait for the iron to become hot before striking it. Life often requires you to heat it by pounding relentlessly.*

3. *Never look back for what was yesterday is passé. It is not yet too late to do it now unwaveringly, without postponing it again.*

It is useful to refer to explanations under 8/5-7 in this context. However, before we close this topic, let us read the brief of *'Eidgah'*, an outstanding story of Munshi Premchand to understand three qualities of **Kartaa**:

"A four-year-old boy named Haamid lost his parents recently. His extremely poor Daadee, the grandmother consoles him telling that since his father was poor, he left him to earn money abroad; and his mother has gone to Allah to fetch lovely gifts for him. Innocent Haamid believes her story and feels happy with the hope of reuniting with his parents one day. His Daadee tells him many inspiring stories.

On the morning of Eid festival, though poorly clad, Haamid cheerfully sets out for Eidgah, the place to offer Islamic prayer, with only three paise given by his Daadee as Eidee, the customary gift of Eid. Compared to this, his friends Mahmood, Mohasin, Noore and Sammi, receive much more Eidee from their parents.

After offering Namaaz, the prayer to God at Eidgaah, the children go to the fair to enjoy colorful rides, eat appetizing sweets and purchase variety of toys. His richest friend Mohasin enjoys all the things one by one, but the less fortunate Mahmood, Noore and Sammi criticize him for his thrifty nature whenever they cannot afford something. However, Haamid just looks on stoically with only 3 paise in his pocket, and considers it unwise to spend his meagre money to get momentary pleasure. Overcoming temptations, he trudges across those attractions, and stops on a hardware shop pondering how to use 3 paise that his Daadee earned by hard labor. After a while, when he sees a Chimataa, a flexible pair of iron tongs, he remembers how his old Daadee burns her fingers while roasting Rotee, the Indian bread for him because she does not have a Chimataa. His eyes glow as he spontaneously decides, 'Yes, I must purchase this Chimataa as a return gift for her on Eid'. He bargains hard with the shopkeeper and finally strikes the deal for his three paise. On their way back home, Haamid's friends ridicule him for his ugly choice, and praise themselves for wisely using their Eidee on rides and sweets, not forgetting to extol the virtues of their beautiful clay toys over his Chimataa. However, before long, as the joy of rides, and the taste of sweets fade away, and their clay toys break on the way, Haamid is still carrying Chimataa proudly in his hands. They now envy his choice, and even offer to exchange their broken toys with it, but Haamid refuses.

As soon as he reaches home, Haamid rushes to his Daadee with the gift; but is momentarily taken aback when she scolds him for spending his Eidee on Chimataa, rather than on rides, or candy or buying some toy. Nevertheless, when he tells her that he bought it to relieve her of the burns she gets daily in cooking, she bursts into tears of indescribable joy and hugs him with profuse blessings for his kind act."

Analysis: The fair symbolizes the world. Everyone offers prayers to God like in **Namaaz** in similar way, but few blessed ones only are truly dedicated to His path. **Eidee** is the material and spiritual resource given by God, the father of everybody. The rides, sweets and toys represent the passions and temptations that pull common persons towards **Raajasik** & **Taamasik Karm**. Burning of fingers in preparing food for an innocent, orphan child is equivalent to old **Daadee** doing **Saattvik Tap**. Mohasin, Mahmood, Noore and Sammi are **Raajasik Kartaa**, until they spend all of their resources in enjoying ephemeral pleasures of life; and then become **Taamasik Kartaa** by discouraging and denouncing Haamid for his good work. Finally, the four-year-old boy Haamid is a **Saattvik Kartaa** because:

1. He is happy and contented with just 3 paise;

2. He stoically looks on his friends and conquers temptation to spend 3 paise on pleasures;

3. He feels pain of his **Daadee** is more important than own joy;

4. He sets his priorities right and selects **Chimataa** as the best buy for the resource at his disposal;

5. Providence helps Haamid by inducing the shopkeeper to accept his offered price of 3 paise instead of his original demand of 6 when the poor boy was about to walk away; and,

6. The happiness & blessings of his **Daadee** is his precious reward.

Moral: *We must develop our Jnaan, the knowledge and intelligence in such a way that we make best use of Karan, the resources available to us to become a Saattvik Kartaa and do a Saattvik Karm. For this, we must overcome lust for pleasures, cultivate the simplicity and purity of heart as that of child Haamid, and place well-being of others above own pleasures and interest.*

৶৽৻

Krishn undertakes to describe three kinds of Buddhi & Dhruti.

(18/29)

बुद्धेर्भेदं धृतेश्चैव गुणतस्त्रिविधं शृणु ।
प्रोच्यमानमशेषेण पृथक्त्वेन धनंजय ॥ १८/२९॥

Buddherbhedam dhruteshchaiv gunatastrividham shrunu I
Prochyamaanamasheshen pruthaktwen Dhananjay II (18/29)

Buddhe: (of intelligence) Bhedam (classifications) Dhrute: (of fortitude) Ch (and) Ev (also) Gunat: (by Guns, Sattv, Raj & Tam) Trividham (of three kinds) Shrunu (listen)I Prochyamaanam (as described by) Asheshen (in totality, entirety) Pruthaktwen (differentiation) Dhananjay (Arjun)II (18/29)

O Dhananjay (Arjun)! I am going to describe to you now the classification of Buddhi, the intelligence; and Dhruti, the steadfastness, as differentiated by three modes of quality, Sattv, Raj & Tam. Listen to Me about them in totality. (18/29)

God first identified **Jnaan**, **Jney** and **Parijnaataa** as **Karm Chodanaa**, the 3 prerequisites that inspire a person to do some work; and **Karan**, **Karm** & **Kartaa** to do the work and accrue **Karm Sangrah** in 18/18. Then He described **Saattvik**, **Raajasik** & **Taamasik** kinds of **Jnaan**, **Karm** & **Kartaa** from 18/19 to 28. Now, He continues His talk on **Karm** until 18/35 by classifying **Buddhi**, the intelligence & wisdom, and **Dhruti**, the steadfastness & determination.

ॐ

Krishn describes three modes of Buddhi, the intelligence.
(18/30, 31 & 32)

प्रवृत्तिं च निवृत्तिं च कार्याकार्ये भयाभये ।
बन्धं मोक्षं च या वेत्ति बुद्धिः सा पार्थ सात्त्विकी ॥१८/३०॥
यया धर्ममधर्मं च कार्यं चाकार्यमेव च ।
अयथावत्प्रजानाति बुद्धिः सा पार्थ राजसी ॥१८/३१॥
अधर्मं धर्ममिति या मन्यते तमसावृता ।
सर्वार्थान्विपरीतांश्च बुद्धिः सा पार्थ तामसी ॥१८/३२॥

Pravruttim ch nivruttim ch kaaryaakaarye bhayaabhaye I
Bandham moksham ch ya vetti buddhi: sa Paarth saattvikee
II (18/30)

Yayaa dharmamadharmam ch kaaryam chaakaaryamev ch I
Ayathaavatprajaanaati buddhi: saa Paarth raajasee II (18/31)
Adharmam dharmamiti yaa manyate tamasaavrutaa I
Sarvaarthaanvipareetaanshch buddhi: saa Paarth taamasee II
(18/32)

Pravruttim (inclination to indulge in an endeavor) Ch (and) Nivruttim (refraining from undesirable works, things) Ch (and) Kaarya Akaarye (in works which must be performed; and which are forbidden works) Bhay Abhaye (worth to be afraid of or of fearlessness)I Bandham (bondage, tie) Moksham (liberation) Ch (and) Yaa (that) Vetti (knows well) Buddhi: (intelligence) Saa (that) Paarth (Arjun) Saattvikee (of the noblest quality of Sattv)II (18/30)

Yayaa (by which) Dharmam (duties & obligations to uphold Dharm) Adharmam (the way of life contrary to Dharm) Ch (and) Kaarya (in works which must be performed as duty) Ch (and) Akaaryam (works which should not be done) Ev (also) Ch (and)I Ayathaavat (improperly) Prajaanaati (knows) Buddhi: (intelligence) Saa (that) Paarth (Arjun) Raajasee (of the quality of Raj)II (18/31)

Adharmam (the way of life contrary to Dharm) Dharmam (duties & obligations to uphold Dharm) Iti (this much) Yaa (by which) Manyate (believe) Tamasaa Aavrutaa (is covered by Tam) I Sarvaarthaan (everything) Vipareetaan (in an opposite way) Ch (and) Buddhi: (wisdom) Saa (that) Paarth (Arjun) Taamasee (of quality of Tam)II (18/32)

O Paarth (Arjun)! The intelligence which decides whether one should indulge in a work or refrain from it; whether it is his duty or not; which work must be feared and not feared; and which work shall cause bondage or liberation; that intelligence is of the noblest quality of righteousness. (18/30)

O Paarth (Arjun)! The intelligence by which one does not know properly what Dharm is and what Adharm is; and also which work is worth doing or not doing; that intelligence is of the quality of passion. (18/31)

O Paarth (Arjun)! The wisdom concealed with darkness of ignorance by which one accepts Adharm as real Dharm; and similarly, everything else in its opposite, negative sense; that intelligence is in the lowly mode of ignorance & darkness. (18/32)

Intelligence of a person always takes the final decision of doing or not doing certain work proposed by his **Man**, the mind & heart. Hence, it is very important for a doer of work to learn about **Saattvik**, **Raajasik** and **Taamasik** kinds of intelligence so that he can train his intelligence to be fixed, equal, quick and dispassionate in order to arrive at proper decisions in right measure, right direction and in the right spirit before undertaking a work.

Saattvik intelligence is free from confusion, bewilderment, doubt, indecision, hesitation, uncertainty in various conflicting situations; and above considerations of 'I & My'. It is for this reason that Gita attached highest importance on steadying intelligence in the very beginning of its teachings under the topic of **Sthit Prajn** (2/55-72). Vidur possesses **Saattvik Buddhi** in Mahaabhaarat. His compilation of morality in the form of 'Vidur Neeti' is worth reading.

Raajasik intelligence confuses the doer by remaining undecided, doubtful about the proper direction. A person with such intelligence has distorted value system as he gives priority to self-interest rather than propriety of work. In Mahaabhaarat, **Buddhi** of Karn is **Raajasik** as he considers it his duty to support every wrong deed of his wicked friend Duryodhan just because he bestowed Ang Desh upon him. He also remains indifferent in his duty towards the subjects of Ang by living in far away Hastinaapur. Dhrutraashtr is another example of **Raajasik Buddhi**.

Taamasik Buddhi is clouded by darkness caused by lack of knowledge, and/or deliberate misconceptions about **Dharm** & **Adharm** i.e. right and wrong, just & unjust, moral & immoral. Negative attitude, inertia, impotence, dullness, fear, pain, weakness, cowardliness, indolence etc. are the attributes of **Raajasik Buddhi**. Such person takes falseness as the law, misrule as the rule; he insists on doing things in his own way as per his liking or disliking.

Taamasik Buddhi of Duryodhan and Shakuni always impelled them to indulge in devious stratagems and mean works.

Clarification: *we have seen, in the beginning of Gita, how Arjun was afflicted by delusive Raajasik Buddhi when well-being of his family & ancestors, and survival of his relatives, became the paramount consideration in deciding his duty. Nevertheless, unlike others, he did not give up the wisdom of consulting a knowledgeable person like Krishn before taking a final decision. His intelligence is strayed temporarily from the path of light due to darkness of delusion, but is alert and courageous enough to rediscover the path of light. Similarly, though Ratnaakar possessed Taamasik Buddhi, he could attain Saattvik Buddhi and become sage Vaalmeeki under the guidance of a guru like Naarad.*

How should we decide what is our **Kaarya** (same as **Kartavya**), a must do duty; and what is **Akaarya** (same as **Akartavya**), a prohibited work? Abraham Lincoln relates it to our emotional state in a practical way:

'When I do good I feel good; when I do bad I feel bad. And, that is my religion'.

The precondition to this simple suggestion however, is to possess a simple and pure heart, free from self-interest to feel good.

Moral: *When we want to check the purity of an ornament of gold, we take it to a jeweler who examines it with the help of Kasautee, the touchstone. We accept the competence of the jeweler and the reliability of his equipment to judge the purity of gold. Similarly, we should refer our dilemmatic Buddhi for doing or not doing certain work, to learned people & saints, and accept their guidance whole-heartedly. Arjun did the same by referring his doubts to Krishn.*

ॐ

Three modes of Dhruti, the steadfastness are described.
(18/33, 34 & 35)

धृत्या यया धारयते मनःप्राणेन्द्रियक्रियाः ।
योगेनाव्यभिचारिण्या धृतिः सा पार्थ सात्त्विकी ॥१८/३३॥

यया तु धर्मकामार्थान्धृत्या धारयतेऽर्जुन ।
प्रसङ्गेन फलाकाङ्क्षी धृतिः सा पार्थ राजसी ॥१८/३४॥
यया स्वप्नं भयं शोकं विषादं मदमेव च ।
न विमुञ्चति दुर्मेधा धृतिः सा पार्थ तामसी ॥१८/३५॥

Dhrutyaa yayaa dhaarayate man:praanendriyakriyaa: I
Yogenaavyabhichaarinyaa dhruti: saa Paarth saattvikee II
(18/33)
Yayaa tu dharmakaamaarthaandhrutyaa dhaarayate∫rjun I
Prasangen phalaakaankshee dhruti: saa Paarth raajasee II
(18/34)
Yayaa swapnam bhayam shokam vishaadam madamev ch I
N vimunchati durmedhaa dhruti: saa Paarth taamasee II
(18/35)

Dhrutyaa (steadfastness) Yayaa (by which) Dhaarayate (sustain) Man: (mind) Praan (the breathe vital for life) Indriyaa (5 sensory organs) Kriyaa: (actions)I Yogen (in Yog) Avyabhichaarinyaa (incorruptible devotion) Dhruti: (Dhruti) Saa (that) Paarth (Arjun) Saattvikee (of the noblest quality of Sattv)II (18/33)

Yayaa (by which) Tu (but) Dharm Kaam Arthaan (for the sake of religiosity, gratification of desire, longing & material wealth, prosperity) Dhrutyaa (Dhruti) Dhaarayate (sustain) Arjun (Arjun)I Prasangen (due to association) Phal aakaankshee (desirous of fruit) Dhruti: (Dhruti) Saa (that) Paarth (Arjun) Raajasee (with quality of passion)II (18/34)

Yayaa (by which) Swapnam (dreaming, sleeping) Bhayam (fear, threat) Shokam (worry) Vishaadam (despair, languor) Madam (frenzy) Ev (also) Ch (and)I n (not) Vimunchati (freed from) Durmedhaa: (person with wicked, bad wisdom) Dhruti: (Dhruti) Saa (that) Paarth (Arjun) Taamasaa (of quality of Tam)II (18/35)

O Paarth (Arjun)! The incorruptible, unpolluted Dhruti, the resoluteness, by which one sustains the actions of his mind, breathes & senses by practising Yog, is Dhruti of the noblest quality. (18/33)

But, O Arjun! **Dhruti** which a person holds fast due to his strong attachment with fruitive results in matters of religious ceremonies, passionate ambitions, and material gains; that resoluteness is of the mode of passion O Paarth (Arjun)! (18/34)

And, O Paarth (Arjun)! **Dhruti** which cannot rid a person from idling & drowsiness, fear, worry & stress and frenzy & pride because of his wicked, pervert, ill-disposed wisdom; that resoluteness is of the quality of ignorance & darkness. (18/35)

Gita repeatedly recommends **Dhruti** as a very important virtue for practising **Yog**. We understood it as fortitude, steadfastness, resoluteness, perseverance & will power first in 2/12-13 as the principal quality of **Dheer**; and then as **Dhruti** in 6/23-26.

Saattvik Dhruti develops the will power to consistently practice, uphold and sustain **Dharm,** and reject temptations to indulge in **Adharm** by not going astray from the due to attractions of **Vishays**, the objects that arouse passionate desires. It strengthens our mind & heart, our instinct of survival and will to act with determination, and hold on to morality & righteousness in normal, as well as, the most trying & testing times of our life. **Dhruti** must be **Avyabhichaarinee**, incorruptible, unpolluted, and undeviating. God used the phrase **Avyabhichaarinee Bhakti**, the singular, incorruptible devotion in 13/10 & 14/26 earlier. **Avyabhichaarinee Dhruti** is the basic requirement for a practiser whether he follows the path of **Jnaan**, **Karm** or **Bhakti** any other. Ekalavya becomes one of the best archers by concentrating on the target by **Avyabhichaarinee, Saattvik Dhruti** though Dron turned down his request to teach him archery.

Raajasik Dhruti chains a person with desire to fulfill ambitions and gain worldly objects of passion. His physical, mental & spiritual faculties remain focused always on achieving favorable results of his every endeavor, whether it is to perform religious rituals, to satisfy a desire, or to earn wealth & prosperity. Bheem possesses **Raajasik Dhruti,** as his sole aim is to please Draupadee by taking revenge of the great insult inflicted on her by Kauravs. He disregards all ethics

& morality of warfare, and single-handedly kills all the hundred Kauravs including Dushaashan & Duryodhan.

Taamasik Dhruti is the worst kind of Dhruti as its practiser is either not interested in doing anything worthwhile, or does something unwillingly under compulsions arising out of **Bhay** i.e. own fears or external threats, **Shok**, the worry for the outcome, **Vishaad**, the depression, and Mad, the false pride. We must remember that God lends us all **Karan**, the material resources needed for performing a good work. It is therefore, our ungratefulness if we take pride in utilizing them in our works. In fact, we have no reason to take pride in giving up materials that were not ours but provided by God.

Persons with **Taamasik Dhruti** are lazy, impulsive and frenzied by nature. Frenzied Ashwatthaamaa kills five unarmed, sleeping sons of Draupadee in night, for his **Dhruti** is **Taamasik** though he is the son and pupil of a Braahman & outstanding teacher like Dron.

SOME ADDITIONAL THOUGHTS ON DHARM, KAAM, ARTH & PURUSHAARTH

Dharm, **Kaam** & **Arth** mentioned here are three types of **Phal**, the fruits a common worldly person aspires to get in his life; and **Moksh**, the liberation is the fourth one targeted by practisers of Yog; collectively designated as **Purushaarth**, the purpose of being a human. Among them, **Arth**, the wealth, assets, property, and money is the coarsest, physically manifested fruit that everyone desires. It comprises of every **Sthaawar**, the stationary and **Jangam,** the moving entity existing in the world. **Kaam** is the desire, longing, ambition born in **Man**, the mind & heart of a person when his **Jnaanendriys**, the sensory organs with their power of sensing **Shabd, Sparsh, Roop, Ras** and **Gandh** encounter **Arth. Kaam** exists in abstract form but manifests as emotions of pleasure or displeasure when sensed by **Jnaanendriys. Dharm** is defines the way to achieve any or all of the four **Purushaarth** including **Dharm** itself.

As no life can come into existence unless **Prakruti** and **Purush** unite with each other, similarly **Arth** & **Kaam** alone cannot yield any fruit unless they unite with each other. Since this statement has great ramification on our way of life let me explain it further:

The bondage of **Karm Phal**, and resultant **Praarabdh**, start ensnaring us the moment **Kaam** and **Arth** join and play havoc with our lives. Creating **Arth**, the wealth for self- sustenance and well-being of the society is not a crime, nor **Kaam**, the desire of librating self and serving the society without attaching undue importance to **Arth** is an evil. The important question therefore before us is how to achieve it? **Dharm** comes in handy here and shows the way. **Dharm** must be the founding principle for all our endeavors for earning **Arth**, and **Kaam**, the ambition to prepare for liberation of soul. Simply stated, we cannot achieve anything befitting a human life without walking skillfully on the tight rope of **Dharm**. Gita teaches us the technique to perform this seemingly difficult task in an easy, simplified way. When **Kaam** & **Dharm** join, they procreate life on earth as proclaimed by God in 10/28, *'I am Kandarp, the lord of Kaam for procreation'*; similarly, when we practise **Dharm** & **Arth** together, they complementing each other's effort to give proper support to life on earth. Readers may refer to 4/7-8 also.

ॐ

Krishn promises to describe three modes of Sukh for which people do any Karm.

(18/36)

सुखं त्विदानीं त्रिविधं शृणु मे भरतर्षभ ।
अभ्यासाद्रमते यत्र दुःखान्तं च निगच्छति ॥१८/३६॥

Sukham twidaaneem trividham shrunu me Bharatarshabh I
Abhyaasaadramate yatr du:khaantam ch nigachchhati II
(18/36)

Sukham (happiness) Tu (also) Idaaneem (now) Trividham (of three kinds) Shrunu (listen) Me (from me) Bharatarshabh (Arjun)

I Abhyaasaat (by practice) Ramate (takes delight) Yatr (where) Du:khaantam (the end of miseries) Ch (and) Nigachchhati (attains, gains)II (18/36)

O Bharatarshabh (Arjun)! Listen now from Me about three kinds of Sukh, the happiness also. A person attains Sukh, the end of all miseries, by repetitive practice (of Yog). (18/36)

God promises to describe **Sukh** also in the light of three qualities of **Sattv**, **Raj** & **Tam** because everybody performs an action to derive **Sukh**, the happiness and comfort from it. We discussed **Abhyaas**, the practice in 6/35.

❧❧

Three modes of Sukh, the happiness are described.

(18/37, 38 & 39)

यत्तदग्रे विषमिव परिणामेऽमृतोपमम् ।
तत्सुखं सात्त्विकं प्रोक्तमात्मबुद्धिप्रसादजम् ॥१८/३७॥
विषयेन्द्रियसंयोगाद्यत्तदग्रेऽमृतोपमम् ।
परिणामे विषमिव तत्सुखं राजसं स्मृतम् ॥१८/३८॥
यदग्रे चानुबन्धे च सुखं मोहनमात्मनः ।
निद्रालस्यप्रमादोत्थं तत्तामसमुदाहृतम् ॥१८/३९॥

Yattadagre vishamiv parinaameʃmrutopamam I
Tatsukham saattvikam proktamaatmabuddhiprasaadajam II (18/37)
Vishayendriyasanyogaadyattadagreʃmrutopamam I
Parinaame vishamiv tatsukham raajasam smrutam II (18/38)
Yadagre chaanubandhe ch sukham mohanamaatman: I
Nidraalasyapramaadottham tattaamasamudaahrutam II (18/39)

Yat (which) Tat (that) Agre (in the beginning) Visham (poison) iv (like) Parinaame (in the end) Amrutopamam (equal to Amrut)I tat (that) Sukham (happiness) Saattvikam (of the noblest quality of Sattv) Proktam (is called) Aatm Buddhi (spiritual intelligence, wisdom) Prasaadajam (propitiated by)II (18/37)

Vishay: Indriy Sanyogaat (by interaction of objects of passion & sensory organs) Yat (which) Tat (that) Agre (in the beginning) Amrutopamam (equal to Amrut)I Parinaame (in the end) Visham (poison) iv (like) Tat (that) Sukham (happiness) Raajasam (with quality of Raj) Smrutam (is regarded as)II (18/38)

Yat (which) Agre (in the beginning) Ch (and) Anubandhe (results in) Ch (and) Sukham (happiness) Mohanam (delusion) Aatman: (of own self)I Nidraa Aalasya Pramaadottham (produced by sleep, indolence & frenzy) Tat (that) Taamasam (of quality of Tam) Udaahrutam (is cited, quoted)II (18/39)

The happiness, that tastes like poison in the beginning, but is actually like Amrut, the Nectar of immortality in the end, and which is propitiated by spiritual intelligence, is said to be of the noblest quality. (18/37)

The happiness that is derived by interaction of sensory organs with objects of passion, and tastes Amrut in the beginning, but is like poison in the end; such happiness is considered as the quality of passion. (18/38)

The happiness which arises due to sleep, indolence & frenzy, and results in bewilderment of the self of a person; that happiness is mentioned as of the lowest quality of darkness & ignorance from beginning to end. (18/39)

We understood **Sukh** as happiness, pleasure, joy, and bliss; and **Dukh** as unhappiness, grief, pain, misery, sorrow, and distress in 2/14 & 2/56 earlier besides many other places. God classifies **Sukh** into three categories according to three modes of nature, **Sattv, Raj** & **Tam** as stated above.

Saattvik Sukh: A **Saattvik Kartaa** earns this kind of happiness with consistent practice and hard labour by channelizing his **Jnaan, Buddhi** & **Dhruti** in doing a **Saattvik Karm. Saattvik** happiness is like that of an old person who plants a seed of mango in his courtyard and feels very happy with the thought that his grand children shall enjoy its fruits one day when it would yield mangoes. Though the labour of planting, nurturing and guarding it is bitter like poison for him, his spiritual joy is like **Amrut**.

Raajasik Sukh: A **Raajasik Kartaa** derives such happiness with the aim of quickly satisfying the demands of passionate **Indriys** and **Man** by channelizing his **Jnaan, Buddhi & Dhruti** in doing a **Raajasik Karm. Raajasik** happiness is like that of a heavy drinker who sells his household things to enjoy a kick of toxic drink every evening.

Taamasik Sukh: A **Taamasik Kartaa** derives such happiness when he channelizes his **Jnaan, Buddhi & Dhruti** in doing a **Taamasik Karm.** Duryodhan deploys all resources at his disposal to build a Laakshaagruh hoping to get **Taamasik** pleasure by burning Paandavs alive in it.

SOME ADDITIONAL THOUGHTS ON SUKH & DUKH (3)

Everybody is in eternal pursuit of **Sukh,** the happiness in life, and afterlife. In his relentless search for happiness, the characteristic qualities he really needs are those of **Saattvik** nature, temperament and inner faculty like intelligence, steadfastness, will, harmony and a perfect order. Chasing happiness while living in **Raajasik** mode is as worthless as trying to catch a rainbow that will not last longer; and in **Taamasik** mode, it is as disastrous as running after mirage in a desert. Leading a **Saattvik** life is like sowing & nurturing a seed of good quality, which would surely sprout and grow into a shady & fruitful tree with proper input of loving care and labour. Mahatma Gandhi thought of happiness thus:

'Happiness is when what you think, what you say, and what you do are in harmony'.

While ranking its member nations on World Happiness Index, United Nations Sustainable Development Solutions Network has set some parameters like GDP per capita, social support, healthy life expectancy, freedom for make life choices, generosity i.e. ability to count on someone in trouble, mutual trust, perceptions of corruption, eudemonia i.e. the sense of meaning and purpose in life. These parameters are important, but in my opinion, parameters more important for people's overall happiness like contentment, tolerance, compassion, spiritual satisfaction, peace of mind etc. should also get their due place.

Sattv, the noble quality of righteousness, illuminates the path of our progress towards **Satat Aanand,** the everlasting happiness. **Raj** the quality of passion attracts towards temporary pleasures on the sideways, and deviates from the path of **Sattv**; whereas **Tam**, the quality of ignorance, frenzy and evil throws a sheet of darkness on us; and we fall into the ditch of sorrow. **Sattv** directs us towards the pond of **Amrut**, the divine nectar of gods; **Raj** tempts us with an intoxicating drink; and **Tam** compels us to drink the poison. Remember we must however, that **Sattv** also is capable only to show the reservoir of **Amrut** from a distance; we have to leave **Sattv** also behind to reach that reservoir and drink **Amrut**. Unless a practiser undertakes this final lap of the journey of life with perseverance & determination, liberation from miseries like death, rebirth, pain, illness, old age etc. shall always elude a practiser. God describes three qualities of **Sukh** only here because no one works to get **Dukh** of any kind in life.

Scriptures also categorize **Sukh** (also **Dukh**), according to its source, as **Aadhidaivik,** Daiv i.e. fate**, Aadhibhautik,** external physical conditions, and **Aadhyaatmik** i.e. spiritual.

৵৽৶

Three modes of nature do not spare anything in the universe from their effect.

(18/40)

न तदस्ति पृथिव्यां वा दिवि देवेषु वा पुनः ।
सत्त्वं प्रकृतिजैर्मुक्तं यदेभिः स्यात्त्रिभिर्गुणैः ॥१८/४०॥

N tadasti prithivyaam vaa divi deveshu vaa pun: I
Sattvam prakrutijairmuktam yadebhi: syaattribhirgunai: II
(18/40)

n (no) Tat (that) Asti (is there) Pruthivyaam (in earth) Vaa (or) Divi (sky) Deveshu (in Demigods) Vaa (or) Pun: (again)I Sattvam (existence) Prakrutijai: (born out of nature) Muktam (free) Yat (which) Ebhi: (these) Syaat (is) Tribhi: (three) Gunai: (from Guns, three modes of nature, Sattv, Raj & Tam)II (18/40)

Nothing that exists in this world, or in the sky, or even in the superior worlds of Demigods or anywhere else, is free from these three modes, Sattv, Raj & Tam of nature. (18/40)

God started describing **Triguns**, three modes of nature in chapter 14, named **Gun Tray Vibhaag Yog**, by explaining **Sattv**, **Raj** & **Tam** in 14/5-20; and told us to be **Gunaateet** i.e. free from the effects of **Triguns** in 14/22-27. However, when Arjun wanted to know more about **Shraddhaa**, the faith in 17/1, He replied that it is of three types. Then He went on to describe three modes of **Yajn** in 17/4; **Aahaar** in 17/7-9; **Tap** in 17/14-19; and **Daan** in 17/20-22; which are very important to develop and firm up one's **Shraddhaa**. Now, in 18/1 when Arjun asked about the difference between **Sannyaas** and **Tyaag**, God classified **Tyaag** into three modes of **Sattv**, **Raj** & **Tam** in 18/7-9. Then He continued to classify **Jnaan** in 18/20-22; **Karm** in 18/23-25; **Kartaa** in 18/26-28; **Buddhi** in 18/30-32; **Dhruti** in 18/33-35; and **Sukh** in 18/37-39 into **Saattvik, Raajasik & Taamasik** qualities. He concludes the topic of **Triguns** herewith saying that there is nothing in the world or even in the celestial space and the superior worlds of gods that is free from **Triguns** i.e. **Sattv**, **Raj** or **Tam** of **Prakruti**, the nature. Classification of entities into three modes of nature ends here.

Clarification: *An accomplished Yogee is an exception to this shlok because he has become Gunaateet by developing the qualities mentioned from 14/22 to 27. He is the only person, in entire universe, not affected by Triguns, Sattv, Raj & Tam of nature.*

ॐ

Krishn proposes to classify people according to characteristic nature of work.

(18/41)

ब्राह्मणक्षत्रियविशां शूद्राणां च परन्तप ।
कर्माणि प्रविभक्तानि स्वभावप्रभवैर्गुणैः ॥१८/४१॥

Braahmankshatriyvishaam shoodraanaam ch Parantap I
Karmaani pravibhaktaani swabhaavprabhavairgunai: II
(18/41)

Braahman (the teacher & preacher in Hindu caste system)
Kshatriy (a warrior in Hindu caste system) Vishaam (Vaishya, the
trader, agriculturist, cowherd in Hindu caste system) Shoodraanaam
(Shoodr, the service provider in Hindu caste system) Ch (and)
Parantap (Arjun)I Karmaani (works) Pravibhaktaani (divided)
Swabhaav (characteristic nature) Prabhavai: (originated) Gunai: (by
Guns)II (18/41)

**O Parantap (Arjun)! Braahman, Kshatriy, Vaishya & Shoodr
are distinguished according to their works and duties, which
originate from the quality of their individual characteristic
nature. (18/41)**

God stated in 4/13:

*"I have created this human society and classified in four groups
as per their natural qualities and duties".*

However, He did not deal with it further due to important issues
there. Now, he elaborates in next three shloks what He meant there.

❧

Qualities and duties of a Braahman are described.

(18/42)

शमो दमस्तपः शौचं क्षान्तिरार्जवमेव च ।
ज्ञानं विज्ञानमास्तिक्यं ब्रह्मकर्म स्वभावजम् ॥१८/४२॥

Shamo damastap: shaucham kshaantiraarjavamev ch I
Jnaanam vijnaanamaastikyam brahmkarm swabhaavajam II
(18/42)

Sham: (control of Man, mind) Dam: (control of Indriys from
Vishays) Tap: (Tap) Shaucham (cleanliness, purity) Kshaanti:
(endurance, forgiveness) Aarjavam (simplicity, uprightness) Ev

(also) Ch (and)I Jnaanam (spiritual knowledge) Vijnaanam (fully realized Jnaan) Aastikyam (belief in theism) Brahm Karm (works and duties of a Braahman) Swabhaavajam (born of characteristic nature)II (18/42)

Tranquility, peace & composure of mind; subduing & control of Indriys from Vishays; penance & austerity for self purification; cleanliness & purity; endurance & forgiveness; simplicity & uprightness; spiritual knowledge; full realization and experience of that knowledge; and finally the faith in God; these are the works and duties of a Braahman born of his characteristic nature. (18/42)

The word **Braahman** is derived from **Brahm**. Accordingly, he who has known **Brahm** i.e. God is Braahman. Krishn specifies nine characteristic qualities a Braahman must possess in this shlok.

Sham & **Dam**: They appeared together in 10/4; and separately in 6/3 & 16/1 where they were explained as a practice of askesis i.e. strict self-discipline and control, particularly for religious and spiritual purposes to calm down mind by restraining, controlling & subduing senses from pursuing the path of passions and gratification of their demands and desires.

Tap: It was explained in 17/17-19 as an ascetic practice, done with great fervor, religious austerity & penance for self-purification.

Shauch: It was explained in 13/7 as habit to maintain cleanliness of body, the household, other surroundings and the environment, purity of inner faculties like heart, mind & conscience, and piety of speech & character.

Kshaanti: It was explained in 13/7 as the virtue of patience, endurance, tolerance, forbearance and forgiveness; and sometimes it includes **Kshamaa**, the forgiveness.

Aarjav: It was explained in 16/1-3 as the virtue of rectitude, simplicity, candour, directness, uprightness, straightforwardness that liberates and declutters us from complications, confusions and doubts arising out of evils like deceit, fraud, and dissembling.

Jnaan & **Vijnaan**: We had understood **Jnaan** & **Vijnaan** in detail in chapters 7 & 9. Though Gita uses **Jnaan** frequently to connote perfect spiritual knowledge in most of its text, it talks specifically of **Vijnaan** as the highest order of spiritual knowledge acquired by constant refinement & perfection of **Jnaan** to realize and experience the eternal truth of soul and its origin **Paramaatmaa**, the Supreme Soul. Besides elementary, theoretical wisdom of prudence & judgment in life, a Braahman must be also very learned, highly educated & knowledgeable about religious matters, scriptures, and most importantly about **Brahm**.

Aastikya: It appears first time in Gita here. It means theism i.e. complete belief and faith in God. I had dealt with theism and atheism in *'Introduction'*. Dhamm Pad states in 399:

'I call him a Braahman who endures insult, assault, & imprisonment, unangered. His army consists of (spiritual) strength and forbearance'.

When someone asked Buddh who is a **Dwij** (Braahman) he clarified:

'A man is never born with a Tilak (a mark put on his forehead by a Braahman), nor with a Yajnopaveet (the sacred thread) on his body. He who performs good deeds is the real Dwij; and he who indulges in bad deeds is base & mean'.

Moral: *Everybody comes in this world equally naked or as clothed (with placenta and umbilical cord). As we start adapting to it, the world begins to teach us to discriminate between ourselves by race, religion, language, caste, geographical boundaries, color, creed, wealth, position etc. whereas the real criterion for it should be good or bad character.*

A person who inculcates above qualities in his **Swabhaav**, the characteristic nature, and leads a **Saattvik** life is a true Braahman. His profession is to guide, teach & preach **Dharm** equally to all sections of society selflessly without expecting any material benefit like remuneration, safety, honor etc. in return.

৯৯৯৯৯

Qualities and duties of a Kshatriy are described.

(18/43)

शौर्यं तेजो धृतिर्दाक्ष्यं युद्धे चाप्यपलायनम् ।
दानमीश्वरभावश्च क्षात्रं कर्म स्वभावजम् ॥१८/४३॥

Shauryam tejo dhrutirdaakshyam yuddhe
chaapyapalaayanam I
Daanamishwarabhavashch kshaatram karm swabhaavajam
II 18/43

Shauryam (valor, heroism) Tej: (energy, brilliance) Dhruti: (Dhruti) Daakshyam (dexterity) Yuddhe (in battle) Ch (and) Api (also) Apalaayanam (not fleeing, deserting a situation)I Daanam (Daan) ishwar Bhaav: (nature of leadership, mastery) Ch (and) Kshaatram Karm (works and duties of Kshatriys) Swabhaavajam (born of characteristic nature)II (18/43)

And the works and duties of Kshatriys, born of their characteristic nature, are valor, energy, steadfastness, dexterity & competence; not fleeing from a battle; donating generously and also exercise Lordship over people as well as situations. (18/43)

The characteristic nature of a **Kshatriy** is to possess these seven qualities:

Shaurya: It means bravery, valor and heroism. A Kshatriy should use his Shaurya to protect the weak, not to oppress them.

Tej: Vigor, energy, high spirit, heat, brilliance, splendor and effulgence with which he can overlord others;

Dhruti: We understood it as fortitude, steadfastness, resoluteness, perseverance, will power in 6/23-26.

Daakshya: It is the quality of capability, proficiency, dexterity, competence, expertise and deftness. It is equivalent to **Kaushalam** in **Yog Karmasu Kaushalam** (2/50). He who possesses it is called **Daksh** (12/16).

440 • GITA for GEN A to Z - Vol III

Yuddhe Apalaayanam: This is the quality of not escaping, fleeing from fighting in a battle for **Dharm**. A common person however, should understand it as bravely facing a difficult situation for a just cause, not running away from it. Conversely, a Kshatriy should never undertake a fight in favor of Adharm even if it is to side a relative, friend, or powerful person. Adharm was at its peak in Mahaabhaarat in which only 7 Akshauhinee Kshatriys had the fortitude to fight under the banner of righteous Paandavs compared to 11 under unrighteous Kauravs. Recall that the whole premise of Gita is based on Arjun wanting to quit his duty of **Apalaayan** from a **Dharm Yuddh** due to his infatuation towards his relatives.

Daan: It was explained as an act of giving, bestowing, endowing, granting, donating, making charities or giving alms to the needy person/s as help, or contributing to soco-religious establishments in 17/20-22.

Ishwar Bhaav: It is the quality of leadership, lordship and mastery on other people. God uses the very powerful word **Ishwar** to describe this trait implying that though the nature of a **Kshatriy** is to dominate and overlord others by his **Shaurya, Dhruti & Daakshya**, he must also take full care of the well-being of his subjects. Raam Raajya, the rule of Raam is the highest ideal for any ruler to this day in India because Raam always considered happiness of His people uppermost even if they demanded banishment of His beloved queen Seetaa.

⊰๏⊱

Qualities and duties of a Vaishya and Shoodr are described.

(18/44)

कृषिगौरक्ष्यवाणिज्यं वैश्यकर्म स्वभावजम् ।
परिचर्यात्मकं कर्म शूद्रस्यापि स्वभावजम् ॥१८/४४॥

Krushigaurakshyavaanijyam vaishyakarm swabhaavajam I
Paricharyaatmakam karm shoodrasyaapi swabhaavajam II

(18/44)

Krushi (agriculture, farming) Gau Rakshya (rearing, breeding and protection of cows, cattle) Vaanijyam (commerce, trade) Vaishya karm (works and duties of Vaishya) Swabhaavajam (born of characteristic nature)I Paricharyaatmakam (rendering various kinds of services) Karm (works and duties) Shoodrasya (of Shoodr) Api (also) Swabhaavajam (born of characteristic nature)II (18/44)

Agriculture; rearing, breeding and protection of cows (and other cattle) And trading & commerce are the works and duties of Vaishya born out of their characteristic nature. And, rendering all kinds of services to others is the duty and work of Shoodr born out of their characteristic nature. (18/44)

The responsibilities and duties of **Vaishya** are to do agriculture, raise cows and other cattle, and trading & commerce of merchandise in the society. In modern context, **Krushi** includes all endeavors like farming, processing, setting up industries, production centers to produce some goods; **Vaanijya** cover activities like trading, selling, marketing, distributing, transporting, financing etc. to promote trade & commerce; and **Gaurakshya** represents keeping animals of all kinds like cows, sheep, goats, camels, buffaloes, honey bees, fisheries, poultry etc. Thus producing things to meet daily needs of the society and creating wealth is the hallmark duty & responsibility of **Vaishya**.

Providing services like household help, cleaning & maintaining private & public places, disposal of waste, driving, assisting other three castes by working under their charge, crafts like building, carpentry, smithy, pottering, dyeing & coloring, spinning & weaving, leather making, tailoring etc., to entire society was the forte of **Shoodr**.

Readers are however, requested to bear in mind the period of Mahaabhaarat and Gita while reading and interpreting shloks related to caste system prevalent in those days in India and stretch their imagination to apply it to present Indian society. My following thoughts may help them to understand this complex topic.

SOME ADDITIONAL THOUGHTS ON HINDU CASTE SYSTEM

Readers may wonder why Gita talks of caste system, which many historians view as a shameful, evil blot of discrimination; and one of the main reasons of downfall of Hinduism. I would prefer to refrain from discussion on merits & demerits of caste system since it is outside our purview. However, some critics of Gita seize upon these shloks as an opportunity to brand it outdated, retrogressive and imposing sanctions upon the concept of a modern society free from discriminating people because of caste. Besides, some orthodox proponents of devolved, distorted and exploitative caste system also try to seek support and justification from these shloks of Gita. Neither of them, in my opinion, has understood Gita. I therefore feel it necessary to remove these ambiguities, which may afflict the minds of some readers of this treatise as well.

Gita laid down the social order of four castes viz. **Braahman, Kshatriy, Vaishya** and **Shoodr** in society in 4/13, but it did not leave the matter just there. It boldly resumes the topic here, and describes the qualities, duties and responsibilities characteristic of each caste. It means that a person does not qualify for a particular caste simply because of being born in the family of that caste; he must possess those specific qualities & perform his duties accordingly to prove him worthy of that caste. Gita, in this way, Gita rejects the theory of caste by birth.

Chaaturvarnya (4/13) of Gita refers to the ancient system of castes that existed in its ideal pure form probably much before Mahaabhaarat when God Himself created human society and classified it into groups of people according to their fundamental attributes, qualities and characters (refer 4/13). It had tremendous positive effect on the spiritual, socio-economical and cultural health of entire society; and on psychological & emotional level of individuals. By these definitions Vidur, a **Shoodr** by birth, is a **Braahman**, and Ashwatthaamaa, a **Braahman** by birth, a **Shoodr**. Vidur Neeti is a scripture highly esteemed for its moral instructions whereas the cursed soul of Ashwatthaamaa restlessly wanders in the universe forever even today. Proponents of caste by birth try to justify saying that parents, family, place, and environment of birth contribute largely in forming **Sanskaar** & **Swabhaav** of a child born in it. they forget that we find two brothers having opposite characters though born in the same family and brought up with same love and care, because **Sanskaar** & **Swabhaav** are inborn traits of a child as per his previous life's performance. The child can however, improve upon these basic traits in a proper environment. Similar classification is broadly applicable in the functioning of modern societies even today:

1. Teaching, training, learning, education, knowledge, religious ministrations, spirituality and morality;

2. Administration, government, law & order, defence, tax collection;

3. Agriculture, production of goods & merchandise, trading and wealth creation; and,

4. Labour and services, artisans, builders and subordinated functions.

Note that the responsibilities and duties of a caste are reducing in numbers, from 9 prescribed for **Braahman** to 7 for **Kshatriy** to 3 for **Vaishya**, and finally one for **Shoodr**. It indicates that the socio-cultural thinking of ancient Indian society was that if it could manage well its first two functions; it should automatically progress in the remaining two areas of economy & service. It is unfortunate for modern world, particularly for India; to tread on the path of consumerism based economical development at the cost of first two functions. It is futile to seek happiness in material growth like chasing a mirage for water. We cannot achieve true happiness without moral education and practice because morality, not punishment alone, can control & vanquish crime from the society.

Caste system based on quality unfortunately degenerated into caste by birth later, as self-seeking powerful people promulgated and enforced it on Hindu society to put shackles and chains of castes in the neck, hands and legs of its members at the time of birth. God said in 4/1-2 that He instructed Sun god with Yog in the beginning of creation but it vanished from this world in course of time. The caste system too deteriorated similarly over a long period. Alas! India freed itself in 1947 from the dreadful shackles of Imperial, colonial and racial powers, but it is still ridden with casteism because of crafty politicians who continue to tighten its shackles by promoting outdated caste-based reservation.

In my personal opinion **Varn** system of Hindu society was one of its strongest foundation pillars on which its culture could survive through many millennia to this day earning the distinction of **Sanaatan Dharm** whereas almost all its contemporary or even some relatively newer cultures and faiths disappeared from the face of earth. It is also noteworthy that description of the functional qualities and characters of people precede the mention of their caste in each shlok thus showing that Gita considers characteristic qualities described in 18/42-44 for each caste important rather than caste by birth. Thus, entire stress of Gita is not on rigid caste system, but on the duties, that suits best to an individual's nature.

Gita once again demonstrates its qualitative modesty in describing caste system as it showed while dealing with **Saamkhya, Paatanjal Yog, Yajn** of **Veds** etc. in its text. It first accepts the basic classification of society into four groups prevalent in the society in its time with due regard, and then gives it a definite, profound turn by attaching the condition of qualities expected in each caste.

Question: Why does Gita mention caste system only and leave Aashram system whereas most of Hindu scriptures mention both together as Varnaashram Dharm?

While describing the caste system, scriptures also club it with four **Aashram**, the system of leading life in four stages called as **Brahmcharya, Gruhasth, Vaanprasth** & **Sannyaas**. This social order of castes & individuals life stages was collectively referred to as **Varnaashram** As far as known to me, the approach of Gita by separating **Varn**, the caste from **Aashram** is unique. It deliberates on caste system in detail but mentions **Brahmacharya** only in 6/14, 8/11 & 17/14 out of four **Ashram**.

Let us first understand the four **Aashram. Brahmcharya Aashram** is the first stage of life when a person strictly observes celibacy to learn from a competent **Guru** the knowledge & skill so that he can perform his duties towards the society and earn his livelihood properly in accordance with **Dharm**. is called **Gruhasth Aashram** is the second stage in which he puts his knowledge & skill into practice, owns a family and contributes to the betterment of society to his mite. The third **Aashram** of **Vaanprasth** (literally meaning departure to forest) is his preparatory by reducing his involvement in worldly affairs in order to finally cut himself off from all his works, go to forest to adopt & lead a life of renunciation, **Sannyaas**, the fourth Aashram. All of it sounds well until **Sannyaas** because Gita considers **Tyaag** superior to Sannyaas as told in 18/4-6. It denounces the idea of renouncing duties of **Gruhasth Aashram** and running away to forest to indulge in painfully rigorous ascetic practices and tells that **Tyaag**, the sacrifice of self-interest while doing a work and detachment from its outcome, is the true form of **Sannyaas**. As per Gita, a man must remain actively, yet dispassionately, involved in performing his duties in the world as long as he is fit and capable. An absconder from his duties is not a **Sannyaasee** but hypocrite, deviated from the path of **Dharm,** because, by running away from his duties, he is doing a great disservice to the cause of society. This seems to be the reason for Gita remaining silent about **Ashram**.

Before we proceed further, I wish to bring an important point to readers' attention that Krishn would speak of **Swadharm, Swakarm, Niyat Karm, Sahaj Karm, Swabhaavaj Karm** and **Swabhaav** in succeeding four shloks. We should understand these terms as **Dharm**, **Karm** and **Swabhaav** of every individual depending on whether his characteristic nature conforms to that of a Braahman, or Kshatriy, or Vaishya or Shoodr mentioned here; and he must perform his duties and fulfill responsibilities accordingly.

॰ॐ॰

Krishn promises to tell how one can achieve success by engaging in his own work.

(18/45)

स्वे स्वे कर्मण्यभिरतः संसिद्धिं लभते नरः ।
स्वकर्मनिरतः सिद्धिं यथा विन्दति तच्छृणु ॥१८/४५॥

Swe swe karmanyabhirat: samsiddhim labhate nar: I
Swakarmanirat: siddhim yathaa vindati tachchhrunu II
(18/45)

Swe Swe (each one of his own) Karmani (duties, activities) Abhirat: (engaged, devoted) Samsiddhim (well ascertained, definite success) Labhate (gets) Nar: (person)I Swakarm (own work & duty) Nirat: (engaged) Siddhim (success) Yathaa (manner in which) Vindati (finds) Tat (that) Shrunu (listen)II (18/45)

A person can accomplish perfection by devoutly engaging in own duties and works. Listen now from Me how a person, committed to his duties as per his characteristic nature, attains the ultimate success. (18/45)

Krishn assures every person that he can achieve spiritual perfection by devoutly following his duties as suited to above-mentioned natural traits of a **Braahman**, or **Kshatriy**, or **Vaishya** or **Shoodr**. Of course, he must perform them with right intention, motive and effort to his full capability. If done in conformity of his **Swabhaav**, the real nature, such action automatically becomes an effective means to progress towards God and attain spiritual liberation. Nevertheless, most of us are unfortunately engaged in deceiving ourselves by working against our nature and trying to do what we ought not to; and appearing what we are not. External considerations, not the internal intuitions, influence our works as they choke our inmost voice very often by compelling factors like family, profession, society, religion etc. surrounding us. Instead being the owner operator of the machine of our life, we ourselves become a machine like ATM in the hands of others. This is in gross violation of the spirit of **Swadharm**.

By asserting that a person devotedly engaged in doing his duties regardless of his caste, creed, or status, shall surely attain the bliss of God, Gita re-affirms what it said in 9/32:

"Devotees fully dependent on Me undoubtedly reach their ultimate destination whether they are women, or trading merchants, or of the lowest caste."

৵৽৶

One can attain God by just doing his duty and offering it to God.

(18/46)

यतः प्रवृत्तिर्भूतानां येन सर्वमिदं ततम् ।
स्वकर्मणा तमभ्यर्च्य सिद्धिं विन्दति मानवः ॥१८/४६॥

Yat: pravruttirbhootaanaam yen sarvamidam tatam I
Swakarmanaa tamabhyarchya siddhim vindati maanav: II
(18/46)

Yat: (from that) Pravrutti: (emanates, originates) Bhootaanaam (all living beings) Yen (by which) Sarvam (all) Idam (this universe) Tatam (is pervaded)I Swakarmanaa (by his own duties & works) Tam (to Him) Abhyarchya (offering, worshiping) Siddhim (success) Vindati (finds) Maanav: (person)II (18/46)

A person can attain ultimate success (of reaching God) by doing his own works and offering them to Him, from whom all beings come into existence, and who pervades this entire universe. (18/46)

What a simple way to accomplish success in life! Just by sincerely performing **Swakarm** i.e. own duties and works in this world, a practiser can attain his desired goal of peace and freedom from stress. The only condition attached to it is that he must faithfully do his duties and offer them to God leaving the result unto Him. He should neither shirk his duties nor look for any fruits for himself;

and direct all of his motives, means, resources, efforts and the acts in the service of God.

Moral: *God returns back to His devotee anything he offers to Him as His Prasaad, the propitious blessing. It implies that nothing can go wrong in our life if we just do our duty and offer it to God.*

Swakarm, appearing for the first time here in Gita is own action done as per **Swadharm** i.e. one's own duty as prescribed and decided by his **Swabhaav**, the characteristic nature conforming to one of the four castes. We discussed it 2/31 to 33; and shall sum up our thoughts later in 18/47.

Clarification: *Krishn used the phrase Yen Sarvam Idam Tatam meaning 'It pervades everything & everywhere' in 2/17 for Aatmaa, the soul but in 8/22 and here, He uses it for God. Since all souls are part of God, the Supreme Soul, they possess the same qualities, including omnipresence, of God except that God is their origin and master.*

Lyricist Majrooh Sultaanpuree writes in film Abhilaashaa:

वादियां मेरा दामन, रास्ते मेरी बाहें ।

जाओ मेरे सिवा, तुम कहाँ जाओगे ॥

जबसे मिलने लगी तुमसे राहें मेरी ।

चाँद सूरज बनी दो निगाहें मेरी ॥

तुम कहीं भी रहो, तुम नज़र आओगे ।

वादियां मेरा दामन .....

{Valleys are My Daaman, the short cloth that covers the breast, and the pathways are My arms. You may start to go anywhere, but without Me, you cannot reach there. From the moment your path starts merging with Mine, you shall constantly remain under the surveillance of My two eyes of the sun and the moon (day & night).}

God only can provide such unconditional assurance of happiness in life.

৵৽৶

Doing own duty is better than doing someone else's duty.

(18/47)

श्रेयान्स्वधर्मो विगुणः परधर्मात्स्वनुष्ठितात् ।
स्वभावनियतं कर्म कुर्वन्नाप्नोति किल्बिषम् ॥ १८/४७॥

Shreyaanswadharmo vigun: pardharmaatswanushthitaat I
Swabhaavniyatam karm kurunnaapnotikilvisham II (18/47)

Shreyaan (meritorious) Swadharm: (an individual's Dharm, duty) Vigun: (faulty) Pardharmaat (than Dharm of another person) Swanushthitaat (perfectly done)I Swabhaav Niyatam Karm (work & duty regulated, prescribed by characteristic nature) Kurvan (doing) N (never) Aapnoti (achieves) Kilvisham (sins)II (18/47)

Engaging in own duties devoutly, even if lacking in virtue, is certainly meritorious than undertaking someone else's duties howsoever perfectly one performs them. He, who sincerely attends to duties & works specified for him as per his characteristic nature, remains unaffected by sinful reactions. (18/47)

Krishn instructed us in 18/10 to not despise the unfavorable nor delight with favorable result; and to continue doing our duties without differentiating them as inferior or superior. He elaborates it further here.

Bewildered Arjun first declared in 2/5 that it would be virtuous for him to live like a beggar rather than kill his relatives but on second thought, he requested Krishn in 2/7 to tell what is best for him. Krishn clearly told him in 2/31 that there is nothing more meritorious for a **Kshatriy** than to fight in a battle for the sake of **Dharm**. When Arjun repeated the same question in 3/2 to tell him clearly, what surely the best is for him, Krishn told in 3/35 **Shreyaan Swadharm: Vigun: Pardharmaat Swanushthitaat** i.e. to act according to **Swadharm** is the most meritorious duty for him than engaging in **Par Dharm**, the duty laid down for someone else. He also warned him of the dire consequences that await him if he indulges in **Par Dharm**. Arjun was too naïve and highly distressed there to take His advice seriously as he wanted to go begging instead of fighting in the war. Krishn therefore, has to repeat the phrase **Shreyaan Swadharm: Vigun: Pardharmaat Swanushthitaat** verbatim in His last speech here before concluding Gita to re-stress the nobility in acting as per **Swadharm**, rather than **Par Dharm**. He assures Arjun further that even by committing a gravely violent action of killing his immoral relatives and massacring others as per **Swadharm** of a **Kshatriy**, he shall remain unblemished from any sin. Thus, in order to practice Gita in life, one must perform his duty well with his best capability & resources even if it is inferior compared to someone else's superior duty. Let us understand it with few examples below:

1. A **Jallaad**, the executioner, who hangs a criminal to death, is in no way inferior to the judge who sentenced him to death, or to the midwife that gave birth to him.

2. Fish must live always in water and not copy a frog or tortoise by going on the shore. If it does so, it is sure to die due to its inferiority complex.

3. The job of the sun and moon is to radiate light but the sun's **Swadharm** permits him to do it in daytime whereas moon must shine in night; moon looks faded when it tries to shine during daytime.

4. We cannot imagine what would happen to the world if seawater decides to flow upstream along the rivers; or air stops blowing, or crops stop growing. If **Achetan**, the inert things in nature do not act whimsically, how **Chetan**, the conscious, intelligent beings like us can violate this rule?

5. **Jnaanee Shoodr** Vidur knew this rule very well, he did not take to sword to fight in favor of his masters; but **Ajnaanee Braahmans** like Dron, Krup and Ashwatthaamaa fought for Kauravs and met their dreadful ends.

The fabric of human societies woven laboriously by great weavers over millennia would become a messed heap of yarn if each of its thread decides whether it should be there in the fabric as warp or weft, at its borders, ends or in between. Please refer to 3/33-35 also.

QUESTION: WHAT IS MEANT BY SWABHAAV NIYAT KARM?

We had discussed **Swadharm, Swabhaav** and **Swakarm** earlier in 2/31-33 and **Niyat karm** in 3/8. Let us sum up our thoughts on **Swabhaav Niyat Karm** combining them here in 18/47. **Swabhaav Niyat Karm** are the activities prescribed and regulated by Scriptures & **Dharm**; or by acknowledged institutions like **Varn**, the caste & **Aashram** in ancient India, or by the government and its constitution in modern times; or by spiritual and religious leaders in a society for its people. They are founded on experience & study of life histories of people of different **Swabhaav**, the basic character. Therefore, the second part of this shlok **Swabhaav Niyatam Karm Kurun n Aapnoti Kilvisham** strengthens our faith & belief in doing **Swadharm** by guaranteeing that no sin would ever accrue to us even if our **Swadharm** appears inferior in quality. For example, if Gabbar severs the arms of Thaakur in film Sholay, his act is highly sinful & punishable; but no sin would accrue to a surgeon who does the same thing while amputating a gangrenous limb of his patient. On the contrary, the doctor's work is **Punya**, a good, meritorious, virtuous act. However, the same surgeon cannot cause even a small cut with his scalpel to a person who is not his patient; applause of a soldier for killing enemies in a war does not authorize him to use his gun on any citizen of his country. Gita highlights that one must be very judicious & honest in deciding and adopting **Swadharm**; and abhor **Par Dharm** depending on his characteristic nature under particular situation, time, person & circumstance. Ashwatthaamaa, being an outstanding warrior by nature, should have performed **Swadharm** by killing his equals in the battle, not by beheading young children of Paandavs while sleeping. It was **Dushkarm**, an evil, cowardly act, which even Duryodhan disapproved.

Moral: *The law of agriculture is to reap more than we sow. Sow a good act, and we reap good Swabhaav, the habit. Sow a good habit and we reap a good character. Sow a good character and we reap the best destiny.*

৶৽৻

Every action is associated with an unavoidable evil also.

(18/48)

सहजं कर्म कौन्तेय सदोषमपि न त्यजेत् ।
सर्वारम्भा हि दोषेण धूमेनाग्निरिवावृताः ॥१८/४८॥

Sahajam karm Kauntey sadoshamapi n tyajet I
Sarvaaraambhaa hi doshen dhoomenaagnirivaavrutaa: II
(18/48)

Sahajam Karm (Karm born together, innate with natural state) Kauntey (Arjun) Sadosham (faulty) Api (even) N (not) Tyajet (should be given up)I Sarv Aarambhaa: (initiating all kinds of endeavors) Hi (because) Doshen (with fault, evil, vice) Dhoomen (by smoke) Agni: (fire) Iv (like) Aavrutaa: (is covered)II (18/48)

O Kauntey (Arjun)! Works & duties, innate with the natural state of being, should not be given up even if they are faulty in quality, because all works are fraught with some fault or the other from beginning as fire is covered with smoke when ignited,. (18/48)

Sahaj Karm means an innate duty born together with a person, with his natural state and disposition. In Gita, it is the same as **Swakarm**, **Niyat Karm**, **Swabhaavaj Karm**, **Swabhaav Niyat Karm** & **Swadharm** mentioned and explained at various places. In ancient times, it meant that the works and duties of a person were innately born with him as per his characteristic nature; and they were closely associated with the caste in which he was born. Nevertheless, with the progress of time and disintegration of the caste system in the modern society, it means the duties & works, which a person should perform as per the profession he chooses depending on his nature, or to which his destiny guides him to undertake in his life.

Lighting a fire and guarding it was a pious and holy work in ancient times as it was not available to people easily. Nevertheless, even such a pious work is fraught with ill effects like smoke, which covers the fire and sometimes even tries to extinguish it. Besides, it also causes discomfort to people, and some insects also burn in it. Many of us must have seen in our childhood how elderly women used to suffer due to smoke while lighting fire for cooking. The second line, **Sarv Aarambhaa hi Doshen Dhoomen Agni iv Aavrutaa** therefore, conveys that all things, works, situations, times and persons in the material world do have their positive and negative sides. One should not give up an activity, which is largely good and beneficial for the society, for the fear of its side reactions. For example:

1. A medicine, meant to cure a disease, is never free from side effects. Still, the doctor must administer it to his patient to relieve him from ailment.

2. A fisherman should not give up his natural duty of catching fish for the fear of killing them.

3. A farmer cannot give up tilling and farming because many creatures will be eventually killed.

4. A woodcutter must not relinquish his duty of cutting and selling wood in order to save the trees whereas a gardener should not stop planting trees because some woodcutter may eventually cut them.

5. A housewife does not stop preparing Chili powder because it causes rash & burning in her eyes, hands etc.

Shailendr writes in film *Dil Apanaa aur Preet Paraai*:

ये रोशनी के साथ क्यूँ धुआँ उठा चिराग से ।

देखती हूँ ख्वाब मैं कि जग गई हूँ ख्वाब से ॥

(Why smoke arises from a lamp with the light? Am I still dreaming or just awakened from a dream?)

He, who made light, smoke and lamp, may answer his question one day. Until that time, let us find a lamp, fill it with oil, fix a wick in it and light it to free us from darkness.

Moral: *All human endeavors are fraught with imperfection, fault, evil and sometimes even a long trail of after effects but that should not deter us from doing our duties in the best possible manner according* *to the situation before us. We are too small like a bolt or pin in the giant machine of universe; trying to change its movements is foolish. Our job is to regulate & synchronize our negligible contribution in keeping this machine operational unless God, its chief operator, wants us to do so.*

Krishn explained **Karm Nishthaa** & **Jnaan Nishthaa** as early as in chapter 3. He concludes **Karm Nishthaa** here and proceeds to conclude **Jnaan Nishthaa** in next five shloks from 18/49 to 53.

৵৵ঌ

Krishn proceeds to summarize and conclude Sannyaas or Jnaan Nishthaa.

(18/49)

असक्तबुद्धिः सर्वत्र जितात्मा विगतस्पृहः ।
नैष्कर्म्यसिद्धिं परमां संन्यासेनाधिगच्छति ॥१८/४९॥
सिद्धिं प्राप्तो यथा ब्रह्म तथाप्नोति निबोध मे ।
समासेनैव कौन्तेय निष्ठा ज्ञानस्य या परा ॥१८/५०॥

Asaktabuddhi: sarvatr jitaatmaa vigataspruh: I
Naishkarmyasiddhim paramaam sannyasenaadhigachchhati
II 18/49
Siddhim praapto yathaa Brahm tathaapnoti nibodh me I
Samaasenaiv Kauntey nishthaa jnaanasya yaa paraa II (18/50)

Asakt Buddhi: (whose intelligence remains unattached in all respects) Sarvatr (everywhere) Jitaatmaa (who exercises self control) Vigat Spruh: (who is without desire, craving for material things)I Naishkarmya Siddhim (success in freedom from reactions of actions) Paramaam (ultimate, supreme) Sannyaasen (by renunciation of worldly matters) Adhigachchhati (attains, achieves)II (18/49)

Siddhim (success in spiritual realm) Praapt: (achieving) Yathaa (in the way) Brahm (Brahm, God) Tathaa (in same way) Aapnoti (achieves) Nibodh (should know) Me (me)I Samaasen (briefly) Ev (only) Kauntey (Arjun) Nishthaa (firm stage) Jnaanasya (of knowledge) Yaa (that) Paraa (ultimate, supreme)II (18/50)

A person whose intelligence is detached everywhere; who does not long for any material thing; and who exercises full control on self; he too attains the ultimate success of freedom from reactions of actions by practising Sannyaas, the path of renunciation. (18/49)

O Kauntey (Arjun)! Understand now from Me briefly also the manner by which one can attain Brahm, the ultimate final stage of knowledge, by accomplishing that success of freedom from reactions of actions through Jnaan Nishthaa, allegiance to the path of perfect spiritual knowledge. (18/50)

A person can achieve **Naishkarmya,** the state of not doing anything, in two ways. Either he decides to do nothing and remain idle fearing that if he does something it would entail a result and some associated evil as said in 18/48; or he evaluates merits and demerits of doing certain work worrying for its result. People of the first kind try to justify their inaction saying that if they should not aspire for results, as preached by Gita, why they should work at all. Gita brands such people as **Taamasik Kartaa** (18/28), the ignorant, indolent doer. If at all they do anything, they evaluate it on the standard of gain and loss for themselves like a **Raajasik Kartaa** (18/27), the passionate doer, and as a result, continue to swing in the cradle of **Sukh** & **Dukh**; birth, death & rebirth. The second kind of people are **Saattvik Kartaa** (18/26), the righteous doer as they have properly understood the message of Gita by taking a work as their *'Must do duty'* and doing it selflessly. Their guiding dictum is *'Virtue is thy own reward'.* Both kinds of people owe their allegiance to the path of **Karm,** knowingly or unknowingly.

Nevertheless, there is a third category of people also called **Akartaa,** the non-doers of works, as **Naishkarmya** also means absence of the pride of being the doer of a work, not giving it up per se. They faithfully believe in **Gunaa Guneshu Vartant** (3/28) and **Gunaa Vartant Ityev** (14/23), i.e. interactions of **Guns,** the three qualities of **Sattv, Raj** & **Tam** of nature, generate all actions. They owe their allegiance to the path of **Jnaan,** also called **Sannyaas** by Gita and **Saamkhya** by Kapil. Krishn promises to summarize the concept of **Jnaan Nishthaa** in next three shloks.

Clarification: *The word Naishkarmya was used in 3/4 with reference to Karm Yog, but here it is applied to Jnaan Yog. Naishkrutik, a word of same family as of Naishkarmya, was used in 18/18 in a very different sense to mean spoilers of own works or of others', also called game-spoilers.*

❦

The path of attaining the same ultimate success through Sannyaas is summarized.

(18/51, 52 & 53)

बुद्ध्या विशुद्ध्या युक्तो धृत्यात्मानं नियम्य च ।
शब्दादीन्विषयांस्त्यक्त्वा रागद्वेषौ व्युदस्य च ॥१८/५१॥
लघ्वाशी यतवाक्कायमानसः ।
ध्यानयोगपरो नित्यं वैराग्यं समुपाश्रितः ॥१८/५२॥
अहंकारं बलं दर्पं कामं क्रोधं परिग्रहम् ।
विमुच्य निर्ममः शान्तो ब्रह्मभूयाय कल्पते ॥१८/५३॥

Buddhyaa vishuddhyaa yukto dhrutyaatmaanam niyamya ch I
Shabdaadeenvishayanstyaktvaa raagadweshau vyudasya ch
II 18/51
Viviktasevee laghwaashee yatvaakkaayamaanas: I
Dhyaanayogaparo nityam vairaagyam samupaashrit: II
(18/52)
Ahamkaaram balam darpam kaamam krodham parigraham I
Vimuchya nirmam: shaanto Brahmabhooyaay kalpate II
(18/53)

Buddhyaa (with intelligence) Vishuddhyaa (highly purified) Yukt: (endowed with) Dhrutyaa (fortitude) Aatmaanam (own self) Niyamya (regulating) Ch (and)I Shabdaadeen (sound etc.) Vishayaan (objects of sensory gratification & passion namely scene, smell, sound, taste & touch) Tyaktvaa (giving up) Raag (infatuation) Dweshau (hatred, aversion, enmity) Vyudasya (laying aside) Ch (and)II (18/51)

Vivikt Sevee (living in an isolated, secluded place) Laghwaashee (one who eats a regulated diet) Yat Vaak Kaay Maanas: (with control on speech, body & mind)I Dhyaan Yog par: (transcended in meditation) Nityam (constantly) Vairaagyam (ascetic practice of detachment) Samupaashrit: (entirely relying on)II (18/52)

Ahamkaaram (ego) Balam (power, strength) Darpam (conceit, arrogance, pride) Kaamam (desire) Krodham (anger) Parigraham (collecting & possessing things more than absolutely necessary for his survival)I Vimuchya (getting delivered from) Nirmam: (free from proprietary Interest, belongingness) Shaant: (calm) Brahm (Brahm) Bhooyaay (be integrally united with) Kalpate (is eligible)II (18/53)

A practiser, endowed with highly purified intelligence, entitles to unite with Brahm if he constantly regulates self by giving up passions of senses like sound etc.; lives in solitude setting aside all feelings of liking & disliking; eats a regulated diet, exercises control on his speech, body & mind; and remains detached by perpetual practice of transcendental meditation. He should be always calm, free from ego, power, pride, desire & anger; desist from accumulating material wealth; and have no belongingness in anything. (18/51, 52 & 53)

Shabd Aadeen Vishayaan: It represents the group of passions like sound etc. of five Sensory organs. Shlok 4/26 also chose **Shabd**, the sound to represent other **Vishays** like scene, smell, taste, and touch, where this phrase appeared earlier. A practiser of **Jnaan Yog** must give up passions of all sensory pleasures or displeasures.

Vivikt Sevee: He is same as a **Jnaanee** described by Krishn in 13/10, as **Vivikt Desh Sevitvam Arati Jan Sansadi** i.e. living in an isolated, secluded place uninhabited by humans and remains aloof from the affairs of nearby human settlements until his duties call on him to intervene when irreligious situations arise there. **Aniket** in 12/19 for God's dear **Bhakt**, a devotee and **Ekaakee** for **Dhyaan** Yogee, a meditator in 6/10 also mean the same.

Laghwaashee: Laghu means very small and **Aashee** means the eater. He is same as **Yuktaahaar** (6/19) and **Niyataahaar** (4/30). He is **Laghwaashee** who takes **Aahaar**, the food in a strictly regulated and controlled way, sufficient only for his sustenance. We already had detailed discussions on **Aahaar** in 17/8-10 earlier. In wider sense, **Aahaar** also includes all other kinds of intakes like water, air, thoughts etc. besides food. Alternatively, if we consider **Aashee** as a derivative of **Aashaa**, the expectation, **Laghwaashee** denotes a person whose expectations are bare minimum.

Yat Vaak Kaay Maanas: A **Jnaanee** person must have full control on his **Kaay**, the body (with its parts & organs), **Vaak**, the speech and **Maanas**, the mind & heart. A practiser can achieve such control by performing three kinds of **Tap, Shaareerik, Vaachik & Maanasik**, described in 17/14-16.

Vairaagyam Samupaashrit: We understood **Vairaagya** in 6/35 as absence of **Raag**, the longing for material objects of passion like wealth, relations, self interests, name & fame; or with prohibited activities like drinking, gambling, womanizing, cheating, overpowering etc. It shall appear in 18/52 also.

Nirmam: We knew him in 2/71 & 12/13 as a person detached from proprietary ownership, interest and/or affection for things a worldly person considers his own. He is **Shaant** who has pacified and controlled three modes of nature, particularly **Raj** and **Tam**, the modes of passion and ignorance in his life. He remains calm and peaceful under all situations. We have learnt enough about **Ahamkaar**, the ego, **Bal**, the power, **Darp**, the pride, **Kaam**, the desire & **Krodh**, the anger in our study earlier. An amusing legend below explains it well:

"Once Lord Brahmaa, the creator of universe, went to visit God to apprise Him of his beautiful creation. Though the receptionist was very polite in asking him to wait, he felt highly insulted. His Kaam, the desire to see God immediately grew intense, his Ahamkaar, the ego started inflating. The fire of Krodh, the anger, fuelled by his Darp, the pride & Bal, the power turned into fury and rage. When he was about to burst on the receptionist, he was astonished to see six persons, attired very much like him, sitting in the waiting room next to the reception desk. Seeing the curiosity in his eyes, the receptionist informed him they were individual Brahmaa of universes from one

to six. Before flabbergasted Brahmaa could react, Devarshi Naarad came there. The receptionist left Brahmaa in surprise, rushed to touch Devarshi's feet and took him straight to God. After he returned, he handed over a token bearing number seven to Brahmaa and told in an apologetic tone, 'Sir! God never likes us to keep His devotee in wait to see Him. I do not know how long Devarshi would take. God shall then meet these six Brahmaa before calling you in. You may kindly relax and have some rest in the meantime until then".

Moral: *It is worthless to live in our own created paradises of ego, power, pride, longing, and anger like a fool. Even Brahmaa, the creator of us all is an insignificant entity, one of the many, before God. Only the ideal persons of Gita described vividly as God's dearest Bhakt, or Sthit Prajn, or Jnaanee, or Sam Darshee Yogee & Yogaaroodh, or Gunaateet in its text, can walk into His abode directly, not anyone else.*

Parigrah: It is the habit of holding, collecting and possessing things more than essential for own sustenance and practice of **Yog** as explained in 4/21. Its opposite **Aparigrah** was discussed in 6/10.

SOME ADDITIONAL THOUGHTS ON PARIGRAH

Parigrah, the habit of collecting things, is a result of greed to possess more. It emanates from either the fear of not getting something when needed or the wicked desire to exercise undue financial power on others. It shows lack of faith in Providence, the foreseeing care and guidance of God for all creatures of the earth; guaranteed by Gita also as **Yog Kshemam Vahaami Aham** in 9/22, and **Bhoot Bhartru** in 13/16. All religions of Indian origin attach very high importance to **Aparigrah** i.e. giving up **Parigrah. Aparigrah** is the spirit behind **Tyaag**, the topic that God started to explain in this chapter; and the thought underlying activities like **Yajn, Karm** & **Daan** that no one should give up as instructed in 18/5. An inspiring anecdote below explains the virtue of **Parigrah**:

"A teacher sent a newly inducted pupil to fetch Bhikshaa, the alms from nearby village. Out of the six Rotees, the Indian bread brought by the pupil, Guru ate two and gave the balance to him. By

the time the pupil finished eating two, he saw a dog wagging his tail and staring intently at the food in his hand. when the boy was about to give those Rotee to the dog, Guru hastily intervened and instructed him to put them for their evening meal in Chheenkaa, the basket hung high from the roof of the hut. The pupil reluctantly complied with his order and came back to him asking his permission to leave his hermitage. When Guru wanted to know the reason for his abrupt decision, the enlightened boy modestly replied, 'Guruji! I came to you to receive proper education from you and to firm up my faith and belief in God. I am very much disappointed to see you preserving two Rotees for your next meal instead of relying on His inexhaustible Providence that provides for everyone's needs. As far as I can see, God made us the means to feed this dog with those two Rotees, but your Parigrah failed Him instead of fulfilling His task."

Caution: We, particularly Gruhasth, the householders, should take care to possess resources and wealth sufficient for a distress free happy life and plan well for future necessities of children's education, own post retirement health, old age etc. The age-old wisdom, 'Save for a rainy day' i.e. to save money for a time when we may need it unexpectedly, should not be overlooked. Over stocking and consumerism should be avoided in the spirit of Aparigrah.

Kabeer requests God to optimise His benevolence:

साईं इतना दीजिये, जा मे कुटुम्ब समाय ।
मैं भी भूखा न रहूँ, साधु ना भूखा जाय ॥

(O Master! Give me only that much, which can sustain my family, feed me as well as a guest.)

Centuries ago, the western world, particularly America, nurtured a dream of 'Plenty for All' to make life better, richer and fuller for every person, with equal opportunity according to his ability. Alas! This dream of establishing high social order in human society is shattered by ¼ of world population engaging constantly in **Parigrah** i.e. collecting more and more wealth in its larder; with the result that the remaining ¾ of 'Have Nots' struggle to make their both ends meet even today while the world is aplenty with materials and resources. Peace eludes the first lot of **Lobh Upahat Chetas** (1/38) **Parigrahee** people, and the second lot interminably awaits alleviation from poverty & hunger in this process of deprivation of humans by humans.

Nurturing ill will, evil thoughts in mind and longing for more things, but not collecting them physically, is the form of mental **Parigrah**. A wise sailor jettisons unwanted loads from his boat to keep it sailing in troubles waters.

Brahm Bhooyaay Kalpate appeared in 14/26 earlier for **Gunaateet**. Like **Gunaateet,** when a practiser of **Jnaan** achieves qualities mentioned here, he too attains **Avyabhichaarinee Bhakti**, the incorruptible, eternal devotion unto God (same as **Madbhakti** in next shlok), and is regarded equal to **Brahm** i.e. God.

Krishn concludes **Jnaan Nishthaa** here.

❧

Krishn summarizes the doctrine of Bhakti, the devotion now.

(18/54 & 55)

ब्रह्मभूतः प्रसन्नात्मा न शोचति न काङ्क्षति ।
समः सर्वेषु भूतेषु मद्भक्तिं लभते पराम् ॥१८/५४॥
भक्त्या मामभिजानाति यावान्यश्चास्मि तत्त्वतः ।
ततो मां तत्त्वतो ज्ञात्वा विशते तदनन्तरम् ॥१८/५५॥

Brahmabhoot: prasannaatmaa n shochati n kaankshati I
Sam: sarveshu bhooteshu madbhaktim labhate paraam II
(18/54)
Bhaktyaa maamabhijaanaati yaavaanyashchaasmi tattvat: I
Tato maam tattvato jnaatwaa vishate tadanantaram II (18/55)

Brahm Bhoot: (unification of individual Soul with Brahm) Prasann Aatmaa (blissful soul) N (neither) Shochati (laments, grieves) N (nor) Kaankshati (desire, wants)I Sam: (equipoise) Sarveshu (all) Bhooteshu (in all beings) Madbhaktim (my devotion) Labhate (gets) Paraam (ultimate knowledge)II (18/54)

Bhaktyaa (with wholehearted devotion) Maam (to me) Abhijaanaati ((knows properly) Yaavaan (as) Y: (who) Ch (and) Asmi (am) Tattvat: (fundamentally)I Tat: (then) Maam (to me) Tattvat: (fundamentally) Jnaatwaa (knowing well) Vishate (enters, merges with) Tadanantaram (immediately, without delay)II (18/55)

The practiser who integrates with Brahm, the Supreme Soul with delighted self; neither laments nor longs (for anyone or anything; and is equipoise in all beings; he achieves My ultimate whole-hearted devotion. (18/54)

By such whole-hearted devotion unto Me, he realizes Me fundamentally as well as completely whatsoever I am. Then, as soon as he realizes Me in this way in entirety, he merges into Me without any more delay. (18/55)

Shlok 15/54 adds freedom from desire to get anything, and from worry for not getting something; delight with own self, and **Samatv**, the equanimity towards everyone as the qualities a practiser of **Jnaan Nishthaa** must cultivate in addition to those mentioned in 18/51-52. God assures such practiser in 18/55 that as soon as he successfully achieves and follows, as preached from 18/51 to 54 in letter and spirit, he is blessed automatically with His pure **Bhakti** and learns everything about Him by attaining oneness with Him. God gave similar assurances from time to time like in 4/12, 39, 5/6, 9/31, 12/7 etc. earlier in similar contexts. God showers His benevolence on such practiser as **Kalp Vruksh**, the divine wish-fulfilling tree, makes available a thing to a person sitting under it the moment he wishes for it. There is no delay between his wish and its fulfillment.

God used the phrase **N Shochati n Kaankshati** earlier in 12/19 while describing the qualities of His most loved devotee. He considers it so important that He repeats it here. It seems to me that He is reminding Arjun of his bewildered condition in chapter 1 where **Vishaad**, the lamentation gripped him, and of the concern (a dormant desire) for victory shadowed his thoughts; and telling him to leave everything unto Him without lamenting for anyone, and/or cherishing a desire to acquire anything. The fact that He addresses Arjun directly from next shlok supports this thought further.

In continuation of 18/51-53, which summarized **Jnaan Nishthaa,** Krishn says here in very clear terms that its practice must ultimately mature into **Madbhakti**, the whole-heated, uncorrupted devotion unto Me for **Bhakti** is the ultimate destination of a practiser of **Jnaan Nishthaa.** It simply means that liberation of a practiser of **Jnaan Yog** can happen only after God bestows him with his **Bhakti** as a reward of achieving perfection in **Jnaan Yog** as shall be clarified in next shloks.

❧✦

God assures of His eternal Pad and instructs Arjun how he should do his duty.

(18/56 & 57)

सर्वकर्माण्यपि सदा कुर्वाणो मद्व्यपाश्रयः ।
मत्प्रसादादवाप्नोति शाश्वतं पदमव्ययम् ॥१८/५६॥
चेतसा सर्वकर्माणि मयि संन्यस्य मत्परः ।
बुद्धियोगमुपाश्रित्य मच्चित्तः सततं भव ॥१८/५७॥

Sarvakarmaanyapi sadaa kurvaano madvyapaashray: I
Matprasaadaadavaapnoti shaashwatam padamavyayam II
(18/56)
Chetasaa sarvakarmaani mayi sannyasya matpar: I
Buddhiyogamupaashritya machchitt: satatam bhav II (18/57)

Sarv Karmaani (all works, duties) Api (even) Sadaa (always) Kurvaan: (doing) Madvyapaashray: (depends exclusively on Me and thinks of Me as the ultimate refuge)I Mat Prasaadaat (by My propitious blessings, grace) Avaapnoti (gets) Shaashwatam (eternal) Padam (rank, status) Avyayam (imperishable)II (18/56)

Chetasaa (consciously) Sarv Karmaani (all works) Mayi (unto me) Sannyasya (by Sannyaas) Matpar: (remain devoted to me)I Buddhi Yogam (with perfect intelligence trying to unite with God) Upaashritya (entirely relying) Machchitt: (conscience, mind & heart engaged in me) Satatam (always) Bhav (be)II (18/57)

He, who does all of his works & duties as usual, and is dependent completely on Me (for results), achieves My eternal, immutable status by My propitious blessings. (18/56)

Detach therefore, yourself consciously from (the results of) all of your works and surrender unto Me with complete devotion. Develop perfect intelligence (of Sthit Prajn) and engage your inner self, the conscience, mind & heart perpetually with Me. (18/57)

In these shloks, Krishn re-asserts the need to continue discharging personal, familial and social duties as per the call of **Dharm** with sincerity and commitment, and leaving the results in the hands of God with undeviating devotion & faith in His Supremacy.

Machchitt, as learnt in 6/14, is concentration of **Chitt**, the mind, heart and soul unto Me i.e. God. **Machchittaa**, the plural of **Machchitt** therefore, are the devotees who have connected permanently and completely their **Chitt** with Me. **Mat Prasaadaat** means by My propitious blessings & grace.

Madvyapaashray: It means complete dependence and reliance on Me for everything. When Krishn goes to Hastinaapur in Mahaabhaarat as an ambassador of peace to try one last time for peaceful settlement, Draupadee and other Paandavs tell Him what they would like him to do there. Arjun is the only one among them who shows his complete dependence on His judgement by telling Him to do whatsoever He considers is the best for them. Dependence on God should however, not push us into **Akarmanyataa** i.e. idleness and not doing anything in the hope that God shall provide us everything. Gita abhors such idleness as **Taamasik**, the lowest trait of human nature. Remember the saying:

'Even a mother does not feed her child unless he cries for it'.

We have arrived very close to the summit of **Samagr Yog,** the wholesome teaching, of Gita. Krishn instructs us in these two shloks through Arjun to:

1. Cultivate perfect, unwavering & steady intelligence by sharpening it on the sharpener of **Abhyaas**, the practice to take proper decisions swiftly. This corresponds to the topic of **Sthit Prajn** elaborated in 2/55-72.

2. Discharge all of our normal and specific duties and responsibilities in the world with no *ifs and buts*. This corresponds to **Karmani ev Adhikaar te**, the first instruction on **Karm Yog** (2/47).

3. Connect our inner faculties like the conscience, mind, heart and soul constantly with God by **Dhyaan**, the meditation. This corresponds to the theme of **Aatm Samyam Yog** of entire chapter 6, more specifically in phrases like **Yat Chitt Aatmaa** in 6/10; **Yat Chittendriy Kriy** in 6/12; **Machchittaa** in 6/14 **Yat Chittasya** in 6/19; and **Anirvinn Chetasaa** in 6/23 etc. Patanjali says, *Restraining Chitt from its natural tendency to sway is Yog.*

4. Relinquish assiduously the desire of results of your works by assigning them unto God with complete devotion. This corresponds to **Maa Phalesu Kadaachan** the second instruction on **Karm Yog** in 2/47. Note the use of word **Sannyasya** that means as properly renouncing, abandoning, and giving up. Gita used it earlier with the same meaning in 5/13 that said:

   'He, who gives up attachment with actions, neither does anything himself nor is the cause of things done'.

This is **Jnaan Yog**.

5. Depend on God for all your needs. This corresponds to **Yog Kshemam Vahaami Aham** in 9/22 and **Maam Ekam Sharanam Vraj** in 18/66.

God says in 18/57 that this is the way to achieve My eternal, immutable status by My propitious blessings.

ॐ

One can overcome all impediments by engaging in God, or perish otherwise.

(18/58)

मच्चित्तः सर्वदुर्गाणि मत्प्रसादात्तरिष्यसि ।
अथ चेत्त्वमहंकारान्न श्रोष्यसि विनङ्क्ष्यसि ॥१८/५८॥

Machchitt: sarvadurgaani matprasaadaattarishyasi I
Ath chettwamahamkaaraann shroshyasi vinankshyasi II
(18/58)

Machchitt: (conscience, mind & heart engaged in me) Sarv (all) Durgaani (obstacles, impediments) Mat Prasaadaat (by My propitious blessings, grace) Tarishyasi (will swim across)I Ath (then) Chet (if) Twam (you) Ahamkaaraat (by false ego) N (not) Shroshyasi (shall listen) Vinankshyasi (shall be lost)II (18/58)

Because, by engaging your conscience, mind & heart in Me, you shall easily cross over all the obstacles (in life) by My propitious grace. However, if you do not listen to My words (and act) according to your false ego, you shall fall from grace (as well as your duty). (18/58)

Sarv Durgaani: Durg is commonly a place fortified by almost impassable impediments, obstacles and difficulties so that enemie cannot enter it. God uses it as a simile to point out that the difficulties a practiser faces on the way to His abode of eternal peace are equal to those faced before conquering a fort. This is the 39th simile in Gita.

Mat Prasaadaat: Derived from **Prasaad**, the propitious blessing of God, it means *'by My Prasaad'*.

Ahamkaaraat: It means due to **Ahamkaar** understood in 7/4 & 5 earlier as misplaced, falsified.

Tarishyasi is same as **santarishyasi** explained in 4/36 as crossing or swimming over the ocean of world. **Vinankshyasi,** its antonym, therefore means getting ruined & lost on the way.

Example of Hanumaan from Raamaayan illustrates this message well:

"Though born as ape, Hanumaan is dedicated to the service of Raam 'Yat Vaak Kaay Maanas' (18/52) i.e. with speech, body, and Man, the mind & heart. In fact, his whole existence, the very purpose of life is for Raam. When Raam entrusts him with the job of finding whereabouts of His beloved wife Seetaa, he has no clue of the obstacles he would have to encounter in his expedition. As it turns out later, he only, among hundreds of apes in his group, could accomplish his master's task single handedly in spite of most difficult situations. He travels hundreds of kilometers through, forests, mountain ranges, caves, rivers to reach seashore, and cross over 100 Yojan vast expanse of sea that lay between him and his goal. In so doing, he brushes aside the tempting offer of Mainaak to rest for a while, wins over the good wishes of Surasaa, the mother of serpents with great wit and acumen and destroys an underwater device set up by Raavan to detect and destroy anyone trying to cross over to Lankaa. He subdues Lankini, in-charge of security at the entrance gate of Lankaa, search for Seetaa whole night in Lankaa and finds her finally in heavily guarded Ashok Vaatikaa. He kills Akshay, a son of Raavan, and hordes of other Raakshas guards. He surrenders voluntarily to Meghanaad, the eldest son of Raavan, faces Raavan in his court fearlessly after capture and advises him to release Seetaa, or face the fury of omnipotent Raam. As Lankan subjects attempt to burn him alive by setting his tail afire, he burns entire Lankaa with that fire, crosses over the sea again, returns to Raam, and informs Him about Seetaa".

No one can imagine, in his wildest dreams, that an ape can surmount with great finesse such unheard obstacles that are impossible even for superhuman beings. When curious Raam asks how he could do it all, Hanumaan replies with utmost humility in Raamcharit Maanas 5/32/9 & 33:

ता कहुँ प्रभु कछु अगम नहिं जा पर तुम्ह अनुकुल।
तब प्रभावँ बड़वानलहिं जारि सकइ खलु तूल॥ ३३॥

(O my Master! Nothing is impossible for him with whom you are pleased. Even a wick of cotton can cause Badawaanal, a fire in the sea with Your blessings.)

Moral: *If an ape like Hanumaan could overcome insurmountable difficulties in performing his duty with unfailing devotion, dedication, faith and selfless, egoless service unto God, a human practiser of Yog can surely achieve liberation, the ultimate goal of life.*

Soor Daas praises mercy of God thus:

चरन कमल बंदौं हरि राई।
जाकी कृपा पंगु गिरि लंघै, अंधे को सब कछु दरसाई॥
बहिरो सुनै, मूक पुनि बोलै, रंक चले सिर छत्र धराई।
सूरदास स्वामी करुनामय, बार-बार बंदौं तेहि पाई॥

(I bow to the lotus feet of Shree Hari, the God. By his gracious kindness, a lame crosses over a mountain, a deaf starts hearing everything, a dumb starts speaking fluently, and a poor walks under a royal umbrella with pride. Soor Daas bows repeatedly at the feet of such gracefully kind master.)

God instills positivity in Arjun by making a general statement that such a **Machchitt** practiser can definitely cross over, by His propitious, benevolent grace, all the impediments erected by **Prakruti** and its **Triguns**, **Sattv**, **Raj** & **Tam**, and **Maayaa**, His power of illusion, on his way to reach Him. Nevertheless, as Arjun shows no response, He cautions him saying that if he chooses to follow not His advice due to ego of being the doer (as per **Karm Yog**) or non-doer (as per **Jnaan Yog**), he is sure to obtain grief in case of adverse result, and inconstant happiness in case of auspicious result.

৶৽৾

Krishn gives another reason that would push him in the war.

(18/59 & 60)

यदहंकारमाश्रित्य न योत्स्य इति मन्यसे ।
मिथ्यैष व्यवसायस्ते प्रकृतिस्त्वां नियोक्ष्यति ॥१८/५९॥
स्वभावजेन कौन्तेय निबद्धः स्वेन कर्मणा ।
कर्तुं नेच्छसि यन्मोहात्करिष्यस्यवशोऽपि तत् ॥१८/६०॥

Yadahamkaarmaashritya n yotsya iti manyase I
Mithyaish vyavsaayaste prakrutistwaam niyokshyati II (18/59)
Swabhaavajen Kauntey nibaddh: swen karmanaa I
Kartum nechchhasi yanmohaatkarishyasyavasho∫pi tat II
(18/60)

Yat (if) Ahamkaaram (ego) Aashritya (relying on) N (not) Yotsya (to fight) Iti (thus) Manyase (believe)I Mithyaa (false) Esh (this) Vyavsaay: (effort) Te (your) Prakruti: (inborn characteristic nature) Twaam (you) Niyokshyati (force you in)II (18/59)

Swabhaavajen (born of characteristic nature) Kauntey (Arjun) Nibaddh: (is tied) Swen (by own) Kaamanaa (of works)I Kartum (to do) N (not) Ichchhasi (wish) Yat (which) Mohaat (due to bewilderment, infatuation) Karishyasi (will undertake) Avash: (under subjection of) Api (although) Tat (that)II (18/60)

Even if you decide to not fight, under the influence of your false ego, your this effort shall be in vain because your Swabhaav, the innate characteristic nature (of Kshatriy), shall forcibly throw you in the battle. (18/59)

O Kauntey (Arjun)! Although you may not be apparently willing to perform this activity of fighting in the war at this moment because of your bewilderment, your own inborn nature (of Kshatriy) would ultimately bind and compel you to undertake your duty. (18/60)

Arjun led the life of a true **Kshatriy** by protecting the weak & just people in conformity of his inborn nature and important part of his personality. Krishn emphatically says here that his instinctive nature shall not allow him to keep away from the war but compel him to jump in it. A soldier, whether on or off duty, shall fight until death to stop an enemy from crossing the border. Krishn is probably reminding Arjun how he almost accused Him in 3/1 for pushing him into a horrific action like war. He tells him now explicitly that it is actually, not He, but his **Swabhaav**, the nature of a **Kshatriy** to fight against **Adharm**, that shall drag him into this war (unless he deliberately & willfully decides to abandon **Swadharm**).

Krishn instructed Arjun in the beginning of his talk in Gita in 2/31:

'Look to your Swadharm; do not falter from fighting for there is nothing more meritorious for a Kshatriy than to fight in a battle for Dharm'.

There, He supported His statement with common worldly reasons like indestructibility of a soul & certainty of the death of its body and availing pleasures of kingdom by a **Kshatriy** upon victory, or heaven after death in the war. He also warned him of the infamy & disgrace, worse than physical death, which shall accrue to him if he runs away from the war. Note the change in the quality of arguments Krishn forwarded there, and now. He puts aside His earlier arguments and tells Arjun now, at the end of Gita, to just do his duty with full faith & devotion, submit it to God's divine, compassionate mercy for delivering judgment on its result, take refuge in Him only, and rise above the pangs of happiness or sorrow in this strife torn world. The aim of Gita is to bring about this transformation in its students and practisers, and lift them from the low level of mundane worldly matters to the superior most world of spiritual realization and eternal bliss.

SOME ADDITIONAL THOUGHTS ON SWABHAAV

As explained earlier in 2/7 and many other places, **Swabhaav** is the characteristic nature of a person. The characteristic nature of water is to remain cool. It may become hot temporarily upon heating with some external resource, but would return to coolness as soon as possible. Similarly, the characteristic nature of an embodied soul is to remain always pure, calm & blissful like his source God, the Supreme Soul. It is natural therefore, for a disheveled, distressed, enraged person to return to his natural state automatically once he liberates his soul from external factors that pushed him in unnatural state. In the same way, even if Arjun is successful in fleeing from the battle, his **Swabhaav** would not let him remain aloof from it even for a short time; it shall certainly drag him back to the war, the place of his duty. It would not be a great surprise if he blames Krishn later why He, his well-wisher friend, mentor and guide, did not exercise His power and prudence to stop him from fleeing.

Swabhaav is not a chain that keeps us captive and grounded with inaction. In fact, it is the motive force, which frees us from the shackles of external world. It provides us with the wings of strength & will, and a bird's eye view so that we can fly in the sky, and identify a place, which requires our decisive action. A teacher must find a place and students to teach. Sun does not know what darkness is and where it lives. Every morning it rises in the sky to give light and warmth to everybody without favor or fear, or ego of doing such noble work because it is his **Swabhaav**.

Though **Swabhaav** is primarily the innate quality born with a person, he can greatly modify or even change it completely by constant practice and perseverance. **Parashuraam** was a **Braahman** by birth, but he transformed his inborn **Swabhaav** into that of a warrior **Kshatriy**. He gave up the duties of **Braahman** to teach and preach, and took to weapons to decimate wicked people, including very powerful kings, from earth. Jesus Christ was born in a carpenter's family, but due to his untiring effort to spread the message of peace and love, entire humanity reveres him as God.

Moral: *To sidetrack Swabhaav is like eclipsing own capabilities & potential, thereby diminishing ourselves and surrendering to external alien environmental forces.*

QUESTION: WHY ARE WE NOT ABLE TO CHANGE OUR SWABHAAV?

Let me answer this question with the help of an amusing story:

"A trader used to travel from village to village to sell his merchandise, which he carried on five camels. One night he halted at an inn. He tied his camels to trees outside, but found that he was short of one rope for the fifth camel. The innkeeper too could not lend him a rope, but advised him to fake the act of tying the camel to the tree with an imaginary rope. As soon as the trader did as told, the restless camel calmed down and went to sleep. Next morning, he untied the camels and shouted them to get up and move. All the camels complied, but the fifth camel did not move. He tried hard but the animal would not budge. The innkeeper saw his predicament

and shouted from his window, 'The camel will not get up unless you untie him'. The merchant followed his instruction once again and played the drama of untying the camel. Surprisingly, the camel got up immediately and started moving along with other camels. The innkeeper came out and explained to the baffled trader thus, 'The camel knew that you tied him to a tree with a rope last evening as you always did, but it did not realize that the rope was missing. Now, when you want him to move, he needs to be untied first as you do every morning. The camel is habituated by his Swabhaav to follow your daily act of tying in the evening, and untying in the morning. The rope for tying & untying may be important for you but it is immaterial for the animal."

Moral: *We too are accustomed to remain tied up with invisible ropes of innate nature, habits, traditions, infirmities, caste, religion, nationality, economic status, family lineage etc. Like the fifth camel, we never realize that the ropes and their bonds are imaginary. We feel pegged down to the ground when someone appears to bind us with them; and when he removes them from our conscience, we feel freed. A worldly person feels insulted if someone disrobes him, but no one can insult a Digambar Saadhu by denuding him. Trees neither are elated when spring covers them with fresh green leaves, nor are they distressed when autumn robs them of leaves.*

Following humurous anecdote illustrates how **Swabhaav** forces a person to return to his normal behaviour:

"A newly wed woman was highly perturbed as her husband used to threaten her of becoming a Sannyaasee on one pretense or other. One day when served him hot meals, he flared up saying it was too hot, and repeated his threat of Sannyaas. Fed up with his daily tantrums, she gathered courage and handed him a bowl saying 'From today onwards, go and beg for your food door to door'. The husband responded immediately with a smile on his face, 'You silly girl! I was just joking. Don't take it seriously.' Even before tasting the food, he appreciated its aroma and called it Amrut."

৺৹৶

Krishn tells Arjun to take refuge in God residing in everybody's heart.

(18/61 & 62)

ईश्वरः सर्वभूतानां हृद्देशेऽर्जुन तिष्ठति ।
भ्रामयन्सर्वभूतानि यन्त्रारूढानि मायया ॥१८/६१॥
तमेव शरणं गच्छ सर्वभावेन भारत ।
तत्प्रसादात्परां शान्तिं स्थानं प्राप्स्यसि शाश्वतम् ॥१८/६२॥

Ishwar: sarvabhootaanaam
hriddesheȷrjun tishthati I
Bhraamayansarvabhootaani
yantraaroodhaani maayayaa II (18/61)
Tamev sharanam gachchh
sarvabhaaven Bhaarat I
Tatprasaadaatparaam shaantim
sthaanam praapsyasi shaashwatam II (18/62)

Ishwar: (God) Sarv Bhootaanaam (all living beings) Hruddeshe (in the region of heart) Arjun (Arjun) Tishthati (remains)I bhraamayan (causes gyration, rotation) Sarv Bhootaani (all living beings) Yantr Aaroodhaani (mounted upon a machine, instrument) Maayayaa (by Maayaa, the divine energy of illusion)II (18/61)

Tam (to him) Ev (only) Sharanam (refuge) Gachchh (go) Sarv Bhaaven (in all respects) Bhaarat (Arjun)I tat Prasaadaat (by His propitious blessings, grace) Paraam (supreme) Shaantim (peace) Sthaanam (place) Praapsyasi (will get) Shaashwatam (eternal)II (18/62)

O Arjun! God, the Supreme Lord resides in the (innermost) region of heart in all beings. Maayaa, God's energy, which creates illusion, gyrates them as if they are mounted on a grand rotating machine. (18/61)

O Bhaarat (Arjun)! Seek refuge unto Him only in all respects. You shall attain supreme peace in His eternal abode by His propitious grace. (18/62)

Bhraamayan: It means to cause something to revolve, roll, whirl round, gyrate, rotate and move. As a derivative of **Bhram**, the doubt and confusion, it also means to lead astray.

Maayaa: We learnt it as God's energy responsible to create illusions about things that have no existence-existent in 4/5-6, and again in 7/13-15.

Yantr Aaroodh: It denotes something or someone mounted on a machine or a wheel. When the machine moves, the object on it also moves with it. Each one of us experienced it in his childhood while riding on a giant rotating wheel. God described universe as **Chakr**, a giant wheel in 3/16 earlier; and we discussed it there.

God said in 6/31 **Sarv Bhoot Sthitam** i.e. He exists in every entity but He did not tell there where and how He lives in everybody. Now, in 18/61, He explains that He resides in the innermost region of heart of every entity; and how He influences his existence through **Maayaa**, His energy in-charge of creating illusions in the world and in an individual's life. A cardiac surgeon may vehemently refute this shlok saying that he cut open hearts of many patients during operations but never found God or anything else in any heart. True! He cannot find God there because the physical appearance of heart with its muscles, blood, veins arteries etc. constrict his eyesight, but ask the patient whose life he saved; he sees God in the heart of surgeon without opening it. It requires the insight of a spiritually accomplished, **Sam Darshee** Yogee to see God in every living being; or the emotional feeling of a lover to find God in the heart of his beloved, or a mother in her children.

SOME ADDITIONAL THOUGHTS ON ISHWAR HRUDDESHE TISHTHATI

Hruddesh: It means in the chamber of **Hruday**, the heart. Anatomically speaking, heart is the most important part of a human body. A person dies when his heart stops pumping blood to the rest of his body. God located it in the safest place in human body beneath the strong cage of ribs. Emotionally speaking, it is the most sensitive part of human existence. Poets write innumerous poetries and songs to express feelings of heart using synonyms **like Hruday, Dil, Man, Jigar, Chitt, Kalejaa** etc. There are hundreds of sayings, idioms and proverbs based on heart in almost every language. However, the most important aspect of heart for our study is spiritual. Let us however, understand its anatomy first:

A human heart consists of two types of compartments: one that receives impure blood from every part of the body, and the second that stores and supplies pure blood to every part of the body by pumping. There are valves that separate the two chambers. The heart wall consists of three layers: the outer, the inner, and the middle. The outer & inner are thin layers whereas the middle one built up of cardiac muscle fibers forms the main bulk of the heart. There is one more, the outermost layer that surrounds entire heart. Arteries carry blood away from the heart to the body, while veins bring it back. The heart beats due to cardiac impulses originated and transmitted in an electrical system, resulting the opening and closing of valves and contraction and relaxation of chambers called a cardiac cycle. The cardiac cycle consists of two steps: systole i.e. contraction of chamber of pure blood and pushing it into the arteries is the first step; and diastole is the second step in which impure blood chamber relaxes and receives it from the veins.

I am aware of my incompetence to describe the anatomy of heart. Still, I have tried to do so in simple words above without technical jargon, with the sole purpose of relating it to our study as follows:

"Heart is the control center and energizer of a human body. the cardiac cycles of Systole, the upper blood pressure and diastole, the lower blood pressure represent the cycles of Dwandw, the duality like happiness & grief, success & failure, gain & loss, victory & defeat, honor & dishonor, hot & cold, fame & infamy, praise & criticism etc. The layers of the heart are like Aavaran, the covers or wraps (explained in 3/38-39) that conceal the soul from us. Our soul continues to suffer due to these Dwandws as long as it remains attached with the outside, not with God inside. God is the electric powerhouse that generates and transmits power to heart, which in turn, energizes and enables the person to function. Akin to heart, a person's life is also compartmentalized into two types of chambers of pure & impure, good & evil thoughts and works. God, sitting in our heart, goes on refining and purifying the impurity in our life but we

never desist from contaminating it repeatedly through contact with outside world; a healthy, happy soul becomes sick as it approaches infectious world. In order to enjoy in the company of God inside, a practiser must introspect often, not be an extrovert."

Maujiraam Mauji expresses it in following beautiful couplet:

'दिल के आईने में है तस्वीर यार की,
जब भी जी चाहा गर्दन झुकाई, देख ली'

{I have framed the portrait of my best friend in the mirror of my heart. I can see (and be with) him whenever I wish by just bending my neck downwards.}

Interpreting it spiritually, God, our best friend, always dwells in our heart. We can see Him whenever we wish provided we bend our head in reverence and humility. Alas! Neither our ego (of being the doer) permits us to bend our neck with humility before Him, nor are we able to see Him within us as the curtains of our interests in outside world hide Him from our view.

Moral: *People often spend a lifetime in search of God with a belief that He plays hide & seek with them, and that they are undeserving of His love. Some others consider themselves as sinners and worship Him out of fear of incurring His anger and condemnation but every such negative thought is meaningless. God loves all of us so much that He dwells in our heart. All that He wants from us is to have faith in His existence there, peep within to experience His presence there, listen to His voice (rationalists may call it inner voice) and act accordingly.*

Raamkrishn Paramhans explains it in a witty manner:

"An avid Chilam[19] smoker approaches his neighbor in dark hours for a cinder for Chilam with a lantern in hand. The neighbor looks at him with a puzzle and replies, 'Brother, you already have what you are looking for. You can light up your Chilam with the flame aglow in the lantern hanging in your hand".

---

19 *Chilam is a small Hukkah like earthen pipe used by villagers in India. They put some tobacco on cinder in it, and inhale smoke.*

Kabeer writes:

कस्तूरी कुंडलि बसै, मृग ढूँढै बन माँहि ।
ऐसैं घटि घटि राम है, दुनिया देखै नाहिं ॥

(Though musk lies in the navel of musk deer, it roams about in the whole forest in search of it. God similarly, resides in everybody but people unable to see Him within themselves, search Him in outside world)

Same idea is expressed by the popular saying, 'बगल में छोरा शहर में ढिंढोरा' i.e. *'A mother searches her son in whole city while carrying him on her side'*.

SOME ADDITIONAL THOUGHTS ON YANTR AAROODHAANI MAAYAYAA

A **Chakr**, the wheel or a machine needs energy for it to rotate and carry out its functions. Here, Gita calls the body of a person as **Yantr**, the machine on which his individual soul is mounted. As the body moves around in the circuitous labyrinths of the world to carry out its various activities under the influence of **Maayaa**, the soul, residing it, also moves with it. It is akin to a fly sitting on a wheel, a passenger in the train, a jockey on a horse moving with those things. Sitting in an airplane, a person thinks he is flying at supersonic speed but in reality, the airplane is flying at that speed carrying him in it. As soon as he lands, he realizes that the jet speed was not his own; he has to drive a few kilometers still to reach his destination. Scriptures give the example of a dog under a cart that thinks the cart is moving due to him. Tulasidaas writes in Raamcharit Maanas 4/11/7:

उमा दारु जोषित की नाई । सब हि नचावत राम गोसाईं ॥

{Lord Shiv tells his consort Umaa, Every soul dances (in the puppet show of world) like a wooden puppet, as per the commands of Raam, the Supreme Master.}

God shapes us as a potter shapes a pot; a weaver weaves a fabric. It is in the best interest of the clay and the yarn to shed their ego, let the master do the work and decide the quality of His product. If the clay and yarn resist him, he shall discard them to make lesser products and take up new materials. Electricity operates appliances like bulb, heater, refrigerator, dishwasher, washing machine etc. but none of them can demand any energy from its source. God said, similarly in 16/19:

'I throw envious, cruel people perpetually into the lowliest species of living beings'

Is God so mean as to make people dance to His tunes, or discard them in trash bin, as He likes? Certainly not! Read the clarification below:

Clarification*: These examples and citations should not generate helplessness of a slave before an autocrat master. God said He is 'Suhrudam Sarv Bhootaanaam' i.e. an intimate friend of everyone in 5/29. A good friend is never expected to threaten or ill-treat his friend, but he should certainly warn and check an errant friend well in time. Suhrud Krishn gives the same treatment to Arjun in Gita by raising an alarm to caution him with dire consequences if he deviates from the path of morality and Dharm. If someone ignores it, it is the law of Karm & Karm Phal stipulated by God that punishes him, not God. All embodied souls are actually puppets in the hands of Praarabdh, the result of their own actions, because nobody can circumvent Praarabdh.*

Krishn described, in 6/2-9 earlier, the qualities of **Yog Aaroodh** i.e. a person who has established himself firmly in the seat of **Yog**, and is most comfortably ensconced in it. A **Yantr Aaroodh** person is exactly opposite of **Yog Aaroodh** because he is ensconced in the machine of world operated by **Maayaa**. **Yantr Aaroodh** is like a tadpole, which has to live in water as long as it has a tail attached to it. He must strive to become **Yog Aaroodh** like a grown up frog that sheds its tail of **Avidyaa** and becomes capable of living in muddy waters of the world as well as on the firm terra of **Yog**. It is equivalent to attaining capabilities of a tortoise mentioned in 2/58.

With an intention to close Gita, Krishn tells Arjun to do what he decides to do.

(18/63)

इति ते ज्ञानमाख्यातं गुह्याद्गुह्यतरं मया ।
विमृश्यैतदशेषेण यथेच्छसि तथा कुरु ॥१८/६३॥

Iti te jnaanamaakhyaatam guhyaadguhyataram mayaa I
Vimrushyaitadasheshen yathechchhasi tathaa kuru II (18/63)

Iti (this much) Te (to you) Jnaanam (Jnaan, knowledge) Aakhyaatam (expounded, explained in detail) Guhyaat Guhyataram (most confidential of all esoteric secrets) Mayaa (by me)I Vimrushya (after properly deliberating) Etat (this) Asheshen (entirely) Yathaa (as) Ichchhasi (you wish) Tathaa (as) Kuru (do)II (18/63)

I have thus expounded to you the ultimate secret of the secret, esoteric knowledge. You may now act as you wish after properly deliberating on it in entirety. (18/63)

Guhyaat Guhyataram Mayaa: Gita is revered as Su-Upanishad, the noble Upanishad. It is a part of Prasthaan Trayee, the three topmost scriptures besides other two, Brahm Sootr and Upanishads. Gita preaches the highest esoteric, philosophical & spiritual knowledge of humanism with the very practical background of a war between two warring factions, where a righteous warrior like Arjun wants to know his proper duty, to fight & kill, or to not fight and save human lives. Thus, Gita acquires the special status of **Guhyaat Guhyataram,** the topmost secret of the secret knowledge taught by God Himself.

The law of universe that everything, whether good or bad, must end, applies to Gita also. After speaking 565 shloks in 28 **Shree Bhagawaan Uvaach** in Gita, Krishn now expresses His intention to conclude His talk. Arjun requested Krishn in 2/7 to be his Guru, accept him as His pupil, and teach & train him so that he can discharge his duty properly. Krishn obliged him by teaching from 2/11 until now. Here, He tells him that He has completed His assigned task of awakening his conscience to know and do his right duty, and simultaneously revealing intricacies of all divine secrets in entirety. He tells him further to decide his duty now and act accordingly.

SOME ADDITIONAL THOUGHTS ON YATHAA ICHCHHASI TATHAA KURU

Simply translated, **Yathaa Ichchhasi Tathaa Kuru** means *'do what you like'*. Some critics of Gita brand Krishn as an autocrat for He talks of Him as God and directs us to take refuge unto Him. Nevertheless, He sets this argument at rest by telling Arjun to do, as he likes. His approach is highly friendly and democratic. Indirectly, it also implies that the critics also may do what they like for He is unaffected by anybody's eloquent praise or harsh criticism of Him. God leaves the ultimate decision of doing or not doing something on the doer even after teaching different aspects of life & afterlife, death & birth, action & inaction, knowledge & ignorance, spirituality & God, nature & its characteristics etc. in Gita, and clearing all possible doubts he may have in his mind. Are we greater than God is, to expect others to follow our instructions, our thoughts and religious faith by coercing, threatening, and overpowering to comply with what we want them to do finally? Teaching, training, guiding, mentoring, counseling, suggesting someone is good, but we have no right to impose our ego on him and control his inborn freedom of leading his life in his own way. A gardener's job is to let the flowers grow and bloom as they wish. **Aakaash**, the sky does not restrict birds from flying in any direction, to any destination; nor does it force them to fly as per its command. Nature allows a honeybee to choose the flowers it likes to collect honey.

God granted the right to act to mankind in the phrase **Karmani ev Adhikaar Te** of 2/47. Albeit, he attached three very important conditions in next three phrases namely **Maa Phaleshu Kadaachan** i.e. *'You have no right on the fruit'*, **Maa Karm Phal Hetu Bhoo** i.e. *'Do not be the cause of the fruit'*, and **Maa Te Sang Astu Akarmani** i.e. *'Do not be inactive'*. This right is accompanied by the responsibility to exercise it wisely with prudence & judgement. Since man is a social living being unlike animals, he must know his **Swadharm**, the duties and responsibilities well towards the society before undertaking an action. The freedom to act in **Yathaa Ichchhasi Tathaa Kuru** is not a license to indulge in anarchy. Trying to become a **Saattvik Kartaa** (18/26) is the first step to enjoy this freedom.

Caution: *Yathaa Ichchhasi Tathaa Kuru is not a license granted by God to everybody to do whatsoever he likes, because one must first listen Gita like teachings as Arjun did from an enlightened person, then consult God residing in his heart before enjoying the freedom to act as he likes. Let us not be like Durdhodhan who did nothing of the sorts, but acted, as he liked.*

࿗

Krishn prepares to tell again the essence of His teachings in Gita.

(18/64)

सर्वगुह्यतमं भूयः शृणु मे परमं वचः ।
इष्टोऽसि मे दृढमिति ततो वक्ष्यामि ते हितम् ॥१८/६४॥

Sarvaguhyatamam bhooy: shrunu me paramam vach: I
Ishto∫si me drudhamiti tato vakshyaami te hitam II (18/64)

Sarv Guhyatamam (topmost esoteric secret) Bhooy: (again) Shrunu (listen) Me (my) Paramam (ultimate) Vach: (speech)I Isht: (dear) Asi (are) Me (my) Drudham (fast) Iti (thus) Tat: (that) Vakshyaami (will tell) Te (to you) Hitam (good)II (18/64)

Listen again to My supreme words that I shall now speak to you to reveal the topmost esoteric secret of all secrets for your benefit, for you are My dearest & fastest friend. (18/64)

Isht Asi Me Drudham: Isht is superlative of **Priy**, the dear and Drudh means very fast & firm. Krishn calls Arjun *'My dearest & fastest friend'* to acknowledge that he possesses all the qualities of His dearest Bhakt mentioned from 12/13 to 20. In this way, He expresses His full faith in his capabilities, and encourages him to decide his duty properly. He assures him:

मैं इसके आगे क्या कहूँ, तू मुझ में है मैं तुझ में हूँ ।

(You are in Me, and I am in you. What more than this,
should I say?)

Krishn talks of His most intimate friendship with Arjun frequently in Gita, and other scriptures like Mahaabhaarat & Shreemad Bhaagawat. They describe Arjun & Krishn as re-incarnation of the inseparable duo of Nar & Naaraayan, earlier incarnations of Lord Vishnu. Practically speaking also, Naaraayan would elope from a place where there is no **Nar**, a human being devoted to Him.

Vakshyaami Te Hitam: God, the best friend of Arjun, instructed whole Gita to him on his request for his benefit. Now, He summarizes it in two shloks that he, as well as everyone can easily remember and practice according to his instructions.

Sarv Guhya Tam: Krishn spoke of knowledge of Gita as **Guhya**, the deep secret for the first time in chapter 9 while teaching it with respect to **Jnaan** & **Vijnaan**. He also told Arjun in 15/20 that the doctrine of **Prakruti**, **Purush** & **Purushottam**, preached in chapter 10, was **Shaastram Guhya Tamam**, the most esoteric secret of Holy Scriptures. Arjun acknowledged the spiritual knowledge imparted thitherto to him by Krishn as **Paramam Guhyam** i.e. a very deep secret in 11/1. In 18/63, Krishn referred to His teachings as **Guhyaat Guhya Taram**, the top most of all esoteric secrets. However, He does not seem fully satisfied and undertakes here to repeat **Sarv Guhya tam** knowledge in most concise manner in just two shloks, 18/65 & 66, once again. Note the degrees of superlatives used progressively from **Guhya** in 9/1, to **Guhaya tam** in 15/20, and **Sarv Guhya Tam** here to extol the importance of entire knowledge of Gita. Since **Sarv** means all, He is going to disclose, in next two shloks, **Sarv Guhya tam**, the apex of all kinds of secret knowledge taught by Him in Gita at different places in different contexts.

❧◈❧

Krishn condenses the essence of His teachings of entire Gita in just two shloks.

(18/65 & 66)

मन्मना भव मद्भक्तो मद्याजी मां नमस्कुरु ।
मामेवैष्यसि सत्यं ते प्रतिजाने प्रियोऽसि मे ॥१८/६५॥
सर्वधर्मान्परित्यज्य मामेकं शरणं व्रज ।
अहं त्वां सर्वपापेभ्यो मोक्षयिष्यामि मा शुचः ॥१८/६६॥

Manmanaa bhav madbhakto madyaajee maam namaskuru I
Maamevaishyasi satyam te pratijaane priyoʃsi me II (18/65)
Sarvadharmaanparityajya maamekam sharanam vraj I
Aham twaam sarvapaapebhyo mokshayishyaami ma shuch:
II 18/66

Manmanaa: (with Man, mind fully engrossed in me) Bhav (become) Madbhakt: (my devotee) Madyaajee (offer everything to me) Maam (to me) Namaskuru (bow with reverence, obeisance)I maam (to me) Ev (only) Eshyasi (shall attain) Satyam (truthfully) Te (to you) Pratijaane (promise, give my word) Priy: (dear) Asi (you are) Me (My) II (18/65)

Sarv (all) Dharmaan (various religious practices) Parityajya (give up) Maam (to me) Ekam (only one) Sharanam (refuge, shelter) Vraj (come, move)I aham (I) Twaam (your) Sarv (all) Paapebhy: (of sins, evils) Mokshayishyaami (I shall deliver, release) Maa (do not) Shuch: (grieve, worry, lament)II (18/66)

Be wholeheartedly engrossed in Me; unconditionally devoted unto Me; offer all sacrificial activities and adorations unto Me; and bow in reverence & obeisance before Me. You shall attain Me in this way (without fail). This is My true & sincere promise to you for you are the dearest to Me. (18/65)

Abandon all kinds of Dharm (what an ignorant person perceives as his personal Dharm), and find shelter in Me alone. I shall deliver you from all sins. Do not grieve. (18/66)

The first part of 18/65, **Manmanaa Bhav Madbhakt Madyaajee Maam Namaskuru Maam ev Eshyasi** appeared ditto in 9/34 earlier in chapter 9 in which Krishn preached **Bhakti**, the devotion at length. He considers it so important that He repeats it while summarizing His teachings of entire Gita in these two shloks. Since we have reached the end of Gita, I wish to remind readers to re-read explanations given under *'Why does Gita use the phrase Shree Bhagawaan Uvaach ...'* in 2/2, and then under, *'Why does Krishn call himself God ....'* in 2/61. I am certain it would enable them to absorb this final message of Gita in proper perspective by relieving them eventually from any scepticism that may still lurk in their minds, preventing from accepting Krishn as God incarnate.

Satyam Te Pratijaane: It means to vouch for some truth to somebody on oath as a Judge expects a witness to speak on oath in his court. By uttering this phrase with the repetition of what He already said in 9/34, Krishn upholds its trueness and reliability on oath with guarantee.

Priy Asi Me: this phrase literally means the same as **Isht Asi Me Drudham** i.e. *'you are dear to Me'* in previous shlok.

Vraj: Besides meaning to move or go, it also means to wander and roam blissfully. Vraj Raaj or Vraj Kishore is a name given to Krishn when He used to roam blissfully in Vraj Bhoomi, the land of wandering with His friends in childhood. Arjun used its derivative **Vrajet** in 2/54 to know how a **Sthit Prajn** roams about in bliss.

Moksh, the liberation was explained in detail after 2/72 in *'What is Mukti or Moksh...'* and in 3/31 as **Mukt**. It is liberation of a person from **Dukh**, the distress, grief, sorrow, and worry in life by practising the teaching of Krishn in Gita.

Maa Shuch: Do not obtain to grief, worry, lamentation. Recall that Krishn started teaching Gita with **Ashochyaan Anvashoch twam** i.e. you are worrying for things that are not worth worrying in 2/11; and He ends it with **Maa Shuch:** i.e. *'Do not worry'* in 18/66. It shows that the prime objective of Gita is to relieve us from **Shoch**, the distress caused by sorrow, worry and lamentation. Rest of Gita teaches us with the ways and means to achieve such liberation, and lead a blissful life.

SOME ADDITIONAL THOUGHTS ON SARV DHARMAAN PARITYAJYA

In very simple words, **Sarv Dharmaan Parityajya** commands us to give up all kinds of **Dharm**. Gita has been teaching us until now to situate firmly in **Dharm** by pondering on it, realizing it and acting according to it in all phases of life. Why, all of a sudden, it commands us now to give up **Sarv Dharmaan** i.e. all religions? Critics of Gita catch hold of this phrase to ridicule Gita as an incoherent, confusing and contradicting religious book of Hinduism. Let us therefore, understand the idea underlying this phrase before going further to grasp the message of these shloks in entirety. Use of adjective **Sarv** indicates that Krishn is not referring here to the only one absolute **Dharm** called **Shaashwat, Sanaatan Dharm** by Him in Gita for entire humanity that is everlasting, immortal, basic, and which continues perpetually since time immemorial. Every human being must protect and preserve this **Dharm** at any cost, even as high as the massacre of Mahaabhaarat. By **Sarv Dharmaan,** He is pointing to various **Dharm** that are qualitatively less meritorious, inferior to **Shaashwat, Sanaatan Dharm**. We can classify **Sarv Dharmaan** into two broad categories:

1. **Vyakti Gat Dharm** i.e. personal duties & responsibilities of every individual towards his family, relatives, friends, teacher, and others closely associated with him; and,

2. **Sansthaa Gat Dharm** that consists of different traditions & rituals, means, practices, methods, that promoters of different sectarian faiths promulgated in the world from time to time them as **Dharm**.

Let us first understand **Vyakti Gat Dharm**. Some of them are:

Kul Dharm: This kind of **Dharm** is limited to one's duties & responsibilities towards his family, ancestors and its lineage in future generations. **Kul Dharm** includes **Dharm** towards relations like husband & wife, parents & children, ancestors & descendents, brothers & sisters, elders & juniors, and all others in the family. Gripped by his familial attachments, Arjun even regards it as **Sanaatan Dharm** in 1/40, and worries that destruction of **Kul Dharm** shall destroy **Sanaatan Dharm** also.

Jaati Dharm: The word **Jaati** broadly refers to various groups based on caste, community, profession, sectarian faith, class of economy etc. Therefore, **Jaati Dharm** consists of the duties & responsibilities that a person should perform for his **Jaati**. Arjun misunderstands it also as **Shaashwat Dharm**, and says in 1/43 that if **Jaati Dharm** ruins, **Shaashwat Dharm** too would destroy.

Arjun talked about **Kul Dharm** & **Jaati Dharm** in 1/40-44 in Gita, and we discussed there. Other kinds **Vyakti Gat Dharm** are like those between **Guru** & **Shishya** i.e. teacher and pupil (2/4-5), **Mitr** i.e. friends, king & subjects, employers & employees, house holder & **Sannyaasee** or guest, **Raashtr Dharm** for a citizen & his country, and the rest in the close circle of an individual.

Sansthaa Gat Dharm: These are the duties & responsibilities instituted by **Sansthaa**, an institutional authority or sect or a body of people. For example, they are prescribed by Holy Scriptures like Ved, Puraan, Meemaansaa, Smruti etc. in Hinduism, Bible & Gospels in Christianity, Quran & Hadith in Islam, Granth Sahib in Sikhism. Founders & preachers of various religious sects instruct their followers in their **Sansthaa Gat Dharm** from time to time. Gita talked about this kind of **Dharm** as **Traividyaa** & **Trayee Dharm** with respect to Hinduism in 9/20-21.

Nevertheless, it is important to know that **Vyakti Gat Dharm** & **Sansthaa Gat Dharm** change with time, situation and priority. Every individual should normally comply and fulfill all kinds of **Vyakti Gat** & **Sansthaa Gat Dharm** as applied to his time, situation & priority. However, if any conflict arises between one kind and another, he should give up the inferior one and carry out the superior **Dharm** by considering greater good for greater number of people. For example, it was forbidden in the period of Mahaabhaarat to kill an unarmed Mahaarathee dismounted from his chariot, but Krishn ordered Arjun to kill Karn when he had dropped his bow in the chariot and got down to pull it from the mud. He explained Arjun that it was more important to kill him in this condition, than to follow normal **Jaati Dharm** of **Kshatriy** in a war. I had explained it in 1/40-44 by shlok 'त्यजेदेकम् कुलस्यार्थे ..... पृथिवीम् त्यजेत्' from Mahaabhaarat 2/61/11. Kahlil Gibran says:

'Religion is a well-tilled field, planted and watered by desire,
Of one who longed for Paradise, or one who dreaded hell fire.
Aye, were it for reckoning, at resurrection, they had not
Worshipped God, nor did repent, except to gain a better lot,
As though religion were a phase of commerce in their daily trade;
Should they neglect it, they would lose, or preserving would be
paid'.

Ralph Waldo Emerson opines:

'Belonging to a particular religion creates an unreligious world'.

Jalaluddin Rumi writes:

'All religions, all this singing, is just for one song. The differences
are just illusions and vanity. The sun's light look a little different
on this wall than it does on that wall, and a lot different on this
other, but it's still one light'.

God, the eternal lover of the soul in us, invites it to come to Him as expressed by Aanand Bakshi in film *Kati Patang*:

आ ये रसमें, ये कसमें सभी तोड़ के ।
तू चली आ चुनर प्यार की ओढ़ के ॥

{Break all the barriers of traditions & obligations (same as Sarv Dharmaan Parityajya) and come to Me O My Darling! Just wearing Choonar (the long cloth that covers the breasts) of love & devotion.}

Gita then introduced, in 2/31-33, the concept of **Swadharm** i.e. one's own inviolable supreme duty saying:

"There is nothing more meritorious for him than to fight in a battle for Swadharm .... If you fail to do so, you would be fallen from your duty, lose your fame and incur sin".

It emphasized the need to perform **Swadharm** without any *'Ifs & buts'* in 3/35 saying:

"Performing Swadharm is more meritorious even if it is qualitatively inferior to someone else's well performed duty. It is frightening to undertake a duty prescribed for someone else".

This statement is so important that Krishn repeats it here though He stated it earlier in 18/47. Please see 3/35 & 18/47 for proper understanding in this context. Thus, **Swadharm**, the duties & responsibilities of an individual towards **Sarv Bhootaanaam** explained in 5/29 as all entities existing in the universe, whether human beings & other living species or inanimate; moving or stationary, must be never abandoned. The doer must accord the highest priority to this kind of **Dharm** and give up **Sarv Dharmaan**, all other kinds of **Dharm** (like few listed above)If the particular situation demands it. He must sacrifice the interests of self, **Kul**, **Jaati**, relationships, friends, sect of personal faith, community & society, and even nation at the altar of humanistic consideration of universal well-being. Gita teaches us to set our priorities right by judging and doing our duties dispassionately as a just a duty, detached from the result of success or failure. Such absolute **Dharm** is founded on universal, perennial qualities described by Gita as **Daivee Sampadaa**, the divine wealth in 16/1-3 and elsewhere.

Arjun was **Dharm Sammoodh Chetaa** in 2/7 as grief afflicted his mind, intelligence, heart and conscience so much that he was unable to decide his right duty. We shall find him completely delivered from this dilemma & confusion in 18/73 after listening to divine message of Gita.

Dear readers! We might have come in this world in different boats carrying banners that bore different colors, marks, sizes, shapes of caste, creed, race, community, religious faith & nationality. Nevertheless, we are now sailing in the same grand ship of universe. It is up to us whether to sail happily together with the spirit of cooperation, co-existence and understanding; or to sink together by fighting with each other.

Gita started with **Dharm** as its very first word in **Dharm Kshetr**, the region of **Dharm** in 1/1. It assured us saying:

1. *'Even an insignificantly small practice of this Dharm shall protect you from great fears in life'* in 2/40;

2. *'The knowledge of Dharm is easy to avail and joyful to practice without any hindrance'* in 9/2; and

3. *'He (the practiser of Dharm) swiftly transforms into Dharmaatmaa, a great righteous soul and attains everlasting peace'* in 9/31.

God declared His mission to protect **Dharm** and uproot **Adharm** in 4/7-8; taught us **Dharmyaamrut**, the nectar of Dharm in 12/13-20; and told in 14/27:

'I am the ultimate refuge of immortal everlasting Dharm; and of constant ultimate bliss'.

Arjun reveres Krishn as **Shaashwat Dharm Goptaa** i.e. *'the protector & savior of eternal Dharm in 11/18'* and Sanjay shall refer to Gita as धर्म्यं संवादम् i.e. the dialogue of **Dharm** in 18/70. These samples from few shloks of Gita prove it beyond doubt that Krishn teaches us **Dharm** through His divine dialogue with Arjun in Gita.

Morals:

1. *One must ultimately set himself free from plethora of laws, regulations & codes of conduct, rituals, traditions and orthodox practices imposed different religious faiths since they entangle him in Karm Bandhan. Even the means & methods of attaining bliss promulgated by different schools of thoughts, philosophies and religions are often intricate, perplexing, confusing and lope sided; sometimes even contradicting and/or condemning other religions.*

2. *One must possess sharp, undulating intelligence of Sthit Prajn to prioritize his duties and works in right order by sacrificing self-interest as well as sectarian interest.*

Clarification: *Since Gita, as well as all other Holy books prohibit Adharm, the antonym of Dharm and Par Dharm, the antonym of Swadharm, I have refrained from discussing them here. Readers, curious to know why they are prohibited, may refer to question, 'What* is meant by Dharm & Adharm' under 4/7-8; and 'Some additional thoughts on Swadharm & Par Dharm' in 3/33-35 respectively.

SOME ADDITIONAL THOUGHTS ON MAAM EKAM SHARANAM VRAJ

The phrase **Maam Ekam Sharanam Vraj** literally means, 'Seek refuge in Me only'. In the beginning of Gita in 2/7, highly deluded & distressed Arjun expressed desire to find his noble duty and sought refuge in Krishn for it by uttering Twaam Prapannam. It seems that Krishn is congratulating him here for his most appropriate decision there to come to His refuge. Through him, He instructs us here that **Sharanaagati** i.e. total refuge in God is the only recourse open to a person afflicted by bewilderment and sorrow. We discussed the spirit of **Sharanaagati** in detail under 'Some additional thoughts on Twaam Prapannam' and 'How does the spirit of Sharanaagati help us in ..... treading on the noble path of our duties' in 2/7 earlier. Let us read those passages and continue to flourish our thoughts about **Sharanaagati** in the light of the knowledge learnt through the study of Gita.

Sharanaagati is not surrender under coercion or compulsion like that of a defeated army general before the victor; it is the willful complete surrender of a person before someone who can help, guidance, support and teach him, in thick & thin situations, in fact, takes full charge of his life. Note the emphasis on **Ekam** i.e. 'The only one, the Supreme Being'. Surrender must be in totality in happiness as well as sorrow and to that Supreme God, not to any other demigod. Remember the warning God gave in 7/23:

'The worshippers of Demigods reach only up to their status.
Only My devotee reaches unto Me'.

Let us learn this spirit of taking total shelter under the divine umbrella of God with few very practical examples as below:

1. A child goes to a fare holding the finger of his father. He can leave his finger and run after attractions of some toys or sweets, and get lost in the mob. Nevertheless, if he lets the father to hold his hand firmly (instead of the child holding his finger casually), the father shall not allow him to run hither

& thither and get lost but take him only to those shops, which he considers beneficial for his child. If the child is suffering with cold, he shall take him to hot chocolate milk vendor instead of his son's choice of ice-cream parlour.

2. A lamb lost his mother. When the innocent lamb came across a lion in the forest, he told him that he has come to him seeking shelter under his gracious patronage since he is the king of forest. The lion felt very kindly towards the orphaned lamb and declared him as his ward. Since that time, the lamb roamed fearlessly in the forest as no other animal could dare to touch the protégé of lion.

3. Scriptures advise a devotee to be like an infant kitten; not an infant baby monkey. The mother cat holds her baby softly by her mouth and carries him wherever she wants. The kitten depends completely on his mother for his existence. On the other hand, the baby monkey is always afraid of falling because he uses his own strength in clinging fast to his mother's breast. The kitten is entirely free from fear, stress, and anxiety whereas the baby monkey is ridden constantly with the fear of losing his grip. Let us learn to be a kitten, not the baby monkey, in seeking refuge in God.

4. Sons, in India, consider it a sacred duty to take their parents on pilgrimage in old age. The parents depend completely on the son for their travel, boarding, lodging, clothing, Darshan, sightseeing etc. The son knows their needs well and takes full care during the pilgrimage.

5. Raamkrishn Paramhans tells a story from Raamaayan to his followers:

"Raam reaches Pampaa Lake during His search of Seetaa and prepares to take a holy dip in it. He pushes one end of His bow in the wet soil on the bank and bathes in the lake. Once ready to move forward in His journey, He pulls the bow from the earth but is aghast to see its tip stained with fresh blood. As He quickly digs the soil with His hands, a wounded frog jumps out. Raam attends to his wound immediately and asks him compassionately why he did not call Him

the moment His bow hit him. The frog replies to Raam thus, 'My Lord! Whenever a snake comes to eat me, I tell him that I am under the protection of Raam; and the snake goes away. Now, when Raam himself hit me for my past Karm, whom other than Him can I ask to protect me? I therefore, waited until You completed Your bath and came for my rescue'. This is the spirit behind Ekam Sharanam, the refuge unto the only One Supreme Being".

6. A factory owner appoints two persons on the same day, a manager for the factory and a personal attendant for himself. At the end of the day, the manger leaves for home, but the attendant does not leave his master even when he enters his car to go home. When the owner tells him to go home, he replies, 'आप ने तो मुझे रख लिया है न. अब मैं आपको छोड़ कर आप कहेंगे तो भी कहीं नहीं जाऊँगा i.e. *you have taken me under your benevolent care. I won't leave you now even if you order me to go'.* Hanumaan must have replied to Raam in the same way when He asked him to return to Kishkindhaa along with other apes, after His coronation.

7. A king once sent an offer to Tulasidaas to join him as an official in his court. Tulasidaas politely replied:

हम चाकर रघुबीर के पटै लिख्यो दरबार ।
तुलसी अब क्या होएंगे नर के मन्सबदार ॥

(I am a humble servant of Raam. He has leased His entire court to me. How can now Tulasidaas serve as an official of a man now?)

8. Meeraa recognizes only Girdhar, nobody else, as her husband:

मेरे तो गिरधर गोपाल दूसरो न कोई ।
जाके सिर मोर मुकुट मेरो पति सोई ॥

{I belong exclusively to Girdhar Gopaal (name of Krishn), none else. He, who adores a crown of peacock feathers, is my Pati, the lord, master & husband.}

God stressed the need of whole-hearted, undivided devotion & total dependence on Him; offer all thoughts, efforts, activities and their results to Him and bowing with reverence before Him in complete surrender, in entire Gita. Nevertheless, shloks like 2/61, 4/10, 6/14, 7/29, 9/13, 25, 34; 11/55, 12/6, 10, 20; 18/56, 18/57 & 65 need specific mention in this regard. I also wish to mention here that God spoke about **Sharan**, the total refuge in Him in 2/49, & 9/18 and even told us in 18/61-62 that we need not search Him here and there, as He is always available within our hearts. With minor variations, He also used the word **Aashray** and its derivatives to stress the need to rely and depend totally on Him in 3/18, 4/10, 7/1 & 29, 9/11, 13 & 32; 12/11, 14/2, 15/14, 16/10 & 11, 18/52, 56, 57 & 59. He also uttered derivatives of **Matpar** i.e. wholly dedicated to Him in 2/61, 6/14, 9/34, 11/55, 12/6 & 20 & 18/57 to teach **Sharanaagati** before 18/65-66. He stated in 7/14:

> *"Only they, who devote wholeheartedly unto Me, are able to swim across (the strong but illusory currents of) this Maayaa."*

He guaranteed in 9/22:

> *"For the devotees who worship Me exclusively and remain constantly united with Me, I bear upon My shoulders entire responsibility of fulfilling their needs and maintain things already gained by them".*

He promised further, in 12/6 & 7:

> *"For those who surrender all of their works unto Me, come to My refuge and worship Me whole-heartedly, I become the savior in the ocean of death and rebirth in the mortal world'.*

The important condition for God to fulfill above assurances and promises is that our **Bhakti**, the devotion unto Him must be:

1) **Ekam** (or **Ananya** in 8/22 & 11/54) i.e. exclusive, undivided, singular, inalienable & whole-hearted;

2) **Avyabhichaarinee** (13/10, 14/26 & 18/33) i.e. incorruptible, unpolluted;

3) **Shraddhayaa Anvitaa** (9/23) i.e. endowed with extreme, undulating, unflinching, perfect faith & reverential belief; and,

4) **Mayi Arpit Man Buddhi** (8/17 & 12/14) i.e. our mind, heart and intellect should be dedicated to God.

Gita dedicates entire chapter 12 and large part of chapter 9 to **Bhakti**, and states in 14/26 that a practiser of **Bhakti Yog** becomes **Gunaateet** equal to **Brahm**. A true **Bhakt** possesses all the qualities described for **Bhakt** from 12/13 to 20, for **Gunaateet** from 14/22 to 27, for **Jnaanee** from 13/7 to 11, and 18/49 to 54 besides **Daivee Sampadaa** from 16/1 to 3. God assures such practiser of **Bhakti** in following lines of a **Bhajan**:

भाव का भूखा हूँ मैं, बस भाव ही एक सार है ।
भाव से मुझ को भजे तो, उसका बेडा पार है ॥

(I am hungry of My devotee's emotional sentiments behind his worship because that only is its essence. His raft, who worships Me with emotional attachment, crosses ocean of the world easily)

जो भी मुझ मे भाव रख कर, आते है मेरी शरण ।
मेरे और उस के हृदय का, एक रहता तार है ॥

(Whoever seeks shelter in Me with full emotional attachment, the wire of his heart is connected with the wire of My heart)

Look at another **Bhajan** by Hari Om Sharan:

तेरा रामजी करेंगे बेड़ा पार, उदासी मन काहे को करे ।
नैया तेरी राम हवाले, लहर लहर हरि आप सम्हाले ।
हरि आप ही उठायें तेरा भार, उदासी मन काहे को करे ॥
सहज किनारा मिल जायेगा, परम सहारा मिल जायेगा ।
डोरी सौंप के तो देख एक बार, उदासी मन काहे को करे ॥

(O my heart! Why do you feel dejected? God shall navigate your boat to the shore.

Your boat is in the expert hands of God. he shall take care of it wave after wave. He carries all your burdens on His shoulders.

(You shall easily reach the shore of His eternal support. All you have to do is just hand over the tug rope of your boat in His hands.)

Naarad praises **Bhakti** thus in Shreemad Bhaagawat:

सत्यादित्रियुगे बोधवैराग्यो मुक्तिसाधकौ ।
कलौ तु केवला भक्तिर्ब्रह्मसायुज्यकारिणी ॥
इति निश्चित्य चिद्रूप: सद्रूपा त्वां ससर्ज ह ।
परमानंदचिन्मूर्ति: सुन्दरीम् कृष्णवल्लाभाम् ॥

{In the first three ions of Satya, Tretaa & Dwaapar, Jnaan, the knowledge and Vairaagya, the detachment were the means of attaining liberation; but Bhakti is the only one in this ion of Kali by which a person can attain Brahm. Lord Vishnu, the ultimate abode of bliss and knowledge, created you (Bhakti) in His own form with this consideration in mind.}

God of Gita is not someone living in a great palace in the sky at a formidable height where one has to reach & knock at His door to seek His grace. Gita's God, and therefore of Hinduism by and large, comes running and knocking constantly on the doors of everyone with the hope that someone would respond to His call someday, be blessed by Him and attain ultimate liberation from distress.

Can anyone of us, the students of Gita, be the lucky & beloved one He is looking for? Definitely yes. All sincere students of Gita shall respond to His constant knocking someday because they are in search of eternal bliss & peace. A wise housewife in search of a good maid knows that the good maid is simultaneously looking for a good mistress. Aanand Bakshi motivates us in film *Kati Patang* to do our part to connect with God:

ज़िंदगी में कई रंगरलियाँ सही,
हर तरफ़ मुस्कुराती ये गलियाँ सही,
खूबसूरत बहारों की कलियाँ सही ।
जिस चमन में तेरे पग में काँटे चुभे,
उस चमन से हमें फूल चुनना नहीं ॥

जिस गली में तेरा घर न हो बालमा,
उस गली से हमें तो गुज़रना नहीं ।
जो डगर तेरे द्वारे से जाती न हो,
उस डगर पर हमें पाँव रखना नहीं ॥

(It is true that life offers much cheerful merriment, and many bylanes welcome me with a smile. Its garden is abundant with beautiful flower buds in springs. Nevertheless, I have resolved to pluck not the flowers from a garden that pricks Your feet with its thorns. I won't ever pass through the lane where You don't live. I won't even set my foot on a track that does not lead me to Your door.)

QUESTION: WHY DOES GITA TALK ABOUT SIN, HELL, HEAVEN ETC. OFTEN?

Gita talks about sinful evil deeds as **Paap** in 1/39 & 45, 2/33, 3/41, 4/36, 5/10, 6/9, 9/32, 10/3 & 18/66; and its synonyms like **Kilbish** in 3/13 & 4/21; and **Agh** in 3/13 & 3/16. Gita also talks of hell as **Narak** in 1/42, 44, 16/16, 21, or **Adh Gati** in 14/18; and of heaven as **Swarg** in 2/37, 43 & 9/20, or **Oordhw Gati** in 12/8 & 14/18.

Existence of **Paap**, the evil, an inevitable counterpart of **Punya**, the goodness is acceptable in dualistic world, as **Dukh** is for **Sukh**, heat is for cold and **Ashubh** is for **Shubh**. Hence, there is nothing objectionable about the mention of **Paap** or its synonyms in Gita. However, the same is not true for the mention of hell & heaven since they are lower or upper worlds than the world we live in.

Some religions and rationalists do not believe in the doctrine of **Punarjanm**, the rebirth in Hinduism after death of a person. Nevertheless, Gita accepts **Punarjanm** and consequential existence of hell and heaven for two reasons. First, it was widely prevalent in its time in India because almost all ancient scriptures preached it. Secondly, Gita is founded on the background of Arjun's **Vishaad**, the fearful delusion described in chapter 1. There, he expressed great concern and worry about accrual of sin, going to hell, not desiring the pleasures of heaven, et al. I advise readers to refer to *Introduction* and 4/9 where I have discussed all related aspects.

Morals:

1. *Even if someone does not believe in the concept of Punarjanm for a while, he would certainly agree me that everybody has to face the consequences of his good or bad deeds in his life sooner or later because he is working against the rules laid down by the society or country in which he lives. Acceptance or non-acceptance of the idea of Punarjanm is irrelevant to the study of Gita.*

2. *Arjun has never been a sinner; nor is anyone amongst us a sinner. Some of us are already on the right path without proper knowledge of destination, and others are strayed from the right path.*

SOME ADDITIONAL THOUGHTS ON SHLOKS 18/65 & 66

These shloks are *'Crème de la crème'* of entire Gita. Here God, the Grand Maestro of the world's greatest symphony of knowledge strikes its crowning note as He shows us the simplest and most effective way to attain liberation from distress in life, and His eternal bliss after death. For this, He delivers His supreme imperative making only one demand from us:

'To unite with Him with total surrender of personal will & ego unto His Supreme Will'.

Thereafter, we need not worry at all because He promises on oath to us to deliver us from reactions of all evil actions and sins by assuming full charge of our lives, and even thereafter. He opens the vast panorama of the world below, the sky above and everything in between the two to let our souls absorb its charm. He throws open the gates of His limitless compassion, grace and energy, lets them flow in us so that we can live blissfully with Him forever. Saahir Ludhiyaanavee expresses it beautifully in film *Naya Daur:*

जब तुझसे न सुलझे तेरे उलझे हुये धंधे ।
भगवान के इंसाफ पे सब छोड़ दे बंदे ॥

खुद ही तेरी मुश्किल को वो आसान करेगा ।
जो तू नहीं कर पाया तो भगवान करेगा ॥
आना है तो आ राह में कुछ फेर नहीं है ।
भगवान के घर देर है अंधेर नहीं है ॥

{Whenever you find it extremely difficult to solve complicated issues, just leave them on the divine justice of God. (The moment you do so), He Himself shall simplify your every problem; Almighty God can do everything that you failed to do. Come to His refuge if you want to; the path unto Him is simple without any twist or turn. His justice might sometimes be delayed (due to your own evil works), but rest assured, there won't be any injustice in His court. Have patience)}.

QUESTION: WHAT DOES ALL THIS TALK OF BHAKTI, SHARANAAGATI AND THE DIVINE PROMISE OF LIBERATION MEAN?

The explanation here is intended for those readers of modern age who may find it hard to accept the concept of **Bhakti** and **Sharanaagati** taught by almost all Scriptures of Hinduism.

Let us first talk about Bhakti.

We discussed **Bhakti** earlier in 9/34 and 12/20 but let us add few more thoughts to it. Shreemad Bhaagawat describes nine ways of doing **Bhakti** of God as listening about Him, singing and dancing in His praise, remembering Him, seeking shelter in His feet, making oblations to Him, bowing to Him in reverence, consider himself as His servant, regard Him as friend, and offering own self to God. People practise **Bhakti** in this manner often at the cost of neglecting their household & social duties and responsibilities. Such misunderstood **Bhakti** is similar to **Sannyaas** i.e. abandoning household duties and responsibilities without giving up attachment towards materials of the world as explained from 18/4 to 9. **Bhakti**, if practised as a routine ritual in this manner without doing **Karm** and acquiring **Jnaan,** becomes as worthless and unproductive as a barren cow that eats fodder without delivering a calf and gives milk. It grows like a **Khejri**, the *Prosopis cineraria* tree found in the Thar Desert of India, which neither yields fruits nor gives useful wood.

God described the qualities of His dearest **Bhakt** in 12/13-20, calling it **Dharmyaamrut**, the essence of **Dharm**. He is His dearest **Bhakt** who is friendly, compassionate & forgiving towards all beings; free from envy, proprietary interest, ego, delight, spite, fear, anxiety, expectation, pain, disliking & liking, desire, and contented with whatever he gets. He must be a regular practiser of Yog, and equipoise with friends & enemies, distress & happiness, defamation & fame, appreciation & criticism, favorable & unfavorable, hot and cold things, and honor & dishonor. He should be temperate, clean, dexterous, stoically indifferent, habitually a non-starter of any activity, dissociated from material things, with mind, heart and intelligence dedicated to God. He should neither be perturbed himself by others, nor cause perturbation to others. He should have firm determination, undulating wisdom and full faith in God. He should speak only when needed, depend entirely on God, and have no belongingness in the household.

My purpose in recapturing above from chapter 12 is to show to readers that Gita does not mention any of the nine kinds of **Bhakti** described in Shreemad Bhaagawat. God is most pleased with a **Bhakt** who practises His teachings in 12/13-20 in letter and spirit in his life.

Caution: *Nine steps of Bhakti, described in Shreemad Bhaagawat, are essential for a believer in God for they initiate him properly in Bhakti during the practising stage. The point that I wish to make here is that he should not be stuck up in any of these steps forever but use them to reach the top in order to get Dharmyaamrut.*

Now, let us also understand Sharanaagati in continuation of above.

As explained earlier, **Sharanaagati** is the spirit of taking refuge wholeheartedly in **Sarv Shaktimaan**, the Omnipotent God. It is good for a person to assign his worries of material and spiritual needs to God and live a worry free life. Nevertheless, **Sharanaagati** should not lead him to inaction thinking that God do everything for him. God is most pleased with a person who discharges all of his duties and responsibilities towards self, family and society with full vigor as per His teachings in Gita. For example:

1. A good teacher does not love a student who touches his feet with reverence, sings in his praise daily and pays good remuneration but neglects his lessons expecting that he would pass him in examination with good marks. On the contrary, the teacher loves most the student that learns and practises his lessons well, but does not try to please him with flattery and high remuneration. Arjun was most liked student of Dron due to this reason.

2. A lioness delivers many cubs and loves them equally but she concentrates on that cub the most that bravely defends himself to his mite without depending on his mother like other cubs that are killed eventually by other animals.

3. Examples of Draupadee, elephant Gajendr etc. in the legends amply prove that God rescues them only after they fully deploy and exhaust their own power to come out of grim situations, not before.

4. An employer prefers to pay well a servant every month rather than want him to run to him for his personal needs daily.

Liberation from miseries in this life, and/or deliverance from **Punarjanm**, becomes easier with the spirit of **Sharanaagati** & **Bhakti; Jnaan** and **Karm** are bound to follow automatically in the life of such practisers. Conversely, the paths of **Jnaan** and **Karm** sans **Bhakti** are tedious, almost impossible to tread upon by a common person. Tukaaraam rightly sums up this concept as:

चतुराई चेतना सभी चूल्हे में जावें,
बस मेरा मन एक ईश चरणाश्रय पावे ।
आग लगे आचार विचारों के उपचय में,
उस विभु का विश्वास सदा दृढ़ रहे हृदय में ॥

(I should consign all my discretions, and awareness to the flames of the hearth. My mind and heart should seek refuge in the feet of the Master. Let all options of rituals and thoughts burn in fire. My only wish is that firm belief in Omnipresent always occupies my heart.)

౿౼౿

God forbids us from sharing this knowledge with some
undeserving people.

(18/67)

इदं ते नातपस्काय नाभक्ताय कदाचन ।
न चाशुश्रूषवे वाच्यं न च मां योऽभ्यसूयति ॥ १८/६७॥

Idam te naatapaskaay naabhaktaay kadaachan I
N chaashushrooshave vaachyam n ch maam yoſbhyasuyati II
18/67

Idam (this) Te (by you) N (not) Atapaskaay (who is not austere) N
(not) Abhaktaay (who is not devoted) Kadaachan (any time)I n (not)
Ch (and) Ashushrooshave (not engaged in devotional service and
unwilling to listen) Vaachyam (spoken) N (not) Ch (and) Maam (to
me) Y: (who) Abhyasooyati (envious)II (18/67)

**You should never impart this knowledge to he who has not
purified himself by Tap, the austerities, nor to he who is not
devoted to Me, not willing to listen to it; and nor to he who is
envious and captious towards Me. (18/67)**

God finished His teachings of Gita in 18/66. He now, prohibits
us from passing the spiritual knowledge of Gita to following types
of persons:

1. **Atapaskaay:** Those who have not purified their **Kaayaa**, the
   body, **Man**, the mind & heart and **Vaak**, the speech by **Tap**,
   the austerities, as preached and explained from 17/14 to
   19 and at many other places like 4/10, 5/29, 10/5, 16/1,
   17/28 & 18/5. It is wise to include **Yajn**, the sacrificial works
   & **Daan**, the charity under **Atapaskaay** as told in 18/3.

2. **Abhaktaay: Abhakt** is the antonym of **Bhakt**. They are
   atheists and non-believers who do not accept the existence
   of God and therefore, have no devotion for Him. They are
   nihilists who reject all religious & moral principles and
   possess **Aasuree Sampadaa**, the demonical wealth explained
   in detail in chapter 16. This category, however, excludes the
   people who do not accept God per se but want to ameliorate

the quality and value of their life and fulfill the purpose of being born as human.

3. **Ashushrooshave:** This category consists of people who are not at all interested in topics dealing with spirituality, liberation, salvation etc. Gita described them as **Kaam Up Bhog Paramaa** (16/11) i.e. grossly absorbed in gratifying passionate desires, **Arth Sanchayaan** (16/12) i.e. who are always after money, and **Aatm Sambhaavitaa** (16/17) i.e. totally lacking in modesty and having false pride of very high opinion about them. The person who hears someone unwillingly & inattentively shall never act according to his advice. He is like the fool who wants to build his house on the sand.

4. **Abhyasooyati:** It is a derivative of **Abhyasooyant** (3/32). They are pseudo-intellectual captious, slanderous people with negative attitude, always to keen to find fault in everything and spreading malice. For them, the sun is simply the hottest fireball in the universe; they see only the black spots in full moon, not its beauty; and think of all spirits as ghosts, all saints as imposters. We had discussed about them in 3/31-32.

QUESTION: WHY DOES GOD, SUHRUD SARV BHOOTAANAAM, EXCLUDE ABOVE PEOPLE FROM DERIVING SOME BENEFIT BY LISTENING TO GITA?

In 5/29, God pronounced Himself as **Suhrud Sarv Bhootaanaam** i.e. a most affectionate, good hearted, well-wisher, benefactor friend, closest to everybody's heart. It therefore, seems He is contradicting His statement here by excluding people mentioned above from the benefits of His teachings.

God made universe with three kinds of people, **Saattvik**, the good, **Raajasik**, the medium and **Taamasik** the bad (18/26 to 28). Scriptures and saints remind and appreciate importance of morality, virtues & nobility to good people and clarify their doubts to reinforce their faith in goodness and improve upon it. Nevertheless, Scriptures and saints have a more important duty to mould the medium quality people by teaching, preaching, and institutionalizing **Dharm** with the example of their own works with the spirit of **Lok Sangrah** (3/20 & 25) so that they shift from the medium path to the path of goodness. If the Scriptures and leaders fail in this paramount duty, the medium people shall stray towards apparently more lucrative path of evil. The balance between **Dharm** and **Adharm** depends on what the medium people choose and follow. God said in 4/7 & 8 that He incarnates bodily on earth to re-establish **Dharm** whenever **Adharm** dominates it by eliminating **Dushkrutaam**, the evil doers, when He finds them beyond redemption. Refer to Analysis of the legend of **Saagar Manthan** with respect to Divine justice under 2/47 where I have explained why demons do not deserve **Amrut**. Gita is **Dharmyaamrut**, the essence of Dharm like **Amrut** as stated in 12/20. It is worthless to try to reform demonic, **Dushkrutaam**, **Aatataayee** people entrenched deeply in **Aasuree Sampadaa**. Following examples explain this point:

1. Howsoever one may try to straighten the tail of a dog; it shall remain always crooked unless he cuts it off.

2. A wise snake charmer knows well that the snake does not swing its hood with joy on the melody of his flute; it is actually trying to find a weak point in him to bite. He therefore, removes the poisonous tooth of the snake before his show.

3. A buffalo follows the stick wielded in the hands of its keeper but it never appreciates if he plays music before it.

4. The fragrance of a sandalwood tree spreads far & wide in whole forest. Even the axe that cuts its branches acquires its good smell, but the poisonous snakes coiled on its branches never give up their poison.

5. My mother used to tell me an inspiring story as below:

"A Bayaa, the weaverbird, constructed a retort shaped nest hanging from a small branch of a tree where predators cannot reach easily. She lived cozily with her offspring in that safe, beautiful nest. On a cold rainy day, she saw a Langoor, the long-tailed big monkey

perched on the same tree and shivering in the downpour. She felt pity on him and advised, 'My dear Sir! God blessed you with hands, legs and a body just like a human being. Why should you suffer in the rain when you can construct a beautiful house for you as men do for themselves?' The frivolous Langoor took the advice of Bayaa as a great offence, and retorted angrily, 'How can a little, frail bird like you dare to insult a mighty monkey like me?' Saying so, he descended from his place and destroyed the nest of Bayaa."

Then, my mother summed up the moral of the story thus:

सीख उसी को दीजिये जो जन सीख सुहाय ।
सीख देवता वानरे को घर बया को जाय ॥

(Advise only to him, who can appreciate your advice. A Bayaa lost her nest in tying to counsel a monkey.)

Caution: Legends describe stories of God and saints transforming wicked persons like Vaalmeeki, Angulimaal etc. A practiser should not be swayed by these exceptions but follow the general rule laid down here for his own good, for any misadventure to do so would either create bitterness & frustration in him, or the wicked person may influence him into his path.

ॐ

God praises on people who teach, study and
listen faithfully Gita.

(18/68, 69, 70 & 71)

य इमं परमं गुह्यं मद्भक्तेष्वभिधास्यति ।
भक्तिं मयि परां कृत्वा मामेवैष्यत्यसंशयः ॥१८/६८॥

न च तस्मान्मनुष्येषु कश्चिन्मे प्रियकृत्तमः ।
भविता न च मे तस्मादन्यः प्रियतरो भुवि ॥१८/६९॥

अध्येष्यते च य इमं धर्म्यं संवादमावयोः ।
ज्ञानयज्ञेन तेनाहमिष्टः स्यामिति मे मतिः ॥१८/७०॥

श्रद्धावाननसूयश्च शृणुयादपि यो नरः ।
सोऽपि मुक्तः शुभाँल्लोकान्प्राप्नुयात्पुण्यकर्मणाम् ॥१८/७१॥

Y imam paramam guhyam madbhakteshwabhidhaasyati I
Bhaktim mayi paraam krutvaa maamevaishyatyasanshay: II
(18/68)
N ch tasmaanmanusheshu kashchinme priykruttam: I
Bhavitaa n ch me tasmaadany: priytaro bhuvi II (18/69)
Adhyeshyate ch y imam dharmyam samvaadamaavayo: I
Jnaanayajnen tenaahamisht: syaamiti me mati: II (18/70)
Shraddhaavaananasooyashch shrunuyaadapi yo nar: I
Sofpi mukt: shubhaanllokaanpraapnuyaatpunyakarmanaam
II (18/71)

Y: (who) imam (this) Paramam (supreme) Guhyam (esoteric secret) Madbhakteshu (to my devotees) Abhidhaasyati (shall explain, teach)I Bhaktim (devotion) Mayi (unto me) Paraam (greatest) Krutvaa (doing) Maam (to me) Ev (only) Eshyati (shall come) Asanshay: (undoubtedly)II (18/68)

n (not) Ch (and) Tasmaat (more than him) Manusheshu (among mankind) Kashchit (anyone) Me (mine) Priy Kruttam: (performer of very favorite task)I Bhavitaa (shall be there in future) N (not) Ch (and) Me (My) Tasmaat (more than him) Any: (else) Priy tar: (more dear) Bhuvi (on the earth, in this world)II (18/69)

adhyeshyate (shall study) Ch (and) Y: (who) Imam (this) Dharmyam (of Dharm, sacred) Samvaadam (dialogue) Aavayo: (ours)I Jnaan yajnen (by performing Jnaan Yajn) Ten (by that) Aham (I) Isht: (worshipped, adored) Syaam (would have) iti (this much) Me (my) Mati: (firm opinion)II (18/70)

Shraddhaa vaan (faithful person who possess undulating faith & reverential belief) Anasooy: (free from Asooyaa, the envy & criticism) Ch (and) Shrunuyaat (listen) Api (even) Y: (who) Nar: (person)I s; (he) Api (even) Mukt: (liberated) Shubhaan (auspicious) Lokaan (superior worlds, heaven etc.) Praapnuyaat (will attain) Punya karmanaam (performers of meritorious, pious acts, works) II (18/71)

He, who will explain this extremely esoteric secret to My devotees, shall be doing greatest adoration unto Me and shall

ultimately come to Me only. There is absolutely no doubt in it. (18/68)

There is no one in entire humanity greater than him who performs this most favorite task of Mine; and there shall be nobody else dear to Me more than him in future also. (18/69)

It is my firm opinion that whosoever shall study this sacred dialogue between us, and realize the essence of Dharm; he would have worshipped Me by way of performing Jnaan Yajn, the path of cultivating perfect knowledge. (18/70)

Besides, he, who faithfully listens to it without envy & criticism, also attains liberation from reactions of his evil works and attains the superior worlds achievable by the doers of pious acts. (18/71)

We have already understood, in 3/31, **Shraddhaa Vaan** as an extremely faithful & reverential believer in God, and **Anasooy** as free from envy, malice, and unwarranted criticism. God forbade us in 18/67 from teaching Gita to those who criticize, averse and detest it. Now, He tells from 18/68 to 71 about those who respect and regard Gita as the source of a **Paramam Guhya**, the ultimate secret knowledge in 18/68. He also mentions what benefits a person can achieve by teaching, studying and listening (and reading) the divine dialogue between Krishn and Arjun that reveals the essence of **Dharm** in Gita.

1. In 18/68-69, He describes those who have accomplished complete understanding of all aspects of Gita in their lifetime, and spend rest of their life in teaching and explaining it to those who do not understand its underlying message but listen to it with faith and devotion. The teachers firm up their listeners' interest in continuing their study of Gita by clarifying their doubts. He appreciates the work of such Yogee as the highest contribution a person can ever make in propagating **Dharm**; and proclaims that there has been nobody dearer to Him than such Yogee until now, nor will there be anybody in future. He guarantees that the person, who faithfully teaches Gita, shall ultimately reach Him. Krishn is the role model for all teachers of Gita.

Caution: *He, who undertakes teaching Gita, should first rise above his individual or sectarian interests & religious faith, and desist from interpreting it any other way to please the audience and earn accolades for himself. He should thankfully acknowledge God's kindness for choosing him to do His task, and always remember that he is doing it not for self or anyone else but God.*

2. In 18/70, God appreciates sincere students and practisers of Gita. He talked of **Jnaan Yajn** for the first time in 4/28 as **Swaadhyaay Jnaan Yajn** i.e. *'knowing own self through study of scriptures'*. Then, in 4/33, He established superiority of **Jnaan Yajn** to all other **Yajns** pronouncing, *'Jnaan Yajn is the most meritorious Yajn as all sacred works finally culminate into Jnaan, the perfect knowledge'*. The serious readers & students amongst us belong to this category.

3. God finally takes up the cause of faithful people who listen to Gita with interest to learn more about it, rather than being skeptical and trying to find faults in it. God assures them also of achieving liberation if they faithfully pursue their interest through **Abhyaas Yog** as taught by Him in 6/35, 8/8 & 12/9; and discussed by us in detail in 6/35 & 8/8.

If students & practisers belonging to category 2, and the devoted listeners of category 3 are able to achieve complete success in their effort, they too attain God like the teachers of category 1. However, if they are not able to do so in current life, they avail the benefits of going to upper worlds of demigods, and come back to this world to resume their practice where they left, as assured by God under the topic of **Yog Bhrasht** from 6/37 to 45.

There are three listeners in Gita viz. Arjun, Sanjay and Dhrutraashtr. Since Arjun listened to it with rapt attention & faith directly from God, he would literally follow His instructions in whole Gita, specifically in 18/65 & 66, for the rest of his life. In Mahaabhaarat, Arjun always seeks advice from Krishn and acts as per His wish & instruction. He has thus attained liberation in his life. Sanjay listened to Gita from a great distance with the primary purpose of narrating it to Dhrutraashtr, but with full faith and devotion towards Krishn. People like Sanjay shall also achieve liberation in their current birth if they spend their remaining life like Arjun, or in next births like a **Yog Bhrasht** if their current practice lacks total dedication. Dhrutraashtr is the third kind of listener who is faithless, not interested at all in its teaching as his interest lay only in knowing what happened in the war (1/1). Such listeners stand no chance of liberation from miseries even in their current lives. Mahaabhaarat states that grief-stricken, repentant Dhrutraashtr left Hastinaapur after the war, went to the forest and died there in a forest fire.

ॐ

Krishn asks Arjun whether His teaching of Gita relieved him from delusion.

(18/72)

कच्चिदेतच्छ्रुतं पार्थ त्वयैकाग्रेण चेतसा ।
कच्चिदज्ञानसंमोहः प्रनष्टस्ते धनंजय ॥ १८/७२॥

Kachchidetachchhrutam Paarth twayaikaagren chetasaa I
Kachchidajnaansammoh: pranashtaste Dhananjay II (18/72)

Kachchit (whether) Etat (this, it) Shrutam (have heard, listened) Paarth (Arjun) Twayaa (by you) Ekaagren (with concentration, attention) Chetasaa (conscience, mind, heart)I Kachchit (whether) Ajnaan (ignorance, lack of Jnaan) Sammoh: (strong bewilderment, delusion) Pranasht: (fully dispelled, destroyed) Te (of you) Dhananjay (Arjun, who amassed wealth by many victorious expeditions)II (18/72)

O Paarth (Arjun)! Have you heard My talk with pointed concentration of conscience, mind & heart? Whether your delusion caused by ignorance, has been completely dispelled now O Dhananjay (Arjun)? (18/72)

It is the last shlok spoken by Krishn in Gita. Arjun requested Krishn in 2/7 to teach him his most appropriate duty as he himself was not able to decide anything properly due to his highly deluded state. In this shlok, Krishn reminds him of his request and asks whether he listened to what He taught him with rapt attention; and whether **Moh**, the delusion caused by his ignorance is destroyed now. Krishn instructed Arjun to start fighting in as many shloks as 2/18, 31 & 37, 3/30 & 35, 4/42, 6/46, 8/7 and 11/34 but he did not respond. Krishn now gives him the last opportunity, as God gives to all of us sometimes in our lives, to finally decide and act, as he likes.

Arjun, by his character, always concentrated on things he regarded more important. Since this was the most crucial time of his life, he did listen to Gita with full concentration and faith; even the threat of impending battle could not distract him from listening to Krishn. Nevertheless, most of us are unfortunately not attentive in our study as passionate situations interrupt us frequently; and some of us are even doubtful and skeptical. Vyaas expresses his disgust for such casual approach of people in the end of Mahaabhaarat:

ऊर्ध्वबाहुर्विरोम्येष न च कश्चित्च्छृणोति मे ।
धर्मादर्थश्च कामश्च स किमर्थ न सेव्यते ॥

(I raise my both hands in disgust and wonder why nobody listens to what I say. I repeat for the last time that you can fulfill your desires and get wealth only by practicing Dharm in life. Why don't you then act according to Dharm?)

It is important to note that Almighty Krishn does not undertake fighting and killing opponents of His best friend Arjun on his behalf. Instead, He asks him to decide and do his duty.

Morals:

1. *There comes a time in everybody's life when he must act decisively without any more delay, because that is the last opportunity given to him by God. When Krishn went to Dhrutraashtr and Duryodhan as a messenger of peace, He gave them the last*

opportunity to give up Adharm and avoid war. Similarly, He gives the last chance to Arjun here to decide and perform his duty of protecting Dharm by fighting in the war against Adharm; or choose to be a crest-fallen coward.

2. *Like Arjun in Mahaabhaarat, we too are engaged in the battle of life. A teacher, a friend, a well-wisher relative can advise us and teach the art of fighting in this battle, but none of them can fight it out on our behalf. The decision to act or to flee from a difficult situation rests entirely in our hands.*

Rumi says:

'It is your road, and yours alone. Others may walk it with you but none can walk it for you'.

I had pointed out under *'Why is Gita located at as unfavorable a place as amidst a battlefield'* in 2/10 that it was a *'Now or Never'* situation for Krishn to speak and relieve His best friend Arjun from his unfounded infatuation. As His teachings from 2/11 have reached an end now, He genuinely asks him to convey his final decision and act accordingly. It is now Arjun's turn to speak *'Now or never'*. Shailendr writes in film *Raat Aur Din*:

दिल की गिरह खोल दो, चुप न बैठो, कोई गीत गाओ ।
महफ़िल में अब कौन है अजनबी, तुम मेरे पास आओ ॥

{This is the time to open the knot of your heart. Do not sit silently in remorse. Sing the song (of your heart) and come to me. We are no more strangers now in this gathering}

৯৩৩

Arjun commits to fight.
(18/73)

अर्जुन उवाच

नष्टो मोहः स्मृतिर्लब्धा त्वत्प्रसादान्मयाच्युत ।
स्थितोऽस्मि गतसन्देहः करिष्ये वचनं तव ॥१८/७३॥

Arjun Uvaach
Nashto moh: smrutirlabdhaa twatprasaadaanmayaʃchyut I
Sthitoʃsmi gatsandeh: karishye vachanam tav II (18/73)

Nasht: (dispelled, destroyed) Moh: (bewilderment, delusion) Smruti: (power of memory, remembrance) Labdhaa (gained, achieved) Twat Prasaadaat (by your propitious blessings, grace) Mayaa (by me) Achyut (Krishn, the infallible One)I Sthit: (firmly situated, fully composed) Asmi (I am) Gat Sandeh: (all doubts cleared) Karishye (shall do) Vachanam (command, instruction) Tav (your)II (18/73)

Arjun said:

"O Achyut (Krishn)! My delusion is destroyed completely. I have regained my memory by Your propitious grace. I am firmly & fully composed now, as all my doubts have been cleared. I shall now perform my duty as per Your command". (18/73)

This is 21st **Arjun Uvaach,** the last one in Gita. At last, Arjun has understood it as **Dharm**, the sacred duty to destroy **Adharm**, the evil before **Adharm** destroys **Dharm** and him with all other righteous people. In 1/46, Arjun resolved to withdraw from the war, dropped his weapons and sat in the rear of his chariot with a heavy heart as terrible **Moh**, the bewilderment, delusion and infatuation gripped him completely in the clutches of his attachment towards his relatives and community. Even in such miserable condition, he consciously submitted to Krishn in 2/7 to guide and recover him from a distressed state, unparalleled in human history. Krishn took his request very kindly, started teaching him from 2/11 until 18/65 & 66, in which He shared the topmost secret of esoteric spiritual knowledge. In his divine dialogue with Krishn, Arjun asked as many as 25 questions in shloks like 2/4, 7 & 54; 3/1, 2 & 36; 4/4, 5/1, 6/33, 34 & 37 to 39; 8/1 & 2; 10/17 & 18; 11/3, 4 & 46; 12/1, 14/21, 17/1 and 18/1. Now, as we reach the end of this divine dialogue between them in 18/73, we find him completely recovered to his original confident self, free from all doubts and delusion due to teachings of Krishn. He manifests his reverence by surrendering to Him, in the spirit of God's final instruction **Maam Ekam Sharanam Vraj** in 18/66, and committing **Karishye Vachanam Tav** i.e. *'Whatsoever I shall do from now onwards, it shall be as per Your Supreme Will & Instruction'*. Recall Arjun's earlier confession in 11/1 where he said **Yat Tvayaa Uktam Vachasten Moh Ayam Vigat Mam** i.e. *'My delusion is dispelled by the explanations given by You'* but it was only about the secret knowledge of **Adhyaatm,** not a wholehearted admission since many doubts and questions still haunted his mind. Now, after seven more chapters at the end of God's teaching, he admits that his delusion has ended, he has regained his intelligence, and clearly states **Sthit Asmi Gat Sandeh** i.e. I am fully satisfied with the replies and explanations given by Krishn in a very calm and compassionate manner (in spite of some agitated postures taken by me). He addresses Krishn as Achyut, the most infallible one as if to assure Him that his commitment is also as infallible as He is. Garud acknowledges to his teacher Kaak Bhushundi in the same way in Raamcharit Maanas 7/129/8:

नाथ कृपा गत मम संदेहा I उपजेउ राम चरण नव नेहा II

(My lord! All of my doubts are cleared now, and my devotion unto the feet of Raam is renewed by your gracious kindness.)

Observe that the steps, in which Arjun confirms his recovery here, descend from **Nasht Moh** i.e. destruction of bewilderment to **Smruti Labdhaa** i.e. regaining lost memory (intelligence) to **Sthit Asmi Gat Sandeh** i.e. I am now firmly positioned beyond any doubt (like a **Sthit Prajn)** to **Twat Prasaadaat** i.e. by Your propitious kindness. These steps are almost in the reverse order of those described by Krishn in 2/62-63 for the downfall of a practiser.

Sandeh is same as **Sanshay** explained earlier as doubt, mistrust, uncertainty, hesitation, apprehension, anxiety, fear and skepticism. **Gat Sandeh** is therefore, synonymous of **Ashanshay**, the doubtless in 6/35, 7/1, 8/7 & 18/68.

Moral: *Shlok 18/73 reflects the deep meaning underlying Bhakti, the devotion and Sharanaagati, the refuge preached by God in His last sermon in 18/65 & 66. Devotion & refuge unto God must ultimately culminate into understanding of own Dharm i.e. duty and* *responsibility beyond any doubt or confusion, performing all works faithfully as the Supreme Command of God, and offering them unto Him for the outcome.*

The divine dialogue between Arjun and Krishn in Gita ends here.

ॐ

Sanjay expresses his joy of listening to the dialogue between Krishn & Arjun.

(18/74)

सञ्जय उवाच
इत्यहं वासुदेवस्य पार्थस्य च महात्मनः ।
संवादमिममश्रौषमद्भुतं रोमहर्षणम् ॥१८/७४॥

Sanjay Uvaach
Ityaham Vaasudevasya Paarthasya ch Mahaatman: I
Samvaadamimamashraushamadbhutam   romharshanam   II
(18/74)

Iti (thus) Aham (I) Vaasudevasya (of Vaasudev Krishn) Paarthasya (of Paarth Arjun) Ch (and) Mahaatman: (a great, venerable soul) I Samvaadam (dialogue) imam (this) Ashrausham (have listened) Adbhutam (wonderful, astonishing) Rom Harshanam (raising of body hairs due to fear, thrill or ecstasy)II (18/74)

Sanjay said:

"Thus, I have heard this conversation between Vaasudev Krishn and Paarth Arjun, the great, venerable souls. This dialogue, never heard before, is so wonderful that my body hairs are raised (in astonishment). (18/74)

This is ninth **Uvaach,** the last of Sanjay. Shlok 1/20 had the word **Ath** that means the beginning. Sanjay started narrating the divine dialogue of Gita between Arjun and Krishn from 1/20 up to this shlok 18/74. He uses the word **Iti** meaning the end of that sacred dialogue here.

ॐ

Sanjay is overjoyed by remembering the dialogue
again & again.

(18/75)

व्यासप्रसादाच्छ्रुतवानेतद्गुह्यमहं परम् ।
योगं योगेश्वरात्कृष्णात्साक्षात्कथयतः स्वयम् ॥१८/७५॥
राजन्संस्मृत्य संस्मृत्य संवादमिममद्भुतम् ।
केशवार्जुनयोः पुण्यं हृष्यामि च मुहुर्मुहुः ॥१८/७६॥
तच्च संस्मृत्य संस्मृत्य रूपमत्यद्भुतं हरेः ।
विस्मयो मे महान् राजन्हृष्यामि च पुनः पुनः ॥१८/७७॥

Vyaasaprasaadaachchhrutwaanetadguhyamaham param I
Yogam YogeshwaraatKrishnaatsaakshaatkathayat: swayam II
18/75)
Raajansansmrutya sansmrutya samvaadamimamadbhutam I
KeshavaArjunayo: punyam hrushyaami ch muhurmuhu: II
(18/76)
Tachch sansmruy sansmrutya roopamatyadbhutam Hare: I
Vismayo me mahaan raajanhrushyaami ch pun: pun: II
(18/77)

Vyaas Prasaadaat (by benevolent grace of Vyaas) Shrutwaan
(by listening) Etat (this) Guhyam (esoteric secret) Aham (I) Param
(ultimate, most)I Yogam (theory, endeavor & practice to bring
embodied soul towards & into union with God) Yogeshwaraat (by
the Supreme Master & Lord of Yog) Krishnaat (by Krishn) Saakshaat
(by my own eyes) Kathayat: (describing) Swayam (Himself)II (18/75)

Raajan (king, Dhrutraashtra) Samsmrutya Sansmrutya
(recollecting, recalling) Samvaadam (dialogue) imam (this)
Adbhutam (wonderful, astonishing)I Keshav Arjun y: (of Krishn and
Arjun) Punyam (auspicious, pious) Hrushyaami (rejoice, delight)
Ch (as) Muhurmuhu: (repeatedly, again & again)II (18/76)

tat (that) Ch (also) Samsmrutya Samsmrutya (recollecting,
remembering repeatedly) Roopam (form and beauty) Ati (too much;

extremely) Adbhutam (wonderful, astonishing) Hare: (of Hari, Lord Vishnu, Krishn)I Vismay: (awe, astonishment) Me (to me) Mahaan (great, grand) Raajan (king Dhrutraashtr) Hrushyaami (rejoice, delight) Ch (and) Pun: Pun: (again & again)II (18/77)

By the gracious benevolence of revered Vyaas, I am fortunate to have heard (and witnessed by my own eyes) this most esoteric secret Yog that Krishn, the Supreme Master & Lord of Yog Himself taught to Arjun. (18/75)

O king (Dhrutraashtr)! I am extremely delighted again & again as I repeatedly recall this wonderful, pious and auspicious dialogue between Krishn and Arjun. (18/76)

O king (Dhrutraashtr)! I am still awed in great amazement when I remember again & again that extremely beautiful, astonishing & grand universal form (Vishw Roop) of Shree Hari i.e. Krishn as an incarnation of Lord Vishnu; while simultaneously rejoicing every moment of it. (18/77)

Vyaas Prasaadaat: Sanjay gratefully acknowledges the kindness of Vyaas in blessing him with divine vision. Though the primary purpose of this boon was to enable Sanjay to witness and report the progress of the war to Dhrutraashtr sitting in Hastinaapur, it inadvertently benefited Sanjay with witnessing Gita word by word, and scene by scene, directly from Krishn as taught to Arjun.

Guhyam Param Yogam: Sanjay also learned **Yog** of Gita with Arjun. He calls it **Param Guhya Yog,** the ultimate most esoteric spiritual knowledge to connect with God as Krishn called it many times earlier.

Yogeshwaraat: Arjun addressed Krishn in 11/4 as **Yogeshwar,** the Supreme Master & Lord of **Yog,** His mystic, divine power to provide things needed for a person's spiritual as well as material well being; and enable him to connect with Him. Sanjay also had used it for Krishn in 11/9. Now, he repeats the same adjective to show his extreme devotion to Him. He shall use it in his last shlok 18/78 also.

Saakshaat Kathyat: God taught Gita to Arjun face to face in the battlefield of Kurukshetr before the war of Mahaabhaarat began. Sanjay says that he too has heard His teachings face to face, and seen with his own eyes though he was sitting far away in Hastinaapur before Dhrutraashtr. It was possible due to the divine vision given to him by Vyaas.

Roopam Ati Adbhutam Hare: Sanjay refers to the Universal form of God manifested by Krishn in chapter 11. Since he too could see it due to divine eyes given by Vyaas, he describes it again here as the most wonderful, miraculous form of God that nobody saw before.

Vismay Me Mahaan: Sanjay expresses his great delightful experience of seeing God's universal form with great awe and astonishment.

QUESTION: WHY DOES SANJAY CALL GITA AS SAMVAADAM IMAM ADBHUTAM?

Samvaadam Imam Adbhutam: It literally refers to the wonderful dialogue of Gita that just took place between Krishn and Arjun. Sanjay calls it **Adbhut** because the dialogue is focused on the most remarkable, esoteric and spiritual knowledge that enables a person to unite with God. **Samvaad** is a kind of **Vaad,** a discussion between two or more people. Some other **Sanskrit** words belonging to this family of words are, **Vaad, Prativaad** & **Vivaad**. Let us examine their relevance one by one with the dialogue between Krishn & Arjun in Gita.

1. **Vaad**: A person adopts this practice generally to force his views and opinions on others. It is also used as a suffix to denote **isms** like in **Adwait Vaad** i.e. monism, **Dwait Vaad** i.e. dualism etc. It resembles **Jalp Vaad** explained in 10/32.

2. **Prativaad**: When a person opposes, refutes and condemns somebody's **Vaad** in an effort to replace it with his own **Vaad,** it is called **Prativaad,** argument for the sake of contradiction. It generates unhealthy competition and one-upmanship. It is a type of **Vitandaa Vaad** explained in 10/32. Approach

of Gita towards different schools of thoughts has been very subtle and gentle.

3. **Vivaad**: A person creates **Vivaad,** the dispute when he puts forth arguments to raise disputes in the subject of discussion without offering any alternate solution. For example, opposition parties in a democratic country raise disputes and obstruct even in the simplest matters with the sole aim of stalling any move of the ruling party. **Vivaad** also a type of **Vitandaa Vaad** explained in 10/32.

4. **Samvaad**: It is the word uttered by Sanjay for the dialogue of Krishn and Arjun in Gita. **Samvaad** is composed of two components, **Sam + Vaad** which, when put together, mean a dialogue or discussion with equanimity and equilibrium of mind. It requires open mindedness, understanding, appreciation and accommodation of each other's viewpoint; use of soft, sweet & simple language; and straight forwardness. It however allows questioning, counter-questioning & even arguing for or against the subject matter but with mutual respect; and occasional use of forceful words in order to drive a truth home. In a **Samvaad,** one does not insist on the other to agree with what he says unless he accepts it with his heart. **Samvaad** leads both parties to arrive together at their common goal of acquiring **Jnaan**, the perfect knowledge about the matter under discussion. A person well versed with the technique of **Samvaad** shall not reject a proposition outright but discuss, modify or amend with specific reasons; and add values to it by extending its scope to greater heights. **Vaad** explained in 10/32 is the same as **Samvaad** here.

Readers must have observed the impressive style of the dialogue in Gita during their study and they shall certainly agree with **Sanjay** to call it a **Samvaad** that brought happiness to all, Krishn, the teacher, Arjun, the seeker of perfect knowledge and Sanjay, the witness. Unfortunately, our modern education system, under the influence of western culture, teaches us to resort to

Vaad or **Prativaad** or **Vivaad** that entangles our lives in worthless discussions. Most of us fail to realize the power and importance of **Samvaad**. A discussion in the style of **Samvaad** resolves disputes, dissolves rivalry & misunderstanding, and strengthens the bonds of camaraderie, as its outcome is a win-win situation for all. Among the four participants in the discussion of Gita Krishn, Arjun and Sanjay emerge as winners but Dhrutraashtr is highly disappointed & dejected looser due to his closed mindedness; he does not participate at all in Gita with the spirit of **Samvaad**. A snake charmer may be able to tame and train a snake but it is impossible for anybody to teach Gita to people like Dhrutraashtr, Duryodhan and Shakuni. This is why God forebade us from preaching Gita to an undeserving person in 18/67.

Moral: *A Prejudiced, biased mind leads a man to futility in life, for, reason quits when obstinacy takes over.*

ॐॐॐ

Sanjay expresses his opinion to Dhrutraashtr fearlessly
about the result of war.

(18/78)

यत्र योगेश्वर: कृष्णो यत्र पार्थो धनुर्धर: ।
तत्र श्रीर्विजयो भूतिर्ध्रुवा नीतिर्मतिर्मम ॥१८/७८॥

Yatr yogeshwar: Krishno yatr Paartho dhanurdhar: I
Tatr shrirvijayo bhootirdhruvaa neetirmatirmam II (18/78)

Yatr (where) Yogeshwar: (the Supreme Master & Lord of Yog) Krishn: (Krishn, the dark complexioned; also who attracts everyone) Yatr (where) Paarth: (Arjun) Dhanurdhar: (supreme, great, expert bowman, archer)I Tatr (there, of those) Shree: (prosperity, wealth, opulence) Vijay: (victory, conquest, triumph) Bhooti: (supreme power, dignity) Dhruvaa (permanent, stable, constant) Neeti: (ethics, morality and statesmanship) Mati: (firm conviction, opinion) Mam (my)II (18/78)

It is my firm conviction that where there is Krishn, the supreme Lord & Master of Yog, and where there is Arjun, a supreme archer, there alone shall rest all the prosperity, wealth & opulence; victory, dignity and stable, ethical morality". (18/78)

This is 700th the last shlok of Gita. Arjun expressed in 1/32 that he has no desire for victory in the war. To this, Krishn replied in 18/59 & 60 that he and his side shall conquer their enemies because even if he does not want to fight at this moment, his **Kshatriy** nature would compel him to involve in fight. Then, He dispelled the doubt he raised in 2/6 as to which side would be victorious, by declaring in 11/32:

'I am the Lord of death, grown to destroy all of your opponents; and shortly shall not exist anymore in near future even if refuse to fight with them'.

Now Sanjay also expresses his firm opinion to Dhrutraashtr that Arjun shall certainly emerge victorious since he is on God's side, and God is on his side. Look at the audacity of Sanjay who is merely a chariot driver in the employment of a mighty king like Dhrutraashtr. He drives such boldness and judgement to forecast the truth by listening to Gita. Vidur also warned Dhrutraashtr in **Aadi Parv**, the first chapter of Mahaabhaarat that in the event of any conflict between his sons & Paandu's sons, the victory would undoubtedly be of Paandavs because **Yato Krishnastato Jay** i.e. victory shall always be on the side where Krishn is. Closed-minded Dhrutraashtr never heeded to his sane advices. Let us understand few important words spoken by Sanjay here for proper understanding of this shlok.

Yogeshwar: Sanjay refers to Krishn as **Yogeshwar**, the Supreme Master and lord of **Yog**, the perfect spiritual knowledge that enables an embodied soul to move towards achieving perfect union with God, the Supreme Soul. Let us also recall God's promise **Yog Kshemam Vahaami Aham** in 9/22, to provide sufficient resources required by His devotee for his sustenance in material world, and to progress in spiritual world. Since Arjun is a wholehearted devotee of Krishn, Sanjay indirectly conveys to Dhrutraashtr that Krishn, being **Yogeshwar** shall definitely ensure his victory in the war.

Dhanurdhar: It literally means an archer. Paarth i.e. Arjun, the son of Pruthaa, is the most outstanding **Dhanurdhar** of his time in Mahaabhaarat. By using the adjective **Dhanurdhar** for Arjun, Sanjay conveys that though Arjun had dropped his bow in 1/47, has now lifted it again, and is ready to fight after the teaching of Gita.

Shree: It is the prosperity, wealth, happiness, splendor, opulence, and beauty. Applied to spiritualism, it projects the blissful status of a soul that unites with Supreme Soul.

Vijay: It is the victory, conquest, and triumph over enemies. It symbolically denotes conquest of our internal enemies like **Kaam**, **Krodh**, **Moh**, **Dwesh**, **Lobh** etc. that obstruct liberation of an embodied soul. We have recognized these spiritual enemies well in our study. Gita teaches us how to conquer them.

Bhooti: It means prosperity, wealth and fame. In terms of morality, **Bhooti** comprises of virtues spelt out in Daivee Sampadaa, the divine wealth from 16/1 to 3. However, spiritual **Bhooti,** for which a practiser of **Yog** aspires, is equivalent to God's **Yogam Aishwaram**, the supreme opulence, grandeur, majesty and mastery of God explained under question *'What is meant by Yogam Aishwaram'* in 9/4-6.

Dhruvaa Neeti: Krishn proclaimed in 10/35:

'I am Neeti, the ethical morality and statesmanship in persons desirous of victory'.

Sanjay uses adjective **Dhruvaa** (feminine of **Dhruv**) to highlight that such **Neeti** is steady and infallible like the **Dhruv**, the North Star in the sky.

Moral*: In order to be successful in any endeavor, we must become simple & pure hearted, clear minded, fully conscious of our Dharm, like Arjun. We must then undertake proposed work with full commitment, vigour & dedication, as Arjun demonstrates here by* *lifting his bow in his hand. It is important to note that instead of requesting almighty Krishn to fight on his behalf, or partake with him, he decides to do his duty by himself since he has thrown away the yoke of his Moh towards Swajan, sacrificed his desire for the kingdom; and learnt the lessons of Swadharm & Swakarm from Gita. We must also have full faith & inviolable, unflinching devotion in God like him, and entrust the outcome in the hands of His Supreme Will. God always stands by such endeavourer in his every move and ensures to deliver such wonderful fruits to him in return that the doer might have never imagined. Arjun attained immortality by listening and acting according to teaching in Gita; his name shall last in this world as long as Gita continues to guide humanity. This is the ultimate success, the culmination of the purpose of human life. Karm based on Neeti, the morality, symbolized by lifting of bow by Arjun, is the most important requirement for a man to achieve success in material world of Shree, Vijay & Bhooti. Nevertheless, if his aim is to achieve the ultimate success of liberation, he must still perform Karm according to Dharm, and detach himself from the desire for favorable result. God shall support him wholeheartedly in achieving the same. If he gives up Karm, he shall miss his goal in the material as well as spiritual world.*

As told in the beginning, Gita starts with **Dharm** in shlok 1/1 and ends here with **Mam** (my) in 18/78. Both words put together mean My **Dharm**. Thus, Gita dwells, deals with and teaches a person to realize his **Dharm** i.e. his duties and responsibilities, and to live by it, and die for it. It shows him the way to lead a blissful life free from misery & distress.

Caution: *At the end of Gita, there is a possibility of someone disagreeing to God's teachings. God would not interfere in his chosen course of action anymore. Nevertheless, such person should bear it in mind that God would stop wasting His time in guiding him (as Krishn did with Bheeshm, Dron, Karn when they did not listen to His counsel), and set out in search of another doer who would love to become His Nimitt (11/33), the agent in implementing His Supreme Will of protecting Dharm.*

CONCLUSION OF CHAPTER 18

It must be clear to us by now that Gita repeatedly insists on **Tyaag** as inward renunciation of desire for fruits, and discards **Sannyaas,** the outward renunciation of the world and work. It clarifies further that such **Tyaag** is the real, sufficient and complete interpretation of **Sannyaas**. The latter without the former is not only worthless but also impossible to attain without practising former, besides being dangerous. A **Sannyaasee** without **Karm Phal Tyaag** is simply an absconder & hypocrite. The real **Tyaag** of Gita is in action, not in running away from it. Gita's **Tyaagee** must relinquish all of his desires to get certain desired results from his work, and the ego of being the doer, not the work per se. **Sannyaas** and **Tyaag** become synonymous when one masters the principle of **Sarv Karm Phal Tyaag** (12/11 & 18/2). The main bone of contention between the two is the expectation or egoistic demand from the work done, because the reward and punishment are beyond the doer's jurisdiction as explained in 2/47 and elsewhere. A **Sarv Karm Phal Tyaagee** looks at success and failure with equanimity; he neither rejoices in success nor laments in failure.

Caution: *Sometimes, the result of a work may not be visible to the doer at all; he should continue doing his Kartavya Karm i.e. duty in right earnest because the result is under the control of Divine Will & Justice and overall Master plan of the Supreme Being. He should not seclude into the immobility and dumbness of stones and trees.*

This chapter has 1 **Shree Bhagawaan Uvaach,** 2 **Arjun Uvaach** and 1 **Sanjay Uvaach**.

We commenced our journey in the great Himalaya of spiritual knowledge, called Gita, with Arjun as our team leader and Krishn as our expert Sherpa & guide from 2/11. Our Initial interest in it might have been casual like site-seeing in any other kind of tourism but we decided very soon to continue further after enjoying the grand panoramic views of some high peaks from a distance while passing through its first lag in plains up to chapter 6. From chapter 7 onwards, the terrain gradually became more difficult but attractive as we entered the region of some snow-clad peaks of medium heights, and the valleys in between them. Though the air became more rarified and thinner, particularly in chapters like 13 & 15, making breathing and communication very difficult, we equipped ourselves with life supporting apparatuses of determination, sincerity and faith, and walkie-talkie (to communicate with God living in our heart), and continued our journey with courage. Nevertheless, it is also true that not every climber can reach the summit as some return from the base camp, others decide to stay back in next camps, but few **Dhruti Utsaah Samanvit** (18/26) persons endowed with steadfastness, fortitude and enthusiasm do reach the final camp. From there, they witness their leader Arjun, along with Sherpa Krishn, climbing the last leg to Mount Everest and waving the flag of **Gita Jnaan** from there to whole world. Arjun could reach Everest in his first attempt due to unflinching faith in his guide and sincere commitment of **Karishye Vachanam Tav** (18/73).

Dear teammates! We too must be glad to reach the final camp and become **Medhaavee** i.e. knowledgeable and **Chhinn Sanshay** i.e. free from doubt (refer 18/10) avout our duty. **Abhyaas Yog** (8/8 & 12/9) i.e. repetitive continuous and sustained study & practice of the rules laid down by expert Sherpa Krishn in Gita shall definitely empower us to climb the topmost summit of its **Samagr Yog** (explained in 2/39 & 40) in our next attempts.

ॐ तत्सदिति श्रीमद्भगवद्गीतासूपनिषत्सु ब्रह्मविद्यायां योगशास्त्रे श्रीकृष्णार्जुनसंवादे मोक्ष संन्यासयोगो नाम अष्टादशोऽध्यायः॥ १८॥

(In the name of God, the ultimate truth thus ends the eighteenth chapter named Moksh Sannyaas Yog of Shreemad Bhagwad Gita, the best Upanishad, Brahm Vidyaa & Yog Shaastr, a dialogue between Shree Krishn and Arjun)

May God bless us with enthusiasm and fortitude to continue our effort to reach ultimate destination as He did for Arjun.

Iti Shree Krishnaarpanamastu.

(I dedicate my entire endeavor to Lord Shree Krishn)